An ITC publication in
FINANCE

The Investment Process

The Investment Process

edited by

JOHN M. LISHAN and DAVID T. CRARY

University of Southern California

INTERNATIONAL TEXTBOOK COMPANY

An Intext publisher

Scranton, Pennsylvania 18515

Standard Book Number 7002 2270 7

Printed in the United States of America by The Haddon Craftsmen, Inc., Scranton, Pennsylvania. Library of Congress Catalog Card Number: 72-105071.

Preface

In recent years the study of investment management has received increased attention from both finance teachers and financial practitioners. This increased emphasis has resulted from the growing realization that approaches to investing and investment management in our economy have changed considerably. Within academia, an earlier emphasis on security analysis has been greatly expanded to include the subject of portfolio management. Throughout the economy, increasing real incomes, intensifying competition for the investor's dollar, applications of automatic data processing to investment management, and the increasing sensitivity of fund users to the benefits of a buoyant equity market are but a few of the many reasons why the subject of investments has become of such great importance to so many. In short, the study of investment is the study of change.

This volume is designed primarily for two groups of readers. The first group, consisting of upper division undergraduate students, should find these papers, selected from the works of writers within the universities and investing community, an illuminating complement to their study of investment management from case materials or from basic texts. Secondly, the book should prove of value to individual investors who ordinarily would not have the time to study the varied sources from which these works were taken.

The diversity of approaches, opinions, conclusions, and recommendations expressed by the authors included in this collection makes it impossible to agree with and endorse them all. In compiling this diverse collection the editors hope to indicate to the beginning student that a knowledge of investment management involves the task of synthesizing an understanding of segments of a variety of disciplines—such as economics, finance, sociology, psychology, mathematics, and statistics into an intelligible, useful framework.

As stated, one objective of the authors is to expose the student to the many facets of investment management. Initially, he is introduced to the relationships of economic policy and the investment process. Secondly, the student is presented several views of the fundamental approach to the determination of security value. This second section encompasses both a description of the analysis used by professional investment advisors and a comparison of current growth stock valuation techniques that are being discussed in the scholarly journals. The third section introduces what is referred to as technical analysis. It concentrates on market analysis and short term price movement forecasting. The concept of random walks in stock market prices is introduced and criticized. In section four the mechanics of the securities markets and brokerage are introduced and examined. The editors attempt to expose the student to the vast body of current literature concerning portfolio management in the fifth section. The last section is devoted to a discussion of the increasingly important role played by the institutional investors.

The materials in this book were selected because of their contribution to the central concepts of investment management. In the aggregate the readings reflect current thinking existing in the market place and in the universities.

The editors wish to express grateful acknowledgement to the authors and publishers of these selections for their permission to use their works. The author and publication source are identified at the beginning of each article.

John M. Lishan
David T. Crary

Los Angeles, California
December, 1969

Contents

The Investment Process

Part I

Economic Policy and the Investment Process

INTRODUCTION

Economics can be defined as the study of how a society chooses to allocate scarce productive resources to produce various products over time and distribute these products among the members of society.

In the first essay in this section Professor William Baumol discusses the allocation of capital resources. He characterizes decisions in this subject area as among the most important to be resolved by any economy. He defines capital as the economy's link with the future and emphasizes that unless the flow of capital goods is responsive to the goals of the members of the public, the community will only be able to exercise a very short-run control over the composition of output. The allocation of real resources is linked to the funds market and the securities markets are conceived as occupying a regulatory role.

The efficiency of the securities market as an allocator is enhanced by those factors which make common stock investment attractive to the public.

Professors Alchain and Kessel clarify one facet of the investment process through their informative discussion of the redistribution of wealth through inflation. Dr. William Freund advances the student's understanding of the relationship of economic activity to investments in his discussion of the price relationships of equities to the profit and fiscal outlook. Professor Weston focuses attention on the past relationships between gross national product and the Dow Jones Industrial Average.

In the last section the editors have attempted to reveal to the student the regulatory role of government in investments. Spatial constraints have limited the coverage of this currently expanding area.

It is hoped that the student will be induced to examine the vast body of literature available in the area. Professor Eiteman discusses the ramifications of recent legislation for the securities markets and Professor Stigler offers a strong criticism of the bases on which parts of this legislation is anchored.

1

The Platonic Shadow: Ideal Markets and Their Imperfect Real Counterparts*

William J. Baumol

The allocation of its capital resources is among the most important decisions which must be made by any economy. In the long run an appropriate allocation of real capital is absolutely indispensable to the implementation of consumer sovereignty (or of the more appropriate concept–public sovereignty–which takes into account *all* of the relevant desires of the individuals who constitute the economy). For unless the flow of capital goods is responsive to the goals of the members of the public, the community will only be able to exercise a very short-run and temporary control over the composition of output and of its activities. After all, capital is the economy's link with the future and unless our desires can influence the apportionment of capital inputs, our wishes can at most effectively control only today's events.

In addition, the allocation of capital resources plays a critical role in the determination of the rate of growth of the nation's output. If capital resources are not provided to those industries the demand for whose products is growing or is at least expandable, if capital is not made available to sectors which are capable of increasing production and productivity and, above all, if there is no investment in research and development, we can be sure that the rate of expansion of the economy will suffer.

Finally, the mechanism which allocates these capital resources can itself play an important economic role. Even if it tends to distribute capital in accord with the wishes of the public, it may do so only slowly to the accompaniment of the discordant squeaking of its rusty gears. The flexibility and speed of response of our capital allocation mechanism affects directly the adaptability of our productive mechanism, and thereby bears on the long-run prospects of our entire economy.

So far we have considered only the nation's real capital, its machinery, its factories, its goods-in-process, its inventories of raw materials and its final

*From *The Stock Market and Economic Efficiency,* The Miller Lectures Number Six, (1965), pp. 1–8. Reprinted by permission of The Fordham University Press and the author.

products. But the apportionment of these real resources among industries and individual firms and, indeed, the selection of the physical forms which constitute the embodiment of our capital resources is largely controlled through the funds market—the market on which *money* capital is provided. Thus the allocation process is heavily influenced by the decisions of the nation's financial institutions, its banks, its insurance companies, and a variety of other bodies many of which will come to mind immediately. In addition the government's monetary and fiscal policies obviously play a highly important role in a variety of ways which need not be gone into here. Finally, as we shall see, one may reasonably attribute a regulatory role to the securities markets, and in particular to the markets for stocks and bonds.

The securities markets are characterized by a number of properties which render them specially suitable to serve as capital resource allocators.

First, they offer guidance to business management—information on the current cost of capital which is so important in determining the level of investment which it is appropriate for the firm to undertake. For example, if its stock prices are high so that the company's securities can be exchanged for relatively generous quantities of resources, this is generally taken to indicate that the cost of capital is low and that the net returns to be expected of any given real investment project will be correspondingly generous. Second, the securities markets offer the advantage of accessibility to vast numbers of capitalists, many of whom possess only minuscule amounts of money and yet who in their aggregate have command over vast quantities of wealth. Third, the markets offer a simple mechanism for the transfer of funds that imposes only a minimum of administrative effort upon the lender. Fourth, markets offer him an easily understood evaluation of the financial condition and future prospects of the borrowing firm as indicated by the market price of its securities and by movements in the magnitude of that price. Finally, the market performs an act of magic, for it permits long-term investments to be financed by funds provided by individuals, many of whom wish to make them available for only a very limited period, or who wish to be able to withdraw them at will. Thus it imparts a measure of liquidity to long-term investments that permits their instruments to be sold at a price that yields a lower rate of return than would otherwise be required. In the words of Professor Machlup

> The fact that from the point of view of the individual saver it [transfer credit] is only intended to be a short-term loan does not limit the possible ways of using it as much as one might first think. For even though the individual savings are only saved for a temporary period, collectively they may in large part be looked upon as long-term savings of the economic system. . . . The probability that. . . new savings will be sufficient to cover withdrawals of old savings is what makes it possible to invest these short-term funds in production. The system whereby this investment is made through the stock exchange has special advantages, for in this case the transformation of what are short-term credits

from the private viewpoint into long-term savings from the social viewpoint can take place to the fullest extent. . . .[1]

For all of these reasons, and no doubt for others as well, one has come to look upon the stock market as the allocator of capital resources *par excellence,* and set aside from some uneasiness about the untoward effects of speculation, one is readily inclined toward the view that the stock market constitutes an allocative mechanism of remarkable efficiency.[2] It is a major purpose of this book to probe somewhat more carefully the efficiency of this piece of machinery.

THE STOCK EXCHANGE AS AN ILLUSTRATIVE PERFECT MARKET

The stock market is among the subjects which have achieved the status of a textbook cliché. Many such volumes have described this institution as a relatively close approximation to a perfect market, indeed, one of the best which is to be found anywhere in our economy. After all, a hasty glance suggests that it possesses all if not most of the characteristics required of a pure competitive market. Its products are homogeneous: if I buy a share of Republic Steel I don't care which share I happen to get or from whom it happens to have been acquired. Anyone's share of Republic Steel is identical with any other. Also there seem to be many sellers, most of whom are relatively small, though we shall note presently that there are some significant exceptions. Finally, the securities markets apparently satisfy the third prime requisite of pure competition, free entry and exit. Anyone who owns a listed security can undertake to sell it and anyone who wishes to acquire one can purchase it. True, entry and exit into the occupations of those who actually operate the market machinery is sometimes restricted. Indeed, in a few cases it is severely limited. It is not easy to become a broker and more difficult to become a floor trader or a specialist. As we shall see, this does have some relevance for the perfection of the market itself. It may mean that the rate of return earned by brokers is somewhat larger than it would have been in the presence of perfect mobility into this occupation. That, in turn, raises the transfer costs incurred in the exchange of securities, and so contributes to the frictions which beset the workings of the market but by itself it need not significantly affect the appropriateness of the stock market as an illustration of pure competition.

[1] Fritz Machlup, *The Stock Market, Credit and Capital Formation* (London: William Hodge & Company, 1940), p. 225. Reprinted by permission of the publishers.

[2] This is not meant to imply that the bulk of the business sector's new funds are obtained through the stock markets or that a large proportion of the markets' operations help directly to supply new capital. As will be indicated in later chapters, neither of these assertions is true. Firms obtain new funds preponderantly from retained earning, not from new stock issues, and the stock exchanges deal in second-hand shares—not in new issues. As such, the exchanges therefore do not supply new capital. But they can control its allocation by determining the terms (prices) on which funds are available, and by making easily available to investors the alternatives open to them.

One of the first conclusions which the student is expected to draw from the competitive model is that (making suitable allowance for the characteristics of the individual product) on such a market prices tend to be set by the forces of supply and demand at the intersection of the supply and demand schedules. . . . Of course, no one denies the presence of deeper motivations which do not reveal themselves in the elementary supply-demand diagram—for example, the role of anticipations of the future, and of the variety of investment opportunities available to the firm whose security is in question. But in the standard model these underlying determinants exert their influence through their effects on the pertinent supply and demand functions which can then still be taken to determine prices in accord with the ordinary procedures described in our basic competitive analysis.

However, at this point a closer look reveals matters which remain somewhat obscure. Just exactly what are these procedures—the series of events and interrelationships whereby the forces of supply and demand are translated into price quotations? On a real market in the real world one encounters no supply-demand graphs and no one reads off the coordinates of their intersection points. In setting price then, one may well ask exactly who does what to whom—what mechanism translates the disorderly parade of data which serve as a substitute for our neat mathematical functions, into a unique determinate price figure? Here, then, is our first reason for looking more closely at the stock exchange as an illustrative competitive market. This reexamination will indicate the nature of the mechanism which gives effect to the forces of supply and demand. We will find that equilibrium does not simply generate itself and that a very special procedure has been instituted to do the job.

Thus, though this portion of our investigation will reveal few significant departures of the workings of the stock market from those of the purely competitive model, an examination of the relationship between the two can nevertheless prove illuminating. It may offer a somewhat increased understanding of the elaborate arrangements which are required for the operation of the competitive mechanism. More important for our central purposes, having discovered the pricing engine we will be able to discuss the effectiveness of the allocation of capital resources produced by this particular arrangement and whether our conclusions on this subject are a matter of the fortuitous organizational details of the operation of the exchange or whether they may be expected to apply generally to competitive markets.

THE STOCK MARKET AND THE THEORY OF RESOURCE ALLOCATION

Thus we return to the central topic with which we intend to deal. Granting that the stock exchange constitutes a reasonably close approximation to a competitive market, it seems all the more reasonable to conjecture that it will serve as a relatively effective allocator of resources. However, a bit more thought can lead us to become somewhat suspicious of this conclusion. The reason is the crucial role played by the market value of a company's securities in the entire process. To serve as an effective resource allocator it would appear that the market should value a stock in some manner on the basis of the capitalized value of the company's expected future earnings as determined by the investment opportunities available to it. For it would seem that only if it does so will funds become most readily available to companies which can best make use of them in light of prospective consumer demands, technological circumstances and other pertinent developments in the future. Apparently, only if stocks are valued in this way will funds be provided most abundantly and at most reasonable terms to the most promising innovator who, according to the classical theory of economic development, has the greatest use for them and who is the one that can obtain the profits which will serve as the investor's reward. Finally, it may seem that only if stocks are valued in this way, that is, if they are priced in terms of the prospective earnings of the company, the market can serve as an effective disciplinary device which punishes managements whose operations are inefficient or unprofitable. For only then will poor performance cause the market to deny funds to the company or to provide them only on extremely unfavorable terms.

In sum, the prices assigned to stocks by the free market[3] are critical to the effectiveness of the market as a resource allocator. And if these prices are perversely or even randomly related to future earnings prospects there is no reason to believe that this function will be performed well and effectively. Yet we have all seen cases where the behavior of prices on the stock market has apparently been capricious or even worse, cases where hysteria has magnified largely irrelevant events into controlling influences.[4] Add to this observation a series of extremely careful and sophisticated statistical studies . . . whose evidence is that random elements in stock price behavior are of dominating importance, and we can no longer remain comfortable with the easy assumption that all will work out well in the end. We shall therefore have to inquire into the manner in which stock prices are determined and examine what theory tells us about the likely relationship between prospective earnings and current market values. As may be expected, the results will be far from categorical. We will see some influences which work one way and some the other. But if the discussion does not settle matters it may at least add somewhat to our understanding of the pertinent relationships.

[3]Sometimes special prices are assigned to some shares by the company itself. For example, a firm may offer shares to its current stockholders at prices below those that the stocks would command on the open market. Neoclassical analysis was never meant to be applied to such special arrangements.

[4]This is a phenomenon which does not occur only on the stock market. Similar events have, for example, occurred on the commodity exchanges.

2

Redistribution of Wealth Through Inflation*

Armen A. Alchian
Reuben A. Kessel

Economists have long speculated about the effects of inflation upon the economic welfare of the owners of business enterprises. This speculation has almost invariably led to the conclusion that business firms gain through inflation. This conclusion has been reached through two independent arguments. One, enunciated by both J. M. Keynes and I. Fisher is that inflation enables business firms to discharge their debts with depreciated money, the creditors' losses being the debtors' gains.[1] Strictly speaking, the validity of this conclusion depends upon two propostions: (i) that business firms are debtors, and (ii) that interest rates reflect biased estimates of the future course of prices when prices are rising. The other argument, advanced by E. J. Hamilton and W. C. Mitchell, is that inflation causes prices to rise faster than wage rates.[2] Consequently workers are systematically underpaid during inflation, this loss by the working class being a gain for the entrepreneurs.[3] This explanation rests upon special assumptions about the character of labor markets that are generally regarded as invalid in other markets.

Practical men of affairs, in particular investment advisers, have been much less confident than professional economists that the owners of business enterprises gain through inflation. They have generally concluded that investors can maintain their capital intact during inflation by investing in common stocks, such as investment being roughly equivalent to an investment in inventories. (Common stocks are ownership or equity shares in a corporation, while bonds

*From *Science,* Vol. 130, No. 3375 (September 4, 1959), pp. 535–539. Reprinted by permission of *Science.*

[1] J. M. Keynes, *Tract on Monetary Reform* (London, 1923), p. 18; I. Fisher, *The Purchasing Power of Money* (New York, 1920), pp. 58–73, 190–191.

[2] E. J. Hamilton, *Journal of Economic History,* 12, 325 (1952); W. C. Mitchell, *A History of the Greenbacks* (Chicago, 1903), pp. 347–348; ——, *Gold, Prices, and Wages under the Greenback Standard* (Berkeley, 1908), pp. 275–276.

[3] Some economists and noneconomists also contend that anyone who holds inventories gains through inflation. Since the price of inventories rises above their cost, this difference is regarded as a real gain in economic welfare. But holders of inventories cannot acquire with their inventories any more of the world's goods and services than they could in the absence of inflation.

represent debt obligations of the corporation.) In other words, an investor in common stock could expect neither to increase nor to decrease his wealth, whereas an investor in bonds and other cash-type investments would suffer a real loss.

This cautiousness of investment counselors is traceable to the experience of investors in equities during the great inflations that have occurred in countries with organized stock markets. It was found during the German runaway inflation following World War I, during the Austrian and French inflations of the 1920's, and more recently during the inflation in Chile that the owners of business firms did not obtain the gains that might have been expected on the basis of the hypotheses set forth by Keynes and Fisher, on the one hand, and Hamilton and Mitchell on the other. These observations are also consistent with the behavior of stock price indexes in the United States during the inflations associated with world wars I and II.

What was especially puzzling was the fate of the owners of banks. Banks are typically enormous debtors, larger debtors, in fact, than most business firms by an order of magnitude. Furthermore, banks employ relatively more labor per dollar of invested capital than is characteristic of business firms generally. Consequently, it is an implication of both hypotheses that banks ought to be enormous gainers through inflation. Yet the available evidence suggests that one of the regular results of inflation is that the owners of bank shares suffer. The experience of the owners of bank shares in the United States, Germany, Austria, Chile, and France suggests that the real value of bank shares declines during inflation. (Real value is simply price divided by an index number reflecting changes in the price level. Consequently, if the price of an asset rises more than the price level, then its real value has increased, and conversely.)

RECONCILING HYPOTHESES WITH EXPERIENCE

How can this evidence be reconciled with either of these hypotheses? A step toward reconciling the Keynes-Fisher reasoning with the lessons of experience as revealed by the stock market was taken by Kessel when he showed that, despite the enormous debts owed by banks to depositors, there exist offsetting credits that are even larger than these debts.[4] These credits are bank assets which are almost entirely (with the exception of bank buildings and business machines) either money or money-type assets such as notes and other obligations payable to banks by either private customers or the government. The existence of these credits led Kessel to argue that one should do more than merely look at the credit that business firms have extended to their customers. What business firms gain from bondholders may be lost to those to whom these firms have extended credit and may never redound to the interests of the owners.

From his analysis emerged a classification for determining whether or not a

[4] R. A. Kessel, *American Economic Review*, 46, 130 (1956).

business firm is on *net* balance, a debtor or creditor. Kessel classified assets and liabilities into categories, monetary and real. A monetary asset was defined as an asset whose market value is independent of changes in the price level. These would include money, accounts and notes receivable, government and corporate bonds, life insurance, prepaid taxes, and so on. A monetary liability was defined as a liability whose amount is independent of changes in the price level; these would include accounts payable, notes payable, mortgages, bonds, preferred stock, and so on. Preferred stock, although called a stock, is typically corporate debt rather than equity. A net monetary debtor was then defined as a firm whose monetary liabilities exceeded its monetary assets; and conversely for a net monetary creditor. The net monetary status would indicate the magnitude of the gain or loss a firm would incur from a given amount of inflation. However, firms with the same amount of indebtedness but of unequal size, where size is measured by the aggregate value of the equity of the owners, would have unequal movements in absolute stock prices. Therefore, in order to compare corporations of unequal size, the ratio of net monetary debt to equity, as measured by the market price of shares times the number of shares outstanding, is used as the measure of net monetary debtor or creditor status.[5] The effects of stock dividends, stock splits, and rights offerings were held constant and did not affect measurements of changes in stock prices. "Stock dividends" and "splits" increase the number of shares of common stock without changing the total investment, whereas "rights" entitle existing stockholders to increase the investment in the corporation by purchasing new shares at a price below existing market prices, thereby also involving some dilution in per-share value. And it was assumed that dividends were continuously reinvested in the shares of the companies that issued them, because this would eliminate variations caused by differences in the extent to which profits were reinvested.

For the United States, Kessel found in his preliminary study that banks were typically net monetary creditors, and that the real value of their shares actually did decline during the World War II inflation, in accordance with the Keynes-Fisher hypothesis. Furthermore, the real value of bank shares seems to have gone down during inflation for every country for which data are available.

Kessel also examined the balance sheets of a small random sample of industrial firms whose stock is traded on the New York Stock Exchange. (Railroads, utilities, and investment companies were omitted. Railroads and utilities were not included because it was supposed that their very close regulation might conceal the effects of inflation upon their stock prices. Investment companies were omitted because of the magnitude of the problems encountered in evaluating the debtor-creditor status of their assets.) In 1939, about 40 percent of the observed firms were creditors and could be expected to lose

[5] This is one of the respects in which the present study is an advance over Kessel's early work. While his concept of net debtor or net creditor was correct, his criterion of *intensity* of debtor or creditor status was wrong, and consequently the measurements based upon his criterion were also wrong.

through inflation, according to the Keynes-Fisher reasoning. After the firms had been divided into the two categories, debtor and creditor, and after the changes in share prices between 1939 and 1946 had been examined, a significant difference was detected between the rise of share prices in the two categories. The share prices of net monetary debtor firms rose significantly more than the prices of net monetary creditor firms. For a period of deflation, 1929–1933, the reverse was found to be true. The share prices of net monetary creditors fell significantly less than the share prices of net monetary debtors.

The behavior of the stock prices of bank shares during the inflation associated with World War II was indistinguishable from the behavior of the shares of equivalent industrial creditors. Other evidence indicates that banks were characterized by large amounts of labor per dollar of invested capital as compared with enterprises generally. This evidence casts doubt upon the validity of the Hamilton-Mitchell reasoning, that inflation causes real wages to fall. If the wage lag had been operative, the value of bank shares would have risen more than the value of the shares of equivalent industrial creditors.

This evidence validated the proposition that during inflation interest rates are systematically lower than they ought to be if inflation is not to transfer wealth from creditors to debtors, but it also challenged the assumption that business firms are, in large part, debtors. The mechanism for redistribution that Keynes and Fisher envisaged was correct, but their assumption that business firms were generally debtors was wrong, and it was this that led them to the erroneous conclusion that business firms gain through inflation. This evidence also explains the behavior of stock-price indexes during inflation. If a substantial fraction of all business firms were net monetary creditors, then an index number of stock prices that was composed of both net monetary debtors and net monetary creditors would not necessarily rise in real value during inflation. Indeed, if the debtors just balance out the creditors, one would expect stock prices generally to keep pace pretty closely with the general price level. These results led to a much larger-scale investigation, designed both to provide stronger evidence of the validity of the mechanism for redistribution envisaged by Keynes and Fisher and to enlarge our empirical knowledge of stock prices.[6]

NEW EVIDENCE FOR MECHANISM OF REDISTRIBUTION

The population of firms investigated includes all of the industrials whose common stock was traded on the New York Stock Exchange at any time between 1914 and 1952. For 1933–1952, the American Stock Exchange was also included. Furthermore, four separate industries were studied for the period 1940–1952–chemicals, steels, retailing, and textiles–in order to hold constant any industry differences. The period of the study, 1915–1952, includes two

[6]This study was undertaken with the aid of a research grant from the Merrill Foundation for the Advancement of Financial Knowledge. The article, from this point on, constitutes the first statement of some of the results of this study.

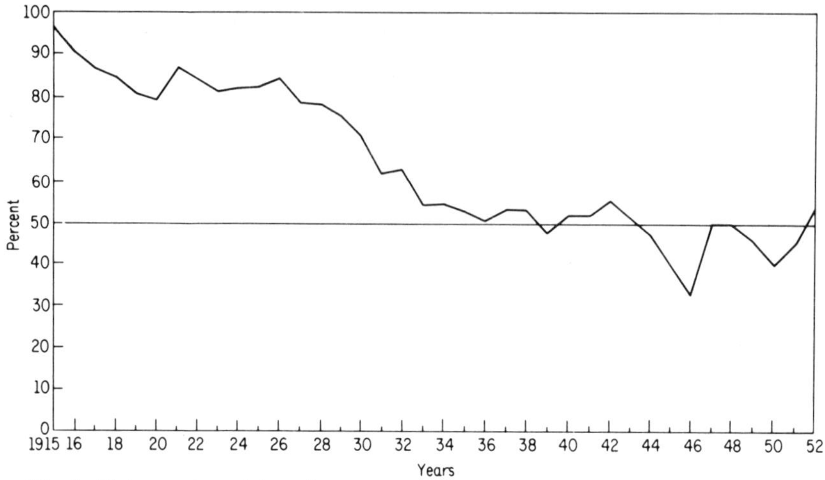

Fig. 1. Net monetary debtor firms as percentage of all firms. [Based on New York Stock Exchange data for 1915 to 1952 and on American Stock Exchange and "over-the-counter" data for 1940 to 1952.]

inflations (world wars I and II), two deflations (1921–22 and 1928–1933), and two periods of relative price stability (1923–1930– and 1933–1940). The number of firms observed in a year ranged from a minimum of 71 to a maximum of 885. In all, nearly 14,000 firm-years of data were observed and analyzed.

What do these data show? The distribution of firms by net monetary debtor and net monetary creditor status has changed spectacularly since 1914. The percentage of firms in each category is shown in Fig. 1. These data are based on the New York and the American Stock Exchange samples. The shift from predominantly net monetary debtor status, around the time of World War I, to a ratio of approximately 50:50 in 1952 may explain why Keynes and Fisher made the assumption they did about business firms being debtors.

Apparently individual firms usually did not shift their net monetary status frequently. A firm that was a net monetary debtor in one year was very likely to be one in the next year, despite a gradual shift of the population as a whole. A classification of firms during the 1915–1920 inflation according to net monetary status shows that 78 of the firms were net monetary creditors during at least 4 years of the 6-year span, while 22 were net montary debtors during at least 4 of the 6 years. A few did not retain their status for as long as 4 years. According to Keynes and Fisher the net monetary debtors should have had an increase in the values of their stocks relative to the net monetary creditors. The observed data show that $1 of equity of the net monetary debtors increased to $2.66, while the net monetary creditors' dollar increased to only $1.60; the superiority is 57 percent and one which would have less than 1 chance in 1000 of occurring by an unusually favorable random selection of firms if there really were no transfers of wealth from creditors to debtors.

Table 1 contains more details, as well as the results for the inflation of

TABLE 1

Observed stock price values (with reinvested dividends) for episodes of inflations, deflations, and stable prices, by exchanges and industries. [From *Moody's Industrials* (1914–1953); *Commercial and Financial Chronicles* (1921–1953); *Bank and Quotation Journals* (1928–1953); and New York *Times* (1915–1953)]

Population sampled	Kind and Number of firms*	Mean resulting equity value† (dollars)	Mean of debtor minus creditor‡ (dollars)	t§	p‖
	Inflations				
1915–1920:					
New York Stock Exchange	Debtors 78	2.66	+1.06	3.27	.001
New York Stock Exchange	Creditors 22	1.60			
1940–1952:					
New York Stock Exchange	Debtors 29	5.93	+1.47	1.80	.05
New York Stock Exchange	Creditors 35	4.46			
American Stock Exchange	Debtors 57	11.30	+3.25	1.65	.05
American Stock Exchange	Creditors 70	8.05			
Over-the-counter	Debtors 22	9.38	+2.93	1.19	.12
Over-the-counter	Creditors 45	6.45			
Steel industry	Debtors 29	6.92	+0.25	.15	.44
Steel industry	Creditors 27	6.67			
Chemical industry	Debtors 19	7.17	+2.53	1.24	.12
Chemical industry	Creditors 19	4.54			
Textile industry	Debtors 29	16.33	+6.67	1.45	.07
Textile industry	Creditors 22	9.66			
Department stores	Debtors 29	8.96	+4.81	2.64	.007
Department stores	Creditors 22	4.15			
New York Stock Exchange wage firms	Debtors 50	7.85	+2.07	1.76	.04
New York Stock Exchange wage firms	Creditors 32	5.78			
	Deflations				
1921–1922:					
New York Stock Exchange	Debtors 118	1.48	−0.30	−1.73	.045
New York Stock Exchange	Creditors 24	1.78			
1928–1933:					
New York Stock Exchange	Debtors 63	.49	−0.60	−3.17	.001
New York Stock Exchange	Creditors 35	1.09			
	Stable Prices				
1923–1930:					
New York Stock Exchange	Debtors 50	2.78	+0.45	1.08	.14
New York Stock Exchange	Creditors 15	2.33			
1933–1940:					
New York Stock Exchange	Debtors 56	4.31	−0.80	− .89	.81
New York Stock Exchange	Creditors 54	5.11			
American Stock Exchange (curb)	Debtors 17	6.44	+1.72	+ .71	.52
American Stock Exchange (curb)	Creditors 20	4.72			

*Number of firms that maintained debtor (or creditor) monetary status during at least 2/3 of the episode.

†Mean price plus reinvested dividends at the end of the episode, per dollar of 1904 stock prices.

‡Mean equity value for net monetary debtors minus mean value for net monetary creditors.

§Student's t test coefficient:

$$t = d \quad \frac{s_1^2}{N_1} + \frac{s_2^2}{N_2} \quad {}^{1/2}$$

‖Sampling probability of t (one-tailed) based on Welch approximation. [B. L. Welch, "The generalization of student's problem when several different population variances are involved," *Biometrika* 34, 28 (1947). Two-tailed test is used for periods of price stability].

1940–1952, for each of the populations of firms studied. In every instance the net monetary debtors did better. In Fig. 2 these results are given in the form of a graph. The probability sampling levels are sufficiently small to make it extraordinarily difficult to attribute such results to random sampling. And when the

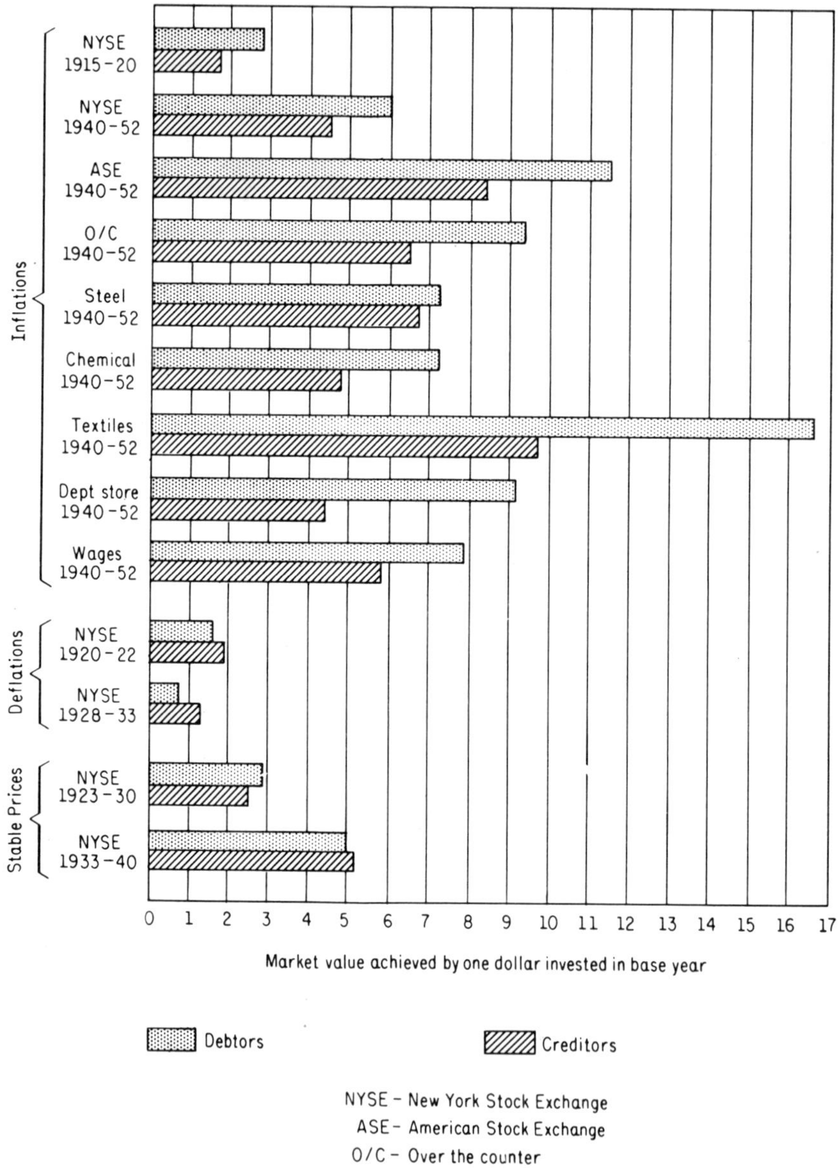

Fig. 2. Market value of equity for debtors as compared to that for creditors (per dollar of base-year common stock value).

probability levels are combined by the R. Fisher chi-square method, the sampling probability falls to below 1 chance in 10,000.

To test whether the results are attributable to inflation rather than to a hidden factor which makes the better firms become net monetary debtors, the deflationary episodes were also considered. In the two deflations of 1921–22 and 1928–1933, the firms were again classified according to whether they were persistently net monetary debtors or creditors. In the short deflation of 1921–22, each firm in the sample maintained its monetary status during the entire period. In the 1928–1933 episode, one deviation was permitted. In both deflations the net monetary creditors did better than the net monetary debtors—just the opposite of the finding for inflations and in conformance with the predictions of the Keynes-Fisher model. The sampling probability levels are small, being less than 5 percent for the short deflation of 1920–22 and less than 0.1 percent for 1929–1932. The combined sampling probability is less than 0.01. Finally, for the periods of price stability of 1923–1930 and 1933–1940, a similar classification of firms revealed no difference in performance between the net monetary creditors and the net monetary debtors, again in conformance with the Keynes-Fisher hypothesis as modified here. These results are also given in Table 1.

But what about the Mitchell-Hamilton wage-lag hypothesis and its implications for business profits? Possibly labor intensiveness is correlated with net monetary status. Under these circumstances, the wage lag, while unrevealed, might yet be operative. To explore this possibility as well as the possibility that growth might be correlated with debtor-creditor status, a sample of 113 firms listed on the New York Stock Exchange was obtained. These firms were the entire population of industrials that reported wage bills some time during the interval 1940 to 1952. Three variables—(i) net monetary debtor or creditor status per dollar of equity, (ii) wages paid per year per dollar of equity, and (iii) yearly sales per dollar of equity—were evaluated for potential predictive content by means of partial correlation analysis. (Equity values were determined by the market price of shares.) And in order to avoid violating assumptions underlying probability tests of significance for correlation analysis, ranks for the three independent variables were used.

The results of this analysis revealed that *only* net monetary status was correlated with relative stock price changes, and that this correlation was in the predicted direction. Moreover, the chance that this observation would be produced by random sampling from a population characterized by an absence of this correlation is less than 1 in 1000. This evidence is completely consistent with the hypothesis that the wage lag is inoperative—that is, that the imperfection of the labor market postulated by the wage lag theorists is nonexistent. Consequently, these results must be regarded as evidence against the hypothesis that a wage lag increases business profits during inflation. However, one must not lose sight of the fact that this is only partial evidence, from a nonrandom sample consisting of 113 firms.

CONCLUSION

These results, reported here for the first time, while constituting overwhelming evidence in support of the Keynes-Fisher reasoning about the bias in interest rates during inflation, fail to support their conclusion that business firms gain through inflation. The frequency of debtors in the business population is not great enough to justify Keynes and Fisher's sweeping statements about the gains of business enterprise through inflation. This evidence also suggests that the Keynes-Fisher theorizing about the effects of inflation is not specific to business enterprises; it is a general theory of wealth transfers caused by inflation and is equally applicable to individuals. What count are monetary asset and monetary liability positions and not the type of economic activity in which one engages.

Especially pertinent to much of the current discussion of the consequences of inflation is that the present evidence, by validating the wealth-transfer effect from monetary creditors to monetary debtors (and rejecting the wage-lag hypothesis), verifies the implication that inflation is basically a "tax" on creditors in favor of debtors. Inflation constitutes a tax on the wealth of individuals to the extent that they are holders of money-type assets rather than savers, wage-earners, businessmen, widows, orphans, or retired schoolteachers.

These results have implications for the adjustment of personal investment and wealth portfolios (including not only stocks, but bonds, life insurance, mortgages, charge accounts, cash holdings, and so on) in order to hedge against inflation or to profit if inflation comes. Similar reasoning applies to the management of investment, pension, and trust funds.

3

Price Relationship of Equities to Profit and Fiscal Outlook*

William Freund

I sometimes think that to forecast the short-run fluctations of the stock market you have to be something more than an economist able to forecast business—that you really need to be an expert in mass psychology. Since I cannot qualify in this field, I am going to refrain from making any predictions as to what stock prices are likely to be next week, next month, or even next quarter. What I hope to do, is to place the market for common stock in some perspective, to discuss the basic factors likely to influence common stock averages during the decade ahead. In particular, my concern will be with the influence of fiscal and monetary policies and the growth of corporate profits on the Standard & Poor's index of 425 industrial stocks. During the past three years, we have been through a period which has required economists to abandon many of their most dearly held maxims of what typically happens in a period of expansion. As you know, the Federal Reserve System has pursued relatively easy money policies in an effort to prolong the present expansion and to push the nation's output nearer the full-employment level. Contrary to other periods of sharp business expansion, long-term rates have fluctuated within an unbelievably narrow channel. Only short-term rates were permitted to edge higher, and this was done not because of any concern about the possibility of an overheating of the economy but to prevent the outflow of short-term funds to money market centers overseas. Short-term rates have come so close to long-term rates that if there is any further narrowing of yields the differential will be wiped out altogether. In the past three years, then, economists have had to learn that a strong economic upswing need not be accompanied by rising long-term rates and that in the present environment short-term rates are more a reflection of international conditions than domestic monetary needs. Relatively easy money in a period of business expansion favors rising stock prices.

*From *The Commercial and Financial Chronicle,* Vol. 201, No. 8458 (March 25, 1965). Reprinted by permission of *The Commercial and Financial Chronicle,* 25 Park Place, New York, New York 10007.

An address by Dr. Freund before the second annual Conference on Basic Forces Affecting Equities, New York University, Graduate School of Business Administration, New York City, Feb 18, 1965. Dr. Edward Zinbarg, Economist, Prudential Insurance Company of America, provided many of the relationships developed in this paper.

But in the past four years, another significant change has taken place, one which has had a profound effect on corporate profits and on stock prices. Again, I think the lessons to be learned are important to anyone considering the future trend of stock prices. During 1964, we cut both individual and corporate income taxes in an amount well over $10 billion. What made the income tax reduction of 1964 particularly significant is that it constituted a major departure from the counter-cyclical tax policy which economists have been recommending for a long time. As you know, economists have generally been agreed that the Federal Government ought to run a deficit in a period of recession if this deficit is later made good through a surplus during the next period of prosperity.

In short, counter-cyclical policy, which had been so widely endorsed, was based on the belief that the Federal budget ought to be balanced not in any one year but over the course of a business cycle. I think the *London Economist* was right when it termed the tax cut of 1964 as "an unrecognized economic revolution." For the first time we cut taxes in a period of prosperity, in a period when the economy was clearly moving upward. The purpose of the tax cut was not to fill in any trough in business activity, but rather to generate a still faster economic growth during the expansion phase of the cycle. It was not a counter-cyclical measure; it was a policy for speeding up the longer-term trend of growth. Clearly, if this policy is pursued in the future it marks a new concept in fiscal policy, one less concerned with a cycle and more concerned with longer waves of growth. As you know, the theory behind the tax cut was simply to stimulate the expansion of wages and profits and dividends to such an extent as to swell Treasury tax receipts. It was hoped that the strong economy would ultimately produce such large Federal revenues as to make the Government's deficit less with a tax cut than it would have been without one. This fiscal experiment proved a brilliant success. Certainly, it has convinced a lot of skeptics that we need not be satisfied with a below-par rate of economic growth.

What does this mean for the future and particularly for stock prices? I think that we will place much less reliance on monetary policy. The Federal Reserve will increasingly become the guardian of our balance of international payments. The Treasury, on the other hand, will show an unprecedented concern for economic stability and growth. From time to time, the fiscal innovation of 1964 will be repeated. I would not be surprised, for example, to see another major tax cut become effective in mid-1966 or early 1967. As a result, we will probably have fewer periods of economic decline or even temporary periods of stagnation. The emphasis will be on growth. As the Queen said in Alice in Wonderland, "If you want to get somewhere, you must run at least twice as fast." How I am not predicting twice as fast a rate of growth—that would be preposterous. But I am forecasting that we will have fewer periods when we merely stand still.

RESURGENCE IN 1967

Let me add at this point that I am particularly optimistic about our chances for a rapid rate of economic growth, spontaneously generated, in the late 1960's and early 1970's. Although we have seen a good rate of growth in the early 1960's, they have, in a sense, been years of transition. From an economic point of view, the postwar period of heavy demands, swollen first by the great depression and then by war came to an end in 1957. A new wave of rapidly rising demands will get underway about 1967 when the so-called "postwar babies" reach marriageable age, form their own households, and enter the market for new homes, television sets, refrigerators, washing machines, home furnishings and the like. This natural strengthening of market forces will also be supported by a heavy replacement demand which will come into the market about that time. The large number of appliances which consumers bought in the late 1940's and 1950's will be in need of replacement. Thus, we are nearing the end of a decade when heavy reliance had to be placed upon the stimulation of accelerated depreciation allowances for business, tax credits for capital investment, and tax reductions for both corporations and individuals. I am optimistic that the proper mix of fiscal-monetary policies, together with these natural market forces, will provide an above-average rate of economic growth during the coming decade.

CURRENT GREAT TRANSITION

There is another reason I am optimistic about the longer-run future of the American economy. A very profound social change has been going on under our noses and it is perhaps because we have been to close to it that so many have failed to recognize it. Professor Kenneth Boulding underscores this development in his recent book *The Meaning of the Twentieth Century*. Professor Boulding calls it "the institutionalization of research and development." We are undergoing, he says, one of the great transitions of mankind, one which is in the same category of fundamental change as the industrial revolution itself. We are developing in the United States a knowledge industry which systematically devotes itself to research, scholarship, and innovation. The search for knowledge is being stressed as never before, not only at the universities, where it has always been taking place, but within American enterprise. Although we are already among the most developed of the world's countries, although we are at an age when one might expect a slowing down in our rate of economic growth, we stand at the brink of an age in which an accelerating rate of economic growth is being fostered through institutionalized research and development. If we can manage to avoid blowing ourselves up, or as Professor Boulding fears, becoming sapped of energy and ambition, we may see the beginning of the brightest period in America's economic history.

CORPORATE PROFITS AND STOCK PRICES

I have talked about fiscal-monetary policies and other influences which are likely to give us an above-average rate of economic growth in the years ahead, but I must still answer the question, "Will the nation's rate of economic growth lead to a parallel increase in corporate profits?"

I am going to assume that over long periods of time the trend of stock prices, earnings, and dividends will be approximately equal. Obviously, they will not be identical because price-earnings, price-dividends, and earnings-dividends relationships do change. Nevertheless, if we fit trend lines to Standard & Poor's prices, earnings and dividends for the past half century, we find that all three growth rates were within six-tenths of 1% of each other. Since we cannot expect to be able to forecast such modest deviations, I assume all three variables —prices, earnings and dividends—will grow at the same rate in the future.

It is also reasonable to assume that over the long run it is earning power which is controlling, that prices and dividends reflect earnings rather than vice versa. The question, therefore, remains, "What rate of earnings growth can be expected in the future?" *Will the expansion in the economy be reflected in a similar growth in corporate earnings?"* This, it seems to me, is the most critical question we must ask in pondering the longer-run outlook for common stock prices.

We cannot assume without further analysis that the trend in corporate earnings and the trend in nation's economy will be parallel. As a matter of fact, Chart 1, which shows the ratio of S & P earnings to GNP for the prewar and postwar years, reveals dramatically the extent to which earnings growth has failed to keep pace with GNP growth. The ratio of earnings to GNP has been trending downward. On the basis of this chart alone, it might be reasoned that

CHART 1
Earnings % GNP
(S and P Industrials)

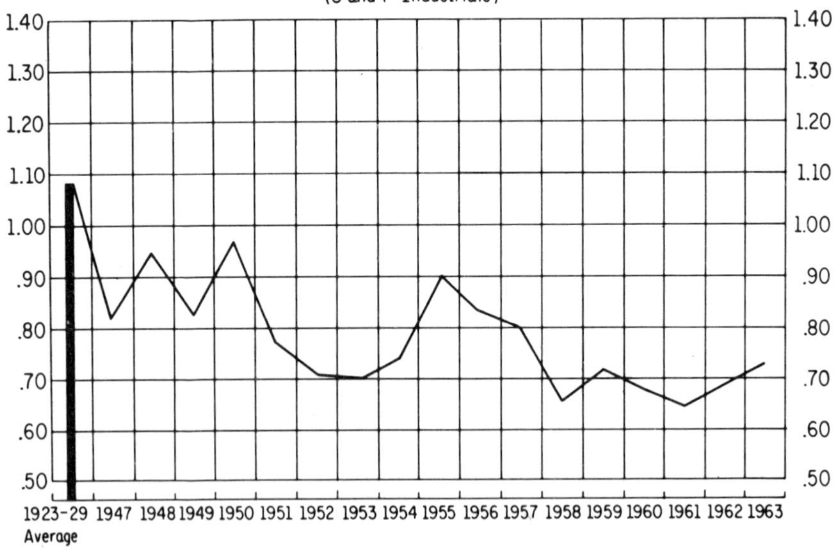

corporate profits will rise less than GNP in the future, and that the same will therefore be true of corporate stock prices. But such an assumption, based solely on a mechanical projection of the past, would be very misleading. Instead of merely assuming that the ratio of corporate earnings to GNP will continue to decline, I want to analyze the factors which have been responsible for the decline and to discuss whether these factors are likely to continue unchanged in the years to come. The succeeding charts are designed to shed some light on the causes of the declining ratio of profits to GNP.

THE EFFECT OF TAXES

One factor which has served as a brake on corporate profits during the postwar years has been the rise in corporate tax rates. Chart 2 shows the ratio of

CHART 2
Federal Income Taxes % Pre-tax Profits
(All Corporations)

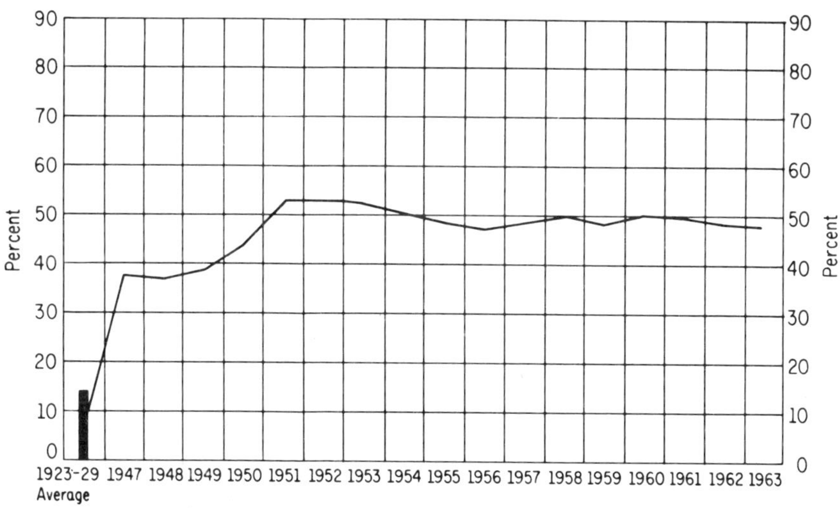

income taxes to pre-tax profits for all U. S. corporations. The postwar average of corporate income taxes to pre-tax profits is more than triple that of the 1920's. Of course, the S&P sample of corporations does not pay actually the same tax rates as all corporations combined, but these are probably fairly good estimates of pre-tax earnings on the index. In Chart 3, the ratio of *pre-tax* earnings, which we have re-calculated, is shown relative to GNP, again for the same time period.

Now quite a different picture emerges. Instead of a down-trend running from the twenties to date, the ratios for the past several years are quite in line with the pre-depression data. The peak ratios of 1950 and 1955 were the abnormal ones!

While stock prices are more a function of after-tax profits, than of pre-tax profits, our concern with the past is primarily as a guide to the future. In the

CHART 3
Pre-tax Earnings* % GNP
(S and P Industrials)

*Estimated

future, corporate income tax rates are not expected to rise—in fact, as I have said, they are likely to be reduced further. Thus, in evaluating the future trend of common stock prices, the trend of pre-tax profits is more relevant than after-tax profits.

But there is another nagging question raised by the chart. Although the recent ratio of pre-tax profits to GNP is similar to that of earlier years, The ratio has declined during the 1950's. Does this connote the beginning of a new long-run problem or is there some factor, not expected to continue in the future, which explains the declining ratio of pre-tax earnings to GNP?

DEPRECIATION

The single most important factor in the poor showing of postwar corporate profits has been rising depreciation charges. Chart 4, which is designed to put the recent magnitudes of depreciation charges into some historical perspective, shows this. It relates depreciation to pre-tax profits, to the book value of stockholders' equity, and to the market value of total plant and equipment. In each case, the ratio rose well above the level of the twenties. Moreover, there has been a recent tendency for the depreciation ratio to level, especially when related to the book values of equity on the S&P industrials.

These data suggest that depreciation charges in the early postwar years were too low for an inflationary economy—lower even than in the noninflationary

CHART 4
Reported Depreciation Charges in Perspective
(All Corporations)

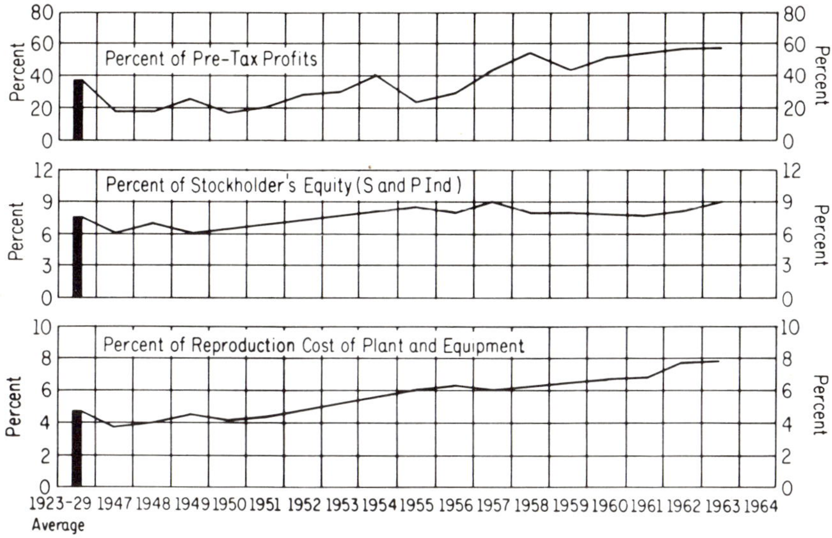

years of the 1920's. Thus, reported profits during the early 1950's were exaggerated.

CASH FLOW

If it is assumed that the ratio of depreciation charges to pre-tax profits have the same pattern for the S&P index as for all corporations–and there is evidence that this assumption is fairly reasonable–an estimate can be made of cash flow on the S&P. This cash flow relationship is shown in Chart 5. Expressed this way, the profit downtrend did not begin in 1950, but in 1955. Let me stress that I am not offering cash flow as a valid measure of profits. Depreciation is a legitimate expense deduction, but it does seem that the postwar trend of *cash flow* is less subject to *artificial* distortion than reported profits and is therefore more pertinent to a discussion of what the future holds in store.

Indeed, it is worth noting that corporate dividends have generally been more closely related to cash flow than to reported profits; and dividends are probably a good reflection of management's views on true profitability.

What these charts show so far is that reported after-tax profits have been declining since the 1920's relative to gross national product, but this trend is largely attributable to rising corporate tax rates which are no longer rising. Pre-tax profits have been declining relative to GNP since 1950, but much of this trend has been due to inadequate depreciation in the early postwar years. Cash flow has been declining relative to GNP only since 1955. Let me focus, therefore, on this most recent period.

CHART 5
Cash Flow % GNP (S and P Industrials)

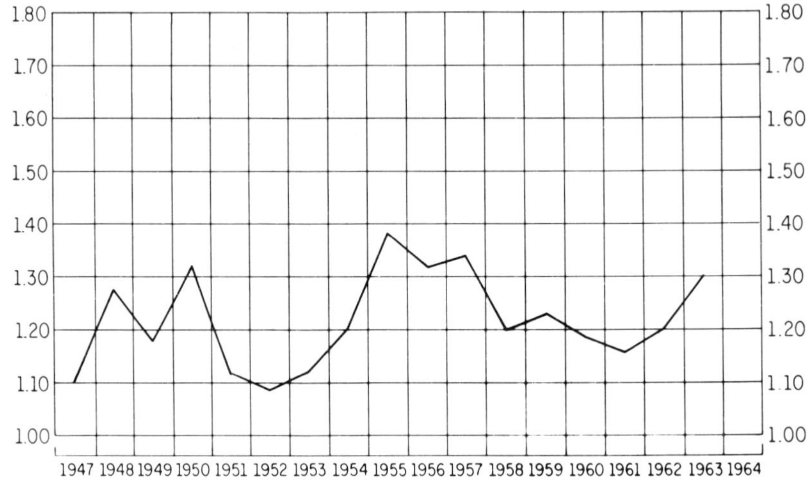

Reported profit plus estimated depreciation

I believe that the declining ratio of cash flow to GNP has been nothing more than a cyclical phenomenon. As you can see from Chart 6, which relates the cash flow to GNP ratio to the rate of utilization of manufacturing capacity, the fit is

CHART 6
Comparison of Cash Flow/GNP Ratio (S and P) with Rate of Utilization of Manufacturing Capacity

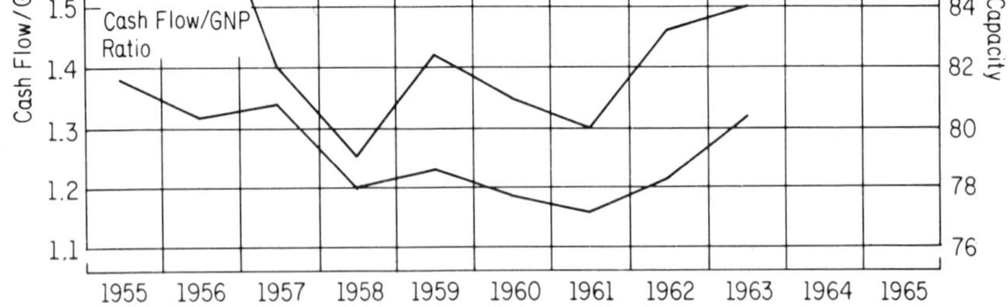

rather good. Thus in the early 1960's, cash flow to GNP declined because our economy was operating too far below its potential. It was largely this under-utilization of manufacturing capacity—not any basic long-run trend—which accounted for the declining ratio of corporate cash flow to GNP. With the upswing in the economy in 1961, corporate cash flow to GNP recovered.

IMPLICATIONS FOR THE FUTURE

This analysis, I believe, is useful not only in explaining some of the factors underlying the behavior of corporate profits during the postwar period but can serve as a guide to the future.

It is true, as many observers have noted in the past, that corporate profits have been a declining percentage of national income during the postwar period. On closer examination, three major factors stand out as causes of the decline: Higher corporate income taxes, rising depreciation charges, and in some years, such as the late 1950's, an underutilization of manufacturing capacity. If all of these factors remained unchanged in the years to come, that is if tax rates and depreciation charges continued to rise and excess productive capacity plagued the economy, one could become pessimistic about the chances of corporate profits keeping pace with the economy. And in turn, one could be pessimistic about the future trend of stock prices.

But I do not believe any of these assumptions are justified and, therefore, my conclusions about the probable trend of stock prices is quite the opposite.

Corporate income taxes in the future will not rise. On the contrary, chances are good that further reductions will be enacted. Depreciation allowances expressed as a percent of pre-tax profits, or stockholders' equity, or the market value of plant and equipment will level. The period of heavily-rising depreciation allowances, stimulated by the postwar boom and depreciation liberalizations, appears near its end. Moreover, I anticipate a rising rate of capacity utilization in the decade ahead. As I have said earlier, I anticipate a full employment economy in the later 1960's sparked by spontaneous forces of consumer demand. Moreover, I anticipate an accelerating rate of productivity and economic growth. For these reasons, I expect corporate profits—that is the dividend-paying ability of U.S. corporations—to rise in line with GNP. In turn, I expect the trend of corporate stock prices to parallel the trend in the nation's economy.

I can put my conclusions into even more specific terms. If my analysis is correct that corporate profits and stock prices will grow at about the same rate as GNP, the *trend* of common stock prices, as measured by the Standard & Poor's Index of Industrials should rise aout 5½% per annum. So as not to be misunderstood, let me underscore that this is a projection of *trend.* We will continue to have fluctuations above and below the trend, much as we have had in the past, reflecting cycles in business activity and occasional excesses in investor psychology. I am not forecasting these cycles. But the long-run trend of stock averages should rise at a rate not far from 5½% per year. This, then, is a measure of the long-run capital gains the patient investor may expect. With dividend yields currently near 3%, the overall return on a large portfolio of common stocks over the long pull be in the neighborhood of 8–8½%, much as it has been for long-term investors in the past.

But, you may ask, why assume a growth rate of 5½%? One of the most impressive features of the American economy has been the stability of long-term economic growth. In real terms, that is apart from price inflation, growth has averaged 3–3½%. For the future, a real rate of growth somewhat above 3½% appears a reasonable assumption. Beyond that, I think we have built enough inflationary biases into our economy that we are likely to get an annual increase of 1½% to 2% in the prices. For these reasons, the total dollar growth of the economy is likely to average about 5½% annually.

SUMMARY

I assume that over the long run earning power will determine equity prices, and that earning power, in turn, will reflect the strong upward momentum of our national economy. Undoubtedly, stock prices will at times become overvalued as optimism and speculative exuberance inflate values to excessive levels. Undoubtedly, too, at other times stock prices will be relatively undervalued as pessimism carries the cycle too far in the other extreme. But over the longer run trend, I believe the broad stock price averages will show a growth trend of about 5½%, of which 3½% will be real growth, 2% inflation. Thus, common stocks will remain a vehicle not only for protecting the investor's purchasing power against the eroding influence of rising prices, but will allow the investor to participate in the long-run expansion of America's economy.

4

A Not-So-New-Era in the Stock Market*

J. Fred Weston †

I. PREVIOUS STUDY

In an article written on the stock market which appeared in early 1956, I made the following statement:

> It would appear that stock prices at the present time are rising in a manner which partakes of both cyclical and secular influences. The cyclical component of current stock market prices is subject to reversal. The secular component, however, promises further growth—a possibility to be recognized by newspaper writers and others dramatizing the stock market whenever it reaches higher levels.[1]

After some statistical analysis and discussion the article concluded as follows:

> In view of the financing needs of corporations in the next decade and the appreciable portion of such external financing that must come from equity sources if balance in the financial structure is to be attained, equity prices must be attractive. While equity financing has increased during the past year relative to previous years, it still has not attained the volume necessary relative to total financial stability needs of corporations. It is reassuring, therefore, to observe that the data presented on the relationship between Gross National Product and stock prices indicate that current stock

*From *Financial Analysts Journal,* Vol. 16, No. 6 (November-December 1960), pp. 57–64. Reprinted by permission of *Financial Analysts Journal.*

†The Bureau of Business and Economic Research of the University of California, Los Angeles, granted research assistance of Robert McKenzie and Rodney Klein to aid in the development of the statistical materials. I am grateful to the members of the Financial Analysts Seminar, under the direction of Marshall D. Ketchum, who invited me to present these ideas while they were not yet fully developed and whose keen criticisms and searching questions contributed greatly to my understanding of the subject. Above all I am indebted to Benjamin Graham who suggested the original topic and whose many insights were drawn upon from numerous discussions.

[1] J. Fred Weston, "The Stock Market in Perspective," *Harvard Business Review* (March-April 1956) p. 75.

prices are not excessively high in terms of long-run secular growth patterns.[2]

The last sentence particularly was ridiculed by well-known and highly regarded financial services shortly after the article appeared. At the time of the article the Dow Jones Industrial Average stood at 442. The article had commented that further rises were likely to be interrupted by cyclical swings of only moderate proportions. The subsequent behavior of the Dow Jones Industrial Average has substantiated this. The average rose from 442 to a level of 525 by early 1957. It dropped back to 420 by the late summer of 1957 and then began another rise which had taken the market to a level of 680 early in 1959 from which position it dropped back to 640 and has since returned to the 680 level at the end of 1959.

Despite the fact that time has dealt kindly with the remarks in that article I should issue a disclaimer. The intent of the article written in 1956 was not to provide a method for forecasting the stock market. The focus of the article was both broader and narrower. It was broader in that it sought to draw upon a wide variety of economic forces which suggested that the performance of the equity markets had to behave in a certain pattern if long-run needs of the economy were to be met. The article was narrower in that it concentrated on only one of the many possible methods that might be used for forecasting the level of the stock market.

The main statistical relationship developed by the article was that the Dow Jones Industrial Average appeared to be related to the total level of business activity in the following manner. The Dow Jones Industrial Average would be equal to 28 points plus .97 Gross National Product. Roughly speaking, in view of the degree of variation in a statistical relationship of this sort, the DJIA appeared to be equal to about the level of GNP plus 28 points. For illustration, with GNP estimated at some 480 billion dollars for the year 1959, one would expect on the basis of the formula the year end average of the DJIA to be roughly in the area of 500.

The DJIA is at time of this writing around 680 which gives us two figures for comparison. However, I wish to underscore and state as emphatically as I can that the purpose of this formula was not to provide a forecasting device as such. The burden of the article and the main function of this formula was simply to emphasize that with the growth in the economy one could expect a growth in corporate earnings, a growth in corporate dividends and a proportional rise in the Dow Jones Industrial Average. The article emphasized that it was not surprising that in 1955 the Dow Jones Industrial Average had risen above its 1929 high, but that the surprising thing was that it took a quarter of a century for the DJIA to accomplish it. The surprising part of this relationship could

[2] Ibid., p. 79.

follow either from the fact that the market was too high in 1929 or that it made its recovery too slowly in the subsequent 25 years.

But the point I sought to emphasize and to underscore was that with the growth in the economy one could expect stock prices to grow and that one could expect that the long term pattern of growth in stock prices would be interrupted from time to time by relatively moderate bear markets. The article suggested also that the experience of 1929–1933 was not characteristic of the cyclical behavior of the economy as a whole nor of the stock market.

But nevertheless, a formula was presented and since there is a difference between the results indicated by the formula and the present level of the stock market, it raises a fundamental and nagging question. Is the stock market at this writing some 200 points too high and if so what will be the consequences? This article, therefore, will be devoted to a forefrontal attack on the question: Are there any basic economic foundations for judging the value of the stock market?

II. BASIC ECONOMIC FACTORS

As background in approaching the subject matter of how to evaluate the level of the market, certain fundamental economic characteristics have to be taken into account. These are set forth in Table 1. Since the nature of the items in Table 1 are relatively familiar, since they have been alluded to in one form or other from time to time in the past, they will not be discussed in detail.

Rather these materials can be organized more briefly in terms of demand and supply factors as set out in Table 2 it is useful to organize the factors influencing the stock market into demand and supply factors as a necessary and valuable reminder that stock market prices are prices and as prices they are subject to the same fundamental influences.[3]

Numerous approaches have been made to price-setting in the securities market. These different methods reflect demand and supply factors in different degrees and to a different extent. The next part of this paper will deal with a

[3]In this connection it might be useful to observe parenthetically, but nevertheless very much to the point a paragraph from Bernard Baruch's autobiography in which he observed that the most valuable course he took in college was a course in economics from Professor Simon Newcomb at the New York University. Professor Simon Newcomb made an observation which Baruch said he remembered in his after years and was the formula by which he became a multimillionaire. The formula was this: when prices go above their historical norms the quantity demanded tends to fall off and the quantity supplied tends to increase and as a consequence prices will fall. When prices are below their historical normal level the quantity demanded is higher and the quantity supplied begins to contract; as a consequence prices will return to their historically normal level. Baruch said that most investors fail to keep this historical perspective and when prices are high they become convinced that they are going to go still higher; when they are low investors become convinced that the country never will recover and stay pessimistic. By having this sense of historical perspective Baruch said he had the courage of his convictions repeatedly and by having the courage of his convictions he became a rich man. This illustrates why I think it worthwhile paying homage to basic factors of supply and demand even when talking about the security markets.

TABLE 1

Fundamental Factors Influencing Market Levels

A. Earnings and Dividends
    1. Dividends (current)
    2. Earnings (current)
    3. Number of shares of common stock outstanding
    4. Trends in profits
        a. capitalization rate changes
        b. relative capital and labor costs
        c. growth rate relative to the industry and other firms in the industry
        d. possible union encroachment upon the profit margins
        e. government policies, general business conditions (i.e. level of GNP) and industry factors as they effect the firm's profit outlook
        f. competitive structure of the industry

B. Market Psychology
    1. Psychological factors as one determinant of capitalization rates
    2. Popularity of various forms of equity (i.e. mutual funds, warrants attached, etc.)
    3. Popularity of romantic growth industries
    4. Attractiveness of small firms for venture capital
    5. Advertisement and notoriety from merger plans

C. Attractiveness of Equities Relative to Other Forms of Real and Financial Investment
    1. Amount of savings
    2. Allocation of savings between debt and equity
    3. Flow of funds to institutional investors (who may or may not be committed to common stock investments)
    4. Potential demand arising from the sale of variable annuities by life insurance companies
    5. Rate of capital investment by business firms
    6. Dividend policies of corporations
    7. Expectations about future price level behavior (inflation)

D. Government Policies
    1. Federal Reserve policy with regard to (1) stock margin requirements, (2) the money supply (i.e. availability of funds), and (3) interest rate
    2. Treasury spending and financing policies
    3. Allocation of funds and credit to designated economic sectors (i.e. housing, small business, etc.)
    4. Tax policies as they effect (1) form of business organization (i.e. corp., partnership, etc.), (2) profit margins directly through rate changes, (3) depreciation and accelerated depreciation
    5. Tax policies influencing the attractiveness of stocks to investors (i.e. capital gain provisions, credit for dividends)
    6. State and local tax policies and attitudes toward industry

E. Foreign Capital Flows
    1. International outlook
    2. Flow of capital between nations
    3. Stock values abroad
    4. Relative growth rates of U.S. vs. foreign countries
    5. Profitability of foreign investment by U.S. firms
    6. U.S. government assistance to developed and underdeveloped foreign countries

TABLE 2

Fundamental Factors Organized as Supply and Demand Influence

A. Demand
   1. Earnings
   2. Dividends
   3. Growth in the economy, industries and firms
   4. Competitive structure of industries
   5. Tax patterns
   6. Price level movements
   7. State of confidence

B. Supply
   1. Interest Rates
   2. Amount and distribution of savings
   3. Capital spending programs by business, government and individuals
   4. Level of disposable income and its distribution
   5. Amount of stock market credit
   6. Money market conditions, especially Treasury and Federal Reserve Policies

summary review of different approaches to setting the normal value of the Dow Jones Industrial Average. I will organize these different methods in terms of the underlying theory or logic involved in the method whether the authors of the method recognized the basic theory implicit or not. One of the functions of this exposition will be to lay bare the theory that is implicit in these methods since every valuation of stock market values or individual business firms does have embodied in it an implicit theory. This presentation shall not give the author of the method because it is not the intention here to criticize anyone or to seek to discredit any security service by referring to its method of calculating the value of the Dow Jones Industrial Average. Furthermore, since the emphasis is simply on different approaches and techniques, it is unessential as to what particular group would be identified with the method.

III. EXTRAPOLATION OF HISTORICAL DATA

One fundamental approach to setting stock market values is a direct extrapolation of historical data. Table 3 sets forth a summary of methods which use

TABLE 3
Direct Extrapolation of the Future Level of the DJIA by Use of Historical Data, 1954 Base

Name of Formula	Formula	1954	1959	1960	1965	1970
Arithmetic	DJIA = 400 + 10n	400	450	460	510	560
Geometric	DJIA = 400 $(1.03)^n$	400	463.7	477.6	553.7	641.9
Moving Average	3% stable growth rate	400	463.7	477.6	553.7	641.9
Warranted Value	2% growth rate	400	441.6	450.5	497.4	549.1
Actual DJIA		400	680			

the technique of extrapolating historical data by a trend line. While most methods actually involve some implicit historical extrapolations, none are so direct in their reliance upon historical data as is this method.

The first method set out in Table 3 is an arithmetic trend line, obtained by fitting a regression line to past data. Starting from a level of 400 in 1954, the equation indicates that the stock market will rise by 10 points a year. This method is clearly invalid, because economic time series conform most generally to geometric growth curves. Witness the frequent references to the growth of productivity or Gross National Product at 2.5 or 3 or 3.5, etc., percent per year.

Accordingly, the geometric growth curve formula in Table 3 appears more applicable. It is in the form of the growth of the DJIA at a compound interest rate of 3%. But even this formula suggests values some 200 points below current levels.

The two remaining formulae in Table 3 are basically the same in concept as the geometric growth curve. A moving average will behave the same as the geometric growth curve, if the cyclical component of prices is regular and the length of the moving average is chosen to coincide with the period of the cycle.[4]

The warranted value formula is based upon an exhaustive study of the relationship between the growth of the economy as a whole and the Standard and Poor's stock index. The relationship was developed for a purpose other than forecasting and is not to be evaluated as a forecasting technique. It is included here only to indicate what its use as a forecasting relationship would suggest for the present and prospective levels of stock prices. Along with the other methods in the group, it suggests that the 1959 year-end level of the stock market is about 240 points too high.

IV. NORMS APPLIED TO HISTORICAL DATA TO AVERAGE CYCLICAL VALUES

This group of approaches is characterized by the application of norms developed on the basis of data and experience to historical averages. The purpose of the averaging is to eliminate cyclical influences.

The leading formulation in Table 4 is the Central Value Theory. The Central Value Theory seeks to calculate a plausible value of the group of stocks in the Dow Jones Industrial Average to provide a basis for judging whether the actual values of the DJIA are too high or too low on the basis of historical standards. The formula is:

The Central Value of the DJIA	equals	Average of the previous ten years' earnings	divided by	2 times the current Aaa bond rate

[4]For an elaboration and illustration of these technical relationships, see J. F. Weston, "Some Theoretical Aspects of the Construction of Formula Timing Plans," *Journal of Business* (October 1949).

TABLE 4

Norms Applied to Historical Data to Average Cyclical Values

Name of Formula	Formula	1954	1959	1960	1965	1970
Central Value Theory	10 yrs Average Earnings / 2 (Aaa Corp. bond yield)	400*	379	398	488	565
Dividend Central Value Theory	Current Dividends / 10 yr Average Yield	400†	464	505	701	896
Intrinsic Value Theory	12.5 (10 yr Average Earnings) + .2 (Current Book Value)	400‡	458	470	572	665
Actual Year-End DJIA		400§	466 680	484	645	859

*Based on 4% corporate bond yield; earnings growth of 4% per annum.
†Based on dividend growth of 4%; growth of DJIA of 6%.
‡Book Value assumed to grow at 3%; earnings at 3%.
§Book Value assumed to grow at 5%; earnings at 6%.

The Central Value Theory has a strong foundation in economic logic behind it. The numerator contains a measure of earnings which is the strongest single influence in determining the demand for common stocks. The denominator is a measure of the competing uses for funds and gets at the supply side of funds that will be in the market for the purchase of equity securities. Doubling the bond rate implies that common stocks should sell at double the yield basis of bonds. Application of formula results in values of the DJIA substantially below recent levels.

A variant of the earnings formula is the Dividend Central Value Theory. While the Central Value Theory employs an average of past earnings and a current capitalization factor, the Dividend Central Value Theory employs current dividends and an average of past capitalization factors. The application of this formula results in values for the DJIA that are about one-fourth higher than the Central Value Theory, but about one-third lower than recent prices.

The Intrinsic Value approach applies a historical norm to an average of past earnings and adjusts this value by adding something for the accounting (historical) measure of the book value of a company's common stock. The method proceeds on the logic of capitalizing past earnings, but recognizes that book values may have some influence. Writers with some economic background are likely to deprecate the influence of book values and emphasize that "future earnings determine current prices and values."

But there is a profound reverse economic logic embodied in the use of the book value element in the Intrinsic Value formula. If earnings on book value have been below some norm (about 12 to 14% after taxes for U.S. industries), stockholders and managements may be expected "to do something about the situation" and earnings may potentially improve. If earnings on book value are much above historical norms, additional investment will be attracted into the industry and earnings are likely to decline. Thus the way the book value element is used in the Intrinsic Value formula, it is an indirect technique for bringing in implicit future earnings forecasts.

The application of the Intrinsic Value Theory results in valuations of the DJIA at about the same levels of the Dividend Central Value Theory.

The methods for valuing common stocks described in this section were developed in the period of the economic development of the United States when the problem of ironing out the business cycle was the paramount intellectual preoccupation. It was difficult to make optimistic assumptions about alternative attractive rates of growth when the problem of secular stagnation preempted the forums of writing and discussion. But if strong long-term growth is at all a realistic postulate, it is erroneous to average past data to calculate plausible current values. The Dividend Central Value Theory is in my judgment the best of the three formulas of this group in that it utilized current dividends and the item averaged, an interest or capitalization factor, is one which does not have a secular growth trend. However, in concept, the other formulas in this section could utilize current or future earnings without affecting the general form of the formula. Such shifts represent a modification of the theory of the price-making forces. We now turn to other types of applications.

V. HISTORICAL NORMS APPLIED TO FUTURE PROJECTIONS

Involved formulas abound for applying historical norms to future projections. When the complex formulae are analyzed, it is found that they in fact represent a relatively mechanical relationship between:

earnings–a multiplier–prices
or
dividends–a multiplier–prices

Present space does not permit a detailed translation of complicated valuation methods into their formal elements, but the basic relationships of these approaches are readily converted to simple underlying elements.[5] Admittedly some of the logic and diversity of forces are not portrayed; on the other hand, often the formulae contain several elements that are jointly correlated, so that only one factor need be used anyhow. Thus the most complicated formulae generally can be approximated roughly by a multiplier relationship representing alternative formulations of applying a multiplier to future earnings or dividends as shown in Table 5.

Table 5 sets forth the application of the Central Value Theory adjusted first for growth in earnings resulting from the growth in the economy and then adjusts for growth in earnings and asset values resulting from price level infla-

[5] For illustrations, see Benjamin Graham, *The Intelligent Investor* (2d ed.; New York: Harper & Brothers, 1959), p. 49.

TABLE 5
Norms Based on Historical Relationships Applied to Projections of Earnings and Dividends for Future Years

Name of Formula	Formula	1954	1959	1960	1965	1970
Capitalizing future earnings	10 X 3% growth	400	383	394	457	530
	5% "	400	398	418	533	680
	12 3% "	400	459	473	548	636
	5% "	400	477	501	640	816
	15 3% "	400	574	591	686	795
	5% "	400	608	645	865	1,154
	5% "	400	608	645	865	1,154
	20 3% "	400	766	788	914	1,060
	5% "	400	811	859	1,153	1,539
Capitalizing future dividends	16 3% "	400	368	378	439	509
	5% "	400	382	401	512	653
	20 3% "	400	459	473	549	636
	5% "	400	477	501	640	816
	25 3% "	400	574	591	686	795
	5% "	400	597	627	800	1,021
Central Value Theory adjusted for growth	Next year's earnings / 2 Aaa rate	3%	438	451	523	606
		4%	451	469	571	694
		5%	464	487	622	794
Central Value Theory adjusted for growth and inflation	Next year's earnings / 2 Aaa − 2		493*	508	589	682
			696†	731	933	1,190
Correlation with GNP	DJIA = 28 + .97 GNPt + 1		475‡	488	562	647
			544§	575	760	1,007
Growth Formula $8(G)^2(E)$	3% growth		510‖	513	560	649
	5% "		661‖	693	923	1,292

*Based on Aaa = 5% and Earnings Growth Rate of 3%.
†Based on Aaa = 4% and Earnings Growth Rate of 5%.
‡Based on 3% growth of GNP.
§Based on 6% growth of GNP.
‖G is the ratio of future decade earnings to past decade earnings. Essentially, it applies a variable multiplier to earnings depending on the growth rate.

tion. Finally, Table 5 sets forth my GNP formula based on a one year's earnings lead and a special type of growth formula which approximates the same results as the GNP formula.

The results of the application of the formulas in Table 5 exhibit a broad set of patterns in which the crucial variables are threefold. (1) The rate of future growth of earnings based on the growth of the economy in real terms, (2) the rate at which price inflation may take place in the country in the future, and (3) the level of interest rates at any particular time and whether the future of interest rates will have any secular long-term growth or secular long-term decline.

An examination of the results set forth in Table 5 indicates that the present levels of common stock prices lean heavily upon the assumption of a strong and uninterrupted rate of future growth in real earnings, substantial price inflation, but without secular growth in interest or capitalization factors. Recent levels of stock prices seem also to have discounted the influence of cyclical movements in common stock prices as well. The movement of stock prices between 1953–1959 represents first a catching up with past movements of GNP of the economy as a whole and then sharply rising above it.

While GNP has grown in a continued strong secular upward pattern, corporate profits after tax have failed to parallel the growth in GNP since 1950. Long-term bond yields are approaching the level which had been experienced in the pre--1930's era. Recent levels of the stock market are based on expectations which depart from patterns which have obtained historically. The basic question arises then as to whether such a departure from past patterns is justified.

VI. INCREASED ECONOMIC STABILITY–INCREASED STOCK PRICE INSTABILITY

Note that there is an important distinction here. The argument is not whether there will be growth in GNP in the future, the argument is not whether there will be some price level inflation, the argument is not that interest rates will have no secular trend or no cyclical fluctuations, the argument revolves over the degree of magnitude of these movements.

Table 6 analyzes the past behavior of the Dow Jones Industrial Average in terms of the amount and percent of changes from year to year as well as compound annual rates of growth over selected time periods. Of all the historical time segments analyzed, only the 1920's including 1929 and the 1950's including the latter years of the 1950's exhibit growth rates of over 10%. Growth rates in the Dow Jones Industrial Average of 4–6% would be plausible, but these are not the kinds of growth rates which have been exhibited in the stock market since 1953. Real questions arise as to the sustainability of growth rates of the order of magnitude of some 14% per annum.

There are many who urge that there is a basis for changing the fundamental approach for looking at the future for earnings dividends and stock prices on the following grounds.

1. There is a growth imperative in the economy which we have never had before.

2. The rise of pension funds with large investments in common stock.

3. The rise of mutual investment funds which brings the small investor into the market on a larger basis.

4. The general tendency of institutional investors to invest in common stock to a greater degree.

5. The Employment Act of 1946 which charges the government with increased responsibility for sustaining a high level of business activity.

These and numerous other factors might be cited in support of the view that

TABLE 6

Growth Analysis of the DJIA, 1920–1959

Year	Year End Value DJIA	Amount of Change	Percent Change	Year	Year End Value DJIA	Amount of Change	Percent Change
1920	72.0	–		1945	192.9	40.6	26.7
1	81.1	9.1	12.6	6	177.2	(15.7)	(8.9)
2	98.7	17.6	21.7	7	181.2	4.0	2.3
3	95.5	(3.2)	(3.2)	8	177.3	(3.9)	(2.2)
4	120.5	25.0	26.2	9	200.1	22.8	12.9
1925	156.7	36.2	30.0	1950	235.4	35.3	17.6
6	157.2	0.5	0.3	1	269.2	33.8	14.4
7	202.4	45.2	28.9	2	291.9	22.7	8.4
8	300.0	97.6	48.2	3	280.9	(11.0)	(3.8)
9	248.5	(51.5)	(17.2)	4	404.4	123.5	44.0
1930	164.6	(83.9)	(33.8)	1955	488.4	84.0	20.8
1	77.9	(86.7)	(52.7)	6	499.5	11.1	2.3
2	59.9	(18.0)	(23.1)	7	435.7	(63.8)	(12.8)
3	99.9	40.0	66.8	8	583.6	147.9	33.9
4	104.0	4.1	4.1	9	680.0	96.4	16.5
1935	144.1	40.1	38.6				
6	179.9	35.8	24.8				
7	120.8	(59.1)	(32.9)				
8	154.8	34.0	28.1				
9	150.2	(4.6)	(3.0)				
1940	131.1	(19.1)	(12.7)				
1	111.0	(20.1)	(15.3)				
2	119.4	8.4	7.6				
3	135.9	16.5	13.8				
4	152.3	16.4	12.1				

Growth Rates (Compound Annual Rates)		Growth Rate
(1920)–(1929)	=3.451	=14.5%
(1920–22)–(1928–29)	=3.269	=17%
(1920–22)–(1946)	=2.112	= 5%
(1920–22)–(1951–53)	=3.444	= 4%
(1920–22)–(1959)	=8.105	= 5.5%
(1946)–(1959)	=3.837	=11%
(1920–22)–(1957–59)	=6.749	= 5%
(1949)–(1959)	=3.398	=13.5%

the future holds new growth and stability in stock market prices. However, the validity of some of these arguments can be seriously questioned.[6] However, whether one agrees or not with the skepticism toward the permanence of some of the recent manifestations in stock market behavior or whether one holds that these are relatively characteristic behavior patterns for middle and advanced stages of a bull market, the following observations must be made. There is a curious paradox of inverse relationships involved here. It might be referred to as the rubber band theorem. If there were indeed a basis for the expectation that there will be greater stability in underlying economic growth patterns including earnings and dividends in the future and even if we agree with the general view that economic recessions in the future may be less violent on the average than they have been in the past, this promise and even assurance of greater general economic stability in the future may in itself be productive of greater instability

[6] Benjamin Graham, "Stock Market Warnings: Danger Ahead," *California Management Review* (Spring 1960), pp. 34–41.

in stock market prices in the future, and provide a basis for very healthy skepticism toward recent levels in the stock market.

For although earnings and dividends growth may continue at a 3 or 4 or 5% rate, there remains the question of how many years of future growth is appropriately reflected in current stock market prices. There is no intellectual foundation for setting an appropriate value.[7] As a consequence, the attainable increased stability in the rate of acutal growth of earnings and dividends in the future *may produce greater instability in stock market prices* becuase the optimistic factors will tend to be over-valued during periods of optimism as they have in the past and tend to be discounted in periods of pessimism.

VII. PROSPECTIVE TRENDS AND CYCLES IN STOCK PRICES

Table 7 sets forth characteristic percent rates of change in leading economic variables over the characteristic postwar business cycles. It indicates the percentage decline during the characteristic recession year, the percentage of rise in the first upswing year, the second upswing year, and the third upswing year, and then the cycle is repeated. The average growth rate per annum for the cycle is also indicated in the table.

TABLE 7

Patterns of Cyclical Change in the U.S. Economy

	FRB Index	GNP	Profits	DJIA Earnings	DJIA Dividends	DJIA
Recession year	− 6%	0	−20%	−20%	−4%	−25%
First up-swing year	10%	10%	30%	30%	8%	30%
Second up-swing year	5%	5%	8%	8%	5%	10%
Third up-swing year	2%	3%	0	0	4%	5%
Average Growth Rate per annum	3%	4.5%	4.5%	4.5%	3.25%	5%

Applying these percentages beginning in 1957 starting with 1958 as a recession year, through 1970 provides the result set forth in Table 8, which sets out trend values of Gross National Product, cyclical values of Gross National Product, the percent change in the cyclical values of GNP, the trend value in the earnings of the Dow Jones Industrial Average, the cyclical value of the Dow Jones Industrial Average earnings, the percent changes in the cyclical value of the Dow Jones Industrial Average earnings and the Triple A bond rate. On the basis of these postulates about the future behavior of these critical variables, the consequences are set forth in Table 9. This table begins with the value of the Dow Jones Industrial Average based on the regression with Gross National Product which would also approximate the value detained by multiplying the

[7]David Durand, "Growth Stocks and the St. Petersburg Paradox," *Journal of Finance* (September 1957).

trend value of expected future earnings on the Dow Jones Industrial Average by some fixed multiplier. Next it sets out a cyclical value of the DJIA based on a modification of the Central Value Theory in which a future growth in cyclical earnings is assumed and in which the cyclical bond rate is employed. Finally, a third element indicates what the level of stock prices would be if the economic values suggested by the first and second column are deviated from through speculative influences.

TABLE 8

Trends and Cycles in Factors Determining Security Prices

Year	Trend Value GNP (.bil.)	Cyclical Value GNP (.bil.)	Percent Change in Cyclical Value– GNP	Trend Value DJIA– Earnings	Cyclical Value DJIA– Earnings	Percent Change in Cyclical Value– Earnings	Aaa Rate
1957	442	442	–	35	–	–	3.8
1958R	464	442	0.0	37	28	–	4.1
1959	490	480	0.9	40	36	29	4.6
1960	517	516	0.8	42	42	17	5.0
1961	545	535	0.4	45	44	5	5.0
1962R	575	535	0.0	47.6	34	(23)	4.0
1963	607	590	1.0	50.6	44	29	4.6
1964	641	635	0.8	53.7	54	23	5.0
1965	676	670	0.6	57	57	6	5.0
1966R	713	675	0.1	60.4	45	(21)	4.0
1967	752	735	0.9	64.1	59	31	4.6
1968	794	780	0.6	67.8	67	14	5.0
1969	837	835	0.7	72	72	8	5.0
1970R	883	840	0.1	76.2	50	(31)	4.0
Growth Rate	5.5%			6%			

This third relationship in Table 9 indicates a value of 700 for the end of 1959, a value which was approximated by the actual behavior of the market in 1959. If characteristic cyclical patterns were followed, the market could potentially drop to a level of 340 by 1961 which would represent a 50% drop from present levels in the Dow Jones Industrial Average.

It would be nice to say that it is not likely that market would have the speculative rises or declines set out in Table 9. It is likewise tempting to conclude as others have done that having had the excess on the upside it is very likely or that history suggests that we will have the speculative deficiencies on the downside.

My position, however, is neither of these. My position is that because of the expectation of increased stability in underlying economic factors the very continued realization of that increased stability and growth are likely to lead to speculative excesses. Increased economic stability and growth set a higher floor to which the Dow Jones Industrial Average is likely to decline on economic

TABLE 9

Trends and Cycles in Security Prices

Year	DJIA Based on GNP*	Cyclical Value DJIA†	Percent Change	Speculative Value of DJIA‡	Percent above and (below) DJIA Based on GNP
1957	478	500		600	20
1958R	503	581	16	697	28
1959	529	583	0	700	24
1960	557	550	(6)	440	(27)
1961	586	425	(23)	340	(72)
1962R	617	733	72	880	30
1963	650	750	2	900	28
1964	684	713	(5)	856	20
1965	720	563	(21)	450	(60)
1966R	757	983	75	1,180	36
1967	798	931	(5)	1,117	29
1968	840	900	(3)	1,080	22
1969	885	625	(31)	500	77

*DJIA = 28 + .97 GNPt + 1

$$\dagger \text{Cyclical DJIA} = \frac{\text{Earnings at t + 1}}{2 \text{ Aaa} - 2}$$

‡Based on 20% overshoot over values based on economic factors in both bull and bear markets.

grounds in the future. However, if we specify some floor in advance, the higher the excess (even if the floor is not lowered through pessimistic excesses) the percentage decline in the market is thereby likely to be greater.

VIII. CONCLUSIONS[8]

A review of the patterns set out in this study makes it possible to set forth two unequivocal conclusions. One of these is that the present levels of the stock market are not excessive if the kinds of expectations which are now held do not change. However, these expectations have been carried to the point where they over-discount the expected future growth and stability. As a consequence on the basis of a reasonable expectation of how firmly investors expectations will be held, I would judge the level of the stock market to be about 100 points too high even from its cyclical norm as of the end of 1959.

My second unequivocal conclusion is that having experienced the kinds of rises that the market has experienced in the past, there is no justification for anything more than an average rate of growth in the Dow Jones Industrial Average of about 5% per annum in the future. The rise of about 35% in 1958

[8]This paper was originally written and circulated among associates on December 18, 1959. Although the material in this section was certain to be historical by the date of publication, it appeared preferable not to alter it, so that the theory behind the conclusions could be tested by events prior to publication date.

may be justified in terms of discounting the expected increase in earnings in 1959 as we were coming out of the 1957–1958 recession. However, for the subsequent cyclical years, a percent rise in the Dow Jones Industrial Average beyond 5–10% would be clearly unjustifiable on economic grounds.

The strong bull market since 1949 may be justifiable through the rise experienced through the end of 1958. The magnitude of the rise experienced in 1959, in my judgment, takes on characteristics of a speculative excess. Furthermore, whatever rises were due to failure of common stock prices to catch up with the growth of the economy through 1956 at the time of the writing of my previous article (and which may have been true even though the end of 1958) have now caught up.

In the future an average rise in the Dow Jones Industrial Average beyond 5–8% per annum would be clearly in the category of excesses. Note this refers to an average rate of increase in the Dow Jones Industrial Average over the cycle. This would imply a characteristic 30% rise coming out of a recession, a 10% rise in the subsequent year, and then a sidewise movement in the market for about a year preceding about a 20–25% drop in the market in any recession year of the magnitude in which the Federal Reserve index drop is about 6% and Gross National Product simply levels out.

5

The S.E.C. Special Study and the Exchange Markets*

David K. Eiteman

Publication of *The Report of Special Study of Securities Markets of the Securities and Exchange Commission*[1] in the Summer of 1963 was both a statement of confidence in the basic structure of the securities markets of this country and a well documented analysis of such weaknesses as remained within the system. Since publication of the *Study,* many changes have been made in operational procedures within the securities markets. It is the purpose of this paper to review those changes which have affected the operations of members of the New York Stock Exchange. Particular attention is given to new procedures for floor trading, specialist activities, and odd-lot operations.

FLOOR TRADING

The Special Study[2]

A "floor trade" is a transaction initiated on the floor of the Exchange by a member for his own account in which he or his member organization has an interest. Certain such transactions carried out by specialists or odd-lot dealers in their official capacities are excluded from the definition of a floor trade. "Floor traders" was a designation applied to certain members of the New York Stock Exchange whose primary activity was floor trading. Thus a floor trader was a member who bought and sold for his own account, taking profits where he could find them and running the risk that the market might suddenly turn against him.

The *Special Study* pointed out that floor traders were the only type of exchange member not assigned and in no way responsible for the execution of public orders. Rather their presence on the floor was motivated only by a personal desire to trade profitably for their own account—a motivation, it was

*From *Journal of Finance,* Vol. 21, No. 2 (May 1966), pp. 311–323. Reprinted by permission of *Journal of Finance.*

[1] 88th Congress, 1st Session, House Document No. 95, Parts 1 through 5, released between April 3, 1963, and September 17, 1963. The Report is commonly referred to as the *"Special Study."*

[2] Floor trading is treated in Part 2, pp. 203–242 of the *Special Study.*

nevertheless conceded, that was in the best tradition of the free enterprise system.

Criticism of floor trading did not originate with the *Special Study*. Indeed, floor trading had been attacked many times previously, usually as a vestige of a bygone era when the Exchange conceived of itself as a private club operating for the benefit of its members rather than as a public market serving the well-being of the nation as a whole.[3]

The *Special Study* raised two major objections to floor trading. Its first objection was that floor traders possess an unwarranted competitive advantage over the investing public. By virtue of their physical presence on the floor, floor traders avoid paying even a minimal floor commission and are in addition so situated as to observe and act upon market developments faster than the investing public.

The *Special Study* estimated that a floor could make a profit buying 100 shares of a $25 stock to resell later the same day if the stock rose by as much as 8 cents a share. Members trading from off the floor, and thus paying a floor brokerage fee would need a price rise of 15 cents to break even, and the public at large would need a price rise of 68 cents to break even.[4] Because of this cost advantage, the *Special Study* argued, floor traders could trade on smaller fluctuations in price than could the general public.

The *Special Study* further argued that a floor trader's location on the floor of the exchange provided a "feel for the market" not available to the general trading public and that this "feel" constituted an unwarranted competitive advantage. Changes in market activity could be observed moments before they appeared on the ticker tape, and the floor trader could react with split-second speed. His intuitive reaction to sudden developments was further sharpened by his ability to listen to the observations and opinions of other members on the floor and by his ability to become familiar with the trading techniques of particular specialists or brokers.

The second main objection raised by the *Special Study* was that floor trading was inimical to the orderly function of the market as a whole because it accentuated price fluctuations both for the market as a whole and for individual

[3]Among the previous studies of floor trading are: S.E.C., "Report on the Feasibility and Advisability of the Complete Segregation of the Functions of Dealers and Brokers" (1936); S.E.C., "Report to the Commission by the Trading and Exchange Division on Floor Trading," January 15, 1945; and Cole, Hoisington & Co., "Report to the New York Stock Exchange on Floor Trading" (May 3, 1945).

[4]The S.E.C.'s cost estimates included, where applicable, brokerage fees, clearance fees, New York and Federal transfer taxes, and the S.E.C. fee. The costs did not include a return to the floor trader on his investments in a seat on the Exchange, which in 1961 would have represented an investment worth from $147 to $225 thousand, or his investment in Exchange dues, floor privilege fees, initiation fee, or other incidental costs. However, the *Special Study* estimated that on the average these additional fixed costs would amount to less than 2 cents per share. *Special Study*, Part 2, pages 208–209.

securities. I.e., floor trading was alleged to be a significant destabilizing factor within the stock market. The *Special Study* reviewed numerous past studies of stock price movements and conducted additional analyses of its own. It concluded that floor traders tend to trade with the price trend in the market as a whole, especially when the market is moving in a pronounced direction. Other tests showed that floor traders followed the trend of price movements to an even greater degree in individual stocks. The *Special Study* also found that floor traders concentrated the bulk of their share volume at any one time in a relatively small number of stocks.

Subsequent Developments–the Registered Trader

In response to the criticism of floor trading, the New York Stock Exchange engaged the management consulting firm of Cresap, McCormick and Paget to conduct a separate study of floor trading and to review the *Special Study's* findings.[5] After four and a half months of study, Cresap, McCormick and Paget submitted a report which recommended continued floor trading on the Exchange on a modified basis to preserve the constructive aspects of floor trading while eliminating the defects. Their report observed that a need exists for mobile capital ready and willing to flow toward market imbalances if this capital can be channeled in a responsible and properly controlled manner. This need, they found, is likely to increase. They found that irreparable harm could come to the auction market from failure to devise an effective means of employing the speculative risk-taking talent and capital on the floor to beneficial ends. In their report, Cresap, McCormick and Paget also took issue with the *Special Study's* criticism of floor traders concentrating on active stocks, pointing out that it was in just such stocks where imbalance of buying and selling most frequently occur. Thus it was in these cases in particular where constructive floor trading was most needed.

Cresap, McCormick and Paget suggested that a new category of member be created to replace those members referred to as floor traders. Such a new category of member would preserve speculative risk-taking and capital mobility, for the new type of member would be available to help maintain continuity and price stability by providing additional support to the specialists when the latters' particular stocks were subject to major imbalances of supply and demand.

Specific recommendations on floor trading in the Cresap, McCormick, and Paget report were as follows:

1. Traders in the newly established category would be registered by the Exchange to deal in all stocks generally after meeting specific qualifications, including (a) familiarity with performance requirements for their classification, attested to by passing an appropriate examination, (b) expressed intent to engage in risk-taking for the objective of improving the continuity and stability of the market, (c) acceptance of an obligation to engage in only such trading

[5] Cresap, McCormick and Paget, *Study of Floor Trading* (February 1964).

practices as are consonant with a fair and orderly market, and (d) possession of a minimum amount of trading capital to ensure adequate performance of their function. Any member's firm would be eligible to register for such a trading account by meeting the above qualifications, including the capital requirement over and above the amount of capital required for any other activities of the member. Trading accounts established under this new classification would be required to meet minimum performance standards, including a certain percentage of their trading volume being against the trend as measured by the Exchange's "tick test."[6] This percentage would have to be met bi-weekly.

2. Trading accounts would be governed by a number of specific regulations, including a requirement that all purchases, whether on the bid or the offer, would be limited to prices below the previous day's high except on minus or zero-minum ticks, on transactions closing out or reducing short positions, on arbitrage transactions, and on transactions intended to correct errors. The effect of this rule would be to remove the possibility that floor trading purchases could contribute to a prolonged or significant rise in the price of the stock. Under already existing rules of the exchange, short sales at minus or zero-minus ticks are illegal.

3. Public orders would receive preferential treatment over floor trading orders by rules denying parity based on time or price, or precedence based on size to a floor trading order over a public order.[7]

4. Members of the Exchange who have not specifically registered to engage in floor trading would not be allowed to initiate orders or effect transactions for their own account while on the floor, except to correct transactions made in error or upon the express invitation of a floor official to assist in a difficult market situation.

Submission of the Cresap, McCormick and Paget report was followed

[6]The "tick test" measures performance in the market in terms of the relationship of a transaction to the last preceding transaction at a different price. A transaction at a price above the last price is a "plus tick," and a transaction at a price below the last price is a "minus tick." A transaction at a price equal to the preceding price but above the last *different* price is a "zero-plus tick," and a transaction at a price equal to the preceding price but below the last different price is a "zero-minus tick." A trader's activities would be regarded as stabilizing if he bought predominantly on minus or zero-minus ticks and sold predominantly on plus or zero-plus ticks. The *Special Study* objected to this measure of stabilization on the grounds that it measured only the relationship of a price to its preceding price, rather than to the longer-term price trend. The *Special Study* also pointed out that whenever the quoted market straddles the last transaction price all purchases on the bid and all sales on the offer are by definition stabilizing. See *Special Study*, Part 2, pages 102–104 for an evaluation of the "tick test."

[7]When two or more bids are made at the same price, the bid to be made first is entitled to priority. If no bid is entitled to priority, then the rules of precedence apply. If all the bids are for amounts of stock less than the amount offered, the bid for the largest number of shares has precedence over the others and will be filled first. Bids for quantities of stock greater than the amount offered have precedence over bids for amounts of stock less than the amount offered. If several bids are made for an amount of stock greater than the amount offered, these bids are considered to be on a parity, i.e., to have equal claim, and the issue is settled by matching a coin.

shortly by the approval of a new class of membership to replace the former floor traders. The term, "registered trader" was applied. The registered trader classification followed the general recommendation of the Cresap, McCormick, and Paget recommendations enumerated above. In addition, registered traders were required to possess at least $250,000 minimum capital by January 1, 1965, and to maintain a stabilization performance, as measured by the "tick test," of 75 per cent, on a monthly basis. The new rules also forbid a registered trader from effecting transactions for his own account while holding an executable order. Any transaction initiated off the floor by a registered trader is regarded as an on-floor transaction if the trader has already been on the floor during that day, and registered traders are required to file daily reports of their trading activities.

The Exchange also clarified existing rules with regard to congregating in or dominating the market in a particular stock by expressly stating that no more than three registered traders could be in the trading crowd for one stock at the same time unless written permission was obtained from a floor governor.

THE SPECIALIST

The Special Study[8]

In a "continuous" market, public customers place market orders to buy or sell shares of stock with the understanding that such orders will be executed immediately on reaching the floor. Public customers furthermore expect that the price at which such orders are filled will be no more than a small variation away from the last previous transaction price. The alternative to a continuous market is for market orders to wait on reaching the floor until a counterpart order arrives—perhaps minutes later but conceivably hours or even days later. A second alternative would be to have a system under which an immediate sale could be achieved only at a substantial reduction from the last price, or under which an immediate purchase could be achieved only by paying a substantial premium.

The New York Stock Exchange provides a continuous market in which investors may expect quick execution of market orders at reasonable prices. The specialist is at the heart of the market mechanizm which ensures immediate and reasonable executions when public counterpart orders are not instantaneously available. Buying and selling for his own account and risk, the specialist assumes the responsibility for quoting at all times both a bid and an offer, while at the same time limiting his transactions in support of his quoted bid and ask in so far as practicable to those reasonably necessary for the maintenance of a fair and orderly market. When buying or selling for his own account, the specialist acts as a dealer, and his profit comes from the difference between the price at which he buys and the price at which he sells.

Specialists combine dealer activities with additional duties as brokers who fill orders left with them by commission brokers for execution. These orders

[8] Specialists are treated in Part 2, pages 57–171 of the *Special Study*.

normally arise from price limit orders which must be held for days or weeks before execution is possible. The customer expects his limit order to be filled when the stated price can be obtained, yet a commission broker could not cover the floor with an accumulation of such orders and still expect to be at the right post at the instant the limit price is first attainable. Limit orders are handed to specialists to hold and execute when the opportune moment arrives. In filling such orders the specialist assumes the position of a fiduciary subagent; his responsibility is to the customer and his remuneration comes from sharing a portion of that customer's commission.

The *Special Study* recognized that the specialist must compromise between his self-interest as a dealer and his fiduciary obligations to the customers of commission brokers. The specialist system itself constitutes a compromise between a desire for a completely free market and a market given continuity and orderliness by a professional market maker.

The *Special Study* concluded that the specialist system "appears" to be an essential mechanism for maintaining continuous auction markets and, in broad terms, appears to be serving its purpose satisfactorily. However, the *Study* did set forth a number of specific improvements in specialist practice, concept, and method which it believed should be adopted to better the market mechanism.

Subsequent Developments

Publication of the *Special Study* was followed by an evaluation of the specialist system by a special Exchange committee of specialists and then by several months of conferences and discussions with S.E.C. staff members. The announced goal of these undertakings was to modify the specialist system so as to improve the over-all liquidity, strength, and vitality of the market for the purpose of serving the public interest, improving the quality of the Exchange market, and strengthening the specialist system. The result of the various meetings, announced in September, 1964, was twofold: a new S.E.C. rule dealing with the specialist system, and a number of modifications of Exchange rules, policies and procedures as they pertain to specialist activities.

The new S.E.C. Rule 11b-1 for the first time embodied formal acknowledgement by the S.E.C. of the dual broker/dealer function of the specialist. The new rule provided for the Exchange establishing rules on capital requirements for specialists, on defining in a positive manner specialists' obligations to maintain a fair and orderly market, on restricting specialists' activities to those reasonably necessary for the maintenance of such a market, on defining the responsibilities of specialists acting as brokers, and on improving methods for the effective and systematic surveillance of the specialist system. Under this S.E.C. rule, the Exchange could alter its own rules without prior approval of the Commission, but the Commission would have 30 days within which it could initiate action intended ultimately to disapprove any Exchange rule changes. The new S.E.C. rule also provided that the S.E.C. could order the suspension or cancellation of a specialist's registration in one or more of his specialty stocks if that specialist were found to have violated any Exchange rules.

As a result of its studies and discussions with the S.E.C., the New York Stock Exchange modified existing rules, policies, and procedures in twelve areas. Four of these modifications, representing the establishment of entirely new procedures, were as follows:

1. In establishing, increasing, liquidating, or reducing positions in specialty stocks, existing Exchange policy was made explicit by additional rules requiring that a specialist's transactions be consistent with his market-making function. The new rules limited a specialist's acquisition of more than 50 per cent of any substantial block of stock offered at the last sale price and further limited his reoffering or rebidding for the stock in the market. Additional limitations were imposed on specialists' liquidating all or substantially all of a position by selling stock at prices below the last different price, or by purchasing stock at prices above the last different price. Specialists were additionally required to avoid failing to re-enter the market, where necessary, after effecting such transactions, and to avoid failing to maintain a fair and orderly market during liquidation of their inventory.[9]

The general tenor of these changes is to put more severe restrictions on a specialist's buying or selling for his own account when such transactions might run counter to the best interest of the market as a whole. The changes were keeping with a *Special Study* recommendation that specialist participation to maintain a fair and orderly market be stated in a more positive manner than previously so that more even standards of performance could be expected from the various specialist units.[10]

2. The *Special Study* recommended that specialists be prohibited from granting "stops" at any price at which the specialist holds an unexecuted customer's order capable of execution.[11] The recommendation was implemented by a new rule affirming that a specialist may "stop" stock for his own account when there is no executable order on his book at the stop price, but that he may not stop stock against the book or for his own account at a price at which he holds an order capable of execution.[12] Exceptions to this rule may occur at an opening or reopening, if there is a competing order in the crowd, and under certain conditions in response to an unsolicited request from a broker that a stop be granted.

3. At certain times a specialist will "clean up" a large block of stock by buying the remainder of the block at a price fractionally lower than the going bid. Under new rules, the specialist is now uniformly required to allocate the

[9] These changes were incorporated into Exchange Rule 104.10(5) and (6).
[10] *Special Study*, Part 2, page 168, recommendation 3.
[11] *Special Study*, Part 2, page 169, recommendation 7 (c).
[12] Exchange Rule 116.30

purchased stock to all executably buy orders in his book. The only portion of the block which need not be so allocated is those shares which would have been acquired at the current bid, either for the account of the specialist or for orders held by him.[13] A similar rule applies in the event of an order to purchase a block for which the specialist supplies all or a portion.

4. The *Special Study* recommended that explicit prohibitions be placed on specialists' servicing accounts of public customers.[14] This recommendation was adopted by the Exchange in the form of a new rule that no specialist may accept a buy or sell order for any stock, in which he is registered directly, from (a) the issuing company; (b) any officer, director, or 10% stockholder of that company; (c) any pension or profit sharing fund; or (d) any financial institution such as a bank, trust company, insurance company, or investment company.[15] In making this change the Exchange noted that it had no indication that specialists had given preferential treatment to their own public customers and that the proposed revision was designed merely to provide additional safeguard against the remote possibility of preferential treatment being given in the future.

In addition, orders given to specialists on the floor may not indicate the account of the originating customer. Exchange rules were also modified to incorporate already existing policy to the effect that it is contrary to good business practice for a specialist to "popularize" the stocks in which he specializes.

The remaining eight changes in specialists' procedures consisted of modification or codification of already existing Exchange rules and policies. These were:

1. Capital requirements for specialists were increased so that each specialist would have the ability to carry 1,200 shares of each 100-share unit stock and 120 shares of each 10-share-unit stock,[16] and the Exchange announced its intention of reviewing specialist capital requirements periodically in the light of price levels, volume and other market conditions. The increased capital requirements were set at the minimum level recommended by the *Special Study*.[17]

2. The Exchange reaffirmed existing policy that, in normal situations, specialists' participation in opening and reopenings should not have the effect of upsetting the public balance of supply and demand, but that nevertheless specific situations may develop when exceptions to this principle are required. This existing Exchange policy was incorporated into rules of the Exchange, along with an affirmation of the specialists' right to buy or sell stock as a dealer to minimize the disparity between supply and demand at an opening or reopening.[18] This addition to the rules followed a *Special Study* recommendation.[19]

[13] Exchange Rule 104.10(7) and (8).
[14] *Special Study*, Part 2, page 170, recommendation 7 (f).
[15] Exchange Rule 113.
[16] Exchange Rule 104.20 and 104.23.
[17] *Special Study*, Part 2, page 168, recommendation 4.
[18] Exchange Rule 104.11.
[19] *Special Study*, Part 2, page 168, recommendation 5 (a).

3. Exchange rules have long required specialists to maintain continuity in the stocks in which they specialize. Continuity has usually been interpreted to mean that the price of succeeding transactions in a changing market should vary no more than 1/8 or 1/4 point from the price of the preceding transaction. In accordance with a request of the *Special Study*[20] the concept of market continuity was broadened to include the requirement that reasonable depth be maintained; i.e., a reasonable volume of shares should be traded at each variation in price.[21] The term "reasonable" is a subjective concept which will vary with conditions in each stock–price range, volume, etc.–and with overall market conditions.

In conjunction with this change, the Floor Department of the Exchange distributed a circular to all specialists calling attention to Exchange policy requiring that specialists' quotations for their own accounts "bear a proper relation to preceding transactions and to anticipated succeeding transactions."

4. The *Special Study* objected to the practice of specialist units maintaining two or more trading accounts in stocks in which they are registered, the purpose of these trading accounts being to segregate purchases and sales for tax purposes.[22] The *Special Study* reported receiving testimony that on occasion specialists trade to adjust inventories kept on a LIFO basis. The Exchange's response to this recommendation was to modify its rules to state that transactions made for the purpose of adjusting LIFO inventory may not be made except as part of a course of dealings reasonably necessary to assist in the maintenance of a fair and ordely market in that stock.[23] The Exchange rejected the *Special Study's* recommendation that specialists should be allowed to maintain only one trading account and went on record strongly favoring the right of specialists to maintain long-term investment accounts in addition to their short-term trading accounts because of the favorable tax considerations involved.

5. The *Special Study* objected to Exchange practice in not printing transactions in "stopped stock" on the ticker tape when a member requested that the print be omitted.[24] The Exchange decided to retain its policy for the present, but to print all such omitted sales on the tape at the end of the day and to include their volume within the total volume reported for the day.[25] The Exchange also agreed to review this decision, with the idea of including all transactions in stopped stock on the tape at the time of transaction after the Exchange's new "900 Ticker" system becomes fully operative.

6. Under Regulations T and U of the Board of Governors of the Federal Reserve System, a member acting as a specialist may finance his transactions on

[20] *Special Study*, Part 2, page 169, recommendation 5 (c).
[21] Exchange Rule 104.10 (1), (2), and (3).
[22] *Special Study*, Part 2, page 169, recommendation 6.
[23] Exchange Rule 104.12.
[24] *Special Study*, Part 2, page 169, recommendation 7 (d).
[25] Exchange Rule 125A.16.

a basis mutually satisfactory to the specialist and the creditor. Exchange rules were revised to require immediate notification by telephone and subsequent confirmation in writing of any intention to terminate or change an existing financial arrangement or to issue a margin call to a specialist.[26] This change, which incorporated an existing Exchange request to specialists into a formal rule, was designed to provide the Exchange quickly with any information relevant to a specialist's ability to maintain a fair and orderly market in the stocks assigned to him. Should it appear that the specialist could not continue in business because of his inability to make satisfactory financial arrangements or to meet a margin call, the Exchange is to notify the S.E.C. The change followed a recommendation of the *Special Study.*[27]

7. In response to *Special Study* requests for the availability of more statistical information on specialist operations,[28] the Exchange amended its rules to require that each specialist organization maintain records showing the breakdown of its income as between commission income and dealer profit and loss in each specialty stock.[29] This information would be available for the confidential use of the Exchange on request. The exchange further agreed to conduct studies to determine the feasibility of using Exchange computer equipment in conjunction with surveillance of the specialist system and to explore the development of more objective standards of price continuity and market depth in assessing the quality of specialists' performance.

8. Lastly, the Exchange codified existing policy to the effect that any substantial or continued failure by a specialist to engage in a proper course of dealings is grounds for the suspension or cancellation of that specialist's registration in any or all of his specialty stocks.[30]

ODD-LOT OPERATIONS

The Special Study[31]

The *Special Study* made two major recommendations in relation to odd-lot operations on the New York Stock Exchange. The *Study* recommended (1) that the Exchange accept the responsibility for regulating odd-lot differentials, and, as a first step, initiate a cost study of the odd-lot business; and (2) that the Exchange study the feasibility of automating odd-lot operations. As will be seen, these two recommendations are interconnected.

[26]Exchange Rule 104.30.
[27]*Special Study*, Part 2, page 170, recommendation 10.
[28]*Special Study*, Part 2, page 170, recommendation 11.
[29]Exchange Rule 104.50.
[30]Exchange Rule 103.
[31]Odd-lot operations are treated in the *Special Study*, Part 2, pages 171–202.

For many years the odd-lot differential was established by the odd-lot houses themselves in conjunction with the commission brokerage firms. The *Special Study* described negotiations between the odd-lot firms and the several regional exchanges at the time of the 1951 increase of the odd-lot differential to ¼ point on stocks priced at $40 and above to illustrate how pressure by New York odd-lot firms could compel the various regional exchanges to raise their odd-lot differential to the same level.[32] The *Special Study* concluded that the odd-lot investor was not in a position to influence the magnitude of the differential because of a lack of price competition in the odd-lot business, and added that if odd-lot firms could reduce some of their costs which were incurred more for the benefit of the commission brokerage firms than for the odd-lot public, a reduction in the size of the differential would be justified.

The *Special Study* also reviewed a 1956 proposal by Ebasco Services, Inc., to automate odd-lot operations. In one plan suggested at that time, data-processing equipment would have been used to match odd-lot orders with reports of round-lot transactions. The computer would then execute the odd-lot order and fill out and route the necessary paper work. The essence of the proposal involved the concept that because the execution of most odd-lot orders (certain unusual types excepted) was an automatic procedure not involving human judgment, the number of associate brokers employed by the odd-lot firms could be reduced. After commenting on the 1956 Ebasco Services, Inc., report, the *Special Study* recommended that the Exchange proceed to make further studies of the feasibility of automating the execution of odd-lot orders and of the impact such automation would have on the costs of the odd-lot business.

The *Special Study* also made recommendations dealing with rules regulating the triggering of round-lot sales by odd-lot dealers, with setting up improved reporting and surveillance procedures, and with disclosure of the odd-lot differential in customers' confirmation of odd-lot transactions.

Subsequent Developments

On June 1, 1964, the New York Stock Exchange formally assumed jurisdiction over the amount of the odd-lot differential to be charged, thus in effect complying with the first recommendation of the *Special Study.*

The Exchange also employed the public-accounting firm of Price Waterhouse to conduct a cost study of the odd-lot business covering the entire year of 1964. At the present writing this study is not available to the public; however, the impact of the various factors enumerated in the recommendations are being evaluated by the Exchange and by the Securities and Exchange Commission. The odd-lot houses report they believe that progress has been made by the Exchange and by the Commission in arriving at a clearer understanding of the principles

[32] *Special Study,* Part 2, pages 181–186.

involved in the odd-lot houses' borrowing of stock and informational services. Possibly as a result of this study and possibly because the odd-lot dealers found themselves in competition with their own commission house customers, the odd-lot dealers withdrew on October 1, 1965, from the practice of arranging stock borrowings between member firms.

Subsequent to the *Special Study,* odd-lot dealers have met with Exchange officials many times to discuss problems inherent in computerized execution of odd-lot orders. In October 1965 the Exchange announced a limited test of off-floor handling and pricing of odd-lot orders to be conducted in early 1966 by Merrill Lynch, Pierce, Fenner and Smith and the major odd-lot houses. Leading up to the ability to conduct this test was the installation by Merrill Lynch of 7740 switching equipment and the advent of post round-lot sale print-out machines on the floor of the Exchange. The 7740 switching machines enable Merrill Lynch to divide odd-lot orders into post categories and to print them at any point deemed desirable. Meanwhile the Stock Exchange print-out machines record round-lot sales at the instant they are recorded at each post in a computerized reading device.

The proposed test will determine if the combined use of these two machines will enable the execution of odd-lot orders at some physical location other than on the floor.

More tests along the same line are contemplated for later in 1966 with additional commission brokerage firms participating. Only after these tests are completed will a final decision be made on automation. Full automation of the odd-lot operation will involve development of additional communication facilities between the auxiliary post and the odd-lot associate brokers for the purpose of informing the associate brokers of odd-lot orders awaiting execution and of the inventory position of the odd-lot firm. The Exchange emphasized in its announcement that odd-lot associate brokers will continue to be required to execute round-lot offsetting transactions for the odd-lot firm.

The Exchange has moved to comply with other recommendations of the *Special Study.* Trading rules covering the execution of odd-lot orders and offsetting round-lot transactions were adopted. At certain times the odd-lot associate broker will find himself holding, say, customers' sell orders totalling more than 100 shares and at the same time wanting to sell against these orders in the round-lot market. If the associate broker's round-lot sale would automatically trigger the execution of odd-lot orders in number greater than the number of shares sold in the round-lot market, the associate broker is now required to deliver his round-lot sale order to the specialist for execution at the highest possible price. Thus, the round-lot sale is made by an agency whose interest is identical with that of the odd-lot sellers.

If this new rule were not in effect, a conflict of interest situation would arise because the odd-lot firms' profit would be maximized by having the offsetting and triggering round-lot sale priced as low as possible—the odd-lot firm would then make its same differential on the first 100 shares purchased from odd-lot customers, but would make additional profit on that portion of the odd-lot- sell orders acquired for existing odd-lot firm inventory. A similar rule applies on the buy side of the market.

The last recommendation of the *Special Study* requested the disclosure to odd-lot customers of the amount of the odd-lot differential paid. At present, practice is to show only the net transaction price (which includes the differential) on the customers' confirmation of transactions, plus or minus appropriate commissions and taxes.

The odd-lot firms maintain that it is a debatable question of fact as to whether or not the odd-lot customers actually bear the cost of the differential. In many cases it is possible that odd-lot market orders will be executed at prices more favorable to the odd-lot customer than would a round-lot market order submitted at the same time.[33] The matter of "disclosure" of odd-lot differentials is currently under study by the Exchange.

CONCLUSIONS

The *Special Study of Securities Markets of the Securities and Exchange Commission* represented the culmination of the most detailed scrutiny of the American securities markets since the 1930's. Unlike many other governmental investigations of economic institutions, the *Special Study* was undertaken at a time of prosperity for both the country and for the institution under study. The decision to make the study was not preceded by major economic, financial, or political scandal; and the study was made and reported with a minimum of recrimination by the parties involved. This timing was probably an excellent thing, for it permitted an invaluable analysis of the American security markets to be made in an atmosphere conducive to unrushed and thorough contemplation of the many interacting complexities in such a market.

In the broadest sense the *Special Study* reached two conclusions. One, it found no major defect in the operations of our securities markets, and two, it found room for continued improvement in a myriad of operational detail. Through the sincere and honest effort of both the Special Study staff, the Securities and Exchange Commission, and the Stock Exchange community, it has been possible in the years since 1963 to improve many aspects of the securities markets without at the same time causing a set-back to confidence in the integrity of these markets.

The importance of the creation of the new registered trader classification to replace the older floor trader grouping is primarily conceptual: the primary

[33]See Eiteman, W. J., Dice, C. A., and Eiteman, D. K., *The Stock Market* (4th ed.; N.Y.: McGraw-Hill, 1966), pages 250–253, for an example of circumstances in which odd-lot customers pay less (or receive more) per share than would have been paid or received on round-lot market orders submitted at the same time.

obligation of the registered trader to help maintain a sound public market now clearly has legal precedence over his self-interests should the two conflict, and rules have been devised and implemented to ensure the fulfillment of this obligation. The benefits which traders do impart to the auction market appear to have been preserved, while the dangers appear to have been removed.

The specialists' dual function of both broker and dealer in the heart of the price-determining mechanism has been officially recognized by a new S.E.C. rule, and many existing Exchange policies and procedures have been incorporated into the official rules of that institution. Greater surveillance of specialists in the light of the new rules should provide for most specialist units achieving the optimal performance attained in the past by the best units; and future market crises should not lead, as they have so often in the past, to a few specialist units being found to have acted other than in accord with the best interests of the investing public.

Implementation of *Special Study* recommendations on automation and cost cutting for odd-lot firms has moved slower than other reforms. However much effort is currently being put into research, and the investing public has every reason to expect significant changes within the next year or so.

6

Public Regulation of the Securities Markets*

George J. Stigler†

It is doubtful whether any other type of public regulation of economic activity has been so widely admired as the regulation of the securities markets by the Securities and Exchange Commission. The purpose of this regulation is to increase the portion of truth in the world and to prevent or punish fraud, and who can defend ignorance or fraud? The Commission has led a scandal-free life as federal regulatory bodies go. It has been essentially a "technical" body, and has enjoyed the friendship, or at least avoided the enmity, of both political parties.

The *Report of the Special Study of the Securities Markets*, which was recently released, is itself symptomatic of the privileged atmosphere within which the S.E.C. dwells.[1] This study investigated the adequacy of the controls over the security markets now exercised by the S.E.C. The study was well endowed: it was directed by an experienced attorney, Milton H. Cohen; it had a professional staff of more than thirty people; and it operated on a schedule that was leisurely by Washington standards. The study was not an instrument of some self-serving group, nor was it even seriously limited by positions taken by the Administration. Such a professional, disinterested appraisal would not even be conceivable for agricultural or merchant marine or petroleum policy, or the other major areas of public regulation. Disinterest, good will, and money had all joined to improve the capital markets of America.

The regulation of the securities markets is therefore an appropriately antiseptic area in which to see how public policy is formed. Here we should be able to observe past policy appraised, and new policy defended, on an intellectually respectable level, if ever it is.

We begin with an examination of certain of the *Special Study's* policy proposals. Cohen presents a vast number of recommendations of changes in

*From *The Journal of Business*, Vol. (37), No. 2 (April 1964), pp. 117–142. Reprinted by permission of The University of Chicago Press.

†I wish to disclose my obligation to Claire Friedland for performing the statistical work.

[1] *Report of the Special Study of the Securities Markets of the Securities and Exchange Commission*, 88th Cong., 1st sess., House Document 95, 1963 (Washington, D.C.: Government Printing Office, 1963), Part I. All citations in text to part, chapter, or page refer to this work.

institutions and practices. Most are minor, and some are even frivolous (market letters should not predict specific price levels of stocks). The content of the proposals, however, is not our present concern; what is our concern is the manner in which the proposals are reached. More specifically: (1) How does the Cohen Report show that an existing practice or institution is defective? (2) How does the Cohen Report show that the changes it recommends (a) will improve the situation, and (b) are better in some sense than alternative proposals? In answering these questions I shall use the discussion of the qualifications of brokers and other personnel in the industry (chap. ii), although the numerous other areas would do quite as well.

1. THE FORMULATION OF POLICY

The Cohen Report tells us that there is cause for dissatisfaction with the personnel of the industry: "From the evidence gathered by the study, it appears that the existing controls have proven to be deficient in some important regards. The dishonest broker-dealer, that 'greatest menace to the public,' to use the words of one Commission official, continues to appear with *unjustifiable frequency.* Also, the inexperienced broker-dealer *too often* blunders into problems for himself, his customers, and the regulatory agencies."[2] So there are too many thieves and too many incompetents.

How does Cohen prove that there are enough thieves and incompetents to justify more stringent controls? After all, one can always find some dishonest and untutored men in a group of 100,000: not all the angels in heaven have good posture.

The "proof" of the need for further regulatory measures consists basically and almost exclusively of four case studies. These studies briefly describe four new firms with relatively inexperienced salesmen who were caught in falling markets and in three cases became bankrupt or withdrew from the business. No estimates of losses to customers are made. The studies were handpicked to emphasize the shortcomings of *new* firms, because this is the place where Cohen wishes to impost new controls. The studies are of course worthless as a proof of the need for new policies: nothing Cohen, the S.E.C., or the United States government can do will make it difficult to find four more cases at any time one looks for them.

Cohen's second, and only other, piece of evidence, is a survey of disciplinary actions against members of the NASD (National Association of Security Dealers) from 1959 through 1961. To quote the report: "The results of this analysis revealed that the association's newest member firms, which are generally controlled by persons having less experience than principals of older firms, were responsible for a heavy preponderance of the offenses drawing the most severe penalties" (Part I, p. 66). Cohen's summary of the statistical study, of which this

[2] *Ibid.*, p. 51. (My italics.)

sentence is a fair sample, would not meet academic standards of accuracy. The study reveals that of 1,014 firms founded before 1941, 223 were involved in disciplinary proceedings between 1959 and 1961; of 1,072 firms founded in 1959–60, only 103 were involved in such proceedings. The data are poorly tabulated (dismissals are included, and duplicate charges against one firm are counted as several firms), but however viewed they do not make a case for the need for more regulation, or for more severe screening of new entrants. [3] Yet Cohen believed that the basis has been laid for his main finding:

> The large number of new investors and new broker-dealer firms and salesmen attracted to the securities industry in recent years have combined to create a problem of major dimensions. . . .
>
> More than a generation of experience with the Federal securities laws has demonstrated, moreover, that it is impossible to regulate effectively the conduct of those in the securities industry, unless would-be members are adequately screened at the point of entry [Part I, p. 150].

These alleged findings lead to a series of policy proposals, such as the following:

1. All brokers should be compelled to join "self-regulatory" agencies (such as the NASD).
2. No one who has been convicted of embezzlement, fraud, or theft should be allowed in the industry for ten years thereafter.
3. A good character should be required for entrants.
4. Examinations should be required for prospective entrants.

The *Report* approves strongly of the six-month training period now required of customers' men in firms belonging to the New York Stock Exchange (NYSE).

Cohen believes that the people dealing in securities with the public should have extensive training and screening such as his own profession requires. My lengthy experience with "account executives" of major NYSE firms has not uncovered knowledge beyond what would fit comfortably into a six-hour course. It would have been most useful if Cohen had investigated the experience of customers of a randomly chosen set of account men with diverse amounts of training and experience: Have differences in experience or training had any effect on the profits of their customers? But he never even dreamed of the possibility—or perhaps it was of the need—of pretesting his proposals.

The report takes for granted not only the effectiveness but also, what is truly remarkable, the infallibility of the regulating process:

> There is no evidence that these practices are typical. . .but regardless of their frequency they represent problems too important to be ignored [Part I, p. 268].

[3] The *Report* discusses only the higher rate of use of expulsion as a penalty against younger firms. The *Report* does not relate sanctions to violations, so that interpretation of heavier penalties is obscure, even the more lenient enforcement against older firms remarked upon by the *Report* is waived.

> The mere fact that there have been any losses at all is sufficient reason to consider whether there are further adjustments that should be made for the protection of investors [Part I, p. 400].

Observe: no matter how infrequent or trivial the damage to investors, the regulatory process must seek to eliminate it (no doubt inexpensively). Surely rhetoric has replaced reason at this point.

As for alternative methods of dealing with the problem of fraud, only one is mentioned: "A number of persons have suggested that a Federal fidelity or surety bond requirement be imposed in addition to or in lieu of a capital requirement. It would seem, however, that such a requirement would present a number of practical difficulties and that more significant protection to the public can be assured through a Federal net capital requirement. No recommendation as to bonding, therefore, will be made at this time" (Part I, p. 92). I must confess to being shocked by this passage. A number of "practical difficulties" exclude the sensible, direct, efficient way to deal with the problem of financial responsibility—difficulties so obvious and conclusive they do not even need to be mentioned.

When one looks at a well-built theater set from the angle at which the audience is to view it, it appears solid and convincing. When one looks from another direction, it is a set of two-dimensional pieces of cardboard and canvas, which could not possibly create an illusion of validity. So it is with the Cohen Report. Once we ask for the evidence for its policy proposals, the immense enterprise becomes a promiscuous collection of conventional beliefs and personal prejudices.

2. A TEST OF PREVIOUS REGULATION

A proposal of public policy, everyone should agree, is open to criticism if it omits a showing that the proposal will serve its announced goal. Yet the proposal may be a desirable and opportune one, and the inadequacies of a proposer are no proof of the undesirability of the proposal. And—to leave the terrain of abstract and unctious truth—the past work of the S.E.C. and Cohen's schemes for its future may serve fine purposes even though no statistician has measured these probable achievements. Quite so. But then again, perhaps not.

The paramount goal of the regulations in the security markets is to protect the innocent (but avaricious) investor. A partial test of the effects of the S.E.C. on investors' fortunes will help to answer the question of whether testing a policy's effectiveness is an academic scruple or a genuine need. This partial test will serve also to illustrate the kind of study that should have occupied the *Special Study*.

The basic test is simplicity itself: how did investors fare before and after the S.E.C. was given control over the registration of new issues? We take all the new issues of industrial stocks with a value exceeding $2.5 million in 1923–28, and exceeding $5 million in 1949–55, and measure the values of these issues (compared to their offering price) in five subsequent years. It is obviously improper to credit or blame the S.E.C. for the absolute differences between the periods in investors' fortunes, but if we measure stock prices relative to the market average, we shall have eliminated most of the effects of general market conditions. The price ratios (p_t/p_o) for each time span are divided by the ratio of the market average for the same period. Thus if from 1926 to 1928 a common stock rose from \$20 to \$30, the price ratio is 150 (per cent) or an increase of 50 per cent but, relative to the market, which rose by 68.5 per cent over this two-year period, the new issue fell 12 per cent.[4]

The prices of common and preferred stocks were first analyzed to determine whether they varied with size of issue after one, three, or five years. In each case there was no systematic or statistically significant variation of price with size of issue. The elusiveness of quotations on small issues makes it difficult to answer this question for issues smaller than the minimum size of our samples (\$2.5 million in the 1920's, \$5 million in the 1950's). One small sample was made of fifteen issues in 1923 of \$500 thousand to \$1 million for which quotations were available, and this was compared with the twenty-two larger issues of the same year. The differences were sufficient to leave open the question of the representativeness of our findings for smaller issues.[5]

The annual averages of the quotations (relative to market) are given for common stocks in Table 1. In both periods it was an unwise man who bought new issues of common stock: he lost about one-fifth of his investment in the first year relative to the market, and another within the years that followed. The data reveal no risk aversion.

The averages for the two periods reveal no difference in values after one year, and no significant difference after two years, but a significant difference in the third and fourth, but not fifth, years. The ambiguity in this pattern arises chiefly because the issues of 1928 did quite poorly, and the number of issues in this year was relatively large—one-third of all issues of the 1920's were made in 1928. It may be that these enterprises did not have sufficient time to become well launched before the beginning of the Great Depression. With an unweighted average of the various years, there would be no significant difference between the averages in the 1920's and the 1950's.

The proper period over which to "hold" a new stock in these comparisons is difficult to specify: presumably it is equal to the average period the purchasers held the new issues. With speculative new issues one would expect the one-year period to be much the most relevant, for thereafter the information provided by

[4]The data are more fully described in the Appendix.

[5]The preferred stocks had almost identical means in the large and small samples, but the small common stock issues had much lower prices than the large issues for the first three years, after which they were essentially equal to those of the large issues. But only the first-year price relatives differed significantly at the 5 per cent level with the small samples available. There were no systematic differences in the variances of the price relatives of large and small issues.

this year of experience would become an important determinant of the investor's behavior.

These comparisons suggest that the investors in common stocks in the 1950's did little better than in the 1920's, indeed clearly no better if they held the securities only one or two years. This comparison is incomplete in that dividends are omitted from our reckoning, although this is probably a minor omission and may well work in favor of the 1920's.[6]

TABLE 1

New Stock Prices Relative to Market Averages, Common Stocks (Issue Year = 100)

	Year after Issue				
	1	2	3	4	5
Pre-S.E.C.:					
1923	92.7	85.0	77.8	62.1	67.0
1924	98.0	76.3	69.1	65.9	51.0
1925	85.0	66.9	54.8	42.2	33.0
1926	90.2	81.8	77.1	62.6	66.9
1927	84.7	69.1	60.1	72.6	103.4
1928	71.6	50.4	40.8	45.0	57.0
Average	81.9	65.1	56.2	52.8	58.5
Standard deviation	43.7	46.7	43.7	48.5	65.1
No. of issues	84	87	88	85	84
Post-S.E.C.:					
1949	93.3	88.1	86.7	86.9	64.9
1950	84.3	76.0	53.0	57.8	46.9
1951	83.6	78.7	76.3	80.4	74.5
1952	87.7	74.3	70.7	70.4	69.8
1953	88.1	79.2	75.4	70.4	93.6
1954	53.2	48.7	56.4	48.1	42.4
1955	71.8	64.9	82.3	77.8	83.4
Average	81.6	73.3	72.6	71.9	69.6
Standard deviation	23.9	27.7	31.0	30.9	38.9
No. of issues	47	47	47	47	47

[6]An estimate of the role of dividends for two years in each period was made as follows: The aggregate dividends received on stocks issued in 1923 and 1924, and in 1950 and 1951, are expressed as rates of return on the initial costs to investors of the issues:

Rate of Return on Initial Cost

Year and Type of Issue	1924*	1925	1926	1927	1928
1923–24:					
Preferred	7.11	7.10	6.77	6.50	6.30
Common	7.11	6.16	6.56	6.77	7.62

Year and Type of Issue	1951†	1952	1953	1954	1955
1950–51:					
Preferred	6.89	4.78	4.81	4.86	4.81
Common	1.62	4.17	4.11	4.08	4.26

*1923 issues only.

†1950 issues only.

This sample suggests that dividends were a larger component of return in the 1920's.

The variance of the price ratios, however, was much larger in the 1920's than in the later period: in every year the difference between periods was significant at the 1 per cent level, and in four years at the 0.1 per cent level. This is a most puzzling finding: the simple-minded interpretation is that the S.E.C. has succeeded in eliminating both unusually good and unusually bad new issues! This is difficult to believe as a matter of either intent or accident. A more plausible explanation lies in the fact that many more new companies used the market in the 1920's than in the 1950's—from one viewpoint a major effect of the S.E.C. was to exclude new companies.[7]

The preferred stocks, which were far more numerous than the common stocks in the 1920's, pose a special problem. We use the market average as the base for measuring investor experience in order to minimize the influence of other factors, but no such market average exists for preferred stocks. The existing preferred stock indexes are actually indexes of the yields of preferred stocks, and exclude defaults or failures, so they do not measure the fortunes of investors in preferred stocks.

The price relatives for preferred stocks are given in Table 2, and it will be observed that the break in the market in 1929 had a decisive influence on the absolute values of these issues. We may in fact summarize the salient numbers:

Year of Issue	Average Price Relative	
	1929	1930
1925	107.2	78.6
1926	94.7	85.7
1927	97.8	91.7
1928	93.7	69.7

As a result of this heavy impact, the price relatives are substantially lower after two years in the 1920's than in the 1950's.

Accordingly we need a deflator, and again use the common stock index (Table 3). The common stock index seems more appropriate than the unsatisfactory preferred stock indexes, especially since most of the recent preferred issues were convertible.[8] The average experience, on this basis, was superior in the 1950's for the first two years after an issue was purchased; thereafter there was no difference.

The undeflated preferred stock experience is the same in both periods for the first two years, and the deflated experience is the same in both periods for the last three years; the opposite indexes show a superior performance in the

[7] Of twenty-six issues of common stock in 1949–54, only six were by companies less than three years old; the corresponding figure for 1923–27 was thirty-eight less than three years old of a total of fifty-three issues.

[8] In the 1920's, thirty-six of 121 issues were convertible and in the 1950's twenty-eight of forty issues were convertible.

TABLE 2
New Stock Prices Relative to Issue Year, Preferred Stocks

	Year after Issue				
	1	2	3	4	5
Pre-S.E.C.:					
1923	95.3	96.9	92.0	97.6	96.2
1924	84.6	71.2	72.9	71.9	56.3
1925	107.6	108.3	118.4	107.2	78.6
1926	101.1	96.2	94.7	85.7	60.5
1927	101.4	97.8	91.7	63.0	44.6
1928	93.7	69.7	50.0	29.9	31.9
Average	97.8	87.0	79.1	65.0	53.2
Standard deviation	20.4	33.4	45.1	53.7	50.3
No. of issues	110	115	117	111	108
Post-S.E.C.:					
1949	112.3	101.7	101.1	97.7	105.2
1950	99.6	96.5	97.5	103.9	105.7
1951	101.1	94.3	101.8	108.8	113.1
1952	95.7	93.6	113.2	95.0	91.2
1953	148.1	117.6	119.5	104.5	n.a.
1954	112.1	102.7	88.5	77.3	88.3
1955	103.6	102.0	109.2	190.5	205.7
Average	107.1	99.0	102.0	107.7	114.3
Standard deviation	18.6	13.7	20.2	51.8	66.5
No. of issues	40	38	36	33	29

TABLE 3
New Stock Prices Relative to Market Averages, Preferred Stocks
(Issue Year = 100)

	Year after Issue				
	1	2	3	4	5
Pre-SEC:					
1923	91.2	72.9	60.0	50.9	37.2
1924	66.5	48.4	39.7	29.0	18.0
1925	93.1	75.1	60.8	43.6	41.6
1926	81.0	57.1	44.5	52.4	57.7
1927	75.1	57.4	70.0	75.1	104.0
1928	74.2	71.8	80.6	94.4	70.9
Average	79.2	66.6	66.9	69.7	65.3
Standard deviation	17.4	24.9	40.0	65.9	42.0
No. of issues	110	115	117	111	108
Post-S.E.C.:					
1949	91.9	67.2	61.2	59.0	52.2
1950	80.5	71.4	62.8	63.0	45.7
1951	92.5	86.1	76.3	58.2	51.5
1952	95.5	76.7	66.2	47.3	47.4
1953	121.6	68.9	59.6	54.5	n.a.
1954	79.9	62.4	56.2	47.4	43.5
1955	88.2	90.8	93.8	131.4	146.8
Average	91.5	76.9	69.6	62.2	59.0
Standard deviation	15.2	14.0	13.6	37.2	49.3
No. of issues	40	38	36	33	29

1950's. This combination of results suggests that our deflators are inappropriate, and we can only repeat our lament at the absence of a relevant preferred-stock index.

Since convertibility is much more common in the later issues, there is an argument for comparing the earlier issues to the base year, and the later issues to the common stock index. The average period these new issues are held may also be longer than common stocks are held. These various considerations combine to suggest that the preferred-stock performance was not significantly better in the 1950's than in the 1920's.

These studies suggest that the S.E.C. registration requirements had no important effect on the quality of new securities sold to the public. A fuller statistical study—extending to lower sizes of issues and dividend records—should serve to confirm or qualify this conclusion, but it is improbable that the qualification will be large, simply because the issues here included account for most of the dollar volume of industrial stocks issued in these periods. Our study is not exhaustive in another sense: we could investigate the changing industrial composition of new issues and other possible sources of differences in the market performance of new issues in the two periods.

But these admissions of the possibility of closer analysis can be made after any empirical study. They do not affect our two main conclusions: (1) it is possible to study the effects of public policies, and not merely to assume that they exist and are beneficial, and (2) grave doubts exist whether if account is taken of costs of regulation,[9] the S.E.C. has saved the purchasers of new issues one dollar.

3. THE CRITERIA OF MARKET EFFICIENCY

So far as the efficiency and growth of the American economy are concerned, efficient capital markets are even more important than the protection of investors—in fact efficient capital markets are the major protection of investors. The *Special Study* devotes considerable attention to the mechanism of the most important single market, the New York Stock Exchange.

One can ask whether this market is competitively organized: are the prices of brokers' services set by competitive forces? The answer is clearly in the negative and the Cohen Report is properly critical of the structure of commissions of the NYSE, which is highly discriminatory against higher-priced stocks and larger transactions. The *Report* explicitly refrains from discussing the

[9]The costs of the program, that is, probably exceed even a reasonably optimistic estimate of benefits. Costs of flotations due to registration have apparently never been estimated even approximately; the S.E.C. data (e.g., *Cost of Flotations*, 1945–49) exclude costs included in commissions of underwriters and costs of the delays imposed by the process, as well as costs of operating the S.E.C. The full costs of registration for new stock issues could be 5 per cent of their value.

compulsory minimum rates set by this self-regulating cartel. The reason for silence is obscure: the present scheme of compulsory private price-fixing of brokers' services seems to me wholly objectionable. The replacement of cartel pricing by competition, with review lodged in the Antitrust Division, would confer larger benefits upon investors than the S.E.C. has yet provided.

The mechanism of response to changing conditions is a more subtle matter, dealt with especially in chapter vi ("Exchange Markets") of the *Special Study*. The task of providing continuity and orderliness of markets in specific stocks is now performed by the specialists, aided or observed (as the case may be) by the floor traders. How well do they presently perform their tasks?

1. The NYSE uses a "tick test" of the effects of specialists on short-run price fluctuations. If a transaction takes place below the last different price, it is called a minus tick, and if above the last different price, it is a plus tick. Purchases on minus ticks and sales on plus ticks are considered stabilizing, and in three sample weeks, 83.9 per cent of specialists' transactions were of this type. The *Special Study* rejects this test on two grounds:

> 1. "A tick by itself does not necessarily represent a change in the public's evaluation of the security." Thus, after a transaction at 35, the specialists will often offer 34½ and ask 35½, and a transaction at either price is a so-called stabilizing tick. This represents "only a random sequence of buy and sell orders."
>
> 2. The specialists' own profit incentive is to buy low and sell high—and presumably (but the *Special Study* does not say explicitly) no virtue attaches to profitable activity.[10]

The *Special Study* demands that the test be applied to a longer sequence of transactions; on individual pairs of transactions the test "can be expected to reveal only cases of grossly destabilizing activity."[11] Specialists engage in only a third of all transactions, but as a rule at least one-third of the ticks in a stock are negative and one-third positive in a day. Hence the specialists could foster market movements while appearing to stabilize them, or so the Report argues. Thus if the specialist sells in the underlined transactions in the following sequence:

35 34 <u>34¾</u> 34 <u>34½</u> 33¾ <u>34</u>,

he is stabilizing by the tick test while riding with a market trend. This prescient behavior is not documented, nor is a specific tick test proposed.

2. The preferred test of the specialist's effect is how his inventory of stock varies as the market price fluctuates: "That is, a member trading pattern which tends to produce purchase balances on declining stock days and sales balances on

[10] *Special Study*, Part II, pp. 102–103.
[11] *Ibid.*, p. 104.

rising stock days would indicate that members exert a stabilizing influence on the stock days in which they traded" (Part II, p. 55). An analysis is made of changes in specialists' stock inventories on four days. In each case inventories moved with the market—that is, they were destabilizing. But if the analysis is performed on stocks classified as rising or falling, balances moved in a stabilizing fashion in seven of the eight cases (Part 2, p. 108). But *within* these eight groups there were a substantial number of cases in which inventories of stocks moved with the market, so specialist performance left something to be desired. Cohen's standards have not flagged: he expects every specialist to do, not his best, but perfectly.[12]

The economist will have observed that the *Report* has no theory of markets from which valid criteria can be deduced by which to judge experience. The tick test and the "offsetting balances" tests are both lacking of any logical basis: these tests assume that smoothness of price movement is the sign of an efficient market, and it is not. Let us sketch the problem of an efficient market.

The basic function a market serves is to bring buyers and sellers together. If there were a large number of people who sent their bid and ask prices to a single point (market), we should in effect observe the supply and demand functions of elementary economic theory. *The* price that cleared this market would be established—it would be a unique price if there were sufficient traders to produce continuity of supply and demand functions—and trading would stop.

This once-for-all, or at most once-per-period, market differs from most real markets in which new potential buyers and sellers are appearing more or less irregularly over time. Existing holders of a stock wish to sell it—at a price—to build a home, marry off a daughter, or buy another security which has (for them) greater promise. Existing holders of cash wish to buy the stock, at a price. Neither group is fully identified until after the event: I would become a bidder for a stock that does not fall within my present investment horizon provided that its price falls for reasons which I believe are mistaken.

So demand and supply are flows, and erratic flows with sequences of bids and asks dependent upon the random circumstances of individual traders. As a first approximation, one would expect the number of holders of a security to be proportional to the total value of the issue. Then the numbers of bids, offers, and transactions would also be proportional to the dollar size of the issue. This is roughly true: the turnover rate of a random sample of one hundred stocks in one month is classified by the total value of the issues, in Table 4, and only in very

[12]The *Special Study* shows particular concern with the specialist who "reaches across" the market, i.e., who initiates transactions by buying stock at the offer or selling at the bid, instead of waiting for someone to trade. This alarm again reflects the Study's identification of the specialist's proper role with strict price stabilization. Suppose the bid is 30 and the ask 30½, and the specialist anticipates that the market will soon go to 32-32½. He buys at 30½ so the effective ask becomes (say) 30¾. He has initiated a price move, but one called for by his function of achieving equilibrium, if his anticipation is correct.

TABLE 4
Turnover Rates of 100 Stocks on the New York Stock Exchange, March 1961

Value of Issue (Millions of Dollars)	No. of Stocks	Ratio of Shares Traded to Total Outstanding
Under 5	9	0.012
5–10	12	.026
10–25	18	.037
25–50	10	.043
50–75	11	.073
75–100	12	.034
100–250	13	.027
250–500	8	.029
500 and over	7	0.008

small and very large issues was there a considerable departure from proportionality.[13]

Let us take a very primitive model of a random sequence of bids and asks, and see what this sequence implies for (1) the level of transaction prices, and (2) the time until a bid or ask is met and a transaction occurs. We start with a demand schedule (Table 5) for a given stock of which 710,000 shares are outstanding, so the equilibrium price is between 29¾ and 30. A sequence of bids and asks now appears. They are truly random: two-digit numbers from a table of random numbers are drawn, and the first digit determines whether it is a bid or ask (even or odd, respectively) and the second digit determines the level of the bid or ask (0–9, or, in market price units, (18¾–31). (This uniform distribution is replaced by a normal distribution later, but it suffices for the present.) The sequence of random numbers (here called "tenders") proceeds:

(1) 28: a bid (2 is even) of 8 (=29¾),

(2) 30: an ask (3 is odd) of 0 (=29¾),

Here a transaction occurs at 30¾ because this highest outstanding bid exceeds the seller's minimum ask. To proceed:

[13]Of course, the frequency of transactions depends upon the size of the individual transactions, but this is not closely correlated with frequency. A short sequence of the transactions of the NYSE was tabulated for November 5, 1963:

No. of Transactions	No. of Stock Issues	Average Transaction Size (Shares)
1	264	225
2	97	181
3	51	199
4	30	190
5	13	192
6	12	303
7	3	200
8	3	196
9	3	144
12–16	9	172
18–67	3	236

TABLE 5
Demand Schedule for a Security

Price	Aggregate Demand
28¾ (0)	800,000
29 (1)	780,000
29¼ (2)	760,000
29½ (3)	740,000
29¾ (4)	720,000
30 (5)	700,000
30¼ (6)	680,000
30½ (7)	660,000
30¾ (8)	640,000
31 (9)	620,000

(3) 95: an ask of 5,
(4) 01: a bid of 1,
(5) 10: an ask of 0.

This last trader sells at 1(=29) to the fourth tender. The process continues, with the further rule that any unfulfilled bids or asks are cancelled after twenty-five numbers. The transaction price and the minimum unfulfilled asking price and maximum unfulfilled bid are shown in Fig. 1.

The transaction prices fluctuate substantially, as will be seen–indeed the mean absolute deviation from the equilibrium price (taken as the closer of 29¾ or 30) is $0.34, or 34 per cent of the maximum possible absolute deviation. The average delay in fulfilling a bid or ask is 3.8 units of (tenders).[14] These particular results depend upon the special distribution of bids and asks we assume, but any reasonable distribution will generate significant fluctuations in price and significant and erratic delays in filling bids or asks.

The time unit involved in the foregoing analysis is the interval between successive bids or asks. If tenders are proportional to transactions, and the latter to dollar size of issue, this time unit will be inversely proportional to the size of issue. The time unit will be roughly 1/1,000 as long for American Telephone and Telegraph as for Oklahoma Gas and Electric common. In addition the effective price unit for trading may be ¼ or ½ dollar for the less active stock where it is 1/8 for the active stock.

In addition to allowing buyers and sellers to deal with one another, an efficient market is commonly expected to display the property of resilience (to use an unfamiliar word for a property whose absence is called "thinness"). Resilience is the ability to absorb *market* bid or ask orders (i.e., without a price limit) without an appreciable fluctuation in price. No market can absorb vast orders without large price changes, so this condition must be interpreted as follows: market buy and sell orders of a magnitude consistent with random

[14]This delay is the average of 7.59 units for the earlier tender plus zero units for the tender that makes a transaction. If we include bids or asks cancelled after twenty-five time units, the average delay is 8.04 units–perhaps a half-hour for an active stock, a week or a month for an inactive stock.

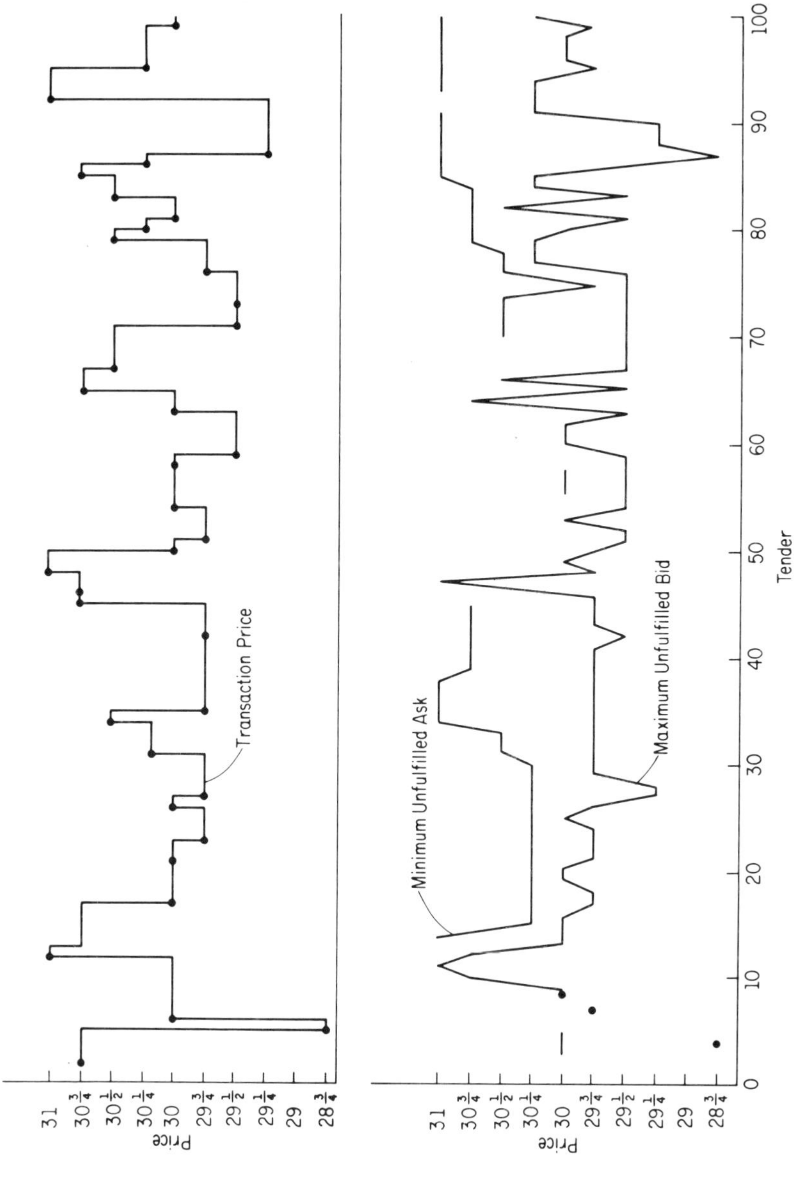

Fig. 1. Hypothetical sequence of transaction prices, generated by sequence of random numbers, and maximum unfulfilled bid and minimum unfulfilled ask prices (equilibrium price of 29¾ or 30).

fluctuation in tenders with an unchanging equilibrium price should not change the transaction prices appreciably.

The reason for making resilience a property of efficient markets may be approached through an analogy. If in a geographical area prices of a product differ, in response to random demand changes, by more than transportation costs, we say that the allocation of the product will be inefficient: A will buy the good for \$6 when B is unable to obtain it for \$7 (including transportation costs). Alternatively, the owners of the good are not maximizing its value.

Similarly, if random fluctuations in price—under our assumed condition of a stable equilibrium price—lead to price changes greater than inventory carrying costs (the cost of transporting a security from one date to another), the allocation of the product will be inefficient among buyers. Alternatively, the sellers are not maximizing the value of their holdings.

If access to the market is free, speculators will appear to provide resilience by carrying inventories of the stock; they are in fact primarily the specialists of the NYSE plus the floor traders. The speculators will charge the cost of carrying inventories and of their personal services by the bid-ask spread they establish, and in competitive equilibrium this spread will be just remunerative of these trading costs. The technical efficiency with which this inventory management is conducted will be measured by the spread between bid and ask prices.

In addition there are costs of the provision of the machinery of exchange, and these are also part of the cost of transactions. The performance of the main function of the exchange as a market place is subject to economies of scale. The greater the number of transactions in a security concentrated in one exchange, the smaller the discontinuities in trading and the smaller the necessary inventories of securities. As a result the price of a security will almost invariably be "made" in one exchange.

Specialists would then alter the price pattern of Fig. 1 by setting fixed bid and ask prices (under the present assumption of fixed supply and demand conditions). They will offer to buy all shares at, say, 29¾ and sell to all buyers at 30, and the difference (the "jobber's turn") will be the compensation for the costs of acting as a specialist.[15]

To summarize: the efficient market under stationary conditions of supply and demand has the properties:

1. If a bid equals or exceeds the lowest asking price (and similarly for offers), a transaxtion takes place.
2. Higher bids are fulfilled before lower bids, and conversely for offers.
3. Prices will fluctuate only within the limits of speculator's costs of providing a market (under competition).

[15] Specialists affect our model in the following ways: (1) the bid of 29¾ effectively eliminates all offers by non-dealers at less than 29¾, so the frequency distribution of offers now ranges from 29¾ to 31, with the lowest offer arising ½ of the time on average; (2) the offer of 20 effectively eliminates all bids by non-dealers at more than 30, with similar consequences.

In this regime the cost of transactions (half the bid-ask spread plus commissions) will be the complete inverse measure of the efficiency of the markets. Bid and ask prices will be (almost) constant through time.[16]

Let us consider now the formidable task of real markets, in which the equilibrium price changes without precise of advance notice. We illustrate the characteristic price patterns in the absence of speculation with Figs. 2 and 3. The sequences of bids, asks, and transaction prices follow the procedure of Fig. 1 with four changes:

1. The random numbers are normally distributed (with $\sigma = \$1.00$).
2. In Fig. 2 the equilibrium price is dropped from \$25.00 to \$23.75 after 50 tenders.
3. In Fig. 3 the equilibrium price begins a linear upward trend of 5 cents per tender after 25 tenders.
4. No tenders are cancelled because of staleness.

In each case, after the equilibrium changes the unfulfilled tenders are alternatively (1) retained, and (2) changed by the amount of the change in the equilibrium price—the two alternatives bracket the most reasonable assumptions. If the reader will compare the equilibrium prices with the observed sequences he will better appreciate the task of the specialist in detecting true changes and avoiding false changes in the equilibrium price (= population value).

If the impacts on equilibrium are sudden and unexpected—as in the examples underlying Fig. 2—the appropriate market response is an immediate and complete shift to the new price level. Under this condition the demand for "continuity" in a market is a demand for delay in responding to the change in demand contitions, and, the *Special Study* to the contrary, there simply is no merit in such delay.

The popular NYSE practice of suspending trading until buy and sell orders can be matched at a "reasonable" price is open to serious objection. To prevent a trade is no function of the exchange, and any defense must lie in a desire to avoid "unnecessary" price fluctuations. An unnecessary price fluctuation is surely one not called for by the conditions of supply and demand of the *week* even though the fluctuation may reflect supply and demand of the *hour*. This

[16]In the absence of specialists, the gains or losses of buyers measured from an expected price of 29 7/8 were exactly offset by the corresponding losses or gains for sellers. (We ignore commissions, which will be the same with or without specialists, at least as a first approximation.) The parties now lose the jobber's "turn" of (say) ¼, which is the price they pay for one of two things: (1) immediate availability of a buyer or seller; (2) the elimination of short run fluctuations in price. These two gains are analytically one: there is always an available buyer at a low enough price, and an available seller at a high enough price, so the gain of immediate marketability is at a price which contains no random elements. (Strictly speaking, we should say a price with much reduced random elements. The specialists' inventory will be exhausted from time to time when unusually long runs of bids or asks arise, since inventories will not be held in quantities sufficient to cope with the longest runs.)

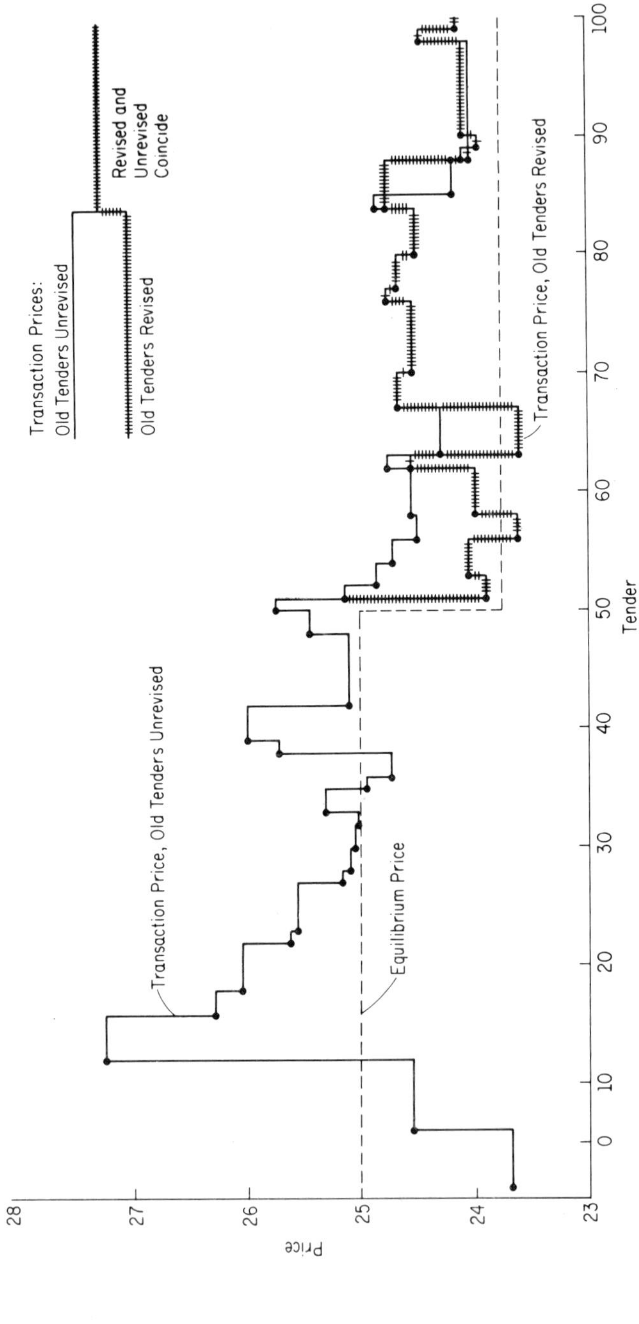

Fig. 2. Sequence of transaction prices generated by random normal deviates: Equilibrium price of \$25 for first 50 tenders; equilibrium price of \$23.75 thereafter.

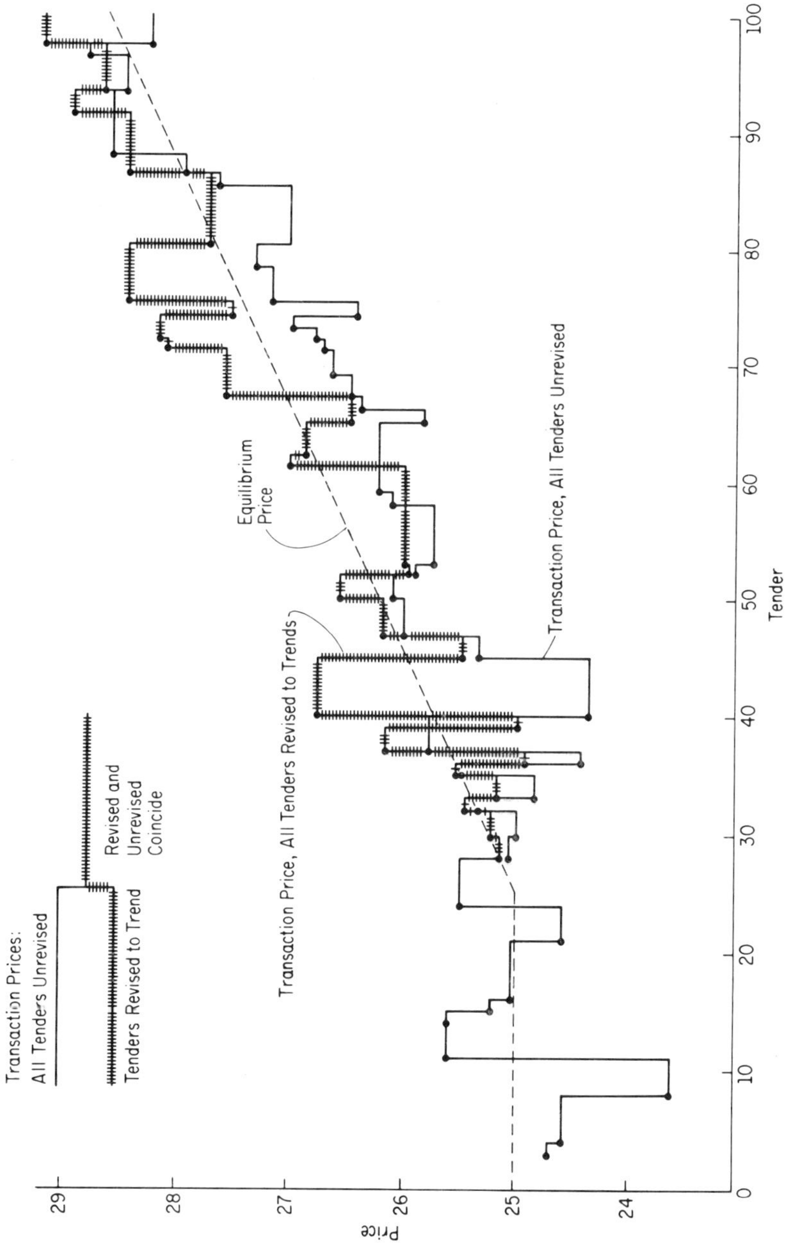

Fig. 3. Sequence of transaction prices generated by random normal deviates: Equilibrium price of $25 for first 25 tenders increasing $.05 per tender thereafter.

suspension of trading means that the exchange officials know the correct price change when there is a flood of buy or sell orders. We need not pause to inquire where they get this clairvoyance; it is enough to notice that the correct way to iron out the unnecessary wrinkles in the price chart is to speculate: to buy or sell against the unnecessary movement. The omniscient officials should be deprived of the power to suspend trading but given vast sums to speculate. Since omniscience can surely earn 20 or 50 per cent a year on the market, there should be no trouble in raising the capital. To disassociate random from persistent changes is sufficiently difficult, however, to make me very admiring of the courage of those who invest in Omniscience Unlimited.

The wholly unexpected shift in market conditions infrequently occurs—as the assassination of President Kennedy and the heart attack of President Eisenhower illustrate. But almost every event casts a shadow before it: the outbreak of war, the expropriation of foreign subsidiaries, the growth of imports of a product, the glowing income statement—all are more or less predictable as to date and import. The speculators then act within a system in which there is a partial anticipation of most events that occur (and many that do not). They will attempt to guess the future course of events, and to the extent that they succeed they will make profits and smooth the path of the price quotations.

In appraising the performance of the market under changing conditions we must abandon our criterion of efficiency in a stationary market that price should be constant over time (p. 129). We now must judge the performance of two functions by the speculator:

1. How efficiently does he perform his function of facilitating transactions by carrying inventories and making bid and ask prices?

2. How efficiently does he predict changes in equilibrium prices, or, in other words, how closely does he keep bid and ask prices to the levels which in retrospect were correct?

The first of these functions is analytically the same as that encountered in the stationary market, but it is now more difficult to discharge or appraise. It is much harder to judge the proper inventories and the proper amount of resources to devote to ascertaining the "true" market price than in the stationary market. The criterion of efficiency is still the cost of consummating a transaction. Much current work on inventory theory, queueing, and related subjects should contribute to the power of our tests of the efficiency of speculators.

The second function, the anticipation of price changes, has one measurable attribute: the trading profits of the speculators are a measure of their skill in anticipating price movements. What is more interesting is that the positive profits of the speculators also demonstrate that their activity stabilizes prices in the sense of reducing the variance of prices over time.[17]

[17] See Lester G. Telser, "A Theory of Speculation Relating Profitability and Stability," *Review of Economics and Statistics* (August 1959).

These profits as reported by the *Special Study* have been quite attractive: on liquid capital of $76.3 million in 1960, specialists made a trading income of $21.2 million (Part II, pp. 371, 373), as well as making $19.6 million in commissions. No profitability data are given for floor traders.

4. CONCLUSION

I have argued at suitable length that the Cohen Report makes poor use of either empirical evidence or economic theory, so its criticisms are founded upon prejudice and its reforms are directed by wishfulness. Full disclosure is the rule of the hour, so I must add that the academic scholars have not given the capital markets the attention they deserve because of their importance and analytical fascination. The area is replete with problems in the economics of information: What over-the-counter transactions should be required to be reported? Should floor traders' orders be delayed in execution to achieve parity with outsiders? and the like. It is an equally attractive area for the theory of decisions under uncertainty: what are the ex post criteria of efficient speculation? The prospectuses of research are glowing–should we start censoring this form of literature too?

APPENDIX

The lists of new flotations of common and preferred stocks are taken from the *Commercial and Financial Chronicle* for the earlier period, and *Investment Dealer's Digest* for the later period. Issues first offered only to stockholders and privately placed issues are excluded, as are public utilities and railroads.

The price quotations are the initial asking price and, at subsequent twelve-month intervals, the averages of the weekly high and low for the week nearest the middle of the month. Averages of monthly highs and lows are employed where weekly quotations are not available. Stock splits and dividends are eliminated, that is, the price of a share is multiplied by the number of shares the original share has become. If an issue of preferred stock is retired, its retirement value is used in the year of retirement, after which it is dropped from the sample.

The price relatives presented here are relative to issue price.

The market index is *Standard and Poor's Annual Industrial Index*. It is said to be biased upward in the early period but not in the later period; this bias would of course exaggerate the influence of the S.E.C. in our tests. *Standard and Poor's Index* covers only common stocks. Tables 1 and 3 of the text summarize information for these price relatives deflated by the relative value of the market index for the same period.

TABLE A–1

Price Relatives of Common Stocks

(Issue Price = 100)

Month of Issue and Stock Name	Value of Issue (Thousands)	Year after Issue				
		1 Year	2 Years	3 Years	4 Years	5 Years
1923						
1–Cuy Amel Fruit Co.	$ 2,942	135.0	99.3	90.6	61.8	99.8
2–Household Products, Inc.	9,350	97.1	105.7	132.4	142.1	195.8
4–Inland Steel	8,006	72.2	85.8	80.8	93.7	115.9
4–Eaton Axle & Spring Co.	4,200	51.7	50.4	91.2	87.5	116.5
5–Munsing Wear, Inc.	3,780	81.2	75.0	84.5	87.2	137.5
11–Wm. Wrigley Jr. & Co.	12,000	111.2	140.5	132.5	165.0	190.0
12–National Dairy Corp.	4,125	129.2	233.7	223.9	195.3	358.2
1924						
3–Transcontinental Oil Co.	$ 8,000	117.2	93.8	112.5	195.2	248.5
6–Game Well Co.	3,000	n.a.	n.a.	112.5	140.1	156.0
11–Brunswick Balke-Callender	6,435	65.4	70.3	67.9	113.5	46.2
12–Long-Bell Lumber Co.	7,912	93.7	80.4	53.1	55.9	24.6
12–(Frank G.) Shattuck Co.	2,750	252.2	229.5	327.3	444.3	460.9
12–The Symington Co.	996	95.0	87.1	87.9	30.1	20.9
1925						
1–Music Master Corp.	$ 3,000	15.6	0.0	0.0	0.0	0.0
2–The Gould Coupler Co.	3,675	82.0	35.0	36.5	30.0	36.5
2–The Cudahay Packing Co.	4,280	85.5	48.7	64.7	61.6	42.1
4–Dodge Bros. Inc.[a]	20,986	110.6	79.2	86.3	75.3	31.8
4–Gabriel Snubber Mfg. Co.	4,950	132.5	138.7	77.5	92.0	34.0
5–Sun Oil Co.	5,767	88.4	91.1	136.5	190.2	218.7
6–Hunt Bros. Packing Co.	2,600	n.a.	89.6	91.4	90.4	81.7
7–Atlas Plywood Corp.	2,500	120.0	104.8	169.5	109.1	37.5
7–Lehn & Fink Products	8,578	99.5	99.0	132.7	140.9	81.5
8–The Maytag Co.	5,000	114.0	158.8	89.4	128.1	56.9
8–Vick Chemical Co.	4,100	118.4	136.7	164.8	175.1	164.6
8–Industrial Rayon Corp.	3,000	42.5	47.8	85.2	99.8	91.9
9–Safety Insulated Wire & Cable Co.[b]	6,250	104.6	133.2	145.0	219.0	72.4
10–Tung-Sol Lamp Works Inc.	2,940	98.0	116.9	142.8	220.5	n.a.
10–American Brown Boveri Electric	13,000	76.5	19.6	28.6	35.2	26.5
10–Gotham Silk Hosiery Co.	2,750	205.4	285.4	280.4	134.2	33.1
10–Western Dairy	3,600	100.0	115.8	129.9	116.9	51.1
11–Fox Theatre Corp.	12,500	95.7	77.2	115.0	50.3	28.0
11–Rice-Stix Dry Goods Co.	2,650	76.9	82.1	71.2	55.7	37.3
12–Consolidated Laundries Corp.	2,750	98.9	71.0	86.1	48.0	59.4
1926						
1–North American Car Corp.	$ 2,588	94.4	106.6	210.7	128.2	95.2

[a] Acquired by Chrysler Motors on July 30, 1928.

[b] Name changed to Safety Cable Co., October 6, 1925, and changed to General Cable Co., November 14, 1927.

TABLE A–1 (continued)

Month of Issue and Stock Name	Value of Issue (Thousands)	Year after Issue				
		1 Year	2 Years	3 Years	4 Years	5 Years
1926						
1–Congress Cigar Co., Inc.	2,800	135.0	200.8	204.2	113.1	56.2
1–Beacon Oil Co.[c]	5,700	105.3	84.2	122.0	78.3	52.0
2–American Home Products Corp.	5,962	120.8	238.2	290.6	221.2	217.9
2–Grief Bros. Cooperage Co.	2,560	105.6	106.9	.100.6	56.2	50.8
2–Amerada Corp.	3,250	141.6	112.5	123.6	74.5	74.5
3–Lambert Co.	7,958	176.5	223.8	234.5	255.7	205.8
7–American Solvents & Chemicals	632	n.a.	158.7	270.5	61.3	9.9
8–Liquid Carbonic Corp.	3,220	102.9	178.6	267.3	205.3	61.5
9–Penn-Dixie Cement Co.	$12,900	59.6	34.0	21.5	15.7	4.0
11–Pacific-Clay Products	2,800	100.9	98.7	105.4	54.9	33.9
12–Patino Mines Enterprises Consol.	5,000	89.8	132.7	117.2	34.0	26.0
12–Fulton Sylphon Co.[d]	3,900	118.4	115.4	64.1	32.2	22.4
1927						
1–National Tile Co.	$ 2,970	n.a.	105.3	82.2	21.2	8.3
3–W. T. Grant Co.	2,688	250.0	267.6	71.3	72.6	60.6
3–Mandel Bros. Inc.	3,638	78.4	71.1	29.8	10.4	5.2
6–Pillsbury Flour Mills, Inc.	3,500	37.2	43.8	30.0	27.5	13.2
8–(John W.) Watson Co.	4,900	27.6	13.5	8.6	1.6	1.3
10–Hershey Chocolate Corp.	3,468	174.3	311.8	243.0	238.4	169.4
11–National Radiator Corp.	2,535	45.2	9.8	3.2	0.3	0.0
11–United Biscuit Co. of America	2,800	181.9	130.8	126.8	95.8	66.5
12–McKeesport Tin Plate Co.	6,000	120.0	106.2	114.4	80.2	74.8
1928						
1–Consolidated Film Industries	$ 1,575	83.1	63.5	46.2	19.0	13.8
2–National Trade Journal Inc.	2,529	29.8	12.3	3.0	0.0	0.0
3–Cutler-Hammer Mfg. Co.	3,088	129.7	219.5	84.6	21.2	13.9
4–Neve Drug Stores, Inc.[e]	4,000	56.2	23.3	14.8	n.a.	n.a.
5–H. W. Gossard Co.	2,588	90.0	64.8	12.8	2.0	4.6
5–Spiegel, May, Stern & Co.	4,060	178.6	57.3	13.4	2.8	10.3
6–Grasselli Chemical Co.[f]	4,700	274.0	155.3	129.2	33.7	112.8
6–International Printing Ink Corp.	4,945	119.8	83.7	18.3	9.3	27.0
6–National Aviation Corp.	3,525	281.7	52.7	27.5	14.6	45.0
6–The Wayne Pump Co.	820	52.1	35.7	8.2	1.2	2.2
6–Consolidated Automatic Merchandising	824	55.9	6.8	2.3	0.7	3.4
7–Kimberly-Clark Corp.	7,280	99.5	102.9	60.9	19.2	41.9
9–Anchor Cap Corp.	4,239	166.5	96.5	46.2	25.3	62.9

[c] Name changed to Colonial Beacon Oil, 1930.
[d] Acquired by Reynolds Metal Co., January, 1929.
[e] Acquired by United Retail Chemists in December, 1928.
[f] Acquired by DuPont Chemical Co., November 1928.

TABLE A–1 (continued)

Month of Issue and Stock Name	Value of Issue (Thousands)	Year after issue				
		1 Year	2 Years	3 Years	4 Years	5 Years
1928						
9–Curtis Flying Service[g]	9,450	146.4	35.7	16.1	11.9	17.9
10–Hershey Corp.[h]	1,338	94.2	18.5	11.4	8.0	9.8
10–Sonora Products	3,000	15.0	0.0	0.0	0.0	0.0
10–Allied Products Corp.	2,500	120.1	33.8	20.0	11.5	12.8
10–Lane Drug Stores Inc.	785	60.5	4.1	1.3	n.a.	n.a.
11–Joseph T. Ryerson & Son	3,900	84.6	66.0	37.7	19.2	31.4
11–Associated Rayon Corp.	3,352	12.7	3.7	6.2	n.a.	n.a.
11–Bellanca Aircraft Corp.	2,972	31.9	16.8	6.4	2.6	17.0
11–United Aircraft & Transport	1,116	112.5	69.0	38.6	59.9	74.1
11–Great Lakes Aircraft Corp.	4,900	32.4	9.2	10.2	2.5	2.8
11–Ranier Pulp & Paper Co.	3,325	81.2	36.1	30.1	19.6	58.6
11–Ritter Dental Mfg. Co.	2,580	102.3	70.4	29.2	20.9	23.3
11–Universal Aviation	4,300	40.7	23.5	16.1	35.3	44.3
11–Pacific Western Oil Corp.	16,080	58.3	38.5	20.8	17.7	32.3
11–Merritt-Chapman & Scott	2,500	84.5	72.0	40.0	1.1	19.2
11–Strauss (Nathan) Inc.	2,695	54.9	20.4	0.2	0.0	0.0
12–Aluminum Goods Mfg. Corp.	4,000	113.1	71.6	49.7	42.2	46.2
12–Helena Rubinstein	3,147	28.4	8.3	3.8	3.2	1.9
12–Hahn Dept. Stores	17,252	39.0	20.7	8.6	4.0	14.1
12–Kroger Grocery & Baking	9,194	51.5	21.8	21.4	18.9	26.4
1949						
1–Bethlehem Steel Corp.	$20,409	99.0	171.0	161.4	172.1	165.8
1–Affiliated Gas Equip., Inc.	9,250	113.5	106.2	97.3	104.8	86.5
1–Koppers Co., Inc.	12,400	94.0	122.8	152.6	128.6	102.6
3–Sylvania Electric Products, Inc.	5,469	99.8	130.6	176.8	162.3	178.2
4–Liggett & Myers Tobacco Co.	38,729	163.9	135.5	128.2	151.8	121.4
1950						
4–Dumont (A.B.) Labs, Inc.	$ 6,250	43.9	46.4	38.8	26.6	40.2
6–Sunray Oil Corp.[i]	9,469	152.5	166.4	139.1	151.5	201.1
9–Canadian Superior Oil of California, (Ltd.)	19,350	145.6	121.2	72.5	108.8	120.0
10–Kaiser Steel Corp.	31,616	104.0	102.5	102.5	112.6	120.2
12–International Min. & Chem.	10,224	75.4	77.6	58.7	77.1	60.4
1951						
3–Jones & Laughlin Steel Corp.	$25,250	92.6	90.4	84.9	139.8	197.0
3–Kimberly Clark Corp.	9,000	102.1	96.1	119.4	202.8	235.6
5–Sylvania Electric Products Inc.	11,650	114.8	121.3	121.9	158.0	177.9
6–Squibb (E. R.) & Sons[j]	15,375	49.5	41.6	53.0	68.3	62.8

[g]Acquired by Curtiss Wright in August, 1929.
[h]Name changed to Houdaille-Hershey Corp. on January 30, 1929.
[i]Name changed to Sunray Mid-Continent Oil Company, 1955.
[j]Merged with (Olin) Mathieson (Chemical) Corp., 1952.

TABLE A–1 (continued)

Month of Issue and Stock Name	Value of Issue (Thousands)	Year after Issue				
		1 Year	2 Years	3 Years	4 Years	5 Years
1951						
10–Aluminium Ltd.	7,095	94.9	87.5	125.8	197.4	237.8
10–Sharon Steel Corp.	7,314	81.9	80.7	69.0	106.9	110.0
10–Lion Oil[k]	14,788	82.7	71.9	98.2	155.8	131.1
12–Federated Dept. Stores	10,030	112.8	99.6	141.9	173.9	157.3
1952						
2–Koppers Co.	$11,250	85.3	76.4	103.9	119.4	120.6
2–Owens-Corning Fiberglass	16,088	125.2	156.6	196.1	281.4	312.6
2–Rheem Mfg. Co.	6,200	89.1	88.3	141.7	110.5	60.1
2–Marathon Corp.	10,900	86.7	80.3	108.9	137.8	107.8
2–Monsanto Chemical Co.	39,200	94.0	86.2	108.2	135.6	96.6
3–Ga.-Pacific Plywood & Lumber Co.[l]	5,250	81.2	53.9	127.4	217.7	292.7
3–Can. Chem. & Cellulose Co.	7,750	81.0	53.6	67.0	64.9	48.0
5–Lion Oil Co.[k]	16,048	86.9	100.3	122.4	156.6	133.9
5–Food Mach. & Chemical	13,425	82.7	95.4	112.0	147.5	139.1
5–Federated Petrol. Ltd[m]	5,175	52.9	38.6	49.6	59.5	100.1
7–Deere & Co.	22,121	81.4	90.1	113.7	86.1	91.2
8–Pillsbury Mills	5,640	107.0	139.7	155.1	143.2	131.8
12–Colorado Fuel & Iron	6,000	89.6	120.6	167.0	180.4	109.0
1953						
2–Sylvania Electric Prods.	$20,141	92.7	135.4	135.9	122.4	108.5
4–Clevite Corp.	5,076	82.7	86.7	84.7	81.8	65.0
4–P. Lorillard	8,290	105.9	96.8	85.0	72.9	226.9
9–Stauffer Chemical	7,750	148.0	221.5	229.4	262.6	343.4
1954						
1–Colorado Oil & Gas	$12,500	108.0	128.0	154.0	108.5	132.5
2–Wagner Electric Corp.	5,400	87.8	95.5	136.1	107.6	143.8
4–American Tide Lands[n]	20,000	11.8	8.8	6.5	1.7	4.2
12–Monterey Oil Co.	10,950	91.1	88.5	58.2	96.1	64.0
1955						
1–United Artists Theatre Circuit	$ 6,802	50.0	34.9	25.7	56.2	50.7
2–Allied Stores Corp.	16,425	96.7	76.6	77.3	102.6	98.1
4–Storer Broadcasting Co.	6,469	99.2	113.7	93.2	130.0	116.3
10–Copperweld Steel Co.	6,000	115.5	109.5	132.5	196.3	135.0
11–Marquette Cement Mfg.	8,688	98.0	84.2	152.9	136.7	139.6
11–Kimberly-Clark Corp.	18,552	93.4	94.1	148.2	144.2	177.2
12–LeCuno Oil Corp.	4,060	61.6	41.0	35.7	17.9	10.7
12–Minute Maid Corp.	6,900	59.8	29.0	100.4	118.0	207.2

[k]Acquired by Monsanto Chemical, September 30, 1955.
[l]Name changed to Ga-Pacific Corp., April 1956.
[m]Merged with Home Oil, December 1955.
[n]Name changed to Marine Drilling Inc., September 1, 1957.

TABLE A–2

Price Relatives of Preferred Stocks

(Issue Price = 100)

Month of Issue and Stock Name	Value of Issue (Thousands)	Year after Issue				
		1 Year	2 Years	3 Years	4 Years	5 Years
1923						
1–(Edward G.) Budd Mfg.	$ 3,000	n.a.	n.a.	n.a.	n.a.	73.7
1–Hammerhill Paper Co.	3,000	101.0	105.0	108.8	108.8	109.0
1–Reliance Mfg. Co.	2,500	96.2	87.1	88.4	99.0	99.2
1–Armour & Co.	60,000	93.6	93.2	98.4	95.2	90.0
1–Lyon & Healy, Inc.	2,500	98.2	103.5	110.0	*	*
1–American Rolling Mill	7,000	100.5	107.2	110.2	112.8	110.0
2–Onyx Hosiery, Inc.[a]	3,500	89.5	80.5	97.5	114.3	122.2
2–National Dept. Stores	5,000	95.5	99.5	95.8	91.5	91.2
2–Rosenbaum Grain Coorp.	3,625	95.1	94.1	7.8	29.4	33.3
3–American Chain Co.	8,750	87.0	93.9	94.6	118.6	*
3–National Cloak & Suit Co.[b]	4,000	93.5	101.0	84.5	90.8	99.9
4–Inland Steel	10,000	98.0	100.6	105.3	108.4	111.4
5–Sherman Clay & Co.	3,000	n.a.	n.a.	94.8	97.7	98.6
9–Remington Arms Co. Inc.	4,000	n.a.	n.a.	100.3	94.1	101.6
11–Palmolive Co.[c]	4,000	n.a.	n.a.	n.a.	107.9	110.0
1924						
9–Franklin Simon & Co.	$ 4,000	101.7	103.9	107.1	104.6	96.4
10–R. Hoe & Co. Inc.	4,000	90.0	59.0	66.0	38.0	52.0
12–Universal Pictures Corp.	3,000	94.9	97.8	99.1	93.5	39.5
12–The Symington Co.	4,504	51.8	24.2	19.4	51.6	37.2
1925						
2–Artloom Corp.	$ 3,000	111.0	113.6	113.0	99.0	60.9
2–First National Pictures, Inc.	2,500	103.7	97.6	107.5	106.0	115.0
2–Spear & Co.	4,500	81.9	78.6	80.4	80.2	79.1
2–General Outdoor Advertising	5,812	118.7	124.2	123.7	109.1	92.3
4–Dodge Bros., Inc.[d]	64,014	108.2	99.2	96.3	152.7	*
7–International Cement Corp.	6,750	101.8	106.8	107.3	*	*
7–International Match Corp.	20,250	144.9	157.9	229.4	203.6	173.2
7–The Outlet Co.	3,500	101.1	110.5	114.5	82.0	105.0
9–(Edward G.) Budd Mfg. Co.	2,500	n.a.	n.a.	n.a.	75.6	61.9
9–Real Silk Hosiery Co.	2,500	n.a.	88.8	93.0	97.1	89.5
10–The Miller Rubber Co.[e]	4,000	96.6	96.6	77.8	42.5	13.1
10–National Tea Co.	3,250	124.8	164.4	287.2	250.0	71.0
10–Gotham Silk Hosiery Co.	4,500	114.9	121.0	111.0	82.9	68.6
11–Firestone Tire & Rubber Co.	10,000	98.8	107.9	108.0	111.1	*
12–St. Maurice Valley Corp.	3,806	n.a.	100.4	96.6	91.0	50.0

*Issue retired.

[a]Acquired by Gotham Silk, December, 1926.

[b]Name changed to Bellas Hess Co., March, 1927.

[c]Name changed to Palmolive-Peet Company, February, 1927, and to Colgate-Palmolive-Peet Company, June, 1928.

[d]Acquired by Chrysler Corp., July 30, 1928.

[e]Acquired by B. F. Goodrich, March, 1930.

TABLE A–2 (continued)

Month of Issue and Stock Name	Value of Issue (Thousands)	Year after Issue				
		1 Year	2 Years	3 Years	4 Years	5 Years
1925						
12–Abraham & Strauss, Inc.	4,250	110.1	110.8	109.6	104.4	106.4
12–New York Canners, Inc.	5,100	89.4	55.0	38.9	27.9	14.5
1926						
1–Chandler Cleveland Motors[f]	$ 3,360	48.0	35.3	40.8	11.2	4.4
1–Crown-Williamette Paper Co.	20,000	99.9	97.8	96.5	100.6	68.0
1–White Sewing Machine Co.	5,000	113.5	109.1	112.8	58.5	13.8
1–Louisiana Oil Refining Corp.	4,000	96.6	90.0	92.2	86.0	55.0
2–Bethlehem Steel Corp.	35,000	107.7	120.6	121.8	126.4	121.4
2–Zellerbach Corp.	5,850	99.0	141.9	98.0	82.3	41.3
3–Collins & Aikman Co.	5,000	152.7	99.9	94.1	83.2	73.9
6–American Seating Corp.	3,000	123.3	99.3	92.7	28.0	12.7
7–American Solvents & Chem.	2,868	69.7	110.5	174.3	69.7	10.9
8–The Halle Bros. Co.	2,500	102.5	102.5	102.0	97.5	90.0
9–Sculling Steel Co.	3,850	85.7	93.8	76.0	45.4	13.0
9–Pacific Coast Biscuit Co.[g]	2,910	99.5	88.7	101.6	359.9	352.5
9–Penn-Dixie Cement Corp.	7,215	94.1	75.8	44.7	40.4	10.1
10–Central Alloy Steel Corp.[h]	6,189	100.5	103.5	104.2	69.5	17.8
10–(Edward G.) Budd Mfg. Co.	3,000	n.a.	32.8	81.1	63.9	23.7
10–Broadway Dept. Stores	3,000	108.4	102.3	93.4	71.7	n.a.
11–Gotham Silk Hosiery Co.	5,000	117.2	117.0	83.1	62.3	58.8
12–Flintkote Co.	2,500	n.a.	110.0	*	*	*
1927						
2–General Motors Corp.	$25,000	104.2	104.6	101.6	83.1	70.2
2–L. Bamberger & Co.	10,000	106.7	105.3	104.1	101.6	91.4
3–American Chain Co.	11,000	100.3	82.0	94.0	35.6	17.5
3–Richfield Oil Co. of Cal.	5,000	111.2	180.5	107.0	24.7	2.5
4–United Cigar Stores of America	20,000	104.7	92.2	40.8	70.0	8.3
5–Crown-Zellerbach Corp.	2,992	127.3	92.0	81.2	21.6	13.8
5–Sun Oil Co.	4,500	109.8	102.9	104.1	95.0	73.4
6–International Paper Co.	15,000	105.2	87.9	78.2	25.0	4.8
6–Pillsbury Flour Mills Inc.	3,000	111.4	109.4	75.0	68.8	33.1
7–Auto Strap Safety Razor Co.[i]	3,762	104.9	99.7	145.4	163.1	157.6
7–Collins & Aikman Corp.	5,500	89.6	90.3	80.3	77.9	55.3
7–Pennsylvania Glass Sand Corp.	3,000	n.a.	115.0	105.0	90.0	n.a.
7–Foster Wheeler Corp.	3,500	n.a.	n.a.	205.0	100.0	75.0
8–National Radiator Corp.	5,850	66.7	15.9	4.0	0.9	0.0
8–Weber & Heilbroner, Inc.[j]	2,500	98.5	90.6	49.0	13.7	4.9
10–Hershey Chocolate Corp. (6 per cent cum. prior pref.)	15,000	104.6	107.6	108.6	*	*
10–Hershey Chocolate Corp. (conv. pref. cum $4/sh.)	22,432	124.4	221.3	143.5	132.6	122.3

[f] Merged with Hupp Motor Car, 1930.
[g] Acquired by National Biscuits, June, 1930.
[h] Merged with Republic Steel, April, 1930.
[i] Acquired by Gillette Safety Razor, November, 1930.
[j] Name changed to Fashion Park, 1929.

TABLE A–2 (continued)

Month of Issue and Stock Name	Value of Issue (Thousands)	Year after Issue				
		1 Year	2 Years	3 Years	4 Years	5 Years
1927						
10–St. Regis Paper Co.	2,740	86.3	99.0	106.4	n.a.	30.9
12–The Cuneo Press Inc.	2,500	92.4	78.7	89.0	65.4	61.7
12–George A. Fuller Co.	4,478	104.9	96.5	82.9	30.2	9.2
12–F. & W. Grand 5-10-25 ¢ Stores	2,500	72.8	38.6	21.4	2.4	0.9
12–Loews Inc.	15,000	101.4	44.3	90.5	59.2	59.6
1928						
1–General Tire & Rubber Co.	$ 3,500	99.5	88.7	82.4	58.3	35.3
1–Consolidated Film Industries	6,375	126.2	92.3	82.1	50.6	43.2
1–Walgreen Co.	4,500	95.5	91.0	85.0	64.7	92.4
2–Hamilton Watch Co.	4,800	100.2	103.5	102.0	64.7	19.9
2–United Piece Dye Works	3,750	103.4	93.7	102.2	88.4	68.0
2–Interstate Dept. Stores Inc.	3,250	128.3	70.8	58.0	46.0	17.4
2–Keith-Albee Orpheum Co.	10,000	112.4	99.5	94.3	24.8	10.9
2–Neisner Bros. Inc.	2,500	178.3	106.5	68.9	2.8	12.8
2–Schulte-United 5¢–$1 Store	10,000	76.0	18.0	1.1	0.0	0.0
3–Spang Chalfant & Co. Inc.	2,500	94.9	96.9	93.4	43.4	20.7
3–Barker Bros. Corp.	3,000	96.0	78.5	55.0	25.0	1.1
3–Standard Dredging Company	4,350	123.3	103.4	33.2	7.8	2.1
4–Brown Co.	10,000	97.4	28.3	34.0	4.7	2.8
4–Cavanagh-Dobbs, Inc.[k]	3,500	96.4	70.2	22.0	7.6	6.0
4–Unit Corp. of America	3,135	98.2	79.0	16.7	0.9	0.0
4–Metropolitan Chain Stores	3,500	99.1	72.6	8.7	0.0	0.0
4–Peoples Drug Store, Inc.	2,500	107.9	100.5	95.6	81.9	60.5
4–Consumers Co.	5,000	79.0	67.4	41.6	4.2	1.6
5–I. Miller & Sons, Inc.	2,500	90.5	77.1	39.3	13.9	5.8
5–Speigel, May, Stern & Co.	7,000	89.2	69.4	17.6	19.8	35.1
6–Borg Warner	3,500	109.8	95.0	95.6	51.7	85.7
6–Hart-Carter Co.	4,480	78.9	56.6	20.3	7.8	25.2
6–International Printing Ink Corp.	7,000	95.7	94.0	59.1	31.7	68.1
6–The Wayne Pump Co.	2,218	78.1	65.9	30.4	5.2	4.7
6–California Dairies Inc.	4,312	50.4	44.9	21.4	4.1	9.8
6–Consolidated Automatic Merchandising	10,176	38.8	6.9	1.0	0.3	1.5
6–Crosse & Blackwell, Inc.	2,704	94.7	71.2	46.8	n.a.	n.a.
6–Leath & Co.	2,642	78.8	65.4	17.3	13.5	8.2
7–Miller & Hart Inc.	2,860	82.0	60.6	33.6	15.4	22.1
9–Anchor Cap Corp.	3,060	139.3	104.9	85.3	69.2	88.0
9–Kendall Co.	3,888	88.7	68.0	40.5	26.2	67.0
9–McKesson & Robbins	9,889	107.4	77.4	57.4	18.1	40.0
10–Houdaille-Hershey Corp.	1,329	97.2	44.2	40.3	19.8	26.9
10–Mullins Mfg. Co.	3,060	83.3	40.3	22.7	15.4	10.4
10–Chase Brass & Copper Co.	2,500	99.4	100.1	87.8	72.2	84.4
10–Mid-Continent Laundries	3,400	65.4	6.6	3.7	n.a.	n.a.
10–Lane Drug Stores, Inc.	1,717	79.5	3.8	2.4	n.a.	n.a.
11–Associated Rayon Corp.	17,648	39.8	48.2	33.1	*	*

[k]Merged with Hat Corp., May, 1932.

TABLE A–2 (continued)

Month of Issue and Stock Name	Value of Issue (Thousands)	Year after Issue				
		1 Year	2 Years	3 Years	4 Years	5 Years
1928						
11–United Aircraft & Trans. Corp.	4,194	112.5	116.3	103.0	118.8	131.6
11–Kraft Phenix Cheese[l]	6,000	96.0	45.5	37.7	30.0	28.6
12–Thompson & Stanet Coo. ...	8,800	67.7	50.6	34.3	30.1	39.7
12–Hahn Dept. Stores	22,700	76.6	54.8	30.3	12.9	24.9
12–Koppers Gas & Coke	20,000	98.5	97.0	63.6	49.5	59.4
12–The Newport Co.[m]	6,500	104.0	70.5	110.2	4.4	14.5
1949						
4–Merck & Co. Inc.	$ 7,192	130.4	n.a.	110.2	98.0	101.7
5–United Biscuit Co. of America	8,280	104.1	103.6	101.4	98.8	102.9
6–Caterpillar Tractor Co.	25,000	105.1	102.9	103.8	98.5	102.5
11–Clinton Industries Inc.	5,025	109.6	98.5	89.1	95.4	113.8
1950						
7–Spencer Chemicals	$ 6,821	100.9	101.2	99.2	102.0	102.5
10–Kaiser Steel Corp.	31,616	104.0	102.5	102.5	112.6	120.2
11–Safeway Stores	6,400	94.0	85.8	90.9	97.2	94.5
1951						
1–City Stores Co.	$ 6,000	86.1	82.1	75.8	96.0	105.8
1–Food Fair Stores, Inc.	8,000	94.2	97.2	93.5	100.0	101.2
6–Minn.-Honeywell Regulator Co.	16,000	108.8	105.4	103.4	*	*
6–Pfizer (Chas.) & Co. Inc.	15,000	110.7	93.8	103.3	113.8	98.7
6–Rheem Mfg. Co.	7,000	92.1	89.7	100.5	118.4	90.2
6–National Tea Co.	12,000	105.0	107.9	125.9	104.0	*
8–U.S. Plywood Coorp.	6,150	94.1	82.6	88.8	99.8	116.8
8–National Distillers Prods.	50,000	101.5	88.8	93.8	99.8	100.6
9–National Container	12,600	87.1	74.3	92.6	141.7	231.4
10–Ashland Oil & Refining	5,045	100.5	97.7	99.5	101.8	97.9
10–Shell Mar Products[n]	5,200	123.2	118.5	127.4	*	*
12–(Olin) Mathieson Chem. Corp.	18,000	109.8	103.9	122.5	120.9	108.1
12–Diamond Alkali Co.	12,000	108.2	100.1	114.1	116.8	103.0*
12–Pittsburgh Coke & Chem. ...	6,000	94.2	78.4	84.0	92.2	90.5
1952						
1–Kaiser Aluminum & Chem. ..	$18,750	92.5	95.2	169.4	104.0	*
1–Consolidated Grocers[o]	9,800	86.2	92.9	99.0	103.6	98.8
1–Atlas Plywood Corp.	5,700	86.3	75.0	82.7	77.9	70.5
5–Elliott Co.	6,000	107.5	102.1	101.8	94.5	104.2
6–Safeway Stores	20,000	106.0	103.0	*	*	*

[l]Acquired by National Dairy, June 4, 1930.
[m]Name changed to Newport Industries, 1931.

[n]Name changed to General Package Corp., July 1953.
[o]Name changed to Consolidated Foods Corp., February, 1954.

TABLE A–2 (continued)

Month of Issue and Stock Name	Value of Issue (Thousands)	Year after Issue				
		1 Year	2 Years	3 Years	4 Years	5 Years
1953						
3–P. R. Mallory	$ 7,500	109.5	109.5	105.5	105.0	*
11–General Precision Equip.	5,408	192.5	106.0	*	*	*
11–Dixie Cup[p]	7,623	142.2	137.2	133.5	104.0	*
1954						
2–Gulf Sulphur Corp.	$ 7,000	111.2	125.0	70.0	31.9	55.0
4–I.T.E. Circuit Breaker	5,000	101.8	97.0	93.0	74.4	92.1
5–Allis-Chalmers Mfg.	35,700	121.6	110.3	113.0	93.6	108.8
9–Spencer Chemical Co.	15,000	99.2	97.0	81.2	91.0	87.2
10–Mead Corp.	7,800	132.9	103.8	*	*	*
11–Tung-Sol Electric	5,000	111.5	103.5	103.6	*	*
11–Penn. Fruit Co.	5,225	106.2	82.3	70.3	95.7	98.6
1955						
3–General Tire & Rubber	$10,225	108.6	126.0	143.8	380.4	428.7
3–Western Auto Supply	5,000	105.0	96.0	99.8	99.1	96.4
5–Minn.-Honeywell Regulator	16,320	102.9	*	*	*	*
9–Kaiser Aluminum & Chem.	35,000	97.8	84.0	84.0	92.0	92.0

[p]Acquired by American Can, June, 1957.

Part II

Fundamental Approaches to Investment Analysis

INTRODUCTION

It is estimated that more than one of every six adults in the United States now owns stock in the nation's publicly held companies. There has been an increase of more than ten million shareowners of the publicly held firms in the past decade. In addition, several million citizens own shares in privately held companies. On the institutional side of the market, the growth of investment companies has been dramatic and well chronicled, mushrooming from four billion dollars in assets in 1946 to more than fifty billion two decades later.

One important reason for this growth in stock ownership seems to be the increased realization that the value of the dollar has fallen steadily since the end of World War II. A second cause may be the widespread evidence that common stocks have been an effective hedge against this inflation. For example, a recent study conducted by the Center for Research in Security Prices of the University of Chicago indicated that anyone who had invested in common stocks broadly from 1926 and had maintained his investment through 1960 would have realized substantial capital appreciation. In other words, increasing numbers of our citizens are becoming aware of the fact that since 1946 the dollar has lost over one third of its purchasing power and during the same time the Standard and Poor's Index of Common Stocks has increased fivefold.

This tremendous increase in the number of stockholders has created the need for more information concerning the investment merits of the many segments of this investment medium.

The articles presented in this section focus on a few of the primary problems encountered in selecting common stocks. The emphasis is on the evaluation of growth. In the first reading William Kurtz discusses those factors which form the basis for determining the 'normal value' of an equity. This valuation method is based on statistical relationships derived from the period 1927–1939. Popular opinions concerning the relationship of growth in earnings and appropriate price-earnings ratios are challenged first by Professors Clendenin and Van Cleave who present data on price appreciation in growth and non-growth stocks for the period 1940–1954, and, secondly, by Professor David Durand who uses a mathematical approach to expose fallacies in many of these opinions.

The reader is introduced to current growth stock valuation methods by Professor Paul Wendt who applies ten approaches prescribed by different scholars to one stock. Professors Heins and Allison examine some of the factors which affect stock price variability. Professor Holt offers an excellent treatise on the relationship between price-earnings ratio, rate of growth, and the duration of growth. Professors Pfahl and Crary examine the relationship of financial leverage to the rate of return anticipated by equity interests. The concluding articles of this section deal with two of the more controversial topics being discussed in the current finance literature. Professors Weil, Segall, and Green discuss premiums on convertible bonds and Professor Mosich considers the impact of merger accounting on post-merger financial reports.

7

Valuation Standards for Investments*

William Kurtz

INTRODUCTION

The interplay of the many factors that combine to make the market price of a common stock at a given moment admittedly does not lend itself to mathematical calculation. However, it is believed that standards can be derived from selected fundamental factors to indicate what might be a "normal value" for a stock at a given time. Establishment of a normal value does not fully answer the investor's question concerning whether or not to buy or sell a particular stock at a given moment but it may be a useful tool in making sound investment decisions. Our studies made over a period of several years suggest that equities tend to fluctuate approximately 20% around their normal value estimates. Volatile stocks may fluctuate 40% around central values while stable issues may be confined to a 10% range of normal value levels. Stocks benefitting from near-term favorable corporate developments or expectations generally sell above their normal values. Conversely, equities that are currently unpopular or face some near-term unfavorable news development tend to sell below normal value estimates. Thus, the valuation methods we have developed are effective only in conjunction with security analysis in depth by industry specialists who provide the fundamental information that may determine whether a stock will sell below or above its normal value. Moreover, valuation studies can be of help to the security analyst in determining to what extent a company's current prospects may be reflected in the price of its stock. For example, highly favorable corporate news releases might have little impact in the market place if the stock were selling 20%-40% above its normal value.

Valuation techniques based upon specialists' fundamental judgments provide the means for establishing the *level* of normal value while current security analysis can be helpful in detecting the *trend* of value. In today's performance-minded environment, it is essential to gauge both the *level* and the *trend* of values. There are numerous examples of high-grade equities selling 20% below

*A paper presented before a Joint Meeting of the Chicago Chapter of the American Statistical Association and The Investment Analysts Society of Chicago at Northwestern University, Evanston, Illinois, April 12, 1966. Reprinted by permission of Hornblower and Weeks–Hemphill, Noyes, 8 Hanover Street, New York, New York, 10004.

normal value for long periods. Conversely, popular issues purchased at or above normal value levels may represent highly successful investments over a shorter period of time.

One should note that valuation techniques and security analysis may reflect only a portion of a stock's price fluctuations in a given period. Numerous random forces and technical market factors may dominate trading activity in popular equities at certain stages of a market's life cycle. It is during such periods that share prices tend to sell 20%-40% above or below normal levels. Recognition of these "outer limits" of probable price performance through the establishment of sound valuation standards could be highly useful at critical market levels.

In general terms, our valuation approach consists of three factors:

1. A price-earnings ratio assuming no growth in earnings.
2. An earnings growth-rate adjustment.
3. An adjustment to reflect relative quality of investment.

The above factors are combined as follows:

$$\text{Normal } P/E \text{ Ratio} = \text{Non-Growth } P/E \text{ Ratio} \times \text{Growth Factor} \times \text{Quality Factor}$$

The non-growth multiple represents the average price-earnings growth equity of average investment quality during the period 1926-1946. It was derived from a correlation of earnings and prices of a large number of stocks for the years indicated and works out to an average price-earnings multiple of 12.8. This ratio will vary inversely with the relationship between current earnings and normal earning power. That is to say, cyclical peak earnings receive a lower earnings multiple than do depressed earnings in our formula.

The growth rate adjustment, called the "growth factor," is obtained from compound interest tables over a five-year period. The five-year term was selected because corporate budgets generally cover this period of time. The adjustment "quality factor" was derived empirically after the other two adjustments were made. The result suggests, and our experience bears out, that investors first separate equities into three broad categories, representing a premium or discount of one-third from standard levels as follows:

Premium = 1.33
Standard = 1.00
Discount = .67

A second approximation for investment quality was noted representing a 10 percentage point variance within each of the three categories noted above as follows:

Premium = 1.33 ±.10
Standard = 1.00 ±.10
Discount = .67 ±.10

The estimate of normal value is not a technical approach but represents a statistical branch of fundamental security analysis. The non-growth earnings multiple is a historic derivative of many years and the five-year growth estimate and quality ratings are determined through discussions with an industry specialist. Only after careful consideration do we arrive at these "judgment" values. The formula is simply the mathematical combination of these judgments.

Derivation of the Non-Growth Multiple

The first and most basic of the three factors in our valuation formula is the non-growth earnings multiple. This represents the price-earnings ratio for a non-growth stock of average investment quality over a long period of time. The non-growth multiple was estimated at 12.8 based upon a correlation analysis between prices and share earnings during the period 1926-1946. The ratio has remained constant during the last ten years of equity market fluctuations. Statistical derivation of the 12.8 multiple is explained below.

At the outset, we note that price-earning ratios are more complex than they appear to be on the surface. This complexity arises from the simple observation that stock prices are not determined by current earnings alone. In other words, if a company's earnings decline to zero in a given year, the price of its stock will not drop to zero but will sell at a significant price level which we shall call "residual" value. In reality, normal market price is composed of two determinants rather than one, namely a basic or residual value plus an appropriate capitalization rate of current earnings. This concept may be expressed mathematically thus:

$$\text{Normal Value} = \text{Residual Value} + (P/E \text{ Ratio} \times \text{Current Earnings})$$

The above assumption was supported statistically by our plotting of the Dow-Jones Industrial earnings against prices for the period 1932-1939 and the first post-war year 1946. The correlation between prices and earnings indicated a residual value of 64 for the DJI average at the point of zero earnings. Chart 1 shows a close correlation between earnings and prices during the decade of the 1930's. The slope of the line of relationship is estimated at 9, which means that a $1.00 increment in DJI earnings will add nine points to DJI prices. Accordingly, the equation of normal value for Dow-Jones Industrial average during 1932-1946 may be expressed as follows:

$$\text{DJI Normal Value} = 64 + (9 \times \text{Current Earnings})$$

Chart 2 shows a plotting of DJI earnings and prices for the years 1927-1931, a period starting with a high level of economic activity and ending with depressed business conditions. The line of relationship drawn through the plotted points may be expressed mathematically as follows:

$$\text{DJI Normal Value} = 94 + (9.6 \times \text{Current Earnings})$$

CHART 1
Dow-Jones Industrial Average
Price vs. Earnings
1932-1939, 1946

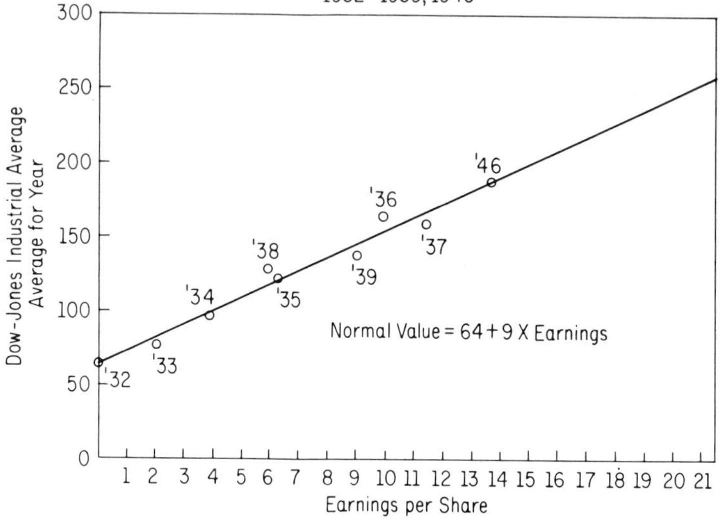

CHART 2
Dow-Jones Industrial Average
Price vs. Earnings 1927-1931

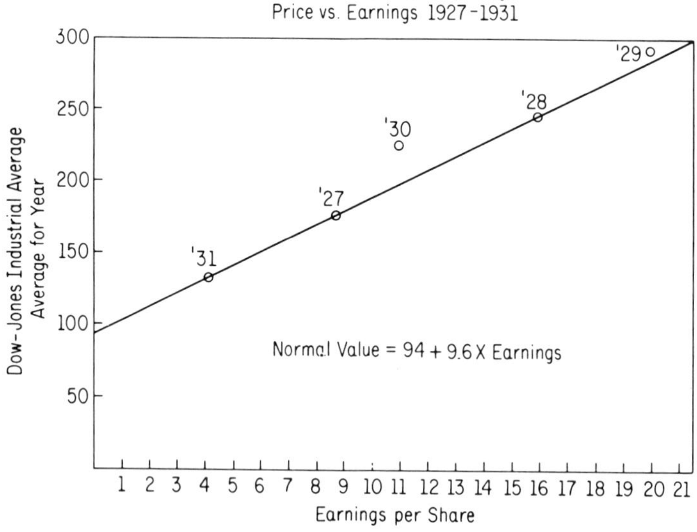

The slope of 9.6 times current earnings is comparable to the one of 9.0 derived from Chart 1. This suggests that there may be a relatively constant capitalization rate for current earnings. In view of the vast difference in economic outlook in the late 20's compared with the depressed 30's, it is surprising to find that, on average, the market capitalized reported earnings at almost the same rate in both periods. It appears that the major difference in market valuation between the two periods is accounted for by the difference in base or "residual" values (94 vs. 64) rather than in earnings capitalization rates.

That the difference in residual values shown in Charts 1 and 2 may reflect lower expectations of normal earning-power during the Great Depression compared with the prosperous period of the 1920's becomes apparent from analysis of historical data. For the years 1920-1931, DJI earnings average $10.37 a share compared with $7.00 a share for the nine years 1932-1939 and 1946. The drop in residual value from 94 to 64 appears to be in direct proportion to the decline in normal earning-power between the two periods as is evidenced by applying the capitalization rate of nine times earnings to normal earning power as follows:

$$\text{Period } 1920\text{–}1931 = 9 \times \$10.37 = 93$$
$$\text{Period } 1932\text{–}1939 + 1946 = 9 \times \$\ 7.00 = 63$$

The similarity between the above figures and the residual value estimates derived from the correlation graphs in Charts 1 and 2 support a conclusion that changes in residual values primarily reflect revised expectations of normal earning power for the Dow-Jones Industrials. Moreover, it would appear that residual values for the DJI average may be estimated by capitalizing at 9 times whatever the "normal earnings" at any time may be.

The analysis thus far seems to confirm the original hypothesis in this study that normal value is dependent on residual value plus a capitalization rate applied to current earnings. Residual value in turn may be estimated by applying the same capitalization rate to normal earnings. In other words, equal weight should be given to current and to normal earnings in establishing a stock's normal value. Thus, the basic valuation formula for the DJI average may be transposed from:

$$\text{DJI Normal Value} = \text{Residual Value} + (9 \times \text{Current Earnings})$$

To:

$$\text{DJI Normal Value} = (9 \times \text{Normal Earnings}) + (9 \times \text{Current Earnings})$$

When current earnings are equal to normal earnings, the above equation indicates that the DJI's normal price-earnings ratio should be 18. This valuation theory is confirmed by historical market data as noted below:

Dow Jones Industrial Average

	Average Earnings	Average Price	Average P/E Ratio
Period 1927–1939 + 1946	$9.45	171	18.1

From the above relationships, the first valuation standard seems to be established, namely a price-earnings multiple of 18 applied to "normal" earnings for the Dow-Jones Industrial Index. As indicated in subsequent sections of this paper, the DJI average contains an estimated 5% annual earnings-growth factor and an investment quality rating that is 10% above the level of the average stock. Since growth factors and varying investment quality characteristics play important roles in the valuation of securities, these two influences must be eliminated from DJI normal multiple in order to derive a basic non-growth multiple for a stock of "average" investment quality. The adjustment factor for a 5% growth rate is 1.28, which represents the impact of compounding 5% annual growth over a five-year period. The DJI investment quality rating is 1.10 or 10% above average on a rating scale which will be discussed in detail later on in this report. These two factors may be eliminated from the normal (and historical) multiple of 18 for the DJI average as follows:

$$\text{Basic Non-Growth Multiple} = \frac{18.0}{1.28 \times 1.10} = 12.8$$

The resulting price-earnings multiple of 12.8 represents the average capitalization rate applied to normal earnings of a stock without growth prospects having standard investment quality characteristics. This basic ratio is multiplied by a growth factor if a stock possesses earnings-growth characteristics and the resulting multiple is either increased or decreased by an investment quality rating before calculating a stock's final "normal" price-earnings ratio as that term is used herein.

The reader may have noticed that the nongrowth multiple of 12.8 is applied only against a company's "normal" earning power. What happens when a company's current earnings deviate significantly from estimated "normal" earnings?

In that case, the non-growth multiple will decline below 12.8 if current earnings are above normal and it will move above 12.8 if earnings drop below normal levels. This characteristic of market valuation explains why price-earnings ratios of cyclical stocks tend to be relatively low at peak earnings and relativley high in a period of depressed earnings. In the final analysis, it reflects the market's tendency to give equal weight to current and normal earnings rather than rely entirely on reported current income, as illustrated by the valuation equations derived earlier.

In other words, half of the 12.8 multiple, or 6.4, is applied to normal earnings and the other half is applied to current earnings in the case of a *non-growth* stock of *average* investment quality.

Analysis of historical market fluctuations strongly suggests that investors keep one eye on current earnings and the other one on average or normal earning power. If current and normal earnings are identical (as is the case with many growth stocks), we start our valuation analysis with the basic 12.8 multiple. In cases where current and normal earnings differ we calculate the appropriate variable non-growth multiple in the following manner:

$$\text{Variable Non-Growth Multiple} = \left[\, 6.4 + \left(\frac{\text{Normal Earns.}}{\text{Current Earns.}} \times 6.4 \right) \right]$$

Thus, if a company's current earnings are 20% *above* normal, its non-growth multiple would be calculated as follows:

$$\text{Variable Non-Growth Multiple } (+20\%) = \left[\, 6.4 + \left(\frac{1.00}{1.20} \times 6.4 \right) \right] = 11.7$$

For a variance 20% below normal earnings the calculations are:

$$\text{Variable Non-Growth Multiple } (-20\%) = \left[\, 6.4 + \left(\frac{1.00}{.80} \times 6.4 \right) \right] = 14.4$$

The following table illustrates the tendency for variability in the non-growth multiple at different relationships of current earnings to "normal" earnings:

% Above Normal Earnings	Variable Non-Growth Multiple	% Below Normal Earnings	Variable Non-Growth Multiple
+20%	11.7	- 0-	12.8
+15%	11.9	– 5%	13.1
+10%	12.2	–10%	13.5
+ 5%	12.5	–15%	13.9
- 0-	12.8	–20%	14.4

In estimating normal earnings for individual companies we rely upon detailed analysis by our firm's industry specialists. These specialists compare projected figures with actual experience during the past few years. However, judgment factors override historical trends in the determination of a company's normal earning power and its assumed growth rate. Revisions in assumptions are made when industry specialists obtain significant information that may affect earlier conclusions about the current or normal earning power of a company.

Derivation of the Growth Factor

It is a well-established fact in financial analysis that investors will pay a premium for a stock with reasonably well-defined growth prospects. We estimate the impact of growth on price-earnings ratios in the following way:

Corporate budgets usually plan ahead in five-year intervals, thus an assumed growth rate is expected to have an impact over this period. Visibility beyond five years, in most cases, is denied even to those who are highly informed about a particular company's prospects. The impact of a given growth rate is determined from the compound interest tables. Thus, an assumed 5% growth rate will have a compounding impact of 1.28 in 5 years. That is to say, $1.00 compounded at 5% a year over 5 years will grow to $1.28. It follows that a 5% growth stock might be worth 1.28 times more than a non-growth stock of similar investment quality. For a 10% growth stock, the growth factor is 1.61. Growth factors at growth-rate intervals of 2.5% are shown below in the scale from 0 to 25% as follows.

Growth Rate	Growth Factor
0%	1.00
2.5	1.13
5.0	1.28
7.5	1.44
10.0	1.61
12.5	1.80
15.0	2.01
17.5	2.24
20.0	2.49
22.5	2.76
25.0	3.05

The method of determining a company's earnings growth rate is fundamental rather than statistical. The long-term demand factors that influence an industry or product group provide important clues regarding a company's basic growth rate. However, a company may be gaining or losing position in its industry, a factor which may modify the growth-rate estimate derived for the industry as a whole. Moreover, the company's past record of growth may be changing as a result of major forces that have not yet influenced its sales but are expected to have an impact over the next several years. A company's past earnings growth may have been derived chiefly from improvement in profit margins rather than increased sales. If so, the industry specialist will discount the record to a large extent and determine the firm's growth rate from sources other than the company's income account. While profit-margin improvement is a desirable characteristic and reflects favorably on a stock's investment quality, it normally is not a sustainable factor over the long term in determining expected growth rates. Similarly, growth through acquisitions may be partly discounted in estimating a company's growth potential.

In actual practice, the impact of varying growth rates on security prices appears to approximate the results obtained by using the compound interest tables over a five-year period. There is a tendency for investment managers to arrive at a consensus regarding any well-known company's secular growth rate over the next five years, although at times there may be a lively debate about the approximate growth rate that should be assumed for a given stock. For example, when IBM encountered delivery problems with its new 360 model computers, some analysts lowered their growth rate designation for the stock from 15% a year to the next notch, or 12.5%. Others maintained the conventional 15% annual growth factor on the assumption that competitors would not be capable of fully capitalizing on IBM's temporary problems. This type of analytical debate occurs frequently and illustrates the importance of access to sound value judgments by industry specialists. In other words, *Valuation Standards* leans heavily on consultations with our firm's industry specialists regarding individual companies.

Derivation of Investment Quality Ratings

The relative investment quality of a security has a major impact on normal value estimates. However, no series of financial ratios or statistical relationships is available that will consistently measure variations in investment quality among leading equities. In this area the analyst must rely on value judgments by industry specialists and attempt to interpret these judgments in a practical manner.

One of the chief determinants of investment quality is the relative reliability of projected future earning power. Thus, highly stable sources of earnings, such as food equities, generally receive high quality ratings, while volatile sources of earnings receive relatively low quality designations. Other significant factors that affect quality ratings include managerial capability, financial resources, capitalization ratios (debt and leverage), return on investment, marketability of the stock, etc. Analysts distill numerous statistical data and intangibles in the process of forming judgments about a stock's investment quality rating. For most leading equities, there usually is a consensus concerning investment quality characteristics that is within fairly narrow limits.

Investment managers initially appear to separate equities into three broad investment quality groups, which may be designated as Premium, Standard (Average) and Discount. There is some evidence that the Premium classification receives an evaluation about one-third over the Standard group, while the Discount class sells at about one-third less than Standard quality equities; in other words, taking Standard as 1.00, Premium would be 1.33 and Discount 0.67.

The above represent group averages; individual stocks are expected to vary around one or the other of these group averages. Empirical observation suggests this intra-group variation may approximate 10 percentage points around the group average. In other words, the highest quality rating in the Premium category is 1.43 (1.33 + .10) whereas the lowest rating in this group is 1.23 (1.33 – .10). The full range of quality variations involve 9 desigations as follows:

Premium = 1.33 ±.10 or 1.23 – 1.33 – 1.43
Standard = 1.00 ±.10 or .90 – 1.00 – 1.10
Discount = .67 ±.10 or .57 – .67 – .77

In effect, this table attempts to simulate the investment manager's practical procedure in groping for a scale of investment quality ratings. The first step involves a choice of one of three main categories. The second step represents a more difficult choice, reflecting a smaller intra-group variation compared with the large variation among the three basic quality groupings. For most well-known equities the selection of an appropriate intra-group rating ± .10 is not too difficult for industry specialists. This two-step rating procedure provides the analyst with nine investment quality ratings which appear to be valid guideposts to the solution of the highly complex problem of determining relative quality.

Statistical support for the above concept of investment quality ratings may be derived from actual experience. In this firm's monthly publication, normal values are calculated for close to 100 leading stocks classified according to the above-mentioned quality-rating concept. Almost all of these equities are in either the Premium or Standard categories. In the March 1965 issue of *Valuation Standards For Investments,* the Premium quality stocks were separated into three lists, based on alphabetical arrangement, in order to obtain three samples of approximately fifteen equities in each of the lists. The same procedure was followed for equities in the Standard quality category. Each stock was assigned an "expected" price-earnings ratio based on its estimated non-growth multiple and its growth rate. A comparison of the actual price-earnings ratios versus expected ratios indicates the extent of premium, or lack of premium, in the actual *p/e* ratio, due to investment *quality* factors.

	Actual *P/E* Ratios As of 2-26-65	Expected *P/E* Ratios (ex Quality Rating)	Premium or (Discount)
Premium Category (1.33)			
Sample 1–(A to G)	25.5	18.7	+36%
Sample 2–(G to N)	24.7	18.8	+31%
Sample 3–(N to Z)	26.2	19.7	+33%
Standard Category (1.00)			
Sample 4–(A to C)	17.9	17.9	–
Sample 5–(C to M)	15.9	16.7	(–5%)
Sample 6–(M to Z)	16.7	16.7	–

The difference in valuation of the price-earnings ratio between the Premium and Standard quality groups is approximately 33%. The impact of growth rates on price-earnings ratios having been removed in both groups, the one-third variance *between* the two groups appears to relate to the differences in quality ratings. It should also be noted that the quality variance appears to be fairly stable among the three samples in each of the two quality categories.

The procedure discussed above was repeated almost a year later using the basic data from the February 1966 supplement of *Valuation Standards.* The results are tabulated below:

	Actual *P/E* Ratios As of 1-31-66	Expected *P/E* Ratios (ex Quality Rating)	Premium or (Discount)
Premium Category (1.33)			
Sample 1–(A to G)	23.4	18.4	+27%
Sample 2–(G to N)	24.2	19.2	+26%
Sample 3–(N to Z)	25.0	20.1	+22%
Standard Category (1.00)			
Sample 4–(A to C)	16.4	18.0	(–9%)
Sample 5–(C to M)	15.0	17.2	(–9%)
Sample 6–(M to Z)	16.6	17.3	(–4%)

While the most recent tabulation shows that issues in the Premium and Standard categories currently sell at prices below their respective "normal" ratings of 1.33 and 1.00, the difference between the two categories remains approximately 33% as expected under this valuation theory. One reason why current prices are below valuation "norms" may be due to optimistic estimates of 1966 corporate earnings in contrast to last year when early estimates of 1965 earnings generally proved to be realistic. In any event, the market in early 1966 has placed a more conservative valuation on recent 1966 earnings estimates, perhaps on the assumption that such earnings estimates may be lowered later in the year. It is significant, however, that the average difference between the Premium and Standard investment quality groups remains 33%, the same as last year. The empirical evidence strongly suggests that investment managers are willing to pay 33% more for a premium investment income than for a standard investment stock in the same growth category. Similarly they appear to demand a discount of 33% for speculative issues with the same growth characteristics. The one-third discount was found in studies made several years ago. In the current *Valuation Standards,* the few speculative issues are all in the upper range of the Discount category.

The investment quality factor has a significant impact on a stock's normal value and must be included as an important variable in any valuation formula. The procedure described above provides a convenient method of quantitatively rating investment *quality* differences that essentially represent value judgments made by informed industry specialists.

VALUATION EXAMPLES

The preceding section discussed the significance of the three variables that affect normal value in this valuation methodology. Below are two valuation examples that illustrate our calculations of normal value:

	IBM
Estimated 1966 Earnings	\$14.75
Estimated Growth Rate	15.0%
Growth Factor	2.01
Quality Factor	1.43
Non-Growth *P/E* Ratio	13.1
Recent Price	530

1966 Normal Value =

$$13.1 \times 2.01 \times 1.43 = 37.7 \times \$14.75 = 556$$

	Anaconda
Estimated 1966 Earnings	\$11.00
Estimated Growth Rate	5.0%
Growth Factor	1.28
Quality Factor	.67
Non-Growth *P/E* Ratio	11.1
Recent Price	94

1966 Normal Value =

$$11.1 \times 1.28 \times .67 = 9.5 \times \$11.00 = 105$$

In the case of IBM, current earnings are below estimated normal earning power, thus its non-growth multiple of 13.1 is higher than the standard 12.8 figure as described on page four. With respect to Anaconda, current estimated earnings are more than 35% above "normal", thus its non-growth multiple is only 11.1. Growth rate and quality designation also are substantially greater for IBM than for Anaconda. By taking into account the wide variations in non-growth multiples, growth rates, and quality ratings for these two disparate equities, it is possible to estimate normal values for both that appear reasonable.

Among the newer electronics firms, Texas Instruments has achieved a good measure of investment acceptance and may be used as an example. It is a leading semiconductor manufacturer, including integrated circuits, an area of exceptionally rapid growth. The impact of integrated circuits on semiconductor companies goes beyond the addition of a new product line. At present, semiconductor devices may account for only 4% of the total value of electronic equipment. In time it has been estimated that integrated circuit producers may contribute as much as 25% of the end product value of electronic systems. With this background it is reasonable to assume an overall company growth rate of 15% yearly, although semiconductor operations account for only one-half of total sales. With respect to investment quality, it may be rated 1.23, or at the lower end of the Premium category. The company's management is highly regarded, its research efforts have been very productive and its financial position is strong. Among electronics equities, Texas Instruments possesses high investment quality characteristics, supporting belief that a quality rating of 1.23 may be generally accepted as reasonable for this issue.

	Texas Instruments
Estimated 1966 Earnings	\$6.75
Estimated Growth Rate	15.0%

	Texas Instruments (cont'd)
Growth Factor	2.01
Quality Factor	1.23
Non-Growth *P/E* Ratio	12.8
Recent Price	225
1966 Normal Value =	

12.8 X 20.1 X 1.23 = 31.6 X \$6.75 = 2.13

This stock has had a substantial advance in price since mid 1965, primarily as a result of expected sharp earnings gains from last year's \$4.92 a share to this year's estimated \$6.75 a share and an upward revaluation of its long-term growth prospects. Thus, the recent price level is not far from estimated normal value despite a doubling in price since last summer. For the near term, it might be expected to fluctuate 20% around its normal value estimate, with the price pattern perhaps significantly influenced by general market conditions now that it is selling near its normal value figure.

Xerox Corporation is another example in the newer rapid-growth stock category that has acquired substantial investment acceptance. The company's latest product additions, including the models 330 and 720 copiers, reflect the increased strength of its position in the office copy field. Xerox now offers a "spectrum of services" in both copying and duplicating and has a marketing organization that exceeds 5,500 people in 120 sales and service offices. Over the longer term, the company expects to diversify by penetrating the rapidly growing computer peripheral equipment market. It is well qualified to participate in this area in view of its special skills in electronics, optics and imaging methods. The valuation assumptions below reflect the general consensus of a 20% annual growth rate and a Premium quality rating of 1.33. Normal earning power for 1966, however, is estimated at \$6.00 a share in contrast to expected current earnings estimated at \$4.00 a share, reflecting deferred income from installation of new products on a lease basis. Thus the stock's non-growth multiple becomes 16.0 instead of 12.8.

	Xerox
Estimated 1966 Earnings	\$4.00
Estimated Growth Rate	20.0%
Quality Factor	1.33
Non-Growth Factor	16.0
Recent Price	245
1966 Normal Value =	

16.0 X 2.49 X 1.33 = 53 X \$4.00 = 212

At recent prices, Xerox sold 20% above its estimated normal value. This stock has a tendency to sell as much as 40% over normal during periods of general market enthusiasm. With respect to near-term downside risk probabilities, a level at normal value or somewhat below appears realistic in the event of a significant general market decline.

Valuation of the Dow-Jones Industrial Average

Charts 1 and 2 furnished the statistical basis for the conclusion that normal value for the DJI Average might be expressed as follows:

DJI Normal Value = Residual Value + (9 × Current Earnings)

The estimates of residual value for the years 1927-1946 were derived from Charts 1 and 2 as discussed earlier. During those years residual value was dependent on expectations of normal or average earning power over a volatile business cycle. The cyclical characteristics of the economy in the 1920's and 1930's almost completely obscured the underlying growth characteristics of that period. As a result, investors regarded normal earning power as an average of several years of widely fluctuating earnings. Thus, residual value remained constant until changed circumtaances resulted in the general acceptance of a new level of average earnings as "normal" for the next business cycle. The sharp drop in average earnings between the 1920's and the 1930's was duly noted by investors, resulting in a decline in residual value of the DJI average from 94 to 64.

In making the transition from pre-war to the post-World War II period, one must take into account changes in the economic structure of our national economy. The wide business fluctuations of the earlier period have been replaced by more stable growth characteristics in the post-war years. Investors are aware of the institutional changes that have occurred in our economy which, on balance, have tended to dampen economic fluctuations and foster long-term growth in total national output.

Under the Full Employment Act of 1946, successive administrations have made deliberate use of fiscal and monetary tools to stimulate economic growth, hopefully with relative price stability. As a result, investors have accepted the hypothesis of well-defined growth prospects modified by occasional moderate cyclical fluctuations in business activity. In other words, investors now recognize the impact of growth potential on normal earnings whereas the dominant cyclical characteristics of the pre-war period produced expectations of a flat trend in earnings accompanied by sizeable year-to-year fluctuations in reported earnings. Thus, one would expect investors to assume a growth curve for normal earnings estimates for the years following 1946 rather than a flat trend as in the more volatile periods of earlier years. This change in investor attitude did occur, although not immediately after World War II ended.

As indicated in Charts 1 and 2, pre-war residual values remained flat until investors revised their expectations to a new level of "normalcy" with respect to average earnings. Thus, residual value remained fixed for a number of years subject to occasional abrupt revaluations. In the post-war period, we believe residual value estimates should reflect a secular growth trend based on the discussion noted above. Moreover, the growth of new industries and services in the post-war period has been pronounced in product groups and services with stable characteristics, thus further reducing the impact of cyclical industries on the economy compared with earlier years. As a result, the investor has come to expect secular growth in normal earnings which, in turn, implies growth in residual values.

Recognition of the growth factor in the post-war equation of normal value helps bridge the gap between the valuation patterns of the 1920's and 1930's and the post-World War II era. There is no assurance that the economy may not revert to a period of activity dominated by cyclical fluctuations instead of one noted for its growth characteristics. However, the available evidence favors the assumption of continued growth subject to moderate interruptions.

The following discussion is directed at devising an *objective* method of estimating residual values which will depict a valid growth trend. The estimating technique may be unorthodox but it has the virtue of being empirical rather than subjective. Stated briefly, it is assumed that the successively higher market lows with respect to the three major market declines in the post-war period may reflect the probable growth trend in residual values for the Dow-Jones Industrial Average. This approach is justified on the assumption that buyers of securities at market troughs probably represent a good cross-section of informed investment opinion about the prospects of corporate earnings several years hence. It follows that successively higher market troughs over the long-term may represent realistic expectations concerning the trend of future normal earning power. As long as knowledgeable investors continue to expect growth in earnings, future market troughs are expected to remain in an upward trend. Interestingly, residual values estimated in this manner in recent years compare favorably with alternate estimates made by multiplying nine times normal earnings derived from a secular trend line.

In the early post-World War II years, however, residual values derived from the trend of prices at market troughs were substantially lower than those derived from earnings trend projections. This difference presumably reflected general expectations of a post-war depression in the years immediately following the end of the war. After corporate earning power was tested during the 1957-1958 recession, *expectations* of post-war normal earning power came in line with actual results. Thus, residual values derived from past market prices "caught up" with those derived from a statistical projection of normal earning power. There may again come a time when investors' expectations may not coincide with the statistical projection of normal earnings. In that event, market history suggests that the expectations may override statistical evidence of normal earning power for a while, to be followed later by a significant revaluation, when investors become convinced about the sustainability of the new "normal" earnings level. This pattern of the lag of investors' expectations behind actual statistical evidence is noticeable in abnormal periods such as during and immediately after major wars.

This method of estimated residual value for the DJI Average is based directly on the trend of prices established at major bear market low points. The reader will recall that 1946 represented the last year in which we used the residual value of 64 as derived from Chart I. Successive estimates of residual values are made by measuring their growth trend as represented by the progression of bear market troughs reported in the table below.

	DJI Troughs
1942	93
1949	162
1957	420
1962	536

The comparison of the first two bear market lows involves the years 1942 and 1949, during which time the DJI gained 69 points over seven years, for an average annual increase of 10 points. Thus we added 10 points yearly to the starting residual base figure of 64 in 1946 as follows:

	Estimated Residual Values		Estimated Residual Values
1946 base*	64	1952	124
1947	74	1953	134
1948	84	1954	144
1949	94	1955	154
1950	104	1956	163
1951	114		

*Chart 1

In 1957, a new market trough was established at 420 which was substantially higher than the low of 162 recorded in 1949. Apparently, investors gained strong conviction about the sustainability of a higher level of earnings than they believed likely during the early post-war years. As a result, residual value estimates increased at a rapid rate as the market attempted to "catch up" with the newly held conviction concerning normal earning power.

1957 DJI Trough	420	
1949 DJI Trough	162	
	258	points
Average gain per year	32	points

Adding the 32 points to successive years following the base year results in values as follows:

	Estimated Residual Values		Estimated Residual Values
1956 base	163	1959	260
1957	195	1960	292
1958	228	1961	324

In 1962, the market established its next trough at 536, which was higher than the low of 420 in 1957. However, the rate of gain in residual values slowed to a more normal rate of 5% a year compared with the preceding period. The difference between 536 and 420 is 116 points for an average increase of 23 points a year.

1962 DJI Trough	536
1957 DJI Trough	420
	116 points
Average gain per year	23 points

Since the market peaked in December 1961 instead of near the middle of the year as in the other two post-war market peaks (1946 and 1956), we added one-half of the 1949-1957 annual growth rate and one-half on the 1957-1962 annual growth rate to establish the residual value for the year 1962, which is centered in the month of June. For the following years, we add the average gain of 23 points per year. The results are as follows:

	Estimated Residual Values
1961 base	324
1962	351
1963	374
1964	397
1965	420
1966	443

We shall continue to add 23 points yearly in future years until the next major market peak and trough have been established to provide us with another market low for comparison with the preceding trough.

In our opinion, the trend of bear market troughs may reflect informed expectations about future earning power and hence reflect valid estimates of residual values for the Dow-Jones Industrials.

This concept may have even more validity today than in earlier periods because the investor has become more sophisticated and information is more readily available to the investing public. In a market decline such as occurred in May 1962, institutional investors witnessed temporary sharp price declines in specific issues despite hard evidence of sustained favorable growth potentials for many individual companies. Strong conviction among knowledgeable investors concerning the probable growth of future earning power of leading corporations may have stemmed the 1962 market break at a level significantly higher than the last bear market low of 1957.

An alternate means of estimating residual value for the Dow-Jones Industrials is one based on capitalizing each year's estimated normal earnings. Chart 3 shows a trend line drawn through the DJI earnings in the post-war years.

Earnings estimated from the trend line are multiplied by the capitalization rate of nine to determine residual value by this approach. In the early post-war years

CHART 3
Dow-Jones Industrial Average
Estimated Normal Value, Residual Value, and Earnings

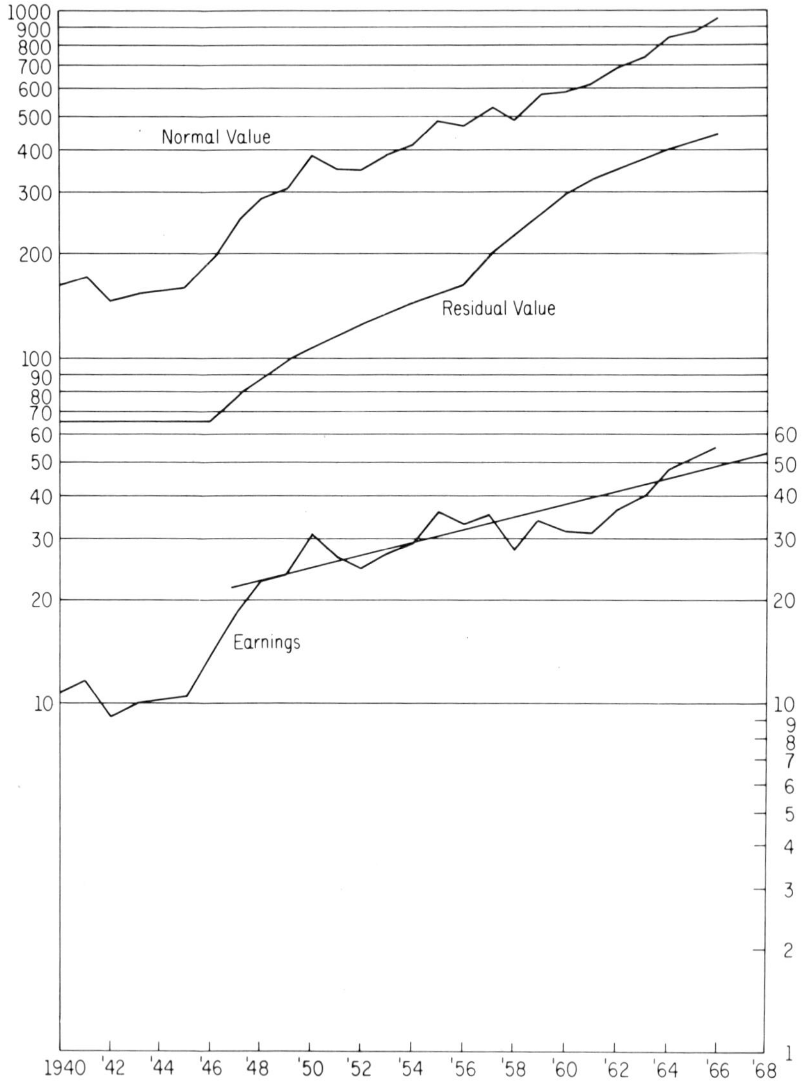

there was a wide gap between values derived from these two methods, but the difference has almost disappeared in recent years.

	DJI Normal Earnings	DJI Residual Value Estimates Based On: Alternate Method (9 X Normal Earnings)	Market Troughs
1962	$41.20	371	351
1963	43.00	387	374
1964	44.80	403	397
1965	46.70	420	420
1966	48.80	434	443

CHART 4
Dow-Jones Industrial Average
Earnings vs. Average Prices Less Residual Values
1927-31, 1932-39 and '46 and 1955-65

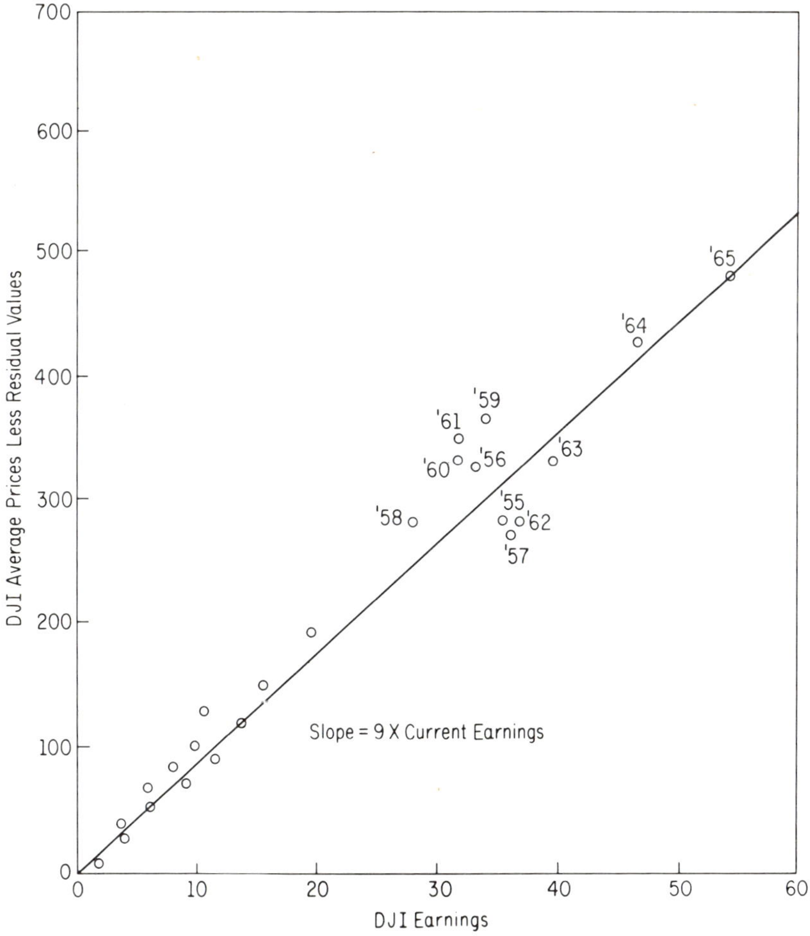

Use of market troughs in estimating DJI residual values introduces the objectivity of the market's realism into the normal value equation. There appears to be an approximate seven or eight-year lag in the actual market trough and its appearance as a residual value estimate later on. It provides an empriical estimate of the market's *expectations* concerning future earning power. In this way a base of market trend is injected into the concept of normal value.

When we subtract estimated residual values from average yearly prices of the DJI, resultant net prices should be equal to approximately nine times earnings based on the valuation equation described earlier. This relationship is shown in the scatter diagram in Chart 4. We plotted data for the years 1927-1939, 1946 and for the years 1955-1965. The early post-World War II years reflected widespread fears of a post-war depression and general lack of confidence in the sustainability of the current earnings level during the conversion period. A more normal relationship between current earnings and prices appears to have been re-established by 1955. During most of the eleven-year period 1955-1965, earnings remained in a relatively narrow range, compared with a wide range of fluctuations during the pre-war period. Therefore, there are larger deviations around the line of relationship in the 1955-1965 period than in the pre-war era. In addition, price levels are significantly higher than in earlier years, thus deviations from the line are larger than before, as would be expected.

The close relationship between net prices (adjusted for residual values) and reported earnings is clearly evident in Chart 4, which in effect extends into a later period the relationships noted in Charts 1 and 2. The slope of the line is nine times current earnings, a relationship which applies not only in the pre-war period but also appears valid over the past eleven years. For the eleven-year period as a whole (1955-1965), estimated normal value (residual value + 9 X earnings) is almost identical with actual average prices as follows:

	Average Residual Value	Average Earnings	Average Price	Est. Normal Value
Period 1955–1965	287	$37.24	628	622
Period 1932–39 & '46	64	6.96	127	127
Period 1927–31	94	11.95	215	202

In summarizing this section, we believe that residual values for the DJI may be independently estimated by referring to past market troughs. With respect to individual securities, however, residual value is estimated by applying the appropriate capitalization rate to normal earnings. In Chart 5 we have estimated DJI normal values for the entire period 1920-1966. In the same chart we also show the levels of residual value and a yearly price range.

Residual value estimates for the years 1920-1926 were derived from the preceding market trough of 53 established in 1914. Residual values for the years 1927-1946 were derived from Charts 1 and 2. The market fluctuations around

	Normal Value	DJI Market Peaks Peak Price	% Above Normal
1937	167	194	+16%
1946	187	213	+14%
1956	463	521	+13%
1959	569	679	+19%
1961	611	735	+20%

	Normal Value	DJI Market Troughs Peak Price	% Below Normal
1938	118	99	–16%
1946	187	163	–13%
1957	520	420	–19%
1960	582	566	– 3%
1962	679	536	–21%

CHART 5
Dow-Jones Industrial Average
Normal Value vs. Actual Prices

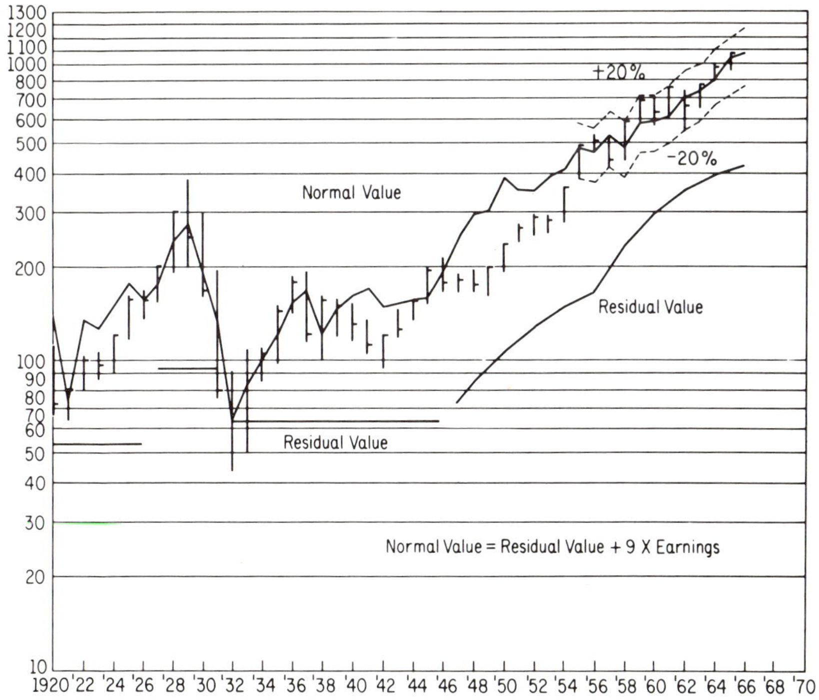

normal value since 1937 are shown above, excluding the war years and the period of abnormal underevaluation that prevailed immediately after the war.

Historically, there appears to be a tendency for DJI prices to fluctuate about 15%-20% around normal value at major peaks and troughs. Based on estimated earnings of $56.50 for 1966 and a residual value of 443, the DJI's normal value for 1966 is estimated at approximately 950.

In the valuation procedure described in this report, we do not include dividend data as an independent variable in calculating normal value. This stems from the fact that dividends depend directly upon the trend of earnings. The point is illustrated by inverting the non-growth multiple of 12.8 to arrive at an earnings yield as follows:

$$\text{Normal Earnings Yield} = \frac{1}{12.8} = 7.8\%$$

Since the price-earnings ratio of 12.8 refers to a non-growth equity, dividend payout is expected to be at least 70%. If a non-growth company earns 7.8% on its equity base, a 70% payout would result in a 5.5% dividend yield. In effect, a non-growth stock that sells at 12.8 times earnings is assumed to provide a yield of at least 5.5% under normal conditions. Dividend yield is a direct function of earnings payout, which in turn is significantly related to a company's earnings growth rate. Growth stocks generally retain a larger proportion of earnings in order to maintain their growth-rate potentials. Since we take into account a company's earnings level and growth rate, we feel that separate statistical inclusion of dividend data is not essential in estimating a stock's normal value under the procedure described herein. In effect, the trend of earnings represents a "lead" indicator of future dividends.

CONCLUSION

Accurate estimates of normal value levels depend upon the validity of the valuation concepts employed as well as upon reliable information with respect to the fundamental "input" data for the valuation formula. Our valuation method is based on statistical relationships derived from the pre-war period covering the years 1927-1939. From the observed statistical relationships we concluded that, over the long range, the market is willing to pay 12.8 times earnings for a non-growth stock of average investment quality. If a stock possesses growth characteristics, the normal price-earnings ratio of 12.8 is increased by the estimated growth factor. In addition, this calculated multiple is either increased or decreased depending on the stock's appraised investment quality rating. We also know that the standard non-growth multiple will vary from 12.8 depending upon whether "current" earnings are above or below estimated "normal" earnings. Once an individual stock's normal value has been established we next attempt to determine its range or degree of volatility in order to estimate the probable fluctuations around "normal" that might be expected. For most stocks, the critical level is ±20%, which also has been the approximate range for the Dow-Jones Industrials in recent years at peaks and troughs. Final decision to buy or sell any individual security depends upon additional analysis provided by industry specialists.

William Kurtz
Institutional Research Department
HORNBLOWER & WEEKS-HEMPHILL, NOYES

WK:pc
April 1966

Dow-Jones Industrial Average
Earnings, Prices, and Normal Value
1920–1966

Year	Earnings	9 X Earnings	Residual Value	Normal Value	Prices			
					High	Low	Close	Avg.
1920	$ 9.12	82	53	135	110	67	72	88
1921	2.10	19	53	72	82	64	81	73
1922	9.11	82	53	135	103	79	99	91
1923	8.25	74	53	127	105	86	96	96
1924	10.88	98	53	151	121	88	121	104
1925	13.89	125	53	178	159	115	157	137
1926	11.39	103	53	156	167	135	157	151
1927	8.72	78	94	172	202	153	202	178
1928	15.97	144	94	238	300	191	300	246
1929	19.94	179	94	273	381	199	248	290
1930	11.02	99	94	193	294	158	165	226
1931	4.09	37	94	131	194	74	78	134
1932	(.51)	–	64	64	89	43	60	65
1933	2.11	19	64	83	109	50	100	79
1934	3.91	35	64	99	111	86	104	98
1935	6.34	57	64	121	148	97	144	123
1936	10.07	91	64	155	185	143	180	164
1937	11.49	103	64	167	194	114	121	154
1938	6.01	54	64	118	158	99	155	129
1939	9.11	82	64	146	156	121	150	139
1940	10.92	98	64	162	153	112	131	132
1941	11.64	105	64	169	134	106	111	120
1942	9.22	83	64	147	120	93	119	106
1943	9.74	88	64	152	146	119	136	132
1944	10.07	91	64	155	153	134	152	144
1945	10.56	95	64	159	196	151	193	174
1946	13.63	123	64	187	213	163	177	188
1947	18.80	169	74	243	187	163	181	175
1948	23.07	208	84	292	193	165	177	179
1949	23.54	212	94	306	201	162	200	182
1950	30.70	276	104	380	235	197	235	216
1951	26.59	239	114	353	276	239	269	258
1952	24.76	223	124	347	292	256	293	274
1953	27.23	245	134	379	294	255	281	275
1954	28.40	256	144	400	404	280	404	342
1955	35.78	322	154	476	488	388	488	438
1956	33.34	300	163	463	521	462	499	492
1957	36.08	325	195	520	521	420	436	471
1958	27.95	252	228	480	584	437	584	511
1959	34.31	309	260	569	679	574	679	627
1960	32.21	290	292	582	685	566	616	626
1961	31.91	287	324	611	735	610	731	673
1962	36.43	328	351	679	726	536	652	631
1963	41.21	371	374	745	767	647	763	707
1964	46.43	418	397	815	892	766	869	829
1965 Est.	54.00	486	420	906	969	841	969	905
1966 Est.	56.50	509	443	952				

8

Growth and Common Stock Values*

John C. Clendenin
Maurice Van Cleave

For almost a generation the identification and appraisal of "growth" stocks has been a topic of absorbing interest to investors. An almost unlimited volume of literature has discussed the features of growth industries and growth stocks and the advantages to be found in them. These advantages are said to include many things, but emphasis is usually laid upon sturdy quality, increasing earnings and dividends, and above all a high probability of substantial capital gains.

It is obvious that an investor obtains satisfactory dividend returns and/or capital gains on stock investments only when he purchases them at reasonable prices. This is especially true of growth stocks, which admittedly should sell at prices which reflect their growth potential but which may be priced high or low because of speculation or uninformed trading. It is the purpose of this article to suggest some criteria for judging the reasonableness of the prices of growth stocks. Our presentation will be made in four steps: (1) We shall illustrate the price-earnings ratios and yields prevailing in April, 1954, on growth and non-growth stocks, and give some examples of price appreciation between 1940 and 1954 in such stocks. (2) We shall reaffirm and comment on some aspects of the theory that the market prices of stocks should be related to the discounted values of probable future dividends to be paid by the stocks. (3) We shall develop evidence on the speed of "growth" which has been attained during the past twenty-five years by major established corporations. (4) We shall present tables which will indicate the mathematical values at reasonable discount rates of stocks which are assumed to pay dividends at increasing rates in future years. These tables will have the function of disclosing the mathematical values of stocks if their dividends tend to grow at various possible rates for specified periods of years, and, conversely, they will disclose the rates of growth and periods of growth which must be expected in order to justify some of the prices now being paid for growth stocks.

*From *Journal of Finance,* Vol. 9, No. 4 (December 1954), pp. 365–376. Reprinted by permission of *Journal of Finance.*

1. PRICE AND PRICE APPRECIATION

The earnings record of such stocks as du Pont, General Electric, and International Business Machines certainly supports allegations of quality, earning and dividend increase, and progressive market appreciation. The record of past price appreciation in these stocks also supplies ample justification for the relatively high prices (in terms of current earnings, dividends, or book values) which investors normally place upon growth isues. Tables 1 and 2 present some comparative data on the earnings and prices of well-known growth and non-growth stocks. Table 1 shows clearly the high price-earnings and price-dividend ratios which characterize du Pont, GE, IBM, and Monsanto, in contrast to the other values presented. Table 2 shows the recent spectacular capital gain records of GE, IBM, Kroger, Sears Roebuck, and Standard Oil of New Jersey, but raises some doubt about the financial miracles allegedly being performed by du Pont and Monsanto. The limited gains of Monsanto and du Pont in this 1940–54 period actually result from their high prices in 1940; this situation illustrates one of the key points to be made in this paper; it will be discussed in connection with our Table 6.

TABLE 1

April, 1954, Prices of Selected Stocks and Stock Groups Expressed as Multiples of 1953 per Share Earnings and Dividends

Stock or Group	Price as a Multiple of Earnings	Price as a Multiple of Dividend
Dow-Jones Industrials	11.6	19.3
Chase National Bank	11.1	23.0
du Pont de Nemours	25.3	31.3
General Electric	20.8	26.7
General Motors	10.3	17.3
International Business Machines	31.0	82.5
International Harvester	9.0	15.5
Kroger Grocery	12.9	21.0
Monsanto Chemical	17.5	34.4
J. C. Penney	17.7	22.9
Sears Roebuck	12.9	21.4
Standard Oil of New Jersey	9.6	18.9
Swift & Co.	7.9	15.0

For the sake of reasonable clarity we shall define a growth stock as a common equity in a corporation whose earnings and/or dividends are expected to increase progressively for a considerable period of time. Presumably a growth equity would "grow" a little faster than the ordinary run of good stocks, since our investigation indicates that most good stocks grow. Furthermore, it is presumed that in the main a growth characteristic implies gains in real terms, hence is not exclusively the product of bigger dollar figures due to price-level inflation. If these conditions are fulfilled, a growth stock would generally represent an equity in a concern which, because of an expanding industry, superior management, successful research, or competitive superiority, is able to earn a wide profit margin and add progressively to its per share resources and earning power.

2. THE PRESENT VALUE THEORY

It seems reasonable to believe that few major corporations will in the next few decades be able or willing to liquidate their assets and distribute their resources in cash to their stockholders. Consequently, the chief advantage in being a stockholder lies in the right to receive cash dividend payments in the future, when and if they are paid. This reasoning has led value theorists to conjecture that under stable "normal conditions" a rational stock market would attempt to appraise a share of stock approximately at the sum of the mathematical present values of all expected future dividends to be paid thereon, using a compound discount rate commensurate with the risk.[1] The theorists have the usual difficulty in translating this subjective approach into a price market, and a number of variants of the basic present-value-of-dividends idea are abroad, but the idea itself seems generally accepted. The argument that the average stockholder expects to receive a few dividends and a sale price instead of an indefinite series of future dividends is usually disposed of by noting that the expected future sale price is simply the market value of the future dividends as evaluated at that time. The basic theory thus remains the same.

TABLE 2
Percentage Increase in Stock Prices April, 1954, Average Compared to 1940 Average

Stock	Increase
Dow-Jones Industrials	135
Chase National Bank	48
du Pont de Nemours	198
General Electric	258
General Motors	194
International Business Machines	600
International Harvester	85
Kroger Grocery	202
Monsanto Chemical	161
J. C. Penney	186
Sears Roebuck	236
Standard Oil Co. of New Jersey	395
Swift & Co.	112

[1] This is standard doctrine. See John B. Williams, *Theory of Investment Value* (Harvard University Press, 1938), or George H. Evans and George E. Barnett, *Principles of Investment* (Houghton Mifflin Company, 1940).

But the busy practitioners of the auction market have little time for conjectural estimates of year-by-year future dividends, and their painstaking conversion into a summated present value. They have developed a quick and simple method, which finds expression in the common practice of estimating a present "normal rate" of per share dividends and earnings, multiplying the dividends by about 20 and the earnings by about 14, and averaging the products as a "normal times" appraisal. If the quality of the stock is unusually high or if future growth in earnings and dividends is expected, the multipliers are increased: if quality lacks or earnings decline is forecast, lower multipliers are used. This process has the merit of giving due wieght to both earnings and dividend rates, which seem sound in both theory and practice. It has the disadvantage of treating both earnings and dividend rates as perpetuities, in a world where change is commonplace. And it has the great disadvantage of making a growth stock seem fantastically high at 20 times earnings or 30 times dividends, when in truth it may not be high at all.

Consider, for example, the case of a strongly intrenched and profitable growth stock now paying $1.00 per year in dividends. Assume that this dividend rate is based on a growing earning power which seems likely to increase at an average rate of 5 per cent (compounded) per year. Assume further that investors require a 5 per cent return on their money, if they undertake risks of this sort. On these assumptions, the dividend rate payable one year hence will tend to be increased by a growth factor of 5 per cent, which will be enough to offset the present-value discount factor at the same rate (1.05^{-1}) thus indicating that the present value of next year's dividend is the same as the immediate cash value of the current one. Similarly, the amount of the dividend two years removed will be $D \times 1.05^2$, and its present value factor becomes 1.05^{-2}, giving this dividend also the present value of the current rate.

Repetition of these calculations leads to the inevitable conclusion that under these assumptions the dividend of each future growth year will have a present value equal to the cash rate of the current year; and to the sum of these must be added the present value of the dividends of the additional future years beyond the growth series. Thus, on the assumptions stated, a $1.00 dividend stock with a prospect of 30 years of growth plus 30 years of stable payments thereafter, may fairly sell at $45¼ today, or at a 2.21 per cent current yield basis (cf. Table 4). More fantastically, a $1.00 dividend expected to increase at 5 per cent *forever* has a present value of $1.00 multiplied by *infinity!*

We have not yet seen any growth stocks marketed at the price of infinity dollars per share, but we shall hereafter be watching. Of course, many investors are skeptical and would probably wish to discount the very large and remote dividends in this perpetually growing series at a high discount rate, thus reducing our computed value per share to a figure somewhat below the intriguing level of infinity.

3. HOW FAST DO THEY GROW?

We turn now to the question of probable percentage rates of increase in corporation earning and dividend-paying power. In making the tests reported in Table 3 below we have concerned ourselves with the "growth" of large and established concerns such as du Pont and IBM. Clearly, long-range average growth rates as they affect most investors are best illustrated by the progress of these established concerns, rather than by the abnormal spurts made by specialized producers in some of the electronics and plastics fields since the war. Secondly, we are not here attempting to predict future growth rates; rather we wish to determine what *average* growth rates have been achieved by large concerns in the past, in order to suggest norms for future estimating. Comparisons with "non-growth" concerns and market averages are added to provide perspective. Third, we have measured the 25-year average growth rates (using a visual inspection method of fitting a constant percentage growth line) of both per share earnings and dividends, and are reporting an average of the growth rates in the few cases in which they differ preceptibly. Due allowance has been made for the effects of stock splits, stock dividends, etc., and for the non-recurring influences of depression, war, boom, price controls, and EPT on the growth trends we are attempting to measure.

TABLE 3
Approximate Average Annual Percentage Growth Rates for Earnings and for Dividends During 1929–53 Inclusive for Selected Shares and Share Groups

	Actual Data	Adjusted to Eliminate Effect of Commodity Price Changes
Dow-Jones Industrials	5	2
Chase National Bank	2	−1
du Pont	7	4
General Electric	7	4
General Motors	6	3
International Business Machines	8	5
International Harvester	5	2
Kroger Grocery	5+	2+
Monsanto	8+	5+
J. C. Penncy	5	2
Sears Roebuck	6	3
Standard Oil Co. of New Jersey	7+	4+
Swift & Co.	4	1

By far the greatest "growth" influence observable on our earnings and dividend figures has been that of commodity price-level changes. We are reporting our measured growth rates both as they actually occurred and as they appear when the basic earnings and dividend figures are divided through by the Wholesale Price Index. We concede the inaccuracy of any such price-adjusting system as this, but we believe that the adjusted growth rates are reasonably related to those which would have been achieved under stable price conditions, hence indicate the "recurring" growth impetus which might be characteristic of a non-inflationary future.

Table 3 shows that there are important differences between the growth rates of different industries and companies. No attempt is made here to single out cases, even those as simple as compounding due to reinvestment of earnings. We simply note that some growth rates are rapid, some are slow, and– significantly–many are immediate, neither fast nor slow. Clearly, some growth is typical, and will have its effect on the long-run value of most stocks.

4. PRESENT VALUES OF GROWING DIVIDENDS

The standard present-value-of-annuity tables provide an easy method of evaluating stocks which seem to promise a stable rate (or average rate) of dividend distribution for periods extending into the distant future. Mathematically, these tables simply provide the sums of the present values of a series of $1.00 annual dividends extending a stated number of years into the future, valued at stated compound discount rates. Thus a $1.00 dividend rate discounted at 5 per cent is worth $12.46 if expected to last for 20 years, $17.16 if expected to last for 40 years, $18.93 if expected to last for 60 years, and $20.00 if expected to continue forever. It should be noted that all of these present-value calculations assume that the future dividends represent the total recovery which the investor will derive from the stock, and must therefore include the recovery of his principal in small installments as well as net income. Thus a $1.00 annual dividend extending over 60 years promises to net 5 per cent on a diminishing balance and amortize an $18.93 present investment as well. But a growing dividend provides an ever increasing annual sum to be discounted, and thus leads to a total (present value) appraisal which can be very large in comparison with the current dividend. Due to the almost infinite variety of assumptions upon which any calculations of the total present values of growing dividends would have to be based, there are no general tables from which the figures can be read. We have attempted to illustrate the impact of growth upon total present values by calculating Tables 4, 5, and 6.[2] In doing so, we have arbitrarily decided to assume that corporate dividends beyond the first 60 years are too conjectural to have value. Our tables therefore all predicate a permanent cessation of dividends after 60 years. This is not a drastic assumption, however; if we assumed that the 60th year dividend continued in perpetuity, our present values would be increased by only 3 per cent to 10 per cent.

[2]The calculations are more laborious than difficult. However, we are indebted to Professor Clifford Bell of the UCLA Department of Mathematics for suggesting several time-saving short cuts which made our task easier.

Table 4 is designed to stress the importance of speeds of growth and of the length of time over which growth is expected to continue. It will be observed that 60 years of dividends at a \$1.00 annual rate have a present value of \$18.93, but if the initial \$1.00 dividend rate is expected to grow for 20 years at 5 per cent (compounded rate) before stabilizing, the total present value is nearly doubled at \$37.00. Expected continuation of the 5 per cent growth rate for the full 60 years would of course lift the present value to \$60.00. Naturally, as the table shows, growth expectations at lesser rates would result in more modest present values.

TABLE 4*

The Present Value of All Future Dividends on a Stock Now Paying \$1.00 per Annum†

(computed values to nearest quarter dollar)

Growth Period (Years)	Stable Dividend Period	Annual Growth Rates Expected					
		5%	4%	3%	2%	1%	0%
0	60	\$18.93	\$18.93	\$18.93	\$18.93	\$18.93	\$18.93
10	50	28¼	26	24	22¼	20½	18.93
20	40	37	32¼	28¼	24½	21½	18.93
30	30	45¼	37½	31¼	26¼	22¼	18.93
40	20	52½	41½	33½	27¼	22½	18.93
50	10	57¾	44¼	34¾	27¾	22½	18.93
60	0	60	45½	35¼	28	22¾	18.93

*The computations used to develop Tables 4, 5, and 6 are all based on the assumption that each year's dividend is received at the end of the year, and includes in full any augmentation of rate due to growth during the year. Hence, any year's dividend during a growth period is the initial rate times $(1 + r)^n$, and its present value is obtained by multiplying by $(1 + i)^{-n}$. The stabilized dividend following a growth period is the amount paid in the last year of the growth series. Computations were made by slide rule.

†*If* the dividend is expected to increase at the indicated compound rate for the indicated period of years and then stabilize until 60 years from today and then cease, and *if* a 5 per cent return is required.

The significance of this table may be illustrated in the case of Monsanto Chemical. This thriving concern has maintained an average growth rate in real terms (see Table 3) of slightly over 5 per cent per year for a quarter century. Its present (late April, 1954) price of \$86.00 represents approximately \$34.40 for each dollar of its \$2.50 annual dividend rate. If the investment assumptions of Table 4 are satisfactory and another 30 years of 5 per cent growth can be anticipated, Monsanto could sell for \$45.00 per dollar of dividends today and not be overpriced. Or to test the actual \$34.40 price in the table, this price evidently anticipates a continuation of the 5 per cent growth rate for about 16 or 17 more years, and if growth beyond about 1970 (1954 + 16) should appear likely, the market price could justifiably rise.

The case of International Business Machines is a little harder to classify. The earnings on this stock are experiencing a sharp upsurge at the moment, and the dividend rate has lagged far behind its normal ratio to earnings. As we read the 25-year growth record, a real growth trend of about 5 per cent per year has been characteristic. However, the present earning power of about $10.00 per share would have been accompanied normally by about $6.00 in dividends, instead of the modest $4.00 which current policy permits. Normal long-range values must be estimated with a normal future payout in view—and if we arbitrarily assume a $6.00 dividend level as of now, we find that the $265.00 price (in May, 1954) represents over $44.00 for each dollar of dividends. (Based on the actual $4.00 dividend, the price is 66 times dividends.) This high price could be justified only by unprecedented growth in the near future, which would provide large early dividends with large present values. However, the company's historic growth rate of 5 per cent per year (computed in real, not dollar, terms) will not justify present prices unless it continues for at least 28 more years—truly a long-range speculation—for it must be assumed that most of the eager buyers at present prices are counting on even further price appreciation. Naturally, these remarks are only applicable if the 5 per cent return and other conditions of Table 4 are accepted, and if further price-level inflation is not projected.

But Table 4 has yet another important message for the income-minded investor. We have already noted that the earnings and dividends of most "mature" strong stocks grow a little with the years, even in real terms—and the probabilities of a politically managed price level have still further implications here when dollar amounts are being considered. Table 4 indicates that even slow growth, at the rate of 1 per cent or 2 per cent per year will justify stock prices ranging from 22 to 28 times dividends. And even the more conservative discount rates envisaged in Table 5 will not completely erase the beneficial effects of persistent slow growth.

In Table 5 we illustrate three principles characteristic of appraisals based on compound discount. First, it should be noted in comparing the 5 per cent and 6 per cent columns that a change in the discount rate makes a very sharp change in the total appraisal. Second, it should be noted that the early dividend years are of high importance in the total appraisal, since they have a relatively high present value, and if they look secure enough to justify a discount rate of only 4 per cent they will compensate for a higher discount rate applied against the larger but more conjectural payments of the later years. Third, when a substantial discount rate such as 8 per cent (see the last column of Table 5) is applied against the truly conjectural expectations of large dividends in far distant years, we find that the results seriously deprecate the long-range wisdom of a price exceeding 30 or 35 times present dividend-paying power. This limit naturally does not apply in cases of expected inflationary price-level change or of imminent very spectacular growth due to unusual circumstances.

Of these three principles the third is clearly the most important. When the last column of Table 5 is checked against the related 4 per cent column of Table 4, the significance of the 8 per cent rate in holding down excessively optimistic appraisals will be apparent. And, after all, the forecasting of a high rate of dividend growth for a period of 30 years or longer is sufficiently conjectural to require a substantial discount rate.

TABLE 5

The Present Value of All Future Dividends on a Stock Now Paying $1.00 per Annum*

Assumed Growth Period (Years)	Stable Dividend Period (Years)	Present Value of Dividends at 4 Per Cent	Present Value of Dividends at 6 Per Cent	Present Value of Dividends First 20 Yrs. at 4 Per Cent Next 20 Yrs. at 6 Per Cent Last 20 Yrs. at 8 Per Cent
0	60	$18.93	$16.16	$17½
10	50	26	22¼	24¼
20	40	32¼	26¾	29
30	30	37½	30½	31¾
40	20	41½	33	33½
50	10	44¼	34¾	34¼
60	0	45½	35½	34¼

**If* the dividend is expected to increase at 4 per cent per annum (compounded) for the indicated period and then stabilize until 60 years from today and then cease, and *if* indicated per cent return is required.

In considering Table 6 we encounter the most magnificent of all obsessions regarding growth stocks—the conviction that huge capital gains are available and normal to holders of growth issues. Table 6 has been constructed to show how the present values of the anticipated dividends of rapidly growing stocks rise as the passing years make larger dividend payments more imminent. However, the indicated capital values do not rise by as much as 1 per cent per year, even when the dividend growth rate is 5 per cent, when the growth period is realistically limited, *and starting from a price base which already recognizes and discounts the growth tendency.* In order to create a capital gain rate of 5 per cent per year, it would be necessary for the market to recognize and discount an *additional* future 5 per cent growth year and an *additional* year of total dividend life every year, thus extending the whole basis of calculations upward and onward. This necessarily implies the discovery of new facts about the company which were not available when the year-earlier estimates were made, an implication which by no means asks the impossible. In fact, it seems reasonable that this might happen for a span of years in such stocks as Monsanto or IBM. But growth may not be assumed to be a perpetual phenomenon in any industry, and as the time of stabilized earnings draws near, the values shown in Table 6 suggest the measure of rational stock price behavior.[3]

But the growth-stock enthusiasts are not impressed even by 5 per cent per year capital gains. What of the 236 per cent appreciation since 1940 in Sears

[3]On this point, cf. Graham and Dodd, *Security Analysis,* pp. 459–60, on "counting the same tricks over," and p. 399.

TABLE 6
The "Present" Values on January 1 of the Years Indicated, of the Remaining Dividends To Be Obtained from a Stock Paying $1.00 per Annum at January 1, 1954*

Year	Growth Rate for the 20-Year Growth Period					
	5%	4%	3%	2%	1%	0%
1954	$37	$32¼	$28¼	$24½	$21½	$18.93
1959	41	35	29¾	25½	21¾	18.63
1964	44¼	37	31	26	21¾	18.26
1969	46	38¼	31¾	26¼	21½	17.77

**If* the dividend is expected to grow at the indicated (compound) rate for 20 years (until 1974) and then stabilize for 40 more years and then cease (in 2014), and *if* 5 per cent return is required.

Roebuck, the 258 per cent in General Electric, and the 600 per cent in IBM? How explain these? The explanations we offer are not specific to the foregoing stocks, but in general we attribute the spectacular capital gains recorded by major growth issues to the following: (1) The commodity price-level rise. If a 15-year doubling in value due to growth is superimposed upon a doubling due to general market strength plus price-level inflation, the result is *multiplication by four,* which makes an impression out of all proportion to the simplicity of its origin. (2) Commencement of growth. When a stock enters a promising long-term growth period its value may rise rapidly from 15 or 20 times current dividends to 30 or 35 times dividends. Thereafter, even as the expected rapid growth takes place, the present value of future dividends (and presumably the price of the stock) will follow the slow-growth patterns of Table 6. (3) Irregular growth. Long-range earnings and dividend progress is often made by "fits and starts" rather than steadily, and market recognition comes in similar eruptive fashion. In consequence, short-term gains of sizable amounts make a false impression of high-average speed. (4) Improved quality. Many spectacular capital gains performances since the war have reflected the "growing up" of the company and/or its industry, with consequent improvement in the investment quality of its stock. Even if earnings and dividend growth continues, the capital gains incident to the shift from an 8 per cent speculative capitalization rate to a 5 per cent investment-grade basis are largely non-recurring, and should not be viewed as a continuous process inherent in growth. (5) Irrationality. We doubt if most stock buyers have done enough thinking and enough arithmetic to know what to expect of a "growth" stock bought for 25 times earnings or 40 times dividends. The term "growth" has been given a sales build-up of enormous scope, and—well, IBM went up, didn't it?

5. CONCLUSIONS

We are well aware that it is possible to prove nonsense with figures, and that some readers will believe that we have done it. However, we have persuaded ourselves of the soundness of several summary propositions, of which the following are the most important:

1. Long-term average growth rates exceeding 5 per cent per annum are very rare among major corporations unless real growth is augmented by price-level inflation.

2. Most good stocks grow as a result of retained earnings and for various other reasons, and the benefits of slow growth in such basically mature concerns as General Motors and International Harvester are substantial (and neglected in the trade literature).

3. Even the most vigorous growth stocks are too high to provide reasonable investment and speculative value if they sell above 25 times earnings or 35 times dividends, unless a spurt of abnormal growth or a price-level inflation is immediately impending.

4. When a strong growth tendency is recognized in a stock, the simultaneous discounting of larger future dividends plus improving quality can justify very great appreciation in its price. This process may reasonably be spread over several years, as the recognition and market response will not be instantaneous.

5. When a growth tendency has been fully reflected in the price of a stock, the stock can probably not thereafter appreciate in value anywhere near as fast as the earnings and dividends grow (as the growth period progresses). Cf. Table 6.

6. If price-level inflation is expected to exert an upward influence on the dividends of the future, a rapid growth tendency becomes doubly desirable, since real growth is compounded with the price-level change to increase dollar dividends and capital values *geometrically.* The converse of this is also true.

9

Growth Stocks and the Petersburg Paradox*

David Durand

At a time like the present, when investors are avidly seeking opportunities for appreciation, it is appropriate to consider the difficulties of appraising growth stocks. There is little doubt that when other things are equal the forward-looking investor will prefer stocks with growth potential to those without. But other things rarely are equal—particularly in a sophisticated market that is extremely sensitive to growth. When the growth potential of a stock becomes widely recognized, its price is expected to react favorably and to advance far ahead of stocks lacking growth appeal, so that its price-earnings ratio and dividend yield fall out of line according to conventional standards. Then the choice between growth and lack of growth is no longer obvious, and the astute investor must ask whether the market price correctly discounts the growth potential. Is it possible that the market may, at times, pay too much for growth?

Most problems encountered in appraising growth stocks seem to fall into two categories. First there are the practical difficulties of forecasting sales, earnings, and dividends. Then come the theoretical difficulties of reducing these forecasts to present values. For a long time it seems to have been assumed, altogether too casually, that the present value of a forecasted dividend stream could be represented simply as the sum of all expected future payments discounted at a uniform rate. Doubts, however, are beginning to manifest themselves. As early as 1938, J. B. Williams suggested non-uniform discount rates, varying from payment to payment.[1] More recently, Clendenin and Van Cleave have shown that discounting forecasted dividends at a uniform rate in perpetuity may lead to absurdities or paradoxes, since implied present values of infinity sometimes result. "We have not yet seen any growth stocks marketed at the price of infinity dollars per share," they remark, "but we shall hereafter be watching. Of course, many investors are skeptical and would probably wish to discount the very large and remote dividends in this perpetually growing series at a high discount rate, thus reducing our computed value per share to a figure

*From *Journal of Finance,* Vol. 12, No. 3 (September 1957), pp. 348–363. Reprinted by permission of *Journal of Finance.*

[1] John B. Williams, *The Theory of Investment Value* (Cambridge, Mass.: Harvard University Press, 1938), pp. 50–60.

somewhat below the intriguing value of infinity."[2] Clendenin and Van Cleave might have made a good point even better had they noticed a remarkable analogy between the appraisal of growth stocks and the famous Petersburg Paradox, which commanded the attention of most of the important writers on probability during the eighteenth and nineteenth centuries.

THE PETERSBURG PARADOX

In 1738 Daniel Bernoulli presented before the Imperial Academy of Sciences in Petersburg a classic paper on probability, in which he discussed the following problem, attributed to his cousin Nicholas: "Peter tosses a coin and continues to do so until it should land 'heads' when it comes to the ground. He agrees to give Paul one ducat if he gets 'heads' on the very first throw, two ducats if he gets it on the second, four if on the third, eight if on the fourth, and so on, so that with each additional throw the number of ducats he must pay is doubled. Suppose we seek to determine the value of Paul's expectation."[3]

One may easily obtain a solution according to the principles of mathematical expectation by noting the sequence of payments and probabilities in Table 1:

TABLE 1

Sequence of Tosses	Probability	Payment
H	1/2	1
TH	1/4	2
TTH	1/8	4
TTTH	1/16	8
TTTTH	1/32	16

Paul's expectation is the sum of the products of probability by payment or

$$\frac{1}{2}+\frac{2}{4}+\frac{4}{8}+\frac{8}{16}+\frac{16}{32}+\ldots$$

If the players agree to terminate the game after n tosses, whether a head shows or not, the series will contain n terms and its sum will be $n/2$; but if they agree to continue without fail until a head shows, as the rules of the game stipulate, then n is infinite and the sum $n/2$ is infinite as well. Thus the principles of mathematical expectation imply that Paul should pay an infinite price to enter this game, but this is a conclusion that virtually no one will accept. A variety of

[2] John C. Clendenin and Maurice Van Cleave, "Growth and Common Stock Values," *Journal of Finance,* IX (1954), pp. 365–76. Quotation appears on p. 369.

[3] Daniel Bernoulli, "Exposition of a New Theory on the Measurement of Risk," *Econometrica,* XXII (1954), pp. 23–36, which is a translation by Dr. Louis Sommer of Bernoulli's paper "Specimen Theoriac Novac de Mensura Sortis," *Commentarii Academiae Scientiarum Imperialis Petropolitanae,* V (1738), pp. 175–92.

explanations have been given to show that the value of the game to Paul is, in fact, only a finite amount–usually a small finite amount; and all of these explanations are relevant to growth stock appraisal. But before considering them, we shall do well to examine an important modification of the original Petersburg problem.

One modification, which is obvious enough, consists in stipulating some figure other than ½, say $1/(1 + i)$, for the probability of tossing a tail and some figure other than 2, say $1 + g$, for the rate of growth; but this has no particular interest for security appraisal. A more extensive modification, which is of interest, provides for a series of increasing payments, instead of a single lump sum. In effect, Peter agrees to pay D ducats if the first toss is a tail, $D(1 + g)$ if the second is a tail, $D(1 + g)^2$ if the third is a tail, $D(1 + g)^3$ if the fourth is a tail, and so on until a head shows–at which point the game ceases. Then, if the probability of a tail is $1 / (1 + i)$, the mathematical expectation is (see Appendix)

$$\frac{D}{1+i} + \frac{D(1+g)}{(1+i)^2} + \frac{D(1+g)^2}{(1+i)^3} + \ldots \tag{1}$$

This series is arithmetically equivalent to a discounted series of dividend payments, starting at D ducats, growing at a constant rate g, and discounted at rate i.[4] The summation of the series is a simple exercise in actuarial mathematics. The sum of the first n terms is[5]

$$D\,\frac{1-(1+g)^n / (1+i)^n}{i-g} \tag{2}$$

provided i is different from g; and the sum of an infinite or very large number of terms approaches the very simply formulated quantity

$$\frac{D}{(i-g)} \tag{3}$$

provided that i exceeds g. If, however, $g \geqslant i$, the sum of an infinite number of terms would again be infinite–as in the original Petersburg Problem–and a reasonable Paul might again object to paying the price.

[4]Possibly the objection may be raised that series (1) is conceptually quite different from a discounted series of dividends on the grounds that the discount rate ordinarily represents the price paid for waiting in addition to the price paid for assuming risk. To meet this objection, it suffices to discount the dividend series twice, first, by an amount just sufficient to cover the price of waiting, and second, by the amount required to cover the risk of dividend termination when Peter finally tosses a head. Then, the growth-rate g in (1) would represent the real-growth rate less an adjustment for waiting, and i would represent only the risk of termination.

[5]See, for example, Ralph Todhunter, *The Institute of Actuaries' Text-Book on Compound Interest and Annuities-Certain*, 4th ed., revised by R. C. Simmonds and T. P. Thompson (Cambridge, England: University Press, 1937) pp. 48–49.

The applicability of formulas (2) and (3) to growth stock appraisal is not new. In 1938, for example, J. B. Williams[6] derived (3), or its equivalent, in order to appraise the retained portion of common-stock earnings. He made the derivation, using quite different notation, on essentially the following assumptions: first, that in any year j, earnings per share E_j bear a constant ratio, r, to book value, B_j; second, that dividends, D_j, bear a constant ratio, p, to E_j. Then,

$$B_j + 1 = B_j + E_j(1-p) = B_j[1 + r(1-p)]$$

Hence, book value, dividends, and earnings are all growing at the same constant rate $g = r(1-p)$ and formula (3) can be rewritten

$$\frac{D_1}{i-g} = \frac{E_1 p}{i-g} = \frac{B_1 pr}{i-g} \tag{3a}$$

Williams realized, of course, that these formulas are valid only when i exceeds g, and he mentioned certain other limitations that are best discussed with some of the proposed solutions for the Petersburg Paradox.

ATTEMPTS TO RESOLVE THE PETERSBURG PARADOX[7]

The many attempts to resolve the paradox, summarized very briefly below, fall mostly into two broad groups: those denying the basic assumptions of the game as unrealistic, and those arguing from additional assumptions that the value of the game to Paul is less than its mathematical expectation.

The basic assumptions of the game are open to all sorts of objections from the practically minded. How, in real life, can the game continue indefinitely? For example. Peter and Paul are mortal; so, after a misspent youth, a dissipated middle age, and a dissolute dotage, one of them will die, and the game will cease–heads or no heads. Or again, Peter's solvency is open to question, for the stakes advance at an alarming rate. With an initial payment of one dollar, Peter's liability after only 35 tails exceeds the gold reserve in Fort Knox, and after only three more, it exceeds the volume of bank deposits in the United States and approximately equals the national debt. With this progression, the sky is, quite literally, the limit. Even if Peter and Paul agree to cease after 100 tosses, the stakes, though finite, stagger the imagination.

Despite these serious practical objections, a number of writers chose to accept the assumption of an indefinitely prolonged game at face value, and to direct their attention toward ascertaining the value of such a game to Paul. First

[6] Williams, *op. cit.*, pp. 87–89, 128–135.

[7] For a general history of the paradox, see Isaac Todhunter, *A History of the Mathematical Theory of Probability from the Time of Pascal to that of Laplace* (reprint, New York: G. E. Stechert & Co., 1931) pp. 134, 220–222, 259–262, 275, 280, 286–289, 332, 345, 393, 470. For a briefer treatment, see John Maynard Keynes, *A Treatise on Probability* (London: Macmillan and Co., 1921), pp. 316 ff.

among these was the Swiss mathematician Gabriel Cramer, who early in the eighteenth century proposed two arbitrary devices for resolving the Petersburg Paradox by assuming that the utility of money is less than proportional to the amount held.[8] First, if the utility of money is proportional to the amount up to 2^{24} = 166,777,216 ducats and constant for amounts exceeding 2^{24}, so that the utility of the payments ceases to increase after the 24th toss, Paul's so-called moral expectation is about 13 ducats. Second, if the utility of money is assumed equal to the square root of the amount held, Paul's moral expectation is only about 2.9 ducats. Cramer believed that 2.9 was a more reasonable entrance fee than 13.

A little later and apparently independently, Daniel Bernoulli devised a solution only slightly different from Cramer's. Assuming that the marginal utility of money is inversely proportional to the amount held, he derived a formula that evaluates Paul's expectation in terms of his resources at the beginning of the game. From this formula, which does not lend itself to lightning computation, Bernoulli estimated roughly that the expectation is worth about 3 ducats to Paul when his resources are 10 ducats, about 4 ducats when his resources are 100, and about 6 when his resources are 1000.[9] At this rate, Paul must have infinite resources before he can value his expectation at infinity; but then, even his infinite valuation will constitute only an infinitesimally small fraction of his resources.

An interesting variant of Bernoulli's approach was proposed about a century later by W. A. Whitworth[10]–at least some of us would consider it a viriant, though its author considered it an entirely different argument. Whitworth was, in fact, seeking a solution to the Petersburg Problem that would be free of arbitrary assumptions concerning the utility of money; and he derived a solution by considering the risk of gamblers' ruin, which is always present when players have limited resources. Thus, for example, if A with one dollar matches pennies indefinitely against B with $10, it is virtually certain that one of them will eventually be cleaned out; furthermore, A has 10 chances out of 11 of being the victim. Accordingly, a prudent A might demand some concession in the odds as the price of playing against B. But how much concession? Whitworth attacked this and other problems by assuming a prudent gambler will risk a constant proportion of his resources, rather than a constant amount, on each venture; and he devised a system for evaluating ventures that entail risk of ruin. Applied to the Petersburg Game, this system indicates that Paul's entrance fee should depend upon his resources. Thus Whitworth's solution is reminiscent of Bernoulli's–particularly when one realizes that Whitworth's basic assumption implies an equivalence between a dime bet for A with $1 and a dollar bet for B

[8] Cf. Bernoulli, *op. cit.*, pp. 33 ff.

[9] *Ibid.*, pp. 32 ff.

[10] W. A. Whitworth, *Choice and Chance* (Cambridge, England: Deighton, Bell & Co., 4th edition, enlarged, 1886), chap. 9.

with \$10. Bernoulli, of course, would have argued that the utility of a dime to A was equal to the utility of a dollar to B. Finally, the notion of a prudent gambler seeking to avoid ruin has strong utilitarian undertones, for it implies that marginal utility of money is high when resources are running out.

But Whitworth's approach—regardless of its utilitarian subtleties—is interesting because it emphasizes the need for diversification. The evaluation of a hazardous venture—be it dice game, business promotion, or risky security—depends not only on the inherent odds, but also on the proportion of the risk-taker's resources that must be committed. And just as the prudent gambler may demand odds stacked in his favor as the price for betting more than an infinitesimal proportion of his resources, so may the prudent portfolio manager demand a greater than normal rate of return (after allowing for the inherent probability of default) as the price of investing more than an infinitesimal proportion of his assets in a risky issue.[11]

Although the preceding historical account of the Petersburg Paradox has been of the sketchiest, it should serve to illustrate an important point. The various proposed solutions, of which there are many, all involve changing the problem in one way or another. Thus some proposals evaluate the cash value of a finite game, even when the problem specifies an infinite game; others evaluate the utility receipts, instead of the cash receipts, of an infinite game; and still others foresake evaluation for gamesmanship and consider what Paul as a prudent man should pay to enter. But although none of these proposals satisfy the theoretical requirements of the problem, they all help to explain why a real live Paul might be loath to pay highly for his infinite mathematical expectation. As Keynes aptly summed it up, "We are unwilling to be Paul, partly because we do not believe Peter will pay us if we have good fortune in the tossing, partly because we do not know what we should do with so much money. . .if we won it, partly because we do not believe we should ever win it, and partly because we do not think it would be a rational act to risk an infinite sum or even a very large sum for an infinitely large one, whose attainment is infinitely unlikely."[12]

IMPLICATIONS OF PETERSBURG SOLUTIONS FOR GROWTH-STOCK APPRAISAL

If instead of tossing coins, Peter organizes a corporation in a growth industry and offers Paul stock, the latter might be deterred from paying the full discounted value by any of the considerations that would deter him from paying the full mathematical expectation to enter the Petersburg game. And again, these considerations fall into two categories: first, those denying the basic assumptions

[11]Section 87 of the New York Insurance Law states: "Except as more specifically provided in this chapter, no domestic insurer shall have more than ten per cent of its total admitted assets invested in, or loaned upon, the securities of any one institution: . . ." Section 81, subsection 13, places additional restrictions on common stock investment.

[12]Keynes, *op. cit.*, p. 318.

concerning the rate of indefinitely prolonged growth; and, second, those arguing that the value of the stock to Paul is less than its theoretical discounted value.

Underlying J. B. Williams' derivation of formula (3) is the assumption that Peter, Inc., will pay dividends at an increasing rate g for the rest of time. Underlying the derivation in the Appendix is a slightly different assumption: namely, that Peter will pay steadily increasing dividends until the game terminates with the toss of a head, and that the probability of a head will remain forever constant at $i/(1+i)$. Under neither assumption is there any provision for the rate of growth ever to cease or even decline. But astronomers now predict the end of the world within a finite number of years—somewhere in the order of 10,000,000,000—and realistic security analysts may question Peter, Inc.'s ability to maintain a steadily increasing dividend rate for anywhere near that long. Williams, in fact, regarded indefinitely increasing dividends as strictly hypothetical, and he worked up formulas for evaluating growth stocks on the assumption that dividends will follow a growth curve (called a logistic by Williams) that increases exponentially for a time and then levels off to an asymptote.[13] This device guarantees that the present value of any dividend stream will be finite, no matter how high the current, and temporary, rate of growth. Clendenin and Van Cleave, though not insisting on a definite ceiling, argued that continued rapid growth is possible only under long-run price inflation.

The assumption of indefinitely increasing dividends is most obviously objectionable when the growth rate equals or exceeds the discount rate ($g \geqslant i$) and the growth series (1) sums to infinity; then formula (3) does not even apply. If Peter, Inc., is to pay a dividend that increases at a constant rate $g \geqslant i$ per year, it is absolutely necessary, though not sufficient, that he earn a rate on capital, $r = E/B$, that is greater than the rate of discount—more exactly, $r \geqslant i/(1-p)$. But this situation poses an anomaly, at least for the equilibrium theorist, who argues that the marginal rate of return on capital must equal the rate of interest in the long run. How, then, can Peter, Inc., continually pour increasing quantities of capital into his business and continue to earn on these accretions a rate higher than the standard rate of discount? This argument points toward the conclusion that growth stocks characterize business situations in which limited, meaning finite though not necessarily small, amounts of capital can be invested at rates higher than the equilibrium rate. If this is so, then the primary problem of the growth-stock appraiser is to estimate how long the departure from equilibrium will continue, perhaps by some device like Williams' growth curve.

If, for the sake of argument, Paul wishes to assume that dividend growth will continue indefinitely at a constant rate, he can still find reasons for evaluating Peter's stock at somewhat less than its theoretical value just as he found reasons for evaluating his chances in the Petersburg Game at less than the mathematical expectation. The decreasing-marginal-utility approach of Cramer and Bernoulli implies that the present utility value of a growing dividend stream

[13] Williams, *op. cit.*, pp. 89–94.

is less than the discounted monetary value, because the monetary value of the large dividends expected in the remote future must be substantially scaled down in making a utility appraisal. Or again, Whitworth's diversification approach implies that a prudent Paul with finite resources can invest only a fraction of his portfolio in Peter's stock; otherwise he risks ruinous loss. And either argument is sufficient to deter Paul from offering an infinite price, unless, of course, his resources should be infinite.

THE PROBLEM OF REMOTE DIVIDENDS

There is, moreover, another important limitation on Paul's evaluation of a growth stock that has not arisen in the discussion of the Petersburg Paradox, namely, the remoteness of the large dividend payments. Conventional theory argues that dividend n years hence is adequately evaluated by the discount factor $1/(1 + i)^n$, but this is open to question when n is very large. The question is, of course, academic for ordinary instruments like long-term bonds or preferred stock, since discounted coupons or preferred dividends many years hence are negligible when discounted in the conventional manner. Thus, for example, if \$5.00 a year in perpetuity is worth exactly \$100.00 (assuming 5 per cent compounded annually), then \$99.24 is attributable to the first 100 payments. But for a stock growing according to series (1) and with $g \geqslant i$, the discounted value of remote dividends, say 10,000 years hence, is anything but negligible; in fact, it may be astronomic. But how should Paul evaluate such remote growth dividends?

If Paul is a real live person without heirs or other incentives for founding an estate, his problem is fairly clearcut. Dividends payable beyond his reasonable life span are useless to him as income, although claims on them may be convertible into useful income through the medium of the market place. At retirement, for example, he might easily be able to increase his income for the remainder of his life by selling long-term securities and buying an annuity. If, however, Paul has heirs, he may look forward several generations and place a very real value on dividends that will be payable to his grandchildren and great-grandchildren. But even here his investment horizon may be limited by the uncertainty of planning for offspring not yet born.

If Paul is a life insurance company, he has a special interest in evaluating remote dividends; for the shades of obligations currently contracted may extend far into the future as the following fanciful though not impossible sketch will indicate. In 1956 John Doe, aged 21, buys for his own benefit a whole life policy containing the customary guaranty of a rate of interest if the insured elects to settle the proceeds in installments. In 2025, aged 90, John Doe decides to settle this policy on his newborn great-grandson Baby Doe and directs the insurance company to accumulate the proceeds at the guaranteed rate of interest until Baby Doe shall reach the age of 21 and thereupon pay them out to him as a life income, according to the table of guaranteed rates in the policy. Encouraged by his monthly checks, Baby Doe now lives to the ripe old age of 105, so that only in 2130 does the insurance company finally succeed in discharging its obligation of 1956, based on the then current forecasts of long-term interest rates.

Even though the case of John Doe may be a bit out of the ordinary, it illustrates forcefully why life insurance companies must concern themselves with dividend income up to perhaps 200 years hence and how a future decline in the earning rate on assets may threaten the solvency of an insurance fund. Although the purchase of long-term bonds is an obvious form of protection against falling interest rates, it is not entirely effective when the liabilities extend too far into the future. To illustrate the difficulty of long-term protection, it will be convenient at this point to introduce a concept called "duration" by Macaulay,[14] which may apply to an individual security, a portfolio of securities, or even to a block of liabilities. Duration, incidentally, must not be confused with a related concept known as "equated time."

The duration of an individual security or a portfolio is the arithmetic mean of the several coupon or maturity dates, each date weighted by the present value at the valuation rate of interest of the expected income on that date. The duration of an E bond or non-interest-bearing note is simply the term to maturity; and the duration of a portfolio consisting, for example, of two \$100 E bonds due two years hence and a \$500 E bond due five years hence would be

$$\left[\frac{2 \times 200}{(1.03)^2} + \frac{5 \times 500}{(1.03)^5}\right] \div \left[\frac{200}{(1.03)^2} + \frac{500}{(1.03)^5}\right]$$

if evaluated at 3 percent compounded annually. The duration of an interest-bearing bond is less than the term to maturity, because the long term of the principal payment at maturity must be averaged against the shorter terms of the various coupons. Macaulay's formula for the duration of interest-paying bonds is somewhat complex; but for perpetuities, such as Canadian Pacific debenture 4's, it simplifies to $(1 + i)/i$.[15] At $i = .03$, the duration of a perpetuity is therefore about 34 years.

In seeking suitable methods for matching the assets of a fund to its liabilities so as to minimize risk of loss from fluctuations in the interest rate, British actuaries have shown that the possible loss is very small when both present value and duration of the assets equal present value and duration of the liabilities; and, indeed, they have given examples where the "loss" is a small gain for fluctuations either up or down.[16] But although the portfolio manager can ordinarily

[14] F. R. Macaulay, *Some Theoretical Problems Suggested by the Movement of Interest Rates, Bond Yields and Stock Prices in the United States since 1856* (New York: National Bureau of Economic Research, 1938), pp. 44–51.

[15] Macaulay, *op. cit.*, pp. 49–50. In Macaulay's formula for perpetuities (p.50) let $R = 1 + i$.

[16] See, for example, J. B. H. Pegler, "The Actuarial Principles of Investment," *Journal of the Institute of Actuaries* (England), Vol. 74 (1948), pp. 179–211; F.

achieve satisfactory matching by merely selecting long- and short-term bonds in such proportions that their average duration equals that of the liabilities, he runs into difficulty when the duration of the liabilities is exceptionally long. Thus, for example, the duration of the liability of a pension fund with many young workers and only a few pensioners can easily exceed 40 years: and this is too long to be matched by a portfolio consisting wholly of perpetuities, whose duration at current interest rates is only about 30 years. In such a difficulty, however, growth stocks offer a possible solution; for when dividends are growing according to series (1), the duration is longer than a perpetuity. In fact, if we define

$$1 + b = \frac{1 + i}{1 + g}$$

then $(1 + b)b$ is the duration of the series.[17] Thus growth stocks provide a possible means of increasing the average duration of a portfolio when the composition of the liabilities requires this. W. Perks has, in fact, hinted as much.[18]

There is, in fact, no theoretical limit to the duration of a stock with dividends growing as in (1). When $g = .05$ and $i = .06$, say, the duration is approximately 100 years; and as the difference between g and i decreases, durations of 1,000 years, 10,000 years, or even 1,000,000 years might result. Moreover, when $g \geqslant i$, $b \leqslant 0$ and formula $(1 + b)/b$ is no longer valid; then the duration is infinite as well as the present value. But although securities with a duration of 100 years might be useful to British life companies for increasing average duration of pension fund assets, or for providing protection against contingencies illustrated by the case of John Doe above, securities with much greater duration would begin to lose appeal. The essential characteristic of a very long duration is that the security holder or his legatees must expect to wait a long time before the security begins to pay a substantial return; and with those hypothetical securities having infinite duration, the legatees must literally expect

---

M. Redington, "Review of the Principles of Life Office Valuations," *ibid.*, Vol. 78 (1952), pp. 286–340; G. V. Bayley and W. Perks, "A Consistent System of Investment and Bonus Distribution for a Life Office," *ibid.*, Vol. 79 (1953), pp. 14–73; A. T. Haynes and R. J. Kirton, "The Financial Structure of a Life Office," *Transactions of the Faculty of Actuaries* (Scotland), Vol. 21 (1953), pp. 141–218; D. J. Robertson and I. L. B. Sturrock, "Active Investment Policy Related to the Holding of Matched Assets," *ibid.*, Vol. 22 (1954), pp. 36–96. Also see Paul A. Samuelson, "The Effect of Interest Rate Increases on the Banking System," *American Economic Review,* XXXV (1945), 16–27, especially p. 19.

Interest of the British in this subject, which seems to be greater than that of the Americans, may be due in part to their relative freedom from liability for policy loans. Although the British companies are prepared to make such loans, they are not forced to do so.

[17] This can be proved by using Macaulay's method of finding the duration of a perpetuity and making the substitution $b = i$.

[18] See his remarks following the paper by Redington, *op. cit.*, p. 327.

to wait forever. Even the most forward looking of investors, who are probably those who leave bequests to such institutions as universities and religious organizations, cannot afford to look that far into the future; for, to paraphase Keynes, it would not be a rational act to risk an infinite sum or even a very large sum for an infinitely larger one, whose attainment is infinitely remote. In effect, the very remote dividends in series (1) cannot be worth their actuarially discounted value when g is large; whether they are worth it when g is small is probably academic, for then the discounted value will be negligible.

To allow for various uncertainties in evaluating dividends in the very remote future, Clendenin and Van Cleave made a significant suggestion, namely, to increase the discount rate applicable to the more remote dividends. The difficulty, of course, is to find some reasonable, objective basis for setting up an appropriate schedule of rates. To illustrate their suggestion, Clendenin and Van Cleave worked out valuations for hypothetical securities by discounting the first twenty years of dividends at 4 per cent, the second twenty at 6 per cent, the third twenty at 8 per cent, and considering all subsequent dividends as worthless. But although such a schedule, totally disregarding all dividends after 60 years, might appeal to a man aged 40 without heirs, it would not appeal to insurance companies and pension managers, who have to look forward 150 to 200 years; and it would certainly not appeal to the loyal alumnus, who wishes to leave a bequest to alma mater. But the essential point is that by setting up a schedule of discount rates that increase fast enough to render very remote dividends negligible, one can assure himself that the present value of any increasing stream of dividends will be finite. An although many investors would object to neglecting dividends after 60 years, few would object to neglecting them after 600.

SUMMARY AND IMPLICATIONS FOR SECURITY APPRAISAL IN GENERAL

There are, to sum up, a number of potent reasons any one of which suffices to dissuade Paul from paying an infinite price for a growth stock under even the most favorable circumstances, namely when $g \geqslant i$ and the sum of series (1) is infinite. Moreover, these reasons do not lose all their force when $g \leqslant i$ and the sum of (1) is finite. In appraising any growing stream of dividends, Paul might wish to make provision for eventual decline and perhaps cessation of the growth rate, as suggested by J. B. Williams; he might adjust large dividends to allow for the decreasing marginal utility of money, somewhat in the manner of Cramer and Bernoulli; or again he might apply Whitworth's reasoning and scale down his valuation to a sum he can afford to risk, given his resources; or finally he might, following Clendenin and Van Cleave, apply a very high discount rate to remote dividends that have no significance to him. And he might, of course, apply a combination of such approaches.

But, oddly enough, the very fact that Paul has so many good reasons for scaling down the sum of series (1) when g is high, and so many ways to accomplish this end, leaves him with no clear basis for arriving at any precise valuation. Thus, the possible adjustments for the decreasing marginal utility of money are many and varied. Cramer's two proposals yielded very different appraisals if applied to rapidly growing growth stocks; and Daniel Bernoulli's proposal would yield yet another result. Or again, there are many ways by which Paul can allow for an eventual decline in the current rate of growth, all of which entail major forecasting problems. Williams' formula, for example, which is stated here in the form[19]

$$V = D \left[\frac{(1+g)^n - (1+i)^n}{(g-i)(1+i)^n} + \frac{(2g+i+2gi)(1+g)^n}{i(g+i+gi)(1+i)^n} \right]$$

after the substitution $D = \Pi_0\ (1 + g)$ and some rearrangement, rests on the somewhat restrictive assumption that dividends grow annually at a constant rate g for n years and then taper off exponentially to a level equal to exactly twice the dividend in the nth year. Even when the assumptions are acceptable in principle, practical application of the formula may require more accurate information on g, i, and n than one could possibly expect to obtain. This is particularly true when n is large and g is only slightly larger than i; then $g - i$ in the denominator of the first fraction is small and tremendously sensitive to errors in either g or i. Nor is this difficulty peculiar to Williams' formula. Table 2, abridged from Clendenin and Van Cleave,[20] gives the present value of 60

TABLE 2

Growth Period	Rate of Growth	
	5 Per Cent	4 Per Cent
0	$18.93	$18.93
10	28¼	26
20	37	32½
30	45¼	37½
40	52¼	41½
50	57¾	44¼
60	60	45½

dividend payments discounted at 5 per cent. It is assumed that the initial dividend rate of $1.00 grows at either 4 per cent or 5 per cent for a period of years and then remains constant for the remainder of the 60-year period, after which dividends either cease or are considered worthless. This table again illustrates the difficulty of making appraisals without an accurate forecast of the growth rate and the length of the growth period.

More conventional securities such as bonds and preferred stocks, though

[19] Williams, *op. cit.*, formula (27a), p. 94.
[20] *Op. cit.*, Table 4, p. 371.

much less troublesome than growth stocks, still present some of the same difficulties of evaluation, and a single example should make this clear. In evaluating bonds–even bonds of supposedly uniform quality–one must make some adjustment for term to maturity. Ordinarily one does this by summing a discounted series of coupons and principal

$$\frac{C}{1+i_n} + \frac{C}{(1+i_n)^2} + \ldots + \frac{C}{(1+i_n)^n} + \frac{P}{(1+i_n)^n}$$

in which the uniform discount factor depends on the number of years to maturity. Alternatively, however, one could follow the suggestion of Clendenin and Van Cleave, which would entail summing the series

$$\frac{C}{1+i_1} + \frac{C}{(1+i_2)^2} + \frac{C}{(1+i_3)^3} + \ldots + \frac{C}{(1+i_n)^n} + \frac{P}{(1+i_n)^n}$$

in which each discount factor i_1, i_2, i_3, etc., depends on the date of the coupon or principal payment discounted. But whether one prefers the conventional method or the alternative, the issue is clear: one cannot apply a standard discount factor i uniformly to all bonds; some adjustment for the length, or duration, of the payment stream is essential.

The moral of all this is that conventional discount formulas do not provide completely reliable evaluation. Presumably they provide very satisfactory approximations for high-grade, short-term bonds and notes. But as quality deteriorates or duration lengthens, the approximations become rougher and rougher. With growth stocks, the uncritical use of conventional discount formulas is particularly likely to be hazardous; for, as we have seen, growth stocks represent the ultimate in investments of long duration. Likewise, they seem to represent the ultimate in difficulty of evaluation. The very fact that the Petersburg Problem has not yielded a unique and generally acceptable solution to more than 200 years of attack by some of the world's great intellects suggests, indeed, that the growth-stock problem offers no great hope of a satisfactory solution.

APPENDIX

PROOF OF FORMULA (1) FOR PAUL'S EXPECTATION IN THE MODIFIED PETERSBURG GAME

The table below lists a few possible outcomes, with associated probabilities, for the modified Petersburg Game, in which Peter pays Paul a series of dividends according to the number of tails that occur before a head finally shows. There is, of course, an infinite number of such possible outcomes, because every finite

Sequence of Tosses	Probability	Dividend	Total Pay (Cumulated Dividends)
H	$i/(1+i)$	0	0
TH	$i/(1+i)^2$	D	D
TTH	$i/(1+i)^3$	$D(1+g)$	$D+D(1+g)$
TTTH	$i/(1+i)^4$	$D(1+g)^2$	$D+D(1+g)+D(1+g)^2$

sequence of tails, no matter how long, has a finite, though possibly very small, probability of occurring. It is assumed, moreover, that throughout even the longest sequence, the probability of a tail remains constant at $1/(1+i)$, leaving $i/(1+i)$ as the probability of a head.

Paul's mathematical expectation is obtained by summing the products of probability in the second column by payout in the fourth. Thus, the sequence TTH, for example, has probability $i/(1+i)^3$ and results in the payout of two dividends, D and $D(1+g)$. The product appears in the table below along with similar products for the sequences H, TH, and TTTH.

Sequence	Product
H	0
TH	$Di/(1+i)^2$
TTH	$[D+D(1+g)]\,i/(1+i)^3$
TTTH	$[D+D(1+g)+D(1+g)^2]\,i/(1+i)^4$

To sum these products, it is convenient to break them up and to rearrange the parts in powers of $1+g$. Thus, for example, all elements containing $(1+g)^2$ form an infinite series

$$\frac{Di(1+g)^2}{(1+i)^4}\left[1+\frac{1}{1+i}+\frac{1}{(1+i)^2}+\ldots\right]$$

where the factor in the bracket is a well-known actuarial form having the sum to infinity $(1+i)/i$. Thus, the sum of all elements in $(1+g)^2$ is $D(1+g)^2/(1+i)^3$, which is one of the terms in series (1). The other terms are obtained in an analogous manner.

10

Current Growth Stock Valuation Methods General Motors— An Illustration*

Paul F. Wendt†

Most modern stock valuation techniques are based upon the present value theory, which was first set forth in detail by John B. Williams, in his *Theory of Investment Value.* Building on the earlier theoretical foundations found in Marshall, Bohm Bawerk and Irving Fisher, Williams argued that the present value of a share of stock is equal to the summation of all dividends expected to be received from it, discounted to the present at an appropriate rate of interest.[1] He argued that tangible income to the investor, dividends, were the only appropriate base for consideration in the valuation of stocks. More recently, others have argued that it does not matter whether one capitalizes dividends or earnings, since price changes in stocks would discount earnings and potential future dividends and since investors could elect to receive income either as dividends or by the sale of stock.[2]

Although most recent writers on the theory of stock valuation have continued to favor the capitalization of future dividends, they have accorded increasing attention to capitalization of earnings for rapidly growing enterprises.[3] The purpose of this article is to describe briefly some of the current

*From *Financial Analysts Journal,* Vol. 21, No. 2 (March-April 1965), pp. 91–101. Reprinted by permission of *Financial Analysts Journal.*

†The author acknowledges the assistance of members of his graduate seminar who aided in the calculations for this article. An early draft was used in the second annual "Seminar on Fiduciary Investment," August 3-14, 1964. sponsored by University Extension and the Graduate School of Business Administration, University of California, Berkeley. The Institute of Business and Economic Research, Berkeley, aided in typing and chart preparation.

[1]Alfred Marshall, *Principles of Economics*, 8th Edition (London, 1925), Vol. 5, Chapters IV, VI, XV; Irving Fisher, *The Nature of Capital and Income* (New York, 1906); John B. Williams, *The Theory of Investment Value* (Cambridge, 1938).

[2]F. Modigliani and M. H. Miller, "Dividend Policy, Growth and the Valuation of Shares," *Journal of Business* (October 1961).

[3]James E. Walter, "Dividend Policies and Common Stock Prices," *Journal of Finance* (March 1956), pp. 29–42; B. G. Malkiel, "Equity Yields and Structure of Share Prices," *The American Economic Review* (December 1963), pp. 1004–1031. See also *AER* (December 1964), "Comment and Reply," pp. 1029–1051.

growth stock valuation techniques and to illustrate the differences in methods, assumptions and resultant valuations by reference to the valuation of General Motors common in mid-1964.

The three methods described briefly in the first part will not be illustrated because of lack of data, similarity to other techniques, or because of other limitations. The seven techniques illustrated in the second part, for which published information is available in sufficient detail to permit calculation, have been selected to provide indication of the range of values which result from alternative assumptions and objectives.

PART I

Building directly on Williams' theoretical foundations, Walter developed the following formula for valuation of the future dividend stream expected from a stock, and illustrated its application to growth, intermediate and so-called creditor stock categories. By his definition, a growth stock is one for which the rate of return on marginal investment (after adjustment for preferential tax treatment of capital gains) was larger than the company's cost of capital or capitalization rate.[4]

$$V_c = \frac{D + \frac{R_a}{R_c}(E - D)}{R_c}$$

where:

D = Annual cash dividends expected per share

E = Earnings per share

R_a = Rate of return corporation will earn on additional investment

R_c = Market capitalization rate

V_c = Value per share

Malkiel, writing in *The American Economic Review* for December 1963, sets forth a formula for calculating the present value of future dividends which is closely similar to the methods employed by Williams and Walter, and to some of the techniques illustrated below. His formula implies the use of the reciprocal of a standard multiplier as a discount rate.[5]

$$P = \frac{D(1+g)}{(1+r)} + \frac{D(1+g)^2}{(1+r)^2} + \frac{D(1+g)^N}{(1+r)^N} + \frac{M_s E(1+g)^N}{(1+r)^N}$$

where:

M_s = Standard earnings multiplier S&P averages

D = Dividend in dollars

[4]Walter, *op. cit.*

[5]Malkiel, *op. cit.* See also Sanford L. Margoshes, "Present Value Techniques of Common Stock Valuation," *Financial Analysts Journal* (March-April 1961), pp. 37–42.

g = Company's growth rate as a percentage
E = Earnings in dollars
r = Standard rate of growth S&P averages or the apparent marginal efficiency of the representative standard share
N = Number of years forecasted
P = Present value of future stream of receipts

The *Value Line Survey*, which might be credited with initiating the econometric analysis of the relationship between stock prices, dividends and earnings at the practitioner level, is based upon a multiple regression analysis of dividend payments, earnings and lagged market prices for a large sample of individual issues. Arnold Bernhard, President, describes the evolution of techniques employed by his firm in his book, *The Evaluation of Common Stocks.* Revisions in technique are published in the "Commentary" to the financial service. The Value Line technique seeks to establish a so-called Quality Rating for each of 1,100 individual issues, a Potential Value five years hence and a Current Value. Using General Motors common stock as an illustration, the author illustrates the technique for establishing these value concepts (pp. 61-76). The most recently published analysis of General Motors common stock published on July 24, 1964 indicated an expected potential value in 1967-69 of $90 based upon an estimated eight -year growth rate of 6.3%. This valuation appears to be based upon the equation V = 8 X 5-year moving average Cash Earnings. (See the "Commentary" of April 3, 1964, describing the revised method of ranking stocks for the next three to five years.)

The estimated normal current value in July 1964 was $70 per share based upon estimates of earnings of $5.75 and dividends of $4.10 for the year ending September 1965. The regression formula used in order to obtain the above normal value was:

$$\log \text{Normal Value} = 1.168 + .750 \log (.68 \text{ Earn.} + \text{Divd.})$$

The constant (1.168) incorporated General Motors' long-term trend and logged price factors.

PART II

The earnings per share of General Motors (shown in Chart I), have been growing at an annual rate of about 5.3% for the last ten years. The dividend growth, however, was almost 9% per annum. Why this difference? In the early years of the last decade the pay-out ratio was only about 50%. In 1963 General Motors reported earnings of $5.56 per share and paid a dividend of $4.00, equivalent to a pay-out ratio of approximately 70%. It is to be expected that future dividend growth will be more in line with earnings growth. In the following illustrations, the assumption is made that dividend and earnings growth will be about 5.3% for the next ten years.

The seven valuation techniques which follow are associated with the writ-

CHART 1

General Motors: Earnings, Dividends, Cash Generated, and Price Range Per Share, and Price/Earnings Ratio

Actual 1954-1963; Estimated 1964-1973

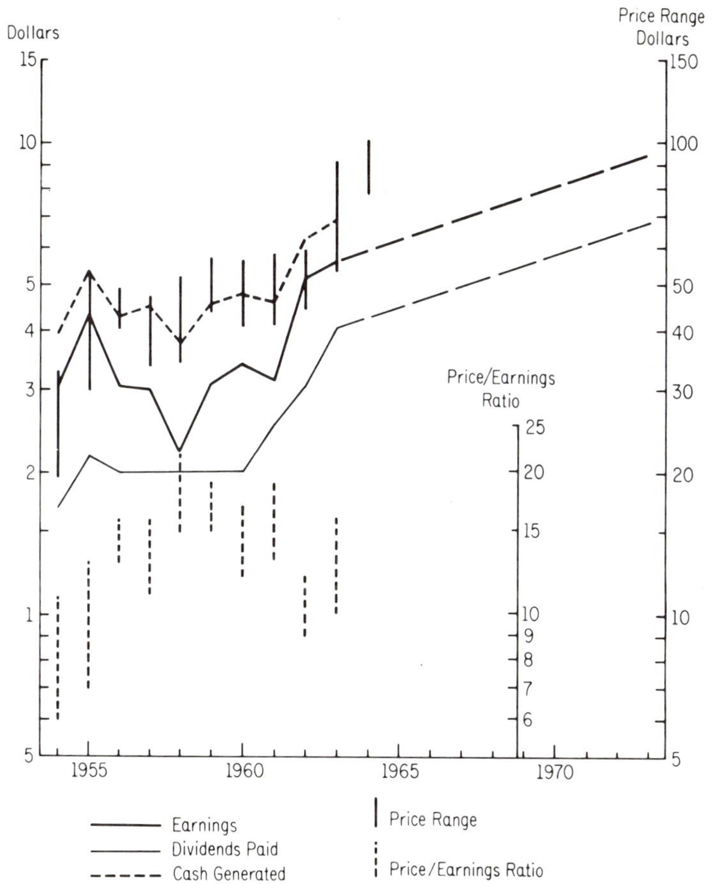

Source: Actual 1954-1963, Standard and Poor's Corp., Standard Listed Stock Reports, General Motors, November 20, 1964. Estimates 1964-1973, estimated by the author, see text.

ings of John C. Clendenin, W. Scott Bauman, Nicholas Molodovsky, Graham, Dodd, Cottle & Tatham, Jeremy C. Jenks, Robert Ferguson and William Kurtz. Although the author has endeavored to follow these various techniques as described in the *Financial Analysts Journal* and elsewhere, it must be emphasized that the assumptions have been made by the author and the resultant valuations represent his interpretation of the values resulting from the application of the different techniques illustrated. Mssrs. Clendenin, Bauman, Jenks, Ferguson, Molodovsky and my colleague, Prof. M. J. Keenan, made many helpful comments and suggestions on the final draft of this article.

TECHNIQUE #1 – CLENDENIN

John C. Clendenin has developed a method for determining the justifiable price-dividend multiplier for a growth stock, given alternative assumptions as to rates of growth, duration of growth and discount rates. He presents a series of present value tables (see Appendix A) which can be used either to determine the assumptions concerning growth rate and duration which are implicit in the current market value of a stock, or for determining the investment value of a stock, given certain assumptions about growth and appropriate discount rates.

Following Williams' theory, Clendenin states:

> Basic theory asserts that the value of a share of stock to a long term investor is contained entirely in the future dividends the share (or its successors following mergers, stock dividends, or spin-offs) may pay, plus the value of occasional rights or small miscellaneous distributions which do not dilute the basic equity.[6]

In describing the use of his technique, Clendenin shows that it can be applied to short-term investment as well. A person who plans to hold a share of stock for only three years, for example, will arrive at today's value by discounting to its present value (a) the dividends he expects to receive during the next three years, and (b) the price he expects to receive at the time of sale, which will be determined by all future dividends the stock is expected to yield from year 3 to infinity.

Three factors are basic to Clendenin's valuation method: (1) the rate of dividend growth, (2) the duration of the growth trend, and (3) the discount or capitalization rates (or yield rates as he calls them). Cautioning investors concerning over-optimism about growth rates and duration, he advocates a system of progressively higher discount rates (with a maximum of 7%) to be applied to expected dividend returns in the distant future. (See Appendix A)

Clendenin suggests that twenty years are "not beyond the scope of reasonable estimation in the case of well-established concerns." Beyond that time he advises caution but illustrates that the largest part of the value of any stock attaches to the dividends of the first twenty years because of the increasing effect of discounting as time progresses. He also suggests application of the method to groups of stocks rather than single issues, to obtain greater reliability in long-term projections.

The analyst using Clendenin's method of growth stock valuation still faces a major task, namely that of deciding what values to assign to Clendenin's basic three factors: growth rate, duration and discount rates. The author offers limited help on how to estimate future growth rate duration. He arrives at a discount rate by checking what the norm is among high-grade stocks, adds 1% to expected real terms growth rate to take into account average inflationary forces, and

[6] John C. Clendenin, "Theory and Technique of Growth Stock Valuation," Occasional Paper No. 1 (Bureau of Business and Economic Research, UCLA, 1957).

suggests a discount rate which depends on the quality of the corporation whose stock is considered. Clendenin avoids being any more specific in assigning values to his factors because "In all instances the investor has a subjective analysis to make. . . ."

Application of Technique #1 to General Motors Common Stock

Reading from Clendenin's Table I in Appendix A (extrapolating to 5.3% growth rate) and assuming that growth will continue for only 10 years, and that earnings remain stable for the ensuing 90 years; General Motors stock is worth:

Multiplier		Dividend		
25.40	X	$4.00	=	$101.60

Its closing price on July 17, 1964 was 94 3/8.

It can be seen from Appendix A that the multiplier rises rapidly as the growth rate and growth period assumed increase. It is interesting to observe from Appendix A that at the July 17, 1964 price of 94 3/8, General Motors common appeared to discount an approximate 4% growth rate for 10 years capitalizing future dividends at the rates shown (i.e., 23.04 X $4.00 = $92.16).

TECHNIQUE #2 – BAUMAN (VARIABLE DISCOUNT RATE METHOD)[7]

Bauman uses, as did Clendenin, the present value concept of arriving at a stock value by discounting at an appropriate yield rate all future cash incomes or dividends. He spells out the factors that determine future dividend income; namely, the growth rate and the growth duration, and argues that a company with a growth rate in excess of the average shown in an industry will sooner or later find its growth rate declining to the average level. How long this "transitional" period lasts depends on the company, the industry, product, competition, etc. A guide to follow is to determine the probable position of the company in its life cycle. For example, if a company has been experiencing an abnormally high growth rate, Bauman suggests, ". . . unless there is sufficient evidence to the contrary, the best earnings and dividend projection is probably one based on a decreasing rate of growth," until it eventually approximates the secular growth rate for the majority of companies in the economy. This secular growth rate of dividends and also earnings plus non-cash charges was found to have been about 4% during the last 36 years. For reasons of convenience, and for lack of evidence to the contrary, Bauman makes the assumption in his model that the growth rate will decline by equal amounts over the span of the transitional period.

According to Bauman, therefore, in order to make a good estimate of future dividends, the investor must ascertain (a) the current growth rate of dividends

[7]W. Scott Bauman, "Estimating the Present Value of Common Stocks by the Variable Rate Method," Michigan Business Reports No. 42 (Bureau of Business Research, University of Michigan, 1963).

(and earnings), and (b) how long will it take until the growth rate has declined to the 4% growth rate average typical for the majority of corporations.

Once the investor has determined the pattern for future dividend incomes, he must discount them to arrive at a present value. What shall be the discount rate? Bauman offers guidelines of from 6 to 10% depending on the risk involved.

The discount rate applied to the first year's expected dividends is usually the lowest, and it increases with time as incomes of more distant years become more and more uncertain. That is, the risk premium added to the discount rate increases with time. Although he does not advise the investor exactly on how much higher future discount rates should be than initial rates, he gives a very strong clue by showing what rates were representative for a majority stock average. The Standard and Poor's Index was shown to be comprised mainly of large companies with medium to high quality. An initial discount rate of 6.5% was held to be reasonable. The average price-dividend ratio for the period 1949-1962 was 24.2 giving an average dividend yield of 4.13% with a 4% annual growth rate. Based on these relationships and using trial and error method, it was mathematically consistent to have the first year's dividend income discounted at 6.5% followed by the second year's dividend income discounted at 6.54875%, the third year's by 6.59750%, with each succeeding year's discount rate increased in a linear manner by the amount of 0.04875 percentage points.

Bauman relies heavily upon historical data, and believes this action is justified by absence at present of any indicators which point to large changes ahead. He reminds the investor, however, to be on guard constantly to recognize signs of changes.

Application of Technique #2 to General Motors Common Stock

How is the present value actually determined by Bauman's method? The same figures for General Motors are applied with the following assumptions:

1. According to Bauman, a discount rate of 6% is applied to the dividend in the first year for a company with a high quality rating. Consequently, this rate is used for General Motors in the first year. Because the discount rates applicable to dividend income in succeeding future years are higher, the average discount rate over the first ten-year period applicable to dividend income is actually 6.2%.

2. The transitional period should be 10 years, since dividends grow at 4% per year beyond the 10 years.

3. Bauman's tables assume that the annual growth rates during the transitional period gradually decrease to 4%. Since we assume that the average annual growth rate over the ten years is 5.3%, a weighted average of approximately 5.3% is obtained if an initial growth rate of 6% is selected.

4. The residual growth rate used will be 4% (as Bauman recommends).

From Variable Rate Table B-6 in Appendix B, the price-dividend ratio applicable for General Motors is found to be 29.9.

The present value of General Motors is then \$4.00 X 29.9 = \$119.60.

Again, it would appear that the stock is underpriced at 94 3/8. Based on

Bauman's Table B-6, shown in Appendix B, if the assumed initial dividend growth rate of 6% declines to 4% over a ten-year period, and if an initial discount rate of 7% is used, General Motors would provide an approximate average yield from dividends of 7.24% at the price of 94 3/8 (i.e., 23.8 X $4.00 = $95.20).

TECHNIQUE #3 – R. FERGUSON[8]

Robert Ferguson presents a method of determining justifiable price/earnings ratios for growth stocks as compared with some standard. His objectives are to answer the following questions:

(a) How many years of the present high growth rate are assumed by today's market price before the growth rate of the company will drop to the "standard" rate?

(b) What price/earnings ratio is justified given a certain rate of growth which is higher than the standard rate for a certain number of years?

The standard can be of any sort, depending upon the kind of company analyzed. The Dow-Jones Industrial Average and Standard and Poor's serve as good examples.

Ferguson takes the market price as a base and then tries to determine what estimates of the basic factors (growth rate and growth duration) the market makes. He then leaves the investor to decide whether these estimates are too low or too high in his judgment. Ferguson develops a nomograph which eliminates the need for complicated calculation on the part of the investor (see Appendix C). The nomograph is a graphical solution to the equation:

$$\frac{P_a}{P^1{}_a} = \frac{(1+R_a)^n}{(1+R_b)^n}$$

where:

P_a = Some standard price/earnings ratio
$P^1{}_a$ = Growth stock price/earnings ratio
R_a = Standard growth rate assumed
R_b = Rate of growth assumed for growth stock

[8]Robert Ferguson, "A Nomograph for Valuing Growth Stocks," *Financial Analysts Journal* (May-June 1961), pp. 29–34. A similar technique was presented by W. Edward Bell in "The Price Future Earnings Ratio–A Practical Guide to Stock Valuation," *Analysts Journal* (August 1958), pp. 25–28. The author contends that his Nomograph is not intended as a "theory of value," but simply as a means of determining current price/earnings ratios which are consistent with assumptions about earnings growth and going market. *P/E* ratios. The author also rejects my view that an adjustment for dividends would represent double counting. My colleague, Professor Michael Keenan, to whom I am indebted for his careful review of this and other points, has pointed out to me that this does not exactly involve double counting, but rather a *very important difference* as to what the price of a share does and does not incorporate. He says, "It seems much more likely to me that the current market price does incorporate some notion of dividend payments but my empirical evidence is not very strong here."

Although it appears that Ferguson ignores the discount rate, closer examination reveals that the use of a standard growth rate in the denominator of his equation (as in Malkiel referred to above), implies that investors will apply uniform discount rates to all common stock earnings, and that differences in price/earnings ratios arise *only* from differences in assumed growth rates and duration.

A further assumption is made implicitly that the quoted growth rates stay on the same level until period T and then drop off suddenly to a rate equivalent to the "standard rate." An analysis based on the foregoing assumption differs, of course, very strongly from Bauman's Variable Rate Method, which assumes evenly declining growth rates and increasing discount rates for incomes with longer futurity. Molodovsky's most recent techniques also assume evenly declining growth rates, as will be observed elsewhere in this Journal.

In the last paragraph of his article describing the nomograph, Ferguson states:

> We have not considered the fact that many stocks pay dividends which are an important source of profit, in addition to price appreciation. This is especially true in situations where the growth rate is of the same order of magnitude as the dividend yield. In these instances, the neglect of dividends may well result in an incorrect calculation. An approximate adjustment for dividend income, useful in many instances, would be to add the yield to the per share earnings growth rate and use the resultant figure in place of the growth rate.

This implicitly assumes that the current market price of stocks completely disregards dividend payments. In my view this procedure would represent double counting and overstate justifiable price/earnings ratios for growth stocks, since dividend payout, in my opinion, is already implicitly reflected in the standard price/earnings ratio used in his equation. (See note 8.)

Application of Technique #3 to General Motors Common Stock

1. To determine length of "transitional" period we use 4% as the standard DJIA growth rate, and assume a standard P/E ratio of 15. For General Motors the P/E is 17, and the growth rate is, of course, 5.3%.

The following instructions are used in the application of the nomograph in Appendix C:

(a) Locate the columns marked "standard growth rates." Choose the one with a growth rate equal to that of the standard, in this case, the $R = 4\%$ column (by interpolation).

(b) Go up this column until you come to the rate of growth of the company being analyzed, in this case, 5.3% (by interpolation). Then, move horizontally to the right until you reach the vertical "*R* line." Mark this spot.

(c) Locate the columns marked "standard price/earnings ratios." Choose the one with the price/earnings ratio equal to that of the standard, in this case, the $P/E = 15$ column.

(d) Go down this column until you come to the price/earnings ratio of the company being analyzed, in this case, 17. Then, move horizontally to the left until you reach the vertical "*P/E* line." Mark this spot, too.

(e) Connect these two marks with a straight line and read the number where the line intersects the diagonal "time line," in this case, 9. This is the length of time, in years, discounted by General Motors' price/earnings ratio (17).

General Motors present market price therefore assumes the current 5.3% growth rate to continue for at least nine years, before it will drop to the 4% average rate as evidenced by the DJIA.

2. To determine the maximum price/earnings ratio which should be paid for the 5.3% growth rate of General Motors as compared with the DJIA rate of 4% if maintained for 10 years:

(a) Locate the number 10 on the "time line." Mark this spot.

(b) Locate the columns marked "standard growth rates." Choose the one with a growth rate equal to that of the standard, in this case *R* = 4% column (by interpolation).

(c) Go up this column until you come to the rate of growth of General Motors, in this case 5.3% (by interpolation). Then, move horizontally to the right until you reach the vertical "*R* line." Mark this spot, too.

(d) Connect these two marks with a straight line and extend the line until it intersects the "*P/E* line." Note the point of intersection.

(e) Locate the columns marked "standard price/earnings ratios." Choose the one with a price/earnings ratio of *P/E* = 15.

(f) Move horizontally to the right from the point noted in (d) until you come to the standard price/earnings ratio column chosen in (e). Read off the price/earnings ratio, in this case 18.5. This is the maximum price/earnings ratio that should be paid for General Motors.

Since the earnings base assumed is $5.56, the maximum price one should pay for General Motors currently (under the growth assumptions stated above) is 18.5 X $5.56 = $102.86.

It can be noted that the alternative selection of a standard price/earnings multiplier of 20 would have resulted in a price/earnings ratio for General Motors of approximately 23 and a resultant value of approximately $128.

TECHNIQUE #4 – MOLODOVSKY[9]

Nicholas Molodovsky has written several articles on the subject of growth stock valuation. He has made a comprehensive historical analysis of the Standard & Poor's and Cowles Commission indexes, and used them as the standard with which to compare all stocks. From the figures of the above mentioned stock indexes (which were carefully adjusted to make them as representative as

[9]Nicholas Molodovsky, "Valuations of Common Stocks," *Analysts Journal* (February 1959), "Stock Values and Stock Prices–Part I (May-June 1960), and "Dow-Jones Industrials–A Reappraisal" (March-April 1961).

possible for the 1871-1959 period studies) the author developed basic historical parameters. The historical growth rate of dividends and earnings has been about 2.5%. The average yield for the period as evidenced by the "Stock Averages" has been about 5%. These two figures combine to show a total effective yield per year of 7.5%, which Molodovsky consequently used as the discount rate in the present value formula in studies contributed to the *Financial Analysts Journal* through 1960. Including later years through 1963, the above parameters respectively changed to about 2.7%; 4.9% and 7.8%.

Molodovsky always took great pains to emphasize that any standardized selections of future periods, such as ten years, for instance, could serve illustrative purposes only. He stressed that in actual analytical practice, projections of future earnings trends of different stocks would have to be made for whatever varying periods might be specifically indicated. Such characteristics of appropriate valuation parameters were already noted, in no uncertain terms, in his 1959 and 1960 studies. He developed his thinking a bit further in his later papers. His article, "The Many Aspects of Yields," which appeared in the March-April 1962 issue of this Journal contained the following statement:

> It is clear that the nature of the industry to which a given company belongs—as well as that corporation's particular characteristics—should in reality determine both the length of the period for which earnings are projected into the future and also the delicate process of the "splicing" with an overall historical rate. Depending on each individual case, such a transition may well take the form of mathematical curves with very different gradations of diminshing rates of growth.

Such gradual transitions can be easily performed by a computer, which could also carry out the valuation formula's requirement of an infinite time horizon. Acording to Molodovsky, this latter condition can be easily met by combining the compound interest formula used for computing a bond's yield to maturity with the expression of a geometric progression for an infinite number of terms which constitutes a mathematical description of a common stock's natural *habitat*. The requisite formulae may be found in any high school textbook of algebra.

It so happens that this issue of the *Financial Analysts Journal* carries an article by Molodovsky and two of his associates discussing the valuations of the DJIA and of its thirty component stocks. Since General Motors is one of the prominent members of this club, I shall let Molodovsky and his associates speak for themselves regarding the valuation of GM.

TECHNIQUE #5—GRAHAM, DODD, COTTLE, AND TATHAM[10]

Messrs. Graham and Dodd, in the most recent edition of their text also get

[10]B. Graham, D. L. Dodd, and S. Cottle, *Security Analysis* (New York: McGraw-Hill Book Co., 1962), Chapter 39.

on the "Present-Value-Band-Wagon" which by now seems to be *"the"* basic principle in all major stock valuation models.

The authors are probably the most conservative of all the writers mentioned in this study so far, because of the limitations placed on growth projections. The maximum growth period which they consider in any of their techniques is ten years. In one method they even bring the limit down to seven years.

The authors present two methods of their own described below and in their text (pp. 536-538). Following Molodovsky, they assume a single discount rate of 7.5% for all companies no matter whether high, medium, or low quality, an assumption criticized by Bauman. The authors also follow Molodovsky in assuming a normal price/earnings ratio. The authors assume a normal pay-out ratio of 60%. They mention, however, that this ratio is fairly high for good growth companies. The higher the growth rate the smaller the pay-out ratio usually becomes. For this reason, the authors do not follow the other writers in capitalizing dividends. Dividends become almost meaningless for good growth stocks, and they consider earnings as much more representative of such a firm's current and future income potential.

Method A

This approach, referred to as their "preferred method," projects earnings growth for only the next seven years. A multiplier is applied to the average of the next seven years' earnings, that is to the fourth year's earnings. The multiplier, of course, depends on the expected rate of growth for the next seven years, but will lie within the range of 13 to 20 because of the limits on the growth rate from 3½% to 20% set by the authors.

The following table, illustrated in their text *Security Analysis,* was developed on the basis of the above parameters:

TABLE 1

Expected Rate of Growth (Four Years)	Multiplier of Average (4th Year Earnings)	Multiplier of Current Earnings
3.5%	13X	15X
5.0	14X	17X
7.2	15X	20X
10.0	16X	23½X
12.0	17X	27X
14.3	18X	31X
17.0	19X	35½X
20.0	20X	41½X

Method B

Graham and Dodd advance two other formulas which yield similar results.

(B-1) Value=8.6T plus 2.1, where T is the tenth-year compound amount of \$1.00 of present earnings growing at any assumed rate. The reader may be reminded that we still work under the assumption of .60 pay-out and 7.5% discount rate. The growth period in this method is assumed to be 10 years.

A 2.5% growth rate will yield T = \$1.28 and here the multiplier is

$$(8.6 \times 1.28) + 2.1 = 13.1$$

and a 10% growth rate will show a multiplier of 24.4 times.

$$(8.6 \times 2.59) + 2.1 = 24.4$$

(B-2) Value=current "normal" earnings X (8.5 + 2G), where G is the average annual growth expected for the next 7 to 10 years. "Normal" earnings are those as they would appear on a smoothed-out earnings curve or "trend line." The authors have arrived at this formula from the finding that a multiplier of 8.5 is appropriate for a company with zero expected growth, and a 2½% growth rate calls for a multiplier of 13.5

A 10% growth rate will show a multiplier of 8.5 + (2 X 10) = 28.5 as compared with 24.4 in the first formula.

As mentioned before, Graham and Dodd's methods for valuing growth issues bear evidence of extreme conservatism in recommending the use of short periods of anticipated growth and relatively low residual growth rates and multipliers. Other writers express conservatism in different ways. Clendenin and Bauman assign a higher discount rate to years in the distant future, rather than limit estimates to 10 years. Graham and Dodd, on the other hand, disregard any higher than "average" growth rate later than 10 years hence.

As with other analysts cited, Graham and Dodd do not advise the reader on how to select the proper growth rate. Whereas past trends definitely are an important factor to consider, they should not be the sole factor. Simple projection of past trends can also lead to results far too optimistic.

Application of Technique #5 to General Motors Common Stock

Method A

A 5.3% growth rate calls for a multiplier of about 14.2 to be applied to the fourth year's earnings, or a multiplier of about 17.4 applied to current earnings (according to Table 1).

17.4 x \$5.56 = \$96.74 is the intrinsic value

Method B

(B-1) 8.6T + 2.1
8.6 (1.68) + 2.1 = 14.45 + 2.1 = 16.55
Value = 16.55 x \$5.56 = \$92.02 Value

(B-2) Current earnings x (8.5 + 2G)
(I assume that \$5.56 is the current normal earnings figure)

$\$5.56 \times (8.5 + 10.6)$
$\$5.56 \times 19.1 = \$106.20$ Value

TECHNIQUE #6–JEREMY C. JENKS[11]

Jeremy C. Jenks, associated with C. J. Lawrence and Sons, a New York Stock Exchange member firm, criticizes existing methods of comparative valuation because they are either based on price/earnings ratios or on price/dividend ratios. He argues that "no *one* approach will give satisfactory results in a wide variety of common stocks . . . because there are *two* 'investment' reasons for owning common stocks . . . dividend income and hope of capital appreciation if the company grows." Thus there really is no sharp dividing line between an "income stock" and a "growth stock."

In this technique, two different multipliers are computed (as in Walter), one to be applied to the dividend from one set of factors, and another multiplier from another set of factors, to be applied to the earnings retained in the business. The two resultant values are added together in order to obtain "the value" of the stock.

The dividend multiplier is based on the assumption that the value of a dividend is a function of:

(1) The yield on high grade, money rate, taxable bonds (Lawrence uses governments)
(2) The quality of the dividend

For quality classifications, the author uses rating scales from A to F (similar to ratings of bonds) applied as follows:

"The best dividend is worth 1% current return basis less than long-term Government bond yields. Each graduation in quality is marked down an additional ½%." (Page 9 of booklet)

A dividend's quality is determined by the following five factors:

(1) Debt + Pref. as % of Capital
(2) Debt + Pref. as % of Working Capital
(3) Pay-out (in %)
(4) Drop in the Net Earnings in 1958 from the 1956-57 peak
(5) Total Plow-back as % of Equity

For the ratings which are assigned by these five factors the author has developed tables (see page 5 of C. J. Lawrence booklet).

The price/earnings multiples used at various levels of yields for long Governments are as follows:

[11] C. J. Lawrence, "Comparative Valuation of Common Stocks" (a booklet published by Cyrus J. Lawrence & Sons, New York, 1959).

Yield Long Governments

Rating	3%	3½%	4%	4½%	5%	5½%
A	27.5	25	22.2	20	18.2	16.7
B	25	22.2	20	18.2	16.7	15.4
C	22.2	20	18.2	16.7	15.4	14.3
D	20	18.2	16.7	15.4	14.3	13.3
E	18.2	16.7	15.4	14.3	13.3	12.5
F	16.7	15.4	14.3	13.3	12.5	11.8

He used an average of several of the long Government issues. The following bonds seemed representative to him at the time of his writing:

	Yield		
	12/10/58	10/23/59	1/7/60
3¼% May 1985	3.73	3.92	4.39
3½% February 1990	3.83	4.05	4.43
3% February 1995	3.59	3.81	4.11

The Retained Earnings Multiple is based on the growth prospects of the business. Lawrence employs three measurements:

(1) The historic rate of growth in earnings. Any large fluctuations are corrected by sales trends.

(2) The 3-year average plowback as a % of equity is designed to show the company's ability to finance growth internally.

(3) The 3-year average expansion factor is intended to measure the company's efforts to grow.

By averaging these three factors the authors hope to get some indication of the growth potential of a company.

The following table of multipliers is derived which corresponds to certain growth rates:

Growth Factor–Price–Retained Earnings Multiples

0	8.9X	8%	14.0X	16%	22.1X
1%	9.5X	9%	14.8X	17%	23.4X
2%	10.0X	10%	15.7X	18%	24.8X
3%	10.5X	11%	16.7X	19%	26.2X
4%	11.1X	12%	17.6X	20%	27.8X
5%	11.7X	13%	18.6X	25%	37.0X
6%	12.4X	14%	19.6X	30%	48.0X
7%	13.2X	15%	20.9X	35%	90.0X

Jenks develops retained earnings multiples by use of compound interest tables but making a 2% negative adjustment.

The Jenks (Lawrence) method employs a final adjustment factor to each valuation, based largely upon the size and relative importance of the company in its industry. In the illustration below, it can be seen that the adjustment factor for General Motors was 130%.

Application of Technique #6 to General Motors Common Stock

An application of the Jenks valuation approach to the stock of General Motors follows: The following valuation can be compared with a 1961 valuation of General Motors by Cyrus J. Lawrence & Sons, which, using a dividend multiplier of 18.1 and an earnings multiplier of 8.6, and applying these to estimated annual earnings of $3.11 for 1961 and $4.00 for 1962 resulted in estimated valuations of $50.50 and $58.10 before adjustment and $65.70 and $75.50 after adjustment.[12]

		Government Yield Basis	
Dividend Rating	%	Rating	4% Multiple
Debt is Pfd. % Cap. (1963 figure)	7.6	B	20
Debt is Pfd. S.C. (1963 figure)	14.6	B	20
Current Payout–(1963)	72.2	E	15.4
Drop in Net '61–'62 to '63	0	A	22.2
Average Plowback % Equity	6.0	D	16.7
Average			18.9

Growth Rating	%	Multiple
Growth in Earnings	5.3	11.9
Average Plowback % Equity	7.0	13.2
Average Expansion Factor	7.9	13.9
Average		13.0
Consistency Factor		70
Adjusted Multiple		9.1

No. of Shares (12/31/63)–Total 286,653,007 Shares

Earnings	Actual 1963	Estimated 1964
Gross Plant	7,967 mil.	7,967 mil.
Sales to Gross Plant	2.08	2.26
Sales	16,495 mil.	18,000 mil.
Net Income	1,592 mil.	2,140 mil.
Pfd. Div.	13 mil.	13 mil.
Net for Common	1,578 mil.	2,127 mil.
Net per Share	$5.56	$6.00
Div. per Share	$4.00	$4.80
Retained per Share	$1.56	$1.50
Div. Cap. at 18.9	$75.60	$85.05
Retained Cap. at 9.1	14.2	13.65
Estimated Values	89.8	98.70
Adjusted Est. Values*	116.7	129.30

* Net income over 200 million. The estimated values are multiplied by 130%.

[12] C. J. Lawrence and Sons, *General Motors Corporation in the World Automobile Market* (New York, May 1962).

It can be seen that the application of the Jenks' technique results in an adjusted value for General Motors of $129.30.

TECHNIQUE #7–WILLIAM KURTZ

William Kurtz, of Hemphill Noyes and Co., has developed a somewhat different adaptation of the present value method described in a company memorandum entitled "Valuation Standards for Investments," which involves three steps:

(1) A price/earnings multiple of 14 as a normal ratio for a non-growth stock.

(2) A growth rate adjustment (five-year compound interest factor at the assumed growth rate) which is multiplied by the standard (14).

(3) An investment quality rating which rates issues as Premium quality (1.33), Standard (1.00), and Discount (.67) and permits intermediate quality rating multipliers.

Application of Technique #7 to General Motors Common Stock

Based on these elements, the value of General Motors common, assuming a 5.3% growth factor (for five years as the maximum growth period allowed) might be estimated as follows:

> 14.0 × 1.28 (compound amount of $1 for 5 years at 5.3%) × 1.10 (quality adjustment factor for General Motors) = $109.58.

This technique has the simplifying advantage of eliminating the selection of a growth period, assuming a standard maximum of 5 years. Its disadvantage, of course, lies in this very assumption, and in the subjective determination of a quality rating. Others may take issue with the assumed normal price/earnings ratio of 14 for a non-growth issue.

SUMMARY

Virtually all the techniques examined have been directed toward the estimation of "intrinsic" value, although some of the methods were more directly aimed toward the determination of price/earnings or price/dividend ratios. Most of the methods require that the analyst make a separate and in most cases a subjective estimate of future growth rates. Jenks' technique is somewhat distinctive in that he relies entirely upon historical data and short run estimates of current earnings.

A wide range of growth assumptions are illustrated in the several techniques discussed, in many cases without providing any guidance for the analyst as to the method of selecting a growth rate to be applied to a particular issue. So-called residual or normal growth rates range from 2.5% to 4% and residual multipliers vary from 13. to 17.1. These differences are frequently the principal factors accounting for the relatively wide range of valuations established by using the various methods shown in Table A, which provides a review of the assumptions and valuation results.

The highest valuations resulted from the methods of Bauman, Jenks and Kurtz, whereas the Value Line approach and the Graham and Dodd methods resulted in the lowest estimated values. Bauman's high figure is a result of three factors, a long "transitional" period, a not very high (the second lowest) discount rate, and a high (the highest of all methods) residual growth rate. A 10-year transitional period with an initial growth rate of 6% was used in order to have a 5.3% average growth rate as in the other methods. A relatively high normal, non-growth price/earnings ratio and the subjective quality rating multiplier account for Kurtz' high estimate.

Two of the techniques (Clendenin and Bauman) are based upon the use of a multiplier applied to future dividends, three methods are based on earnings, while the third, Jenks', uses a combination of earnings and dividends. The techniques examined reveal an implied pay-out ratio in the dividend multipliers similar to that for General Motors (70%). It is obvious that the differences in the resultant valuations would have been greater if the pay-out ratio on General Motors were subsequently different. The important question appears to be, not whether a multiplier should be applied to earnings or dividends, but whether it can anticipate the relative weight which will be given to dividends and earnings in the market.

It should be pointed out that the discount rates shown in Table A are not strictly comparable, since in some cases (Molodovsky, Graham and Dodd), they apply to both dividend income and price appreciation, while in others (Clendenin and Bauman), they apply only to dividend income. In the case of the Ferguson and Kurtz models, the multipliers are applied to total earnings and represent the reciprocals of discount rates.

The Ferguson technique makes no explicit assumptions about growth rate, growth duration, or discount rates. Ferguson merely examines the growth rate and duration inherent in the current market price and compares them with the components contained in a standard such as the DJIA. By his method, relative to the standard, General Motors' growth potential warrants a maximum price of $102.86, slightly more than $8 over the current market price. Much depends, in his method, upon the so called standard growth rate assumed.

Jenks' method also does not lend itself to a simple check on the basic assumptions as the majority of approaches do, since it is largely based on historical data. Since his technique is not based upon long-term projections, the method does not employ present value techniques. It can be noted that the so-called adjustment factor used in the Lawrence technique adds $25 to $30 to the resultant share value. This factor adds an important element of subjectivity to Jenks' technique. Mr. Jenks reports that new simplified valuation methods have been developed by his firm using Standard and Poor's Compustat tapes.

CONCLUSIONS

It is apparent that widely differing values can be assigned to growth stocks by varying the assumptions concerning future growth rates and duration of growth and by applying different discount rates to future dividend returns. None of the valuation techniques discussed provide any accurate method for estimating future growth rates or duration.

What then is the operational usefulness of these techniques? It can be argued that the application of these valuation methods will provide rough guidelines to a "range of values" for growth stocks under consistent assumptions. Assuming that an analyst is prepared to establish his own discount rates and time horizon for estimating future growth, the range of indicated values will be relatively narrow, as can be noted in Table 2. The values for General Motors assuming a ten-year growth period at 5.3% per annum and a 7.5% discount rate

TABLE 2

Comparison of Assumptions and Valuations for Seven Growth Stock Valuation Techniques

Technique	Growth Rate	Growth Duration	Discount Rate	Residual Growth Rate	Value
1. Clendenin	5.3%	10 years	4%, 5%, 6%, 7%	None	$101.60
2. Bauman	5.3%	10 years (trans. period)	6.2%	4%	$119.60
3. Ferguson	5.3%		Current Market P/E multiplier		$102.86 (maximum)
4. Molodovsky	See text of Molodovsky's article in this issue.				
5. Graham & Dodd Method A	5.3%	7 years	7.5%	3.5%	$ 96.74
Method B-1 (8.6*T*+2.1)	5.3%	10 years	7.5%	2.5%	$ 92.02
Method B-2 (8.5+2*G*)	5.3%	10 years	7.5%	2.5%	$106.20
6. Lawrence (Jenks)	5.3%		Variable Rates for Dividends and Retained Earnings		$129.30
7. Kurtz	5.3%	5 years	Basic Market Multiplier of 14 X Earnings		$109.58

are in a very close range. The differences noted are due to the varying assumed residual growth rates, which will influence the multipliers applied to earnings at the conclusion of the growth period. This element of prediction involves a high degree of uncertainty, since it not only requires judgment with respect to long-term growth, but also implies that the analyst can forecast price/earning ratios which will prevail in the distant future. Graham and Dodd maintain that the use of a short-growth period and a long-term average multiplier for residual earnings adds a "safety factor" to security analysis, which by its very nature involves a high degree of uncertainty.

Viewing the difficulty of forecasting long-term future corporate earnings, it would appear that the weight of evidence should favor the use of growth periods of 10 years or less. This has the further advantage that it should make less uncertain and difficult any forecast of residual growth rates and multipliers, since it brings them closer. The assumption of a gradual rather than an abrupt decline in growth rates, as Bauman and Molodovsky recommend, also seems warranted. It must be recognized, however, that adherence to these relatively conservative assumptions leaves the more distant future to be eyed with varying degrees of optimism by professional and amateur crystal gazers, and thus leaves the final judgment as to over- or under-valuation to the market place.

The recent availability of Standard and Poor's Compustat tapes has opened up new horizons for multiple regression analysis of stock market data. Economists at the Bank of New York and Trust Company have assumed a leading role in cross-section multiple regression analysis of stock prices, earnings and dividends based on the Compustat tapes. Whitbeck and Kisor describe this analytical technique in the *Financial Analysts Journal* for May-June 1963.[13] Regressing current average market price/earnings ratios on estimated growth rates, dividend pay-out (supplemented by indexes of stability and marketability), they derive an average multiple regression equation for 135 representative issues. Using the coefficients from this equation, they derive theoretical price/earnings ratios for individual issues, based upon their current estimates of growth, dividend pay-out, etc. By comparing these with actual prevailing price/earnings ratios (assuming "normalized" earnings), they derive indexes of relative under- or over-pricing in the market for individual stocks.

The most significant potential for stock valuation techniques embodied in this cross-sectional multiple regression analysis of stock prices (and price/earnings ratios) lies in the comparison of changes over time in the relative weights accorded in the market to expected growth in earnings and dividend pay-out. It is of further consequence, of course, to examine the relationship between price/earnings ratios, estimated growth rates and dividend pay-out by individual

[13]Volkert S. Whitbeck and Manown Kisor, Jr., "A New Tool in Investment Decision Making," *Financial Analysts Journal*, Vol. 19, No. 3 (May-June 1963), pp. 55–62. The authors illustrate the derivation of a theoretical price/earnings ratio and an estimated value for General Motors Common Stock ($51), based upon estimated market parameters as of June 8, 1962, page 58.

industries or groups of industries to shed further light upon the diversity of investor expectations over time and among different stock groups. This should provide a test of the validity of the valuation technique described above. Such analysis may pave the way to greater insight into the behavioristic characteristics of security investors over time and shed more light on the never-ending academic discussions concerning the relative weight attached by investors to dividends versus earnings.

APPENDIX A

TABLE 1

Approximate Present Values of All Future Dividends on a stock now paying $1.00 per annum, if the dividend is expected to increase at the indicated compound rate for the indicated period of years and then remain stable until 100 years from today, and if the payments of the first decade are discounted at 4%, those of the second at 5%, those of the third at 6%, and those of the remaining 70 years at 7%.

Growth Period	Annual Growth Rates 5%	4%	3%	1%	0%
None	$17.01	$17.01	$17.01	$17.01	$17.01
10 years	24.85	23.04	21.37	18.37	17.01
20 years	31.21	27.51	24.27	19.12	17.01
30 years	35.97	30.55	26.08	19.51	17.01
40 years	39.65	32.67	27.22	19.69	17.01
50 years	42.63	34.23	27.99	19.80	17.01

TABLE 2

Approximate Present Values of the Future Dividends on a stock now paying $1.00 per annum, if the dividends are expected to grow at the indicated rates for 20 years and then remain stable for the next 80 years, and if the dividends of the first decade are discounted at 4%, those of the second at 5%, those of the third at 6%, and those of the remaining 70 years at 7%.

Growth Rate per year	Present Values First Decade	Second Decade	Third Decade	Next 70 Years	Total
6%	$10.85	$11.36	$ 7.36	$ 5.96	$35.53
5%	10.35	9.84	6.09	4.93	31.21
4%	9.87	8.53	5.03	4.08	27.51
3%	9.40	7.37	4.14	3.36	24.27
2%	8.96	6.39	3.41	2.76	21.52
1%	8.53	5.52	2.80	2.27	19.12
0%	8.11	4.74	2.30	1.86	17.01

Note: These tables and similar appendix tables are calculated on the assumption that each year's dividend is received at the year end, and that it contains the full year's growth element. The short-cut calculation methods which were used may underestimate some of the values by as much as 1½ per cent. Slide rule computations were used.

APPENDIX B

Variable Rate Table B-6

10-Year Transitional Period Price-Dividend Ratios

Initial Growth Rates (Per Cent)	Initial Discount Rates 5%	6%	6½%	7%	8%	9%	10%	12%
Depressed								
0	29.6	22.4	20.0	18.1	15.1	13.0	11.4	9.1
1	31.1	23.6	21.0	18.9	15.8	13.5	11.9	9.5
2	32.6	24.7	22.0	19.8	16.5	14.2	12.4	9.9
3	34.3	25.9	23.1	20.8	17.3	14.8	12.9	10.3
Constant								
4	36.0	27.2	24.2	21.7	18.1	15.5	13.5	10.8
High								
5	37.8	28.5	25.3	22.8	18.9	16.2	14.1	11.2
6	39.7	29.9	26.5	23.8	19.8	16.9	14.7	11.7
8	43.6	32.8	29.1	26.1	21.6	18.4	16.0	12.7
10	48.0	36.0	31.9	28.6	23.6	20.1	17.4	13.7
12	52.7	39.4	34.9	31.3	25.8	21.9	19.0	14.9
14	57.9	43.2	38.2	34.2	28.2	23.8	20.6	16.1
16	63.4	47.3	41.8	37.4	30.7	26.0	22.4	17.5
18	69.5	51.7	45.7	40.8	33.5	28.2	24.3	18.9
20	76.1	56.5	49.9	44.5	36.5	30.7	26.4	20.5
25	95.1	70.3	61.9	55.2	45.0	37.8	32.4	24.9
30	118.2	87.1	76.6	68.1	55.4	46.3	39.6	30.3
35	146.1	107.4	94.3	83.7	67.8	56.6	48.2	36.6
40	179.9	131.8	115.5	102.4	82.8	68.8	58.5	44.2
50	268.7	196.0	171.3	151.6	121.9	100.9	85.3	63.8
60	394.8	286.7	250.2	220.8	176.9	145.8	122.7	91.1
70	570.7	413.2	359.8	317.1	253.1	207.9	174.4	128.6

APPENDIX C

CHART 2
Growth Stock Nomograph

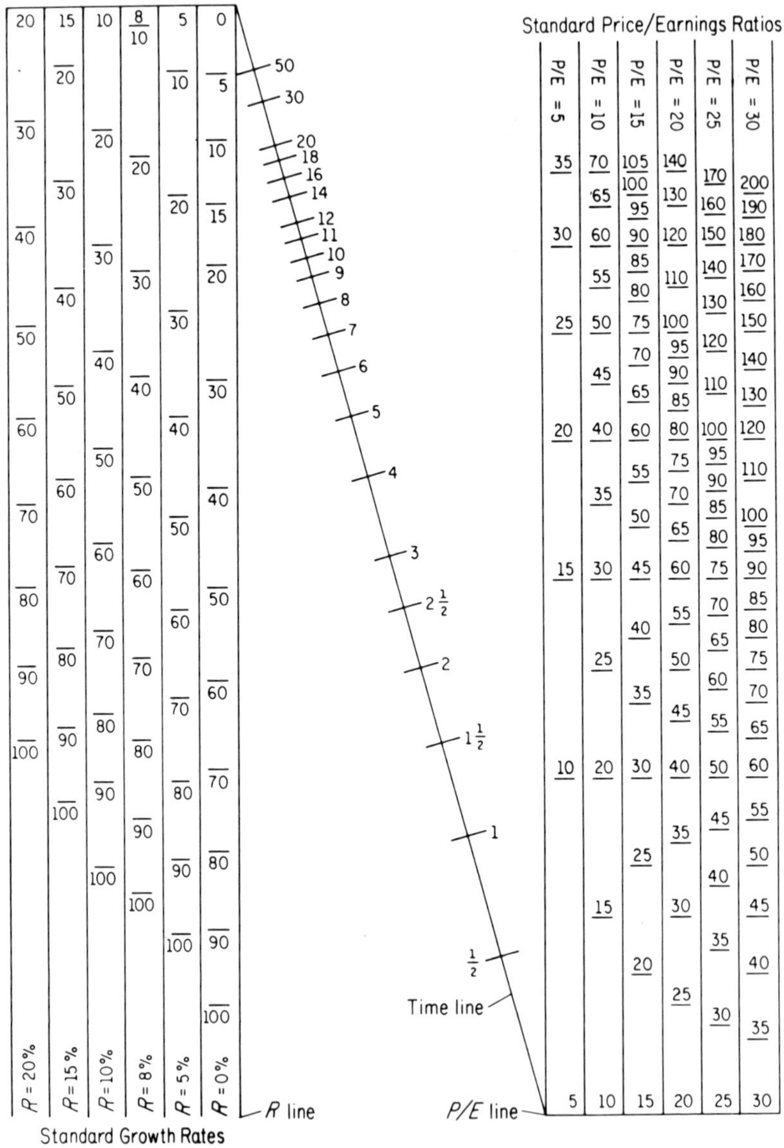

11

Some Factors Affecting Stock Price Variability*

A. James Heins
Stephen L. Allison

One would have thought that John Clendenin's 1951 article would have laid to rest the notion that there is a relationship between the level of stock prices and the relative amount of variability in stock prices.[1] Although he does not employ a statistical analysis, and uses only two independent variables, Clendenin's findings strongly indicate that low-price stocks do not fluctuate more widely than high-price stocks, other factors being constant.

Nonetheless, some writers in the area cling to the notion that low-price stocks have greater variability. In the third edition (1951) of the monumental *Security Analysis*,[2] the authors state clearly that low-price stocks have a probability of advancing or declining more than higher-priced stocks, and cite a 1936 study by Louis Fritzemeier[3] as authority for this claim. This statement is reproduced exactly in the fourth edition (1962),[4] and the Fritzemeier study is again cited. No mention is made of the Clendenin study and its findings to the contrary. Other post-1951 writers have similarly referred to the great variability of low-price stocks without accounting for the findings in the Clendenin article.[5]

The Fritzemeier study has two faults that cast doubt upon its findings: (1) while selected stocks were limited to lower grades, no attempt was made to control the quality variable within the grades allowed; and (2) the findings were

*From *The Journal of Business*, Vol. 39, No. 1, Part 1 (January 1966), pp. 19–23. Reprinted by permission of The University of Chicago Press.

[1] John C. Clendenin, "Quality versus Price as Factors Influencing Common Stock Price Fluctuations," *Journal of Finance* (December 1951).

[2] Benjamin Graham and David L. Dodd, *Security Analysis* (3d ed.; New York: McGraw-Hill Book Co., 1951), p. 563.

[3] Louis H. Fritzemeier, "Relative Price Fluctuations of Industrial Stocks in Different Price Groups," *Journal of Business* (April 1936).

[4] Benjamin Graham, et al., *Security Analysis*, 4th ed. (1962), p. 649. In particular, the authors say: "It is a commonplace of the securities market that an issue will rise more steadily from 10 to 40 than from 100 to 400." As with many *commonplaces* of the securities market, this statement is inaccurate, or at least inadequate.

[5] E. F. Renshaw, "A Note on Behavior in the Stock Market," *Financial Analysts Journal* (August 1958); Henry Allan Latane, "Price Changes in Equity Securities," *Journal of Finance* (September 1954); and others.

based upon variability of groups of low-price and high-price stocks rather than individual stocks.

The Clendenin study avoided both of these pitfalls by introducing a risk variable, measured by investment grade, and by examining frequency distributions of individual stock price movements. The only shortcomings are that more variables were not incorporated in the analysis and that a more formal analysis was not used. These shortcomings can be remedied today because of advances in computer technology.

THE MODEL

In an orderly market one would not expect that the price of a stock, which is determined by the market valuation of stockholders equity in corporate assets divided by the number of shares of stock outstanding, would have any effect on the variability in that price. The authors of *Security Analysis* refer to an "arithmetic advantage" of low-price stocks, but that is merely an expression of the fact that if one buys one share of a \$4.00 stock he can lose less than if he buys one share of a \$40 stock, a fact which is quite obvious–but one which avoids the also obvious fact that if one buys ten shares of a \$4.00 stock he can lose as much as if he buys one share of a \$40 stock. One would expect \$40 worth of equity in a corporation to have a likelihood of becoming worth \$80 or \$20 that is independent of the number of shares into which that equity is divided. Only by appealing to some sort of irrational investor can one justify the notion that low-price stocks, *ceteris paribus,* will behave differently than high-price stocks. The problem is to determine whether stock investors are indeed this irrational.

Our general hypothesis thus can be stated as: the relative price variability of a common stock is not related to the average price of the stock, other factors held constant. In order to test the hypothesis, we have assumed a functional relationship between the relative variability in a stock price and the general level of that price and other control variables. We have further assumed a linear function and estimated the parameters by the technique of multiple regression. One of the crucial control variables, the investment grade of the stock, is highly correlated with the average price. It is this correlation that has probably led to the commonplace that low-price stocks are more volatile; the volatility is due to the low grade or high risk of the stock and not the low price. In order to avoid the problems of collinearity, the observations were restricted to stocks rated A and B by Standard and Poor's Corporation, and separate regressions were run for each of the two rating categories. A regression was not run on the C group because virtually all stocks in that rating group had low prices, and the narrow range of prices did not permit us to test for the effect desired.

Relative price variability was measured as the difference between the high and low price of the stocks for the year under study as a percentage of the average price for the year. The average price of the stocks was taken as the arithmetic average of the high and low price.

In addition to the investment grade of stocks, the following control variables were employed in the regression analysis:

1. Variability in per share earnings of the stocks was measured by the difference between the high and low annual earnings per share for the previous 4 years as a percentage of the average annual earnings for the 4-year period. A 4-year period was used because we felt it provided an adequate indication of the degree of earnings variability and yet was recent enough to provide a reasonable indication of future variability.

2. The price-earnings ratio of the stocks was measured by the average price divided by the latest annual earnings per share. We employed this variable to allow for possible price variability arising because the market price reflects an expected large increase in future earnings.

3. Activity or turnover in the stock was measured by the total shares traded during the year as a percentage of the number of shares of the stock outstanding during the year.

4. Principal exchange on which the stock was listed was measured by the dummy-variable technique. It was considered possible that the nature of the exchange itself might lead to more or less price variability.

THE REGRESSIONS

Most of the data was obtained from the *Security Owner's Stock Guide* by Standard and Poor's Corporation for the year 1959. The samples for the A and B rated groups contain forty-eight and sixty-two observations, respectively, and represent one-fourth of the stocks in each group which were listed on either the New York or American Stock Exchanges. Since the effect of average price on price variability was the essential factor being tested, stocks that incurred splits or substantial stock dividends during 1959 were rejected from the samples. Because only four observations in the A group were listed on the American Stock Exchange, control variable (4) was not used in the regression equation for the A rated stocks.

The following regression equations were then formed:

$$V_a = \mathrm{A} + b_p x_p + b_e x_e + b_r x_r + b_a x_a$$
$$V_b = A + b_p x_p + b_e x_e + b_r x_r + b_a x_a + b_c x_c$$

where

$$\left.\begin{array}{l} V_a = \text{relative price variability of A rated stocks} \\ V_b = \text{relative price variability of B rated stocks} \end{array}\right\} \frac{\text{High-Low}}{\text{Average Price}}$$

A = constant term

x_p = average price of the stock

x_e = earnings variability

x_r = price-earnings ratio of the stock

x_a = activity or turnover of the stock

x_c = principal exchange on which stock is listed (0 if New York; 1 if American).

The resulting parameters are presented in Tables 1 and 2. The *b* coefficients were accepted as significant if they were at least 1½ times their standard error, that is, if the absolute value of the *T*-ratio was 1.50 or greater. The matrices of the simple correlation coefficients between the variables, and the means and standard deviations are shown in Tables 3 and 4.

TABLE 1

Results of Multiple Regression: A Rated Stocks

Independent Variable	*b* Coefficients	*T*-Ratio
x_p	.0022	0.31
x_e	.0182	0.22
x_r	.4122	1.54
x_a	.5738	2.33

Constant term (A)	13.30
Coefficient of determination (R^2)	0.19
Coefficient of multiple correlation (R)	0.44
Unexplained variance	0.81
Sample size	48

TABLE 2

Results of Multiple Regression: B Rated Stocks

Independent Variable	*b* Coefficients	*T*-Ratio
x_p	.0056	0.29
x_e	.1077	2.21
x_r	−.1033	−0.61
x_a	.2315	2.37
x_c	2.6472	0.47

Constant term (A)	23.97
Coefficient of determination (R^2)	0.26
Coefficient of multiple correlation (R)	0.51
Unexplained variance ($1 - R^2$)	0.74
Sample size	62

As shown by the regression results for both A and B rated stocks, Clendenin's findings are substantiated; the variability of stock prices is not significantly related to the average price of stocks. In other words, low-price stocks exhibit no tendency to experience relatively wider price fluctuations than high-price stocks with similar characteristics.

Some of the other results are also of interest. Apparently, more active stocks experience greater price variability than less active stocks. Although this result confirms our expectations, a few colleagues indicated surprise when shown the results. Their belief was that the greater activity would tend to stabilize the price by offering support when large blocks of stock were sought for purchase or offered for sale. Our expectation was based upon the notion that the greater activity reflected relatively large purchases and sales and, hence, led to instability.

TABLE 3
Matrix of Simple Correlation Coefficients, Means (M), and Standard Deviations (SD) of Variables: A Rated Group

	V_a	x_p	x_e	x_r	x_a	M	SD
V_a	1.00	0.07	0.06	0.27	0.34	28.5	10.9
x_p	....	1.00	0.23	0.45	−0.30	59.0	26.8
x_e	....	....	1.00	−0.06	0.10	28.8	19.2
x_r	....	....	....	1.00	0.02	17.8	6.5
x_a	....	....	....	....	1.00	10.5	6.7

The indicated relationship between price variability and the price-earnings ratio offers room for speculation. The results show that A rated stocks with a higher price-earnings ratio tend to experience greater price variability than their lower-ratio counterparts. This was not altogether unexpected, since stocks priced on the basis of optimistic predictions as to future earnings may be subject to more severe price shocks if earnings do not increase in any short-run period. What was somewhat puzzling is that this effect does not show up in the B rated group. Upon reflection and not in anticipation, the answer to this conundrum probably lies in the relation of price-earnings ratios to earnings variability. Since earnings in A stocks are much more stable, the price-earnings ratio, as we measure it, indicates investors' estimates of future earnings trends; whereas in the more unstable B group, a high price-earnings ratio might indicate an "off year" in earnings and not expectations of a long-term upward trend in earnings. This is in part substantiated by the high positive correlation of the price-earnings ratio and earnings variability in the B group; there is little such correlation in the A group. If price-earnings ratios had been based on average earnings in the past few years, the results might have been more compatible.

Exactly the opposite effect shows up in the relationship between earnings variability and price variability; a significant relationship exists between these

TABLE 4

Matrix of Simple Correlation Coefficients, Means (M), and Standard Deviations (SD) of Variables: B Rated Group

	V_b	x_p	x_e	x_r	x_a	x_c	M	SD
V_b	1.00	0.02	0.43	0.16	0.44	0.05	43.2	19.2
x_p	....	1.00	−0.12	−0.03	0.12	−0.40	25.1	12.6
x_e	....	....	1.00	0.40	0.47	0.06	91.8	54.5
x_r	....	....	....	1.00	0.34	0.05	18.1	14.5
x_a	....	....	....	....	1.00	−0.02	39.8	26.5
x_c	....	....	....	....	....	1.00	0.3	0.4

variables in the B group, but not in the A group. In this case again, the problem may lie in the intercorrelation of earnings variability and the price-earnings ratio in the B group. About all one can say here is that somewhat more confidence can be shown in the findings for the A rated group with respect to the effect of earnings variability and the price-earnings ratio on stock price variability.

As expected, the results of the regression on B stocks show that the exchange listing the stocks has no significant effect on price variability.

CONCLUSIONS AND CAVEATS

Although the subsidiary results of the regressions are of interest in explaining stock price variability, the fundamental conclusion of this effort remains that stock price variability bears no relationship to the average price of stocks, if other factors are held properly constant. This is not a new finding, but it does formalize and reinforce the findings of the Clendenin study of 1951. Furthermore, it is hoped that future expositors of stock-pricing theory will either adopt the findings here and in the Clendenin study or else offer a measure of evidence which points to contrary relationships.

Despite the confidence with which we espouse our results, a major limitation in our analysis must be noted. The coefficients of multiple correlation are relatively low and the unexplained variances correspondingly high. In other words, a good deal remains to be done to explain why some stocks fluctuate more widely in price than do other stocks. It does seem, though, that the level of stock prices plays no part in this explanation.

12

The Influence of Growth Duration on Share Prices*

Charles C. Holt†

INTRODUCTION

The spectacular investment performance of "growth stocks" in recent years has focused attention on the problem of evaluating the securities of fast-growing companies. Unfortunately, methods for placing valuations on such securities are not yet adequately developed, and investors make their buy-and-sell decisions as best they can.

That a company's high rate of "growth" may come to an end is an important, but little-emphasized, investment consideration in the evaluation of growth stocks. To call attention to this point, we present in this paper an exploratory analysis of the relationship between price-earnings ratio, rate of growth, and the duration of growth. In omitting risk from the present analysis, we are explicitly neglecting the fact that investments in growth stocks are often riskier than in non-growth stocks. Consistent with this, the capitalization rates for both kinds of securities are assumed to be the same, and hence any differences in their price-earnings ratios are attributable to differences in their growth of earnings.

The obvious investment success of growth stocks has led investors to seek out these securities for purchase, with the result that their prices have been driven up so that growth stocks now generally carry high price-earnings ratios. But just how high it is wise for investors to drive price-earnings ratios is not clear. If a growth stock is evaluated by discounting future growing dividends back to the present, the paradoxical result is obtained that an infinite price earnings ratio is justified for a stock whose dividends per share are expected to grow at a (per cent per annum) rate that is higher than the discount rate. This clearly untenable result comes from the implicit assumption of an *indefinite* continuation of exponential growth and may be avoided by limiting the assumed

*From *Journal of Finance,* Vol. 17, No. 3 (September 1962), pp. 465–475. Reprinted by permission of *Journal of Finance.*

†Conversations with M. H. Miller and F. Modigliani supplied much of the stimulation for writing this paper.

growth period.[1] Another method[2] has received considerable attention in investors' literature and seems to have had considerable influence. The growth in earnings per share of a company is extrapolated, say five years into the future, at the growth rate indicated from the recent past. The current price of the stock is divided by this forecast of earnings five years hence, to obtain a price-earnings ratio. In this way, more normal, i.e., lower price-earnings ratios are obtained for growth stocks and some useful indication is given on whether the existing price of the security is justified or not. However, this method is rather crude in ignoring any dividends that might be received during the five-year period or growth that might occur after this arbitrarily selected period.[3]

DURATION OF GROWTH

If investments in the common stocks of growth companies were expected to continue growing indefinitely at a constant exponential rate, then the investor's problem would be largely one of selecting the companies with the highest forecasted growth rates.[4] But before anyone chose to follow such an investment policy, he would be well advised to question seriously the assumption of indefinitely continued growth. Studies of the past growth in the applications of inventions and in the sales of companies and industries show growth curves in which very high rates of growth are achieved initially, but ultimately the growth rates tend to slow down or stop as maturity is reached. This logistic type of growth curve is rather complicated, and the forecasting of its leveling-off is quite difficult from both the statistical and the forecasting points of view. Although we shall not attempt this degree of refinement, it does seem desirable to assume that the growth opportunities of a "growth" company are likely at some point in time to slow down to the rate that is normally achieved by companies generally. Presumably, this more modest growth rate can be maintained indefinitely. As the period of high growth passes, the price-earnings ratio of a company will drop back to the normal level characteristic of "non-growth

[1] O. K. Burrell, "A Mathematical Approach to Growth Stock Valuation," *Financial Analysts Journal,* XVI (May-June 1960), 69–76; John C. Clendenin and Maurice Van Cleave, "Growth and Common Stock Values," *Journal of Finance,* IX (1954), 365–76.

[2] Julian G. Buckley, "A Method of Evaluating Growth Stocks," *Financial Analysts Journal,* XVI (March-April 1960), 19–21.

[3] The more subtle point that the dividend returns from a growth stock are farther in the future than those from non-growth stocks and hence that forecasts of the dividends are riskier has not been adequately treated as yet, nor will it be considered here. See David Durand, "Growth Stocks and the Petersburg Paradox," *Journal of Finance,* XII (September 1957), 348–63; and Henry Allen Latané, "Individual Risk Preference in Portfolio Selection," *Journal of Finance,* IV (March 1960), 45–52.

[4] For a more refined analysis of growth see M. H. Miller and F. Modigliani, "Dividend Policy, Growth, and the Valuation of Shares," *Journal of Business,* XXXIV (October 1961), 22. Growth in earnings of itself does not necessarily justify a high price-earnings ratio, if dividends are correspondingly low–i.e., the growth requires some form of expanding opportunities for profit. The present paper will not analyze the source of "growth" but only the problem of determining its value.

stocks." This perhaps distant, but almost inevitable, decline in price-earnings ratio constitutes one of the important risks of investing in a growth stock, especially since the termination of rapid growth is so difficult to forecast.

To simplify matters, we shall make the assumption that the growth in earnings per share (adjusted for stock dividends and splits) of a company will continue at a high constant exponential rate until some point in time when the rate drops abruptly to the average rate for non-growth companies. Under this assumption, the *duration of growth* for a company becomes a simple concept, i.e., the time duration of the high growth rate. Clearly, companies with long durations of growth should be valued more highly than those with short durations of growth, other things being equal. Also companies with high growth rates of earnings should be valued higher than companies with low growth rates, other things being equal.

Both the duration and the rate of growth need to be taken into account in valuing a growth stock. One way to do this is to consider the following question. How long, at a minimum, will the present high rate of earnings growth of a company have to continue in order to attain the same level of earnings that can be achieved by an alternative investment in non-growth stocks of comparable risk? Assume that beyond this time the high growth rate drops to the normal rate, the low dividend pay-out rises, and the high price-earnings ratio falls so that the two investments become virtually equivalent. In saying this, we have, of course, roughed over the uncertainty problem by assuming comparable risk for both investments. This time is the *minimum* required growth duration for the growth stock to justify its high price-earnings ratio. Of course, in both cases we need to take into account the dividend yields.

If we can formulate an analysis for determining the duration of growth estimate that is implicit in the market price of a growth stock, this may be useful to investors in making judgments as to whether the high price-earnings ratio of the growth stock is justified or not. We can obtain the market's estimate of duration of growth as follows: If we let $E'(t)$ be the earnings per share (adjusted for stock splits and stock dividends) of a common stock in the year t (measured from the present, when $t = 0$) and let ΔE be the per cent per annum growth rate of earnings per share, then an estimate of future earnings per share as long as this growth rate continues is given by the following expression:

$$E'(t) = E'(O)\,(1 + \Delta E)^t \qquad (1)$$

It is convenient for analysis to assume the reinvestment of dividend income to obtain additional "growth" so that it can be combined simply with the above expression.[5] This is done by pretending that the dividends are used to buy more

[5] There is little meaningful distinction between dividend income and capital gains aside from factors that we are not considering now, namely, risk, taxes, brokerage commissions for odd-lot transactions, and administrative convenience.

(perhaps fractional) shares of the same stock. This assumption is purely for analytical purposes, to put all securities on a common "no dividend payment" basis.

Thus if D is the constant per cent per annum dividend yield (i.e., ratio of dividends to market price), the number of shares $N(t)$ at the end of year t is

$$N(t) = (1 + D)^t \tag{2}$$

assuming that one share was bought originally when $t = 0$. The total earnings $E(t)$ at the end of year t on the original and purchased shares combined are

$$E(t) = E'(t)\,N(t) = E'(0)\,[(1 + \Delta E)(1 + D)]^t \tag{3}$$

Since D and ΔE are "small" and for the one original share $E'(0) = E(0)$, we obtain

$$E(t) \approx E(0)(1 + \Delta E + D)^t \tag{4}$$

This growth measurement of investment return is equally applicable to growth and non-growth stocks. We apply it to both and introduce the subscript g to indicate a growth stock and the subscript a to indicate an alternative non-growth stock of comparable risk.

After the *duration of growth,* which we designate as τ, we have assumed that the growth stock has the *same* general characteristics as the non-growth stock. Hence in the year τ their market values will be in direct proportion to their earnings of that year.[6] Since uncertainty has been left out of our analysis and since no dividends are withdrawn, we would expect that the market would tend to value the shares of the two stocks for current purchase in direct proportion to their value in year τ and hence in direct proportion to the forecasted earnings in the year τ. If this proportionality condition were not satisfied, investors would tend to buy the relatively underpriced stock, in order to be in a better position in the year τ, thereby driving up the low price. Thus the market will tend to satisfy this relation between the current share prices of the growth and the non-growth stocks, $P_g(0)$ and $P_a(0)$, respectively:

$$\frac{P_g(0)}{P_a(0)} \approx \frac{E_g(0)\,(1 + \Delta E_g + D_g)^\tau}{E_a(0)\,(1 + \Delta E_a + D_a)^\tau} \tag{5}$$

or, equivalently,

$$\left(\frac{P_g(0)\,/\,E_g(0)}{P_a(0)\,/\,E_a(0)}\right) \approx \left(\frac{1 + \Delta E_g + D_g}{1 + \Delta E_a + D_a}\right)^\tau \tag{6}$$

[6] *$E(t)$ is given by substituting* τ for t in expression (4).

Here we see that the ratio between the price-earnings ratios of the two stocks is equal to the ratio of their composite growth rates raised to the τth power. The compounded growth offsets the high price-earnings ratio of the growth stock.

We may solve for τ by taking logarithms. For simplicity, we have dropped the time parentheses indicating current prices and earnings but without changing the meaning:

$$\ln\left(\frac{P_g / E_g}{P_a / E_a}\right) \approx \tau \ln\left(\frac{1+\Delta E_g + D_g}{1+\Delta E_a + D_a}\right) \tag{7}$$

Since this equation is linear in the logarithms, we may graph it on semilog paper to obtain the simple relation shown in Fig. 1. Fortunately, the log scales on the graph avoid any necessity of dealing with logarithms. The intersection of a horizontal line representing the relative price-earnings ratio with a sloping line representing the relative growth rate determines a point. Dropping vertically, we can read the market estimate of growth duration τ. In this way, by plotting the point of intersection, we can obtain τ for a security. An example will clarify the results of the analysis. Suppose that the current price-earnings ratio for a growth stock is 45 and for a non-growth stock of comparable risk is 15. Then the relative price-earnings ratio is $(P_g/E_g) \div (P_a/E_a) = 45/15 = 3$, as shown by the heavy horizontal line on Figure 1. Suppose, further that the growth in earnings per share of the growth stock is expected to continue at the rate of 30 per cent per year but the dividend yield is only 1 per cent per year. The non-growth stock, on the other hand, is expected to have only a 5 per cent growth in earnings but has a 5 per cent divident yield. Thus the relative growth rate is $(1 + \Delta E_g + D_g) \div (1 + \Delta E_a + D_a) = (1 + 0.30 + 0.01) \div (1 + 0.05 + 0.05) = 1.31/1.10 = 1.2$, as shown by the heavy sloping line through the origin of Fig. 1. The intersection of these two lines determines a point labeled A. Dropping vertically, we can read from the horizontal scale that the market estimate of duration of growth is evidently 6 years. That is to say, the market is valuing the growth stock *as if* its present high rate of growth would continue for 6 years and then decline sharply to the normal level. The graph has made it easy to find that $\tau = 6$. This value, of course, satisfies equation (6) for this example:

$$\frac{45}{15} \approx \left(\frac{1 + 0.30 + 0.01}{1 + 0.05 + 0.05}\right)^6$$

Another way to interpret the six-year growth duration is in terms of total growth potential. A 30 per cent growth rate is, say, 25 per cent above the normal growth rate, taking the non-growth stock as the standard. If this rate continues for 6 years, we would have a total growth potential of $(1.25)^6 = 3.82$ or 382 per cent. This amounts to forecasting that the ratio of earnings per share of the growth stock to the non-growth stock will ultimately improve by almost a factor of 4.

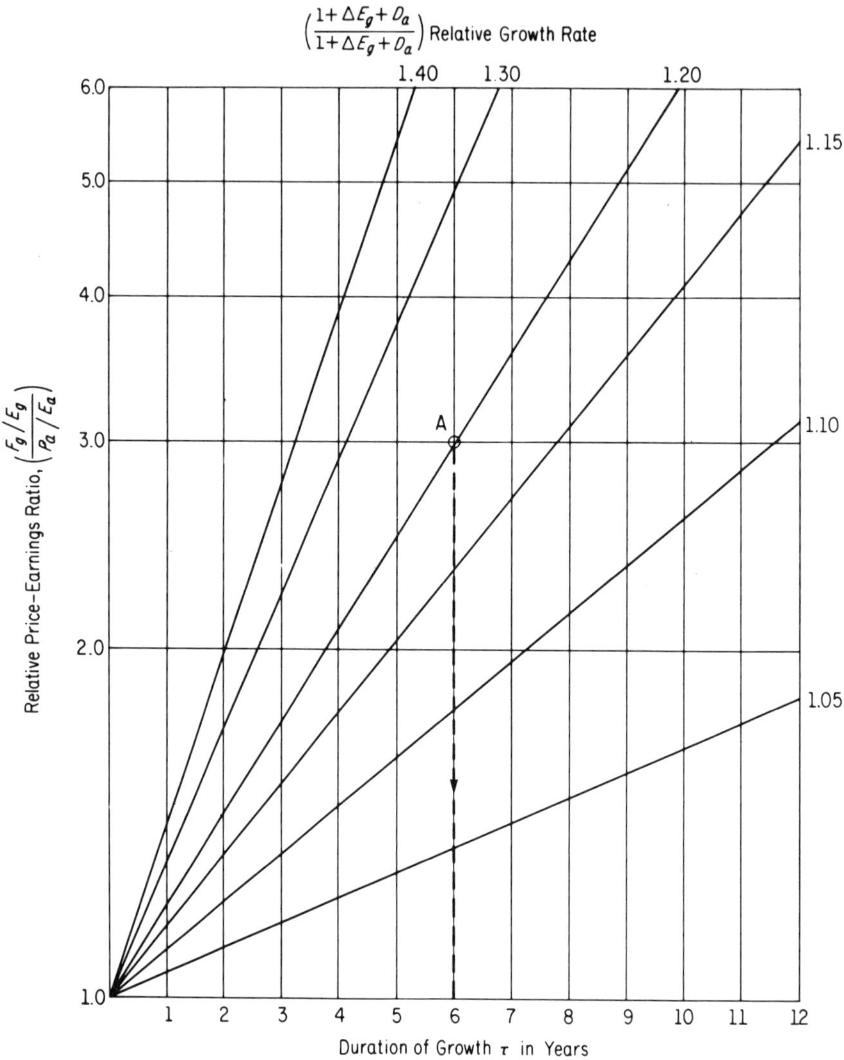

Fig. 1. Growth versus non-growth companies

AN ILLUSTRATION USING MARKET DATA

The use of this analysis may be illustrated by selecting the Dow-Jones index as a representative alternative non-growth investment, and selecting the following growth common stocks: Ampex, International Business Machines, Litton, Polaroid, and Texas Instruments. The dividend yields and price-earnings ratios for May, 1960, were used.

For the Dow-Jones index, the price earnings ratio P_a/E_a was 18, D_a was 3 per cent per year, and ΔE_a was 5 per cent per year. These forecasts were extrapolations of the previous 5 years' history. We have obtained ΔE_g for each of the growth companies by plotting on semilog paper the earnings per share, adjusted for stock splits and stock dividends, for 1956 through 1959 and estimated the slope.

Before plotting points for each growth company, Fig. 1 was modified by changing its scales to incorporate the Dow-Jones index as the standard non-growth alternative[7] (see Fig. 2). Plotting these data on Fig. 2 indicates the

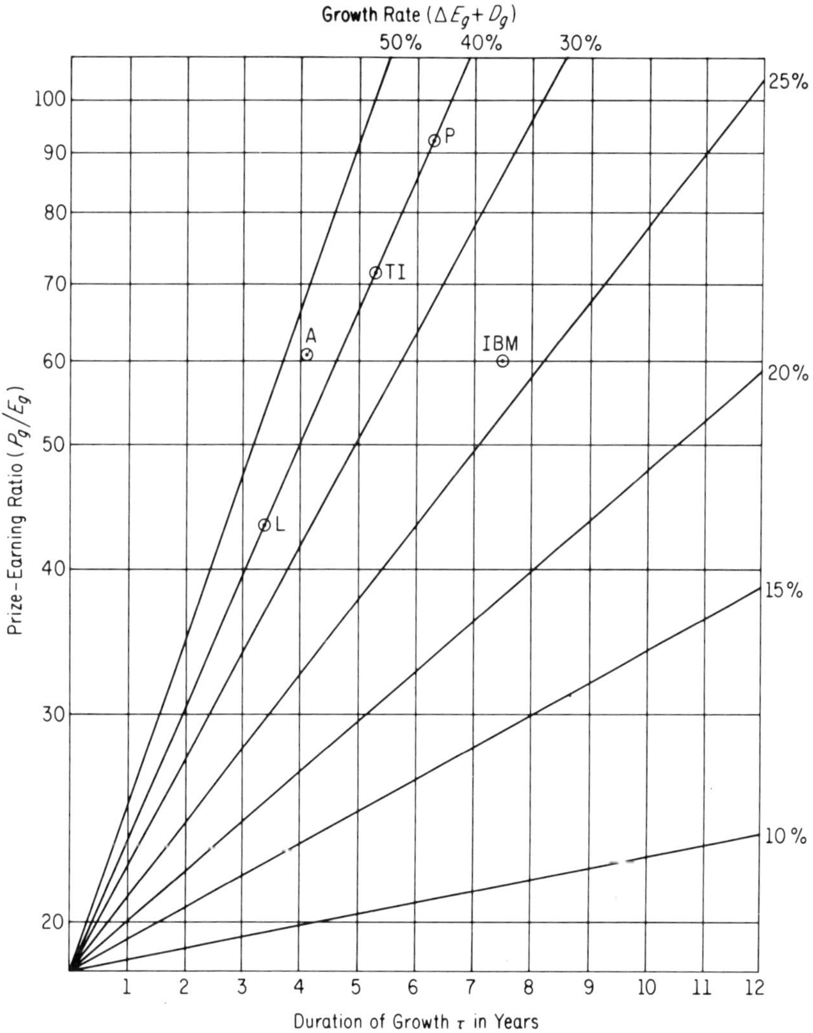

Fig. 2. Growth companies versus Dow-Jones investment (as of May, 1960)

[7]The growth-rate scale on Fig. 2 plus 1 equals the relative growth-rate scale of Fig. 1 multiplied by (1+0.30+0.01).

growth duration periods shown in the second column of Table 1. In interpreting these results, one is tempted, at first blush, to say that Litton is the better buy because it will justify its high price-earnings ratio relative to a Dow-Jones investment in a shorter period of time than the other companies. However, valid conclusions require a comparison for each company between the market estimate of duration of growth and the investor's own estimate. The investor can compare his judgments with those of the market and act accordingly where he feels the market is in error. Clearly, if growth duration actually proves to be longer than the market's estimate, the stock will have proved to be a bargain purchase. A stock with growth duration shorter than the market estimate will prove to have been a poor investment. As always, the investor must bet that his forecast is better than that of the market. If he can forecast growth durations successfully, growth stocks may offer important investment opportunities.

TABLE 1

Company	Market Estimate of Duration of Growth (Years)	Adjusted for Taxes (Years)
Ampex	4.1	4.2
International Business Machines	7.5	7.5
Litton	3.4	3.4
Polaroid	6.3	6.8
Texas Instruments	5.3	5.7

This analysis may be used in another way. An estimate of the growth duration for a company may be made by the investor and the corresponding line drawn vertically on Fig. 1 or Fig. 2 until it intersects the sloping growth-rate line and then move left horizontally to read the price-earnings ratio. This is the price-earnings ratio that would be warranted by this duration of growth. This could be compared with the price-earnings ratio existing in the market and purchase-sell decisions made accordingly.

ADJUSTMENT FOR TAXES

An extension of the analysis might well take into account the fact that long-term capital gains are taxed at an advantageously low rate, so that income through price appreciation is more desirable than dividend income. An exact adjustment for taxes would greatly complicate the analysis, but, by ignoring the fact that capital gains taxes are postponable, we may make an approximate adjustment. By making the simplifying assumption that capital gains are taxed in the year in which they occur, we can modify formula (7) to reflect growth after taxes.

The growth from dividend reinvestment is reduced by taxes to $(1 - K_D)\,D$, where K_D is the marginal tax rate applicable to dividend income. Similarly, the growth of earnings is reduced to $(1 - K_C)\Delta E$, where K_C is the marginal tax rate applicable to capital gains income. A person whose marginal income tax rate was 30 per cent would be taxed at half that rate on capital gains, i.e., $K_D = 0.3$ and $K_C = 0.15$. The maximum K_C is, of course, 0.25.

Recalling that the price-earnings ratio of the growth stock falls as the termination of the high growth rate approaches, we need to recognize that all the gain in earnings is not reflected in gain in market price of the shares. Since we have applied the capital gains tax to the full earnings appreciation, we need to make an offsetting adjustment by applying the capital gains tax to the decline in price-earnings ratio. If we rewrite the left parentheses of formula (7),

$$\frac{P_g/E_g}{P_a/E_a} \approx \frac{P_a/E_a + (P_g/E_g - P_a/E_a)}{P_a/E_a} \tag{8}$$

we can interpret the right parentheses in formula (8) as the capital "loss" component for the growth stock as the result of the reduction in price-earnings ratio to that of the non-growth stock. We apply the capital gains tax to this "loss" adjustment by multiplying the "loss" term by $(1 - K_C)$:

$$\frac{P_a/E_a + (P_g/E_g - P_a/E_a)(1 - K_C)}{P_a/E_a} \approx 1 + \left(\frac{P_g/E_g}{P_a/E_a} - 1\right)(1 - K_C) \tag{9}$$

Incorporating the above adjustments in formula (7), we obtain

$$\ln\left[1 + \left(\frac{P_g/E_g}{P_a/E_a} - 1\right)(1 - K_C)\right] \approx \tau \ln\left[\frac{1 + (1 - K_C)\,\Delta E_g + (1 - K_D)\,D_g}{1 + (1 - K_C)\,\Delta E_a + (1 - K_D)\,D_a}\right] \tag{10}$$

The inclusion of the tax adjustment does not complicate the graphs, but it does complicate somewhat the computation step before entering the graphs. The effect of the adjustment will be to reflect the preference of the high-income person for companies that do not pay out their growth in the form of dividends. Applying this adjustment to the companies that we have already considered and assuming an investor whose tax rates are $K_D = 0.5$ and $K_C = 0.25$, we obtain the overtake periods shown in the third column of Table 1. In this case, the overtake periods were not greatly affected by the adjustment for taxes.

CONCLUSION

Four limitations of this analysis need to be noted. First—and most important—the uncertainty of forecasting earnings in the distant future is a much more important consideration for growth stocks than for non-growth stocks. Hence, ignoring the risk inherent in probabilistic forecast errors is an important omission which will tend to make growth stocks appear more attractive than they really are. Second, the analysis rests on forecasts of constant earnings-per-share growth rates and constant dividend-per-share yields. Such forecasts on a per share basis need to be made critically because past data may reflect purely financial transactions, such as increasing leverage, etc., which may reflect increasing risk rather than growth. Third, the relative tax advantage of capital gains income, which is the principal return from growth stocks, is somewhat understated by neglecting the deferred collection of the capital gains tax, so that growth stocks appear less attractive than they really are—especially for high-income investors. Fourth, we hardly expect the growth of earnings to terminate sharply but, rather, would expect the growth rate to decline gradually as the special advantages enjoyed by the growth company are whittled away by increasing competition, expiration of patents, appearance of substitute products, etc. Thus the high growth rate would tend to last longer than the above analysis would indicate, but the rate of growth would be reduced.

The need for a really adequate theory of investment under certainty is emphasized by the gross approximations that were used in this exploratory analysis. Granting these limitations, the analysis does offer a systematic framework for evaluating growth stocks that includes many of the relevant variables with a minimum of complexity and computation. Hopefully, the analysis is simple enough—even using the adjustment for taxes—to be useful to investors.[8]

[8] An independent, but equivalent, analysis by Robert Ferguson has recently yielded a nomograph which reduces the computations to a simple mechanical procedure ("A Nomograph for Valuing Growth Stocks," *Financial Analysts Journal,* XVII (May-June 1961), 29–34). Unfortunately, the underlying assumptions of his analysis are not fully explicit.

13

Leverage and the Rate of Return Required by Equity

John K. Pfahl
David T. Crary

An examination of the finance literature of the past decade would have led even the casual observer to conclude that a great deal of confusion exists concerning the cost of capital and the ramifications of this concept for the suppliers of capital as well as financial managers.

An indication of this confusion is the complete disagreement in the literature concerning the cost of the various sources of funds, the optimal use of leverage, investment decisions and financing decisions.[1]

The authors intend in this article to challenge some of the assumptions contained in recent works in the area of finance and to question the wisdom of some of the conclusions that have followed them. The authors plan to show that:

1. The cost of capital to the firm is dependent on the investment decisions of the firm.
2. Leverage does not affect the cost of capital to the *firm.*
3. From the point of view of the *equity* interests, a minimum acceptable degree of leverage exists.

This paper is confined to a consideration of the effects that a change in financial leverage has on a company's cost of capital and on the rate of return anticipated by the suppliers of capital.

In order to isolate the effect of leverage from the myriad other factors that may be involved in the judicious use of debt, this analysis will be conducted in terms of a "model." This model, consisting of an attempt to explicitly represent reality, is necessarily less complex than the reality itself, but it is hoped that it is

[1]For example, see: Roland P. Soule, "Trends in the Cost of Capital," *Harvard Business Review* (March-April 1953), p. 33; J. Fred Weston and Eugene F. Brigham, *Managerial Finance* (2d ed.; New York: Holt, Rinehart and Winston, Inc., 1966), p. 284; Richards C. Osborn, *Business Finance the Management Approach* (New York: Appleton-Century-Crofts, 1965), p. 159; Richards C. Osborn, *Corporation Finance* (New York: Harper and Brothers, 1969), p. 157; Franco Modigliani and Merton Miller, "The Cost of Capital, Corporation Finance and the Theory of Investment," *The American Economic Review* (June 1958), pp. 268–9; and Ezra Solomon, "Leverage and the Cost of Capital," *The Journal of Finance* (May 1963), p. 279.

sufficiently complete to approximate those aspects of reality which are being investigated. In this presentation, as in every analysis utilizing abstraction, the authors have drastically over simplified the complex reality of the problem in an effort to explain certain of its salient aspects.

The model assumes that one is dealing with firms which possess or acquire assets of only one quality. The assets are such that for each dollar invested, a flow of operating earnings is generated which provides a rate of return of k per annum of a given quality with respect to the certainty or uncertainty with which it can be expected to occur. The specific quality inherent in the assets of this model firm is immaterial so long as all assets possess the same quality. Quality then, in this sense, is related only to the certainty of earnings. In other words, it is assumed that the risk inherent in the assets of the firm, or the business risk, is held constant. Financial risk, on the other hand, will be allowed to vary. Business risk is not affected by the manner in which the firm raises its capital but only by the economic factors which govern the success of the firm as a producing unit. Since the assets of each firm are assumed to be of a given quality, changes in risk will occur solely as a result of changes in leverage. It should be clear that assuming a given level of risk is not the same as assuming no risk. The model merely identifies a risk level and holds it constant for purposes of analysis. In the real world it is quite true that the risk level of a firm will not be known or constant.

In addition, it is assumed that the model firm may acquire a capitalization structure composed of only two kinds of financing, externally-derived equity in one case and debt in the other. Though this assumption is maintained throughout the analysis it can be illustrated that the use of more than two types of financing would not change the conclusions.

The structure of market capitalization rates is assumed as given and not subject to change during the immediate planning horizon. The market is assumed to consist of rational investors who conceive of return to capital as being remuneration for the acceptance of risk—and it is assumed that there are no taxes.

The final assumption is that the capital market is reasonably perfect. Since the buyers in a perfect market have equal knowledge concerning products, it is assumed that a given commodity cannot consistently sell at more than one price.

DEVELOPMENT OF THE MODEL

There are two ways in which leverage[2] can be altered in a model. It can be assumed that the model company substitutes debt for equity in its capital structure, i.e., it issues debt and uses the proceeds to redeem outstanding stock. This approach has the virtue that it keeps the asset structure constant as leverage changes. An alternative method for analyzing changes in leverage is to permit the

[2] For the purposes of this analysis leverage is defined as the market value of debt/the market value of debt plus the market value of equity.

model company to expand, i.e., to issue more and more debt, using the proceeds to acquire additional assets. In order not to contaminate the leverage effect, however, it is necessary to assume that each new asset acquired generates operating earnings of a same size and quality as those produced by existing assets. Although both approaches yield the same conclusions, in this paper the method which changes leverage by substitution is used.

As mentioned previously, it would seem that the leverage question can most easily be resolved by thinking in terms of a model. Those aspects of the model most relevant to this discussion will be presented as a graph with the vertical axis representing the rate of return and the horizontal axis representing the degree of leverage. The model firm is assumed to be a ten percent firm. In other words, the capital market is in agreement that a ten percent return to the owners of the firm's assets is completely commensurate with the risk of success or failure inherent in the assets of the firm. A ten percent rate of return is adjudged by the suppliers of capital as commensurate with the business risk accepted. Therefore, with a capital structure consisting solely of equity, stockholders would demand a ten percent return.

RETURN TO THE SUPPLIERS OF DEBT CAPITAL

What rate of return should the suppliers of debt capital demand as the capital structure approaches a one-hundred percent debt position? It would seem that as the capital structure approaches a total debt position, rational investors in a reasonably perfect market would continue to demand a rate of return commensurate with the risk confronting them. The risk to debt holders at any point in this capital structure which is less than one hundred percent debt is a risk level less than that commensurate with a ten percent return and approaches that point only as debt becomes one hundred percent of the capital structure. Below a one hundred percent debt capital structure, the risk to debt holders, as a class, is less than that contained in the business risk of the assets because of the protection afforded by equity. The claims of the suppliers of equity capital are defined as subordinate to those of the suppliers of debt capital by law. As the capital structure approaches one hundred percent debt the practical value of this legal right disappears. The safety which creditors possessed vis-a-vis equity interests at lower levels of leverage ceases to exist. The advantages, in fact, continue to exist but become meaningless for practical purposes.

Thus, as the total debt position is approached it would appear that the risk assumed by the debt interests would approach that level of risk assumed by the equity interests when the firm possessed no debt claims in the capital structure. With an all-equity capital structure the owners are confronted with only one class of risk–business risk. As the firm approaches an all-debt capital structure the suppliers of debt capital are confronted with only one class of risk–the business risk inherent in the bundle of assets for which they have supplied capital.

Therefore, as the firm approaches a one hundred percent debt position, rational suppliers of debt capital in a relatively perfect market would demand the same rate of return as was demanded by the suppliers of equity capital when the firms possessed an all-equity capital structure. Investors at both points would seem to occupy the same position vis-a-vis risk. Solomon seems to suggest this position when he states: "For extreme leverage positions, i.e., as the company approaches an all-debt situation, it is clear that k_i (the demands of the suppliers of debt capital) will be at least equal to k_o (the overall cost of capital).[3]

Since in a reasonably perfect market a given commodity cannot consistently sell at different prices, it would be expected that rational investors would demand the same return from this bundle of assets which they possess both at one hundred percent equity and one hundred percent debt. As the capital structure approaches one hundred percent debt, the total risk assumed by debt holders would be commensurate with the risk inherent in the assets of the firm or ten percent. The rate of return demanded by the suppliers of debt capital would approach ten percent as the capital structure approached one hundred percent. In line with this approach Solomon writes: ". . . at one hundred percent leverage, the bondholders are simply owners with no senior securities ahead of them, i.e., the total value of the company cannot be below its hypothetical zero-leverage value. . ."[4]

In line with this thinking the return demanded by the suppliers of debt capital at varying levels of leverage is represented in the following graph. The symbol k_i is used to represent the average cost of debt capital (see Fig. 1).

What should be the demands of debt holders as the debt position approaches zero? It was established earlier that for the purposes of this paper there is assumed to be a relationship between risk and return. It was assumed that rational investors would demand more return for assuming more risk. The demand for return is assumed to vary continuously with risk. It was indicated that debt suppliers because of their legal contractual claims have, at any point in which the capital structure contains less than one hundred percent debt, a lower risk than that assumed by the suppliers of equity capital. It was assumed that as the firm approaches an all-debt position the demands of the suppliers of debt capital would approach ten percent. As the debt position of the firm approaches zero, the risk to the suppliers of debt approaches zero and their demands should approach zero.

It is recognized that debt capital is not available at rates of return approaching zero and this situation is dealt with in a later section. In addition, it is important to note that while return is assumed to vary continuously with risk, this does not imply a linear relationship. For the purposes of this analysis and in

[3]Ezra Solomon, "Leverage and the Cost of Capital," *Journal of Finance*, Vol. XVIII (May 1963), p. 277.

[4]Ezra Solomon, *The Theory of Financial Management* (New York: Columbia University Press, 1963), p. 105.

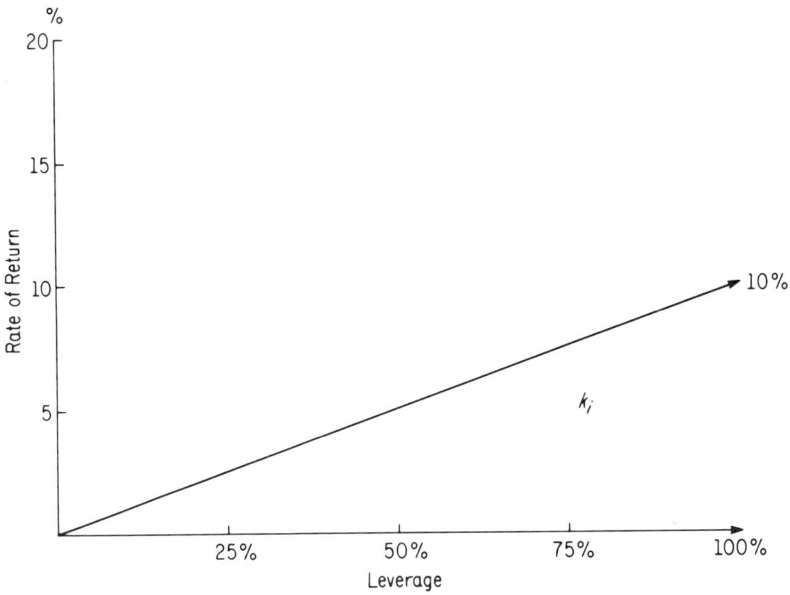

Fig. 1. The cost of debt capital in a changing capital structure.

the interest of initially utilizing a simple model, it is assumed that the k_i line is a straight line beginning at zero at the zero level of leverage and approaching ten percent as debt approaches one hundred percent. While the return to debt could be assumed to follow some curvilinear pattern, the justification for this does not seem to be greater than that yielding a straight line. A perfect correlation between required return and risk would lead to a linear relationship.

While in the graph the k_i line appears to be continuous, it is true that in reality it is a discontinuous function because of the fact that debt issues are offered with yields which vary in discrete amounts. Therefore, the graph of the k_i function could be more accurately portrayed as in Fig. 2.

This discontinuity has led some observers to believe that in reality the k_i line appears as in Fig. 3. An indication of this thinking is found in the many finance texts in which the examples purporting to explain the concept of leverage assume that the cost of debt capital remains constant for varying degrees of leverage.

This graph represents a situation in which a firm is able to secure a relatively large amount of debt financing at a fixed rate. The rate of return demanded by the debt suppliers remains constant as the percentage of debt in the capital structure increases. There may be several reasons to explain this action. Perhaps one reason is that governmental regulations restricting the investments of certain financial institutions to debt securities have increased the supply of debt funds and, in effect, lowered their price. Another possible explanation might be that

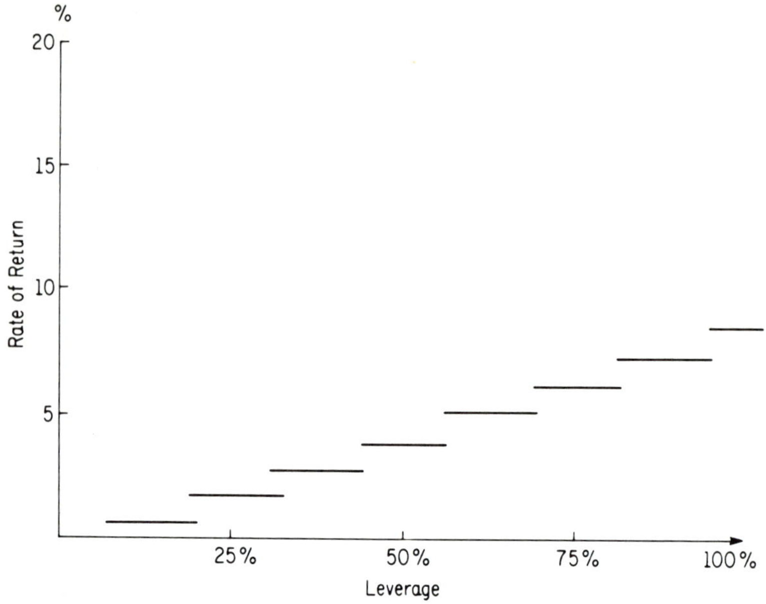

Fig. 2. The incremental cost of debt capital.

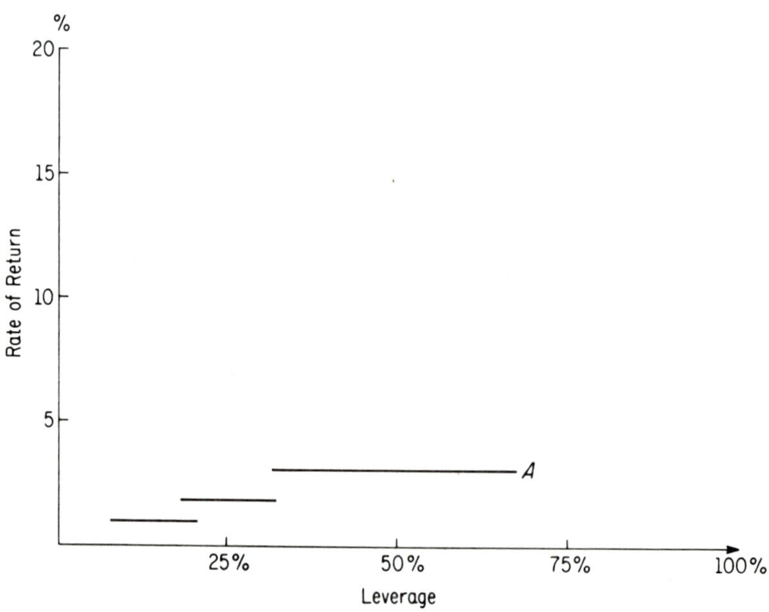

Fig. 3. The perceived costs of increments of debt.

the primary concern of a firm whose commitments are in fixed dollar claims is to get its funds invested at a rate higher than it is paying on its commitments rather than seeking to maximize rate of return. In addition, it is possible that the suppliers of debt capital are unable to accurately evaluate the increase in risk involved in a relatively small increase in leverage. Factors of this nature could combine to create an imperfect market.

When factors of this nature affect the debt capital market the k_i function does not appear to be continuous and the firm is able to secure debt financing at rates that are advantageous to equity interests. The debt holders are at a disadvantage at point A because the quantity of risk they are assuming has been increasing continuously while their rate of return has not. While it is clear that situations of this nature exist, it would be difficult to construct a model based on innumerable possible market imperfections.

RETURN TO THE SUPPLIERS OF EQUITY CAPITAL

What rate of return should the suppliers of equity capital demand as leverage is increased? It would be expected that the rate of return demanded by equity interests would increase with the introduction of debt into the capital structure since the risk to the equity interests has been increased by the addition of financial risk to the business risk they formerly possessed.

As stated previously, it is assumed that the suppliers of capital under consideration are not risk lovers but rational investors who demand increased return when subjected to increased risk. If one is not considering the case of risk lovers, then it can be assumed that at any level of leverage B which is more levered than any degree of leverage A, no matter how small the difference between A and B, the rate of return demanded by each class of security holder (debt and equity) will be higher for level B than for level A. If the preceding propositions are assumed and the upper limit for debt is established, then, whether the function describing the return demanded by debt is continuous or discontinuous, it will be an increasing function. Since it is assumed that, except for their different positions resulting from different combinations of business and financial risk, both debt and equity holders perceive increased risk identically, equity will demand an increased rate of return as leverage increases in the same manner that debt does. If these propositions are extended to their logical conclusion, an increase in leverage from A to B should increase the rates of return demanded by debt and equity by the same amount. By a series of steps proceeding from a low level of leverage A to a high level of leverage B, it can be shown that as the return to debt approaches the rate of return demanded by equity when there is no leverage, equity will be demanding twice that rate as debt approaches one hundred percent.

This relationship is depicted in the graph in Fig. 4. The symbol k_e represents the cost of equity capital.

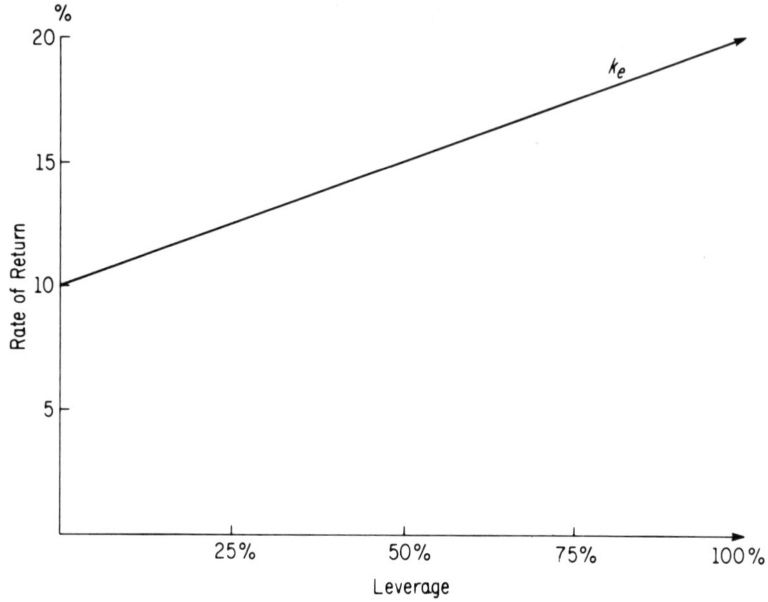

Fig. 4. The cost of equity capital in a changing capital structure.

The only conditions under which this conclusion regarding the cost of equity capital would not be reached are: (a) if one postulates that the rates of return demanded by debt and equity holders do not increase in the same way and by the same amounts, (b) if one postulates that the rate of return to debt is something other than zero at zero degree of leverage and at the same time holds the writer's assumption that both types of capital suppliers evaluate increased risk as calling for equal increases in return, or (c) if one postulates that the rate of return demanded by debt at one hundred percent leverage will be different from that rate demanded by equity at zero degree of leverage.

To suggest that the demands of equity would exceed the rates shown on the k_e line is to suggest that the inherent risk of the assets has been changed by the financing of such assets. This assumption is not rationally supported.

The rate of return demanded by equity interests approaches but does not reach twenty percent because leverage only approaches and does not reach one hundred percent. This is true because legally a corporation cannot exist with a one hundred percent debt capital structure.

Earlier the equity interests were described as residual claimants. It is true that because of the legal position of debt, equity has a secondary claim to the earnings of the firm. If the cost of capital were defined in an ex post sense as many current authors deal with it, it could easily be demonstrated that the returns available to equity interests in this situation would approach twenty percent.

THE AVERAGE COST OF CAPITAL

The symbol k_o is used to represent the over-all cost of capital to the firm. Once the k_i line and the k_e line are derived, the resultant is a constant k_o for any and all levels of leverage. The completed graph containing k_e, k_i, and k_o appears as in Fig. 5.

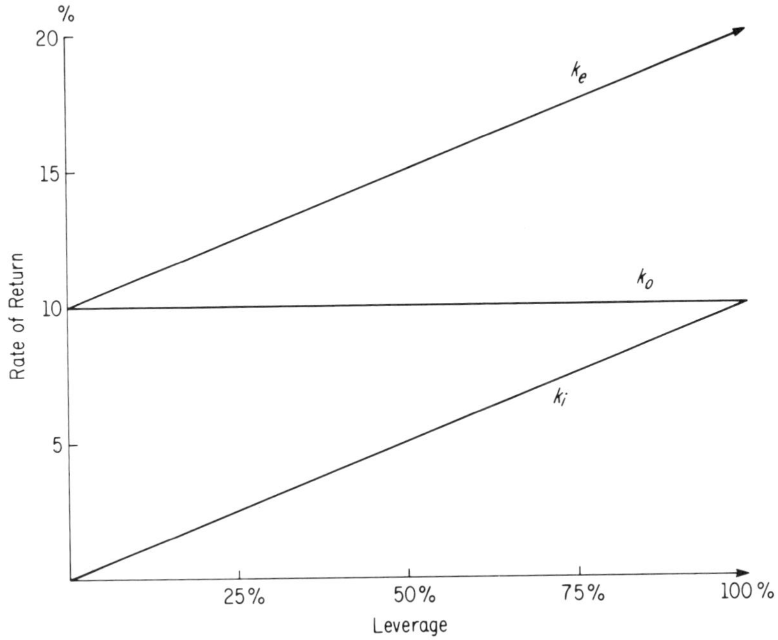

Fig. 5. The average cost of capital in a changing capital structure.

One must conclude that, given the assumptions of the model, an increase in leverage can neither raise nor lower a company's cost of capital no matter how "judicious" or "excessive" this increase may be. For example, representative levels of leverage yield the following values for k_i, k_o, and k_e:

25% debt	50% debt	75% debt
$k_i = 2.5\%$	$k_i = 5.0\%$	$k_i = 7.5\%$
$k_o = 10.0\%$	$k_o = 10.0\%$	$k_o = 10.0\%$
$k_e = 12.5\%$	$k_e = 15.0\%$	$k_e = 17.5\%$

With the cost of capital to the firm remaining constant under varying degrees of leverage one might inquire as to the incentive for equity interests to increase leverage. At this point, one must recall that it is k_e which varies with leverage and that this is of most relevance to the equity interests. From the stockholder's point of view, it would seem that the sole reason for an increase in the leverage of a firm is that owners have arbitrarily decided that they would prefer to take on additional risk with its commensurate increase in dollar income. It is recognized that many times the decision is made not by stockholders but by the management of the firm which could be pursuing objectives such as growth rather than increased return to equity interests. While it can be assumed that investors are generally interested in increasing their dollar income, the various reasons involved in a stockholder's decision to assume additional risk are as yet ill defined.

After arbitrarily deciding to assume more risk, is an investor indifferent as to the type of investment he selects so long as the return is commensurate with the risk assumed? No! It seems that a preference could exist between two situations from which an investor has decided to demand the same return in the next time period. For example, one is confronted with the problem of deciding what has gone into the determination of the return to be demanded. If the investor feels that *all* variables were accounted for in deriving this return, then the two investments would be conceived as equal and the investor would be indifferent as to the one chosen. In all probability, however, an investor would feel that he had not taken all variables into consideration—possibly because of the large number and complexity of the variables—and he probably could not be certain that he had appropriately weighted all the variables considered. Therefore, even though an investor feels that he may receive the same interest-rate-like return from two stocks in the next time period, he may prefer one to the other. This preference may be based on the expectation that one firm is in a growing industry and the other in a declining one. It could be based on the expectation of stability in one company over the long run as compared to volatility in the other, or, feeling that he cannot accurately weigh all variables, an investor could prefer a position in a levered firm with its lower risk inherent in the physical assets to one promising the same return in an unlevered situation. In other words, an investor may prefer a levered position in a nationally known firm in a stable industry returning 12 percent to an unlevered position in a local pizza shop yielding the same return.

It would seem that this logic could explain an increase in leverage. Some investors might be willing to take a higher risk for a higher yield. And it is possible that investors could possess a preference for one investment alternative among several expected to yield the same returns in the next time period. In other words, certain investors might prefer to increase their financial risk in a line of business with a relatively low business risk, for example, public utilities, rather than switching their capital to a firm with a higher level of business risk offering the same rate of return.

MODIFICATION OF THE MODEL

Given the assumptions of the previous section concerning the absence of corporate income taxes, the presence of rational investors who demanded a rate of return that varied directly and continuously with risk, and relatively perfect capital markets, it was concluded that a firm's cost of capital is independent of its capital structure.

In the hypothetical world posited by this model, the answer to questions concerning the most satisfactory composition of a firm's capital structure would be that any and all combinations of debt and equity are equally satisfactory. The model suggests that there is no optimum capital structure. Differences in capital structure for firms in the same risk class would necessarily be explained in terms of factors other than cost.

However, it is readily noted by even the casual observer that great differences in capital structure do exist. These variations are not explained by the model as it now exists. It would seem that if this model is to be useful to operating financial managers it should be modified in an attempt to make it more applicable to the real world. One way to accomplish this would be to relax some of the assumptions that differ most from the real world.

At this point, the assumption concerning perfect capital markets is relaxed. It is observed that no one offers to lend funds at the lowest rates shown on the k_i line. John Maynard Keynes explained this phenomenon in terms of the concept of "liquidity preference."[5] Since it is impossible to secure funds in this interest rate range one could deal with the problem by assuming an instantaneous rise in the real k_i line.[6] In other words, instead of assuming that interest rates would approach zero as leverage approached zero, one would recognize that a minimum rate of interest equivalent to something near the pure rate of interest would exist.

Once this market imperfection is introduced, it would seem that the implications for equity interests are clear. If any leverage is contemplated, equity interests must push leverage to that point where the real k_i line coincides with the theoretical k_i line. While it is recognized that ex ante[7] returns and ex post[8] returns are in equilibrium in an all-equity capital structure, ex ante and ex post results with leverage will be in equilibrium for equity interests *only* at those points where the real k_i line coincides with the theoretical k_i line. So long as equity interests find the ex ante and ex post situation in disequilibrium, they should adjust leverage. In the case under consideration, equity interests should increase leverage at least to the point where k_i and theoretical k_i intersect or

[5] John Maynard Keynes, *The General Theory of Employment, Interest and Money* (New York: Harcourt, Brace and World, Inc. 1930), p. 168.

[6] The expression "theoretical k_i line" is used to identify the k_i line representing the earlier assumptions of perfect markets and rational investors. The term "real k_i line" identifies the market level of interest confronting the firm.

[7] ex ante; planned or anticipated

[8] ex post; realized

decrease leverage to the zero level where they are also in equilibrium. At any point, where the real k_i is above the theoretical k_i, equity interests will be receiving a rate of return that is less than commensurate with the amount of business and financial risk that they have accepted.

As shown in Fig. 6, when a degree of leverage not sufficient to make the real k_i intersect the theoretical k_i is contemplated, it would seem in an ex ante sense that the k_o line is rising and then declining while in an ex post sense it is the k_e line which dips. In other words, equity's anticipated returns coupled with the required payments to debt would make it seem, when viewed in an ex ante sense, that the returns to the suppliers of capital would exceed the ten percent return on total assets assumed for the model firm. However, in an ex post or realized sense, it can be seen that when the required payments are made to debt the remaining returns available to equity are less than the amount anticipated.

In the situation portrayed by Fig. 6 it is assumed that the minimum cost of debt capital is 4 percent. If it is assumed that the suppliers of both debt and equity capital continue to behave rationally, demanding a rate of return that varies directly and continuously with risk, and that the capital market remains relatively perfect except for the liquidity preference, then it can be seen that the ex ante and ex post positions of the equity suppliers will be in disequilibrium (except at zero leverage) until leverage reaches 40 percent. Equilibrium then exists from 40 percent leverage to the point where it approaches 100 percent.

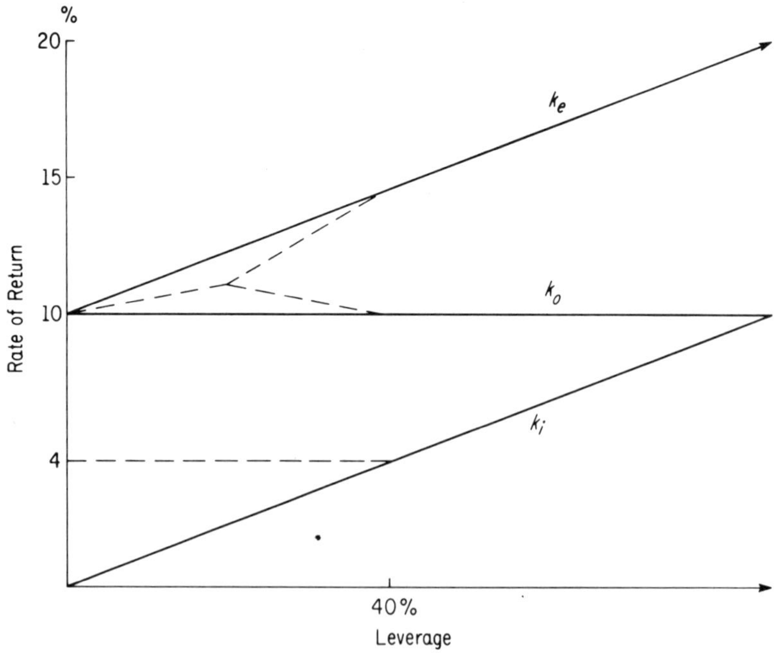

Fig. 6. The minimum acceptable degree of leverage.

The figures shown below show k_e in both an ex ante and ex post sense at different degrees of leverage with the market imperfection included. For example, with a capital structure consisting of 1 percent debt, equity interests anticipate a 10.1 percent return; however, only 10.03 percent is realized. In other words, from a realization point of view, the k_i and the k_o are given and k_e is the dependent variable.

Equity interests have an incentive to increase leverage until equilibrium is reached. In this example, equity interests will not receive payment commensurate with the risk they are taking until 40 percent of the capital structure is represented by debt. In the area beyond the market imperfection (40 percent debt in this case), the ex ante and ex post equilibrium for equity interests would seem to connote management indifference as to the type of security to issue to secure funds. In this situation, cost is not a factor and management is concerned with the less easily quantified factors of control, flexibility, and availability.

Capital	Structure	Payment to Capital Bonds First	k_i and k_e Ex ante	k_o Ex ante	k_i and k_e Ex post	k_o Ex post
Bonds Stocks	100 9900	\$ 4.00 996.00	4.0% 10.1%	10.03%	4.0% 10.0%	10.0%
Bonds Stock	500 9500	20.00 980.00	4.0% 10.5%	10.175%	4.0% 10.31%	10.0%
Bonds Stock	1000 9000	40.00 960.00	4.0% 11.0%	10.30%	4.0% 10.66%	10.0%
Bonds Stock	2000 8000	80.00 920.00	4.0% 12.0%	10.49%	4.0% 11.50%	10.0%
Bonds Stock	3000 7000	120.00 980.00	4.0% 13.0%	10.30%	4.0% 12.57%	10.0%
Bonds Stock	4000 6000	160.00 840.00	4.0% 14.0%	10.0%	4.0% 14.0%	10.0%

This approach to the leverage question would appear to contain powerful implications concerning the appropriate degree of leverage for various types of industries.

For example, assume a very stable industry with a 6 percent risk inherent in the assets and a capital market demanding a minimum of 4 percent on debt instruments. In this situation, equity interests must extend leverage to 67 percent in order to have ex ante and ex post conditions in equilibrium.

On the other hand, in a higher risk firm, such as one with a sixteen percent risk inherent in the assets, it seems that leverage would be pushed only to twenty-five percent in order to reach the point of indifference with the same market imperfection. Equilibrium between ex ante and ex post conditions is attained with a lower percentage of debt in the capital structure.

Traditionally, finance texts have indicated that the optimal range of leverage was higher for low risk companies than for high risk ones. The authors' approach to the leverage question indicates why the preceding statement is valid.

Earlier it was mentioned that firms are sometimes able to secure large amounts of debt at a constant rate of interest. These occurences appear to

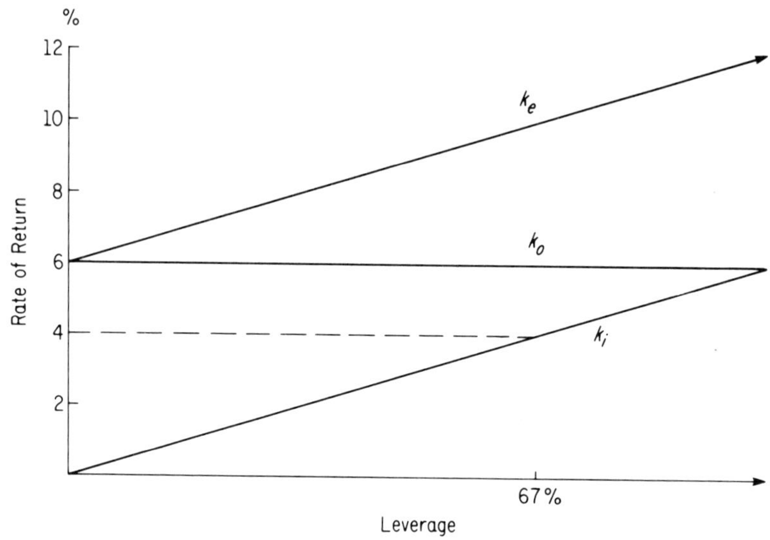

Fig. 7. The minimum acceptable degree of leverage in a low risk firm.

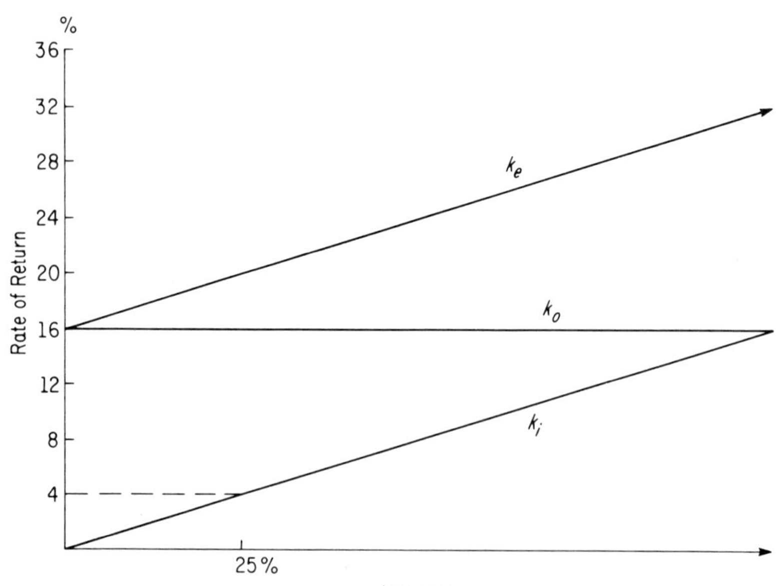

Fig. 8. The minimum acceptable degree of leverage in a high risk firm.

violate one of the assumptions of the model in that the rate of return demanded by debt suppliers remains constant as the percentage of debt in the capital structure increases.

There seem to be valid explanations for this seeming market imperfection. Chief among these would appear to be the effect of government regulations on the investment practices of some of the largest suppliers of debt capital. Whatever the explanation, equity interests are at an advantage whenever the real k_i lies below the theoretical k_i. This relationship is depicted in Fig. 9.

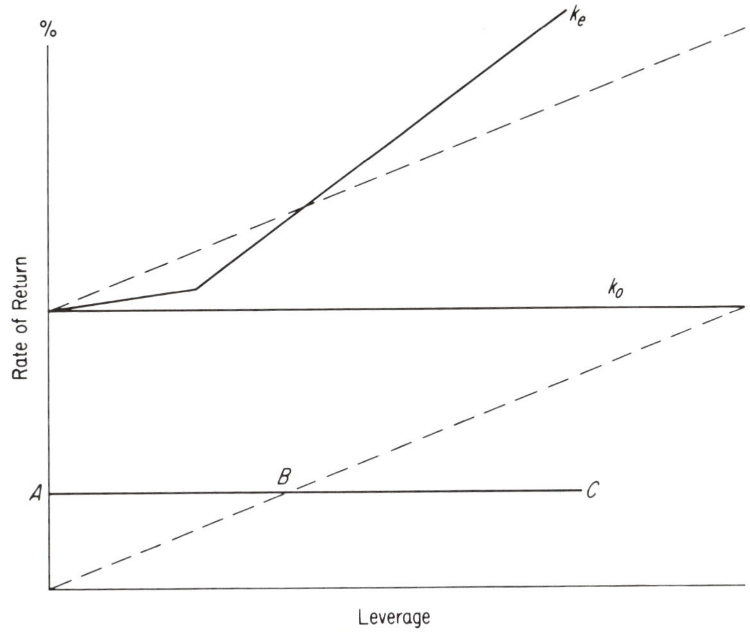

Fig. 9. Unfavorable, indifferent, and favorable ranges of leverage.

If any leverage is contemplated, equity interests have an incentive to extend it to at least point *B*. If both business and financial risk are considered then leverage at any level between point *A* and point *B* is less desirable than the point of zero leverage. However, if the firm is able to secure debt at rates that will intersect the k_i line and lie below it, as in line segment *B* - *C*, equity returns are greater than anticipated or demanded. The rate of return to equity will exceed the ex ante demands that were derived from a consideration of both business and financial risk. These returns will follow the pattern of the k_e line in Fig. 9.

CONCLUSIONS

The recent finance literature suggests that some confusion exists concerning the effect of a change in leverage on a firm's cost of capital. This paper has been an attempt to resolve some of the questions surrounding several aspects of this problem area. The model developed to examine the problem is normative. It deals with the rates of return that should be demanded by the suppliers of capital when confronted with different levels of risk.

In this approach the cost of capital would appear to be dependent on the investment decisions of the firm. Given the assumptions of the model, leverage does not affect a firm's cost of capital. In addition, it would seem that certain implications for financial management exist. From the point of view of equity interests, a minimum acceptable degree of leverage exists. This view contrasts with that of many authors of the traditional school who seem to conclude that the use of any amount of debt is beneficial to equity interests so long as the earnings realized through the use of debt capital exceed its cost. For example, Hoagland states that:

> . . . borrowing may be used as a device to increase earnings on stock whenever the cost of the loan is less than the amount it earns for the borrower.[9]

This same line of thought is suggested by Husband and Dockeray who state in discussing the use of leverage that:

> It is anticipated that there will be a differential between the rate of interest and the rate of earnings which would add further to the profits of the stockholders.[10]

Guthmann and Dougall also seem to convey the idea that leverage can be advantageous at any level in writing:

> The customary reason for trading on the equity is the hope of employing these "senior" funds at a rate of return higher than their cost in order to increase the return on investment of the residual owners.[11]

The model used in this paper suggests that, contrary to traditional thought, the utilization of debt in the generation of earnings that exceed the cost of this debt is not always advantageous to equity. Authors of the traditional school appear to have ignored the effect of increased financial risk on the suppliers of equity capital. From the point of view of equity interests there is a minimum acceptable degree of leverage. This amount of leverage is that necessary to force the real k_i line to coincide with the theoretical k_i line. If the real k_i lies above the theoretical k_i line as in line segment A - B shown in Fig. 9, the equity

[9]Henry E. Hoagland, *Corporation Finance* (3d ed.; New York: McGraw-Hill Book Company Inc., 1947), p. 170.

[10]William H. Husband and James C. Dockeray, *Modern Corporation Finance* (3d ed.; Homewood, Ill.: Richard D. Irwin, Inc., 1962), p. 216.

[11]Harry G. Guthmann and Herbert E. Dougall, *Corporate Financial Policy* (4th ed.; Englewood Cliffs, New Jersey: Prentice-Hall., 1955), p. 102.

interests are at a disadvantage relative to the zero leverage position. If the real k_i line intersects and lies below the theoretical k_i line, as in segment B - C in the same figure, the equity interests are at an advantage relative to their position at the point of zero leverage or at any point where the real k_i line coincides with the theoretical k_i line. From the point of view of equity interests, point C is the most advantageous position at which to maintain debt in this firm. The returns to equity are maximized at this point. It is recognized that in perfect capital markets debt capital at the rates shown by line segment B - C would not exist in the long run. When the real k_i line is below the theoretical k_i line, equity interests are receiving more return than anticipated or required.

This analysis suggests that given capital market imperfections, leverage, at worst, forces equity suppliers to a point of indifference as to the rate of return on their investment and, at best, proves very beneficial to them. If potential benefits to equity resulting from increasing leverage exist, one might wonder why the use of debt on the whole is relatively low. It seems apparent that very few firms possess leverage in the upper ranges discussed in this paper.

The authors find no theoretical or practical reason for attaining less than the maximum amount of leverage that capital markets will allow when the analysis is confined to the cost of capital. Since the empirical evidence indicates that these levels of leverage are not attained, further research seems indicated.

The reader may feel that the assumption of no taxes could explain some of the differences between the results of the model and reality. However, in a separate study, the authors relax this no tax assumption without changing the basic conclusions of this paper.

One factor in this seeming paradox is that management, not owners, makes the decisions concerning the amount of leverage the firm will possess. In many cases, it seems, management is more sensitive to risk at the higher levels of leverage than are owners. One apparent explanation for this is that for management the risks of increased leverage include the possible loss of salary as well as a lower return on investment on a portion of personal assets. In other words, conflicts arise in situations where there is a separation of ownership and management in that, while the decisions to increase leverage must be made by management, any increased returns accrue to the suppliers of equity capital.

The entire decision process might include factors of control which are important to management and at the same time do not seem to be important to the economics of the corporation. As suggested before, many decisions relating to leverage are not entirely economic. Perhaps a few of the decisions in this area are made on the basis of tradition alone. Therefore, it seems that any firm which does not carry leverage to the maximum levels discussed in this paper must justify its action on some basis other than the cost of capital or return to equity interests.

14

Premiums on Convertible Bonds*

Roman L. Weil, Jr.
Joel E. Segall
David Green, Jr.†

The conversion parity of a convertible bond is the product of the number of common shares for which the bond can be exchanged and the market price per share. Alternatively, the conversion parity of a particular convertible bond is the market value of the stock for which the convertible bond can be exchanged. The difference between the market price of the bond and its conversion parity is usually called the premium. In theory, the premium is the difference between the present values of the cash stream expected to accrue to convertible bondholders and the cash stream expected to accrue to the holders of the stock into which the bond is convertible. It is clear that such precise specification is, in the present state of knowledge, impossible. Indeed, recent papers on premiums do not pretend to attempt careful and complete specification, nor does this one. Rather, the objective of this study is to ascertain the degree to which observed premiums can be explained or predicted from obtainable data. This study explains about one-half of the variance in bond premiums.

Section I is a description of what appears to be the extant theory and a criticism of that theory on operational and theoretical grounds. Incorporated in Section I is a mathematical model which, though not currently testable, suggests some serious deficiencies in the extant theory. Section II describes the statistical tests employed to examine the theory and the results of these tests. Section III reports the conclusions.

I. THE DETERMINANTS OF THE PREMIUM

As we interpret the literature, the premium may be explained by the following factors.

*From *Journal of Finance,* Vol. 23, No. 3 (June 1968), pp. 445–463. Reprinted by permission of *Journal of Finance.*

†We thank David Duvel, Eugene Fama, Lawrence Fisher, Lester Lave, Richard Roll, and Hodson Thornber for comments, and the Ford Foundation which, through its grant to the Graduate School of Business of The University of Chicago, supported this research. An earlier version was presented to the Seminar on the Analysis of Securities Prices of the Center for Research in Security Prices (sponsored by Merrill Lynch, Pierce, Fenner and Smith, Inc.), May 11, 1967 at the University of Chicago.

1. *Transaction Costs.* Broker's commissions are lower on bonds than on stocks. The commission for a bond is $2.50; to buy equivalent stock, the commission is likely to be at least $15 and may, in principle, be arbitrarily high.[1] For example, if the bond is convertible into 100 shares of stock and has no premium, the investor who desires 100 shares of stock could save by buying the bond and converting it. The bond deserves a premium to reflect this saving.

2. *Income Differences.* The owner of a convertible bond (CB) is promised a specific interest stream and principal repayment, although he may expect something less than the promised stream. The owner of the equivalent stock is promised nothing but maintains some expectation about a dividend stream or increasing share prices. If the present value of expected bond income exceeds the present value of expected stock income, bonds should merit a premium on that account and vice versa. Negative premiums are, of course, limited by arbitrage possibilities which are discussed below.

3. *Financing Costs.* The Federal Reserve Board margin requirements currently permit borrowing of 30 per cent of the cost of a stock purchase while current banking practices allow borrowing of 70 to 90 per cent of the bond purchases. Kleine [1966] and Hershey [1966] argue that CB's deserve a premium for this additional borrowing capacity.

4. *Anti-dilution Clauses.* Kaplan [1965] points out that CB's do not have uniform anti-dilution clauses. Among the many ways in which the CB holders' interest may be diluted and his security cheapened are:

a. the sale of common stock below market price,
b. the payment of stock dividends (a particular form of (a) where the sale price is zero),
c. the distribution of "capital" in the form of large dividends or partially liquidating dividends, and
d. the issuance of options, rights, warrants, or other convertible securities.

To protect the bondholder, various anti-dilution clauses are usually provided. Kaplan reports a surprising variance in these provisions. All modern convertibles include provisions for stock splits and stock dividends above some small percentage, but the provisions for the more subtle forms of potential dilution vary greatly. Consequently, the premium should reflect the strength and coverage of the anti-dilution clause.

5. *Price Floors.* It is widely accepted that the CB has a safety feature which the equivalent stock does not have. The CB pays a relatively certain coupon and has a relatively certain value of $1000 at maturity. It has, therefore, a value as a bond which is in some measure independent of the value of the conversion

[1] As the price of the stock rises, the commission paid to buy the stock rises to a limit of $75 per hundred shares, but the number of shares obtainable from one bond may, because of stock splits, increase without limit. The commission paid to buy the bond remains a constant $2.50.

feature. If the stock price falls, the bond price may also fall but only to a price somewhat above the prices of nonconvertible bonds of similar quality. This minimum price is regarded as the *floor* for the CB. Since there is no such floor for the stock, the CB warrants a premium. The floor is the more valuable the closer it is to the bond price. The premium, then, should be inversely related to the difference between the floor and the bond price. Explicit consideration is not given to the quality of the bond since quality is largely summed up in the floor.

6. *Volatility of Price.* It has been alleged that the larger the variance in the price movements of the stock, the more valuable will be the conversion option on the bond; and the more valuable the conversion option, the greater will be the premium on the bond.[2] Also, the more volatile the price of the stock, the more likely is the bond floor to be reached, and the more relevant the floor, the higher will be the premium.

7. *Duration.* In general, the longer the life of an option the more valuable it must be. Therefore, the premium should be positively associated with time to maturity or expected time to call or, perhaps, expected time to dilution.[3] Some bonds may be exchanged for successively fewer shares of stock over time according to a schedule set forth in the indenture. For such bonds, duration must incorporate changes in the exchange ratio.

These seven variables are alleged to be important in the determination of premiums on convertible bonds; preliminary investigation, intuition, and convenience have persuaded us to disregard or at least defer consideration of four of these.

Financing costs seem quantitatively unimportant. Changes in margin requirements appear to have little impact on stock prices even though changes in margin requirements are associated with marked changes in the volume of stock market credit.[4] Apparently, substitute credit sources are readily available at small differences in cost. On statistical grounds, the financing cost variable is likely to be useless in predicting premiums. Assume that a trader may borrow 30 per cent of a stock purchase and 80 per cent of a bond purchase. The gross financing cost difference (*FCD*) will be:

$$FCD = B(.2\mathrm{I}_p + .8\mathrm{I}_m) - S(.7\mathrm{I}_p + .3\mathrm{I}_m) \qquad (1)$$

[2]Poensgen [1965/66] demonstrates that the value of the conversion option is an increasing function of the bond price variance. Poensgen's "value of the conversion option" is not identical with our premium, but his statement is the only one on this subject we can find in the scholarly literature.

[3]Brigham [1966] reports that 23 per cent of the firms in his sample follow a policy of encouraging conversion by increasing common stock dividends. We have described this policy earlier as dilution.

[4]See, e.g., Moore [1966].

where

B	is the cost of the convertible bond,
S	is the cost of the same amount of stock as can be obtained from converting the bond into stock,
I_p	is the cost of capital of the individual trader or the rate of interest he charges himself for money, and
I_m	is the interest rate the trader must pay his banker or broker to borrow.

Now define Δ so that $I_p = I_m + \Delta$; that is, Δ is the difference between the two interest rates. We expect that Δ is greater than zero for most individuals but the following analysis is independent of the sign of Δ. Substituting $I_m + \Delta$ for I_p in (1) we obtain

$$FCD = I_m(B - S) + \Delta(.2B - .7S)$$

or

$$FCD = (I_m + .2\Delta)(B - S) - .5\,\Delta S \tag{2}$$

At any time $(I_m + .2\Delta)$ is approximately the same for all stock-bond pairs.[5] Observe that the coefficient of $(I_m + .2\Delta)$ on the right-hand side of (2) is $B - S$, exactly the premium that we are concerned with. If Δ were zero, the *FCD* would be exactly proportional to the premium we wish to predict or explain. Even as Δ becomes different from zero, the *FCD* is by its definition almost proportional to the premium. In preliminary studies it was found that as Δ ranged from zero to .06, the simple correlation between *FCD* and the premium dropped only from 1. to .85. Since such a large component of the financing cost difference is proportional to the premium itself, it is unreasonable to hope to infer the impact of holding costs on the premium. The inclusion of a financing cost variable in a model to predict the premium guarantees excellent but uninteresting results. A different methodology or a different form of the variable might yield more reliable inferences about the significance of financing costs but a suitable methodology or form has not occurred to us.

Anti-dilution clauses also seem relatively unimportant in the determination of the premium. In a more formal analysis, the strength and coverage of these clauses would be incorporated in an expected income variable; indeed, some sources of dilution, e.g., stock dividends, are automatically captured in any sensible measure of income accruing to stockholders. Still, it could be helpful to

[5] At least one New York brokerage firm, Garvin Bantel and Co., charges different rates of interest depending upon the security. In the quotations we have seen, the spread between the largest and smallest rates is only .0075.

quantify the existence of anti-dilution clauses. Unfortunately, such quantification is costly and there is no *a priori* notion of either the correct form of the variable or, given the form, what a reasonable coefficient might be. Accordingly, anti-dilution clauses are not treated in this study.

The standard analysis of *price volatility* seems faulty; if it is correct to regard a stock price as the present value of some expected cash stream, and if the market is not indifferent to price volatility, an allowance for that volatility is incorporated in the stock price, presumably through the rate used to discount the cash stream. But if the bond price is influenced mainly by the stock price, then the bond price will also incorporate an allowance for volatility and there should be no additional premium on the bond. If the bond price is influenced mainly by the floor (i.e., the premium is very high), volatility can be very important since only a volatile stock will provide a large probability that the bond price will move above the floor. For bonds whose prices are close to the floor, the more valuable bonds will be those whose underlying stocks are the more volatile and, for such bonds, the premium will be positively associated with volatility. But bond prices can be well above the floor only because they reflect the value of the underlying stock. Such bond prices will already include the volatility allowance and there should be no association between the premium and volatility. For reasons to be explained in the Appendix, our sample consists only of bonds selling well above the floor and so volatility will not enter the analysis.

The possibility remains that volatility is important even for bonds selling well above the floor because volatility makes the floor more likely to be called into play. Preliminary tests (on data not reported in this article) involving a regression of the premium on the floor *and* a measure of volatility suggest that volatility is unimportant. Another preliminary test of the volatility notion is based on the same data used in this article.[6] For each of the 18 observation dates of Table 1 the premiums for the bonds in the sample data were ranked and for each bond in the data a measure of volatility of the underlying stock price was calculated. This measure is the coefficient of variation of stock price relatives over the last n months for n=3, 6, 12, 24, 60, and as many months back to January 1, 1926 as are available.[7] These measures were ranked and the

[6] A tabulation of the results of this test appears in Table 8, Report 6724 of the Center for Mathematical Studies in Business and Economics, Graduate School of Business, University of Chicago, Chicago, Illinois, 60637. Report 6724 is the study preliminary to this article and will be furnished free on request.

[7] The volatility index is constructed as in the following example for n = 6. Suppose the closing prices of the stock in the last six months were

100 120 80 100 75 100.

Then the price relatives (price at time t divided by price at time $t-1$) are

6/5 2/3 5/4 3/4 4/3

The mean price relative is 1.04. The standard deviation of the stock price relatives is about .277 and the coefficient of variation is about .277/1.04 or about .27.

Spearman rank correlation coefficient computed for the two sets of ranks, one on premiums measured both in dollars and as a percentage of bond price, and the other on volatility. There is no significant over-all relationship between volatility and premium and the volatility variable is not further considered.[8]

The *duration* of the conversion privilege seems of great importance, but little can be done in specifying the empirical counterpart. Ideally, duration would be measured by the length of time traders of CB's expect the privilege to last. Although the privilege expires with maturity or call or other forced or encouraged conversion, maturity dates and call provisions provide little information. All bonds in our sample were callable and all matured at least six years after the relevant dates—a longer period than is generally contemplated for the investor's horizon.[9] There is some information on the conversion policies of issuing firms,[10] but nothing that permits assigning a duration value to each of the CB's. For lack of an operational measure, the duration variable is omitted.

The concept of the *price floor* involves some theoretical difficulties which are discussed below, but is accepted by most writers as being of great importance in determining the premium. A preliminary test also suggests that a floor variable be included. Since the premium is expected to vary inversely with the difference between the bond floor and the bond price, and since the floor does not change equally with the bond price, the premium should vary inversely with the bond price. The correlation coefficient between the ranks of bond prices and the ranks of their premiums was −.60 in that preliminary test. The size of the premium was significantly inversely correlated with the bond price.[11]

Three variables remain with which to explain premiums on convertible bonds: transaction costs, income differences, and the floor. The omitted variables were omitted because empirical counterparts of reasonable form could not be found or because of theoretical inconsistencies; where possible, tests were employed to assess the wisdom of the omissions.

A less pragmatic, more rigorous approach to explaining premiums is possible, of course, and the following model is one example. The model is not readily testable, but does demonstrate what must be made operational before a more cohesive theory can be tested. The model treats the principal repayment feature of the bond as a component of the cash flow to the bondholder, but differentiates the principal from coupon payments and values the two separately. The model shows that the principal repayment is the equivalent of an option to sell.

Assume without loss of generality that the bond is convertible into one share of stock.

[8] We recognize a danger in this treatment. Volatility could be important once the other relevant variables are taken into account. The simple rank correlations are sufficiently unimpressive, though, to suggest that the danger is more apparent than real.

[9] Cf. Baumol, Malkiel and Quandt [1966].

[10] Cf. Brigham [1965].

[11] Data for this test are shown in Table 1, Report 6724, *op. cit.*

TABLE 1
Calculated Bond Premiums Where Stock Price Exceeds Conversion Price, Bimonthly, 1961–1963
(for $1000 bonds)

		1961						1962					1963						
		1/9	3/13	5/8	7/10	9/11	11/13	1/8	3/12	5/14	7/9	9/10	11/12	1/3	3/11	5/13	7/8	9/9	11/11
Aldens	5-80	112	44	14	−3	73	−6	*	−18	−18	57	119	64	56	*	20	101		129
Am Dist	4 3/8-86	–	–	–	–	11/1[i]	*	157											
Am Op	4.40-80			203	55	132	136	60	*	86	127		125	130	*	113	86	*	15
Ashland Oil	3 7/8-93	–	–	–	–	–	–	–	–	–	–	–	–	2/21[i]		107			
Atl Ref	4 1/2-87		160	121	126		137	120	135										
Avco	5-79	96	5	46	−38	−4	3	56	*	−28	−7	−7	−26	−10	37	−11	−35	*	25
Balt G & E	4 1/4-74	*	10	*	−23	−9	−27	−12	13	−12	14	6	−1	−22	4	*	−23	1	*
Boeing	4 1/2-80				195	155			149										
Bruns Corp	4 1/2-81	N	355	440	*	335	368												
Burroughs	4 1/2-81							208	166	152									
Chad Goth	5.90-71xw			29	*	41	60	*	35	−41	54	59							
Chad Goth	6-74xw			39	54	*	55	*	20	−71	*	*							
City Pdts.	5-82	–	–	6/14[i]														63	*
Comb Eng	3 3/8-81			106	53		109												
Cons Electro	4 1/2-84	38	17	*	13	34	23	154	200										
Crow Coll	5-83	–	–	–	–	–	–	–	–	–	–	–	–	–	5/13[i]	123	149	64	107
Det Ed	3 3/4-71	*	*	*	*	*	*	*	*	43	*	*	−44	−126	−39	*	*	*	*
Dow	3-82	14	2	−1	−4	−24	−7	20	26	5		119	55	43	*	4	44	12	32
Fan Stl	4 3/4-76	91	*	19	*	*	232												
Food Fair	4-79			*	*	*	77	37	128										
Gardner Denver	4 1/4-76	*	*	32	−27	−47	*	*	60	77	*	*	25	*	*	−28	*	7	−23
Gen Am Oil	4 3/4-84									93									
Gen Am Tr	4-81	10	*	*	*	*	*	*	*	*	*	−20	3	N	N	N	N	N	N
Gen T & Elec	4-71	3	−26	*	36	93	93	174	*	35	25	55	68	26	*	8	51	−11	−6
Gen T & Elec	4 1/2-77	19	−26	61	28	84	74	13	22	−4	43	87	74	41	6	22	57	−11	−2
Grace	3 1/2-75		81	14	23	−8	−1	23	8	*	−3	11	−3	−7	−8	−2	3	2	*
Grand Union	4 1/8-78		73	42	−18	*	32	37											
Gt West Fnl	5-74	47	*	*	*	−74	−4	−58	*	−88	60	122	171	196	135	*	97	148	*
Hal Xerox	4 1/2-81	–	5/8[i]			*	*	*	257	113	317	166	189	152	175	136	58	*	11/29[c]
Hunt Food	4 3/8-86	–	–	7/14[i]		54	44	135	193										
Int Min & Chem	3.65-77								121									*	76

Int Silver	5-81	–	–	–	7/3[i]		260	235	70	4	95	83	102	27	*	77	*	*	71
Int T & T	4 7/8-83	14	–16	57	–11	–40	16	–62	–34	–45	*	–63	142	–13	24	–15	*	–35	–26
Ints. Dept. Str	4 5/8-81	–	–	–	8/17[i]	148	8	23	–10	–26	60	142		126	108	61	66	13	24
Kayser Roth	5 1/2-80		49	41	3	39	18	42	43	–45		109	177	N	2/1[c]	–	–	–	–
Libby McN	5-76								113							*	87	112	52
Lionel	5 1/2-80		204	192															
Lock Air	3 3/4-80	56	13	*	–32	–51	*	*	11	–8	–24	*	4	6	–20	–12	–3	*	–11
Macy	5-77	*	–7	*	*	9	–38	7	–88	–23	*	–19	*	–26	*	–26	*	*	*
Metro Brd	6-75	*	*	*	*									160	*	–3	*	5	*
National Airlines	6-76	–	5/15[i]						200	70		*	73	14	8	–8	–13	–8	–18
Natl Tea	3 1/2-80	*	102	*	–5	–7	7	38	89										
Northrop	4-75	*	–2	*	6/19[c]	–	–	–	–	–	–	–	–	–	–	–	–	–	–
Northrop	5-79	71	73	33	12	61	3	*	25	27	10	34	–19	50	42	66	*	75	91
Ox Paper	4 3/4-78							144	178										
Pan Am Air	4 7/8-79															69	49	2	–1
Phillips	4 1/4-87	98	58	103	45	49	35	48	33	91						125	110	65	
Potomac El Pw.	3 3/4-73	–20	–45	*	*	–70	11/15[c]	–	–	–	–	–	–	–	–	–	–	–	–
Richfield Oil	4 3/8-83	55	54	3	21	23	53	55	48	79	115	81	103	76	34	30	51	3	38
Rohr	5 1/4-77		127	–38	–1	*	*	49	40	85									
Scott Paper	3-71	–11	–39	–26	16	–4	–27	–30	–6	–9	32	57	70	61	3	–3	5	–11	18
Smith Corona	5 1/4-79			147					*	*									
Spiegel	5-84	5	–27	13	7	134	158	124	149							160	164	175	
Sym Wayne	4 3/4-82	–	–	–	–	–	–	–	–	5/21[i]				124	145	*	81	86	51
Talcott	5-79	8	6	–40	*	–25	*	*	–40	*	*	*	35	*	*	*	*	*	*
Thom Ramo	4 7/8-82		203	*															
Union Oil	4 1/4-91	–	–	6/10[i]				168	186					165		115	64	*	–6
United Airl	4 7/8-85	*	187	48	62	172	203	201						204		128	7/29[c]	–	–
U.S. Freight	5-81	–	4/1[i]		173	93	124	121	79	49	*	142	129	37	24	–1	12	4	36
Vendo	4 1/2-80		280	179	285		335												

* No market transaction on observation date
N Not on Moody's List
Blank space when stock price below conversion price
[i] Issued
[c] Called
– Not outstanding

Sources: Moody's Bond Survey, "Convertible Bonds," various dates.

Let $f(p, t)$ be the probability that the stock has a price of p at time t;
$h(p, t)$ be the premium that the bond buyer must pay at time t when the stock price is p; at time t the stock costs p and the bond costs $p + h(p, t)$;[12]
P_0 be the price of the stock at time $t = 0$;
Y_S, Y_B be the income streams from the stock and the bond, respectively;
C_S, C_B be the transaction costs to buy the stock and the bond, respectively;
$PV(\cdot)$ be the present value operator.

The horizon for this derivation is T, the earlier of:

a) the time the bond matures or
b) the time the bond is called.[13]

For the moment, assume the bond is not called. The expected value at T of holding the convertible bond is represented by[14]

$$B_T = \int_0^{1000} 1000 f(p, T)\, dp + \int_{1000}^{\infty} pf(p, T)\, dp$$

where the first integral represents the value of the bond if the stock price is below \$1000 and the second integral represents the bond value for stock prices above \$1000.

$$= \int_0^{1000} 1000 f(p, T) dp + \int_0^{\infty} pf(p, T) dp - \int_0^{1000} pf(p, T) dp$$

$$= \int_0^{\infty} pf(p, T) dp + \int_0^{1000} (1000 - p) f(p, T) dp$$

The first integral above is just the value of the stock at T and the second integral is the value of an option to sell the stock for \$1000 at T. Thus we can write

[12] It is recognized (see, for example, Harbaugh [1963]) that the premium is dependent upon the time the bond matures as well as the price of the stock.

[13] We recognize that an individual bondholder may contemplate selling the bond before T, so that the individual bondholder's horizon may conceivably be shorter than T. The price at which he can sell, however, must reflect the expected price at T, properly discounted. Alternatively, the individual bondholder who contemplates owning a 10 year bond for one year considers the expected price at the end of one year to be highly relevant; but the expected price at the end of one year is in turn a function of the expected prices in the future up to ten years. It is possible, of course, that an individual bondholder can expect the price of the bond to rise during the first year and fall during the remaining years at a rate which more than covers transaction costs. It seems impossible, though, for the investment community to hold such an expectation and not have the expectation contradicted by market action designed to take advantage of the expectation.

[14] This analysis was first suggested to us by David Duvel in an unpublished manuscript.

$$B_T = E[\text{stock}] + E[\text{option}]$$

The bond buyer pays

$$P_0 + h(P_0, t_0) + C_B \tag{3}$$

and his expected present value from horizon T is

$$PV(E[\text{stock}] + E[\text{option}]) + PV(Y_B) \tag{4}$$

The stock buyer pays

$$P_0 + C_S \tag{5}$$

and his expected present value from horizon T is

$$PV(E[\text{stock}]) + PV(Y_S) \tag{6}$$

The difference between what the buyer of the stock and the buyer of the bond pays is (3) – (5) or

$$h(P_0, t_0) + C_B - C_S \tag{7}$$

and the difference between the expected present value of their wealth at T is

$$PV(E[\text{option}]) + PV(Y_B - Y_S) \tag{8}$$

Equating (7) and (8) we see that

$$h(P_0, t_0) = PV(E[\text{option}]) + PV(Y_B - Y_S) + (C_S - C_B)$$

Thus the premium the bond buyer expects to pay at any time is the present value of the difference in income streams plus the difference in transaction costs plus the present value of an option to sell the stock for \$1000 at maturity.[15]

II. ANALYSIS OF THE DATA

The data used in the tests, Table 1, include all observations that satisfy the requirements listed in the Appendix. The Appendix also discusses the reliability of the data.

The Equations

A general form of the equation employed is:

$$\frac{P}{B} = f(F) + \beta \frac{Y_d}{B} + \gamma \frac{T}{B} + \delta \frac{1}{B} \tag{9}$$

[15] When the possibility of call is allowed, this option becomes the present value of an option at the call price at time t multiplied by the probability of call t plus the probability of the bond's maturing multiplied by the value of the option for \$1000 at T.

where

P = calculated premium,

B = bond price,

F = floor variable; the difference between the bond price and the straight debt value of the bond as reported in the *Bond Survey*; the form of the floor variable is not yet specified,

Y_d = difference in current income streams; bond income (coupons) less stock income (dividends per share multiplied by number of shares into which the bond is convertible); the present value of the expected income difference over the expected life of the bond would be preferable, but for obvious reasons, the study uses current income difference,

T = transaction cost difference; cost to buy the stock into which the bond is convertible less cost to buy the bond including all transfer taxes.

To reduce the effect of measurement errors all variables are divided by the bond price. For any one bond-stock pair, this transformation is neutral, but when the transformation is applied to two or more the measurements are placed on the same basis.

The Form of the Floor Variable

The extant theory on the floor variable implies that the premium is inversely but nonlinearly related to the floor. That is, as the price of the bond rises above the straight debt value, the value of the floor declines[16] but the value of the floor declines less the higher the increase in the bond price. Thus, as a bond price rises from 1,000 to 1,250 the insurance value of the bond decreases more than when the bond price rises from 2,000 to 2,250 (the same absolute increase) or even to 2,500 (the same percentage increase).

This analysis suggests that the premium is a monotonically decreasing function of the floor variable. Our test of this suggestion was as follows: the observations of the floor variable were divided into 10 ranges, [0-10], (10-20], (20-30], (40-50], (50-75], (75-100], (100-150], (150-200], and (above 200)—the square bracket indicates inclusion of the end point of the range and the parenthesis indicates exclusion of the end point. Ten dummy variables were specified, one for each of the 10 ranges: the *i*th dummy variable for a given bond observation is set equal to 1 if the floor variable of that observation falls in the

[16]The floor probably increases as the value of the common stock increases since the debt-equity ratio declines with an increase in the value of the common stock. Alternatively, the floor increases with the value of the stock because the promised cash flow of the bond becomes more certain. The upper limit to the floor will be reached when the floor is sufficiently high to make the cash flow equivalent to the pure rate of interest. We shall ignore changes in the floor arising from changes in the value of the common stock.

ith range while all other dummy variables for that observation are set equal to zero. For example, if a bond with a straight debt value of 95 sells for 130, the floor variable is 35; thus the fourth dummy variable is set equal to 1 and all other dummy variables are set equal to zero. This standard technique is often used to test a variable which is hypothesized to affect a regression model in some unspecified nonlinear fashion. For the results of this test to be fruitful, R^2s as least as high as in the other tests, significant coefficients, and coefficients which decrease in some pattern over the 10 ranges are required. That is, we expect the coefficient of the first dummy floor variable [0-10] to be the largest, the coefficient of the last dummy variable (above 200) to be the smallest with a pattern of more or less decreasing coefficients in between to justify the hypothesis that the smaller the floor variable, the larger the premium on that account. The slight pattern of the floor dummy variables showed increases over the range, not decreases. Ideally, a complete nonlinear regression analysis on (9) is required to determine the best nonlinear function for $f(F)$, but aside from the analysis above, the investigation was initially confined to the following forms: $1/F^2$, B/F^2, B^2/F^2, $1/BF^2$. The form $1/BF^2$ gave the best initial results; therefore $1/BF^n$ was examined for n between 1.5 and 16. Since the best fit was obtained for n almost equal to 2, $f(F)$ was taken to be $1/BF^2$,[17] and the equation becomes

$$\frac{P}{B} = \frac{a}{BF^2} + \beta\frac{Y_d}{B} + \gamma\frac{T}{B} + \delta\frac{1}{B} \qquad (10)$$

Test 1. The data consist of 452 observations on the convertible bond prices for 18 different dates over the three-year period. The data were split into two sets using a random-number series. Then one-half of the data were used to find the coefficients of equation (10) and the other half of the data were tested using the coefficients previously estimated. If the theory is valid, then the estimate of the parameters α, β, γ and δ derived from part of the data would successfully predict the premiums on other bonds which were not included in the sample used to estimate the coefficients. Since the 18 sets of data represent 18 different dates and since market conditions in general are not constant, 18 constant terms were used, one for each month rather than one as indicated in equation (10). The first equation fitted was

$$\frac{P}{B} = \frac{a}{BF^2} + \beta\frac{Y_d}{B} + \gamma\frac{T}{B} + \frac{1}{B}\sum_{i=1}^{18}\delta_i m_i \qquad (11)$$

where m_i for each observation was equal to one if the observation were from the

[17]In the full study of all 18 sets of data we tried both the form B/F^2 and $1/F^2$ and found little difference in the results.

ith set and was equal to zero otherwise.[18] The results of this regression are shown in Table 2, column 1; R^2 was .57. After the coefficients were estimated, they were used to predict the premiums on the observations in the other, "held-out," sample and the quasi-R^2 was .36. As should be expected, the estimated coefficients did not perform as well on the test data as they did on the data from which they were derived, but they are clearly not useless. Observe from the t-values that all the coefficients except that for the floor are significantly different from zero. A similar regression was fitted omitting the floor variable:

$$\frac{P}{B} = \beta \frac{Y_d}{B} + \gamma \frac{T}{B} + \sum_{i=1}^{18} \frac{1}{B} \delta_i m_i \tag{12}$$

The results of this regression are shown in Table 2, column 3; again the estimated coefficients did not do as well in predicting the premiums for the test data as they did in predicting the premiums for the data from which they were derived but the results are as good on the test data as when the floor variable was included. Columns 2 and 4 of Table 2 are included to help delimit the power of the 18 dummy variables in equations (11) and (12). For the two regressions shown in these columns there is but one constant term for all bonds—no distinction is made between bonds of different periods. The R^2s are slightly worse but the predictive power of the coefficient is as good with one constant term as with 18 dummy variable constants.

The results of Test 1 are not particularly conclusive; we have been only moderately successful in predicting premiums in the test data.

Test 2. As a further test, the data were split into 18 sets, each set including all the observations for a given date, and equation (13) was fitted to each set.

$$\frac{P}{B} = \frac{a}{BF^2} + \beta \frac{Y_d}{B} + \gamma \frac{T}{B} + \delta \frac{1}{B} \tag{13}$$

Consider equation (13): if the extant theory is valid, the 18 α coefficients from the 18 regressions will be significant, and more or less the same; similarly, the 18 β coefficients and the 18 γ coefficients will be significant and more or less equal. The δ coefficients need not remain constant over all dates because of variable market conditions, in particular market rates of interest.

The results of fitting equation (13) to the 18 sets of observations are shown in Table 3 regression 1.

The Results

Income Differences. The extant theory does not explicitly predict the size

[18]The m_i, commonly called dummy variables, are in this context interpreted as constants for each month.

TABLE 2

Results of Regressions

1. $P/B = \alpha/BF^2 + \beta Y_d/B + \gamma T/B + 1/B \sum_{i=1}^{18} \delta_i M_i$

2. $P/B = \alpha/BF^2 + \beta Y_d/B + \gamma T/B + \delta/B$

3. $P/B = \beta Y_d/B + \gamma T/B + 1/B \sum_{i=1}^{18} \delta_i M_i$

4. $P/B = \beta Y_d/B + \gamma T/B + \delta/B$

Using One Half of Observations and the Resulting Coefficients to Predict the Other Half

Regression Coefficients (t-values)

	1. With Floor Variable	2. With Floor Variable	3. Without Floor Variable	4. Without Floor Variable
FLOOR (α)	589.89 (1.37)	269.22 (0.66)	....	....
YDIFF (β)	1.62 (8.77)	1.73 (9.43)	1.70 (9.56)	1.76 (10.01)
TRCDF (γ)	−6.84 (9.65)	−6.78 (9.58)	−7.11 (10.41)	−6.88 (10.00)
CONSTANT (δ)	....	12.80 (11.94)	....	13.15 (14.23)
MONTH 1 (δ_1)	8.52 (4.46)	....	9.38 (5.19)	....
" 2 •	14.27 (8.09)	....	14.83 (8.62)	....
" 3 •	9.79 (5.16)	....	10.60 (5.86)	....
" 4 •	11.06 (6.62)	....	11.72 (7.31)	....
" 5 •	10.57 (6.39)	....	11.24 (7.11)	....
" 6 •	15.90 (9.41)	....	16.46 (10.01)	....
" 7 •	12.45 (7.08)	....	13.27 (8.01)	....
" 8 •	15.47 (9.52)	....	16.09 (10.29)	....
" 9 •	11.05 (5.89)	....	12.29 (7.47)	....
" 10 •	13.16 (6.27)	....	14.17 (7.18)	....
" 11 •	15.47 (7.69)	....	16.49 (8.80)	....
" 12 (δ_{12})	15.49 (7.87)	....	16.27 (8.62)	....
" 13 •	14.72 (7.47)	....	15.45 (8.12)	....
" 14 •	11.66 (5.35)	....	12.48 (5.94)	....
" 15 •	12.03 (6.48)	....	12.91 (7.39)	....
" 16 •	13.09 (6.88)	....	14.03 (7.89)	....
" 17 •	11.51 (4.97)	....	12.91 (6.21)	....
" 18 (δ_{18})	11.55 (5.69)	....	12.30 (6.29)	....
First Half: R^2	.57	.50	.57	.50
Second Half: Quasi-R^2 (1-b/a where a is variance of P/B and b is residual variance)	.36	.37	.35	.36

TABLE 3
Results of Fitting Regressions

1. $P/B = \alpha/BF^2 + \beta Y_d/B + \gamma T/B + \delta/B$
2. $P/B = \qquad \beta Y_d/B + \gamma T/B + \delta/B$

Separately for each of the Observation Dates and Testing the Stability of the Coefficients Over Time

		1. With Floor					2. Without Floor					Degree of Freedom for F
Row	Observation Date	R^2	α (t)	β (t)	γ (t)	δ (t)	R^2	β (t)	γ (t)	δ (t)	F*	n_1/n_2
1.	1/16/61	.70	2570.	1.30	1.79	−1.04	.65	1.26	−.37	3.57	. . .	. . .
			(1.42)	(2.34)	(.74)	(.26)		(2.18)	(.18)	(1.46)		
2.	3/20/61	.69	2164.	2.54	−3.94	7.64	.67	2.50	−5.51	11.18	2.07	3/44
			(1.35)	(3.54)	(1.27)	(1.68)		(3.43)	(1.88)	(2.95)		
3.	5/15/61	.59	130.	1.98	−8.00	13.48	.59	2.00	−7.99	13.54	1.25	6/71
			(.04)	(2.41)	(2.85)	(3.59)		(2.77)	(2.92)	(3.85)		
4.	7/17/61	.52	2763.	1.61	−5.81	7.94	.50	1.72	−6.22	10.18	.98	9/99
			(1.08)	(2.32)	(2.56)	(2.23)		(2.47)	(2.77)	(3.50)		
5.	9/18/61	.55	−2267.	2.01	−6.04	12.03	.54	1.85	−5.47	10.14	.75	12/129
			(.83)	(2.83)	(2.53)	(3.15)		(2.72)	(2.41)	(3.34)		
6.	11/20/61	.62	1116.	2.08	−7.62	14.73	.62	2.06	−8.16	16.32	.92	15/162
			(.64)	(2.53)	(2.70)	(3.41)		(2.53)	(3.06)	(4.69)		
7.	1/15/62	.73	−125.	1.86	−6.15	14.01	.73	1.88	−6.07	13.77	.94	18/192
			(.10)	(2.07)	(2.20)	(3.25)		(2.21)	(2.32)	(4.04)		
8.	3/19/62	.86	776.	2.20	−9.28	16.57	.85	2.22	−9.83	17.90	1.10	21/227
			(.87)	(5.41)	(5.72)	(6.78)		(5.49)	(6.59)	(9.45)		
9.	5/21/62	.65	854.	.54	−7.17	11.32	.63	.62	−8.19	13.86	1.42	24/255
			(1.11)	(1.33)	(3.92)	(3.54)		(1.54)	(5.16)	(6.16)		
10.	7/16/62	.85	−757.	1.97	−9.85	18.63	.85	1.92	−9.75	17.57	1.35	27/271
			(.44)	(3.74)	(5.03)	(5.03)		(3.85)	(5.18)	(6.47)		
11.	9/17/62	.84	−467.	1.93	−6.22	14.75	.84	1.84	−6.26	14.45	1.36	30/291
			(.29)	(3.44)	(3.38)	(5.22)		(3.98)	(3.51)	(5.66)		
12.	11/19/62	.82	2244.	1.97	−3.26	8.06	.80	1.99	−4.56	11.88	1.35	33/314
			(1.58)	(4.33)	(1.44)	(2.16)		(4.20)	(2.09)	(4.02)		
13.	1/21/63	.88	4839.	1.67	−5.07	8.99	.83	1.97	−6.97	15.13	1.34	36/339
			(2.98)	(4.08)	(2.84)	(2.83)		(4.29)	(3.59)	(5.38)		
14.	3/18/63	.71	3819.	1.24	−2.70	5.40	.65	1.19	−4.66	11.31	1.30	39/355
			(1.52)	(2.18)	(.92)	(.95)		(2.00)	(1.69)	(2.59)		
15.	5/20/63	.85	3637.	1.13	−4.60	7.98	.77	1.09	−7.26	14.38	1.28	42/382
			(3.46)	(3.11)	(2.88)	(3.01)		(2.49)	(4.28)	(6.24)		
16.	7/15/63	.79	1893.	.60	−2.81	7.53	.73	.88	−3.86	10.73	1.27	45/405
			(2.18)	(1.35)	(1.50)	(2.64)		(1.93)	(1.97)	(4.02)		
17.	9/16/63	.63	1185.	.61	−2.24	5.72	.56	1.16	−4.77	10.52	1.23	48/427
			(1.74)	(.99)	(.72)	(1.21)		(2.13)	(1.65)	(2.61)		
18.	11/18/63	.62	1091.	.47	−1.37	4.75	.59	.80	−1.38	5.66	1.30	51/449
			(1.17)	(.90)	(.81)	(1.83)		(1.82)	(.80)	(2.27)		

*Null hypothesis for F shown on row i: $\beta_1 = \beta_2 = \ldots = \beta_i$ $\gamma_1 = \gamma_2 = \ldots = \gamma_i$, and $\delta_1 = \delta_2 = \ldots = \delta_i$. The numbers in this column show that none of the seventeen null hypotheses can be rejected.

of the coefficients but some reasonable guesses can be made. The coefficient of the income difference should be positive, a number equal to the present value at some appropriate discount rate of an uncertain annuity of $1 to be received for as long as the bond is held. A coefficient within the range, say, 1 to 10 would not be surprising. The actual coefficients, ranging from 1.6 to 1.8, are on the low side of our range.

Transaction Costs. The sign of the coefficient of the transaction cost difference is hypothesized positive since it costs more to buy the stock than the bond.[19] One hypothesis is that the coefficient of the transaction cost difference should be nearly +1, reflecting an expectation of buying the bond, later converting it to stock, and then selling the stock so that the transaction cost difference is realized exactly once. A coefficient between 1 and 2 would be a

[19]The transaction cost difference variable is measured as the cost of buying the stock minus the cost of buying the bond. This variable is positive and the larger it is, the greater the advantage of buying the bond.

reflection of the reasonable possibility of sometimes once realizing the difference and sometimes twice. In both tests the coefficient of the transaction cost difference is not even close to its "reasonable" value; indeed, the sign is negative.[20] One seemingly relevant aspect of the transaction cost difference is not, to our knowledge, discussed in the literature: the spread between bid and asked prices for both the bond and the stock. Since the trader buys at approximately the bid and sells at approximately the asked, the greater the spread the greater the transaction cost. The spreads on the bonds and the underlying stocks were computed for the 17 bonds for which quotations were available from market data[21] on November 11, 1963. The difference between the stock spread and the bond spread was divided by two to approximate a one-way (either purchase *or* sale) trading cost and so make the spread component of the transaction cost consistent with the commission and taxes component of the transaction cost. The spread component was added to the transaction cost as previously defined to form a new transaction cost variable and the regression was recomputed for the 17 bonds. If the spreads were useful in explaining the premium, the coefficient of the redefined transaction cost variable would conform more closely to what a "reasonable" coefficient might be and R^2 would not fall. The coefficient does become more "reasonable," 1.14 as compared to –3.11 for the old transaction cost variable, but the t-value was such that the coefficient is not significantly different from zero; coefficients of other variables are reduced in significance, and R^2 drops from .69 to .63. The addition of the spread adds nothing to the explanation of the premium.

The Floor Variable. As noted under Test 1, the floor variable adds little to the results obtained. In Test 2, with three exceptions, the coefficients of the floor variable are not significantly different from zero.[22] Sixteen of the other fifty-four coefficients are not significantly different from zero. When the floor variable is omitted, however, the results shown in Table 3 regression 2, are very much more encouraging. The R^2s are only slightly smaller than in the regression

[20]As discussed below, the floor variable really adds nothing to the regression. It is empirically demonstrable and theoretically understandable that there is a strong inverse relation between the actual price of the bond and the size of the premium. As bond price gets higher, the premium gets lower. As bond price gets higher, the transaction cost savings get larger. The negative coefficient on the transaction cost variable may indicate only that the higher the bond price the lower the premium.

[21]The data came from Francis Emory Fitch, Inc., *Stock Quotations on the New York Stock Exchange* and *Bond Quotations on the New York Stock Exchange*. The stock quotations are reported at 11:30 A.M. and the bond quotations at 11:00 A.M.

[22]One should not be misled by the magnitudes of the coefficients for the floor variable. Although these coefficients are sometimes 1000 times as large as the coefficient of the income difference variable, the coefficient of the income difference variable can be significantly different from zero while the coefficient of the floor variable is not. The "*t*-value" is used to test the significance of a coefficient. Each coefficient in our results is shown with its *t*-value. Unless that *t*-value is as large as or larger than 2, the associated coefficient is not significantly different from zero. By reference to standard statistical tables of *t*-values, the reader can ascertain the exact size the *t*-value must exceed in order for the associated coefficient to be different from zero for a given significance level.

with the floor variable and of the fifty-four coefficients, only ten are not significantly different from zero. Furthermore, when the null hypotheses that all β γ and δ for all the observation dates up to and including a given date are equal, the hypotheses cannot be rejected.[23]

III. CONCLUSIONS

It seems clear that our tests do not strongly support our interpretation of the received theory of the premium on CB's. This result could arise because of the nonsimultaneous transactions from which the data are gathered (see Appendix), from insufficiently refined tests, from a mistaken interpretation of the theory, from a faulty theory, or from some combination. The main finding of the paper is that the floor is of negligible importance in explaining the premium. Yet, the most commonly accepted source of the premium is the price floor. Brigham [1966], for example asserts

> . . . the convertible bond usually commands a premium over its conversion value because, by holding convertibles, an investor is able to reduce his risk exposure. To illustrate, suppose a particular bond is convertible into 20 shares of stock with a market price of \$70, giving a conversion value of \$1,400. If the stock market turns sharply down and the stock price falls to \$35 per share, a stock investor suffers a 50 per cent loss in value. Had he held a convertible bond, its price would have fallen from \$1,400 to the bond value floor. . . which is probably well above \$700. Hence, holding the convertible entails less risk than holding common stock, and this causes convertibles to sell at a premium above their conversion value.

Similarly, Baumol, Malkiel, and Quandt [1966] observe

> But our security holder also knows (assuming he has not actually converted his security in the interim) that if it turns out that his forecast was mistaken and that stock price has in fact fallen sharply, he has the option of disposing of a security whose market price will be largely governed by its value as a bond rather than a stock. Thus the "bond value" of the convertible may provide a cushion limiting the risk assumed by the convertible holder vis-a-vis the outright owner of common share. Consequently, the determination of the value of a

[23] There are exactly 17 different null hypotheses tested in Table 7 for regression 2. For example, the fourth null hypothesis is that

$$\beta_1 = \beta_2 = \beta_3 = \beta_4 = \beta_5$$
$$\gamma_1 = \gamma_2 = \gamma_3 = \gamma_4 = \gamma_5$$
$$\delta_1 = \delta_2 = \delta_3 = \delta_4 = \delta_5$$

where β_i γ_i δ_i, are the coefficients in the ith row of the table. None of the seventeen null hypotheses is rejected by the F test. If only the β_S and γ_S are simultaneously tested for equality, the F's are even smaller; most in fact are less than one. (In general, the smaller the F's, the more likely is the null hypothesis.) The F tests are not shown for regression 1 in Table 3 because they are irrelevant in view of the unimportance of the floor variable.

> convertible comes down to the analysis of the values of these two components—the expected value of the security and the insurance value of the convertibility feature.

Both papers recognize that the higher the price of the bond, the less important is the floor since the higher the price the lower is the likelihood of a fall to the floor. But even so, the importance of the floor is exaggerated. The owner of one $1,400 bond convertible into 20 shares of stock now selling at $70 has a floor of, say, $1,000 and the owner of 20 shares of stock worth $1,400 does not; but establishing an identical floor for the stockholder is easy and the cost seems trivial. A stop-sell order at $50 for 20 shares is an obvious device.[24] It is true that stop-sell orders are sometimes not executed at the trigger price, but then the cost of the floor per share becomes only the difference between the stop-sell trigger price and the price at which the order is finally executed plus commissions and the other transactions costs—all multiplied by the probability of a price fall to $50 and the probability of the market price going through the stop-sell price.[25] A second way for the stockholder to establish a floor for himself might be the purchase of a put for 20 shares at $50 of the same duration as the conversion privilege. Such an option could be costly, but it also conveys more possibilities for gain to the purchaser than does the simple floor. We think it appropriate, then, to regard the owner of one $1,400 convertible bond as standing in the same position vis-a-vis the floor as the owner of 20 shares of stock with a stop order at the straight-debt value.[26] Since a stop order is cheap, the floor should play little role in determining the premium.

Indeed, the notion of a floor for the bond may be entirely without merit even when the price of the stock is less than its conversion price. Suppose the price of the stock in our example were $40 and the price of the bond $1,000. A bondholder has little or no downside risk, but will gain from an increase in the price of the stock. Now consider the owner of $1,000 worth of stock (25 shares) with a stop-loss order at, say, $39.50. He, too, has little downside risk and will gain even more than the bondholder from an increase in the price of the stock. It seems to us that a convertible bond is almost completely described as a claim to a fixed and relatively certain cash stream plus an option to exchange that claim for another claim to a variable and relatively uncertain cash stream. There is no place in this description for a floor any larger than the expected cost of executing a stop-sell order. The determination of the premium depends, we suggest, entirely on the differences in the expected cash streams, but the calculation of the expected cash streams is the whole problem of security evaluation.

[24] We are indebted to Eugene F. Fama for his suggestions in this area.

[25] To make the stock plus a stop-sell order even more like the bond, a buy order for the bond may be entered for execution simultaneous with the stop-sell execution.

[26] *More precisely, if* S is the straight-debt value and N the number of shares into which a bond is convertible, the stop order should be placed at S/N.

APPENDIX: THE DATA AND RELATED PROBLEMS

The data of Table 1 were employed in our tests. These data include all New York Stock Exchange *CB's* that

a. are listed in the odd-numbered months, 1961-1963, in *Moody's Bond Survey*, "Convertible Bonds,"

b. have actual transaction prices rather than bid prices shown in the *Bond Survey*,

c. do not require additional cash payments to convert the bond,[27] and

d. have a conversion value (market value of the stock into which the bond is convertible) greater than par.

The last criterion, d, requires further explanation. Typically, publicly sold CB's are offered at about par, the conversion ratios set so that the conversion value is less than par value at time of issue, and the coupon rate is lower than the yield on nonconvertible debt issues of similar quality.[28] This set of circumstances implies a trade-off between the ratio of conversion value to par and the ratio of nonconvertible yields to CB coupon rates. The actual ratios are said to be determined in light of market preferences for the relatively certain interest income and the relatively less certain capital gain. The burden of this exposition is that the premiums on many CB's will be determined primarily by the terms of issue, most notably the issuer's choice of trade-off between coupon rate and conversion value. If the market value rises above par, however, the analysis ceases to be valid; the premium will be less sensitive to the terms of issue and more sensitive to the intrinsic differences between the asset forms. We may put this issue differently: a cross-section of *all* CB's will include many CB's whose premiums are large and whose premiums differ mainly because of differences in issuing terms; if the cross-section includes only those CB's whose conversion value exceeds par, premiums will tend to be smaller and the impact of the happenstance of issue terms will be reduced; hence, criterion d.

Ideally, the data employed for this study should be derived from simultaneous bond and stock transactions. The prices shown in the *Bond Survey* are closing prices and are not likely to be simultaneous. Table 4 shows the import of this problem. The premiums as calculated from the *Bond Survey* data of February 11, 1963 are shown next to premiums calculated in the following way: for each of the twenty bonds for which data are available we look at transaction prices quoted in the *Wall Street Journal* for the 5 business days preceding February 11 and for the 5 business days following February 11; we pick the one

[27] Bladen [1966] points out that securities such as the United Air Lines 4s of 1990, which require an additional cash payment to convert, provide the bondholder with an advantage in the form of an interest-free loan and a reduced likelihood of a margin call. This kind of convertible bond carries an additional premium, Bladen says, because of its added attractiveness and is, therefore excluded from our sample. During the time from which our data are gathered, there were less than six such bonds.

[28] Cf. Brigham, [1965].

TABLE 4

Comparison of the Feb. 11, 1963, Calculated Premiums with those Calculated from the Near Date with Minimum Stock Price Fluctuation

	Premiums in Dollars		Premiums as Per Cent of Closing Bond Price	
	Near Date	Feb. 11	Near Date	Feb. 11
Balt G & E	− 10	12	− .67	.82
Int T & T	6	21	.24	.85
Natl Airlines	8	19	.48	1.19
Scott Paper	14	14	1.09	1.09
Intl Silver	17	9	1.19	.62
Richfield Oil	46	58	3.61	4.53
Gen T & Elec 4-1/2	47	23	3.01	1.45
Avco	49	59	2.25	2.76
Northrop	56	48	4.41	3.76
Gen T & Elec 4	58	38	3.75	2.43
Dow	68	71	5.13	5.36
Aldens	75	28	5.60	2.12
U.S. Freight	85	93	6.25	6.90
Int Dep Str	98	150	8.28	12.50
Hal Xerox	120	113	7.50	7.24
Sym Wayne	120	125	10.43	10.68
Nopco	134	134	11.45	11.45
Union Oil	154	172	13.29	14.62
Metro Bdcast	165	155	12.22	11.57
Gt West Fnl	187	120	13.17	8.76
	1497	1462		
Rank correlation coefficient	.902		.925	

day when the price range over which the stock traded is the smallest; we calculate the premium for the bond from the prices quoted on that day and call it the "Near Date" premium. "Near Date" premiums are less sensitive to the simultaneity problem and are more accurate estimates of the true premium, although the "Near Date" premiums are not necessarily calculated from transactions closer together in time. The differences in calculated premiums suggest the extent of the unreliability of our basic data. Since we have only a rough estimate of the "true" premiums we can not expect a highly satisfactory statistical explanation.

Some negative premiums may be noted in Table 2. A negative premium implies the existence of an arbitrage possibility: the investor could buy the bond, sell short the underlying stock, and then convert the bond to stock in order to cover the short sale. The negative premiums in the data are anomalies reflecting either nonsimultaneous transactions or transaction costs too large to warrant the arbitrage operation. Floor traders, of course, pay no commissions and could be expected to exploit arbitrage opportunities that are unprofitable for the outside buyer. At least some of the negative premiums result from observation error.

REFERENCES

1. W. J. Baumol, B. G. Malkiel, and R.E. Quandt. "The Valuation of Convertible Securities," *Quarterly Journal of Economics,* LXXX, No. 1 (February 1966), 48-59.
2. Ashby Bladen. "Time to Buy?" *Barron's* (October 10, 1966), 9ff.
3. Eugene F. Brigham. "An Analysis of Convertible Debentures: Theory and Some Empirical Evidence," *Journal of Finance,* XXI, No. 1 (March 1966), 35-54.
4. Allan W. Harbaugh. "Operations Research in the Stock Market." El Segundo, Calif.: Computer Sciences Corporation (650 N. Sepulveda Blvd.), 1963. (Multilith.)
5. Robert D. Hershey. "Bond Men Start Hunting," *New York Times* (August 21, 1966), Section F, p. 1.
6. Stanley A. Kaplan. "Piercing the Corporate Boilerplate: Antidilution Clauses in Convertible Securities," *University of Chicago Law Review,* XXXIII, No. 1 (Autumn 1965), 1-30.
7. Alexander E. Kleine. "Address to the Illinois Society of Certified Public Accountants," June 30, 1966. (Distributed by Harris, Upham and Company, Chicago.)
8. Thomas Gale Moore. "Stock Market Margin Requirements," *Journal of Political Economy,* LXXIV, No. 2 (April 1966), 158-167.
9. Otto H. Poensgen. "The Valuation of Convertible Bonds," *Industrial Management Review,* VII, No. 1 (Fall 1965), 77-92, and *ibid.,* No. 2 (Spring 1966). 83-98.

15

Impact of Merger Accounting on Post-Merger Financial Reports*

A. N. Mosich

Corporate mergers are a frequent and important occurrence in the modern business era. The competitive advantages and other economic benefits to be achieved from mergers have been given wide attention. Considerably less light has been shed, however, on the potentially dramatic impact on the post-merger financial condition and earnings of companies involved in mergers.

The accounting method used to record a merger has no current effect on the economic position of the merged units. It can, however, have an immediate and significant effect on the financial reports following the merger. Consequently, the accounting method used has a very important and direct bearing on the future financial direction of the enterprise.

When the merger is treated as a purchase, acquired assets are recorded at the purchase price and there is no transfer of the acquired corporation's retained earnings to the surviving company's balance sheet. Under the pooling method, by way of comparison, the acquired company's assets and retained earnings are generally transferred to the records of the acquiring unit at the acquired company's book value. Since the valuation of acquired assets usually has a material effect on future earnings and financial ratios, this distinction (how to value the acquired assets) between accounting methods for mergers is a very basic and important factor in making the decision to use purchase or pooling accounting.

CHOICE BETWEEN PURCHASE AND POOLING ACCOUNTING

According to the definitions of the applicable accounting methods, the circumstances surrounding a particular merger transaction govern the choice of merger accounting method. Presumably, the proper method will be clearly determined by the pertinent facts. However, the choice is generally not that clear. In many merger situations, management may select either method, and the accountant's responsibility is to assist in the selection by recommending the

*From *Management Accounting,* Section 1, Vol. 47, No. 4 (December 1965), pp. 21–28. Reprinted by permission of *Management Accounting.*

method which will best serve both the immediate and the long-range interest of all concerned.

Application of the alternate methods to a fictitious Akquirer Corp.-Zeller, Inc. merger will serve to illustrate the extent to which the resultant reports of a company's financial condition will differ. The pertinent financial data for both companies just prior to their merger on January 1, 1965, are shown in Exhibit 1.

EXHIBIT 1

Pre-merger Financial Data

	Akquirer Corp.	Zeller, Inc.
Cash and receivables	$ 7,000,000	$ 1,250,000
Inventory (LIFO basis)	8,000,000	2,000,000
Equipment (net) remaining life, 10 years	5,000,000	1,750,000
	$20,000,000	$ 5,000,000
Current liabilities	$ 5,000,000	$ 1,000,000
Equipment purchase contracts	2,000,000	500,000
Capital stock, $10 par	5,000,000	1,000,000
Premium on capital stock	—	500,000
Retained earnings	8,000,000	2,000,000
	$20,000,000	$ 5,000,000
Shares outstanding prior to merger	500,000	100,000
Total earnings for 1964	$ 2,000,000	$ 500,000
Earnings per share for 1964	$4.00	$5.00
Sales for 1964	$15,000,000	$10,000,000
Market value per share December 1964	$60.00	$150.00
Price-earnings ratio December 1964	15 times	30 times
Book value per share December 1964	$26.00	$35.00

The terms of the hypothetical merger call for Akquirer Corp. to issue 250,000 shares of its common stock to the shareholders of Zeller, Inc., in exchange for their Zeller stock. The total value of the stock to be issued by Akquirer is $15 million, based upon an evaluation of the Zeller's assets as follows:

Cash and receivables	$1,200,000
Inventory	3,250,000
Equipment (net), remaining life—ten years	4,250,000
Patents and goodwill, estimated remaining life—ten years	7,800,000
Less liabilities assumed by Akquirer Corp.	(1,500,000)
Total value of assets acquired	$15,000,000

Since the Akquirer-Zeller merger could probably be treated as either a purchase or a pooling of interests, Exhibit 2 shows both the entries which

Akquirer Corp. would make under each method and the respective post-merger balance sheets. The significant differences will be covered in ensuing discussion of analyses considered in choosing between the two methods.

EXHIBIT 2

Alternative Entries for Merger
(000's Omitted)

	As Purchase		As Pooling	
	Debit	Credit	Debit	Credit
Cash and receivables	$1,200		$1,250	
Inventory	3,250		2,000	
Equipment (net)	4,250		1,750	
Patents and goodwill	7,800		—	
Current liabilities		$ 1,000		$1,000
Equipment purchase contracts		500		500
Capital stock, $10 par		2,500		2,500
Premium on capital stock		12,500		—
Retained earnings		—		1,000

Post-merger Balance Sheets
(000's Omitted)

Assets	As Purchase	As Pooling
Cash and receivables	$ 8,200	$ 8,250
Inventory	11,250	10,000
Equipment (net)	9,250	6,750
Patents and goodwill	7,800	—
	$36,500	$25,000
Liabilities and Capital		
Current liabilities	$ 6,000	$ 6,000
Equipment purchase contracts	2,500	2,500
Capital stock, $10 par	7,500	7,500
Premium on capital stock	12,500	—
Retained earnings	8,000	9,000
	$36,500	$25,000

EFFECTS OF THE CHOICE ANALYZED

Exhibit 3 has been prepared to reflect financial data, ratios and earnings rates after the merger. The information in this exhibit will be referred to a number of times in subsequent paragraphs.

Pooling. Zeller's assets are recorded at historical costs less accumulated depreciation, and Akquirer's postmerger balance sheet shows the addition of $3,500,000 in stockholders' equity, that being equal to the total amount of the Zeller shareholders' equity. Therefore, under the pooling method, the future financial performance of the corporation will be directly comparable to the combined past records of the two merged companies.

Purchase. When, as in this case, the price paid for the acquired company exceeds the book value of its assets, the acquiring corporation can apportion the

EXHIBIT 3

Financial Data After Merger

	As Purchase	As Pooling
Total assets	$36,500,000	$25,000,000
Total stockholders' equity	28,000,000	16,500,000
Current assets	19,450,000	18,250,000
Current liabilities	6,000,000	6,000,000
Net working capital	13,450,000	12,250,000
Current ratio	3.2 to 1	3.0 to 1
Total liabilities as percentage of assets	23.3%	34.0%
Book value per share	$37.33	$22.00
Ratio of equipment to equipment contract payable	3.7 to 1	2.7 to 1
Projected earnings per share for 1965	$2.28	$3.65
Projected cash flow per share for 1965	$4.55	$4.55
Projected earnings rate on sales	6.84%	10.96%
Projected rated earned on beginning assets	4.68%	10.96%
Projected rate earned on beginning stockholders' equity	6.11%	16.61%
Price of Akquirer Corp. stock at end of 1965 if price-earnings ratio remains at 15 times earnings	$34.20	$54.75

purchase price on the basis of appraised values, and, by use of the purchase method, record the acquired assets at "actual cost." Upon inspecting the post-merger balance sheet on Exhibit 2, some obvious results are the increases in stockholders' equity and in the ratio of assets to liabilities. Equally significant will be the increased reported cost of doing business because of the additional depreciation on equipment and the amortization of patents and goodwill. Those favoring this method of recording the merger will reason, at least in part, that Akquirer Corp. has thus committed itself to reporting future operating results on the basis of the true value of the acquired assets.

COMPARATIVE EFFECTS ON FUTURE FINANCIAL PERFORMANCE

Effect on Earnings

The probable effect of the alternate methods of recording the merger must be based on certain assumptions. First, it can be expected that annual sales volume of the new company will not show any immediate increase over the $25 million pre-merger volume of the two constituent companies. It is also to be expected that the merger will result in some cost reduction due to consolidation of certain functions. Based on these probabilities, the effect of the two accounting methods on earnings in the first year following the merger can be projected as shown in Exhibit 4.

EXHIBIT 4

Post-merger Projection of Earnings

	Earnings (000 Omitted) Pooling	Purchase	Shares	Earnings per Share
A-Z Combined				
Pre-merger earnings	$2,500	$2,500	750M	$3.33
Cost (increase) or decrease, 1965				
A. Cost savings by consolidation	$ 240	$ 240		
B. Depreciation of increment in equipment	—	(250)		
C. Amortization of goodwill and patents	—	(780)		
Net cost difference	$ 240	$ (790)*		
A-Z earnings, 1965:				
Pooling	$2,740			$3.65
Purchase		$1,710		$2.28

*NOTE: The revaluation of inventories, shown in Exhibit 2, had no effect on 1965 earnings because inventory consumption is valued by the LIFO method, and the inventories did not drop below 1964 year-end levels.

The issuance by Akquirer Corp. of 250,000 new shares of stock, while adding Zeller's contribution to profit of only $500,000 ($2 per share), has diluted the $4 per share earning rate of pre-merger Akquirer to $3.33 per share, and it is to this rate that the comparative effects on earnings must be related.

Under the purchase method, the cost reduction produced by consolidation is far less than the added cost of amortizing the increment in asset values, and the result is a reduction in reported earnings to $1,710,000, or $2.28 per share. Compared to this, the pooling method produces earnings of $3.65 per share, which is almost ten percent above the prior year's combined rate of $3.33. Such a difference in projected post-merger earnings is obviously a strong inducement to management to choose the pooling method of recording a merger.

Effect on Cash Flow and Rate of Return

The cash flow, defined for this purpose as net income after adding back noncash expenses, would be the same in each case because the additional charges to income using purchase accounting are noncash deductions.

Since reported earnings are lower and total assets and stockholders' equity are higher using purchase accounting, the internal rates of return on sales, assets, and stockholders' equity are substantialy lower, as can be noted from an analysis of data in Exhibit 3. The rate earned on stockholders' equity, for example, is 16.6% if pooling is used, and only 6.1% when purchasing is used. These factors can have significant meaning to the investor and affect the future market value of stock.

The rate of return on investment, when pooling is used, is inflated because the pooling method does not reflect amortization of the excess of the market value over the book value of Akquirer Corp.'s net assets. Unless this reporting effect of the pooling method is discounted by the investor and his financial analyst (presuming they are supplied the needed information), erroneous conclusions may be reached.

Potential Effect on Market Value of Stock

Under the assumption that the market value of common stock is directly related to earnings, and that the price/earnings ratio for Akquirer Corp. stock remains unchanged at 15 times earnings subsequent to the merger, the market value of Akquirer Corp. shares at the end of 1966 would amount to $34.20 per share (purchase) or $54.75 per share (pooling). However, post-merger stock prices do not necessarily follow a predictable price/earnings pattern and, furthermore, post-merger market value of stock is not completely controlled by the accounting method used for the merger.

Effect on Raising Additional Funds

For purposes of the Akquirer-Zeller example, it is assumed that the average cost of capital after taxes is computed by taking a weighted average of the after-tax interest rate on bonds and the reciprocal of the price/earnings multiplier as the cost of equity funds. Assuming a post-merger price earnings multiplier of 15 and the current corporate tax rate, the average cost of capital under purchase and pooling would be 6.4 percent and 6.2 percent, respectively.

The proximity of these two figures is illusory. Lower earnings per share accompanied by a probably lower market price of stock under purchase accounting is assumed to result in identical price/earnings ratios of 15 times earnings. By using pooling, Akquirer Corp. would probably be able to sell additional shares at a higher price than if it recorded the merger with Zeller, Inc. as a purchase. The cost of additional equity funds, then, would not be the same. Using the extremes of the prices of stock as projected (purchase, $34.20; pooling, $54.75), the cost of raising equity funds may be much higher under purchase accounting than under pooling accounting.

The cost of raising additional funds through borrowing may also differ, since the stockholders' equity would be much higher if purchase accounting is used. Creditors may view this as a favorable factor and would lend money at lower interest rates than if pooling accounting were used. However, lower earnings reported as a result of the use of purchase accounting may more than offset this favorable factor.

DISCLOSURE IN FINANCIAL STATEMENTS

Mergers of any financial significance require the approval of both the acquiring and selling shareholders. The details of the merger, as well as proforma financial statements showing a post-merger balance sheet and a summary of earnings for the past five years, as if the merger had been in effect, is required by the Securities and Exchange Commission to be included in the proxy statements to the shareholders which are distributed prior to the shareholders' meeting called to approve the merger. These pro-forma statements must be prepared using the accounting method that is to be adopted if the merger takes place.

Subsequently, management still has a responsibility to disclose the pertinent details of the merger in its post-merger financial statements. Among the facts regarding the merger which should be mentioned are the method of accounting which has been adopted as well as the following:

1. If the merger is a purchase:

Operations of the acquired company are combined with the operations of the acquiring company only from the date of acquisition. (Significant full-year totals for sales and other items may be reported in a footnote.)

2. If the merger is a pooling:

Operations of the acquired company are combined with the operations of the acquiring company for the entire year, and financial statements of prior years must be restated as though the companies have been a single unit from inception.

OPPORTUNITY FOR MANIPULATION

An interesting opportunity to increase reported earnings artificially through a merger is often referred to as a "bargain purchase." In cases where the price paid for a going concern is lower than the recorded asset values, the assets should be recorded at no more than the price paid. However, inability to apportion total cost to specific assets has resulted in recording assets acquired at the high book value of the acquired company, thus resulting in a credit account on the balance sheet of the acquiring company.

Accounting Research Bulletin No. 51 of the AICPA states that the balance in this credit account "would be taken into income in future periods on a reasonable and systematic basis." This has prompted the observation that this practice could seem quite tempting to companies that might like to increase their reported pershare earnings substantially through acquisition of enterprises in financial difficulty.

While it does not appear likely that such a practice will become widespread, management accountants should be aware of this effect and, therefore, be able to assist management in selecting the accounting method that would not bring about such a variation in per-share earnings.

WHY ALL THE UPROAR ABOUT PURCHASE OR POOLING ACCOUNTING?

The use of purchase accounting requires an appraisal of assets in order to allocate the actual price paid to assets acquired. In view of the increasing price-level trend established during the past quarter century, the recording of assets at current rather than historical cost will continue to reduce post-merger earnings. When this is unexplained, the lower rate is unattractive to management because good performance and efficiency are related to increases in the earnings rate Nevertheless, factual presentation of the negotiated terms of the merger must be made. When the increase in the value of assets to be amortized or depreciated is determined, any false conclusions that can be drawn from the increased charges against income should be offset by full disclosure of the other related data in order to justify the merger.

During a period of inflation and high stock prices, the use of pooling has a certain appeal– it is simple because it does not require appraisal of assets for accounting purposes, and it offers balance sheet conservatism and uniformity since all of the assets are stated at historical cost. The argument has sometimes been advanced that an otherwise desirable acquisition would not reach fruition if the pooling approach could not be used. The choice of method, however, is relatively unimportant if the proposed acquisition is not capable of producing a satisfactory rate of return based on the total economic consideration paid for the acquired business.

At present, accountants are being criticized for the latitude in making the choice between the purchase and pooling methods which allows too much inconsistency and diversity in reporting. Only the clearest understanding of the problems and results of each method can bring about the desirable degree of agreement among accountants and consistency in their reports. The reason for the uproar is that management's integrity will be jeopardized unless a reliably consistent basis for choosing between methods becomes generally recognized and used.

MANAGEMENT ACCOUNTANT'S INCREASED RESPONSIBILITY

The impact of corporate acquisitions and mergers on financial statements and comparative analyses will vary depending upon which accounting method is used. The differences that result from using either the purchase or pooling method require responsible and thorough study to properly quanify a merger or acquisition for financial reporting purposes.

All the aspects of the comparative effects of purchase and pooling must be reviewed before accepting the apparently favorable results of pooling when a merger proposal is being ranked and compared with other growth projects. When a discounted cash-flow analysis is made, the inflated return on investment disappears. Upon complete analysis, the risk and nature of the proposed transaction can be seen in full perspective.

With an increasing number of stockholders being involved when mergers occur, management accountants must be able to (1) provide clear guidance by understanding postmerger effects of the accounting methods available, and (2) convey this understanding to the managements responsible for the resulting financial statements. The more completely the facts are disclosed to readers of the statements, the better prepared all concerned will be to make decisions.

Management and financial officers must face up to the consequences of choosing between these two accounting methods. So long as unnecessary inconsistency and diversity exist, improvements must be sought. Until reporting on mergers and post-merger results is understandable to readers of financial statements, management accountants will subject their companies to criticism. Their responsibility to improve both general understanding and the usefulness of their reports must start with their own understanding.

Part III

Stock Market Analysis and Forecasting Short Term Price Movements

INTRODUCTION

The objective of the editors in this section is to introduce the student to so-called, "technical analysis." In this approach internal stock market data is examined in an attempt to identify recurring patterns of price movements or recurring interrelationships between stock price movements and other market variables. The members of this school of thought believe that information concerning future price movements can be found by studying historical market data.

In the first segment of this section Daniel Seligman presents the subject of charting, Professor Seneca examines the usefulness of short-interest data in forecasting market movements and the advance-decline line is discussed by George Freeman. Professor Edward Zinbarg explains the concept of the confidence index and criticizes its record as a leading indicator of stock market price movements.

One of the most heated controversies in the current investments literature is presented in the second part of this section. One school of investment thought, introduced in the first part of this section, is persuaded that past movements of stock prices and related internal market data can prove useful as an indicator of future price movements. A second school, random walk, has developed, which bases its thinking on the premise that securities markets are examples of "efficient" markets. An efficient market is defined as containing relatively large numbers of rational investors and where information is relatively freely available to all participants. As the writers of the second school explain, competition among many well-informed investors would eliminate the recurrence of systematic historic patterns of price movements and preclude meaningful predictions of stock prices.

In the first article Professor Harry Roberts questions the basis for using historical market patterns to predict the future behavior of security prices and suggests that changes in certain stock market indexes behave as if they had been generated by a simple chance model. Professor Sidney Alexander surveys price changes in speculative markets. His research indicates that these price changes appear to follow a random walk over time, but a move, once initiated, tends to persist. Professor Fama contributes a brief and simple description of the theory of random walks along with some of the important issues it presents concerning the work of market analysts.

In an attack on the random walk theorists, Professor Leo Barnes attempts to support the traditional view that knowledge and intellectual training will increase one's chances of investment success. In the concluding article in this section Professor Robert Weintraub argues that the random walk hypothesis flies in the face of common sense. In particular, he challenges the usefulness of the definition of the term "the next move" employed by the random-walk school.

16

Playing the Market with Charts*

Daniel Seligman

The charting of stocks, once a recondite art practiced only by a few Wall Streeters, is becoming the recondite preoccupation of masses of investors. All over the U.S. tens of thousands of chartists are peering at their charts, trying to discern in the patterns and configurations of the past a clue to the future—the future of their stocks, that is, not the future in general. Though not all of them use the same system, the chartists will tell you, to a man, that the system they use works. And they must believe it, since many of them spend hour after hour every night keeping charts and interpreting them. Chartists sometimes speak of their wives as "chart widows."

Charting is also a growing profession. Virtually every substantial brokerage firm uses some charts, either because they are an effective selling device with certain customers or because the research department thinks that charting is an effective aid in stock forecasting. And there is a sizable business done in providing chartists of all types with ready-made charts and interpretations. Chartcraft, Trendline, Graphic Stocks, Trend & Value, Securities Research, Trendex, Marketlines—all these and many other services have attracted thousands of customers. Several of them charge fairly hefty fees: Marketlines offers a custom service for $2,500 a year. Wyckoff Associates in Chicago gives a correspondence course in charting that has attracted some 5,000 students over the years; they pay $500 and, because the lectures arrive on tape, must equip themselves with a tape recorder. The New School for Social Research in New York last fall offered a Monday-night course in charting that outdrew virtually everything else the school had to offer in literature, philosophy, psychology, and the social sciences. A book called *Technical Analysis of Stock Trends* by Robert D. Edwards and John Magee, first published in 1948, has gone through four editions and eleven printings and sold nearly 50,000 copies—at $12 apiece. The book is used as a text in a number of business schools.

A chartist is, to begin with, a "technician." And he ordinarily explains what a technician is by contrasting himself with a "fundamentalist." A fundamentalist is a man who tries to estimate the present value and future course of stocks by looking for information about the companies' assets, net worth, past and

*From *Fortune*, Vol. 65, No. 2 (February 1962), p. 118. Reprinted by permission of *Fortune*.

prospective earnings, etc. A militant technician regards this kind of information as only secondarily useful, if of any use at all. He argues that all such information has been taken into account in the market and so is already reflected in the recent movements of the stock, which he sees on his charts. The man who gets "fundamental" information can never be certain that what he knows is complete, and maybe it isn't even accurate. A chartist, however, feels that *everything* about a stock–not only its earnings prospects, but also the emotions that people bring to it, the influence of tax selling and of other extraneous forces–is subsumed in the chart configurations. His task is to figure out what the configurations mean.

THE WONDERFUL WORLD OF CHARTS

Charting was generally in bad odor during the 1920's and early 1930's. It was associated with stock manipulations–i.e., the manipulators kept charts of price and volume activity, looking for ways to control the prices of stocks on minimal investments; at the same time a few traders tried to use charts in an effort to detect manipulations. Aside from these shady connotations, there was always a widespread suspicion that the chartists were all a little crazy. It is apparent that charting has now become respectable.

Charting appeals to investors at several different levels of sophistication. Securities Research of Boston includes among the subscribers to its charts the First National City Bank, the prestigious investment-counseling firm of Scudder, Stevens & Clark, and the Rockefeller Brothers organization; until he went to Washington Securities Research also had Defense Secretary McNamara on its list. It is, of course, unclear to what extent these sophisticated clients are real chartists; some of them, undoubtedly, use the charts only as handy reference works. Many of the most dedicated and least critical chartists are small investors. They may feel that they do not have access to good information, feel remote from "the insiders," and despair of their ability to understand complex financial information even if they had access to it. Retired business and professional men are also likely to be avid chartists: they have investments to watch over and time on their hands, and besides, living in California or Florida, they may feel a long way from the fundamentals of Wall Street.

It is also fair to conclude that charting has a special appeal for a certain personality type– the collector. Listening to one such chartist describe the satisfaction he derives from sitting down after dinner with his charts for a few hours, one is reminded of the philatelist or lepidopterist. Finding certain patterns on the charts gives chartists satisfaction that transcends the possibilities of turning the patterns into money. In his book, *The General Semantics of Wall Street*, Magee writes rhapsodically about "the wonderful world of the logarithmic spirals [which] contains so much of beauty and so much of the sheer wonder of pattern and rhythm. . . "

Some chartists reject any fundamental information about stocks, on the ground that earnings, book-value figures, and the like only tend to blur the big picture. This group includes Magee, whom many regard as the leading chartist theoretician today; the window in his workroom in Springfield, Massachusetts, is boarded up, symbolizing and reinforcing Magee's unconcern with the outside world–the world in which real, live investors pay money for the securities of companies that sell their products to real, live customers. Recently Magee's charting service recommended Colonial Corp. stock. A visitor to Magee's windowless workroom, looking at the Colonial charts with him, asked what business the company was in. "I haven't the faintest idea," Magee said, aggreeably. (Colonial makes low-priced apparel.) Some chartists are opposed even to reading the business news in the daily papers. "It puts poison in the mind," says Robert G. Evans, proprietor of the Wyckoff organization. The more reasonable-sounding of the chartists, among whom is Edmund Tabell, head of institutional research for Walston & Co., the brokerage firm, take the view that charts are mainly useful for spotting interesting stock-market situations, but that investors should not act in these situations until they have gone out and examined the fundamentals.

There are, in general, two main charting techniques, or schools of thought. One school works with bar charts, like the one below, the other with so-called "point and figure" charts. This article will examine the techniques and claims of the bar chartists; next month's article will examine the "p. and f.'ers." Before discussing either one, however, it may be well to gain a perspective on Dow Theory, the first of any "technical approach" to gain a wide following.

Some of the underlying concepts of Dow Theory may be detected in the thinking of chartists today–especially bar chartists. Unfortunately, a certain vagueness enshrouds Dow Theory. The vagueness begins with the question of whether is really *is* a theory. Is Dow Theory a hypothesis tested by events and found useful in predicting the future? Or does it merely supply us with a handy vocabulary for describing the past?

WHERE THE DOW THEORY CAME FROM

Charles H. Dow himself, the editor of the *Wall Street Journal* around the turn of the century, did not seem to believe that he had a method of forecasting. He once wrote that "there is no way of telling when the top of an advance or the bottom of a decline has been reached until some time after such top or bottom has been made." But around 1910 a *Journal* editor named William P. Hamilton began to interpret Dow's ideas somewhat more ambitiously, and to use them in forecasting. Hamilton's interpretations, as set forth and further embellished by another writer, Robert Rhea, in a 1932 volume called *The Dow Theory,* have come to be accepted as the definitive statement of the theory.

Dow theorists draw a vivid analogy between the movements of the stock market and those of the sea: there are tides (the major trends), waves (intermediate corrections), and ripples (minor fluctuations). Dow, Hamilton, and Rhea all believed that investors should ride with the major trend. But how is one to tell the tides from the waves? Hamilton offered several clues. He suggested that major trends are characterized by three distinct phases. A bull market, for example, begins with a reaction against the panic selling at the end of a bear market. The second phase is a long, persistent rise as the news of improved profits begins to come in. The third phase is marked by wildly speculative and emotional buying as the uniformed public begins climbing aboard. A reaction against this buying is the first phase of a bear market, in which the whole process is reversed.

In retrospect, most bull and bear markets can be fitted into this pattern. But at the time it is happening it is ordinarily hard to tell the difference between, say, a "correction" of the trend and the beginning of a major reversal. Hamilton laid down several rules in an effort to help the perplexed investor. The most important rule is that the market can be considered in a major upward trend when—and only when—the Dow-Jones industrial and rail averages both hit important new highs, and in a major downtrend when both hit important new lows. Rhea explained that "the validity of the last primary trend confirmation stands until countermanded by an equally valid countermovement."

How well does the method work? Hamilton himself incorrectly called a bear market in 1926, but later he achieved fame by proclaiming a bear market four days before October 29, 1929. Since then Dow theorists have often had more difficulty, or perhaps less luck, in applying the method. In 1946 the industrial and rail averages both hit new highs just before a setback; in the fall of 1957 the averages signaled a bear trend just before a major advance; and in March, 1960, the averages again signaled a bear market that did not materialize.

At least, the averages signaled these turns to *some* Dow theorists. One of the maddening perplexities about the theory is that it does not say how to tell which highs and lows are truly significant. There is also no agreement as to the exact duration and extent required of an advance or decline before it shall be construed as a major trend rather than an intermediate correction. For these reasons, practicing Dow theorists often disagree with one another about the present character and future prospects of the market. A majestic simplicity marks their reconstructions of the past, but their formulations about the future are often elaborately woolly—e.g., "In coming years the stock market may be in for a tumble of major proportions, possibly before the year 1962 is out." (This warning was delivered by E. George Schaefer, who publishes "The Dow Theory Trader" out of Indianapolis; he has generally sounded bullish in the past decade.) One of the few Dow theorists whose predictions have been unambiguous is Richard Russell, who publishes the "Dow Theory Letters" out of San Diego. Writing in *Barron's* at the time of the March, 1960, "bear signal," Mr. Russell stated categorically that "the great bull market which began on June 13, 1949, ended on July 8, 1959." In the fall of 1960, just before the market began to rise, Mr. Russell wrote that the bear signal had been "confirmed." For a while he viewed the rise as an intermediate correction of a major downward trend, but as the market kept right on rising he abandoned this line and allowed that he had been wrong.

GET THEM WHILE THEY'RE GOING UP

Dow Theory, of course, has been concerned only with the market as a whole. But in the 1930's, Richard W. Schabacker, a financial editor of *Forbes,* wrote several books that attempted to apply some of the Dow-Hamilton ideas in forecasting the prices of individual stocks. He was helped by his brother-in-law, Robert D. Edwards, a professor of meteorology who later began to write about stocks himself, and in 1948 combined with John Magee to write *Technical Analysis of Stock Trends.* This book is pretty much the bible of modern chartists.

The chartists' indebtedness to Dow and Hamilton is considerable. In *Technical Analysis* one may, for example, rediscover the old Dow doctrine of riding with the trend until it is countermanded. To many nonchartists, this doctrine may sound like an ideal and obvious objective rather than a program for action, but virtually all chartists attach great weight to the doctrine. In practice, it seems to lead them to prefer stocks that *have been rising* and to frown on stocks that have been falling–stocks that a fundamentalist might regard as "oversold." Bar chartists tend especially to prefer stocks that are at their all-time highs–stocks that a fundamentalist might regard as "overbought." The chartists' view of these stocks has a certain hard logic to it. When a stock is well below its high, they reason, there are always a certain number of investors who have losses and who will try to recoup by selling as the stock gets back to the price at which they originally bought. These sales create "resistance areas" that impede the advance of the stock; and the greater the volume of trading near the high, the greater the resistance is presumed to be on the way back up. A stock at a new high has no such impediment; the chartists would say that it has "clear sailing."

The opposite of a resistance area is a "support area"–i.e., a price level at which a falling stock may expect to be supported by buyers. Ordinarily, a support area exists at a level where a rising stock had earlier been accumulated by investors. As the stock goes up from, say, 25 to 30, the investors feel that their original judgment has been vindicated, but they wish they had bought more–and vow that they *will* buy more if the stock ever comes back down. At the same time, the sellers who had earlier "given up" on the stock now find their interest in it rekindled, and they decide to get back in if they can at around the price they sold at. And so plenty of support for the stock will turn up when it falls back to 25. Again, the extent of the support depends on the volume of trading that took place when the stock was earlier at that level.

Still, when you buy stocks that have been rising, and sell stocks that have been falling, you would appear to face the danger of buying at the top and selling at the bottom. The bar chartists say that this problem is manageable, however. For one thing, they maintain, strong trends are not apt to be reversed suddenly. Says Edwards in *Technical Analysis*: "One does not bring instantly to a stop a heavy car moving at seventy miles an hour and, all within the same split second, turn it around and get it moving back down the road in the opposite direction at seventy miles an hour." Before a stock turns around, its price movements will usually form one of a number of "reversal patterns" on the chart. The basic assumptions of the chartists here are that the big, sophisticated insiders are "distributing" their stock at the top (or "accumulating" at the bottom); that the entire operation is too complex to complete in a day or two; and that, for these reasons, reversal patterns tend to involve a fairly extensive sideways movement.

Unfortunately, no chartists have ever got around to demonstrating statistically that these patterns really do presage reversals in the trend of a stock's price. Edwards and Magee have festooned *Technical Analysis* with examples of reversal patterns being followed by reversals, but a skeptic has no trouble finding reversals without patterns and patterns without reversals. To begin with, it is not hard to find stocks that reversed their major trends suddenly, without slowing down from 70 mph. From the end of 1958 to the summer of 1960, Amerada Petroleum fell steadily, to a low of 55. It then turned around and rose sharply, forming a "V"; recently it has been around 110. An "inverted V" was formed about a year ago by Kerr-McGee Oil, which rose sharply from about 40 to 120, was split two for one, then fell sharply to around 40. To be sure, not all chartists will be discomfited by such examples. There are, indeed, some who regard V's, whether erect or inverted, as significant reversal patterns themselves. William Jiler of the Trendline Corp. has recently completed a book *(How Charts Can Help in the Stock Market)* in which V formations are said to "spark the most dynamic of all price swings." He notes that because "the V-turn strikes with little warning," it is "among the most difficult to analyze."

A "head-and-shoulders formation" coming after a sustained rise is supposed to signal a "top"—i.e., that the rise is over. Bar chartists are always watching out for this formation. When it appeared in Texas Instruments in 1960 many chartists sold out at around 200. The head and shoulders on Litton proved to be a "false signal," however; after a brief decline in September, 1960, that stock resumed its long upward trend. Among those led astray on Litton was the charting advisory service run by John Magee, a leading chart theorist, who had been right on the T.I. downturn. He advised his subscribers to sell Litton if the stock closed below 76; fortunately, he advised them to buy back in at 82. (The weekly charts shown here were supplied by the Mansfield chart service.)

PICASSO, MOVE OVER

But Jiler agrees with Magee and Edwards about the reliability of one major reversal pattern, the so-called "head-and-shoulders formation." As this is described in *Technical Analysis,* it has four main elements when it is a "top":

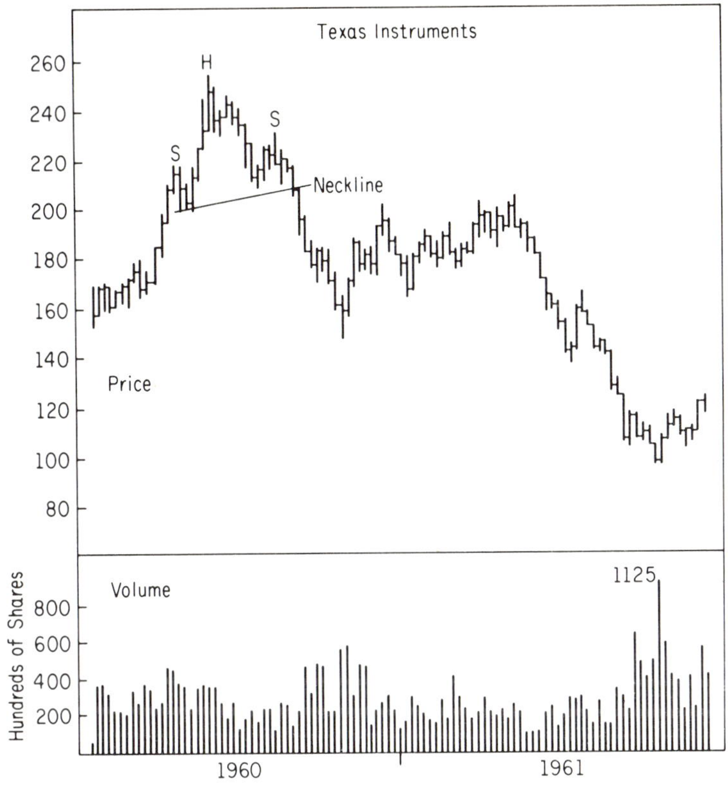

A. A strong rally, climaxing a more or less extensive advance, on which trading volume becomes very heavy, followed by a minor recession on which volume runs considerably less than it did during the days of rise and at the top. This is the "left shoulder."

B. Another high-volume advance which reaches a higher level than the top of the left shoulder and then another reaction on less volume which takes prices down to somewhere near the bottom level of the preceding recession, somewhat lower perhaps or somewhat higher but, in any case, *below the top* of the left shoulder. This is the "head."

C. A third rally, but this time on decidedly less volume than accompanied the formation of either the left shoulder or the head, which fails to reach the height of the head before another decline sets in. This is the "right shoulder."

D. Finally, decline of prices in this third recession down through a line (the "neckline") drawn across the bottoms of the reactions between the left shoulder and head and the head and right shoulder, respectively, and a close below that line by an amount approximately equivalent to 3 per cent of the stock's market price. This is the "confirmation" or "breakout."

This sounds clear enough, but unfortunately stock movements fitting this

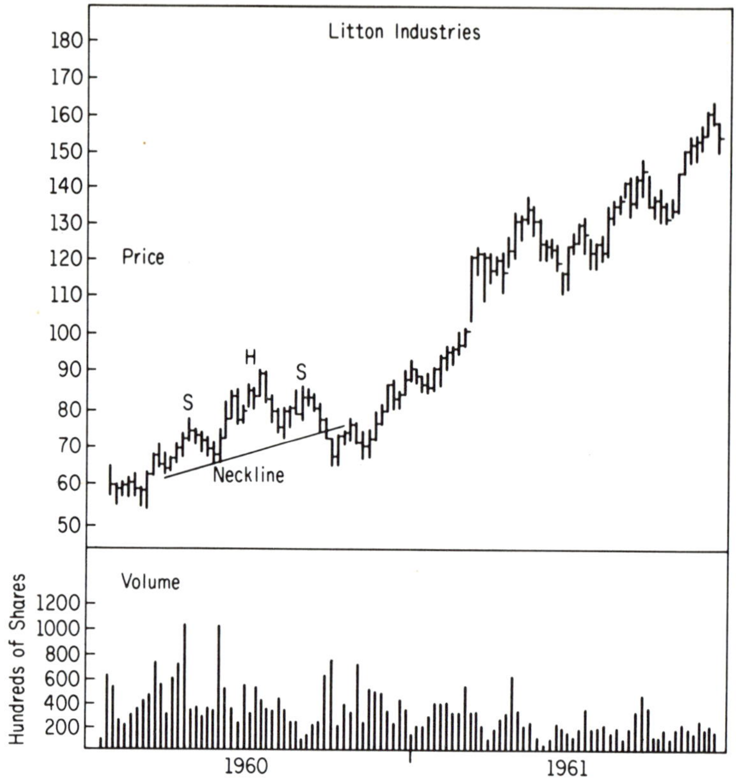

pattern unambiguously are hard to find. Practicing chartists are sometimes nagged by the question of whether to construe small ripples on their chart lines as "shoulders" or to ignore them. Sometimes a stock whose movement is ambiguous on a daily chart will look like a neat head-and-shoulders on a weekly chart; which one is the perplexed chartist to follow? Chartists are fond of citing the beautiful head-and-shoulders top on Texas Instruments in mid-1960, when the stock hit its high of 256 (see page 231); a lot of chartists sold out of T.I. or went short at that point—or rather, at about 200, where the "downside breakout" was "confirmed." (T.I. later went on down to 95.) But now observe that Litton Industries also formed a nice head-and-shoulders top in 1960. This induced some chartists to sell or go short around 70; and Litton's recent price has been over 150.

The T.I. and Litton patterns were relatively close to the ideal. But a head may have more than two shoulders and still be allowable, and the shoulders may have more than one head between them. Says Jiler: "This need not frighten a public that pays fortunes for paintings by Picasso." *Technical Analysis* reproduces, with evident pride, a chart of Marshall Field & Co. in the spring of 1946. On this chart the authors have drawn *three* heads between the two shoulders, whose neckline slants upward. The price was at 52 when the neckline was broken; the authors remark proudly that M.F. was selling at 23 a year later.

THOSE UNTRUSTWORTHY TRIANGLES

Of all the reversal patterns, triangles are among the hardest to cope with. The authors of *Technical Analysis* warn that "a downside breakout from a Symmetrical Triangle which is attended right from the start by conspicuously heavy volume is much more apt to be a false signal rather than the start of a genuine downtrerend. . . Here is a very pretty technical pattern and it cannot always be trusted." Worst of all, the triangle may turn out to be a *consolidation pattern,* rather than a *reversal pattern;* in other words, the triangle may represent a breathing spell on the way up rather than the end of a rise.

Magee and Edwards identify many other reversal patterns: rectangles, double and triple tops and bottoms, rounding turns, diamonds, wedge formations, etc. Their book is profusely illustrated with bar charts on which all these patterns have been exemplified by the authors. But the dismaying fact is that many of the patterns could, without doing any great violence to the authors' definitions, be construed as other patterns. The same holds true, unhappily, of the "consolidation formations" identified by Magee and Edwards: flags and pennants, ascending and descending triangles, scallops, etc.

It is apparent, then, that in seeking to identify the configurations on their charts investors often find themselves adrift on a sea of ambiguities. But the ambiguities do not end with the configurations formed by price patterns. There is also a problem about the trend lines and channels in which stocks allegedly move. All bar chartists–indeed *all* chartists–pay a great deal of attention to trend lines, which are straight lines drawn along the successive tops and bottoms of stocks' price fluctuations (see the A.T.&T. chart on page 235). Chartists register the delight of discovery whenever they can draw lines showing that a stock has moved between two trend lines–i.e., within a single channel–for a considerable period of time. But just what is it that is discovered by the trend lines? This is not so clear. Says *Technical Analysis:* "[Trend lines] are all always broken ultimately and some very shortly after they are set up. The problem is to decide which breaks (i.e., penetrations by a price movement) are of important technical significance and which are of no practical consequence."

This appears to be a sizable problem indeed, for the book goes on to say that a "break" may be followed by several different patterns. When the price has, for example, broken an "intermediate up trendline," drawn off several recent bottoms, several things may ensue: there may be "a full intermediate recession or a period of consolidation"; in other words, the stock may go down or go sideways. In addition, it may go up: "a more immediate but less important probable consequence" is the so-called "pullback." In any case, what should the investor *do* when his up trend line has been broken? Should he sell? Or sit tight and hope for a pullback? Or draw another trend line, off other bottoms? Which trend lines really count? Magee and Edwards are invincibly vague on these matters.

IT'S FUN, BUT IS IT TRUE?

Bar charts have certain obvious and indisputable uses. First of all, they give a clear and concise picture of the past, and enable an investor to get a quick sense of the stability or volatility he might expect in a certain stock; they are certainly useful as *records* in the same way that an ordinary sales or profits chart is. And the record of the volume of trading, which ordinarily appears at the bottom of a bar chart, is a handy clue to the extent of public interest in a stock. Moreover, it is often relevant for an investor to know whether a sharp rise or decline on a certain day was on heavy or thin volume; a two-point rise on only 200 shares is presumably just a temporary aberration in the market; but if the rise was on 20,000 shares, the investor might legitimately wonder whether the big "insiders" know something that has not reached the public, and are beginning to accumulate. The chartists' general view that volume fluctuations can be used to identify support areas and resistance levels also seems to be built on fairly sturdy underpinnings. Finally, it might be repeated that bar charting is obviously *fun* for a lot of people, and on this count alone it is apt to continue attracting fans. Indeed, it is possible that the technique will get so many followers that it will itself become an important influence on the market. If everyone were a chartist, Magee observed recently, "it would become self-defeating."

But right now investors interested in bar charting might well have some other concerns about it. The major concern is the fact that the scores of claims made for different chart patterns are simply unproved. They have not been tested and, in fact, are probably untestable–i.e., because they are so vaguely formulated and so thoroughly hedged. Joseph Mindell, a partner in the specialist firm of Marcus & Co., and the author of *The Stock Market,* says that he spent years studying the patterns but finally gave up on them. He asks: "What's the use of a pattern that works except when it doesn't work?"

FLAGS UP AT A.T.&T

Fortune recently asked William Jiler, who publishes the Tredline and Commodity Research Bureau charts, to analyze a daily chart of A.T. & T. Ordinarily, chartists spend a lot of time looking for "reversal patterns," which are presumed to signal a change in direction. But the important configurations on this chart, as Jiler sees it, are the "consolidation patterns"–flags and pennants denoting a breathers on the way up. Jiler finds a swing objective by noting the difference between a breakout point (A.T. & T. at 97) and the top of the next important consolidation pattern (the highest point in the first "up flag," (117); this distance (twenty points) is then added to the lowest point in the flag (110) to

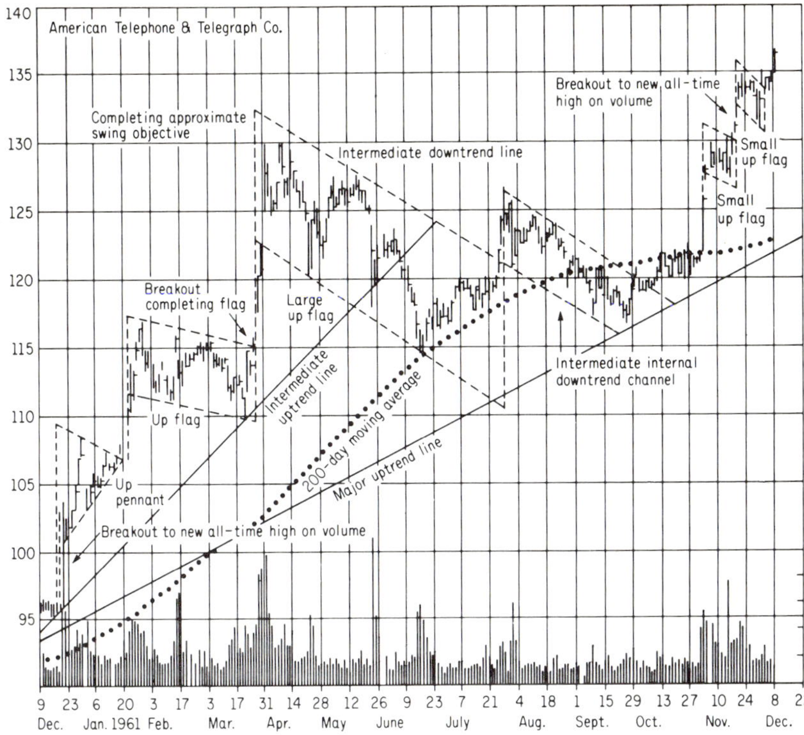

get the objective in the next move. A.T. & T. did indeed make it to 130 on the next move.

Jiler regards A.T. & T.'s pattern as distinctly bullish because the company has not yet broken its major uptrend line. Jiler drew it off some earlier "bottoms" not shown on this chart. Unfortunately, there is no general agreement among chartists as to which trend lines are significant.

17

The Mystique of Point-and-Figure*

Daniel Seligman

Burton Crane, who writes a daily report on the stock market for the New York *Times,* noted one day last October that chartists were enthusiastic about Brunswick Corp., then selling at 64: "Brokers said that the stock had pushed through the tops attained on the last two rallies. . . and therefore had been attractive to chart readers." Unfortunately for the chart readers, the stock then fell back below 60, and Crane was reporting that "its failure to behave as predicted probably brought selling." He later added that "all the reported company news was good but that the chart readers. . . were exerting a heavy influence on the stock." Toward the end of October, with Brunswick at 57, he said that the chartists felt it was just above "a major support area." But early this year it fell through this support area and then through another one even lower, and Crane reported that the chartists were taking the news hard: "It broke through the 50-51 range that chart readers have described as a support area. This touched off stop orders. . . the stock touched a low of 46 1/8 before making a slight recovery." Later in January, Brunswick was still giving chartists a rough time. "Brokers said that customers were watching the chart action of the stock," Crane reported, "and that the break through the 40-41 level had brought selling." The following day the stock hit a low of 38 5/8, and chart readers were beginning to talk of support in *that* area.

Whatever the foregoing may suggest about the acumen of stock chartists, it is at least clear that they are becoming hard to ignore; by sheer weight of numbers they often seem able, at least temporarily, to affect the market prices of some stocks. The brokerage community itself is obliged to heed the chartists. Although many brokers are skeptical of chart interpretations, investor demand for them is so great that virtually all big brokerage firms today have at least one or two chartists on hand. These days most of them use the so-called "point-and-figure" technique.

Students of stocks, an article in these pages observed last month (see "Playing the Market with Charts"), are of two kinds: There are "fundamentalists," who try to foresee the future of a stock by analyzing financial and operating data about the company; and there are "technicians," who try to

*From *Fortune,* Vol. 65, No. 3 (March 1962), p. 113. Reprinted by permission of *Fortune.*

foresee the future by analyzing the behavior of the stock itself. Technicians are usually chartists, and chartists, as the article last month also observed, may themselves be divided into two main camps. There are those who draw bars showing the daily (or weekly or monthly) high, low, and closing prices, and attempt to discern in the patterns formed by successive bars a guide to the future. Last month's article was concerned principally with these bar chartists. This month's is concerned with the point-and-figure men.

THE METHOD, WITH A CAPITAL M

At first glance, point-and-figure charts are a mysterious proposition, and indeed they are harder to read than ordinary bar charts. Yet p. and f. is actually the oldest of all charting techniques; it was probably in use as early as 1880. It picked up a lot of followers after 1933, when a man named Victor de Villiers wrote a booklet about it called *The Point and Figure Method of Anticipating Stock Price Movements;* he said he was presenting what he had learned about the Method (he always capitalized it) after twenty years' study of market movements. It was his hope that many investors would start using p. and f., and his expectation that, if they did, "the peaks and valleys of booms and depressions" would be "moderated," because investors would recognize and avoid technically weak markets and, conversely, prop up oversold markets.

What makes p. and f. initially confusing to the beholder is that the time represented on the chart is not divided into regular intervals. P.-and-f. scholars believe that many significant patterns may take months, or even years, to develop, and that their identity is obscured on a bar chart, where a given unit of time takes up a given unit of space, moving from left to right. To make the patterns clearer, p. and f. "compresses" them. So long as a stock is moving in one directions, the record of the price changes is made by marking x's in a line straight up or down. Only when the direction changes—and the change must be at least from one whole number to another—does the chartist move to the right, where in the next vertical column he starts another row of x's. Most p. and f. men keep such "one-point-reversal" charts; however, chartists trying for an especially broad view, or dealing with unusually high-priced stocks, may keep three-point-reversal or even five-point-reversal charts. This may mean that they will not make an entry on their charts for weeks at a time; chartists plotting, say, General Motors on a three-point chart recently would not have made an entry from January 8 to January 25, because the stock, in the mid-50's, scarcely moved at all in either direction. Conversely, charts recording changes of less than one point are ordinarily reserved for low-priced stocks, although some chartists say that to get to really close quarters with *any* stock you should chart it in fractions.

Point-and-figure technicians look for several things in the patterns formed by their columns of x's. To some extent they look for "reversal patterns" similar to those on bar charts; a booklet of *Study Helps in Point and Figure Technique,* published by Morgan, Rogers & Roberts, Inc., a publishing firm catering to p. and f.'ers, suggests, for example, that the following patterns are useful in identifying so-called "tops": Inverse Fulcrum, Inverse Compound Fulcrum, Delayed Ending, Head and Shoulders, Inverted V, Inverted V Extended, Duplex Horizontal, and Inverse Saucer. The booklet, written by Alexander H. Wheelan, also includes questions and answers for students. Question (accompanied by chart data): "Does this look like reaccumulation preparatory to a new upthrust? If so, why? If not, why not?" Answer: "No—because fulcrum characteristics are not present. Furthermore, to be bullish the decline from 42 should have held at 40 or 39 instead of sinking to the bottom of the congestion area. . ."

WHERE DOES THE COMPASS POINT?

But in practice, p. and f.'ers attach less significance to major reversal patterns than to the congestion areas referred to in Wheelan's answer. A congestion area is formed by a lateral movement of columns of x's—i.e., instead of a pronounced vertical trend, there is a series of reversals after only brief advances or declines. The extent of this lateral movement is held by p. and f.'ers to be a clue to the extent of the next major upward or downward move. Their operating equipment often includes a compass like those used by geometry students; the stock's "price target" is ordinarily found by opening the compass to measure the lateral congestion area, then swinging the compass upward (or downward). Disheartening as the fact may appear to "fundamentalists," at least some of the investment recommendations coming out of Wall Street these days are made by men whose principal equipment for the task is a compass.

Thus far, p. and f. doubtless seems terribly arbitrary and mysterious. Why should the width of the congestion area determine the upward or downward prospects of the stock? What proof is there of any such relationship? The mystery deepens when you discover that the leading exponents of p. and f. do not agree on how to answer these questions. Before getting at their answers, it may be advisable to meet some of the men. Among the big names of p. and f. in the brokerage community:

Edmund W. Tabell, fifty-eight, a former actor, is a partner of, and head of institutional research for, Walston & Co. His weekly market letter has a circulation of 30,000, and is a major source of new business for Walston, from which he draws around $100,000 a year.

Kenneth Ward, sixty-two, senior vice president of Hayden, Stone & Co., writes a weekly *General Technical Survey* with a circulation of 60,000. "Charting has been very good to me." Ward remarked recently. "People are always asking why, if I'm such a good chartist, I'm not rich. I always tell them that I *am* rich."

James Dines, thirty, began writing a market letter for A. M. Kidder & Co. less than two years ago, has already got 12,000 circulation, is bringing in a lot of business.

Eugene Peroni, fifty-one, is a partner of Hill, Darlington & Grimm, for which he writes a market letter; it appears to be responsible for a large part of the firm's recent growth. Peroni is a graduate architect and businessman who retired in 1949, then spent seven years trading and studying the market, and working out his own refinements of charting (which he refuses to disclose).

John W. Schulz, forty-three, is a partner and major asset of Wolfe & Co., and the author of a market letter that, unlike those mentioned above, is not free; it comes as part of the service called Trend & Value, published by a corporate affiliate of Wolfe, that sells for $175 a year and goes to "several hundred" subscribers. Schulz gives his readers heavy doses of charting theory, along with logorrheic (some people think) reconstructions of his thinking about individual stocks. Here, for example, is Schulz writing about Kern County Land some months back, when the stock was at 73 (it has lately been around 80):

> Long-term three-point-unit base targets can now be plotted in the 90's, as shown. The major-trend base of 1959-60 yields a "first" one-point target at 85, suggesting an uptrend potential that has now been realized in large part. Secondary major-trend targets projected from the 1960 base structure on the one-point chart stand at 72-75 and have been liquidated. Since March, a mild deceleration of the advance (into channel D) seems to have taken place. A top reversal of any consequence has not so far materialized, but allowing for vulnerability to pressure from profit-taking sales, it may be reasonable to allow for penetration of potential support indicated by the chart in the 68-72 range and thus to hypothesize an intermediate-trend top-reversal structure with *H*-targets as shown. Allowing for a possible 50 per cent retracement of the 30-point advance to 77, the H-targets in the lower 60's would seem to be a reasonable description of latent reaction risks. Nevertheless, given a favorable general-market climate, the above-mentioned support potential astride the 70 line could remain intact and further major-uptrend development could materialize within either channel C or D.

It is probably fair to say that all of these men have had successful forecasting records. Some of them maintain an updated list of buy and sell recommendations on individual stocks, and the records look pretty good. If, for example, you had put $1,000 on every recommendation Dines made since he began his letter in June, 1960, and sold when Dines told you to, then by January, 1962, you would have realized gains in seventy-two stocks and losses in only twenty-six; your maximum investment at any one time would have been around $40,000; and your over-all profit today would be $12,800. Some p.-and-f. letters put out by independent services have also shown good results. Take, for example, the Marketlines service, founded by Walter Goldberg, forty-three, an ex-lingerie salesman who got fascinated by charts about ten years ago. In 1961 Marketlines closed out 153 positions in the imaginary portfolio it runs for its subscribers; all together, it had a net profit of 323½ points.

But if Dines, Goldberg, and other luminaries of the point-and-figure community are generally successful, it does not exactly follow that the technique itself works. Blurring the picture is the fact that (like many successful bar chartists) they are students of the fundamentals too, and it is often hard to say on which grounds they are basing their recommendations. Ward stresses the primacy of fundamentals and Tabell thinks they are important too, even while insisting that p. and f. is useful for "bird-dogging" interesting stocks. Peroni maintains that p. and f. is the single most important element in his forecasting success, but he is also a close student of the fundamentals. And even Schulz, for all his elaborate exegeses on the charts, turns out in conversation to know a lot about company operations. How, then, is one to ascertain the value of p. and f. by itself? The problem is complicated by the experts' resolute lack of precision in describing the technique; words like "usually" and "perhaps" keep getting into their descriptions of what it is they do, and efforts to pin them down to rigorous definitions that would enable an outsider to test their systems are met with protestations that the systems cannot be applied mechanically—that they require "interpretation." To the outsider, it may seem that what they really require is faith.

WHAT'S MY LINE?

Take, for example, a fairly crucial question about the central operation of p. and f.: measuring the width of the lateral movement, or "congestion area." In theory, a breakout from this congestion area suggests that a significant vertical move is about to take place; whether it is to be a rise or decline is indicated by the direction of the breakout, and its likely extent is suggested by the width of the congestion area. Actually, however, most lateral movements may be measured at several different price levels, and picking one rather than another usually gives you a different target. For example, in analyzing the chart on page 235, John Schulz got a target of 160 for A.T. & T. by measuring the lateral trend along the 120 line and another target of 146 by measuring along the 117 line; in addition, he got two "near-term" targets by measuring shorter segments of the main trend. But how is one to know which measurements are valid? In short, what are the rules of this game? Schulz himself is not very helpful on this point; he has written that "on the question of where in actual practice, measurements of lateral action should be taken, we are far from doctrinaire . . . we advocate the utmost flexibility because this tends to obviate the dangerous rigidity of preconceived notions." It would also seem to obviate any test.

There is also a maddening problem of definition about the "price target" itself. Does it represent a flat prediction that a certain price will be reached by a certain date—a prediction that can be put to the test? Unfortunately, it doesn't seem to be that specific. Tabell was asked recently how long a target could remain unfulfilled before the chartist should acknowledge that he had gone wrong; the answer was that no time limit could be put on a target's fulfillment.

Schulz is especially mysterious on this subject. "Price targets," he has written, "may generally be presumed to imply a degree of probability that the price level they identify will, in due course, be reached." If the targets are not reached, in other words, nothing has really gone wrong with the system. In retrospect, the chartist will say that he should have measured the lateral trend differently; or possibly he will blame things on a "false breakout." According to Dines, "a false breakout is the curse of the chartist."

WAITING FOR FINER MINDS

Beyond these operating difficulties, there is a larger problem. Why *should* p. and f. work? Specifically, why should the width of a lateral movement suggest anything at all about the extent of a subsequent vertical move?

Anyone who raises this interesting question with the leading p.-and-f. technicians is apt to arrive at an interesting conclusion: most of them haven't thought much about it. Tabell, for example, said recently that the method "works" 70 per cent of the time, but "I know of no valid rationale for it. The scientific reason it works just is not known." Dines observed that "when people with finer minds than mine come into the market, they will be able to determine the forces at work here." Meanwhile, Dines just doesn't know any good reason for relating the lateral and vertical moves—except that the system works, he says.

The only p.-and-f. technician who seems to have thought seriously about a rationale for the system is Schulz. He has not been completely consistent on the subject, but the drift of his recent thinking is clear. He believes that the lateral movement represents a redistribution of the floating supply of the stock; the longer the lateral trend remains in effect—i.e., the wider the congestion area—the more stock is presumed to change hands. Thus the width of the congestion area is related to a drying up of the floating supply of the stock. This means, Schulz wrote in a *Forbes* column last year, that when the stock begins to move up, "the normal deficit of supply that prevails in any uptrend is temporarily made more acute " And by the same token, "the deficit of demand that characterizes a downtrend is temporarily increased when a lateral trend in concluded."

This sounds plausible, but note several facts about it. Different stocks have different numbers of shares outstanding, of course, and also have floating supplies of widely varying size. A lateral movement that "dries up," say, 10 per cent of the floating supply will obviously have much less effect in a price advance than a movement that dries up 80 per cent of the supply. This suggests that the system, if it has any validity at all, depends on a close analysis of stock turnover. Yet in practice most p. and f.'ers pay no attention to volume; or rather, they insist that it is somehow implied by the number of price reversals—though why there should be a precise relationship between the two is quite unclear. Schulz himself has been paying more attention to volume in his recent analyses.

There is, it happens, one point-and-figure technique that is testable. This is the technique used by Chartcraft, Inc., a service operating out of Larchmont, New York. The Chartcraft service has about 5,000 customers, perhaps 40 per cent of whom are brokers. It is run by A. W. Cohen, fifty-two, a lawyer who formerly owned the William-Frederick Press, and got interested in charting when he published a book called *Stock Market Trading,* by Ernest J. Staby. He and Staby set up Chartcraft in 1948; Staby has since retired.

Like many other p.-and-f. technicians, Cohen has a few wrinkles that are all his own. He keeps three-point-reversal charts, but does not pay as much attention to congestion areas or price targets as other p. and f.'ers do; instead, his emphasis is on short-term trading and modest (but fast) profits. "Being a pig," Cohen has written, "often leads to disaster." His followers are supposed to buy, or go short, on certain "signals" that are clearly defined; there are five buy signals and five sell signals. Most of these signals may be viewed as "breakouts" similar to those that other p. and f.'ers look for, except that Chartcraft's are apt to come fairly soon in a lateral movement. With each new commitment, the Chartcraft follower is advised to place a stop order to limit possible losses; the stop is placed at the point where a change in direction would cancel the previous signal. The fundamentals are ignored entirely. In short, the entire system is defined in unambiguous terms, and anyone who pleases can go off and test it.

Oddly enough, Chartcraft itself has never run a test of the technique. The service claims that "trades established on the Chartcraft formations should yield a 10 per cent profit 85 per cent of the time." Cohen was asked recently for the evidence behind this claim; he replied that the statement was based "on what brokerage firms have told us."

10 PER CENT OR BUST

To test the claim, FORTUNE examined every buy and sell signal given on every one of the more than 700 New York Stock Exchange stocks that Chartcraft routinely covers. (The firm also offers American Stock Exchange, over-the-counter, and commodity services.) The time period covered was the first nine months of 1961; this period was selected instead of the full year because many of the signals given in the last quarter of 1961 were not resolved when this article was being written–i.e., the signals had neither led to a 10 per cent profit (at which point a sale was assumed) nor touched off a stop order. Ninety per cent of the signals given in the ninth-month period were resolved.

For the nine months, Chartcraft's record may be called disappointing, to say the least. Of the stocks tested, nearly 300 gave no signal at all. The remaining stocks gave a total of 855 signals. A trader who acted on these signals would have made his 10 per cent profit on 342 trades, or 40 per cent of the time. He would have touched off a stop-loss 426 times (50 per cent), and the average loss would have been 9.98 per cent–i.e., virtually the same as the average profit. One stock, Carter Products, gave Chartcraft fans an especially hard time: it gave off four buy signals and four sell signals; all but one were losers.

On the whole, however, Chartcraft did better on buy signals than on sell signals, perhaps because it was in a rising market. Of the 421 buy recommendations, 220 (52 per cent) made the 10 per cent profit and 180 (43 per cent) were stopped out; of the 434 sell recommendations, only 122 (28 per cent) were profitable, and 246 (57 per cent) were stopped out.

Other p.-and-f. technicians will surely argue that, because of special features of the Chartcraft system, these results suggest nothing about their own systems. Perhaps not But meanwhile Chartcraft is the only point-and-figure technique available for testing–and the results of one test inspire no special confidence in p. and f.

18

Short Interest: Bearish or Bullish?*

Joseph J. Seneca†

The interpretation of the influence of a large volume of short interest on general stock market behavior has been the subject of much disagreement. Essentially the issue is whether large short positions have a net bullish or bearish effect. Some traders see a favorable reaction, claiming that increases in short sales represent a boost to potential demand because eventually these positions must be covered. They add that increases in short interest are a natural reaction to advances in trading volume. Others see a bearish effect and view high short interest conditions as a signal of pessimism and a judgment that a downturn is likely. It seems appropriate, therefore, to study the market reaction to varying short interest situations on a formal basis.

I

Regression analysis will be used to isolate the effect of the short interest variable in an equation together with indicators of the general economic climate. The equation used to test this problem is one that relates the behavior of stock prices jointly to corporate dividends and short interest position. The form of this relation was chosen after initial research with a variety of explanatory variables (corporate profits, the index of industrial production, unemployment rates, margin requirements, and seasonal variables) indicated that dividends provided the best measure for the general state of the market and the economy.[1]

The initial estimate is

$$\underset{}{ASP_t} = \underset{(0.870)}{49.322\,ADV_t} - \underset{(0.297)}{2.333\,SIL_{t-\frac{1}{2}}} + \underset{(6.065)}{75.631}$$

Coefficient of determination = .9362
Variance = 241.405
Durbin-Watson Statistic = .5042

*From *Journal of Finance*, Vol. 22, No. 1 (March 1967), pp. 67-70. Reprinted by permission of *Journal of Finance*.

†This paper is an outgrowth of problems raised in the Econometrics Seminar, University of Pennsylvania. The author wishes to thank Professor Lawrence R. Klein for suggesting the problem and his interest in the resulting work, and Professor Phoebus J. Dhrymes and C. I. Higgins for helpful discussions concerning the theoretical estimation methodology.

[1] There is some evidence that capital values adjust fairly rapidly (in three to four days) to changes in earnings and dividends. J. W. Ashley, "Stock Prices and Changes in Earnings and Dividends," *Journal of Political Economy* (February 1962), pp. 82-85.

where *ASP* is the deflated Standard and Poors "500" composite stock price index; *ADV* is deflated corporate dividends (in billions of dollars) and *SIL* is the volume of short interest outstanding on the fifteenth day of each month divided by the volume of transactions from the previous fifteenth and then lagged a fortnight. The dividend figure is for the current month while the stock price index is an average centered on the fifteenth of the calendar month.

The timing of the variables is of the utmost importance, with the short interest position preceding the price variable. To achieve insight into real behavioral phenomena, both the dividend and stock price variables are deflated by the wholesale price index, and since the problem is one of short term behavior the period of observation is monthly from January 1946 to July 1965, a total of 235 observations.[2]

Essentially, the equation removes the overall conditions of the economy by including the corporate dividend variable, which generally parallels price movement, and thus measures the net effect of short interest within this basic framework. It is evident from the results that the marginal effect of short interest is negative. The coefficient is markedly significant, being almost eight times its standard error, and points to the conclusion that increases in the volume of short interest positions are actually bearish phenomena.

II

However, it is also apparent that the equation is strongly subject to autocorrelation, with a Durbin-Watson statistic of .5042 being well below the level required to indicate a random error structure (1.74).[3] The presence of auto--correlation in residuals leads to inefficient estimators and at times also disturbs the consistency properties.[4] Therefore, to obtain a better estimate of the relation between short interest and prices, this autocorrelation problem must be solved.

After several approaches were explored, the adjustment process best suited to this equation was found to be a second order autoregressive scheme.[5] The

[2] The idea is to observe short run movements in prices as related to short interest since a short sale is concerned with the holder's view of the immediate future. Some observers believe the market does not move in causal patterns. C. W. J. Granger and O. Morgenstern comment, "Stock market prices in New York do not follow any cyclical pattern of the conventional kinds, but are mostly random fluctuations superimposed upon very long term upward or downward movements," in "Spectral Analysis of New York Stock Market Prices," *Kyklos*, Vol. XVI (January 1963), pp. 1-27.

[3] Several studies dealing with the autocorrelation problem in stock prices in the context of the random walk theory can be found in P. H. Cootner (ed.) *The Random Character of Stock Price Behavior*, MIT Press, 1964. For a thorough empirical study of stock prices using spectral analysis see Benjamin F. King, "Market and Industry Factors in Stock Price Behavior," *Journal of Business* (January 1966), pp. 139-90.

[4] This occurs when the autocorrelation is induced by a distributed lag estimation process or generally when lagged endogenous variables are used.

[5] A first order scheme, $y_t - \rho_1 y_{t-1} = a_o + a_i(x_t - \rho_1 x_{t-1}) + \epsilon_t$ yielded a minimum for the residual sum of squares at the boundary of $\rho_1(+1)$. Although an improvement in the Durbin-Watson statistic was achieved, a continually falling variance is not an acceptable result; thus at the suggestion of P. J. Dhrymes, second order schemes were used.

equation becomes an adjusted relation of the form

$$y_t - \rho_1 y_{t-1} - \rho_2 y_{t-2} = \alpha_o + \alpha_1 (x_t - \rho_1 x_{t-1} - \rho_2 x_{t-2}) + \epsilon_t$$

with an error structure

$$u_t - \rho_1 u_{t-1} - \rho_2 u_{t-2} = \epsilon_t \qquad \text{where} \qquad \epsilon_t \sim N(O, \sigma^2 I)$$

The estimation of this relationship is a non-linear problem, and the technique used below yields the classical maximum likelihood properties for the resulting estimators.[6] The procedure, formulated by P. J. Dhrymes, is to scan simultaneously on the autoregressive coefficients (ϱ_1, ϱ_2) covering their entire admissible range and select that equation which minimizes the residual sum of squares. Alternatively, this process can be viewed as maximizing the log likelihood function

$$L(a_i, \sigma^2 \mid \rho_1, \rho_2, x, y) = -\frac{T}{2} \ln(2\pi) - \frac{T}{2} \ln\sigma^2 - \frac{1}{2\sigma^2} \sum_{t=1}^{T} (y_t - \rho_1 y_{t-1} - \rho_2 y_{t-2} - a_0 - a_i (x_t - \rho_1 x_{t-1} - \rho_2 x_{t-2})^2$$

and thus yields the maximum likelihood properties for the coefficients. The form of the equation that meets these criteria is

$$ASP_t = .68\, ASP_{t-1} + .32\, ASP_{t-2} + \underset{(2.571)}{4.041} (ADV_t - .68\, ADV_{t-1} - .32\, ADV_{t-2})$$

$$\underset{(.159)}{-.460} (SIL_{t-1/2} - .68\, SIL_{t-1.1/2} - .32\, SIL_{t-2.1/2}) + \underset{(.419)}{.770}$$

Coefficient of Determination = .9894
(in terms of the original variance)
Variance = 40.27
Durbin-Watson Statistic = 1.9333

This adjusted equation, as before, shows a statistically significant negative effect of short interest upon stock prices, and the Durbin-Watson statistic indicates that the autocorrelation has been removed.

[6] See Discussion Paper No. 21 by P. J. Dhrymes, "On the Treatment of Certain Recurrent Non-linearities in Regression Analysis," and also Discussion Paper No. 22 by P. J. Dhrymes, "On Some Characteristics and Applications of the kth Order Autoregressive Process," both papers July 1966, Economics Research Services Unit, University of Pennsylvania.

A further adjustment process that is an approximation to a second order scheme proposes an error structure of the form

$$u_t - u_{t-1} - \rho_2 u_{t-2} = \epsilon_t \text{ with } \epsilon_t \sim N(O, \sigma^2 I)$$

This method, while restricting the ρ_1 coefficient to unity, did yield the desired statistical property of a glóbal minimum for the residual sum of squares.[7]

The computed relationship is

$$ASP_t = ASP_{t-1} - .31664\, ASP_{t-2} + \underset{(3.56)}{4.03}\,(ADV_t - ADV_{t-1} + .31664\, ADV_{t-2})$$

$$\underset{(.159)}{-.459}\,(SIL_{t-1/2} - SIL_{t-1.1/2} + .31664\, SIL_{t-2.1/2}) + \underset{(3.17)}{5.84}$$

Coefficient of Determination = .9895
(in terms of the original variance)
Variance = 39.91
Durbin-Watson Statistic = 1.934

It is interesting to note that the Durbin-Watson statistic again indicates a random error structure, while the coefficient of the short interest variable remains significantly negative. It is still a bearish factor.

III

Recent behavior of the market has supported the results of this analysis. Short positions were substantial in the fall of 1965 and remained high in 1966. Although dividends were at record levels during this period, the market has since experienced a significant downturn. The view of this paper is that the portrayal of short interest as a bullish factor overlooks the very nature of a short sale. It is true that a short position is a committment to buy, but it is more fundamentally a judgment on the near future behavior of prices, and this judgment is simply that prices are going to fall. Changes in short positions can be thought of as changes in expectations where these expectations are based on current economic and social conditions. In this sense, a large volume of short sales does not precipitate subsequent stock price behavior; rather it is a prediction based on many issues–economic, political and psychological–that present conditions point to a price downturn. That is, simply, short sales act as a predictor rather than a causal variable on stock price.

In September, 1965, when a short interest had risen for the third consecutive month and was nearing a figure of eight million shares, a trader commented in the *Wall Street Journal* that this rise indicated that "a lot of people are convinced that the market is headed for lower prices."[8] Both the behavior of the market since that time and the results of this analysis support this judgment.

[7] Both a Cochrane-Orcutt and scanning process led to identical results in this part of the analysis. See D. Cochrane and G. H. Orcutt, "Application of Least Squares Regression to Relationships Containing Auto-correlated Error Terms," *Journal of the American Statistical Association*, Vol. 44 (1949).

[8] *Wall Street Journal*, September 21, 1965.

19

Advance - Decline Line: A Clue to the Underlying Strength or Weakness of the Market*

George K. Freeman

One of the most respected of all "technical" indicators—those based on the action of the market itself—is the Advance-Decline Line. The *A-D* Line not only is logical in construction and application, but also, unlike many indices which require complex calculation and occult interpretation, it possesses the beauty of simplicity. Even investors who have scant interest in the technical approach to the stock market undoubtedly could profit by a study of the *A-D* Line's behavior patterns.

Most investors find it hard to recognize that the underlying trend of the stock market is not always represented accurately by the well-known "averages." Toward the end of a bull market, for instance, the performance of the broad list of stocks increasingly lags behind that of the Dow-Jones Industrials. Brokers naturally hear complaints about this discrepancy every day; the typical customer refuses to believe that only his stocks are failing to keep up with the Average. Nevertheless, it is an elemental fact that nearly every bull market ends, for most stocks, long before the averages reach their ultimate peak. The time during which the odds are on the side of the securities' buyer often is less than half the full duration of the bull market.

THREE-PHASE MARKETS

Even the Dow Theory, which is based wholly on the trends of the Dow-Jones Industrial and Railroad Averages, gives a tacit nod to the internal deterioration of a bull market—and the strengthining of a bear market—before the Averages signal any such change. Under Dow Theory, both bull markets and bear markets are divided into three broad phases. Only in the middle phase do the Averages faithfully depict the sub-surface condition of the market. The third and final phase of a bull market is a "distribution" area, wherein farsighted investors oblingingly sell stocks to feverish late-comers; the comparable phase in a bear

*From *Barron's* (January 21, 1963). Reprinted by courtesy of *Barron's National Business and Financial Weekly*.

market is an "accumulation" area, in which the more astute element buys stocks from a discouraged public. Clearly, the third phase of one and the first phase of the opposite trend overlap.

Technical analysts devote a large part of their energies—and devise scores of statistical indices—to identifying these periods of disparate movements. The simplicity of the Advance-Decline Line is only one of the qualities which commend it for the task. Most major newspaper accounts of the day's market action include the total number of stocks the price of which gained from the previous day's close (Advances); the number which posted losses (Declines); and the number which closed at the same price as the day before (Unchanged).

While these figures can be grouped, charted, and analyzed in many ways, the Advance-Decline Line is derived simply by subtracting Declines from Advances. These differentials, which naturally will be minus numbers whenever Declines exceed Advances, are added each day to form a continuous, cumulative total. Plotted on a chart as a series of connected daily totals, these cumulative differentials between Advances and Declines form the Advance-Decline Line.

CLEARCUT BAROMETER

What single statistic could describe the underlying condition of the market better than this relationship between the number of stocks advancing and the number declining? The trend of the Advance-Decline Line reveals whether the number of stocks which are rising is growing larger or smaller—a readily intelligible barometer or the strength of bull markets and the weakness of bear markets.

To illustrate the computation of the Advance-Decline Line, let us suppose the index was started on December 24. That day, 472 issues rose and 566 fell. Thus, the first *A-D* Line entry would be –94 (472 – 566 = –94). On the following trading day, 718 issues advanced and 291 declined, a difference of +427. This figure would be added to the previous *A-D* Line reading, –94, for a new reading of +333 (–94 + 427 = +333).

The next day, 428 issues advanced, 597 declined: net difference, –169. When this minus number is added to the previous cumulative total, +333, the *A-D* Line entry becomes +164 (+333 – 169 = +164).

Next day saw 494 advances, 509 declines. Net difference, –15. New index reading, +149 (+164 – 15 = +149). The following day's trading brought 594 advances, 459 declines. Difference, +135. Index reading, +284 (+149 + 135 = +284).

WEEKLY TABULATION

As simple as it is, this daily calculation—and its plotting on a chart—may constitute a more rigid regimen than an investor cares to undertake. Also, in a very short time the cumulative total may run to extreme figures, making the choice of a scale for the chart a difficult problem. A weekly tabulation, based on

Friday-through-Friday price changes, appears in Barron's and in many Sunday newspapers. Calculated from these data, the Advance-Decline Line conforms closely, in its general pattern, to a daily index; at the same time, the mathematical work and the chart scale are reduced by four-fifths.

Several services present this as a weekly index, and the accompanying chart, showing the *A-D* Line from 1960 to the present, is drawn from weekly calculations. (From 1950 through 1955, the weekly average of the daily Advances and Declines was used in the computation; from 1956 to the present, the full week Friday-through-Friday tabulation was employed.)

MOMENTUM PEAKS

As the chart indicates, bull markets generally reach a "momentum peak" well before a final top in the Averages. Only in early 1953, in the span of our graph, did the Average make a significant peak (this one preceding a 9-month, 13% drop in the Industrials) while the *A-D* Line continued upward. This was one

Fig. 1. The advance-decline line.

of the rare occasions–not seen since–when the market actually was stronger than the Average around a top area.

In early 1951, early 1955, early 1959 and in mid-1961, the Advance-Decline Line revealed a weakening of the market coincidentally with, or slightly ahead of, minor intermediate tops, but substantially ahead of far more important peaks in the Average. Indeed, though complete studies are not available, it seems certain that practically every salient market top would have showed up early in this index. Except for reactions caused by unexpected news events–which usually do not alter the underlying trend for very long–bear markets result from the gradual deterioration of investment support. The waning interest is bound to show up in the Advance-Decline Line.

The typical pattern, as revealed in the chart, runs something like this. The absolute peak in the *A-D* Line ordinarily occurs very shortly before a market peak of intermediate importance. However, the first *A-D* peak seldom coincides with the final top in the Average. The market rebounds from its correction and goes on to new highs, but the *A-D* Line, which also has retreated on the correction, fails to reach new highs on the upswing. This disparity means that some stocks already have passed their bull-market peaks.

The sequence may recur for many months, with each subsequent move into new high territory on the part of the Average finding fewer and fewer stocks participating. Eventually, the bull market facade no longer can be maintained. The trend of the Average reverts to down–as the Advance-Decline Line had done long before.

TIME TO SELL

Which top is the final one? Unfortunately, the Advance-Decline Line does not ordinarily furnish this information (though some analysts, by means of refinements of their own, have come up with the answer). However, in practice it is not essential to identify the ultimate top; few investors own all 30 Industrials and no other stocks. In most cases, when waning momentum shows up in the Advance-Decline Line, the proper investment procedure depends on the relative strength of the issues in the investor's own list. If they all should be weak holdings, conceivably they all should be sold at the first sign of ebbing market momentum.

Contrariwise, a portfolio might comprise the relatively few stocks which are destined to rise for many more months, in which case their relative strength (a simple comparison of their action with that of the Average) would show that they all should be held. Sooner or later, of course, when the market plainly is a dying swan–as shown, among other ways, in a long series of lower tops in the *A-D* Line, against higher tops in the Average–profits should probably be taken. Most commonly, however, the investor will hold some strong stocks and some weak ones, so that the sensible course simply is to weed out the softer issues as the *A-D* Line signals the onset of general weakness.

WATCHING THE TREND

In other words, it doesn't especially matter what the Average does after the *A-D* Line makes its peak. The investor who is alert to the Line's signal merely gears his program to the Line's trend, rather than that of the Average, and refuses to be deceived by the apparent strength of the market.

Like many character-of-the-market indicators, the Advance-Decline Line does not "lead" at market bottoms. A low in this index usually will synchronize–to the very day–with a low in the Average. However, in some cases the Line actually will make its absolute low well after the nadir in the Industrials; this happens frequently after a severe break in the market, when popular sentiment is at a low ebb. At such times, with the public largely out of the market, the Average well may be more buoyant than the overall list of stocks.

In 1962, for example, the Average bottomed in late June. However, the *A-D* Line, after an initial bounce, fell to a deeper trough in October, at which time the Average held above its comparable June level.

Absolute lows in the Average are reasonably easy to recognize, by numerous technical signs; yet, except for trading purposes or the purchase of a few top-grade securities at rock-bottom prices, there is no great premium on identifying those points. In the aftermath of a bear market, there customarily is a long readjustment before most stocks make their final lows. The Advance-Decline Line is an excellent guide in this often tedious period.

DESCRIBES ACTION

In his book, Strategy of Daily Stock Market Timing (Englewood Cliffs, N.J.: Prentice-Hall, 1961), Joseph Granville describes the action of the Advance-Decline Line on the 1958 market upturn (the figures are based on a daily computation begun on January 2, 1958):

"On February 4, 1958, the Dow-Jones Industrial Average reached a minor recovery high of 458.65 and the advance-decline line (cumulative differential) was up to 5,593. This was followed by a decline in the market but on March 24, 1958, the advance-decline line got up to 5,982 (a new recovery high) while the Dow-Jones Industrial Average was still under the February 4th high at 453.75. This was followed by another decline in the market but on April 18, 1958, the advance-decline line rolled through the previous top of 5,982 and reached a new high of 6,270 while the Dow-Jones Industrial Average was simultaneously down to 449.31. That second breakthrough by the advance-decline line above a previous top marked the prime buy point of the massive 1958-59 market upswing."

The Advance-Decline Line is not only a useful key to the market's long-term position, but also a fine-focusser on lesser turning points. In fact, no other technical indicator is quite so consistent in picking market tops, whatever their eventual dimension. From even a very short-term standpoint, disparate movements by the *A-D* Line and the Average call for trusting the message given by the Line.

Thus, on January 2, 1963, the Industrials fell 5.31 points, while the daily *A-D* Line rose +108. Next day the Average was up 10.63 points, showing in microcosm how the *A-D* Line may disclose the underlying trend of the market better than the Average.

Not every disparate movement brings such fast results. From the longer view, the Average and the *A-D* Line may be out of harmony for years, before the Average gets in tune; observe the patterns of 1955-57 and 1959-60 or, in even broader perspective, 1959-62. This same sort of lag, on a much smaller scale, may appear at shorter-term junctures. In general, the longer the disparity lasts, the more violent is the eventual catching-up.

There are many short-term variations on the Advance-Decline concept. Most are built on moving averages, of such length as the technician finds best suited to his purpose. Since any length might be selected, an almost infinite variety of Advance-Decline indices could be developed; however, seldom does an *A-D* moving average index cover a period shorter than 10 days or longer than 25 weeks. Additional variations arise from the use of two lines—one for Advances and one for Declines—oscillating around a "zero" line between overbought and oversold extremes.

Moreover, whether a one- or two-line index is chosen, the use of percentages rather than raw figures gives further opportunity for variation on the theme. The object of any of these indices is merely to place the Advance-Decline data under a sharper microscope, so that short-term and intermediate-term trend changes may be pinned down more precisely.

If analysts were allowed only one set of statistics from which to draw their market judgments, it seems certain that most would select the Advance-Decline data. It is literally impossible for distribution and accumulation, signifying fundamental changes in investors' sentiments, not to show up in the Advance-Decline indices—particularly in the Advance-Decline Line.

The *A-D* Line is a simple yet highly sophisticated indicator, which tells more about the condition of the market than any price average possibly could. The less reliance an investor places on outward appearances—on "averages"—the brighter are his chances for stock market success.

20

A Vote of No Confidence in the Confidence Index*

Edward D. Zinbarg

Along with many other technical indicators on Wall Street, the validity of the Confidence Index has rarely been tested. Appearing weekly in Barron's since the early 1930's, it is designed to show the relationship between yields on high-grade and low-grade bonds. Those who think the Index is a leading indicator of stock prices assume that changes in this relationship reflect changes in the risk preferences of professional investors—or "smart money." They further assume that these changes will be reflected in the common stock operations of professional investors and, with a time lag, in overall common stock price indexes.

Given the now widespread awareness of the Confidence Index, it is understandable that much confusion and consternation occurred among its adherents in 1966. After having been on a plateau for two years, the index dropped sharply in May, rose equally sharply in July through September, and then began falling again in October and November. What were these gyrations of the index saying about the future of the market?

The purpose of this article is to argue that people who believe that the Confidence Index says something worth listening to about the future of the stock market—either in 1967, 1968, or at any other time—are more likely than not to be misguided. It challenges the contention that the Confidence Index is a valuable leading indicator of stock market turning points for two basic reasons:

1. The underlying theory of why the Confidence Index should be a good stock market barometer is ill-conceived in several respects.

2. Whether the theory is right or wrong, in actual practice during the full postwar period, the Confidence Index has had a rather poor record as a stock market prophet.

THEORETICAL SOUNDNESS

The Confidence Index is a ratio of two yield series—the average yield on 10 highest-grade corporate bonds, divided by the average yield on 40 bonds of a substantially lower median quality. Since high-quality bond yields are less than

*From *The Institutional Investor,* Vol. 1, No. 1 (March 1967), Reprinted by permission of *The Institutional Investor.*

lower-quality bond yields, a rise in the ratio of high-grade to lower-grade bond yields represents a narrowing of "yield spreads." That is, the two yield series are coming closer together. Likewise, a fall in the ratio represents a widening of yield spreads. The two series are growing further apart.

Recognizing that yields move in the opposite direction from prices, it is possible to think of the Confidence Index in terms of price. The Confidence Index rises when lower-grade bond prices outperform (rise more than or fall less than) high-grade bond prices. The Confidence Index falls when high-grade bond prices outperform lower-grade bond prices.

Followers of the Confidence Index reason as follows:

The corporate bond market is dominated by professional investors, especially large life insurance companies and bank-administered pension funds.

These investors have access to the best available information on prospects for economic and capital market conditions. They represent what we have called smart money.

When these investors are relatively gloomy about business and financial prospects, they tend to shift their bond investments toward higher-grade issues, causing high-grade bond prices to outperform lower-grade bond prices. This leads to a fall in the Confidence Index. Likewise, when smart money is optimistic, it tends to shift its emphasis toward lower-grade bonds. This causes lower-grade bond prices to outperform high-grade bond prices, and the Confidence Index rises.

Being sophisticated professionals, these investors try to anticipate economic slow-downs and recoveries rather than wait until turning points actually are at hand. Therefore, the Confidence Index should normally change direction before the economy does.

When smart investors become cautious, and shift their relative bond preferences away from lower-grade bonds, they also shift away from common stocks. And before long, their wisdom should be borne out and common stock prices should decline. Likewise, when smart investors become optimistic, and shift their relative bond preferences toward lower-grade bonds, they also shift toward common stocks. And before long, common stock prices should rise.

Thus, changes in the trend of the Confidence Index should occur in advance of both the economy and the stock market. The typical lead time of the index over the popular stock price averages is believed to be two to four months.

This line of reasoning has several weaknesses. In the first place, the assumption that professional investors as a group are astute enough to pinpoint economic turning points a given number of months in advance is debatable. They may, on the whole, do a better job of economic forecasting than the proverbial man-in-the-street. But professional economists who work for large financial institutions would be the first to admit that the precision of their timing skills still leaves much to be desired.

Second, even assuming accurate forecasting, it is a mistake to assume that there is a precise relationship between bond investors' economic forecasts and their relative preferences for high-grade versus lower-grade bonds. It is doubtless true that prosperity causes investors to mentally upgrade lower-quality securities and to be satisfied with smaller risk premiums when they judge the adequacy of lower-grade bond yields versus yields on high-grade bonds. This reduction in demanded risk premiums is reflected in a general tendency for yield spreads on bonds of different quality to narrow during prosperous times. Similarly, it is doubtless true that an opposite reaction occurs during recessions—risk premiums increase and yield spreads widen. But to abstract from these general tendencies, which are evident during booms and recessions, and argue that institutional attitudes toward risk shift markedly in anticipation of economic turning points, is not at all realistic

Large financial institutions are at least as much influenced in their investment operations by considerations of long-term portfolio balance, by customer relations, and by the competitive striving for improved yields as they are by anticipated short-term changes in the economic environment. Therefore, their relative preferences for high-grade versus lower-grade bonds, or indeed for stocks versus bonds, should not be expected to be very closely attuned to their transitory attitudes regarding the state of the business cycle.

Another oversimplication, that of focusing only on investors' attitudes, ignores the fact that prices—of bonds or of anything else—are determined by supply as well as by demand. The theory of the Confidence Index does not allow for any impact on yield spreads of shifts in the relative supply of bonds of varying quality.

For example, suppose that at a particular period of time, investors' risk preferences did indeed shift en masse toward higher-quality. Other things being equal, this would tend to widen yield spreads—that is to depress the Confidence Index. But suppose that simultaneously many giant, blue-chip, high-quality corporations were engaged in heavy debt financing. Might not the pressure of supply in the high-grade sector of the market offset the increased demand in that sector, causing corporate bond yield spreads to remain constant or perhaps even to narrow?

If there were a consistent tendency for the supply of high-grade bonds to diminish relative to low-grade bonds prior to economic downturns and to increase prior to upturns, considerations of supply would reinforce Confidence Index theory. But Chart I, showing a weighted average of Moody's quality ratings of publicly-offered corporate bond new issues, suggests no such tendency. The chart was constructed by assigning the number 1 to a new Aaa bonds, 2 to Aa, 3 to A, and 4 to Baa (issues of less than Baa quality were ignored). Each rating category was weighted by the volume of new issues in that category each month, and a weighted average rating was calculated. To delineate trends more clearly, a 6-month centered moving average of the monthly average ratings is plotted on the chart in addition to monthly data. Downward move-

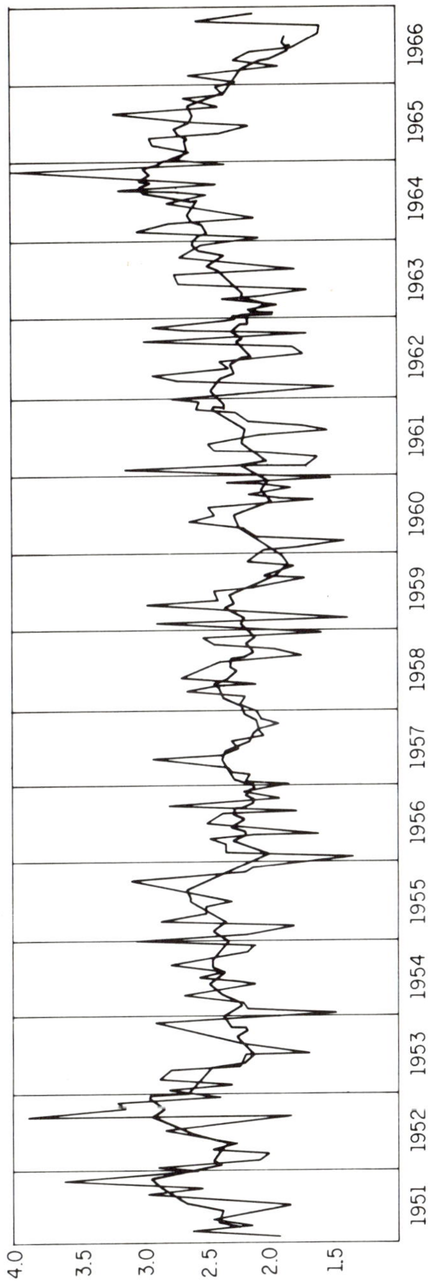

CHART 1

Weighted Average Moody's Rating of Publicly Issued New Corporate Bonds

ments represent increasing quality of new issues, and upward movements represent reductions in quality.

Note that average quality of new bond issues tended to fluctuate within a rather narrow band (2.0-2.5) during most of the period covered. Such significant upward or downward movements which did occur, however, surely do not reinforce Confidence Index theory.

If anything, the chart suggests that changing supply pressures may often offset such changes in demand forces as are postulated by Confidence Index theorists. For a year prior to the 1953-54 recession, for example, the average quality of new issues increased rather than diminished. And as the economy emerged from that recession, average quality diminished rather than increased. In 1963-64, the average quality of the supply of new issues became progressively poorer, thus tending to offset rather than reinforce the yield spread impact of a presumed shift of demand toward lower quality bonds. And from late-1964 until signs of the economy's vulnerability appeared in 1966, average quality increased sharply.

Thus, if smart money was getting nervous during this period, and increasing its preference for high quality issues, high-quality corporate borrowers were obliging them. This changed supply pattern would tend to prevent the widening of yield spreads-– decline in the Confidence Index–which might have occurred prior to the 1966 stock market slide. But, as we shall see, this did not in fact occur.

Finally, if the reasoning of Confidence Index enthusiasts were essentially sound, other ratios of high-quality to lower-quality bond yields should move parallel to Barron's Confidence Index. Yet a comparison of the Confidence Index with a ratio of, say, Moody's Aaa to Baa corporate bond yield averages reveals several periods of divergent movement at a time when followers of the Confidence Index might well have been reading "signals" into their data. This is highlighted in Chart 2.

EMPIRICAL SUCCESS

When all is said and done, of course, "the proof of the pudding is in the eating." If the Confidence Index really has worked fairly consistently as a stock market barometer, theory can stand aside or be modified.

Chart 3 presents the full postwar record of the Confidence Index. Using monthly averages of weekly data. Admittedly, the averaging process might tend to shorten slightly any lead time of the index over the market, but there is no reason to think that the use of monthly rather than weekly data obscures any underlying relationships. Indeed, weekly data confirm the conclusions presented below. Alongside the Confidence Index is shown the movement of aggregate stock prices, as measured by the Standard & Poor's 425 Industrial Stock Price Index. Thus, the "hits and misses" of the Confidence Index can be tallied readily.

CHART 2

Disparities Between Confidence Index and a Ratio of Moody's Aaa/Baa Yield Averages

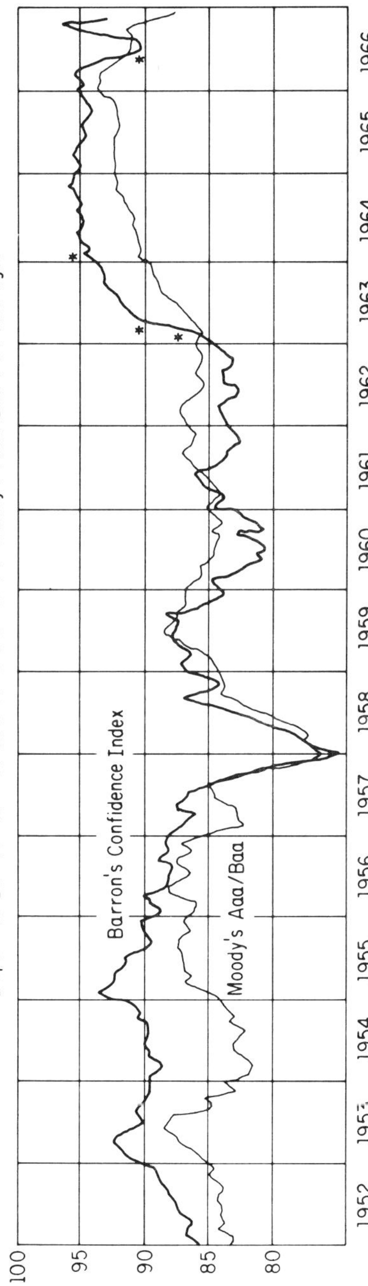

*Components of confidence index revised

CHART 3

Stock Prices and Confidence Index

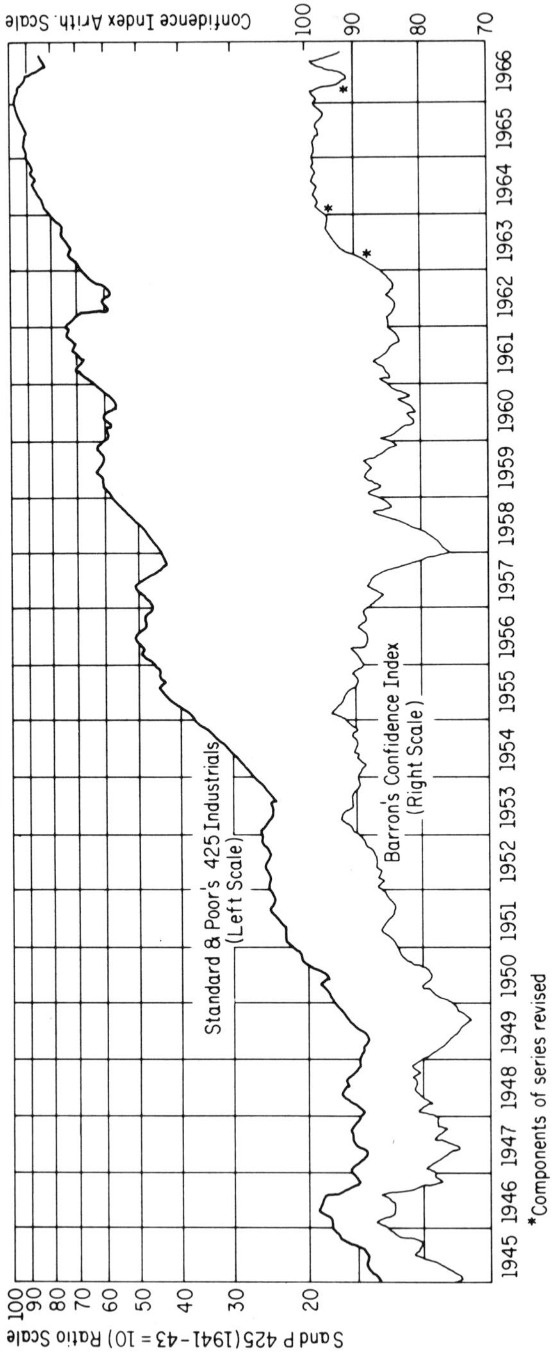

RECORD IN SIGNALLING BEAR MARKETS

1946: The Confidence Index peaked in January, 1946, four months in advance of the stock price peak which occurred in May. It should be noted, however, that the initial downturn of the Confidence Index was very shallow. The index in August was only slightly lower than in January. Thus, it is not at all

	Good Leading Indicator	Equivocal Leading Indicator	Misleading Indicator*
STOCK PRICE PEAKS			
1946		●	
1948			●
1953			●
1956-57			●
1959-60	●		
1962		●	
1966			●
STOCK PRICE TROUGHS			
1947			●
1949			●
1953			●
1958			●
1960	●		
1962		●	

*Coincident, lagging or extremely long lead.

clear that one would have recognized at the time that the index was indeed in a downtrend. The really sharp decline in the index did not occur until September, when the stock market was also falling sharply. Perhaps the fairest judgment is that the Confidence Index gave a correct, but not unequivocal, bear market signal during this period.

1948: Since the market's recovery from 1947 to 1948 did not carry the averages to a new high, some people classify the 1948-49 stock price decline as merely a continuation of the 1946 decline rather than as a separate bear market. However, the obvious relationship of the stock price decline to the general economic recession of 1949 seems to warrant a separate bear market classification. If so, then the Confidence Index clearly did not lead this bear market. In fact, it lagged the June stock price peak by several months.

1953: The third postwar bear market (defined here as a decline extending over several months and amounting to more than 10 percent occurred in 1953. Again the Confidence Index lagged by several months.

1956-57: The stock market made a double-top in August, 1956 and July, 1957. Whichever date one chooses as the beginning of the bear market, however, the associated peak of the Barron's Confidence Index was in February, 1955—far too early to have been of much value in reaching timing decisions.

1959-60: Although the stock market peaked on a monthly average basis in July, 1959, the major decline was delayed until 1960. Thus, the peaking of the

Confidence Index in September, 1959, and its fairly pronounced downtrend thereafter, can be viewed as a correct bear market signal.

1962: The stock market peaked in December, 1961, and the Confidence Index in June, 1961. However, the decline of the Confidence Index was very shallow, and it was already rising when stock prices first began to decline. Like the 1946 experience, we can classify this as a correct signal, but not unequivocally correct.

1966: The behavior of the Confidence Index prior to the 1966 bear market surely was not that of a good leading indicator of stock prices. As the bull market proceeded, the Confidence Index rose to near its maximum theoretical level of 100 percent by early 1964, and then moved horizontally for almost two years. It declined in May, several months after the peak of stock prices, rebounded to its previous high level during the summer, and then began to ease again.* It is extremely difficult to determine objectively how a follower of the Confidence Index would have timed his purchases and sales during this period, but the likelihood of his having been "whipsawed" (that is, selling and then buying back at a higher price level) seems great.

RECORD IN SIGNALLING BULL MARKETS

1947: The turn of the Confidence Index was coincident with the turn of stock prices.

1949: The Confidence Index lagged the trough of stock prices.

1953: The Confidence Index lagged the trough of stock prices.

1958: The turn of the Confidence Index was coincident with the turn of stock prices.

1960: The Confidence Index correctly signalled the stock price trough several months in advance.

1962: The Confidence Index had hit bottom and started to rise before stock prices even began to decline. Thus, while it might be said that the index led the market trough, from a practical point of view it did not.

1966-67: Not yet determinable.

The conclusion is evident. The Confidence Index has not exhibited the characteristics of a good leading indicator of the stock market during the past twenty years. More often than not it was coincident or lagging.

NO CONFIDENCE

If the Confidence Index is used simply as the take-off point for a thorough analysis of supply and demand factors in the capital market, we can have no particular quarrel with it, except to point out that many other series of data could serve the same purposes equally well. But if, as has typically been the case, the index is used mechanically, a vote of no-confidence in the Confidence Index should be the rule.

21

Stock Market "Patterns" and Financial Analysis: Methodological Suggestions*

Harry V. Roberts †

INTRODUCTION

Of all economic time series, the history of security prices, both individual and aggregate, has probably been most widely and intensively studied. While financial analysts agree that underlying economic facts and relationships are important, many also believe that the history of the market itself contains "patterns" that give clues to the future, if only these patterns can be properly understood. The Dow theory and its many offspring are evidence of this conviction. In extreme form such theories maintain that *only* the patterns of the past need be studied, since the effect of everything else is reflected "on the tape."

A common and convenient name for analysis of stock-market patterns is "technical analysis." Perhaps no one in the financial world completely ignores technical analysis–indeed, its terminology is ingrained in market reporting–and some rely intensively on it. Technical analysis includes many different approaches, most requiring a good deal of subjective judgment in application. In part these approaches are purely empirical; in part they are based on analogy with physical processes, such as tides and waves.

In light of this intense interest in patterns and of the publicity given to statistics in recent years, it seems curious that there has not been widespread recognition among financial analysts that the patterns of technical analysis may be little, if anything, more than a statistical artifact. At least, it is safe to say that the close resemblance between market behavior over relatively long time periods and that of simple chance devices has escaped general attention, though the role of chance variation in very short time periods have often been recognized. One possible explanation is that the usual method of graphing stock prices gives a picture of successive *levels,* rather than of *changes,* and levels can give an artificial appearance of "pattern" or "trend." A second is that chance behavior itself produces "patterns" that invite spurious interpretations.

*From *Journal of Finance*, Vol. 14, No. 1 (March 1959), pp. 1-10. Reprinted by permission of *Journal of Finance.*

†I am indebted to Lawrence West and Arnold Moore for help in the preparation of this paper.

More evidence for this assertion about stock-market behavior is still needed, but almost all the fragmentary evidence known to me is consistent with it. The major published evidence from recent years is a paper about British stock indexes (and American commodity prices) by the British statistician, M. G. Kendall, which appeared in 1953.[1] I have done similar, though less comprehensive, work with recent American data, for both indexes and individual companies, which has been entirely consistent with Kendall's findings. If, for example, weekly *changes* of the Dow Jones Index are examined statistically, it is apparent that these changes behave very much as if they had been generated by an extremely simple chance model. The history of market *levels* behaves very much as if levels had been generated by a *cumulation* of results given by the chance model.

These general conclusions have been reached, probably repeatedly, long before Kendall's study. Thus Holbrook Working, writing in 1934, said:

> It has several times been noted that time series commonly possess in many respects the characteristics of series of cumulated random numbers. The separate items in such time series are by no means random in character, but the changes between successive items tend to be largely random. This characteristic has been noted conspicuously in sensitive commodity prices. . . . King has concluded that stock prices resemble cumulations of purely random changes even more strongly than do commodity prices.[2]

Indeed, the main reason for this paper is to call to the attention of financial analysts empirical results that seem to have been ignored in the past, for whatever reason, and to point out some methodological implications of these results for the study of securities.

From the point of view of the scholar, much more research is needed to establish more precisely the limits to which these generalizations can be carried. For example, do they apply to changes for periods other than weekly? (In my own explorations they have worked fairly well for both longer and shorter periods.) How well do they apply to individual securities? (Most work has been done on indexes.) What slight departures from the chance model are detectable? Perhaps the traditional academic suspicion about the stock market as an object of scholarly research will be overcome, and this work will be done.[3] This paper, however, is concerned with the methodological problems of the financial analyst who cannot afford to ignore evidence that is easily obtainable from the most casual empirical analysis. From his point of view there should be great interest in the possibility that, to a first approximation, stock-market behavior may be statistically the simplest, by far, of all economic time series.

[1] Maurice G. Kendall, "The Analysis of Economic Time Series. I," *Journal of the Royal Statistical Society* (Ser. A), CXVI (1953), 11-25.

[2] Holbrook Working, "A Random-Difference Series for Use in the Analysis of Time Series," *Journal of the American Statistical Association* XXIX (1934), 11.

[3] Holbrook Working has worked for many years on the behavior of commodities markets, and full publication of his findings is still forthcoming.

This paper will describe the chance model more precisely, discuss briefly the common-sense interpretation of the model, and outline a number of methodological suggestions for financial analysts.

THE CHANCE MODEL

Kendall found that changes in security prices behaved nearly as if they had been generated by a suitably designed roulette wheel for which each outcome was statistically independent of past history and for which relative frequencies were reasonably stable through time. This means that, once a person accumulates enough evidence to make good estimates of the relative frequencies (probabilities) of different outcomes of the wheel, he would base his predictions only on these relative frequencies and pay no attention to the pattern of recent spins. Recent spins are relevant to prediction only insofar as they contribute to more precise estimates of relative frequencies. In a gambling expression, this roulette wheel "has no memory."

The chance model just described insists on independence but makes no commitment about the relative frequencies, or probabilities, of different outcomes except that these must be stable over time. A frequency distribution of past changes is a good basis for estimating these probabilities, so long as the independence assumption holds. For concreteness in demonstration, we shall assume that weekly changes of a particular index behave as if they were independent observations on a normal distribution, with mean +0.5 and standard deviation 5.0. The details of constructing such a roulette wheel need not concern us here. We shall, in fact, employ for our purpose a published table of random numbers that can be modified easily to conform to the specifications stated above.[4] Assuming that the series starts at 450, we obtain a hypothetical year's experience graphed in Figs. 1 and 2.

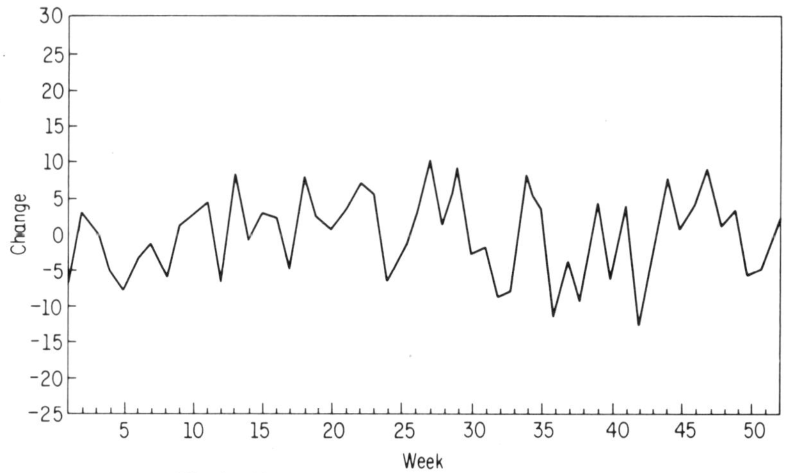

Fig. 1. Simulated market changes for 52 weeks.

[4]The RAND Corporation, *A Million Random Digits with 100,000 Normal Deviates* (Glencoe, Ill.: Free Press, 1955).

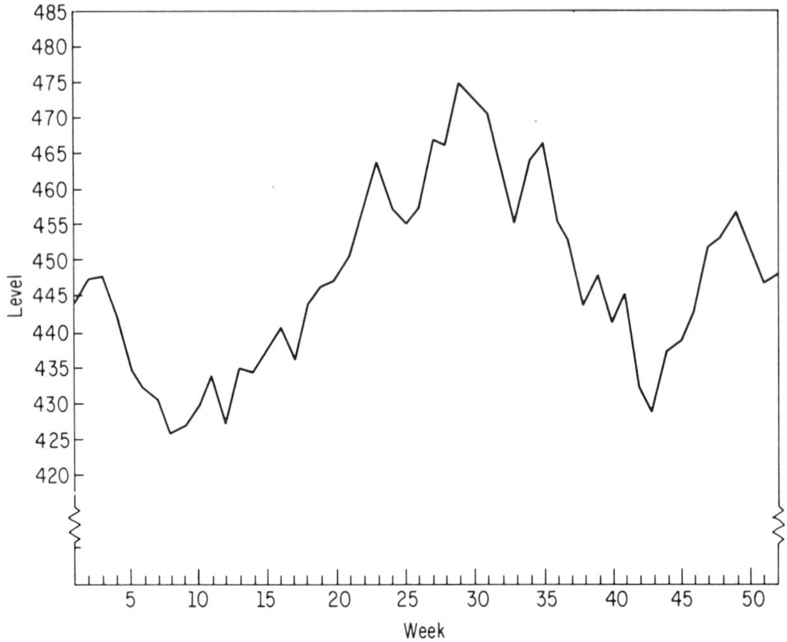

Fig. 2. Simulated market levels for 52 weeks.

To even a casual observer of the stock market, Fig. 2 is hauntingly realistic, even to the "head-and-shoulders" top. Probably all the classical patterns of technical analysis can be generated artificially by a suitable roulette wheel or random-number table. Fig. 1 gives much less evidence of patterns, although intensive and imaginative scrutiny would undoubtedly suggest some. The only *persistent* patterns of Fig. 1 (and its continuation beyond 52 weeks) are (1) the relative frequency of different outcomes and (2) the clustering tendency for similar outcomes. The clustering phenomenon runs contrary to intuitive feelings about chance and raises temporary hopes about predictability. These hopes, however, can be crushed by theoretical analysis that shows clustering to give no information beyond that contained in the relative frequencies.

Figures 3 and 4 give the corresponding diagrams for the Dow Jones Industrial Index for 1956. The general resemblance between Figs. 3–4 and Figs. 1–2 is unmistakable, although no pains were taken to devise a "roulette" wheel that would simulate closely the actual history of 1956. The major difference in detail between Figs. 1 and 3 is that Fig. 3 shows greater dispersion. We probably could have imitated Fig. 3 more closely by using a somewhat larger standard deviation than 5 in constructing the artificial series. It is well, however, to avoid giving the wrong impression by showing *too* striking a parallel in all details. Two artificial series constructed by precisely the same method typically differ from each other just as would two brothers or two years of market history. To put it differently, the chance model cannot duplicate history in any sense other than that in which one evening in a gambling casino duplicates another. For relatively short periods of history like 52 weeks, there can be substantial differences. In fact, however, the dispersion of Fig. 3 is almost surely greater than that of Fig. 1 by more than we would expect from the same chance mechanism. We subsequently obtained a better simulation by using a standard deviation of 7 rather than 5.

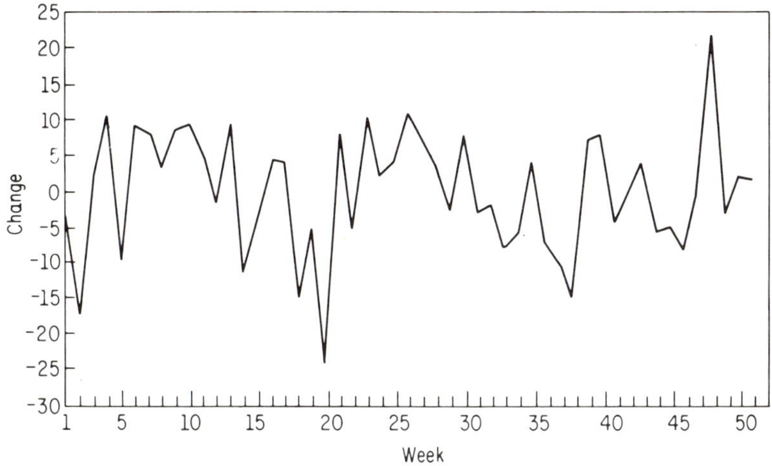

Fig. 3. Changes from Friday to Friday (closing) January 6, 1956–December 28, 1956. Dow Jones Industrial Index.

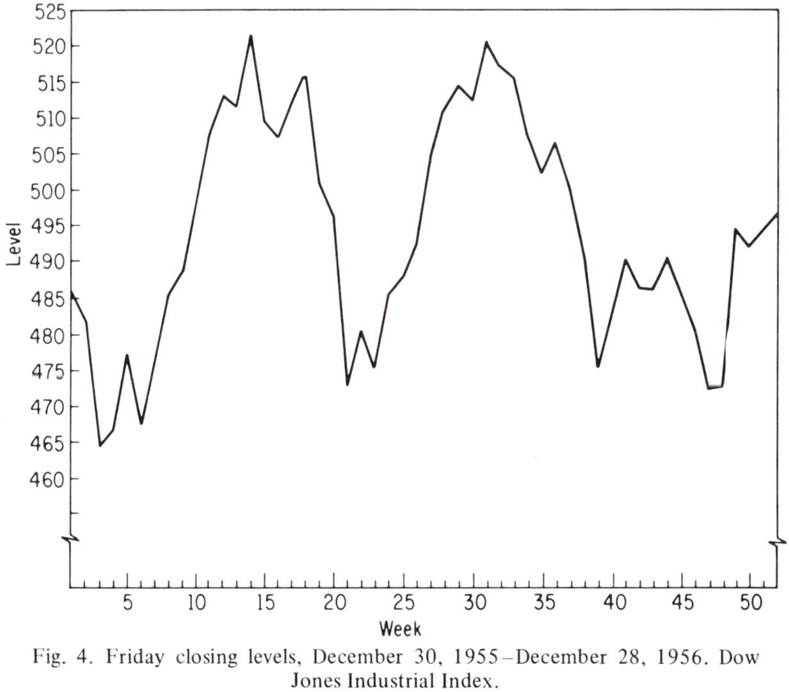

Fig. 4. Friday closing levels, December 30, 1955–December 28, 1956. Dow Jones Industrial Index.

MEANING OF THE CHANCE MODEL

There are two common reactions to this chance model: (1) while "chance" may be important in extremely short-run stock-market movements, it is inconceivable that the longer-term movement should be a cumulation of short-term "chance" development; (2) once one reflects on the situation, it is obvious that a simple chance model must hold. We shall discuss each reaction briefly.

The first reaction stems partly from a misunderstanding of the term "chance." The chance model of the previous section was meant to illustrate the possibility of constructing a simple mechanical device that would duplicate many of the characteristic features of stock-market movements. Even if the statistical behavior of the market and the mechanical device were completely indistinguishable, it might still be possible to attain a degree of predictability better than that given by knowledge of past relative frequencies alone. To attain such predictability, however, more would be needed than the past history of market prices: e.g., economic theory and knowledge of economic facts might suggest relationships of market prices with other economic variables that might be of predictive value. It seems more likely that economic analysis could give predictive insight into stock-market behavior than that physical analysis could help with a real roulette wheel. Even completely deterministic phenomena, such as the decimal expansions of irrational numbers (e.g., e and π), appear to be "chance" phenomena to an observer who does not understand the underlying mechanism. Phenomena that can be described only as "chance" today, such as the emission of alpha particles in radioactive decay, may ultimately be understood in a deeper sense.

In another sense the reaction against "chance" is sound. Much more empirical work is needed, and it seems likely that departures from simple chance models will be found—if not for stock-market averages, then for individual stocks; if not for weekly periods, then for some other period; if not from the independence assumption, then from the assumption of a stable underlying distribution: etc. Indeed, the analytical proposals of this paper are based on the assumption that such departures will occasionally be found. Holbrook Working has discovered such departures in his commodity market research.[5]

As to the second reaction, that the chance model is obvious, there is a plausible rationale. "If the stock market behaved like a mechanically imperfect roulette wheel, people would notice the imperfections and by acting on them, remove them." This rationale is appealing, if for no other reason than its value as counterweight to the popular view of stock market "irrationality," but it is obviously incomplete. For example, why should not observation of market imperfection lead to greater imperfection rather than less? All we can do is to suggest the importance of the study of such questions.

[5] Holbrook Working, "New Ideas and Methods for Price Research," *Journal of Farm Economics,* XXXVIII (1956), 1427–36.

SUGGESTIONS FOR FINANCIAL ANALYSIS

This section is devoted to statistical suggestions to financial analysts and others who make their living by the study of the market. The fundamental suggestion, of course, is to analyze price *changes* as well as price *levels.* Initially, the weekly change seems worth using, but other time periods may also be useful. This suggestion seems trivial, but it is not. If the simple chance hypothesis is correct, then the statistical behavior of changes, which are independent, is much simpler than that of levels, which are not. There already exists, for example, a body of statistical techniques for analysis of independent data: in fact, modern statistical theory has been largely built up on the assumption of independence. Much of it also assumes, as we did for convenience in the artificial example, that the underlying distribution is a normal distribution in the technical sense of that term. The assumption of normality usually seems far less crucial to the applicability of statistical methods than does that of independence, and some statistical techniques, called "non-parametric," do not make the normality assumption.

If one graphs weekly changes without any formal statistical analysis, he will have taken the most important single step. So long as the stock or stock index behaves like a reasonably good roulette wheel, the visual impression will be similar to that of Figs. 1 and 3. If there is a really fundamental shift in the underlying situation, it can be detected visually more readily by an analysis of changes than of levels. Conversely, if there has been no fundamental shift, a graph of changes will be much less likely to give the impression that there has been a shift.

There are formal statistical techniques to supplement visual analysis (though never to replace it entirely, since graphical study is always partial insurance against misapplication of statistical analysis). The most popular field of applied statistics–industrial quality control–draws on these techniques extensively. Though there would undoubtedly be many differences in detail, a financial analyst should find much of interest and relevance in methods of quality control.[6] We shall illustrate briefly how these ideas might be applied in financial analysis. For concreteness, we begin with the data given graphically in Fig. 3.

1. The first question is that of independence: Can we regard these weekly changes as independent? Purely to illustrate one test of independence, we shall apply a test based on runs above and below zero. If we denote a positive change by "+" and a negative change by "–", Fig. 3 yields the following sequence of +'s and –'s.

– – + + – + + + + + + – + – – + + – – – + – + + + + + +
– + – – – – + – – – + + – – + – – – + + – + +

[6]W. Allen Wallis and Harry V. Roberts, *Statistics: A New Approach* (Glencoe,Ill.: Free Press, 1956), chaps. 16, 18; A. Hald, *Statistical Theory with Engineering Applications* (New York: John Wiley & Sons, Inc., 1952), chap. 13; Eugene L. Grant, *Statistical Quality Control* (rev. ed.; New York: McGraw-Hill Book Co., Inc., 1952).

A "run" is a consecutive sequence of the same symbol: e.g., – –, + +, –, and + + + + + + are the first four runs. We count 24 runs, which does not differ significantly from the expected number of 26.41.[7]

There are many tests for independence, and experience will show the most useful ones for this kind of application. I would guess that the mean-square successive difference[8] would prove useful. This has the virtue of providing a descriptive measure of the degree of independence or dependence, as well as a test that gives simply an all-or-none verdict or a significance level. A slight degree of dependence may not invalidate subsequent analysis of the kind proposed here, while substantial dependence may open the way for forecasts that exploit the observed pattern, just as one might do by careful study of a defective roulette wheel.

The idea of "rational subgroups" commonly used in industrial practice may be useful,[9] particularly in relating changes for different intervals of time, such as days and weeks.

2. If substantial dependence is found, it may be directly useful for forecasting, using the well-known methods of autoregression. Dependence may also suggest useful avenues for investigation. A sharp jump in the level of price changes for a particular stock, for example, might be found to coincide with a change in management. The company's history since that change would then be the object of an analysis like that described in the preceding paragraph.

3. If a close approximation to independence is found for any moderately large number of weeks (say at least 52, as a rule of thumb), set up "control limits" to aid visual analysis in the future. These limits can be calculated in many ways.[10] If a point falls outside the control limits, this gives a signal for the analyst to search for an explanation beyond the series itself: e.g., company developments, economic changes, governmental actions. So long as points stay within the limits, there is no need for special attention, although there may also be supplemental warning signals based on gradual shifts that cause trends but do not immediately throw points outside control limits. There will be risks of failing to search when a search is warranted and of searching when nothing is to be found. These risks can be evaluated and the control limits determined accordingly. The aim of the procedure is to economize the time of the financial analyst, who cannot possibly be simultaneously in close contact with the many individual companies that he must be familiar with. It should tend to avoid the numerous false signals that are so strongly suggested by examination of levels rather than changes.

This outline of statistical procedure is meant only to be suggestive. The general nature of the statistical attack is obvious, but the details will be supplied

[7]For mechanical details see Wallis and Roberts, *op. cit.*

[8]*Ibid.*

[9]Grant, *op. cit.*

[10]Wallis and Roberts, *op. cit.*; Hald, *op. cit.*; and Grant, *op. cit.*

with practical experience guided by sound statistical theory. It may be found, for example, that it is wiser to analyze changes of logarithms or square roots of levels than absolute changes, especially when long periods of time are examined. But much is to be gained simply by viewing a familiar problem from a new vantage point, and minor statistical refinements or blemishes may not be crucial.

These statistical suggestions are only a preliminary to the real work of the financial analyst, which extends far beyond the tape itself and draws on knowledge and skills, including statistical knowledge and skills, that are not discussed here. There is every reason to believe, however, that this method of looking at the tape will facilitate all that takes place afterward. Further statistical analysis, such as multiple regression, will be sounder if based on independent changes rather than dependent levels. Judgment and intuition will proceed more soundly if not hindered by an unnecessary grappling with market "patterns."

22

Price Movements in Speculative Markets: Trends or Random Walks*

Sidney S. Alexander †

There is a remarkable contradiction between the concepts of behavior of speculative prices held by professional stock market analysts on the one hand and by academic statisticians and economists on the other. The professional analysts operate in the belief that there exist certain trend generating facts, knowable today, that will guide a speculator to profit if only he can read them correctly. These facts are believed to generate trends rather than instantaneous jumps because most of those trading in speculative markets have imperfect knowledge of these facts, and the future trend of prices will result from a gradual spread of awareness of these facts throughout the market. Those who gain mastery of the critical information earlier than others will, accordingly, have an opportunity to profit from that early knowledge.

The two main schools of professional analysts, the "fundamentalists" and the "technicians," agree on this basic assumption. They differ only in the methods used to gain knowledge before others in the market. The fundamentalist seeks this early knowledge from study of the external factors that lie behind the price changes. In a commodity market he tries to estimate the future balance of supply and demand for that commodity. In the stock market he studies general business conditions and the profit prospects for various industries, and for the individual firms within those industries, with special attention to new developments.

The "technician" operates on the same basic assumption, that facts existing at one time will govern the prices at some future time, but he operates in a different manner. He leaves to others the study of the fundamental facts in the reliance that as those others act on their knowledge there will be a detectable effect on the price of the stock or commodity. The technician, accordingly, studies price movements of the immediate past for telltale indications of the movements of the immediate future.

*From *Industrial Management Review,* Vol. 2, No. 2 (May 1961), pp. 7–26. Reprinted by permission of *Industrial Management Review.*

†The data gathering and processing underlying this research were supported by the Sloan Research Fund of the School of Industrial Management, Massachusetts Institute of Technology.

Both schools of analysts thus assume the existence of trends which represent the gradual recognition by the market of emergent factual situations–trends which, if they exist, must depend for their existence on a lagged response of the market prices to the underlying factors governing those prices. It might, at first blush, seem possible that the trends arise not from a lagged response of the market price to the fundamental circumstances, but rather from a trend in those underlying circumstances themselves. Thus, although a stock's price might at all times represent a given multiple of its earnings, its earnings might be subject to a long run trend. If, however, there are really trends in earnings, so that an increase in earnings this year implies a higher probability of an increase next year than do stable or declining earnings, the stock price right now should reflect these prospects by a higher price and by a higher ratio of price to current earnings. Consequently, if there is no lagged response there should be no trend in prices. By a trend in this connection we mean a positive serial correlation of successive changes or, more generally, a probability of future price change dependent on present price change.

The professional analysts would certainly not subscribe to the notion that the best picture of the future movements of prices can be gained by tossing a coin or a set of coins. Yet that is just what the academic students of specualtive markets say is the best way. The academic students of speculative markets have come to deny the very existence of trends in speculative prices, claiming that where trends seem to be observable, they are merely interpretations, read in after the fact, of a process that really follows a random walk. A price can be said to follow a random walk if at any time the change to be expected can be represented by the result of tossing a coin, not necessarily a 50-50 coin, however. In particualr, a random walk would imply that the next move of the speculative price is independent of all past moves or events.

This probabilistic view of speculative prices is consistent with the theoretical bent of economists who like to talk about perfect markets. If one were to start out with the assumption that a stock or commodity speculation is a "fair game" with equal expectation of gain or loss or, more accurately, with an expectation of zero gain, one would be well on the way to picturing the behavior of speculative prices as a random walk. But in fact, this picture of a speculative price movement is as much based on empirical findings as on theoretical predispositions. In a pioneer work Bachelier,[1] a student of the great French mathematician Poincaré, derived, in his doctoral thesis in 1900, a theory that speculative prices follow random walks, largely from the assumption of zero expectation of gain. He then compared the statistical distribution of price behavior expected from this theory with observed distributions of price changes of certain government securities (*rentes*) on the Paris *Bourse*, and he found a close correspondence between the observed distribution and that to be expected from his theory.

[1] M. L. Bachelier, *Théorie de la Speculation,* Gauthier-Villars, Paris, 1900.

The most impressive recent findings confirming the random walk hypothesis are those of Kendall.[2] He calculated the first twenty-nine lagged serial correlations of the first differences of twenty-two time series representing speculative prices. Nineteen of these were indexes of British industrial share prices on a weekly basis. (See Table 1.) Two of the remaining three were cash wheat at Chicago, one weekly and one monthly, and the last was the spot cotton price at New York, monthly. Essentially, Kendall was asking with respect to each weekly series: How good is the best estimate we can make of next week's price change if we know this week's change and the changes of the past twenty-nine weeks and correspondingly for the monthly series?

Contrary to the general impression among traders and analysts that stock and commodity prices follow trends, Kendall found, with two or three exceptions, that knowledge of past price changes yields substantially no information about future price changes. More specifically, he found that each period's price change was not significantly correlated with the preceding period's price change nor with the price change of any earlier period, at least as far as he tested, up to twnety-nine periods. Essentially, the estimate of the next period's price change could have been drawn at random from a specified distribution with results as satisfactory as the best formula that could be fitted to past data. In the case of weekly wheat prices, that distribution was studied in detail and it turned out to be very close to a normal distribution.

There was one notable exception, however, to this pattern of random behavior of price changes. That was the monthly series on cotton prices in the United States since 1816 with, of course, a few interruptions for such events as the Civil War. For this series there did appear to be some predictability, and Kendall felt impelled to draw the moral that it is dangerous to generalize even from fairly extensive sets of data. For, from the behavior of wheat prices and the stock prices, one might have concluded that speculative markets do not generate autocorrelated price changes—and here was cotton providing a notable exception.

Alas, Kendall drew the wrong moral. The appropriate one is that if you find a single exception, look for an error. An error there was, for the cotton price series was different from the others investigated by Kendall. Almost all the others were series of observations of the price at a specified time—say, the closing price on Friday of each week. Each observation of the cotton series was an average of four or five weekly observations of the corresponding month. It turns out that even if the original data—the Friday closing prices—were a random walk, with successive first differences uncorrelated, the first differences of the monthly average of four or five of these weekly observations would exhibit first-order serial correlations of about the magnitude Kendall found for cotton.[3]

[2]M. G. Kendall, "The Analysis of Economic Time Series—Part I: Prices," *Journal of the Royal Statistical Society (Series A)*, Vol. 96 (1933), pp. 11–25.

[3]This point was independently discovered by the author and by Holbrook Working.

So Kendall's exception vanishes, and we are left with the conclusion that at least for the series he investigated the serial correlations were not significantly different from zero.[4]

But the question immediately arises whether a week is not an inappropriate period of observation. The market analysts might protest that when they speak of a trend they are speaking of a smooth underlying movement on which is typically superimposed a lot of short-term fluctuation. With weekly observations the short-term fluctuations might very easily swamp the underlying trends. In particular, the give and take of the market leads to a phenomenon, recognized by all analysts, of reactions, usually called technical reactions, presumably associated with profit taking. These reactions are, of course, negatively correlated with the main price swings. That's what makes them reactions. Kendall's correlations, close to zero, could possibly be a consequence of the combination of the negative contributions of the reactions and the positive contributions of the trends.

The path of a speculative price might, accordingly, be represented by a sum of two components, a smooth underlying trend or cycle changing direction only infrequently, and a much shorter cycle of action and reaction. Under this hypothesis the first-order serial correlations of daily price changes might be negative, the first order correlation weekly changes might be close to zero, while the first order serial correlations of monthly or bimonthly changes might be significantly larger than zero.

We can test this possibility by studying the first order serial correlations of Kendall's data using successively longer intervals of differencing. As we do so, and consider first the first order serial correlation of one week changes, then of two week, four week, eight week, and sixteen week changes, the influence of the reactions should become smaller and smaller and the trend effect, if there is one, should become dominant. The corresponding correlations, roughly calculated,[5] are given in Table 1.

While an occasional high value correlation occurs in Table 1 for intervals greater than one week, it must be remembered that for the given total time period under study, the number of observations drops in proportion to the length of the differencing interval. Since the variance of the correlation coefficient is inversely proportional to the number of observations, it is directly proportional to the length of the differencing interval. An occasional high

The latter, however, had the pleasure of first publishing it in "Note on the Correlation of First Differences of Averages in a Random Chain," *Econometrica,* Vol. 28, No. 4 (October 1960), pp. 916–918.

[4]Another possible exception may be noted for Kendall's Series 3, Investment Trusts, whose first five serial correlations were 0.301, 0.356, 0.158, 0.164 and 0.066. This series will be mentioned again below.

[5]Roughly, because they were computed, not from the original data, but from the serial correlations published by Kendall. Since successive serial correlations are based on fewer observations because of the necessity of sacrificing end terms, a certain "end term error" is introduced by this procedure.

TABLE 1

Serial Correlations of First Differences of Kendall's Stock Price Indexes, 1928-1938, for Various Intervals of Differencing

Kendall's Number	Industry Group	First Order Serial Correlations. Differences Taken over Interval of:					Second Order Serial Correlations
		1 Week	2 Weeks	4 Weeks	8 Weeks	16 Weeks	8 Weeks
1	Banks and discount companies	0.058	0.092	−0.067	−0.059	0.191	0.136
2	Insurance companies	.052	.048	− .056	− .169	−.035	.049
3	Investment trusts	.301	.450	.279	.020	.066	.064
4	Building materials	.125	.044	− .087	− .075	.345	.271
5	Coal	.148	.156	− .014	− .186	−.074	.032
6	Cotton	.087	.179	.036	− .227	−.075	.123
7	Electric light and power	.181	.145	− .024	− .130	.219	.232
8	Gas	.096	.235	.103	.119	.360	.232
9	Iron and steel	.088	−.005	− .028	− .122	−.009	.057
10	Oil	−.013	.027	.015	− .015	.073	.061
11	Total industrial productive	.195	.155	− .016	− .149	.055	.110
12	Home rails	.010	−.030	− .002	.162	.072	−.019
13	Shipping	.053	.032	− .017	.111	.388	.325
14	Stores and catering	.230	.145	− .082	− .218	.104	.199
15	Total industrial distributive	.237	.179	− .008	.033	.303	.241
16	Breweries and distilleries	.034	.102	.046	.020	.152	.078
17	Miscellaneous	.200	.191	− .011	− .101	.267	.267
18	Total industrial miscellaneous	.177	.190	.033	− .069	.291	.252
19	Industrials (all classes combined)	.234	.207	.018	− .063	.279	.246

computed value of the correlation becomes increasingly probable as the differencing period is lengthened, even if the true correlation is zero.

It must be concluded that the data of Table 1 do *not* give any substantial support to the hypothesis that, as differences are taken over longer and longer intervals, the first order serial correlations of the first difference generally increase.

Once again, Series 3, investment trusts, is an exception. It seems to have a particularly high level of serial correlation on a two-week period of differencing. Other occasional higher values among the various series, for changes at sixteen week intervals in particular, have to be seriously discounted although they suggest intriguing possibilities for further study.

These higher correlations for sixteen week changes (for Series 4, 8, 13, 15, and possibly 17, 18, and 19) proceed from a rather curious relationship that holds for 18 of the 19 series. The first order correlations on an eight-week basis tend to be algebraically smaller than the second order correlations (see Table 1). The implication of the existence of an eight week half cycle may be an interesting suggestion, although it could hardly be said to be established by the data.

One further attempt was made, in spite of Kendall's findings that the serial correlations were not significantly different from zero, to see if some nugget of systematic trend behavior might still be found in his data. It is possible that while the lagged autocorrelations of any series were not found to be significantly different from zero when taken one at a time, they might jointly form a pattern that is significant. A simple test of this possibility was attempted. A trend was fitted to the first differences of each stock price series by a Spencer 21-term moving average.[6] Then the ratio of the variance of the moving average to the variance of the first differences themselves was computed.

The variance ratios given in Table 2 are to be interpreted as follows. If each first difference lay exactly on the moving average trend line, that is, if the trend line were a perfect fit, the variance ratio would be unity. If on the other hand, all the serial correlations of order greater than zero were identically zero, the expected values for a random walk, the variance ratio would be 0.143, the sum of the squares of the coefficients in smoothing formula. It is, of course, possible for the ratio to be even less than 0.143.

Except for Series 3, the trend variance is not a much larger proportion of the original variance of the first differences than would be expected in the case of a random walk. It must be concluded that, with this exception, if trends exist in the first differences, they are very weak.

[6]See E. T. Whitaker and G. Robinson, *The Calculus of Observations* (4th ed.; London: 1944), p. 290, for the formula used. Actually, it was not necessary to fit the trends to the series themselves, but the variance of the moving average, expressed in units of the variance of the first differences, could be computed by applying the smoothing coefficients of the Spencer formula directly to the lagged serial correlations.

TABLE 2

Ratios of the Variance of Smoothed First Differences to the Variance of Unsmoothed First Differences. Kendall's Stock Price Indexes*

Series	Industry Group	Ratios
1	Banks and discount companies	0.161
2	Insurance companies	.158
3	Investment trusts	.525
4	Building materials	.162
5	Coal	.202
6	Cotton	.210
7	Electric light and power	.206
8	Gas	.230
9	Iron and steel	.158
10	Oil	.145
11	Total industrial productive	.212
12	Home rails	.138
13	Shipping	.151
14	Stores and catering	.212
15	Total industrial distributive	.219
16	Breweries and distilleries	.171
17	Miscellaneous	.221
18	Total industrial miscellaneous	.218
19	Industrials (all classes combined)	.232

*Smoothing performed by 21 term Spencer Moving Average.

All in all, Kendall's data do seem to confirm the random walk hypothesis. Further work by Osborne[7] strengthens the random walk hypothesis from a different point of view. While Kendall worked with serial correlations for each series separately, Osborne worked with ensembles of price changes. Roughly stated, he found that the changes in the logarithms of stock prices over any period in a given market, principally the New York Stock Exchange, constituted an ensemble which appeared to be approximately normally distributed with a standard deviation proportional to the square root of the length of the period. This proportionality of the standard deviation of price differences to the square root of the differencing period is a characteristic of a random walk and had been pointed out much earlier by Bachelier. In Bachelier's case, however, the differences were arithmetic, while in Osborne's they were logarithmic.

It must be noted that Osborne's measurements do not concern trends in the prices of stocks but merely the statistical distribution of the changes in the logarithms, which, as Osborne pointed out, correspond quite closely to percentage changes. That they do not correspond exactly to percentage changes has an important bearing on one of Osborne's principal findings, as we shall see.

[7]M. F. M. Osborne, "Brownian Motion in the Stock Market," *Operations Research,* Vol. 7, No. 2 (March-April 1959), pp. 145–173. See also comment and reply in *Operations Research,* Vol. 7, No. 6 (November-December 1959), pp. 806–811.

Osborne also supplied a theoretical mechanism that *could* explain the observed pattern of price movements. The mechanism is a random walk in the logarithm of prices with each step being a constant logarithmic value, depending on the time length of the step. The basic step is a transaction of which there might be ten or a hundred a day. The compounding of such steps in familiar probability sequences would, over any period of time, yield a normal distribution of changes in the logarithms of price, with standard deviation proportional to the square root of the period over which comparison is made.

One peculiar result of Osborne's proposed mechanism merits further study. Bachelier, the pioneer in regarding speculative price behavior as a random walk, derived the theoretical properites of the distribution of changes in the prices of *rentes* on the assumption of a "fair game," that is a zero expectation of gain. A price change in either direction of a given amount was equally probable in Bachelier's model. Osborne made a somewhat different assumption with a radically different result; he assumed that a change in either direction of a given amount in the logarithm of price was equally likely, no longer a fair game.

Thus, under Bachelier's assumption, given an initial investment value, say \$100, it would be equally probable, at the end of time T to be worth \$100 + k or \$100 − k. Exactly how large k would be for any stated probability would depend on the fundamental constant of the distribution and the square root of the length of time T. But whatever the value of k, so long as the probability of a gain of k is equal to the probability of a loss of k for all k within the permitted range, the expected value in any future period remains \$100 and the expected gain 0.

Under Osborne's assumption, however, there will be an expectation of gain. Suppose, using logarithms to base 10 and starting from \$100, a gain over some particular period of time, say five years, is equally likely to be a gain of logarithm 1 or loss of logarithm −1. These would correspond to an equal probability that the price at the end of five years would be either \$10 or \$1,000. The mathematical expectation in this case would be \$505, or an expected gain of \$405. This example illustrates the familiar difference between the arithmetic and the geometric mean. Over the long run, then, it makes a great deal of difference whether there is an expectation of zero arithmetic gain or zero logarithmic gain. In the latter case there will be a tendency for an investment value to grow, independent of any growth in the economy other than the growth implicit in the existence of a random walk in the logarithms.

How clearly established an empirical finding is the logarithmic rather than the arithmetic step in the random walk? Osborne was led to the logarithmic form, while Bachelier was not, because Bachelier considered only a single type of security at a time, whereas Osborne considered an ensemble of prices, usually all the common stock prices on a particular exchange. Osborne assumed, without much explicit consideration, that it was appropriate to try to fit one distribution of expected change to all common stocks, whether priced at \$100 or \$10 or whatever. Very little empirical investigation is required to show that the relative frequency of price rises of \$10 in one month is much smaller among stocks selling at \$10 than among stocks selling at \$100. On the other hand, it is quite reasonable to expect that the relative frequency of a \$1 price rise in a month among \$10 stocks would be about equal to the relative frequency of a \$10 price rise in a month among \$100 stocks. And rough empirical tests seem to be in accord with the latter case.

If then we have to choose a single distribution that will fit stocks of all different prices, and if our only choice were between equal probabilities of dollar amount changes and equal probabilities of proportional changes, we are necessarily led to choose the latter. The assumption of equal probabilities of given changes in the logarithm of price falls in the latter class.

But there are other possible models which yield equal probabilities of changes of given proportions. One is of particular interest to us in that it certainly fits the data as well as the logarithmic model and does not imply a built-in growth of values as does the logarithmic. It postulates equal probability of given percentage changes, almost the same as equal probability of given logarithmic changes, but not quite. On the tiny difference hinges the existence or nonexistence of the remarkable property of speculation being a game biased in favor of winning.

In both the logarithmic form and the percentage form of the hypothesis it is equally probable that a \$100 stock rises by \$10 in a month or that a \$10 stock rises by \$1. Under both schemes it is equally probable that a \$100 stock declines by \$10 in a month or a \$10 stock by \$1. But under the percentage form it is equally probable that a \$100 stock goes to \$101 or to \$99 in a given time, whereas in the logarithmic form it is equally probable that a \$100 stock goes to \$101 or \$99.01 in a given time. This difference of one cent in a dollar change from \$100 spells the difference between zero expectation of gain and positive expectation.

If, then, the percentage hypothesis is adopted instead of the logarithmic hypothesis, the expectation of gain disappears. The difference between the distributions generated by the two hypotheses would, over most time periods of practical interest, be so fine that any test delicate enough to distinguish between them is likely to throw them both out.

In fact, both hypotheses would generate normal distributions of the changes in the logarithms of prices, differing only their means and standard deviations. In testing various models of this sort we generally infer the mean and the standard deviation from the data and assume that the mean was influenced by general economic conditions separate from the random walk. Under these circumstances we can say whether the observed distribution is or is not close to normal, but we cannot say whether it is closer to the percentage hypothesis or to the logarithmic. To discriminate between these hypotheses we would need an independent measure of the random step, or of the standard deviation. Bachelier actually derived such an independent measure from the price of options, but Osborne merely showed that the distribution resembled a normal distribution and the standard deviation increased with the square root of the differencing period. To whatever extent his findings support the logarithmic hypothesis, they also support the percentage hypothesis.

But Osborne did not rigorously test the normality of the distribution. A rigorous test, for example the application of the chi-square test to some of the data used by Osborne, would lead us strongly to dismiss the hypothesis of normality. (See Table 3.) It yields a chi-square of over 60 for 8 degrees of freedom, although almost all of the discrepancy between actual and expected frequencies arises from the extreme classes of increases or decreases greater than 10 per cent.[8] It may be presumed that special factors operated to produce far more large price changes than are characteristic of a normal distribution. This sort of situation (leptokurtosis) is frequently encountered in economic statistics and would certainly overshadow any attempt to test fine points such as the difference between a logarithmic and a percentage scheme.

TABLE 3

Changes in Prices of Listed Common Stocks (NYSE) Observed Compared with Expected*

Percentage Price Change	No. of Issues	
	Observed†	Expected‡
+10% and over	54	21
+ 8% to +10%	30	30
+ 6% to + 8%	50	54
+ 4% to + 6%	71	87
+ 2% to + 4%	119	127
− 2% to + 2%	346	328
− 4% to − 2%	149	157
− 6% to − 4%	100	121
− 8% to − 6%	74	79
−10% to − 8%	31	43
−10% or over	51	28
Total	1075	1075

*Month ending November 15, 1956.

†Source: *The Exchange* (NYSE), Dec. 1956, back cover.

‡On the assumption of normal distribution with mean equal to the median of the observed distribution, with standard deviation equal to the semi-interquartile range divided by 0.6745, and with total frequency equal to observed total frequency.

In any case the requirement that equal proportional gains for stocks of different prices should have equal probability does not imply a nonzero expecta-

[8]It should be noted that Osborne remarked that the tails of the observed distribution did not appear to correspond to those of the normal distribution.

tion. The nonzero expectation follows specifically from the assumption of unequal steps, measured in dollars, in the random walk, as between steps up and steps down. For small steps, equal logarithmic changes imply *almost* equal percentage changes, but the very small difference eventually grows to a very large one, another demonstration of the wonderful power of compound interest.

But more to the point than the difference between logarithmic and percentage schemes is the question: How far do Osborne's findings go to show that stock market prices really follow a random walk? Osborne, at best, merely showed that stock price changes might, to a rough approximation, have been generated by a random walk type of model. He suggests conditions that are sufficient to generate the observations, but not necessary. In plain language, he has a scheme which could gave generated his observations; maybe it did and maybe it didn't.

It does seem that the principal clash between the analyst and the academic concerns not the nature of the statistical ensemble of price changes but rather the question of the existence of trends. For, if the implication of Kendall's findings are indeed general, it would make as much sense to try to predict the outcome of a coin toss as to predict movements of the stock market. The prime issue is, therefore, whether there is some way in which speculative price behavior is not random.

In order to attack this problem, the author ran off a set of simple tests of randomness of successive monthly or weekly changes of speculative prices. The technique may be illustrated by a weekly series on wheat (Wednesday closing prices of cash wheat over the period 1883–1934, excluding 1915–1920, a total of 2,379 weeks). Each week was classified as being a week of price rise or price fall, and the lengths of the runs were tallied. A run is defined as a sequence of successive weeks in which the price moves in the same direction. Table 4 shows the resulting table of runs and compares it with the distribution to be expected on the assumption of a random walk with equal probability of rise or fall. The correspondence is very close indeed, suggesting that at least the sequence of directions of changes in weekly wheat prices might have been produced by a random walk. Kendall[9] previously showed that, except for a few extreme items, the distribution of the size of these weekly wheat price changes is normal and independent of the movement of the preceding week.

The distribution of the runs of Standard and Poor's monthly composite index of stock prices,[10] 1918–56, is, however, inconsistent with the assumption of a random walk of equal probability of rise or fall. (Expectation 1 for 1918–56 in Table 5.) We may note, however, that for this stock average for the period 1918–56:

(a) The relative frequencies of rising and declining months were 0.58 and 0.42, respectively;

[9] Op. cit.
[10] The index is a monthly average of weekly observations.

(b) The relative frequency of rising months among all months for which the preceding month was rising, $p(+ \mid +)$, was 0.67, and the relative frequency of declining months for which the preceding month was declining, $p(- \mid -)$, was 0.50.

TABLE 4

Distribution of Lengths of Weekly Cash Wheat Prices at Chicago*

Length of Run (Weeks)	Observed		Expected† Up or Down
	Up	Down	
1	280	295	297
2	147	132	149
3	86	77	74
4	38	42	37
5	15	18	19
6	13	12	9
7 or longer	7	8	9
Total	586	584	595‡

*1883–1934, Excluding 1915–1920. Source: Holbrook Working, "Prices of Cash Wheat and Futures at Chicago Since 1883," *Wheat Studies*, Vol. II, No. 3 (November 1934), pp. 75–124. See also Kendall, op. cit., Table 1 for frequency distribution for these prices, of differences between week t and t + 1 against differences between weeks t + 1 and t + 2.

†Expected on assumption of 0.5 probability of rise or fall, and 2,379 monthly observations.

‡Expected total differs from sum because of rounding.

A new set of expected runs based on these contingent relative frequencies for 1918–56 did fit the observed runs quite well. (Expectation 2 for 1918–56 in Table 5.) Furthermore, expectations based on these relative frequencies derived from the 1918–56 data fit the 1871–1917 data for upruns quite closely, but downruns only fairly well. (Expectation 2 for 1871–1917 in Table 5.) Actually, the simpler hypothesis (Expectation 3) that the probability of continuation of a run is 0.6 and of termination 0.4 fits the 1871–1917 data very well and also the 1918–56 upruns. It does imply a much higher frequency of long downruns than was observed in 1918–56, however.

Unfortunately, this evidence of the probability of one month's movement depending on the previous month's is entirely the result of using an average of weekly prices for each month's observation. Distributions of runs of industrial stock prices for 1897–1929 and 1929–59 are given in Table 6, based on a single-point observation for each month, the last trading day of the month. These distributions are very close to those to be expected on the assumption of each month's change being independent of the previous month's, with a 0.57 probability of a monthly rise and 0.43 of a decline. (Expectation 4, Table 6.) The same probabilities seem to fit both periods equally well, and the hypothesis of trends seems to be blown sky high.

One notable exception to the rule that statisticians have not found trends in

TABLE 5

Lengths of Run of Standard & Poor's Monthly Composite Stock Price Index,*
Observed (Obs) vs. Expected (Ex)

Length of Run (months)	January 1918 to March 1956								January 1871 to December 1917					
	Up				Down				Up			Down		
	Obs	Ex 1†	Ex 2‡	Ex 3§	Obs	Ex 1†	Ex 2‡	Ex 3§	Obs	Ex 2‡	Ex 3§	Obs	Ex 2†	Ex 3§
							(number of runs)							
1	31	58	30	37	39	58	45	37	41	37	45	40	56	45
2	21	29	20	22	27	29	23	22	29	25	27	30	28	27
3	16	15	13	13	15	15	11	13	15	17	16	17	14	16
4	10	7	9	8	9	7	6	8	11	11	10	9	7	10
5	5	4	6	5	1	4	3	5	4	7	6	4	4	6
6 or longer	9	4	12	8	1	4	3	8	9	15	8	10	4	8
Total	92	117	90	93	92	117	90¶	93	109	112	112	110	112¶	112

*Monthly averages of weekly indexes. SOURCE: 1918-1956. Standard & Poor's *Trade & Securities* (Security Price Index Record). Number of Monthly observations: 467 for 1918-56, and 559 for 1871-1917.

†Based on probability of 0.5 for rise or fall, successive months independent, derived from *a priori* hypothesis.

‡Based on $p(+|+) = 0.67$ and $p(-|-) = 0.50$, derived from 1918-56 relative frequencies.

§Based on $p(+|+) = p(-|-) = 0.6$, derived from 1871-1917 relative frequencies.

¶Expected total, differs from sum because of rounding.

stock market prices is furnished by the work of Cowles and Jones.[11] They found an excess of sequences over reversals in stock market prices, but they used, at least for monthly data, averages of weekly observations. Their findings presumably derive principally from this error, plus a second effect, the influence of more frequent movements up than down.

TABLE 6

Distribution of Lengths of Run of Monthly Industrial Stock Prices,* Observed (Obs) vs. Expected (Ex)

Length of Run (Months)	Jan. 1897–Jan. 1929				Feb. 1929–Dec. 1959			
	Up		Down		Up		Down	
	Obs	Ex 4†	Obs	Ex 4†	Obs	Ex 4†	Obs	Ex 4†
1	42	40	58	53	38	38	49	50
2	24	23	18	23	22	22	19	22
3	16	13	14	10	9	12	10	9
4	6	7	4	4	7	7	4	4
5	1	4	1	2	3	4	2	2
6 or longer	7	6	1	1	8	6	2	1
Total	96	93	96	93	87	88‡	86	88

*End of month closing prices. Dow Jones Industrials, Jan. 1897 to Jan. 1929 with break from July 1914 to Jan. 1915 (379 months). SOURCE: *The Dow Jones Averages,* Barron's, New York 1931; Standard & Poor's Industrials, Feb. 1929–Dec. 1959 (362 months). SOURCE: see fn. (*), Table 5.

†Based on assumption of independence of successive monthly changes, and on the probability of 0.57 of a rise, and 0.43 of a fall, derived from entire period 1897–1959.

‡Expected total differs from sum because of rounding.

The first effect is illustrated by the data in Table 5, based on monthly averages of weekly observations. For these data there is a ratio of 1.56 of sequences to reversals for 1871–1917, and 1.54 for 1918–56. The ratio of sequences to reversals shrinks to 1.045 for the 1897–1959 end of month data of Table 6. The second effect can largely be explained on the basis of a 0.57 relative frequency of monthly rises and 0.43 of monthly falls for 1897–1959. For each monthly movement were drawn independently at random with these probabilities of rise and fall, we should expect a ratio of sequences to alternations of 1.040, almost identical to that observed.

In a revision of his findings designed to eliminate the first effect, Cowles still found some evidence, though weaker, of the existence of an excess of sequences over reversals, a ratio of 1.07 for monthly one point observations as compared with an earlier figure of 1.33 for the monthly averages of weekly observations.[12]

[11] Alfred Cowles and Herbert E. Jones, "Some a Posteriori Probabilities in Stock Market Action," *Econometrica,* Vol. 5, No. 280 (July 1937), pp. 280–294.

[12] Alfred Cowles, "A Revision of Previous Conclusions Regarding Stock Price Behavior," *Econometrica,* Vol. 28, No. 4 (October 1960), pp. 909–915. The data cover about 1,000 months over the periods 1834–1865, 1897–1922, 1928–1958.

But he did not make any allowance for the effect of a higher relative frequency of rises than declines. If the relative frequency of monthly rises were between 0.59 and 0.60 in the period covered by Cowles' data, as is likely, the ratio of 1.07 would be expected even if monthly movements were independent.

It must be concluded that the month to month movement of stock prices, at least in direction, is consistent with the hypothesis of a random walk with about a 6 to 4 probability of a rise. Evidence to the contrary was spurious, arising from the correlations introduced by monthly averaging or neglect of the unequal probability of rise and fall.

Lest the reader take undue comfort from the bullish implication of the 6 to 4 probability of a rise, it must be noted that declines, though less frequent than rises, are sharper, so that the average decline is substantially larger than the average rise. Nevertheless, there has been a well recognized upward trend of stock market prices of the order of 5.6% a year over the period 1897–1959, (Table 7).

One final test may be reported that should give great comfort to the analyst and encouragement to those who would use statistical studies to guide their speculative efforts, for it furnishes evidence that stock price changes could not have been generated by a random walk. Suppose we tentatively assume the existence of trends in stock market prices but believe them to be masked by the jiggling of the market. We might filter out all movements smaller than a specified size and examine the remaining movements. The most vivid way to illustrate the operation of the filter is to translate it into a rule of speculative market action. Thus, corresponding to a 5% filter we might have the rule: if the market moves up 5% go long and stay long until it moves down 5% at which time sell and go short until it again moves up 5%. Ignore moves of less than 5%. The more stringent the filter, the fewer losses are made, but also the smaller the gain from any move that exceeds the filter size. Thus with a 5% filter there will be a loss on any move between 5% and 10.53% and a gain on any move larger than 10.53%. For if the move is just a 10.53% move, say from 100 to 110.53, then we would go long at 105 (100 plus 5%) and sell at 105 (110.53 minus 5%) and so just break even. With a 10% filter most of the moves which entailed a loss with the 5% filter would be filtered out. But a 20% move, which would yield a 9% profit with a 5% filter (computed on the lower vertex of the move, actually about 8.6% of the purchase price), would yield a 2% loss on a 10% filter.

Thus, as the filter size is increased, the number of transactions is reduced, and losses on small moves are eliminated, gains on large moves are reduced, and some moves which would yield gains with a small filter will yield losses with a large. This example illustrates the familiar tradeoff between reliability of the information and the cost of the information. The more stringent the filter, the higher the reliability, but the more of the move that is sacrificed in identifying it both in getting in and in getting out.

The results of the application of various filters to the Dow Jones and Standard & Poor's industrial averages from 1897 through 1959 are shown in Table 7. If stock price movements were generated by a trendless random walk, these filters could be expected to yield zero profits, or to vary from zero profits, both positively and negatively, in a random manner. Given an underlying long term trend, they might be expected to produce some profits, the greater profits being associated with the greater filter, but in any case, profits smaller than could be expected from just buying and holding.

In fact, medium filters uniformly yield profits, and the smallest filters yield the highest profits, and very high they are.

The retrospective gains from the filter rule (before commission) are compared in Table 7 with the gains that could be achieved over the corresponding period by just buying and holding. The results uniformly favor the smaller filters over the buy and hold method. Thus, the filter method derives its success from a characteristic of stock price behavior other than that implied by the upward long term trend alone. This conclusion is also confirmed by the fact, apparent from inspection of the work sheets, that the filter method made gains on the declines as well as on the rises.

From a practical standpoint these profits would be substantially reduced, but by no means eliminated, by the payment of commissions. I leave to the interested reader the computation of allowance for commissions.

It must be concluded that there *are* trends in stock market prices, once the "move" is taken as the unit under study rather than the week or the month. That is, the nonrandom nature of stock price movements revealed by Table 7 proceeds not only from filtering out small moves, but also from transforming the measure over which changes are considered. The many statistical studies which have found speculative prices to resemble a random walk have dealt with changes over uniform periods of time. The filter operation, however, deals with changes of given magnitude irrespective of the length of time involved. In short, it substitutes the dimension of the "move" for the dimension of time.

The findings surveyed in this paper can be summarized by the statement that in speculative markets price changes appear to follow a random walk over *time*, but a move, once initiated, tends to persist. In particular, if the stock market has moved up x per cent it is likely to move up more than x per cent further before it moves down by x per cent. This proposition seems to be valid for x ranging from 5 per cent through 30 per cent. It will require further study to find out if it is valid for x smaller than 5%.

The riddle has been resolved. The statisticians' findings of a random walk over the time dimension is quite consistent with nonrandom trends in the move dimension. Such a trend does exist.

I leave to the speculation of others the question of what would happen to the effectiveness of the filter technique if everybody believed in it and operated accordingly.

TABLE 7

Profits from Filters of Various Sizes Compared with Buy and Hold,* 1897–1959†

Period	Filter Size‡ (Percentages)											Buy and Hold
	5	6	8	10	12.5	15	20	25	30	40	50	
	Average move (%)§											
1897–1914	13.8	15.8	19.8	22.8	30.7	39.6	62.6	62.6	82.5	80.2	97.0	
1914–1929	12.8	14.9	19.7	25.4	33.3	43.0	69.4	115.8	115.8	115.8	115.8	
1929–1959	14.5	16.4	22.3	26.3	31.6	36.1	52.9	72.3	188.9	199.0	291.0	
	Average profit per transaction (%)¶ (before commissions)											
1897–1914	2.9	3.0	2.7	1.5	3.2	5.4	12.2	4.0	7.7	(9.2)††	(15.5)	75.3
1914–1929	2.0	2.2	2.6	3.6	5.2	7.8	16.3	32.5	24.7	9.6	(5.7)	596.6
1929–1959	3.5	3.6	4.8	4.3	3.9	2.9	6.0	9.8	11.2	43.2	57.3	154.1
	Number of transactions#											
1897–1914	117	95	67	53	32	22	12	12	8	7	7	1
1914–1929	112	93	59	40	28	19	10	6	6	6	6	1
1929–1959	274	228	144	113	86	70	40	26	20	8	6	1

	Average transactions per year											
1897–1914	6.5	5.4	3.8	3.0	1.8	1.2	0.7	0.7	0.4	0.4	0.3	
1914–1929	6.6	6.3	4.0	2.7	1.9	1.3	0.7	0.4	0.4	0.4	0.4	
1929–1959	9.0	7.5	4.7	3.7	2.8	2.3	1.3	0.8	0.6	0.3	0.2	
	Average profit per year (%)** (before commissions)											
1897–1914	20.5	17.4	10.5	4.6	5.8	6.6	7.8	2.6	3.2	(3.3)	(3.9)	3.2
1914–1929	15.8	14.7	10.7	10.0	9.9	9.9	10.3	11.1	8.6	3.4	(2.1)	14.1
1929–1959	36.8	30.0	24.5	16.8	11.4	6.9	7.8	8.2	7.0	9.3	8.5	3.0

*Based on Dow Jones Industrials, 1897–1929 and Standard & Poor's Industrials, 1929–1959. See fn. (*), Table 5, and fn. (*), Table 6 for source references.

†Periods: January 2, 1897 to July 30, 1914
December 12, 1914 to September 3, 1929
September 7, 1929 to December 31, 1959.

‡5% filter here designates 5% in either direction, others designate indicated percentages upward and equal *logarithmic* moves downward. E.g., 10% filter implies 10% upward or 9.09% downward.

§Calculated as follows: for each move, as defined by a specified filter, let the variable, M, denote the difference between the logarithms of the upper and lower endpoints of the move. The figure given as the average move is 100 (antilog $\overline{M} - 1$) where M is the arithmetic mean of the M's.

¶Let R be the average logarithmic profit defined as $\overline{R} = \overline{M} - 2F$. $\overline{M}$ is defined in fn. (§) and F is log $(1 + f)$ where f is the filter expressed as a ratio, e.g., f is 0.10 for a 10% filter. The quantity $2F$ corresponds to the portion of the move that is used up in getting in or out. On an upmove of average size $\overline{M}$ the percentage profit would be $P_u = 100(\text{antilog } \overline{R} - 1)$; on a downmove, $P_d = 100P_u/(100 + P_u)$. The average profit centered in Table 7 is $P = (100 + P_u)^{1/2}(100 + P_d)^{1/2} - 100$.

#A transaction is defined as a purchase and sale, so that each transaction would require two commissions. In each period there is one terminal transaction, such as for Dec. 31, 1959, terminated not by a filter signal but by the period limits. The corresponding terminal move was counted as half a move in the computation of $\overline{M}$, and of the number of transactions per year.

**Computed as $100[1 + (\overline{P}/100)]^{\overline{q}} - 100$, where $\overline{q}$ is the average number of transactions per year, and $\overline{P}$ is defined in fn. (¶).

††Numbers in parentheses signify losses.

23

Random Walks in Stock Market Prices*

Eugene F. Fama †

For many years economists, statisticians, and teachers of finance have been interested in developing and testing models of stock price behavior. One important model that has evolved from this research is the theory of random walks. This theory casts serious doubt on many other methods for describing and predicting stock price behavior–methods that have considerable popularity outside the academic world. For example, we shall see later that if the random walk theory is an accurate description of reality, then the various "technical" or "chartist" procedures for predicting stock prices are completely without value.

In general the theory of random walks raises challenging questions for anyone who has more than a passing interest in understanding the behavior of stock prices. Unfortunately, however, most discussions of the theory have appeared in technical academic journals and in a form which the non-mathematician would usually find incomprehensible. This article describes, briefly and simply, the theory of random walks and some of the important issues it raises concerning the work of market analysts. To preserve brevity some aspects of the theory and its implications are omitted. More complete (and also more technical) discussions of the theory of random walks are available elsewhere; hopefully the introduction provided here will encourage the reader to examine one of the more rigorous and lengthy works listed at the end of this article.

COMMON TECHNIQUES FOR PREDICTING STOCK MARKET PRICES

In order to put the theory of random walks into perspective we first discuss, in brief and general terms, the two approaches to predicting stock prices that are commonly epoused by market professionals. These are (1) "chartist" or "technical" theories and (2) the theory of fundamental or intrinsic value analysis.

The basic assumption of all the chartist or technical theories is that history tends to repeat itself, i.e., past patterns of price behavior in individual securities will tend to recur in the future. Thus the way to predict stock prices (and, of

*From *Financial Analysts Journal,* Vol 21, No. 5 (September-October 1965), pp. 55–59. Reprinted by permission of *Financial Analysts Journal.*

†The author is indebted to his colleagues William Alberts, David Green, Merton Miller, and Harry Roberts for their helpful comments and criticisms.

course, increase one's potential gains) is to develop a familiarity with past patterns of price behavior in order to recognize situations of likely recurrence.

Essentially, then, chartist techniques attempt to use knowledge of the past behavior of a price series to predict the probable future behavior of the series. A statistician would characterize such techniques as assuming that successive price changes in individual securities are dependent. That is, the various chartist theories assume that the *sequence* of price changes prior to any given day is important in predicting the price change for that day.[1]

The techniques of the chartist have always been surrounded by a certain degree of mysticism, however, and as a result most market professionals have found them suspect. Thus it is probably safe to say that the pure chartist is relatively rare among stock market analysts. Rather the typical analyst adheres to a technique known as fundamental analysis or the intrinsic value method. The assumption of the fundamental analysis approach is that at any point in time an individual security has an intrinsic value (or in the terms of the economist, an equilibrium price) which depends on the earning potential of the security. The earning potential of the security depends in turn on such fundamental factors as quality of management, outlook for the industry and the economy, etc.

Through a careful study of these fundamental factors the analyst should, in principle, be able to determine whether the actual price of a security is above or below its intrinsic value. If actual prices tend to move toward intrinsic values, then attempting to determine the intrinsic value of a security is equivalent to making a prediction of its future price; and this is the essence of the predictive procedure implicit in fundamental analysis.

THE THEORY OF RANDOM WALKS

Chartist theories and the theory of fundamental analysis are really the province of the market professional and to a large extent teachers of finance. Historically, however, there has been a large body of academic people, primarily economists and statisticians, who adhere to a radically different approach to market analysis—the theory of random walks in stock market prices. The remainder of this article will be devoted to a discussion of this theory and its major implications.

Random walk theorists usually start from the premise that the major security exchanges are good examples of "efficient" markets. An "efficient" market is defined as a market where there are large numbers of rational, profit-maximizers actively competing, with each trying to predict future market values of individual securities, and where important current information is almost freely available to all participants.

In an efficient market, competition among the many intelligent participants leads to a situation where, at any point in time, actual prices of individual

[1] Probably the best known example of the chartist approach to predicting stock prices is the Dow Theory.

securities already reflect the effects of information based both on events that have already occurred and on events which, as of now, the market expects to take place in the future. In other words, in an efficient market at any point in time the actual price of a security will be a good estimate of its intrinsic value.

Now in an uncertain world the intrinsic value of a security can never be determined exactly. Thus there is always room for disagreement among market participants concerning just what the intrinsic value of an individual security is, and such disagreement will give rise to discrepancies between actual prices and intrinsic values. In an efficient market, however, the actions of the many competing participants should cause the actual price of a security to wander randomly about its intrinsic value. If the discrepancies between actual prices and intrinsic values are systematic rather than random in nature, then knowledge of this should help intelligent market participants to better predict the path by which actual prices will move towards intrinsic values. When the many intelligent traders attempt to take advantage of this knowledge, however, they will tend to neutralize such systematic behavior in price series. Although uncertainty concerning intrinsic values will remain, actual prices of securities will wander randomly about their intrinsic values.

Of course intrinsic values can themselves change across time as a result of new information. The new information may involve such things as the success of a current research and development project, a change in management, a tariff imposed on the industry's product by a foreign country, an increase in industrial production or any other *actual or anticipated* change in a factor which is likely to affect the company's prospects.

In an efficient market, *on the average,* competition will cause the full effects of new information on intrinsic values to be reflected "instantaneously" in actual prices. In fact, however, because there is vagueness or uncertainty surrounding new information, "instantaneous adjustment" really has two implications. First, actual prices will initially overadjust to changes in intrinsic values as often as they will underadjust. Second, the lag in the complete adjustment of actual prices to successive new intrinsic values will itself be an independent, random variable with the adjustment of actual prices sometimes preceding the occurrence of the event which is the basis of the change in intrinsic values (i.e., when the event is anticipated by the market before it actually occurs) and sometimes following.

This means that the "instantaneous adjustment" property of an efficient market implies that successive price changes in individual securities will be independent. A market where successive price changes in individual securities are independent is, by definition, a random walk market. Most simply the theory of random walks implies that a series of stock price changes has no memory—the past history of the series cannot be used to predict the future in any meaningful way. The future path of the price level of a security is no more predictable than the path of a series of cumulated random numbers.

It is unlikely that the random walk hypothesis provides an exact description of the behavior of stock market prices. For practical purposes, however, the model may be acceptable even though it does not fit the facts exactly. Thus although successive price changes may not be strictly independent, the actual amount of dependence may be so small as to be unimportant.

What should be classified as unimportant depends, of course, on the question at hand. For the stock market trader or investor the criterion is obvious: The independence assumption of the random walk model is valid as long as knowledge of the past behavior of the series of price changes cannot be used to increase expected gains. More specifically, if successive price changes for a given security are independent, there is no problem in timing purchases and sales of that security. A simple policy of buying and holding the security will be as good as any more complicated mechanical procedure for timing purchases and sales. This implies that, for investment purposes, the independence assumption of the random walk model is an adequate description of reality as long as the actual degree of dependence in series of price changes is not sufficient to make the expected profits of any more "sophisticated" mechanical trading rule or chartist technique greater than the expected profits under a naive buy-and-hold policy.

EMPIRICAL EVIDENCE ON INDEPENDENCE

Over the years a number of empirical tests of the random walk theory have been performed; indeed, so many that it is not possible to discuss them adequately here. Therefore in describing the empirical evidence we limit ourselves to a brief discussion of the different approaches employed and the general conclusions that have evolved.

The main concern of empirical research on the random walk model has been to test the hypothesis that successive price changes are independent. Two different approaches have been followed. First there is the approach that relies primarily on common statistical tools such as serial correlation coefficients and analyses of runs of consecutive price changes of the same sign. If the statistical tests tend to support the assumption of independence, one then *infers* that there are probably no mechanical trading rules or chartist techniques, based solely on patterns in the past history of price changes, which would make the expected profits of the investor greater than they would be with a simple buy-and-hold policy. The second approach to testing independence proceeds by testing directly different mechanical trading rules to see whether or not they provide profits greater than buy-and-hold.

Research to date has tended to concentrate on the first or statistical approach to testing independence; the results have been consistent and impressive. I know of no study in which standard statistical tools have produced evidence of *important* dependence in series of successive price changes. In general, these studies (and there are many of them) have tended to uphold the theory of random walks. This is true, for example, of the serial correlation tests of Cootner [4],[2] Fama [5], Kendall [9], and Moore [10]. In all of these studies, the sample serial correlation coefficients computed for successive price changes were extremely close to zero, which is evidence against important dependence in the changes. Similarly, Fama's [5] analysis of runs of successive price changes of the same sign, and the spectral analysis techniques of Granger and Morgenstern [8], and Godfrey, Granger, and Morgenstern [7] also support the independence assumption of the random walk model.

We should emphasize, however, that although the statistical techniques mentioned above have been the common tools used in testing independence, the chartist or technical theorist probably would not consider them adequate. For example, he would not consider either serial correlations or runs analyses as adequate tests of whether the past history of series of price changes can be used to increase the investor's expected profits. The simple linear relationships that underlie the serial correlation model are much too unsophisticated to pick up the complicated "patterns" that the chartist sees in stock prices. Similarly, the runs tests are much too rigid in their manner of determining the duration of upward and downward movements in prices. In particular: in runs-testing, a run is considered as terminated whenever there is a change in sign in the sequence of successive price changes, regardless of the size of the price change that causes the change in sign. The chartist would like to have a more sophisticated method for identifying movements—a method which does not always predict the termination of the movement simply because the price level has temporarily changed direction.

These criticisms of common statistical tools have not gone unheeded, however. For example, Alexander's filter technique [1, 2] is an attempt to apply more sophisticated criteria to the identification of moves. Although the filter technique does not correspond exactly to any well-known chartist theory, it is closely related to such things as the Dow Theory. Thus, the profitability of the filter technique can be used to make inferences concerning the potential profitability of other mechanical trading rules.

A filter of, say, 5 percent is defined as follows: if the daily closing price of a particular security moves up at least 5 percent, buy and hold the security until its price moves down at least 5 percent from a subsequent high, at which time simultaneously sell and go short. The short position is maintained until the daily closing price rises at least 5 percent above a subsequent low, at which time one should simultaneously cover and buy. Moves less than 5 percent in either direction are ignored.

It is, of course, unnecessary to limit the size of the filter to 5 percent. In fact, Professor Alexander has reported tests of the filter technique for filters ranging in size from 1 percent to 50 percent. The tests cover different time periods from 1897 to 1959 and involve daily closing prices for two indices, the

[2] See references at article's end.

Dow-Jones Industrials from 1897 to 1929 and Standard and Poor's Industrials from 1929 to 1959. In Alexander's latest work [2], it turns out that even when the higher broker's commissions incurred under the filter rule are ignored, the filter technique can not consistently beat the simple policy of buying and holding the indices for the different periods tested. Elsewhere I have tested the filter technique on individual securities. Again the simple buy-and-hold method consistently beats the profits produced by different size filters. It seems, then, that at least for the purposes of the individual trader or investor, tests of the filter technique also tend to support the random walk model.

IMPLICATIONS OF THE RANDOM WALK THEORY FOR CHARTIST AND INTRINSIC VALUE ANALYSIS

As stated earlier, chartist theories implicitly assume that there is dependence in series of successive price changes. That is, the history of the series can be used to make meaningful predictions concerning the future. On the other hand, the theory of random walks says that successive price changes are independent, i.e., the past cannot be used to predict the future. Thus the two theories are diametrically opposed, and if, as the empirical evidence seems to suggest, the random walk theory is valid, then chartist theories are akin to astrology and of no real value to the investor.

In an uncertain world, however, no amount of empirical testing is sufficient to establish the validity of a hypothesis beyond any shodow of doubt. The chartist of technical theorist always has the option of declaring that the evidence in support or the random walk theory is not sufficient to validate the theory. On the other hand, the chartist must admit that the evidence in favor of the random walk model is both consistent and voluminous, whereas there is precious little published discussion of rigorous empirical tests of the various technical theories. If the chartist rejects the evidence in favor of the random walk model, his position is weak if his own theories have not been subjected to equally rigorous tests. This, I believe, is the challenge that the random walk theory makes to the technician.

There is nothing in the above discussion, however, which suggests that superior fundamental or intrinsic value analysis is useless in a random walk-efficient market. In fact the analyst will do better than the investor who follows a simple buy-and-hold policy as long as he can more quickly identify situations where there are non-negligible discrepancies between actual prices and intrinsic values than other analysts and investors, and if he is better able to predict the occurrence of important events and evaluate their effects on intrinsic values.

If there are many analysts who are pretty good at this sort of thing, however, and if they have considerable resources at their disposal, they help narrow discrepancies between actual prices and intrinsic values and cause actual prices, on the average, to adjust "instantaneously" to changes in intrinsic values. That is, the existence of many sophisticated analysts helps make the market more efficient which in turn implies a market which conforms more closely to the random walk model. Although the returns to these sophisticated analysts may be quite high, they establish a market in which fundamental analysis is a fairly useless procedure both for the average analyst and the average investor. That is, in a random walk-efficient market, on the average, a security chosen by a mediocre analyst will produce a return no better than that obtained from a randomly selected security of the same general riskiness.

There probably aren't many analysts (in fact, I know of none) who would willingly concede that they are no better than the "average" analyst. If all analysts think they are better than average, however, this only means that their estimate of the average is biased downward. Fortunately, it is not necessary to judge an analyst solely by his claims. The discussion above provides a natural benchmark with which we can evaluate his performance.

In a random walk - efficient market at any point in time the market price of a security will already reflect the judgments of many analysts concerning the relevance of currently available information to the prospects of that security. Now an individual analyst may feel that he has better insights than those that are already implicit in the in the market price. For example, he may feel that a discrepancy between market price and intrinsic value exists for some security, or he may think the intrinsic value of the security is itself about to change because of some impending piece of new information which is not yet generally available.

These "insights" of the analyst are of no real value, however, unless they are eventually borne out in the market, that is, unless the actual market price eventually moves in the predicted direction. In other words, if the analyst can make meaningful judgments concerning the purchase and sale of individual securities, his choices should consistently outperform randomly selected securities of the same general riskiness. It must be stressed, however, that the analyst must *consistently* produce results better than random selection, since, by the nature of uncertainty, for any given time period he has about a 50 percent chance of doing better than random selection even if his powers of analysis are completely non-existent. Moreover, not only must the analyst do consistently better than random selection, but he must beat random selection by an amount which is at least sufficient to cover the cost of the resources (including his own time) which are expended in the process of carrying out his more complicated selection procedures.

What we propose, then, is that the analyst subject his performance to a rigorous comparison with a random selection procedure. One simple practical way of comparing the results produced by an analyst with a random selection procedure is the following: Every time the analyst recommends a security for purchase (or sale), another security of the same general riskiness is chosen randomly. A future date is then chosen at which time the results produced by the two securities will be compared. Even if the analyst is no better than the random selection procedure, in any given comparison there is still a 50 percent chance that the security he has chosen will outperform the randomly selected security. After the game has been played for a while, however, and the results of many different comparisons are accumulated, then it will become clear whether the analyst is worth his salt or not.

In many circumstances, however, the primary concern is with the performance of a portfolio rather than with the performance of individual securities in the portfolio. In this situation one would want to compare the performance of the portfolio in question with that of a portfolio of randomly selected securities. A useful benchmark for randomly selected portfolios has been provided by Fisher and Lorie [6]. They computed rates of return for investments in common stocks on the New York Stock Exchange for various time periods from 1926 to 1960. The basic assumption in all of their computations is that at the beginning of each period studied the investor puts an equal amount of money in each common stock listed at that time on the Exchange. This amounts to random sampling where the sampling is, of course, exhaustive. Different rates of return are then computed for different possible tax brackets of the investor, first under the assumption that all dividends are reinvested in the month paid, and then under the assumption that dividends are not reinvested.

A possible procedure for the analyst is to compare returns for given time periods earned by portfolios he has managed with the returns earned for the same time periods by the Fisher-Lorie "randomly selected" portfolios. It is important to note, however, that this will be a valid test procedure only if the portfolios managed by the analyst had about the same degree of riskiness as the Fisher-Lorie "market" portfolios. If this is not the case, the Fisher-Lorie results will not provide a proper benchmark. In order to make a proper comparison between the results produced by the analyst and a random selection policy, it will be necessary to define and study the behavior of portfolios of randomly selected securities, where these portfolios are selected in such a way that they have about the same degree of riskiness as those managed by the analyst.

If the claims of analysts concerning the advantages of fundamental analysis have any basis in fact, the tests suggested above would seem to be easy to pass. In fact, however, the only "analysts" that have so far undergone these tests are open end mutual funds. In their appeals to the public, mutual funds usually make two basic claims: (1) because it pools the resources of many individuals, a fund can diversify much more effectively than the average, small investor; and (2) because of its management's closeness to the market, the fund is better able to detect "good buys" individual securities. In most cases the first claim is probably true. The second, however, implies that mutual funds provide a higher return than would be earned by a portfolio of randomly selected securities. In a separate paper [5] I reported the results of a study which suggest that if the initial loading charges of mutual funds are ignored, on the average the funds do about as well as a randomly selected portfolio. If one takes into account the higher initial loading charges of the funds, however, on the average the random investment policy outperforms the funds. In addition, these results would seem to be consistent with those of the now famous Wharton study of mutual funds [11].

These adverse results with respect to mutual funds have tended to lead random walk theorists to feel that other financial institutions, and most professional investment advisers as well, probably do no better than random selection. Institutions and analysts can only dispel such doubts by submitting their performance to a rigorous comparison with a random selection procedure.

CONCLUSION

In sum the theory of random walks in stock market prices presents important challenges to both the chartist and the proponent of fundamental analysis. For the chartist, the challenge is straightforward. If the random walk model is a valid description of reality, the work of the chartist, like that of the astrologer, is of no real value in stock market analysis. The empirical evidence to date provides strong support for the random walk model. In this light the only way the chartist can vindicate his position is to *show* that he can *consistently* use his techniques to make better than chance predictions of stock prices. It is not enough for him to talk mystically about patterns that he sees in the data. He must show that he can consistently use these patterns to make meaningful predictions of future prices.

The challenge of the theory of random walks to the proponent of fundamental analysis, however, is more involved. If the random walk theory is valid and if security exchanges are "efficient" markets, then stock prices at any point in time will represent good estimates of intrinsic or fundamental values. Thus, additional fundamental analysis is of value only when the analyst has new information which was not fully considered in forming current market prices, or has new insights concerning the effects of generally available information which are not already implicit in current prices. If the analyst has neither better insights nor new information, he may as well forget about fundamental analysis and choose securities by some random selection procedure.

In essence, the challenge of the random walk theory to the proponent of fundamental analysis is to show that his more complicated procedures are actually more profitable than a simple random selection policy. As in the case of the chartist, the challenge is an empirical one. The analyst cannot merely protest that he thinks the securities he selects do better than randomly selected securities; he must demonstrate that this is in fact the case.

REFERENCES

1. Sidney S. Alexander. "Price Movements in Speculative Markets: Trends or Random Walks," *Industrial Management Review,* II (May 1961), 7-26.
2. Sidney S. Alexander. "Price Movements in Speculative Markets: Trends or Random Walks, Number 2," *Industrial Management Review,* V (Spring 1964), 25-46.

3. Paul H. Cootner (ed.). *The Random Character of Stock Market Prices.* Cambridge: M.I.T. Press, 1964. An excellent compilation of research on the theory of random walks completed prior to mid-1963.
4. Paul H. Cootner. "Stock Prices: Random vs. Systematic Changes," *Industrial Management Review,* III (Spring 1962), 24-45.
5. Eugene F. Fama. "The Behavior of Stock Market Prices," *Journal of Business,* XXXVIII (January 1965), 34-105.
6. L. Fisher and J. H. Lorie. "Rates of Return on Investments in Common Stocks," *Journal of Business* (January 1964), 1-21.
7. Michael D. Godfrey, Clive W. J. Granger, and Oskar Morgenstern. "The Random Walk Hypothesis of Stock Market Behavior," *Kyklos,* XVII (January 1964), 1-30.
8. Clive W. J. Granger, and O. Morgenstern, "Spectral Analysis of New York Stock Market Prices," *Kyklos,* XVI (January 1963), 1-27.
9. M. G. Kendall. "The Analysis of Economic Time Series," *Journal of the Royal Statistical Society* (Series A), XCVI (1953), 11-25.
10. Arnold Moore. "A Statistical Analysis of Common Stock Prices." Unpublished Ph.D. dissertation, Graduate School of Business, University of Chicago (1962).
11. "A Study of Mutual Funds," prepared for the Securities and Exchange Commission by the Wharton School of Finance and Commerce. Report of the Committee on Interstate and Foreign Commerce. Washington: U.S. Government Printing Office, 1962.

24

What Difference Does Knowledge Make to Investors?*

Leo Barnes†

A new breed of scepticism has hit the investment world. It is the rather startling view that knowledge of securities, financial fundamentals, and investing techniques makes little if any difference to the results achieved.

No little responsibility for spreading this cult of ignorance must, regretfully, be attributed to the Center for Research in Security Prices of the Graduate School of Business of the University of Chicago, as a result of the widespread publicity sought–and obtained–in 1964 and 1965 for its extensive computerized studies on rates of return for stocks listed on the New York Stock Exchange from 1926 to 1960.[1] A second, though often misinterpreted influence contributing to this new scepticism emanates from the learned mathematical demonstrations in recent years by eminent scholars that, statistically, *short-term* stock price moves are just a "random walk."[2] In this paper I shall be dealing exclusively with the former, major influence.

It is a triple irony that this latest revolt against reason in investments springs, of all places, from the academic community; that it comes at a time when the postwar and post-Sputnik knowledge explosion and a revolutionary computerized technology have begun to take hold in the areas of security analysis and portfolio management; and that, by the same causation, the weaponry of the revolt bristles with technical mathematical formulae and is wrapped in yards of computer-generated statistics. What vast reasoning power is being used to demonstrate the futility of reasoning!

*From *Financial Analysts Journal,* Vol. 21, No. 5 (September-October 1965), pp. 60–68. Reprinted by permission of *Financial Analysts Journal.*

†The author wishes to thank fellow members of the Ford Foundation's workshop in Research in Business Finance and the Harvard faculty advisers for valuable suggestions. Special appreciation is due to Professors John Lintner, Eli Shapiro, and James Ludtke.

[1] James H. Lorie and Lawrence Fisher, "Rates of Return on Investments in Common Stocks," *Journal of Business* (January 1964); and Lawrence Fisher, "Outcomes for 'Random' Investments in Common Stocks Listed on the New York Stock Exchange," *Journal of Business* (April 1965).

[2] An impressive collection of essays, mostly espousing this view, can be found in *The Random Character of Stock Market Prices* (edited by Paul H. Cootner), M.I.T. Press, 1964. See also Professor Fama's article in this issue.

My purpose here is counter-revolutionary—to restore, if possible, the traditional rationalist view that knowledge is power, even in investments; that wisdom and intellectual training increase one's chances of investment success in the not too long run (always assuming, of course, the guts and gumption to act on one's theoretical findings). So despair not, ye scholars, students, and budding or triumphant C.F.A.'s, but carry on!

HAS THE PRESS DISTORTED THE SCHOLARS?

It is, of course, necessary to distinguish between the facts, allegations, and inferences as presented in scholarly studies and as interpreted in the business and public press. All too often, communications media exaggerate and sensationalize. Thus, some of the more extreme conclusions paraded in the press do not appear, as such, in either of the two articles by Professors Lorie and Fisher, director and associate director of the University of Chicago Center. However, it has to be assumed that the latter do hold the striking views attributed to them, by direct quotation at press conferences or otherwise. For these personalized views have been proclaimed far and wide, over radio and TV as well as in the press; and no denials or retractions from either the Center or its directors have come to my attention.

Moreover, since the bolder statements in the business press and other media are far more influential than the more cautious conclusions in the learned journals, the publicized findings deserve to be answered on their own terms in any case.

Accordingly, I begin with (1) a summary, via selected quotations, of the findings of the Center for Research in Security Prices, as attributed to the directors of the Center by the business and financial press, or as interpreted by leading business writers and editors. Then I present (2) my own summary of the procedures and more restrained factual conclusions of the Center's second published study by Lawrence Fisher, together with a critique of the methodology, terminology, and some of the major implications drawn by Professor Fisher in this article.[3] I conclude with (3) an evaluation of some exuberant interpretations of the Center's two studies, which are, unfortunately, likely to endure as the public and business image of their message and meaning.

THE PUBLIC IMAGE OF THE CENTER'S FINDINGS

Starting in late May, press reports about the findings of Professor Fisher's 1965 article were, as I have indicated, much more forthright, unqualified, and enthusiastic than the article itself—as it subsequently became available to subscribers to *The Journal of Business* early in July, in an unusually delayed April,

[3]The April, 1965 article by Professor Fisher serves the useful supplementary purpose of clarifying uncertainties and answering question about the procedures used and conclusions reached in the January, 1964 article by Professors Lorie and Fisher.

1965 issue. To illustrate, I cite first the authoritative *Wall Street Journal* of May 25, 1965:

> Close your eyes and pick any common stock on the New York Stock Exchange by jabbing a pin at the list. If you had done so between 1926 and 1960, the odds are better than 3-to-1 that the selected issue would have been a profitable investment.
>
> And, if your buying was done in the immediate postwar years, the chances are less than 1 in 10 that you would have lost money.
>
> Further, any stock market investor, using nothing but pure chance in making his selection, would have had a 50-50 chance of earning a combined capital-gain and interest return of 9.8% yearly, or better, compounded over the 35-year period.
>
> If three or four additional stocks had been selected, the percentage of profitability was "substantially" in excess of 80%, James H. Lorie . . . said.
>
> He added, "There is no evidence that mutual funds select stocks better than by the random method."
>
> An individual able to buy 15 or 20 different stocks "might do better than a mutual fund," he said.

Newsweek adds this tidbit in its issue of May 31, 1965:

> . . . the evidence is growing," Lorie warned, "that it's hard for anybody to do much better—or much worse—than he'd do with random selection.

And *Business Week* amplifies the same point on May 29, 1965:

> For a sizable area of Wall Street—mutual funds, security analysts, investment analysts, investment advisers, and the like—the study could prove unsettling. Everybody in this area makes his money, to one degree or another, by selling his skill to less expert investors. Now, the Chicago study says that a random investment, one where no skill at all is applied, will prove profitable most of the time. And Lorie thinks the market pros would do little better—or worse—than the average for investments selected at random.

Sylvia Porter, in her nationally syndicated business column, contributes these challenges, presented in the *New York Post* of May 25, 1965:

> What do these astounding statistics mean to you?
>
> First, they pulverize most of the technical stock investing theories by which so many Streeters swear and they mock the mythology of stock selecting and investment timing by which so many millions of U.S. investors live.
>
> Second, they raise deep questions about the widely accepted economic theory that a high rate of annual return implies a high degree of risk.

Finally, M. J. Rossant, of the editorial board of *The New York Times,* on June 1, 1965, draws the ultimate "know-nothing" conclusion suggested by the Fisher-Lorie findings:

> Mr. [Keith] Funston, who has long held that investors should investigate before they invest, hailed the growing maturity of investors

> and called for a continuing attack on economic illiteracy. But Chicago University's Center for Research in Security Prices has reported that the average investor, whether mature or immature, literate or illiterate, stands a good chance of making money just by buying stocks. . . . Economic illiteracy poses no handicap.
>
> Professional investment managers, who are economically literate and allegedly astute in the ways of the stock market . . . have presented no evidence to demonstrate that their highly developed skills are clearly superior to the know-nothing approach of random selection.

THE FACTUAL FINDINGS OF FISHER'S 1965 ARTICLE

What manner of report is this which leads respected business journals and analysts to such bold, provocative conclusions? Especially for those readers who have not yet had the opportunity to read Fisher's article in the original, it will be useful to summarize his key procedures and conclusions that are most relevant to our topic.

1. The article enumerates "the results for all possible combinations of purchases and sales of individual common stocks for which we have data available at the Center . . . [Included are] the results obtained by buying a stock at the market price at the end of each month and selling it at the end of each subsequent month for the period of its listing on the New York Stock Exchange between January, 1926 and December, 1960. For the 1,715 common stocks, 56,557,538 combinations [or transactions] are tabulated."[4]

All cash dividends on any stock are assumed to be reinvested in the same stock at the closing price on the last business day of the month in which they are paid. Wherever subscription rights are received, enough of them are sold for cash to exercise the remaining rights. The usual customary adjustments are made for all stock splits and stock dividends. A standard round lot brokerage commission of 1% of the net value of either a purchase or a sale is arbitrarily assumed for all transactions.[5] Similarly, on reinvestment of cash dividends, a standard commission of 1% is also assumed. Unlike the first Center study by Professors Lorie and Fisher, no adjustment for income, capital gain, or transfer taxes is attempted.

2. Fisher goes on to report the frequency distribution of the *ratio of final proceeds to initial cost* for every one of the 56,557,538 transactions made during the 35-year period. Here are the landmark percentiles, as summarized by Fisher in popular form:[6]

> (a) "Profits were made more than three times out of four" [78.3% of the time].
>
> (b) More than half of the initial investments at least doubled in value [50.4% of the time].

[4] *Op. cit.*, p. 149.

[5] *Historically, it may be noted that the 1% figure is on the high side for most round lots* during the 1926-1960 period; but the differences in results obtained by using more precise commission rates would, of course, be small.

[6] *Op. cit.*, p. 151.

(c) Losses of more than 50% of the initial investment occurred in about 1 out of 13 transactions [7.9% of the time].

(d) Losses of more than 25% of the initial investment occurred in about 1 out of 8 transactions [13.2% of the time].

Total losses were suffered only in about 1 out of each 20,000 transactions.

Professor Fisher's presentation of his findings, summarized above, is probably the most widely publicized portion of his study (a typical example is the quotation from the *Wall Street Journal* cited above). It is therefore unfortunate that the concept of "profit" and "loss" employed in this section of the article (and picked up in hundreds if not thousands of newspapers and magazines) is somewhat naive. For, in the investment field, the term "profit" ordinarily implies a *capital* gain—not just *any* increment of total final return over initial cost. Thus, cash banked at 4% compounded annually will double in less than 18 years with no capital appreciation. But it is a rather loose use of words to say that an investor who saves his money at this rate of interest will show a "profit" of 100% over such a period.

Similarly, if the total proceeds from an initial investment in a stock *and from all its reinvested dividends* amount to 10% over initial cost (or even 40% or 50% over such cost) after 10, 15, 20, 30, or more years, it will frequently be inaccurate for tax purposes to say that a "profit" has been made. For the Internal Revenue Service, such transactions will often involve a capital loss—even though the compounded accumulated income from reinvested dividends more than offsets that loss.

There must be literally millions of hypothetical transactions in the Fisher-Lorie stock universe that show a "profit" in the loose sense but a capital loss in the strict legal meaning. Similarly, there are millions of transactions in which the capital loss, in the strict sense, is larger than the loss in total proceeds, as reported by Fisher. For investors, in the real world, these are important practical differences.

3. Professor Fisher uses more neutral language in presenting a second table of results. This shows, for the same 56-million-plus transactions, the frequency distribution of *annually compounded rates of return* (once again not distinguishing between capital appreciation and dividend income). Here are some of Fisher's findings about the extraordinarily high returns from common stocks during the 35-year period, 1926-1960, restated in this form:[7]

The 56.6 million transactions yielded an *annually compounded rate of return* of:

At least 4%—more than 69.8% of the time.
At least 5%—more than 66.6% of the time.
At least 8%—more than 56% of the time.
At least 12%—more than 41% of the time.
At least 20%—more than 18% of the time.

[7] *Op. cit.*, p. 153.

At least 30%—more than 8% of the time.
At least 50%—more than 3% of the time.
At least 100%—exactly 1% of the time.

4. Professor Fisher next analyzes such annually compounded rates of return *over various different holding periods* from 1926 through 1960 for all stocks listed on the New York Stock Exchange during those periods. For this purpose, it is assumed that equal dollar amounts of each stock are initially purchased. The rest of the procedure is the same as in (1) above. Table I shows these results in Column A for most of the major longer term holding periods used by the Center.

HOW USEFUL FOR INVESTORS ARE FISHER'S FINDINGS AND IMPLICATIONS?

In this section, I propose to analyze and evaluate some of the procedures, factual conclusions, generalizations, and implications found in Professor Fisher's 1965 article. In particular, how unbiased and how useful are the total portfolio rates of return, cited in Table I, as criteria for individual and institutional investors?

1. *What exactly does the Center's* 1926-1960 *universe represent* It is not entirely accurate to call it a "universe of *stocks.*" Rather it is primarily a universe of hypothetical *transactions*. The difference is quite significant with respect to the "randomness" of the Center's universe. *For the repeated random selection of individual* stocks *listed on the New York Stock Exchange for monthly purchase and sale from* 1926 *through* 1960 *results in a highly one-sided or skewed selection of* transactions *over this same time span*. This fact is very clearly developed by Professor Fisher. He states:

> Such a sampling process implies that more results will be obtained for stocks which were listed for many years during the period than for stocks that were listed for only a few years.[8]

Thus, we learn from Professor Fisher that, while there are a total of 1,715 stocks involved in the transactions simulated by the Center's big computer, only 241 of these 1,715, or 14.1%, were listed on the New York Stock Exchange through the entire 1926-60 period; and of these 241, a complete series of end-of-the-month prices was available for only 201 stocks (or 11.7% of the 1,715 total). These 201 issues accounted for over 31% of the 56.6 million transactions tabulated over the 35-year period. Similarly, 366 issues whose prices were available for over 33 years, or 21.3% of the 1,715 total, accounted for more than 50% of all the transactions.[9]

In other words, what starts out as a random process of picking *any* NYSE *stock* and *any* end-of-the-month purchase or sale date winds up as a highly one-sided collection of *transactions* heavily weighted by a hardy band of about

[8] *Op. cit.*, p. 150.
[9] *Ibid.*

one-fifth of all the stocks represented, that account for more than half of the individual transactions.

Of course, this blue-chip bias is no fault of Professor Fisher or Professor Lorie; it is simply inherent in the terms of their total experiment. Professor Fisher recognizes that, to avoid such bias, "it would have been desirable to have had an equal number of buying and selling dates for each stock . . . and an equal number of holding periods ending at each month. Unfortunately, meeting these qualifications would have also required data for an infinitely long period of time rather than for the 420 months which were available."[10]

The nature of the bias resulting from the Center's method of selecting transactions can be indicated by answering this question: *Which stocks make up the roster of those durable* 366 *issues that are involved in more than* 50%, *or almost* 29 *million, of the* 56.6 *million transactions?* Clearly, many if not most of them are from the aristocracy of American business—the older, well-established companies, the institutional favorites that traditionally sell at higher price-earnings ratios than the average stock. High price-earnings ratios have been especially prevalent in the closing decade covered by the Center's studies, 1950-60, during which period institutional investing became increasingly important in the acquisition and accumulation of common stocks.

As a result of this blue-chip bias, "random" selection from the Lorie-Fisher universe of transactions means picking a pretty exceptional stock perhaps 50% of the time—a process more akin to the evolutionary "survival of the fittest."

2. *Besides the blue-chip bias described above, the Center's universe of transactions involves still another statistical skewness resulting from the same successful survival of the strongest companies over the 35-year period.* Most investors (and all analysts) are familiar with the phenomenon of how one or a few highly successful choices can enormously improve the statistical results of a portfolio. Thus, it has been known to happen that a mutual fund holding 100 or so stocks has outperformed its competitors and the averages very largely because two or three of its selections have appreciated more than 1,000%, even while most of its other holdings have fared rather indifferently.

Exactly the same phenomenon—intensified by the power of annually compounded reinvestment over long periods—has greatly skewed the Lorie-Fisher results. The enduring, successful companies repeatedly show up in the millions of transactions, and their gains pile up and compound over the years. Thus, while the dollar value of any initial purchase is the same for all stocks, *by the end of the 35-year period 1926-60, just 4 stocks out of 1,715—less than ¼ of 1%—account for 27% of the dollar value of the closing portfolio!* (Interestingly, for 1926-60, the four stocks are IBM, Brunswick, Jewel Tea, and National Lead.)[11]

What all this means to the Center's published rates of return is clearly

[10] *Op. cit.*, pp. 150–151.

[11] *Op. cit.*, p. 158.

indicated for us by Professor Fisher. The *"total portfolio" rate of return* for all the Center's portfolios for different time periods is in every instance higher than the *average* of the particular rates of return on the individual stocks in each of these portfolios. The more the skewness in any portfolio, the larger is the difference between the total and the average rate of return. The comparisons shown in Table 1 illustrate this phenomenon of "skewness from success." Note especially, from the last two columns of the table, how many more N.Y.S.E.-listed stocks show rates of return below the total porfolio return in Column A than show rates below the average rate of return in Column B.[12]

3. Another important relationship emerges from Table 1. It appears that the S & P Composite Index[13] in Column C almost always outperforms the Column B average rate of return, but only infrequently outpaces the Column A total portfolio rate of return. This has some significance for our subsequent discussion of mutual fund performance.

TABLE 1

Total Portfolio Rates of Return, Average Rates of Return, and Rates of Return on the S & P Composite Index for Various Holding Periods, 1926–1950

Holding Period	Rate of Return*			Per Cent of Stocks in Portfolio With Rate of Return Below	
	A	B	C		
	Total Portfolio	Average Rate of Return	S & P Composite Index	A	B
1/26– 9/29	18.9	12.1	32.2	63	50
1/26– 6/32	−16.6	−24.0	−10.3	70	52
1/26–12/40	3.4	− 3.3	4.1	69	45
1/26–12/50	7.3	4.6	7.6	67	46
1/26–12/55	9.0	6.4	9.2	68	43
1/26–12/60	9.7	6.5	9.9	75	46
9/29–12/60	8.3	5.4	7.5	75	44
6/32–12/60	18.0	14.6	15.6	75	47
12/40–12/50	18.8	16.1	13.0	67	55
12/40–12/55	18.7	16.0	16.1	68	53
12/40–12/60	16.6	13.8	13.2	71	51
12/50–12/55	18.0	15.8	22.6	59	51
12/50–12/60	15.0	11.9	15.8	65	48
12/55–12/60	11.2	7.9	8.8	64	50

*Per cent per year, compounded yearly, in terms of final proceeds per dollar initially invested.

Note: Figures are from Fisher, *op. cit.*, page 158.

[12] *Op. cit.*, pp. 157–158. As Fisher notes, this type of skewness would not develop if simple rather than compound interest had been used in the computations.

[13] The S & P Composite Index consisted originally of 90 stocks, but since March, 1957 the coverage was extended to the present total of 500 stocks.

The basic implication to be drawn from our critique—which, as the reader will have noted, is based largely on Professor Fisher's own analysis—is the following: *An average rate of return on individual stocks, as shown in Column B of Table 1, is to be preferred as a measure of success when investing in one or a few stocks—rather than the mean proceeds per dollar initially invested for a twice-biased collection of hypothetical transactions over a long period of time, as shown in Column A of Table 1.* The statistical validity of this position can be verified in the percentages shown in the last two columns of the table. Note that (a) the proportion of individual stocks with rates of return below the column B averages ranges from a low of 43% for the 1926-1955 holding period to a high of 55% for the 1940-1950 holding period; and that (b) the percentages for quite a number of holding periods are very close to 50%.

ON THE ALLEGED BLESSINGS OF IGNORANCE—AND THE PRACTICAL FUTILITY OF WISDOM

What are professional investors and investment advisers, in or out of Wall Street, to do about some of the more bizarre facts, figures, conclusions, and implications apparently drawn from the Center's studies by Professors Lorie and Fisher and by the business press, as previously summarized?

I submit that the first task is to try to demonstrate that most of the conclusions and implications simply do not follow from the facts and figures. If that can be done much of the battle against these strange views—so contrary to our daily experience—will be won. My own contribution, concentrated in this section, is as much logical and epistemological as financial.

There seem to be two quite different main ideas running through these views: (1) Investment success comes pretty easily—all you need is a little cash stake and one or two sharp darts. In addition, (2) almost any investor can do about as well as any other—it's all pretty much a matter of chance. So why bother to investigate before you invest? Why, indeed, take the trouble to become an expert or a professional? (Stock market firms that are delighted by the first proposition must be a bit embarrassed by the second.)

It is helpful to expose more of the logical scaffolding behind these two quite different themes—if only to wonder at how truly absurd conclusions can follow with impeccable logic from only slightly erroneous premises. Here is the syllogistic reasoning that seems to be involved:

Premise #1: Random selection in the stock market (at least on the N.Y. Stock Exchange) does very well indeed.

Premise #2: The average investor does (or can do) as well as random selection.

Premise #3: Many "expert" individual and institutional investors do little if any better than random selection, while many don't even do as well.

Conclusion: "Expertness" does not pay, knowing little or nothing does not hurt.

Sometimes there are one or two additional premises used to cement this cult of ignorance:

Premise #4: Not much, if any, improvement in the performance of the "experts" can be expected. And/or–

Premise #5: The difference between a successful and an unsuccessful investor is largely a matter of luck, not skill.

My position is simply that all five premises are either dubious, clearly false, or irrelevant to the important issues; so the conclusion is invalid. I know it will be charged that I am setting up and knocking down straw issues. But are they not the very issues that the Center for Research in Security Prices and other advocates of the random choice philosophy have provided us in the press and other publicity media?

"RANDOM CHOICE" MAY BE GOOD–BUT NON-RANDOM INVESTMENT CAN BE BETTER

Let us begin with Premise # 1, implying that random stock selection is the path to fortune. Not only, it seems, is "any time a good time to buy a 'good' stock,' as some brokers tell us, but any time is a good time to buy any stock listed on the New York Stock Exchange. If "good" and "time" are construed broadly enough, this premise certainly *was* true for the great majority of stock transactions in the 1926-1960 period covered by the Center's studies, as Professor Fisher's figures amply demonstrate. But from this broad historical truth alone it does not, of course, follow either (a) that this happy state of affairs will continue indefinitely in the future; or (b) that, more specifically, it will continue to be true for "random" N.Y.S.E. investments made in 1965-66; or that non-random selection of stocks (c) could not have produced *even better* results in the past, and/or (d) will not do so in the future.

Point (c) is most easily demonstrated. Fisher's own findings clearly show how proper non-random investment–non-random both as to timing and as to the individual stocks selected–would have produced much better results than his random method. Looking at Table I, it is simple hindsight to note that it would have been much more profitable to buy in 1932 than in any other starting year shown, and least profitable to buy in 1929. For sales at the end of 1960 the order of profitability of the starting years (as one might expect even without a computer) are 1932, 1940, 1950, 1955, 1926, and 1929. To the extent that at least some long-term investors managed to skew their starting times even partly in line with this pattern, the better were their results apt to be compared with random timing.

As for non-random *selection,* we have already noted the remarkable effects on any portfolio of a few spectacular issues. Since the Center is dealing with hypothetical transactions anyhow, it may not be too inappropriate to compare the results of its *random* choices on the New York Stock Exchange from 1926 to 1960 with an equally hypothetical pair of *totally omniscient* choices for a somewhat longer period. It has been estimated by Arthur Wiesenberger & Co. that; had one been able to time precisely all the turns on the Dow-Jones Industrial Average since 1915, one could have parlayed a paltry starting investment of $100 in the DJIA into over $765,000 by the end of 1964, for a return of 19.6% compounded annually (without even taking, let alone reinvesting, dividends). And if one also had the benefit of perfect *industry* selection as well as omniscient timing, so that one were smart enough to invest fully in the single best- acting industry group at all times, one could have pyramided that trifling $100 in 1915 up to the fantastic total of over $171 *billion* at the close of 1964, for a compounded annual rate of return of 53% (again, ignoring all dividends).[14] Drool, if you wish, at the potentials from adding perfect *individual stock* selection to these two other hypothetical perfections, and from the additional profit that could accrue from promptly reinvesting all dividends received.)

Such purely theoretical comparisons serve the practical purpose of illuminating the magnitude of the opportunities for improving on the results of random selection by thorough investigation and systematic techniques—in short, by knowledge. They are vast indeed.

Our second criticism of Premise # 1 is that it cannot possibly provide truly intelligent investment advice for any particular "here and now," like 1965-66. These years are not just "any time" to the investor putting his dollars at risk into the stock market. They are a specific time for which the most effective investment action would seem to depend at least as much (or more) on the financial, economic, and political conditions prevailing in 1965 and expected in 1966-67 than on what happened to listed stocks in the 35 years from 1926 to 1960—or on what, perhaps, may therefore be inferred to happen to listed stocks in the 35 years from 1965 to 2000. Even to imply, let alone boldly assert, that probably the most useful advice the typical investment counsellor can give a client in 1965 is just to pick any ten or twenty stocks listed on the New York Stock Exchange—on the assurance, based on the Center's computer-spawned findings for 1926-60, that all will be well by 1980, 1990, or 2000—seems to me to make the investment profession a wholly owned subsidiary of the "theater of the absurd."

Indeed, the entire position seems to wind up in paradox if not self-contradiction. For, if we are to use stock market results for 1926-60 as a model for 1965-2000, need we not also assume that the United States will once again experience the biggest depression, the greatest war, and the most sustained economic boom in its history? And, if that is the presumption, may we not ask whether we are now at the 1926, the 1929, or some other stage of the recurrent pattern? In short, if we are to be guided by any stock market history at all and are permitted to project the results of random selection for 35 years in the past into the future, we can hardly avoid opening the door to *all other relevant*

[14] Arthur Wiesenberger, *Investment Companies,* 1965 edition, p. 67. See also Leo Barnes, *Your Investments,* 1965 edition, p. 160.

history and experiences as well– and for periods longer (or shorter) than 35 years. And with that, the random selection approach would seem to get lost in the rush.

In this connection, some comment on the obvious importance of the time period selected for comparison purposes is relevant for proper perspective. Clearly, if one's terminal year happens to end with the level of stock prices at or near a market high, while one's beginning year happens to start at or near a market low, phenomenal results will invariably be shown. (Conversely, if the reverse relationship prevailed, investment disaster would inevitably result.) Professors Lorie and Fisher do not, of course, succumb to such transparent self-delusion. *But they have, I think, tended to minimize the impact of an essentially similar historical bias involving their terminal decade rather than their terminal year.*

THE PHENOMENAL '50's–A REVOLUTIONARY REVALUATION

If the last ten years of a selected long-term period are extraordinarily good, merely phenomenal results become simply stupendous, thanks to the power of annually compounded interest. I submit that the 1950-60 decade–the last ten years of the University of Chicago Center's 35-year span on which most eyes are focused– *is not only such an extraordinarily good period but, indeed, a unique decade in U.S. stock market annals.*

This historical bias in the Lorie-Fisher long-term universe can be most readily demonstrated by examining the trend of U.S. stock prices for as far back as we have reliable data–to 1871. Table 2 gives the score by decades (and one half-decade, 1960-64) since that year, showing the price change and the annually compounded rate of return for each period (ignoring dividends) on Standard & Poor's comprehensive stock indexes and suitably linked predecessor indexes.

Note how the net gain of 257% for 1950-59 not only far exceeds the two next best decades–1920-29, plus 140%; 1900-09, plus 71%–*but actually comes close to matching the total gain of 276% for all the preceding 79 years from December 1870 to December* 1949!

The verdict of history for stock prices is, accordingly, that the decade 1950-59 is highly atypical and unlikely to recur. It represents a revolutionary revaluation of common stocks by investors, especially by institutions. If the extraordinarily high 1950-59 rates of return are ever to be duplicated over a future ten-year period, that would seem possible either as another reaction to another prior drastic downgrading of common stocks by investors, such as occurred in the 1930's and 1940's; or (less likely) as part of a wild era of runaway inflation.

In short, the exceptional rates of return for longer term periods which terminate with (or include) 1950-60 cannot be accepted as suitable investment norms for the years ahead. As our last bit of evidence in closing our discussion of Premise # 1, notice in Table 2 the definite decline to a less extreme rate of return during the latest five years, 1960-64. This decline continues a trend

TABLE 2

Stock Prices and Rates of Return Since 1871

Decade or Period	Per Cent Price Change in Period	Annual Rate of Return*
1871–1879	+ 11.8%	1.2%
1880–1889	+ 8.1	0.8
1890–1899	+ 13.2	1.3
1900–1909	+ 71.1	5.5
1910–1919	– 13.4	– 1.4
1920–1929	+ 140.0	9.1
1930–1939	– 42.2	– 5.3
1940–1949	+ 33.7	2.9
1950–1959	+ 257.1	13.6
1960–1964	+ 42.2	7.3
*	*	*
1871–1919 (49 years)	+ 102.7%	1.4%
1871–1949 (79 years)	+ 275.9	1.7
1871–1964 (94 years)	+1,808.2	3.2
1920–1949 (30 years)	+ 85.4%	2.1%
1920–1959 (40 years)	+ 562.1	4.8
1920–1964 (45 years)	+ 841.3	5.1

*Percent per year, compounded annually.

Note: Figures are computed by the author from data for Standard & Poor's 500-stock index and its predecessor 90-stock index, linked to Cowles Commission indexes prior to 1918. Computations are in terms of December average prices. See Standard & Poor's Corp., *Security Price Index Record,* 1964 edition, page 112.

The figures shown do not include dividends, treated either as cash or as reinvested. Either treatment would have made long-term price gains considerably larger and price losses considerably smaller.

toward lower, and more erratic, returns begun in the previous five-year period (as clearly shown in the last three lines of Table 1).

AMATEUR INVESTORS ALL TOO OFTEN FARE WORSE THAN RANDOM

Now let us turn to Premise # 2–to wit, that the average or typical investor does (or can do) as well as purely random selection. There is, of course, no gainsaying the fact that he *can* do as well (if some generous foundation supplied him with the money) simply by buying and selling at random–say, a la Lorie-Fisher. But the plain fact is that (a) he has not; (b) he does not; and (c) he almost certainly will not.

Available empirical evidence, plus some elementary theoretical analysis, suggests that the typical, relatively uniformed investor does not do nearly as well as a random selection of New York Stock Exchange issues. The assumption that he does is perhaps the Achilles heel of the sceptical random choice position. For it seems to lead directly to the erroneous inference that, since *expert* investors often do not seem to do any better than a random selection, then they are not doing any better than unskilled investors can do.

However, everyday stock market experience, plus volume and odd-lot figures, show that most investors typically buy more and sell less at or near market highs, and sell more and buy less at or near market lows. It is a truism that, when stock prices are really low, most investors think they are too high; and that, when stock prices are really high, most investors think they are still low. Thus, most investors are likely to do worse than random in *timing.*

Moreover, anyone who has ever reviewed many individual investor portfolios will not require much persuasion to agree that the typical investor is also likely to do worse than random in *selection.* It is amazing how partial many investors still are to hot tips, new issues, skilfully touted unlisted stocks, high yielders, non-producing Canadian mines, etc. In their efforts to make a killing and beat the averages, they often wind up faring much worse than the averages—or a random choice. The average investor *would* probably be a bit better off in the long run if he picked his stocks by throwing darts at a newspaper page of N.Y.S.E. issues.

Even when individual investors act prudently rather than rashly, they are not moving randomly. Thus, S.E.C. statistics—when joined to New York Stock Exchange figures on the number of shareholders in U.S. business—tell us that, from 1961 through 1964, a steadily rising total of individual investors have, collectively, been selling stocks, while institutions have been buyers on balance. Net sales of stocks by individuals maounted to $2.3 billion in 1961, $3.8 billion in 1962, $4.1 billion in 1963, and $2.8 billion in 1964.[15] While a good deal of this money was probably transferred to mutual funds (especially in 1961 and 1964), the figures clearly indicate that many individual investors did not fare as well in the 1962-65 bull market as a purely random investment mechanism would have done.

All in all, in terms of his psychological as well as financial limitations, it is very hard to see how the typical individual investor could be persuaded to invest randomly; and how, failing this, he could do as well in the market as a random selection of Big Board issues.

WHY SOME EXPERTS DO MUCH BETTER THAN RANDOM

We now look at Premise # 3, claiming that expert investors do little if any better than a random walk, while many don't do as well. Here, of course, adequate statistical evidence is sadly lacking. As is well known, the best data we have are for mutual funds and other regulated investment companies reporting their results regularly to the S.E.C. The accumulated evidence indeed suggests that most investment companies do *not* perform quite as well as either the Dow-Jones Industrial Average or Standard and Poor's Composite Index. This performance discrepancy narrows but is not overcome when appropriate adjustments are made for the non-stock holdings of many funds.[16]

[15] Securities and Exchange Commission Statistical Series, *Volume and Composition of Individual's Savings,* Release No. 2042, April 7, 1965. New York Stock Exchange, *Institutional Shareownership,* June 1964.

[16] See Leo Barnes, *Your Buying Guide to Mutual Funds and Investment Companies*

Now I freely grant that mutual fund performance could—and should—improve. But the available evidence does *not* imply that quite a number of mutual funds do not perform better than a random selection, or that many more mutual funds do not outperform most individual investors. If one looks again at Table 1, it will be seen that, for almost all the holding periods listed, the S & P Index (Column C) outperforms, usually by a substantial margin, the average rate of return shown in Column B (though not the statistically skewed total portfolio rate of return in Column A).

Thus, to the extent that at least some mutual funds or other institutional investors "keep up with the averages," they would seem to do at least somewhat better than the "average" stock on the New York Stock Exchange—and probably considerably better than the "average" investor. To this limited extent, at least, investment knowledge and experience can be shown to pay off.

Obviously, too, there are many individuals who also outperform purely random selection. Is there anything (besides a smattering of luck) that distinguishes these particularly prospering investors? *I submit that it is specialized knowledge— methodically and firmly applied.* If the reader looks closely at those investors in his acquaintance who have consistently and persistently outperformed the averages, I believe he will usually find them to fall into one or another of the following categories—all illustrating the importance of some kind of particular knowledge:

1. *The corporate insider, especially in fast-growing companies.* Here, of course, luck or happenstance plays some part, in that the people involved happen to be connected with one company rather than some other.

2. *Other investors with special knowledge*—who, by tip or by wit, become very familiar with opportunities in specific companies or industries and make the very most out of them. These are usually people with fast reaction times as well as intellectual insight. Mr. Billy Rose is a widely publicized modern instance of this type.

3. *Investment specialists.* Here I mean not only stock exchange floor members, but also many professional or amateur investors who systematically specialize in a particular area, industry group, or specialized investment instrument like convertible securities or warrants. It is common experience in Wall Street that, over any respectable period of time, such specialists do better financially than the generalist who tries to cover the whole waterfront.

4. *Followers of consistently effective investment approaches or techniques.* There is respectable theoretical evidence (which I do not have the space here to explore) suggesting that, if a limited number of investors properly utilize various approaches or techniques for improving investment timing, investment selection, or both, they *could have done* better than average in the past, or *could do* better than average in the future. However, there is little useful information available

---

(1960), pp. 47–48; Irwin Friend et al, *A Study of Mutual Funds* (prepared for the Securities and Exchange Commission by the Wharton School of the University of Pennsylvania), U. S. Government Printing Office, 1962, Chapter V.

about how many investors have actually taken advantage of such approaches or techniques–like sophisticated variable ratio formula plans, various "cut-losses-short, let-profits-run" devices, or systematic concentration on "fast-growth" and other types of special situations. But some there obviously are.

LUCK DOESN'T HURT–BUT BRAINS HELP, TOO

I shall bring my "counter-revolutionary" excursion to a close by considering very briefly the two supplementary Premises # 4 and # 5–namely, that not much if any improvement in the performance of the experts can be expected; and that, in any event, the difference between investment success and failure is more a matter of luck than of skill.

Premise # 4 is particularly intriguing because of the postwar knowledge and technological explosions referred to at the start of this article. As a result, higher educational achievement than formerly required is now demanded as a matter of course by most investment firms. The exchanges themselves and Federal and State regulatory agencies are also introducing higher intellectual requirements for staff positions. The MBA degree–and now the achievement of the C.F.A. distinction–will increasingly become a prerequisite for professional advancement.

Are we to concede to the view that all this educational enrichment is for naught? Or should we not rationally expect more investors to raise their comparative batting averages as a result of it?

A basic stumbling block to answering these questions is the very composition and structure of the measures by which investor performance is judged. Since many of the so-called "institutional" stocks wiegh heavily in the Dow-Jones Industrial Average and the Standard & Poor's indexes, price changes for such stocks are apt to raise or lower these standard measures about as much as they do the performance record of the institutions. (I offer the designation "bootstrap effect" for this phenomenon.) As the eminent author and investor, Benjamin Graham puts it: "It may be that the professionally managed funds are too large a part of the total picture to be able to outperform the market as a whole."[17]

What is obviously needed better to appraise the performance of all investors is an *unweighted* average of a very large number of stocks–an index that is unskewed either by capitalization (as in the S & P indexes) or by price (as in the Dow-Jones and many other price averages). In such an index, an equal per cent price change for any stock would have exactly the same effect as for any other stock.

The Value Line Investment Survey has developed such an index for the approximately 1,100 stocks it regularly supervises. And its overall average has performed conspicuously poorer for most periods since the middle of 1961 to

[17]Benjamin Graham, "Some Investment Aspects of Accumulation Through Equities," *The Journal of Finance* (May 1962), p. 204.

the middle of 1965 than has either the DJIA or the S & P 500. The per cent of capital appreciation for this four-year period (dividends not considered) is 16% for the Value Line Average, 28% for the DJIA, and 31% for the S & P 500.[18]

A similar disparity prevails for another unweighted index—the 800-stock average maintained by the American Investors Service. In most years since 1946—the period in which institutional participation in the stock market has become steadily more important—the AIS average has shown substantially less capital appreciation than either the DJIA or the S & P 500.[19] A year-by-year comparison of the lag behind the DJIA since 1961 is especially interesting:

	1960	1961	1962	1963	1964
DJIA	−8.4%	+19.2%	−10.9%	+16.7%	+14.6%
AIS	−5.7%	+22.3%	−23.2%	+11.2%	+ 9.3%

Such disparities suggest that comparisons with unweighted indexes will show investment superiority or inferiority compared to "average" performance more clearly and consistently than comparisons with the blue-chip-loaded yardsticks. In these days of instant "real time" computer information, it should be relatively simple (and inexpensive) for the New York Stock Exchange, the American Stock Exchange, Standard & Poor's—or the University of Chicago's Center for Research in Security Prices—to provide speedy computation and publication of truly comprehensive unweighted averages of stock prices. Presumably, only such indexes will enable us successfully to test Premise # 4.

As for Premise # 5, it cannot, of course, be disproved statistically. Luck is a matter of the long run and, in the long run, as John Maynard Keynes remarked, "we are all dead." Thus, for example, we obviously cannot *prove* that the management of frontrunning mutual fund A is smarter, not just luckier, than that of lagging fund B; or that Mr. B. Baruch was brainier, not merely luckier, than Mr. B. Zeckendorf. But with all due apologies to the latter, the hypothesis that the former gentleman was smarter is surely pragmatically more acceptable and useful than the view that he was just luckier (say, by being on the scene a generation or two earlier).

Consider for a moment the logic of applying the same "cult of ignorance" or luck hypothesis to the many other important branches of human activity in which certainty is conspicuous by its absence. Are all of our more successful business forecasters merely luckier than their less successful confreres? Are physicians no smarter but only luckier than witch doctors?[20] What about our fiscal (or military) policy makers in government? Should they just toss coins

[18] *The Value Line Investment Survey,* issue of July 9, 1965.

[19] George A. Chestnutt, Jr., *Stock Market Analysis: Facts and Principles,* American Investors Service, 1965, pp. 30–48.

[20] The view that witch doctors are as smart as physicians is, incidentally, widely believed—and legally affirmed—in several of the new African States like Kenya and Nigeria. See *The New York Times,* August 2, 1965, p. 2.

when deciding to cut taxes or to curb the dollar outflow (or to send troops to Southeast Asia or Central America)?

Finally, it must be noted that we have less than 100 years of accurate stock price records, and much less of a backlog for other financial information. That is only about five generations of investors on whose actions we can base our generalizations. Pragmatically, however, we have no choice but to live and act as if our all too limited investment generalizations and practical decisions, based on "the best of our knowledge and belief," have some validity—*unless and until they are decisively disproved.* And this, it is submitted, the findings of the University of Chicago's Center for Research in Security Prices have failed to do.

25

On Speculative Prices and Random Walks: A Denial*

Robert E. Weintraub†

INTRODUCTION

Do speculative price movements follow some systematic and hence predictable pattern or class of patterns? Can information about tomorrow's price movements be gained by studying today's price data? Professional traders or speculators would have to answer these questions in the affirmative, for they operate as if this period's price movements can be used to their advantage. But today it is respectable, if not fashionable, for the professional economist and statistician to answer these questions in the negative. In the past few years a number of academic papers have concluded that speculative price movements are random walks.[1]

How should we interpret the claim that speculative prices move randomly? Following Hendrik S. Houthakker, randomness in speculative price data may be defined negatively as the "absence of any systematic pattern."[2] Alternatively, following Harry V. Roberts, the random-walk hypothesis may be taken to mean that speculative price movements "behave very much as if they had been generated by an extremely simple chance model."[3] Whether randomness is defined negatively following Houthakker or positively with Roberts, the implication of the random-walk hypothesis is that the speculators cannot know what they are doing when they study this period's price movements by way of seeking some sign of the next period's movements. I shall argue that the random-walk

*From *Journal of Finance,* Vol. 18, No. 1 (March 1963), pp. 59–66. Reprinted by permission of *Journal of Finance.*

†I am indebted to Thelma Lubkin, a former student, for help in preparing this paper.

[1]See, for example, Harry V. Roberts, "Stock 'Patterns' and Financial Analysis: Methodological Suggestions," *Journal of Finance,* XIV (1959), 1–10; M. F. M. Osborne, "Brownian Motion in the Stock Market," *Operations Research,* VII (1959), 145–73; Holbrook Working, "New Ideas and Methods for Price Research," *Journal of Farm Economics,* XXXVIII (1956), 1427–36; and Maurice G. Kendall, "The Analysis of Economic Time Series. Part I. Prices," *Journal of the Royal Statistical Society,* Ser. A, CXVI (1953), 11–25.

[2]Hendrik S. Houthakker, "Systematic and Random Elements in Short-Term Price Movements," *American Economic Review,* LI (1961), 164.

[3]Roberts, *op. cit.*, p. 2.

hypothesis flies in the face of common sense and the facts and, moreover, suggests a degree of naïveté on the part of its advocates as to the rules of the game which professional speculators are playing.

How valid is the random-walk hypothesis? No one has disagreed in full, but some economists have found elements of non-randomness in speculative price movements. Houthakker presented evidence that stop orders give rise to a non-random profit.[4] Sidney S. Alexander also has published results[5] that would appear (at least at first glance) to confirm that common-stock prices follow discernible paths. According to Alexander, these trends can be brought into common view by "filtering" out random variability in common-stock prices. The filtering process consists simply of ignoring changes of less than–at a first approximation–5 per cent and betting that larger changes are more likely to continue than to reverse.

Alexander's results will please the adherents of all schools of thought on speculative prices save one. "Fundamentalists," "technicians," and supporters of the random-walk hypothesis will be pleased. But professional speculators–men who adhere to the view that it pays to study the past (e.g., "the tape")–will be confused by and also disdainful of Alexander's findings. Fundamentalists will be pleased because the existence of major non-random moves tends to affirm their contention that fundamental developments in underlying supply and demand factors must bring major price changes. They will not care that moves of less than 5 per cent appear to follow random walks; for they would not regard moves of this order as being fundamental in any sense whatever. Technicians also will be delighted by the existence of major non-random moves and will not be bothered by Alexander's failure to find trends in the cases of moves of less than 5 per cent. Their charts are usually drawn so that traders may ignore minor fluctuations and concentrate on formations and patterns showing major price movements. Also, adherents of the random-walk hypothesis will not be displeased because Alexander's results corroborate their contention that moves occur that are independent of previous price trends–even though such moves evidently do not exceed 5 per cent. But there is nothing in Alexander's results to comfort professional speculators–men who survive and prosper by exploiting price movements that more often than not are considerably less than 5 per cent.

It is a fact that there are professional traders who earn incomes from speculating on price movements. It is also true that these earnings are high enough frequently enough that licenses to speculate where trades are executed often can be sold for thousands of dollars. The "seats" of floor traders on the New York Stock Exchange are the clearest and purest example of such licenses. The existence of floor traders or, more to the point, of the value that the market has attached to their licenses to speculate where trades are executed is difficult

[4] Houthakker, *op. cit.*, pp. 164–72, esp. 164–68.

[5] Sidney S. Alexander, "Price Movements in Speculative Markets: Trends or Random Walks," *Industrial Management Review*, II (1961), 7–26.

to reconcile with random-walk hypothesis on speculative prices, including the modified version suggested by Alexander's results. These men, in effect, earn their incomes by betting against the applicability of the random walk hypothesis to price moves of less than 5 per cent.

THE NEXT MOVE

The fallacy or delusive quality of the probabilistic view of speculative prices arises from the very peculiar definition of the term "the next move," which is employed by those who claim that the next move is independent of past moves.

The most important and impressive study tending to corroborate the random-walk hypothesis of speculative prices was published by Maurice G. Kendall in 1953.[6] Kendall calculated lagged serial correlations of the first differences of series of observations of speculative prices existing at specified moments in time, e.g., series of Friday closing prices. Graphically, Kendall plotted the difference between the closing prices on the first and second Fridays observed against the difference between the second and third Fridays; and the latter difference against the difference between closing prices on the third and fourth Fridays, etc. Thus Kendall defined, implicitly if not explicitly, the next move as the difference between the prices existing at the ends of two adjacent finite time periods. To date, no one has questioned the usefulness of this definition, even though it is obviously irrelevant. Kendall's definition is a non-operational concept and hence irrelevant because professional traders do not operate only at specified moments in time such as on Fridays at 3:30 E.S.T.

Conceptually, the next move is simply the difference between the current price and the very next one. But to define the next move in this way is also to impose a non-operational time horizon upon speculators. They are not compelled to sell on the trade immediately after they buy or to cover on the trade immediately following their making a short sale. The next move must be defined so that the abstract speculator of statistical research has the same, or nearly the same, opportunities to speculate which real-world speculators have. In terms of satisfying this requirement about opportunities, either one of two definitions of the next move would appear to be appropriate. First, the next move of a price may be defined as equal to the difference between the *highest* price reached in time period t_1 (e.g., Wednesday) and the closing price of t (Tuesday), provided that the difference between the closing prices of t (Tuesday) and the preceding period t_{-1} (Monday) is positive. But if the previous trend (i.e., the difference between the closing prices of t and t_{-1}) is negative, then the next move is the difference between the *lowest* price reached in t_1 and the closing price of t. It should be realized that the use of the *highest* and *lowest* prices of t_1 in the definition is essential to provide the abstract speculator of statistical research with the same opportunities that real-world speculators have, for the latter have opportunities to sell at the highest price and to cover at the lowest price.

[6] Kendall, *op. cit.*

Speculators using the above formulation of the next move will buy whenever price in t closed above the closing price of t_{-1}. They sell sometime during period t_1, hopefully at the highest price in t_1 and in the hope that the highest price in t_1 is above the closing price of t. Conversely, they sell whenever price in t closed below the closing price of t_{-1} and buy (cover) during t_1, hopefully at the lowest price in t_1 and in the hope that the lowest price in t_1 is below the closing price of t. Thus speculators using this definition are betting on the existence of monotonic day-to-day trends.

Alternatively, it would be appropriate to define the next move as follows: the next move is the difference between the *lowest* price reached in t_1 and the closing price of t, provided that the closing price of t is higher than that of t_{-1}. But if the preceding trend is negative, the next move is the difference between the *highest* price reached in t_1 and the closing price of t. Speculators using this definition of the next move are betting against the existence of trends or, if the reader prefers, on the existence of zigzag patterns. They will sell short whenever price in t closed above the closing price of t_{-1} and cover during t_1, hopefully at the lowest price in t_1 and in the hope that the lowest price in t_1 is below the closing price of t. Conversely, they buy whenever price in t closed below the closing price of t_{-1} and sell in t_1, hopefully at the *highest* price of this period and in the hope that the highest price of t_1 is above the closing price of t.

It is useful to iterate that, unlike the Kendall definition, our formulations of the next move are operational concepts for professional speculators. The definition of the next move that is employed by the probabilistic school requires speculators to cash in their bets at a specified moment in time. There is no such rule or limitation on speculative activity, and hence this definition is not operational for professional speculators. Unlike the Kendall definition, our formulations of the next move permit speculators, whether they are betting on or against trends, to cash in their bets at the most opportune moment in time (i.e., at the most advantageous price) between the close of t and the close of t_1. Thus our formulations permit testing for trends in speculative prices under rules that give speculators no more and no less freedom than they actually have.

EVIDENCE THAT SPECULATIVE PRICES FOLLOW TRENDS

The existence of trends in speculative prices was tested for by computing three lagged serial correlations from *daily*[7] price data on the *New York Times* Industrial Stock average for November, 1961, and also from daily price data on the more familiar Dow-Jones average for the June 1, 1961, through July 31, 1961, period.[8] These data are presented in Tables 1 and 2.

[7] The choice of daily price data to test for serial correlation is arbitrary. However, it should be realized that a day is not an unreasonable approximation of a speculator's time horizon; certainly it appears a better approximation than an hour or a week.

[8] Choices of indexes and time periods were made haphazardly, not by design—random or other.

On October 31, 1961, the *Times* stock average closed at 673.80. On November 30, 1961, it closed at 680.91. Thus there was little, if any, over-all trend in this period. Similarly, there was little over-all trend in the summer period. On June 1, the Dow-Jones average closed at 611.05 and on July 31 it closed at 597.93. Both series are therefore taken from periods without over-all trend. Since (presumably) it is easier to speculate successfully in periods marked by over-all trend than in periods without steady up or down price movements, testing for serial correlation in periods without over-all trend eliminates a possible bias in the results.

Also it should be noted that the tests made using the summer data involve 41 observations, whereas the tests made from the fall data involve only 23 observations. If the results of the two series of tests differed markedly, it would

TABLE 1

"The Next Move" Calculated from *New York Times* Industrials (25 Common Stocks) Daily Prices for November, 1961

Date Nov.	High	Low	Close	"The Next Move"		
				Under Kendall's Definition	For Speculators' Betting	
					On Trend	Against Trend
1	678.54	670.59	674.85	1.05*	....	....
2	681.11	671.81	677.80	2.95	6.26	3.04
3	682.11	672.73	678.79	0.99	4.31	5.07
6	687.20	675.40	683.52	4.73	8.41	6.06
8	696.96	683.39	692.35	8.83	13.44	0.12
9	696.70	686.80	691.26	−1.09	4.35	5.55
10	696.84	687.47	694.27	2.96	− 3.79	−5.58
13	702.64	690.90	698.34	4.12	8.37	3.37
14	705.88	693.60	702.55	4.21	7.54	4.74
15	709.46	700.00	703.14	0.59	6.91	2.55
16	706.17	694.59	701.01	−1.23	3.03	8.55
17	704.31	693.57	698.39	−3.52	− 8.34	−2.60
20	704.20	693.84	698.80	0.41	− 4.55	−5.81
21	702.80	689.86	693.58	−5.22	4.00	8.94
22	696.27	687.54	691.76	−1.82	− 6.04	−2.69
24	697.13	688.01	693.32	1.56	− 3.75	−5.37
27	698.86	689.01	693.38	0.06	5.54	4.31
28	695.82	684.80	689.45	−3.93	2.44	8.58
29	692.29	683.04	687.02	−2.43*	− 6.39	−2.84
30	687.34	677.70	680.91	−6.11*	− 9.98	−0.32

*The first number in this column, 1.05, is *not* a number in the series termed "The Next Move under Kendall's Definition." But this number is the first number in the previous trend series. Conversely, the last number in this column, −6.11, is not a number in the previous trend series but is the last number in the series termed "The Next Move under Kendall's Definition." The last number in the previous trend series is the next to last number in this column, −2.43.

TABLE 2
"The Next Move" Calculated from Dow-Jones Industrials (30 Common Stocks) Daily Prices for June 1–July 31, 1962

Date	High	Low	Close	"The Next Move"		
				Under Kendall's Definition	For Speculators' Betting	
					On Trend	Against Trend
June						
1	616.54	603.58	611.05	– 2.31*	....	....
4	608.82	591.37	593.68	–17.37	–19.68	2.23
5	603.37	584.12	594.96	1.28	– 9.56	9.69
6	611.82	595.50	603.91	8.95	16.86	0.54
7	608.14	599.27	602.20	– 1.71	4.23	– 4.64
8	607.30	598.64	601.61	–00.59	– 3.56	5.10
11	603.20	592.66	595.17	– 6.44	– 8.95	1.59
12	593.83	580.11	580.94	–14.23	–15.06	– 1.34
13	586.42	572.20	574.04	– 6.90	– 8.74	5.48
14	579.14	560.28	563.00	–11.04	–13.76	5.10
15	579.90	556.09	578.18	15.18	– 6.91	16.90
18	583.08	567.05	574.21	– 3.97	4.90	–11.13
19	575.21	566.59	571.61	– 2.60	– 7.62	1.00
20	574.59	561.28	563.08	– 8.53	–10.33	2.98
21	561.87	549.15	550.49	–12.59	–13.93	– 1.21
22	551.99	537.56	539.19	–11.30	–12.93	1.50
25	541.24	524.55	536.77	– 2.42	–14.64	2.05
26	548.61	533.46	535.76	– 1.01	– 3.31	11.84
27	539.28	528.73	536.98	1.22	– 7.03	3.52
28	559.32	541.49	557.35	20.37	22.34	4.51
29	569.06	555.22	561.28	3.93	11.71	– 2.13
July						
2	576.63	557.31	573.75	12.47	15.35	– 3.97
3	582.99	570.53	579.48	5.73	9.24	– 3.22
5	586.30	577.39	583.87	4.39	6.82	– 2.09
6	582.58	571.28	576.17	– 7.70	– 1.29	–12.59
9	582.28	569.65	580.82	4.65	– 6.52	6.11
10	599.02	583.50	586.01	5.19	18.20	2.68
11	590.94	580.36	589.06	3.05	4.93	– 5.65
12	596.59	586.68	590.27	1.21	7.53	– 2.38
13	592.99	583.87	590.19	– 0.08	2.72	– 6.40
16	591.23	582.41	588.10	– 2.09	– 7.78	1.04
17	588.77	576.59	577.85	–10.25	–11.51	0.66
18	577.39	568.02	571.24	– 6.61	– 9.83	– 0.46
19	578.68	568.98	573.16	1.92	– 2.26	7.44
20	579.86	570.78	577.18	4.02	6.70	– 2.38
23	582.24	574.50	577.47	0.29	5.06	– 2.68
24	579.31	572.02	574.12	– 3.35	1.84	– 5.45
25	576.55	568.10	574.67	0.55	– 6.02	2.43
26	582.87	574.08	579.61	4.94	8.20	– 0.59
27	586.80	577.14	585.00	5.39	7.19	– 2.47
30	593.03	583.87	591.44	6.44*	8.03	– 1.13
31	601.15	591.78	597.93	6.49*	9.71	0.34

*See the footnote in Table 1.

make sense to attach more significance to the results pertaining to the summer period than to those pertaining to the fall period. But, insofar as the results are consonant, no special importance should be placed on the results for the summer period. Finally, it should be noted that all of November was characterized by relative day-to-day price stability, whereas the first half of the summer period was marked by fairly wide price swings from day to day. On the common-sense hypothesis that the task of predicting tomorrow's price movements is more difficult in periods of wide daily price swings than in periods of relative price stability, it appears reasonable to expect somewhat less serial correlation in the summer period than in the fall period. The results are as follows:

1. Using Kendall's definition of the next move, the serial correlation is 0.42 for the November period and 0.31 for the summer period.

2. Using the definition of the next move that would be employed by speculators betting on the existence of zigzag patterns (i.e., against trends), the serial correlation is –0.55 for the November period and –0.61 for the summer period.

3. Using the formulation that would be employed by professional traders betting on the existence of monotonic trends, the serial correlation is 0.77 for the November period and 0.69 for the summer period.

The results cannot be tested for significance with standard statistical techniques, since serial correlation is present and, in fact, predicted by hypothesis. Doubtless it would be desirable to test for trend in the way suggested by this paper, using different time periods and different price series, such as individual stock prices, for example, before accepting the suggestion of these results that speculative prices follow trends.

ECONOMIC IMPLICATIONS

One of the implications of my results is that speculators have opportunity to make capital gains. A corollary implication is that it is an error to infer, as many have done, from the lack of lagged serial correlation between first differences of closing prices that speculators have little or no opportunity to win. Instead, it would appear that this lack of serial correlation between first differences of closing prices simply means that speculators who are supposed to smooth out price movements over time are doing their job well.

Part **IV**

Investment Mechanics — The Securities Markets and Brokerage

INTRODUCTION

Part IV of this book focuses on the subject of investment mechanics. In the first essay Ralph and Estelle James explain the role played by the stock exchange specialist and detail recent criticism of the performance of this function. The major benefits of the specialist system in providing a brokerage for those orders placed "away from the market" and maintaining a close, continuous, and orderly market are weighed against their costs. The authors suggest that the brokerage function of the specialist requires little skill or individual discretion and could be provided by an attendant of the exchange or by a computer. In addition, they question the combination of brokerage and trading activities.

In the second work of this section, Professor Thomas Moore provides an excellent essay on stock market margin requirements. He examines the reasoning used by Congress in the enactment of this legislation. In presenting data on the efficacy of margin requirements, he concludes that available data indicate that not one of the aims of the legislation establishing margin requirements has been accomplished.

The market for put and call options is examined by Professor Charles Franklin and Marshall Colberg. James Dines reminds the reader that at one time or another, nearly everybody in the stock market, whether short or long, is faced by a large loss. To prevent small losses from becoming big ones, the fourth article of the section presents the stop loss order in theory and practice.

The Third Market is composed of over-the-counter trading of securities listed on a national exchange. The origin, rapid growth and future of the third market are discussed in the article written by Douglas Campbell. He suggests that lower costs and the absence of ticker tape announcements that accompany exchange dealings were important in the more than twenty-fold growth of the third market in the period 1941–1961. David Hoddeson's article concludes the section with a discussion of the factors contributing to the growth of the regional exchanges.

26

The Disputed Role of the Stock Exchange Specialist*

Ralph and Estelle James

Are the services of the specialist on the stock exchange really as valuable as they are alleged to be?

What are the four major costs or disadvantages of the present specialist system, and how do they compare in importance with the advantages?

What changes and reforms in the specialist system should the financial community be considering now?

The current Securities and Exchange Commission (SEC) investigation of the stock exchanges has fast become the most sweeping in scope and penetrating in purpose since those of the 1930's. Increasingly central to its concern are a few hitherto obscure but powerful men, the "specialists," who in the words of George Keith Funston, the president of the New York Stock Exchange, provide "the guts of the whole market system."[1]

Disclosures of gross malfeasance on the part of at least two major American Stock Exchange specialist firms have brought this system under sharp attack. Its refashioning or even total elimination is emerging as a serious public policy issue on which the Special Study Group of the SEC is commissioned to report to Congress by January 3, 1963. In spite of the obvious dramatic appeal and political hay to be made of such exposés, it may be hoped that the SEC will not unduly emphasize the ferreting out of evildoers, but will, with broad theoretical and empirical perspective, carefully reassess the basic structure of the organized exchanges and the economic functioning of the specialist therein.

The specialist clearly provides some real benefits to the operation of the market, but these services are not cost-free. Aside from the well-publicized possibility of deliberate wrongdoing there are, as we shall show, more subtle and seldom mentioned dangers. Such effects are an inevitable by-product of the activities of the most honest and conscientious of specialists. This preliminary analysis, relating primarily to the New York Stock Exchange, suggests that

*From *Harvard Business Review,* Vol. 40, No. 3 (May-June 1962), pp. 133–146. Reprinted by permission of *Harvard Business Review.*

[1] *Wall Street Journal,* July 11, 1961, p. 1.

substantial room for improvement does indeed exist. However, information gaps abound. As a result additional research, particularly including some intensive case-by-case studies of stock-price movements, is needed to establish the basis for minor changes, major overhauling, or complete rejection of the specialist system.

NATURE OF THE JOB

The New York Stock Exchange is not, as it appears superficially, a free and open auction market with price determined by the interplay of numerous buyers and sellers, but rather a closely controlled and highly regulated system with the specialist serving as day-to-day manager. One or more specialists have been appointed for each issue to perform in two broadly defined capacities:

1. As a *broker*, the specialist fills market or limit orders for other brokers or floor trading members. When an individual investor places a buy-or-sell order "away from the market" with his account executive, his order is typically recorded in the "book" of the specialist in that issue, to be executed by the specialist in return for a small fee should the market reach the specified level.

2. As a *dealer*, the specialist trades whenever this appears "reasonably necessary" to create "a fair and orderly market" in his stock, an ambiguous phrase which has been interpreted to mean "the maintenance of price continuity and the minimizing of the effects of temporary disparity between supply and demand."[2] In this process he supposedly imparts liquidity and stability to the market and, without directly seeking it, earns a profit for his own account.

Information is not available on the current volume of the specialist's *brokerage* activities, although we are told that in the 1930's he performed this function for approximately 33% of all exchange transactions.[3] There is no reason to believe that the same figure applies today, however, for the relative importance of limit orders may well have changed since the 1930's.

Aggregate data on the specialist's *trading* operations for his own account have been published by the SEC and the New York Stock Exchange, and from these it is possible to compute the changing "specialist participation rate" (SPR) over the past 25 years. Now we define the SPR as the sum of all transactions in which the specialist is involved as dealer (either as buyer or seller), divided by the total stock exchange volume for the relevant period. Other studies have doubled the denominator, defining the SPR as specialist purchases plus sales divided by all purchases plus sales, thereby obtaining percentages which are exactly half of those in Exhibit 1. Such an index, which at its highest point can

[2]New York Stock Exchange, Department of Floor Procedure, *Rules and Practices Governing Dealings in Stocks* (New York, 1958), pp. 62-63.

[3]Raymond Vernon, *The Regulation of Stock Exchange Members* (New York: Columbia University Press, 1941), p. 76; *The Securities Markets* (New York: The Twentieth Century Fund, Inc., 1935), p. 414; U.S. Securities and Exchange Commission, *Report on the Feasibility and Advisability of the Complete Segregation of the Functions of Dealer and Broker* (Washington: Government Printing Office, 1936), p. 141.

EXHIBIT 1

Annual Specialist Participation Rate at the New York Stock Exchange, 1937-1961

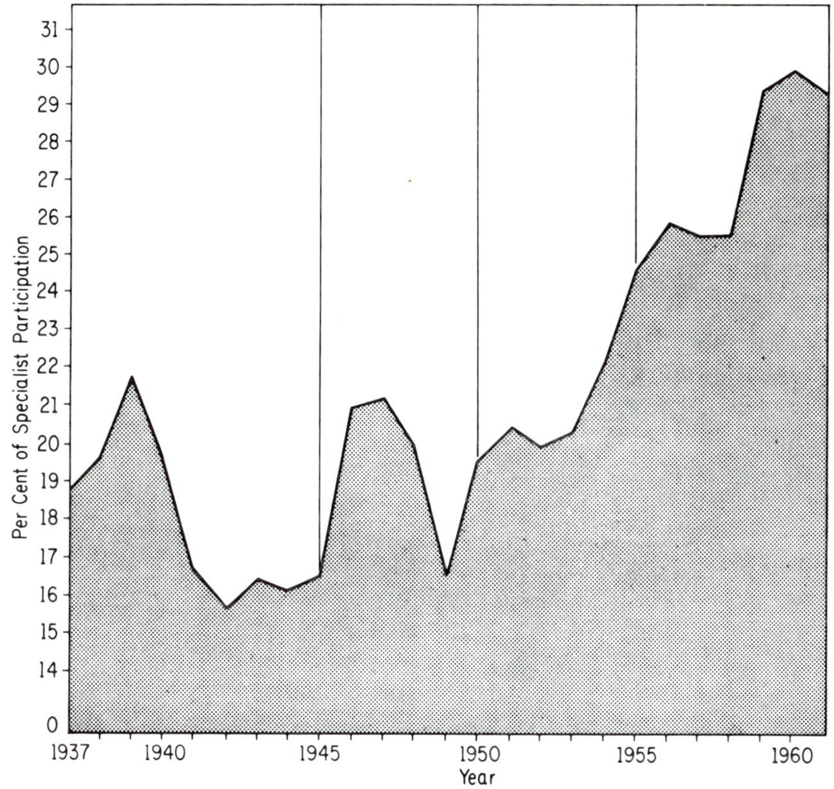

Notes:

$$\text{Specialist participation rate} = \frac{\text{Specialist purchases + sales for his own account}}{\text{Total volume of transactions (all purchases or sales)}}$$

The figure for 1961 is from January 1 to July 1; the figure for July 1, 1959, to July 1, 1961, was 29.8%.

Source: New York Stock Exchange, *Fact Book, 1961,* p. 45; and U.S. Securities and Exchange Commission, *Statistical Bulletin* (Washington, Government Printing Office, 1951-1961).

equal only 50%, understates the actual participation of the specialist in the market by focusing on the percentage of purchases *or* sales which he accounts for rather than on the proportion of transactions to which he is a party in *either* capacity. As can be seen from the exhibit:

The SPR was reasonably stable in the 19% to 22% range between 1937 and 1954 except for a moderate drop to 16% during World War II and again in 1949.

In 1954–1955 the index began its upward climb, becoming stabilized at 25% to 26% for 1956–1958.

Another spurt came in the latter part of 1958, the index moving from 25% in October to over 30% by July and August, 1959, and finally settling in the 29% to 30% range where it remains today.

Thus, at present, the specialist is either buyer or seller for three out of every ten transactions. And for relatively inactive stocks the SPR is higher still, probably reaching 50% for certain types of issues. (A higher SPR for relatively inactive stocks, although with a drop-off at the extreme end of the continuum, was revealed in the leading surveys of the 1930's. The unavailability of disaggregated data makes it impossible to test their specific applicability to current circumstances, but discussions indicate that the general tendencies and broad rationale of the foregoing conclusion are probably still valid.)

How can this precipitous rise of almost 50% in less than six years (1953–1959) be explained? Certainly a major factor has been the active intervention of the New York Stock Exchange in demanding greater specialist participation—an influence proudly claimed by William K. Vanderbeck, head of the Big Board's Floor Procedures Department, who uses the daily SPR as one of three major criteria for evaluating a specialist's performance.[4] One would expect a priori that a small number of individuals engaged in so large a proportion of all trades must have a significant impact on market behavior, perhaps not all completely desirable. And this indeed turns out to be the case, as we shall try to show later in this article.

ALLEGED BENEFITS

A number of benefits are supposed to result from the specialist system. There are, in fact, some very real benefits, but they are not as numerous or significant as is sometimes claimed.

Brokerage Function

By recording and eventually executing limit orders in his stock, the specialist renders an undeniable service. He provides a much-needed central clearinghouse for buy-and-sell orders placed "away from the market" as well as a fair and systematized first-come, first-served determination of priority when several identical orders have accumulated. In so doing, he relieves the original broker of a worrisome and time-consuming responsibility, and assures the individual investor that his limit order will not be forgotten or lost in a bureaucratic file when the strategic moment arrives.

At the same time, it should be recognized that this clearest and most uncontroversial of the specialist's functions is also the one requiring the least skill and individual discretion, and could be carried on by an easily trained attendant of the exchange, or even by a new computer.

Furthermore, the effectiveness of the specialist's acting as a broker would be

[4] *Wall Street Journal,* July 11, 1961, p. 17.

little hampered if he were separated from his questionable trading activities, although the reverse is probably not the case.

Continuity and "Liquidity"

The specialist is expected to maintain a close, continuous, and orderly market, trading for his own account whenever necessary to narrow (a) the spread between bid and asked prices and (b) the difference between two consecutive transactions. The former supposedly makes it possible for an investor to buy at a lower price or sell at a higher price than would otherwise obtain. Note, however, that this is a two-edged sword, with one man's gain being the other man's potential loss. For example:

If the bid and asked prices are 40 and 41, respectively, and are narrowed to 40¼ and 40¾ by the specialist, one party may gain (e.g., the buyer, if he were about to capitulate at 41, for he can purchase at the lower price from the specialist), but only at the other party's expense (the private seller, underbid by the specialist, has lost a potential customer for his stock).

At present, in some cases the party to suffer is the controversial floor trader; in others the loser is the patient investor with a registered limit order, and it is hard to understand why his impatient counterpart with an order to buy or sell at the market price should be explicitly favored.

As for narrowing the price difference between consecutive transactions, this imparts liquidity in the very limited sense which may be induced from the exchange's rules and usage of the term – i.e., making it feasible at any moment for an investor to receive for his stock a value similar to that established by the previous transaction. In so doing, the specialist is highly successful as evidenced by the second of three major evaluative criteria employed by the New York Stock Exchange: 88% of all trades analyzed from this perspective in 1960 were executed ¼ point or less away from the preceding sale.

Such provision of liquidity is believed to encourage public participation in the market and to enhance the safety of investments once made. But may not this liquidity protection be more illusory than real in some instances? May not an artificially contrived continuity, by concealing information about a stock's potential volatility, at times diminish rather than add to the safety of an investment? These perplexing questions will be dealt with later.

Effect on Stability

One might speculate that stability is more important than continuity in determining the liquidity and safety of an investment. In the exchange's words, the specialist is supposed to dampen short-run fluctuations in the value of his stock by "minimizing the effects of a temporary disparity between supply and demand." Precisely what is meant by this phrase, however, is hardly clear, and the degree to which this function has been fulfilled is even less apparent.

The attention of the exchange seems to center on two aspects of stability.

The first and most dramatic involves the market's reaction to a sudden unanticipated piece of news, such as a new discovery by a particular corporation, an unforeseen dividend cut, or an intensification of the Cold War. For example, the New York Stock Exchange often points proudly to the large balances accumulated and the risks assumed by specialists on September 26, 1955, the first market day after Eisenhower's heart attack, in an effort to mitigate the 32-point drop in the Dow-Jones industrial average. (Incidentally, the market had substantially recovered by the end of the week, enabling the specialists to make impressive profits on the entire operation. Virtue is rewarded!)

The second aspect concerns an extremely short-run concept of stability. The specialist is said to be stabilizing his market if he buys on a "downtick" (meaning that the second of two consecutive transactions takes place at a lower price than the first) or sells on an "uptick." This is the last of the three primary criteria used to police his performance. In 85% of all trades for his own account he did indeed pass the test in 1960, according to the New York Stock Exchange. However, such an index conceals the fact that, while doing all his buying on downticks, the specialist may be accumulating on a day when the price of his stock is rising, and vice versa, thereby accentuating rather than counteracting fluctuations in its value. In fact, the available evidence suggests that the day following Eisenhower's heart attack was not at all representative; that the specialist does not, as some sources maintain, generally perform the stabilizing function of "slowing rapidly declining markets by buying stock for his own account . . . [and] rapidly rising markets by supplying stock, selling short if necessary."[5] Thus:

A number of surveys conducted in the 1930's tested the relationship between daily stock-price movements and changing specialist positions. The SEC observed a slight tendency to trade against the trend, and a Twentieth Century Fund study suggested the opposite, with both results largely inconclusive.[6]

Using a somewhat different (aggregative) approach, Raymond Vernon found a clear positive relationship between the two variables, with respect to both direction and size.[7]

We have collected data on price changes and specialists' purchases and sales for the two-year interval July 1, 1959 to July 1, 1961, a period clearly set off from earlier years by the degree of specialist participation but quite heterogeneous with respect to range of daily volume and alternating dominance of "bulls" and "bears." Since one might expect that the stabilizing function of the specialist would be most apparent and most needed to counteract wide price movements, we have selected all days (about 20% of the total) on which the Standard & Poor's industrial average closed more than 0.5 or more away from its

[5] *Changing Times,* August 1955, p. 30.

[6] U.S. Securities and Exchange Commission, op. cit., pp. 35-36 and Appendix H-1 and H-2, pp. 142-143; Twentieth Century Fund, Inc., op. cit., pp. 418-424.

[7] Op. cit., pp. 82-88, 95-96.

previous close. (Standard & Poor's was chosen as a readily available average using a broader base of reference than the highly selective Dow-Jones average does.) Out of a total of 107 observations, 55 were days of upward movement and 52 of downward movement. We then calculated for these two groups the number of days on which specialists' purchases exceeded sales, and vice versa.

The results are presented in Exhibit 2. Specialists purchased more than they sold on about half of the upward-moving days, and sold more than they purchased on a clear majority of downward-moving days – although for the few most extreme price movements they were more likely to trade against the market.

How was the specialist behaving on wide-price-movement days which proved to be part of a major rally or decline? Here, especially, he seemed to play an accelerating rather than a stabilizing or neutral role. For example, during the bear market of January to March 1960 (a market decline of over 10%), he sold on 10 out of 13 sharp downward-moving days, including all 7 such days in January when more than two-thirds of the total drop took place. Similarly, specialists were buying on 13 out of 22 sharp upward-moving days during the prolonged revival of October 1960 to May 1961 (a rise of over 20% in market values). A particularly crucial subinterval lasted from late February to mid-April 1961, a time of exceedingly high volume (a procession of five-million-plus-share days), remarkably narrow daily price variations, and generally tumultuous indecisions as the market approached and successfully challenged its historic "685 Dow-Jones ceiling." Significantly, on all 5 rising wide-price-movement days

EXHIBIT 2

Daily Relationship Between Direction of Wide Price Movements and Specialists' Trading on the New York Stock Exchange, July 1959 - July 1961

	Number of Days on Which Specialists' Purchases Were Greater Than Sales	Number of Days on Which Specialists' Sales Were Greater Than Purchases	Total
Wide Price Movement Upward	28	27	55
Wide Price Movement Downward	22	30	52
Total	50	57	107

Note: For a definition of "wide" price movement, see text.

Source: Standard & Poor's *The Outlook*, 1959-1961; U. S. Securities and Exchange Commission, *Statistical Bulletin*, 1959-1961.

during this hectic period, specialists were buying on net and thereby adding to instead of mitigating the "bullish" trend.

Need for Further Study

We do not mean to argue that the specialist *should* be stabilizing over-all market movements. Rather, we simply point out that the often-heard statement claiming he does produce this effect is not supported by the (admittedly inconclusive) foregoing data. Indeed, it appears that at times his position-taking actions may actually broaden the amplitude of the swing. Of course, this does not rule out the use of other techniques and procedures by the specialist to achieve stability – for example, strategically placed buying and selling which may prevent a stock from breaking through a "hold point" (a price, on the upside or downside, to which the stock repeatedly rises or falls and then holds, thereby developing resistance to passing through that point when approached in the future). As we shall see presently, shrewdly handled operations of this sort may prove extremely powerful in today's market, more so, in fact, than the specialist's limited capacity to take a position regarding the stock. But a determination of the extent of such influences, and therefore any real evaluation of the specialist's impact on stability, must await more intensive, case-by-case studies of particular stocks and times.

COSTS OF SYSTEM

The net advantages of the specialist system can only be determined by weighing its benefits against its costs. As indicated, the major benefits provided are the brokerage function and, in a limited sense, the continuity-liquidity function; the evidence does not demonstrate that the stability function has been successfully performed. What are the major types of costs offsetting these advantages?

Conflict of Interest

The specialist's commitment to "maintain an orderly market" as a quasi-public servant and his brokerage duties to his clients may at times run counter to his own private profit-making interests. This is illustrated by the recently disclosed American Stock Exchange cases of the father-son team, the Res, which helped to set off the current SEC investigations and of the Gilligan, Wills firm featured in the first published report of the Special Study Group. By touting, bribery, setting up bogus accounts for trading purposes, and using discretionary orders, the Res created an illusion of frenzied activity and to their own benefit manipulated the sometimes wild price movements of their stocks. Gilligan, Wills and other American Exchange specialists have resorted to such questionable practices as holding for long-term investment purposes; advising and executing private orders for friends, relatives, and insiders; disclosing the "book" to brokerage firms before a secondary offering; purchasing stocks prior to listing; and off-board purchasing after listing.[8]

Both exchanges attempt to circumvent these dangers by numerous and highly detailed regulations which govern specialist behavior in potential conflict-of-interest situations. However, these rules are only as good as the procedures which enforce them. And on the American Stock Exchange the enforcement practices have been exceedingly lax: the violations of the Res and of Gilligan, Wills extended over several years, apparently undetected or at least unpunished by the American Stock Exchange, whose board of governors has, incidentally, long been dominated by specialists.

The Big Board proudly considers its standards more stringent and foolproof. Its checks (which outsiders are not permitted to examine) include weekly trading reports from specialists, surprise spot checks, market studies of individual stocks, and a computer geared to detect unusual price movements. Unfortunately, these policing procedures, particularly concerned with the specialist's participation rate and his continuity function, may not be well suited for detecting some of the more ingenious of rule-evasion techniques in conflict-of-interest cases.

Privileged Position

The specialist's privileged position constitutes a second cost of the present system. His unique access to information which no one else may possess legally may, in itself, be regarded as unfair and therefore undesirable. By consulting his "book" (which must be kept in total secrecy), he can make a reasonably accurate estimate of the current supply-and-demand schedules for his stock (although these of course are subject to rapid change) before deciding whether to buy or to sell. In addition, he is often provided with "inside" information by the management of "his" corporation before an official announcement is made. Yet his dealings are not open to the same public scrutiny as are those of more formal "insiders."

It has been argued that the specialist deserves these unique privileges, as partial compensation for the risks he must inevitably assume in the course of his stabilizing activities; in other words, that he enjoys no excess profits beyond the remuneration just necessary to keep him at his job. This is an empirical problem which can only be evaluated on the basis of further information. What is the size of an average specialist's income, in contrast with that which he would receive as a regular broker or floor trader? What percentage of these earnings stem from his

[8] For detailed accounts of these activities, see U.S. Securities and Exchange Commission, *Brief of the Division of Trading and Exchange In the Matter of Re, Re, and Sagarese* (Washington: Government Printing Office, April 28, 1961); and U.S. Securities and Exchange Commission, *Staff Report on Organization, Management, and Regulation of Conduct of Members of the American Stock Exchange* (Washington: Government Printing Office, January 3, 1962).

brokerage as compared with his dealership functions? The SEC's preliminary findings on the American Stock Exchange suggest that between 65% and 80% of total profits arise from trading, but as yet no such data are available for the New York Stock Exchange. How greatly do profits vary from stock to stock, from year to year, and so on? Do numerous brokers clamor for the specialist's position when an opening occurs? The answers to some of these questions would help in making a final judgment on the equity of the current system.

Illusions Created

A third, more subtle, and little recognized cost involves the creation of certain volume and volatility illusions by even the most incorruptible and well-meaning specialists. Were all specialists suddenly inactivated, everything else being equal, the total volume on the New York Stock Exchange would fall by 15%. For, instead of Investor A selling to a specialist who in turn sells to Investor B, a procedure which now accounts for about 30% of all trades, A would sell directly to B (perhaps after waiting a short while for B to appear), thus eliminating the intermediary transaction. And for the less active stocks, whose SPR is probably as high as 50%, 25% of all trades may stem from this "inflationary" effect; that is, they are actually much more inactive (both absolutely and relative to other stocks) than they seem.

The volume illusion is especially great with respect to short sales, more than 60% of which stem from the specialist's account. In other words, if there were no specialists, short sales would total less than half of their currently small amounts. This leads one to wonder about the percentage of published monthly short sales outstanding in each stock which are charged to the specialist. The actual figure is probably much smaller, for the specialist is presumably a rapidly covering in-and-out trader with purchases very nearly equaling sales each week, and even on most individual days.

Potentially more important than the absolute aggregate volume illusion are stock-by-stock differences and day-to-day changes in volume arising merely from a participation rate which varies between specialists and over time. At present, in contrast with 20 years ago, the distortion of day-to-day changes appears negligible, the daily SPR falling within the 27% to 31% range with remarkable consistency; but the current interstock diversity is substantial, the SPR for some issues being as much as 200% to 300% higher than for others, in the extreme.

Closely related to the volume illusion is a phenomenon which might be termed the "volatility illusion." Market analysts distinguish between a "good" market in a stock where trading is active over a narrow price range, and a "thin" market where trading is slower and the spread between transactions is greater. A rational investor might expect to find a correlation between the degree of "fullness" on a day when market orders to buy and sell are roughly in balance, and the resistance of the stock to price changes when a disparity between supply and demand develops. However, under the current system this hypothesis is not valid for the specialist's activity increases volume and forces on all stocks a similarly narrow spread. Therefore, the investor implicitly assuming a connection between "fullness" and price-change resistance will be misled, induced by an artificially contrived continuity into believing that a given stock, or the market in general, is safer and more stable than is actually the case.

If, in the absence of the specialist, the "fullness" of the market would indeed provide a better index of susceptibility to sharp price fluctuations (which seems like a reasonable expectation), the present system has closed off an important avenue of information about true differentials in volatility potential among stocks. It should be recognized, though, that if the specialist were eliminated, the initially wider spread for some stocks would no doubt narrow somewhat in time because of the increased use of limit orders among investors, a market technique whose use has unquestionably been discouraged over the last decade by specialist-induced continuity.

Price Distortions

The whole of the market is not necessarily the sum of its parts. Each individual transaction by a specialist may have little impact on intermediate-term price trends if, as the New York Stock Exchange proclaims, he acts merely to narrow the spread. On the other hand, his overall impact is not necessarily neutral. This is particularly so to the degree that technicians dominate the market, when specialists may set the tone for price movements weeks ahead by strategic buying and selling, even without taking a significant long or short position.

One of the major features of the market in recent years, many analysts claim, is the growing importance of technical as compared with fundamental considerations, i.e., the attentiveness of both investor and speculator to price patterns as guidelines for decision making, in place of (or, more often, in addition to) their own current knowledge and future anticipations concerning fundamental economic data. Newspaper advertisements galore testify to the systematic indoctrination of the public with the technician's reliance on chart patterns, hold points, "bull signals," "bear signals," and so on, culminating in the best-selling book by Nicholas Darvas, which attributed positive harm to any basic economic information concerning a stock on the basis that all important data are telescoped into its price movement by insiders' transactions.[9]

Other writers, such as Harry V. Roberts,[10] suggest that the manifestations of alleged technical markets cannot be demonstrated or even disproved. To the extent that this is correct, the potential costs of the current specialist system are correspondingly reduced. However, it should be realized that our discussion,

[9] *How I Made $2,000,000 in the Stock Market* (Larchmont, New York: American Research Council, 1960). An excellent survey of the technicians' approach and influence may be found in Daniel Seligman's "Playing the Market with Charts" and "The Mystique of Point-and-Figure," *Fortune* (February 1962 and March 1962).

[10] "Stock Market 'Patterns' and Financial Analysis," *Journal of Finance* (March 1959), pp. 1–10.

unlike Roberts', is predominantly concerned with individual stocks, not with the market as a whole, and that the dominance of "technical" considerations for certain not-too-rare stocks on certain not-too-infrequent occasions is quite sufficient to endow the role of the specialist with a high level of significance.

Where fundamentals are the major determinants of market decisions, the specialist can exercise little influence on intermediate-term price movements. But when technical factors assume a dominant role for individual stocks, he becomes more than a mere catalytic intermediary. By helping to build a chart pattern, by "reinforcing a hold point" or permitting his stock to "penetrate a support level," he can alter, as well as simply react to, an externally determined supply and demand, and can be instrumental in mapping its future price course for the forthcoming weeks.

Nature of Power

The explanation for this power lies in the contrasting dynamic nature of market equilibriums under these two conditions:

1. When fundamentals control, a stable equilibrium point will exist for any given set of anticipations and underlying data, with amount of stock demanded decreasing and amount supplied increasing as price rises, and conversely as price falls. Should the specialist temporarily overshoot or undershoot this equilibrium value, he will be propelled backward by these natural market forces (unless he is willing to alter these curves personally by taking a long-term position in his stock). Thus, they hold in close check the discretionary impact of his fallible judgment.

2. But a technician's market may be dynamically unstable, with numerous buy orders just above and sell orders immediately below the stock's current narrow range of movement. These instructions may take the form of limit orders now on the specialist's books, and of which he therefore is well aware, or of currently unplaced orders which investors are merely considering until the stock breaks through its hold point. The specialist cannot be sure of the precise size or even the existence of the latter, but based on his past intensive experience with the stock he is in an enviable position for making an estimate.

This situation is depicted in Exhibit 3, with the stock trading between 19 and 22 but unstable both above and below. Excess demand is negative below 19 due to the prevalence of stop-loss orders, and positive above 22 because of a multiplicity of buy-stops. If the price should start to move in either direction, it will therefore continue in that direction until a new equilibrium range has been reached, about which the forces of supply and demand will then temporarily regroup themselves once again.

While the specialist may not set off a chain of stops by trading for his own account, the decision to permit others to do so or, on the other hand, to stabilize and strengthen the hold point by buying and selling against the trend, has necessarily been left to his momentary discretion, which consequently

EXHIBIT 3

Unstable Equilibrium in a Technical Market

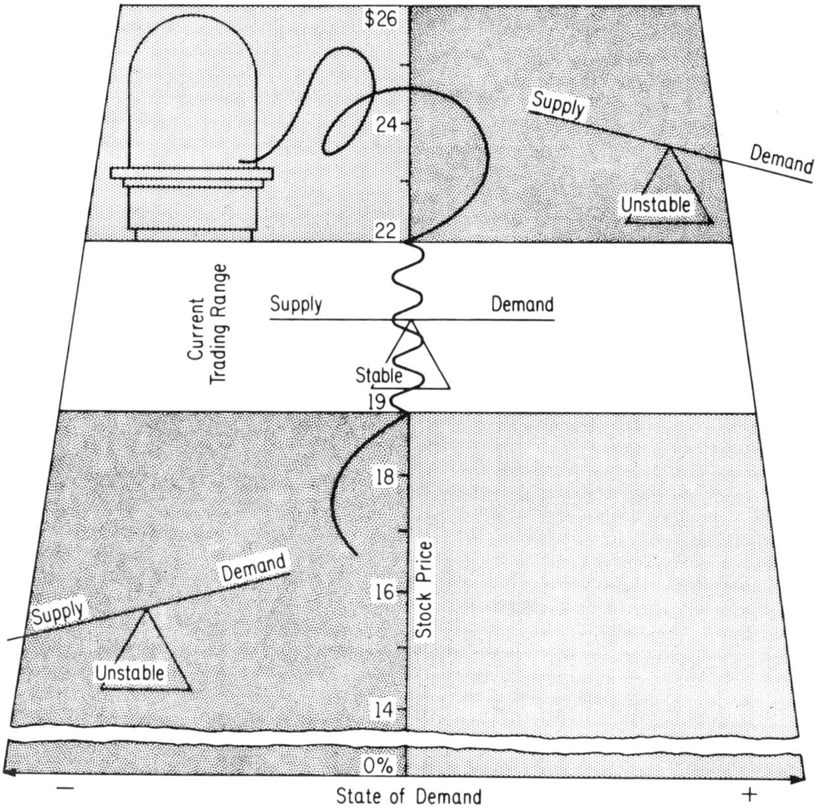

assumes extraordinary significance at crucial turning points in the chart history of his stock.

To what extent are exceptionally clear price patterns supported or even explicitly designed by specialists? Although some may be unaware of their stock's chart history, many, if not most specialists, must be cognizant and at least unconsciously affected thereby. Given the 30% SPR, it is hard to believe that particularly well-defined patterns would not undergo significant disruption were specialists switched or completely eliminated. The degree of this distortionary effect could only be determined by a case-by-case intensive examination of specialists' activities as their issues approached the vicinity of what was then or later became a major hold point.

The moral to be emphasized is that these price movements do not all develop as the result of independent spontaneous decisions of numerous buyers and sellers. Instead, they stem, to an unknown and varying degree, from the deliberate (although not necessarily ill-intentioned) behavior of a small group of men invested with special authority and knowledge by the New York Stock Exchange.

POLICY QUESTIONS

As the foregoing analysis doubtless indicates, we think that the financial community should take a hard look at the specialist system as it is and consider the possibilities of improving it. In doing this, four main sets of questions strike us as important.

Overparticipation?

If one's policy bias runs in terms of minimum regulation but maximum diffusion of market information to which supply and demand are free to react, one would favor very restricted participation by the specialist as a trader. A low SPR would tend to dampen the various illusionary and distortionary effects discussed earlier, and reduce the privileged-position cost and conflict-of-interest danger as well. Yet current exchange policy operates explicitly to the contrary, with strong attempts to increase the participation rate. As indicated in Exhibit 1 the SPR has risen precipitously to 30% largely as a result of such prodding.

Is today's high rate essential for effective performance of the specialist's duties? To test if the SPR is need-induced or simply exchange-induced, let us examine whether it varies with conditions which would change the usefulness of the specialist's service:

Taking an extreme example, one would anticipate, a priori, the necessity of specialist intervention to be much greater on low-volume, wide-price-movement days than it would be on high-volume, narrow-price-movement days when natural market activity should be more capable of adequately supplying both continuity and stability.

Accordingly, for the period July 1, 1959 to July 1, 1961, we selected those days in which volume exceeded 5 million (high) or fell below 2.5 million (low), a total sample of 102 days, or 20% of all days in the two-year interval. Days of exceptionally wide and narrow price movement were further stratified within this sample, the former defined as a change of 0.5 or more and the latter 0.15 or less from the previous day's close in Standard & Poor's industrial average. (Thus, for example, there were 11 days of high volume and wide price movement.) The SPR was then computed for each group and subgroup, with the results summarized in Exhibit 4.

The contrasts in SPR between categories are in the expected direction: the high-volume SPR is less than that for low-volume when compared for each price-movement type, and similarly the wide-price movement SPR is consistently greater than that for narrow movements. The largest SPR is consequently found in the low-volume, wide-price-movement box, and the smallest SPR in the

EXHIBIT 4

Market Volume, Price Movement, and SPR at the New York Stock Exchange, July 1, 1959-July 1, 1961

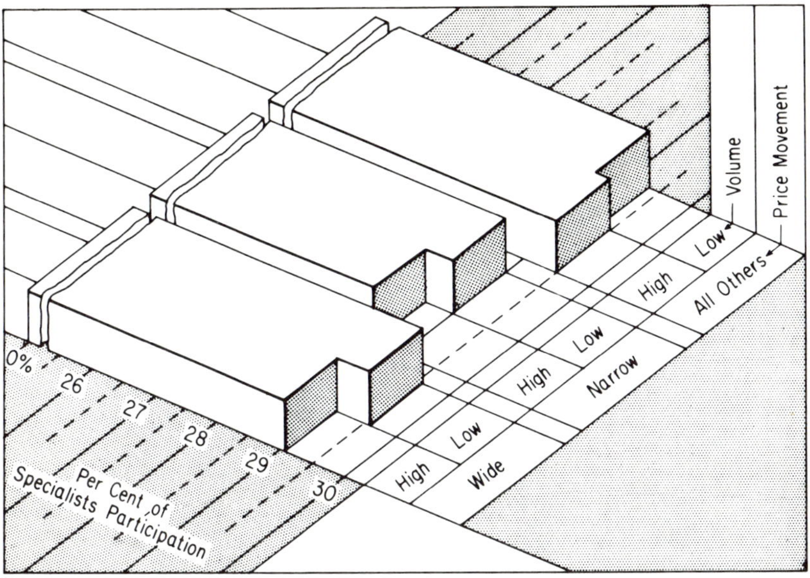

Note: For definitions of "high" and "low" volume and of "wide" and "narrow" price movement, see text. The high-volume group was concentrated in 1961, whereas the low-volume days were scattered throughout the two-year interval. Since the average SPR was relatively stable over the whole period, this pattern should not have distorted the results.

Source: Standard & Poor's *The Outlook, 1959-1961;* U.S. Securities and Exchange Commission, *Statistical Bulletin,* 1959-1961.

high-volume, narrow-price-movement box. However, the most striking finding is the very slight degree of variation among the different categories—fully consistent with the overriding regularity of daily SPR during this period.

The remarkable insensitivity of the SPR to differences in degree of need strongly suggests that it is largely dictated by external rather than by spontaneous endogenous forces, and that the specialist, prodded by exchange directives, may be participating more than is necessary for him to fulfill his responsibilities successfully. It might be argued in rebuttal that a highly fluctuating SPR would accentuate the illusionary effect on day-to-day changes in volume and is not desirable for this reason. It would seem, though, that the various costs inherent in excessive specialist intervention are much more consequential, and that the daily SPR variation could be much greater than the current negligible rate before reaching harmful proportions.

Change Entry Restrictions?

About half of the stocks on the exchange utilize the services of only one specialist; most of the others have two or three.[11] Entry is completely controlled; when an opening is created by admission of a new issue or retirement of an old specialist, the exchange selects, from among its brokers who apply, the member it feels can most effectively perform the duties involved. Given these severe restrictions on access to job and privileged information, it would be surprising if monopoly profits failed to develop.

The validity of this proposition can be established only by empirically examining some of the questions outlined earlier in the article on the specialist's privileged position. If found to be true, it raises several interesting policy alternatives. For example, the exchange might:

Auction off the opportunity to become a specialist among its otherwise qualified members, thus appropriating these monopoly profits for its own use.

Charge a flat fee for the right to act as specialist, just as it requires a person to purchase a "seat" to become an ordinary member of the exchange.

Reduce the specialist's monopoly profits and stimulate competition by increasing the number assigned to a particular issue. This would have the further advantage of weakening his conflict-of-interest potential and his power to influence a stock's chart pattern; on the other hand, it might result in harmful confusion, undefined responsibility, and a higher aggregate participation rate with its resulting illusion of market activity. Once again, we need more factual evidence, such as a case-study comparison of price movements for stocks with single and multiple specialists.

Separate Broker-Dealer Roles?

Segregation of the broker-dealer functions, long in effect on the London stock market, was considered, almost adopted, and finally discarded by federal legislators in the 1930's. This has been a recurring theme of investigations since then and obviously should and will be a central focus of any current study, particularly in view of the likely concentration on conflict-of-interest malfeasance. However, this emphasis has tended to obscure the fact that the other and possibly more significant costs of the present system–the illusion of activity and price distortion–would be negligibly affected by such a policy decision, while the conflict danger, its primary target, might be circumscribed simply by more stock exchange regulations. Therefore, it is imperative to explore other policy alternatives, and only cursory attention will be given here to this proposal.

The immediate and chief impact of separating the broker-dealer functions would be to remove from the specialist-trader any privileged access to the "book" and any monopoly profits resulting therefrom. This is at once its most desirable characteristic and the feature around which most objections center. For access to privileged information purportedly enables the specialist to perform his duties more effectively, gives the exchange moral justification for demanding that his behavior conform to certain rules, and (by clearly distin-

[11] New York Stock Exchange, Department of Floor Procedure, *Stocks and Specialists* (New York, revised to November 15, 1960).

guishing him from other floor traders) increases the practicality of policing his actions. In addition, it has been claimed that access to the "book" and to brokerage fees is necessary to offset the risks that the specialist is called on to assume in the name of "public service."

Certainly, specialists who today receive only the opportunity costs of their services would refuse to fulfill the more unprofitable of their social responsibilities were any advantages of their current privileged position removed. Perhaps for certain groups of stocks (the inactive or highly speculative) there is justification for combining the two functions, while for others there is no need to do so.

But should we not consider a bolder, more imaginative move? Just as the broker function—the recording and eventual executing of limit orders—could be performed effectively by clerical personnel who are not permitted to trade for their own account, why could not a well-trained employee of the exchange or even a clever electronic computer carry out the dealer function of "maintaining an orderly market"? In so doing, this quasi-specialist would not buy and sell for his personal account; instead, he would trade for the "bank," i.e., for the stock exchange itself, which could establish a kind of stabilization fund for this purpose. The capital requirements thus incurred by the exchange would be quite small, because one would expect these operations to be largely of an in-and-out nature, with purchases roughly equaling sales over periods as short as a week or less, and net purchases of one stock ordinarily cancelling out against net sales of another.

The practical difficulties in implementing such a radical reorganization are obviously very great because of the incentive problem, the need to place constraints on the quasi-specialist, the vagueness of the "orderly market" concept, and so on. At the same time, it should be realized that many of these same definitional and motivational problems exist today in less explicit form and are therefore more easily overlooked, to the detriment of the entire system.

More Information?

Probably the most workable and the most needed step of all is to increase greatly the diffusion of information about the specialist—his activities and impacts—to the general investing public and more particularly to professional market analysts. Here is what might be done:

1. One simple yet powerful reform could be effected merely by marking the tape in some manner to indicate for any given transaction whether a specialist as trader was involved and, if so, as buyer or seller. This would help to clarify, for example, whether a stock with a "good market" was distinguished from a "thin" one mainly by the degree of specialist intervention; whether support offered to a stock at a particular hold point was forthcoming from the stabilizing specialist or from private investors; whether the specialist played an active role in building a stock's chart pattern; and so on. Thus the various illusions and distortions described earlier would be publicly recognized and evaluated, and hence lose much of their special significance.

Such a measure would also serve the function of instantaneously revealing suspicious behavior by specialists which might otherwise go unnoticed for months or even years, thereby tending to protect investments from the danger of dishonest manipulation. Although the specialist who is guilty of malpractice today may eventually be discovered, many individual investors will have suffered in the long interim period; there is only limited value in declaring a foul three months after all bets have been collected.

"Painting the tape" in this manner might, to be sure, encourage an entourage of specialist imitators who try to copy his transactions as they come across the tape. Whether this would help to stabilize the market or would result in a hopelessly confused situation and thereby negate the gains brought about by the reform is, however, difficult to predict without further investigations. Incidentally, other forms of information might also be conveyed by coded marks on the tape. For instance, short sales could be indicated in this way.

2. A second valuable reform might be to require that disaggregated data on the participation rate and changing position of each specialist be made available to financial newspapers every month, just as are data on short sales outstanding and "insider" transactions. Currently, only figures aggregated over the whole market are published. These may conceal more than they reveal in many ways, and few "informed" analysts are even aware of their existence in the SEC *Statistical Bulletin.* This step, too, would help to illuminate the precise and varying influence of the specialist on market activity and price movements of different stocks.

3. Some perquisites of the specialist's privileged position could be removed by making available, to anyone requesting it, data culled from his book of limit orders on amounts supplied and demanded over relevant price ranges. At present, only the totals attached to the best bid and offer prices may legally be revealed. Other than the unknown cost of implementing such a plan (which, it is true, might turn out to be prohibitive), there seems to be little reason for withholding information from the public that may clearly be crucial to formulation of intelligent investment decisions.

CONCLUSION

This article is as much a bid for further research as a report of research already done. Unfortunately, given the paucity of public information, particularly the highly aggregative level of the accessible statistics, this is about as far as we can go. A more adequate economic analysis must await the availability of better data, for the specialist's impact is primarily on individual stocks, not on the market as a whole.

We may *hope* that the investigation-prone SEC, having access to information which is closed to the private researcher, will expand the area of its malfeasance inquiry and seek a more general comprehension of market function and behavior. Central to such a broadened focus should be an assessment of the costs and benefits of the specialist system along the lines suggested in this article. In the course thereof, new standards and tests for regulating the specialist's actions would no doubt emerge. For example, to what extent does he destabilize by buying on balance when the price of his stock is rising, and vice versa?

It certainly seems inappropriate to contemplate major revisions in the current specialist system, thereby moving still further into unchartered waters, without first obtaining a clear understanding of how the existing mechanism operates. But what if, as appears likely, the legalistically minded SEC Special Study Group, working under its rigid time schedule and limited budget, fails to provide the needed economic appraisal? Then it becomes incumbent upon the stock exchanges themselves both to encourage and to enable private research. And this means making available the basic data researchers require. The financial community's public posture can only stand to benefit from forthright public disclosure, accompanied by academic scrutiny and evaluation.

27

Stock Market Margin Requirements*

Thomas Gale Moore

In my judgment," maintained William McChesney Martin, Jr., Chairman of the Board of Governors, Federal Reserve System, "we can never under the present margin regulations have the same result that occurred in terms of a financial crash in 1929 through undermargined accounts, low margins resulting in a financial debacle."[1] A widely used elementary economics textbook claimed, "Margin requirements have exercised an important restrictive influence on security speculation, as contrasted with the uncontrolled period of the late 1920's. . . . Nearly everyone agrees that Federal Reserve margin requirements exercise a healthy restraint on speculative stock purchases in a boom" (Bach, 1963, p.116). But what evidence is there that margin requirements have the effects claimed? At the December meetings of the American Economic Association, George J. Stigler, in the Presidential address, called on economists to test their assumptions that state regulation of private activity has indeed been successful (Stigler, 1965). This article brings together some data on the efficacy of margin requirements. While the figures can only be considered preliminary, and more data should be collected to test margin requirements, the data that are available and presented here indicate that not one of the aims of the legislation establishing margin requirements has been accomplished.[2]

An examination of the congressional hearing on the bill to allow the Federal Reserve to control margins indicates three major objectives: to reduce "excessive" credit in the stock market and leave more for productive uses; to protect buyers of stock from going too far into debt and suffering therefrom; and to reduce fluctuations in the stock market due to forced selling of securities when prices drop and to overly easy purchases when prices rise. While different writers on the subject of margin requirements have placed various emphases on these objectives, no one, to this writer's knowledge, has suggested a new one. In this paper we will first examine each of these reasons and then test whether the

*From *The Journal of Political Economy,* Vol. 74, No. 2 (April 1966), pp. 158–167. Reprinted by permission of the University of Chicago Press.

[1] In *Stock Market Study* (U.S. Senate, 1955), pp. 580–81.

[2] For a contrary view, see Jules I. Bogen and Herman E. Krooss (1960).

objective has been satisfied. Preliminary to examining the reasons for the requirements, let us clarify what the law actually permits.

THE LAW AND THE FEDERAL RESERVE REGULATIONS

The law[3] permits the Board of Governors of the Federal Reserve to establish the maximum amount of credit that any exchange member, and any broker or dealer who transacts a business through the medium of an exchange member, can provide to a customer for the purpose of purchasing or carrying any security (except exempt securities) registered on a national security exchange. It also provides that the board can limit the amount of credit that a bank can offer on the same securities. The board has varied its requirements from cash purchases (100 per cent margin) to a 40 per cent margin (60 per cent can be borrowed). In recent years margin requirements have fluctuated between 60 and 90 per cent. The regulations issued by the board have been detailed and complicated and have varied from time to time with regard to undermargined accounts–those in which the credit extended is greater than would be permitted under the regulations then in force. Undermargined accounts come into existence when there is a decline in the market price of the stock being held or when the board raises margin requirements. Normally, the board has permitted individuals with undermargined accounts to sell their stock and replace it with another in the same day, as long as the net liability in the account and the net value of the assets in the account do not change by the exchange.

The law and regulations exempt certain securities from the margin accounts. Purchasers of governmental securities can borrow up to 100 per cent of the value from brokers or from banks. While brokers are not permitted to lend on unregistered stock, banks are free to lend any amount they see fit on such stock for the purchase of them or as collateral for the purchase of registered bonds. Moreover, both brokers and banks are permitted to lend as much as they deem safe of any registered security for any purpose except the purchase of securities. These exemptions necessarily weaken the effectiveness of the regulations. It is permissible for a firm (or individual) to invest the working capital of its business in the stock market and then borrow up to 80–90 per cent of the value of the securities to use as its working capital. It would be possible for a determined speculator to pyramid his investments by lying as to the purpose of stock loans. In effect, he could operate in the stock market on the same margin as his bank or broker will give him for purposes other than buying stock. No one yet knows how extensive such practices are, but Martin believes that "the relative amount . . . cannot be large in the aggregate."[4] The Federal Reserve requires banks and brokers to secure signed but not sworn statements as to the purpose

[3]Sections 7 and 8 of the Securities Exchange Act of 1934.
[4]U.S. Senate (1955), p. 553.

of any loan secured by a listed security. The board also requires the banks and brokers to exercise "reasonable diligence" in preventing customers from avoiding the margin requirements in this way.

THE PURPOSE OF THE REQUIREMENTS

Selective controls, with the exception of margin requirements, traditionally have been instituted only in times of national emergencies such as wars, when Congress has felt that the government should have more power over the allocation of resources. Normally, when the emergency has passed, the controls have been abandoned. Yet since the establishment in 1934 of margin requirements, there has been almost no agitation for their removal, and there has been some talk of extending the controls to the purchase and carrying of government securities (U.S. Treasury and Federal Reserve Board, 1959).

The reasons for the lack of opposition to these controls probably lie in the small number of individuals affected and in a belief that the controls protect the community from "excessive" speculation. The quotations at the beginning of this paper reflect the typical belief that the objectives of these regulations are desirable and are being fulfilled. Let us examine these objectives in detail.

EXCESS CREDIT DEVOTED TO THE PURCHASE OR CARRYING OF SECURITIES

One of the major purposes of the law is to prevent "the excess use of credit for the purchase or carrying of securities."[5] The House of Representatives report reads, "The main purpose [of the margin provisions] . . . is to give a Government credit agency an effective method of reducing the aggregate amount of the nation's credit resources which can be directed by speculation into the stock market and out of other more desirable uses of commerce and industry–to prevent a recurrence of the precrash situation where funds which would otherwise have been available at normal interest rates for uses of local commerce, industry, and agriculture, were drained by far higher rates into security loans and the New York call market" (U.S. House of Representatives, 1934).

Thus one of the objectives is to divert loanable funds from the stock market to other uses. I will leave it up to the reader to decide whether the government should try to regulate the quantity of credit in different markets. While it is clear that imposing margin requirements will tend to diminish credit for those securities regulated, it is desirable to know the magnitude of the effect. This is especially important since some securities are not covered. An individual who could not borrow as much as he wished on listed stock might turn to over-the-counter securities or government securities, in which case loanable funds are not being shifted in the desired direction.

[5] Loss (1961), pp. 1242–43.

In any case, most of the credit used to purchase stock will work its way into "more productive channels." If the user of credit buys a new issue of a stock, the issuer will receive the funds and put the money to work. If the user buys them from another individual, the seller will have the funds and be able to spend them on consumer goods. The point is that when stocks are bought on credit, the funds change hands and eventually will be spent on goods and services.[6]

Clearly, the major sources of credit for the stock market are bank loans. It is these funds that Congress and the Federal Reserve felt were being diverted into the stock market from "more productive" uses. There are other sources of credit for the stock market, many unregulated. Savings and loan associations, finance companies, and foreign sources have at times loaned funds to brokers or to individuals for the purpose of financing security purchases. When margin requirements are imposed or raised, the use of these uncovered sources of credit can only rise. Hence, any relationship found between bank credit and margin requirements would only overstate the effect on the total quantity of credit involved.

To quantify the effects of margin requirement on the amount of credit, let us consider a formal model. An estimate of the model's parameters will indicate the magnitude of the effect. Our model is that demand for bank loans to carry securities, L, is a function of stock prices, P (the higher prices, the more that can be borrowed), the cost of borrowing, i_b (interest rate on security loans), and margin requirements, M. The supply of loans is a function of the charge for such loans, i_b, and possible alternative earnings from these funds, i_o. The basic model is:

$$\text{D}: L = f(P, i_b, M) \tag{1}$$

$$\text{S}: L = g(i_b, i_o) \tag{2}$$

Because we are interested only in the net effect of changes in margin requirements, only the reduced form of this model was run. The basic data (January, 1947–January, 1965) on bank loans to brokers for carrying securities and to others comes from the *Federal Reserve Bulletin.*[7] Naturally, the appropriate figures are the loans for covered securities, that is, non-governmental securities. However, during the period from February, 1953, to June, 1959, governmental security loans were lumped with non-governmental. Therefore, a dummy variable, $G(0\text{–}1)$, has been added to the regression run to take this factor into account. Thus the regression fitted was:

$$L = L(M, P, i_o, G) \tag{3}$$

[6]Of course, ease of credit may affect transactions and prices on the exchange, but that's not the point here.

[7]The data on bank loans are for reporting banks in leading cities. These banks make about 80 per cent of the total of such loans of commercial banks.

TABLE 1
Demand for Stock Market Credit

	Margin Requirements	Stock Prices*	3-Month Treasury Bill Rates	Dummy	R^2	F
Loans to brokers . .	–5.002 (3.131)	4.510 (.648)	18.067 (78.312)	480.91 (121.15)	.318	24.611
Loans to others . . .	– .739 (.472)	2.534 (.098)	3.185 (11.806)	169.05 (18.26)	.848	293.69
Total loans	–5.741 (3.371)	7.044 (.698)	21.252 (84.319)	649.96 (130.44)	.480	48.69

*Standard & Poor's Index of all stock prices.

After an adjustment of the variables through an iterative procedure to remove the serial correlation in the residuals,[8] the results show (see Table 1) that if margin requirements were lowered from the average requirement during this period (67 per cent) to 25 per cent, which was the usual requirement during the late twenties (Bogen and Krooss, 1960, p. 76), loans to brokers would rise by about $209 million and to others by about $33 million.[9] Or, to put it another way, it would shift about 0.3 per cent of banks loans and investment from the security markets to other uses.

The equation fitted was:

$$L_t - \delta L_{t-1} = a(1 - \delta) + b_1(M_t - \delta M_{t-1}) + b_2(P_t - \delta P_{t-1}) + b_3(i_t - \delta i_{t-1}) + b_4(G_t - \delta G_{t-1}), \tag{4}$$

where δ was estimated by regressing:

$$u_t = \delta u_{t-1} + \epsilon_t \tag{5}$$

And u_t is the error term in the simple regression:

$$L_t = a' + b'_1 M_t + b'_2 P_t + b'_3 i_t + b'_4 G_t + u_t$$

PROTECTING BUYERS

The report of the Senate Banking and Currency Committee (1934, p. 11) on the bill to establish legal margins says that they are also intended "to protect the margin purchaser by making it impossible for him to buy securities on too thin a margin." Certainly they do prevent him from buying securities on as small margins as he might. Presumably the objective is to protect the buyer from the consequences of his own "folly."

[8] See J. Johnston (1960), pp. 193–94, for a description of the method employed.

[9] Assuming that the effect of margin requirements is linear and constant down to 25 per cent.

In a market economy there are certain market forces which prevent people from building up too many liabilities. The lender is anxious to insure the safety of his loan. A broker making a loan to a customer for purchasing securities will naturally require what he believes to be a safe margin. The more risky the broker considers the transaction, the more margin he will require and/or the higher interest he will charge.

With or without legal minimum margin requirements, certain individuals will suffer losses when stock prices decline. With or without the legal requirements (assuming margins are less than 100 per cent), certain loans for stock purchases will be defaulted, and hence the interest charged on the loans must include a premium for risk. If legal margin requirements have diminished the risk appreciably for borrowers, they must also have diminished the risk for lenders. Hence, one result of the imposition of margin requirements should be a reduction in loan rates for purchasing and holding securities relative to other interest rates for loans and investments whose risk has not changed over this period.

To test whether risk has been measurably diminished by the imposition of margins, the ratio of the interest charge on ninety-day stock exchange time loans to ninety-day prime bankers' acceptances has been computed for the years 1919–33, and 1946–57.[10] The mean ratio for the 1919–33 period was 1.354, while the mean ratio for the later period was 1.568–the premargin period charged relatively *lower* rates for the stock exchange loans than the postmargin period.[11] The difference is insignificant statistically. What is important is that the riskiness of stock market loans relative to prime bankers' acceptances appears to have remained unchanged. It is possible, of course, that both bankers' acceptances and stock exchange loans have become safer, the latter due to margin requirements and the former due to other changes. Yet there is no obvious evidence that bankers' acceptances (always relatively safe) have become an even safer investment over this period. Hence the evidence fails to support the proposition that margin requirements have made borrowing for security purchases safer for buyer or lender. This objective of margin requirements thus appears to be unfulfilled.

Moreover, correlating the ratio of stock exchange time-loan interest rate to prime bankers' acceptances with margin requirements for the period 1946–63 indicates no relationship. That is, higher margin requirements do not reduce interest rates on stock exchange loans. In fact the coefficient is positive but not significantly different from zero. This test is inconclusive, however, since a rise in speculative demand for loans might push up interest charges and also might

[10]Data are from Bureau of the Census (1960). These two series (X305 and X309) were used because both were for loans of the same length–thus abstracting from variations in short-term versus long-term interest rates–and because both were available for the whole period.

[11]This test is not proof, since it is possible that in the twenties the relatively safe security loans were made by banks and the risky ones by brokers. Hence the risk to banks might not have been appreciably affected by margin requirements, but the risk to brokers might have been diminished. Thus bank-loan rates on securities might be unaffected.

induce the Federal Reserve to raise margins; thus a positive correlation is unsurprising.[12] In any case, there is no support for the proposition that margin requirements diminish the risk to investors (and lenders) of borrowing for stock market purchases.

This conclusion is unsurprising since brokers and banks in granting credit for the purchase of stocks will undoubtedly investigate the credit status of the borrower and will refuse to lend to those with much risk. Thus the regulation may be redundant. The requirements might even have a perverse effect. They might encourage lenders to relax their standards since they can refuse to lend the borrower as high a proportion of the purchase price of the stock as they might be asked for were there no requirements. Thus, more risky loans may be encouraged.

REDUCING FLUCTUATIONS IN THE STOCK MARKET

"The task of the Board, as I see it, is to formulate regulations with two principal objectives. One is to permit adequate access to credit facilities for security markets to perform their basic economic functions. The other is to prevent the use of stock-market credit from becoming excessive. The latter helps to minimize the danger of pyramiding credit in a rising market and also reduces the danger of forced sales of securities from undermargined accounts in a falling market," said William McChesney Martin, Jr., at a congressional hearing.[13]

But do margin requirements act this way? Federal regulations apply only to the initial purchase of a security and do not require more security when a stock declines. However, most exchanges and brokerage houses have minimum requirements considerably lower than the purchase margins.[14] If a stock declines enough so that the owner's equity falls below that level, more margin will be called for; and if it is not forthcoming, the stock will be sold. It is clear that the higher maintenance margins are, the more calls there will be for more margin. Encouraging low maintenance margins would eliminate much of the danger of forced sales.

When a stock declines in value, the incentive for a speculator to sell it depends partly on the regulations affecting undermargined accounts. For most of the period in which the Federal Reserve has regulated margins, it has allowed an individual with an undermargined account to swap stocks if the sell and buy orders are carried out within a short period and if the exchange does not result in either a more valuable portfolio or in more credit being secured. Thus high margins create no particular incentive for staying with a stock. But for one brief period (July 5, 1945–April 1, 1948) the Federal Reserve refused to allow funds

[12] I am grateful to an anonymous referee for this point.
[13] U.S. Senate (1955), pp. 550–51.
[14] The New York Stock Exchange requires a maintenance margin of 25 per cent, and some brokerage houses require even higher maintenance margins.

to be withdrawn from undermargined accounts or substitutions to be made. The effect of such regulations is to reduce the incentive to sell a stock when its price has declined. Hence this would tend to reduce selling on the downswing. It is clear that the lower margin requirements are, the less desirable a sale would be to the speculator. Thus to reduce selling during a downswing, policy should be directed to having low margins without allowing substitutions or cash withdrawals from undermargined accounts. This has not been the policy of the Federal Reserve.

TABLE 2
Demand for Credit with Changes in Stock Prices*
($N = 215$)

	Margin Requirements	Stock Prices	Changes in Stock Prices	R^2	F	D
Total loans	−5.918 (3.620)	7.437 (.496)	−4.379 (1.628)	.526	58.19	2.138
Loans to brokers	−5.205 (3.340)	4.728 (.458)	−3.157 (1.502)	.350	28.21	2.218
Loans to others	− .713 (.532)	2.709 (.073)	−1.223 (.239)	.870	352.37	1.562

*The coefficient for the dummy has no economic interest and is not shown, although it is significantly different from zero in all cases.

The theory that stock market credit is destabilizing rests perforce on the assumption that speculators are irrational. When prices rise, so the theory goes, the public wishes to buy more and bids the price up farther; when prices fall, investors panic or are forced to sell. The idea that they are forced to sell assumes that they have no other assets and no other way of raising cash in a hurry. Yet a broker would hardly grant credit to such an individual. Those with margin accounts must have some other liquid assets or they would not be given credit. Credit buying can also be a stabilizing influence, since credit makes it easier to buy when prices have declined as well as when prices have risen.

The question is empirical: do users of credit operate to destabilize the market? If they do, then when prices rise, credit purchasers should increase their demand for securities and credit. A positive correlation, then, between changes in stock prices and the amount of credit would support the destabilization hypothesis.

The model for the demand for stock market credit discussed above then will be expanded to include changes in stock prices. Demand for credit will be a function of the stock prices, interest charges on the loans, margin requirements, and changes in stock prices. If borrowers act in a destabilizing fashion, the coefficient for changes in stock prices should be positive; a rise in stock prices leads to a rise in borrowing, and a fall in stock prices leads to a fall in borrowing. If, on the other hand, the use of credit is stabilizing, the coefficient will be negative. In estimating the parameters, the reduced form only has been run.

The reduced-form equation fitted is:[15]

$$L = f(M, P, G, \Delta P) \tag{6}$$

or more specifically because of the serial correlation:

$$L_t - \delta L_{t-1} = a(1-\delta) + b_1(M_t - \delta M_{t-1}) + b_2(P_t - \delta P_{t-1})$$
$$+ b_3[P_t - P_{t-1}] - \delta(P_{t-1} - P_{t-2}) + b_4(G_t - \delta G_{t-1}), \tag{7}$$

where δ is estimated as in equation (5). The results are given in Table 2.

It is apparent from the results in Table 2 that borrowing on securities tends to be a stabilizing influence. That is, when the stock market has risen, loans are lower than if the stock market had declined. Certainly this does not suggest that investors use credit in a destabilizing way. If investors with credit increase stock price fluctuations, loans should be higher when the stock market has been rising than when it has been declining. But this is the reverse of what actually happens. This suggests that margin requirements may actually inhibit the stabilizing influence of investors.

Let us look at the market before and after legal requirements were imposed, as an additional test. If margin requirements prevent pyramiding and forced selling, they should have reduced the variance in stock prices. Stock prices, however, will fluctuate for other reasons besides speculative activities. In the long run, stock prices should move with corporate profits. As a simple test, then, profits after taxes of the large corporations were used as an independent variable in a simple linear regression to standardize for the difference in business conditions. Table 3 shows the results.

Three factors should be noted in Table 3: the standard deviation of stock prices of the later period is larger than the standard deviation of the earlier period; the variance of the residual for the postlegal margin period is larger than for the prelegal margin period; and the Durbin-Watson statistic indicates more serial correlation in the 1946–60 period than earlier. While the higher standard deviation in prices for the 1946–60 period means little before adjusting for the movement of profits, the higher variance suggests that there has been no reduction in fluctuations in the stock market. But even after adjusting for fluctuations in the profits of major corporations, stock prices had more variance in the 1946–60 period.[16] Moreover, if speculators are destabilizing, then a rise in price of stocks will lead them to push the price up more, and a fall in price will increase the probability of a further fall in prices. Hence in a simple regression such as this, if margin requirements have decreased this type of activity, serial correlation should have been reduced. Note, however, that the

[15] Because stock prices and treasury bill rates were very highly correlated ($r = .82$), and since the treasury bill rate added nothing to the variance explained, it was dropped.

[16] The difference, however, is insignificant.

Durbin-Watson ratio is lower for the later period, indicating more serial correlation.

TABLE 3

Regression of Stock Price Profits, 1919–33 and 1946–60*

	Mean of Stock Prices†	Standard Deviation	Regression Coefficient and S.E.	Variance of Residual	Durbin-Watson Statistic	R^2
1919–33 . . .	1.000	.4950	.00081 (.00016)	.0905	1.090	.657
1946–60 . . .	1.000	.5186	.00026 (.00006)	.1053	.729	.636

*Profits of large manufacturing corporations for the period 1919–33 come from the Bureau of the Census, *Historical Statistics of the United States*, V-236. For the 1946–60 period, they come from various issues of the *Statistical Abstract*, Table 661, "Sales, Profits and Dividends of Large Manufacturing Corporations."

†Stock prices are Standard & Poor's index of industrial prices normalized to have a mean of 1 for each fifteen-year period. Stock prices are taken from the *Statistical Abstract* for various years and from *Historical Statistics of the United States*.

The above test, it might be argued, is irrelevant to the issue. While speculators might push prices away from the appropriate level in the short run, in the long run such increased dispersion will wash out. In other words, it seems plausible that on an annual basis the effect of margin requirements might be undetectable, though in the short run it might be pronounced. Hence it is necessary to examine daily fluctuations in the stock market. For this purpose, a three-month period, June through August, has been selected for analysis. In some years there might be a considerable trend, while in other years no trend at all would be observable during a three-month period. *Ceteris paribus*, more variance would be found in the year with the trend than in that without the trend. Hence we have also included in the analysis a linear trend factor and regressed industrials stock prices, daily, on a time variable. The results are given in Table 4.

Table 4 indicates that there is no measurable difference in variance in stock prices in the period before there were legal margins and in an eleven-year period after the war. For all three measures, 1928 falls within the range found during the later period.[17] The standard deviation of daily stock prices was higher in 1949, 1950, and 1955 than it was in 1928. After adjusting for any linear trend during the three months, the variance around the trend was much higher in 1950 than in 1928, and almost as high in 1955. The Durbin-Watson statistic also shows more serial correlation in five postmargin periods than in 1928. And, as argued above, if margin requirements reduce destabilizing activity, they should also reduce serial correlation. Thus daily price data produce no evidence that margin requirements reduce fluctuations or non-stabilizing buying and selling.

[17]The daily Standard & Poor's index of industrial prices is not readily available before 1928. Since one year was sufficient to establish the point, no effort was made to compile figures for earlier years.

TABLE 4

Stock Prices for Three Months: Trend Removed*

Year	Standard Deviation (10^{-1})	Variance of Residuals (10^{-3})	Durbin-Watson Statistic
1928	.3384	.684	.165
1946	.2795	.295	.261
1947	.2913	.595	.126
1948	.2776	.222	.358
1949	.4182	.232	.244
1950	.3993	1.590	.114
1951	.3146	.210	.252
1952	.1955	.180	.092
1953	.1420	.194	.178
1954	.2815	.179	.292
1955	.4118	.674	.118
1956	.2923	.500	.101

*For each three-month period the mean of stock prices is set equal to 1.

The statistics therefore indicate that margin requirements have failed to satisfy any of their objectives. Two reasons probably account for their failure. First, most people wishing to avoid the law can easily do so by borrowing on securities for other purposes. The funds normally devoted to these other uses can then be turned into the stock market. It is not impossible that someone might mislead his banker in borrowing on securities by claiming to use the funds for one purpose, while actually using the loan to purchase securities. The second reason for the failure of the law probably stems from the rationality of the public. If users of stock market credit are rational, there will be no pyramiding on the upswing or large amounts of selling on the downswing. The data suggest that credit users are rational and that they do not use credit as freely on the upswing, given the value of stocks, as they do on the downswing. The failure of the law probably stems from the loopholes in it and/or from the incorrect assumption it makes about borrowers.

It is, of course, possible that had there been very high margin requirements in 1929 (they were about 25–30 per cent for the large accounts and higher for the smaller ones), the stock market crash would not have been so precipitous. One Monday, October 26, 1929, the market dropped 12.5 per cent and the next day, 10.5 per cent. That was essentially all the drop for that year. The market actually rallied and finished higher at the end of the year than it closed on "Black Tuesday." It seems possible that some of the fall the second day might have been due to forced selling by those on margin. Thus, had there been higher requirements, it is possible that the fall might have been slower. (Note, however, that low margins also made it easier for speculators to buy when the price fell and hence might have prevented an even greater drop.) But considering the decline in corporate earnings of the next few years, it seems impossible to believe that, even if all sales on the exchange had been for cash, stock prices would not have declined to the same extent.

CONCLUSION

Margin requirements add to paper work and to the costs of stock market transactions; they discriminate against brokers in favor of bankers; they discriminate against those who are lawabiding; and, most important, they fail to fulfil their stated objectives. However, they do give the Federal Reserve a way of expressing its concern with movements of the stock market. But statements by the Federal Reserve setting forth its view might be substituted for changes in margin requirements, if the Federal Reserve feels a need to voice its view of stock market activity. Certainly in light of these findings it might be well to consider whether the margin requirements should be dismantled. Better data might indicate they are valuable, but it seems unlikely that if they have marked effects, these effects would not have been detected by the above tests.

REFERENCES

Bach, George Leland. *Economics*. 4th ed. Rev. Englewood Cliffs, N.J.: Prentice-Hall, Inc., 1963.

Bogen, Jules I., and Herman E. Krooss. *Security Credit*. Englewood Cliffs, N.J.: Prentice-Hall, Inc., 1960.

Bureau of the Census. *Historical Statistics of the United States, Colonial Times to 1957*. Series X305 and X309. Washington: Government Printing Office, 1960.

Johnston, J. *Econometric Methods*. New York: McGraw-Hill Book Co., 1960.

Loss, Louis. *Security Regulation*. Boston: Little Brown & Co., 1961.

Stigler, George J. "The Economist and the State," *A.E.R.*, LV (March 1965), 1–18.

U.S. House of Representatives. *Security Exchange Bill of 1934* (73d Cong., 2d sess., report no. 1383). Washington: Government Printing Office, 1934.

U.S. Senate. Committee on Banking and Currency. *Stock Exchange Practices* (73d Cong., 2d sess.). Washington: Government Printing Office, 1934.

U.S. Senate. Committee on Banking and Currency. *Stock Market Study* (84th Cong., 1st sess.). Washington: Government Printing Office, 1955.

U.S. Treasury, and Federal Reserve Board. "Margin Requirements," *Treasury–Federal Reserve Study of the Government Security Market*. Part 3, suppl. 2. Washington: Government Printing Office (1959), pp. 47–64.

28

Puts and Calls: A Factual Survey*

Charles B. Franklin
Marshall R. Colberg†

The market for Put and Call options on stocks is a relatively unpublicized, but not unimportant, American financial institution. Although the use of such options has been increasing, little reliable up-to-date information is available on the subject. Pamphlets published by Put and Call brokers provide a general picture of their nature and uses, some textbooks have brief descriptions, and some articles have appeared on the subject in financial publications. These are seriously incomplete, however, and often misleading in some respects. The main purpose of the present article is to give a rather detailed description of the present-day market for Puts and Calls, the information having been secured chiefly from recent interviews with leading Put and Call brokers in New York City and Securities and Exchange Commission officials in Washington, D.C. In addition, a preliminary statistical investigation of option pricing will be described and some appraisal of the usefulness of these options will be made.

NATURE OF PUTS AND CALLS

A Put in the stock market is an option contract in which the purchaser or holder has the right to sell a specified number of shares (usually one hundred) at a fixed price within a specified period of time. A Call gives the holder the right to purchase a specified number of shares (also usually one hundred) at a fixed price within a specified period of time. The corresponding obligation of the seller (maker) of a Put option is to buy the stock at the specified price if the option holder chooses to "put" it to him. The maker of a Call contract has the responsibility of selling the stock at the specified price if the option holder chooses to "call" it from him. Thus the buyer of the option pays for the privilege of possibly being able to sell the stock at a higher price than its market value or to buy stock at less than its market value, while the option seller is paid for the risk that he may be forced to buy stock at a price above the market value or to sell stock at less than its market value.

A "Straddle" is a simultaneous Put and Call on a given stock at the same

*From *Journal of Finance,* Vol. 13, No. 1 (March 1958), pp. 21–34. Reprinted by permission of *Journal of Finance.*

†The authors are indebted to the Research Council of Florida State University for a grant which made possible the interviews on which this paper is largely based.

price. The buyer of the Straddle acquires the option of either selling or buying the stock at the market price existing at the time the option contract was made, while the maker of the Straddle incurs the corresponding contingent legal obligation of either buying or selling the stock or, if both parts of the option are exercised, of both buying and selling the stock during the period for which the options are valid. "Spreads" are similar in nature to Straddles except that the specified selling and buying prices are not the same. The Put price is below the current market price of the stock while the Call price is above the going market price. This makes the selling price of a Spread lower than that of a Straddle, with the price differential depending greatly on the number of "points away" from the market price at which sale and purchase of the stock can be made. Little use is made of Spreads, but Straddles are popular.

THE BROKERS

Practically all of the Put and Call business in the United States is handled by about twenty-five option brokers and dealers located in New York City. These brokers operate through an association. All the contracts in which they deal are guaranteed or indorsed by member firms of the New York Stock Exchange. This indorsement guarantees the performance of the contract and makes options negotiable bearer instruments. The owner of the option may sell to anyone he chooses and the terms of the option remain unchanged. The purchaser of the option is not required to know anything about the maker of the option or about his financial standing because of this indorsement. Put and Call options can be bought and sold through a local broker, or one may place an order directly with a Put and Call broker.

Some of the mystery surrounding dealings in Puts and Calls stems from the absence of published price quotations for this market. Although some Put and Call prices are published in the *New York Times*, the *New York Herald Tribune*, and the *Wall Street Journal*, the quotations are usually "away from the market" and, furthermore, are not firm offers, but only invitations to bid. Options advertised in the newspapers for sale are usually brokers' surplus Puts and Calls resulting from their disposition of either the Put or the Call side of a Straddle. That is, a broker who has an opportunity to sell a Call may instead acquire a Straddle on favorable terms. He then sells the Call and is left with a surplus Put which he may advertise for sale. It is possible to be placed on the mailing list for quotations on Puts and Calls "at market," but these again are not firm offers. An individual may find them useful for purposes of comparison, but in order to determine the actual market price, it is necessary to make an inquiry either directly to a Put and Call broker in New York or through a local stock broker.

THE SELLER OF OPTIONS

Options can be, and sometimes are, sold by small investors. Most Puts and Calls originate, however, with large individual stockholders, particularly those who hold a "continuous portfolio." Such stockholders are in a position quickly to write most of the options for which a demand may arise because they are able to furnish stock which may be called for and to purchase stock which may be put to them. Institutional investors in stocks participate in writing options, but not to a large extent. In part this lack of participation probably stems from conservatism and a lack of information of the options market on the part of portfolio managers.

According to brokers, regular option writers can realize from 16 to 18 per cent per year on funds devoted to the sale of Puts and Calls. The actual average is not ascertainable by the authors from available information, but when it is considered that the average ninety-day Call retails for about 10 per cent of the price of the stock, and the average six-month and ten-day Call sells for about 15 per cent of the price of the stock, typical percentage earnings can be seen to be substantial. Calculation of such average earnings is complex because an "opportunity cost" is involved which must be deducted from gross returns to option sellers. That is, the seller of a Put will be deprived of the opportunity of acquiring stock at a lower market price when it is put to him at the higher price specified in the option. The seller of a Call which is exercised loses the opportunity of making a capital gain which would otherwise have existed. In order to compute the actual average percentage return to options writers for any past period it would be necessary to deduct these opportunity costs. This would require extremely detailed price information and the use of rather moot assumptions as to what would have been done had options not been sold. There is, of course, no certainty that future earnings would be similar to past earnings, especially because of the unpredictability surrounding the option seller's alternative opportunities.

A seller of options may be long, short, or have no position in stocks. For the most part, the options brokers recommend that if a potential seller has no position he acquire one by selling Puts. If the stock is not put to the writer he can continue to write Puts. These will provide him with income, but if they are not exercised it is likely that it is because the stock is increasing in market price and that the potential investor will eventually have to pay a higher price by deferring his purchase. Once the stock is put to the option seller he can sell a Call against his newly acquired long position. Alternatively, he may sell a Straddle if he is in a financial position which would permit him to acquire additional shares which might be sold to him under such an option. If stock is put and not called while the Straddle is in force the option maker will then be long on twice the original number of shares and then may sell two Calls. If, instead, the Call side only is exercised, the option maker will no longer have a position in stock so he may well decide to sell Puts until he again acquires a long position.

If both sides of the Straddle are exercised (which will happen only if the stock both falls below and rises above the price which existed when the Straddle was made) the option writer may sell another Straddle. Usually options will provide for purchase or sale of stock at the market price in force when the option is written, but they may be sold "away from the market" at lower prices. In addition, an option writer in a sufficiently strong financial position may decide to sell against the same position when an option has partially expired but has lost so much value to the purchaser as to be virtually unexercisable. For example, if the option writer were long on a stock and had sold a Call which had not yet expired but which would probably not be exercised due to a decline in the market price of the stock, it might appear to be quite safe to sell another Call against the same shares. (The stock broker indorsing the second option sale would have to be assured that the protection against the possible exercise of both Calls was sufficient.)

THE BUYER OF OPTIONS

Since no reports are required by, or rendered to, the Securities and Exchange Commission on this subject, and since brokers and dealers in Puts and Calls are likely to guard closely the source of their business, one may only speculate as to the geographic location, financial size, and other characteristics of the purchaser of options, However, an examination of available information permits some inferences regarding the nature of the purchaser.

Some brokers maintain that the real economic function of options is to provide protection against loss of value of stock through a hedging operation. This hedge can be effected by an investor or speculator who is long on a stock through the purchase of a Put; one who is in a short position on a stock may hedge through the purchase of a Call on the same stock. The possible loss of the first man is limited to the cost of the Put option and the possible loss of the short seller is limited to the cost of the Call. If most purchases of options were for protection of this sort there would probably be many more Puts sold than Calls because many more people are in a long position than in a short position.[1] This is not the case. In fact, during most periods the volume of Calls traded is several times that of Puts.

An additional clue to the identity of the purchaser is to be found in the volume and content of advertising placed by Put and Call brokers and dealers. Most of this advertising is designed to reach the potential *buyer* of Puts and Calls, although a small part is slanted to bring in new *sellers*. This would seem to be a paradox, since the dealers are disposed to state that the market for options originates from the demand of buyers who are anxious to secure protection against adverse price movements in the stock market.

The evidence indicates, therefore, that Puts and Calls are bought mainly for speculative purposes. Usually the options themselves are not the main vehicle in speculation; instead, actual purchases and sales of stocks ordinarily take place

[1] This conclusion does not follow with certainty, however, since it is possible that those who sell short are more anxious to protect themselves from loss or are more familiar with options than the typical investor who is long on stocks.

when options are worth exercising. Their use permits speculation with limited capital, with the potential loss restricted to the cost of the option plus commission and taxes. The inference is consistent with the remark of one veteran broker, as reported by *Barron's*, that speculation accounts for probably 80 per cent of option trading.[2] It appears that the emphasis usually placed by the Put and Call brokers on the "protection" which can be afforded by the use of such options is designed to secure for the trade the public acceptance generally enjoyed by commodity hedging and by many types of insurance.

As a general rule it is probably true that options are too expensive to purchase frequently for protection against either a long or short position. Stop-loss orders placed below or above the market provide a similar sort of protection without expense. If conditions affecting the stock market are unusually uncertain, or if a particular stock in which an interest is held is particularly volatile, the purchase of a Put or Call may be worthwhile. This is especially true when the investor does not wish to make frequent decisions with respect to buying and selling stock. A wealthy widow with substantial stockholdings, for example, may not wish to be "stopped out" of the market whenever her securities decline a few points in price since this will require frequent "agonizing reappraisals" of her holdings. If, nevertheless, she is fearful of a stock market crash, the purchase of a rather long period Put will provide protection without much supervision.

QUANTITATIVE IMPORTANCE OF PUTS AND CALLS

Members of the Put and Call Brokers and Dealers Association regularly report the volume of transactions in these options to the Securities and Exchange Commission. (Price information is not fully reported to the SEC, however.) Table 1 shows the yearly volume of Puts and Calls traded from 1939 through 1955, the quantity being measured by the number of shares on which options were written. Total shares traded on the New York Stock Exchange are also shown and the percentage of Puts and Calls to total shares traded is computed. The calculation is not strictly valid since some stocks on which options are written are traded on the other exchanges; the volume of such stocks, however, is rather small.

The volume of Puts and Calls traded was considerably higher in fiscal year 1955 than in any previous year, increasing even more rapidly than the volume of stock traded. Compared with the volume of stock bought and sold, Puts and Calls appear to have been used about twice as much in the year ending June 30, 1955, as in the 1938–39 period. Actually, the importance of Puts and Calls has increased in greater measure than this because of the pronounced shift to longer-term options during the period. This shift is visible in Table 2. Data in this table are not continuous because they are not available for all years.

[2] "Puts and Calls, An Old Investment Technique Wins New Popularity " *Barron's*, XXXV, No. 36 (September 5, 1955), 13.

TABLE 1
Trading in Puts and Calls and Stocks
1939–55

Year Ending June 30	Puts and Calls Traded* (Thous. Shares)	Stock Traded† (Thous. Shares)	Puts and Calls Traded as Percentage of Stock Traded
1939	1,320	321,831	0.41%
1940	1,222	384,239	0.32
1941	965	196,076	0.49
1942	747	211,504	0.35
1943	1,197	315,222	0.70
1944	1,319	306,683	0.43
1945	2,040	429,447	0.47
1946	2,173	516,093	0.42
1947	1,090	391,599	0.28
1948	1,664	387,568	0.42
1949	1,333	322,449	0.41
1950	1,946	204,112	0.95
1951	3,242	324,756	1.00
1952	3,157	223,000	1.41
1953	3,045	431,821	0.70
1954	2,550	339,327	0.57
1955	5,540	694,258	0.80

*Unpublished data of the Securities and Exchange Commission.
†*Annual Reports of the Securities and Exchange Commission* (Washington, D.C.: Government Printing Office).

TABLE 2
Sales of Options of Various Duration as Percentages of Total Option Sales*

First Six Months	7-day Options	30-day Options	60–90-day Options	Over 90-day Options
1938	14.7%	70.5%	14.8%	None
1940	3.9	59.2	36.9	None
1942	0.9	45.2	53.9	None
1944	1.1	20.2	78.7	None
1955	None	5.4	50.0	44.6%

*Unpublished data of Securities and Exchange Commission.

It can be seen that seven-day options have disappeared and that thirty-day options, once the traditional trading medium, are now rare. Options of sixty- to ninety-day duration are popular, but are being replaced to some extent by options of more than ninety-day duration. Durations of six months and ten days are now quite popular, the period being designed to take advantage of the capital gain provisions of the federal income tax law.[3]

[3]The income-tax situation with respect to options is interesting. However, no attempt will be made in this paper to describe the tax law because of its complexities and the likelihood of error due to amended interpretations by the Internal Revenue Service.

OPTION ARBITRAGE

Because of the fact that over a considerable period the demand for Calls has far surpassed the demand for Puts while the supply of both types of options has been approximately equal, there has developed over the past fifteen years a specialized operation known as "conversion" or "option arbitrage." This is a rather complex operation about which little is believed to be known except by those in the trade and the options specialists in the Securities and Exchange Commission.

Suppose a broker has a chance to sell a ninety-day Call on one hundred shares of some stock for $475, and that he would have to pay $450 for such a Call. At the same time, however, he may be able to buy a Put of similar duration on the same stock for $350. The broker may then simultaneously sell the Call (which he has originated), buy one hundred shares of the same stock (in order to be able to deliver on the Call), and buy the Put (to protect his position in the stock). Let us assume that a price of $60 a share for the stock applies to all of these transactions.

If during the currency of the options the price of the stock should decline to $55, the owner of the Call will not exercise it and, as the option approaches maturity, the broker puts the stocks to the writer of the Put at a price of $60. The broker has protected himself at a cost of $350 spent on a Put and has collected $475 for the Call which a customer wanted. The larger the spread between Put and Call prices the greater his arbitrage profit will be.

Suppose, instead, that the stock rises to $65 during the option period and that as a consequence, the stock which he has acquired is called away from the broker. His net cost is again only $350, the cost of the Put, if we disregard other fees and taxes connected with the transactions. The broker does not exercise the Put, but it has been available for use in the event of an otherwise dangerous decline in the price of the stock.

Many of the Put and Call brokers prefer not to, or are financially unable to, originate options and, consequently, do not engage regularly in the sort of arbitrage operations described above. This has led to the development of the "conversion house." Such a firm is a member of the stock exchange and is also better able financially to carry the necessary securities. Most of the conversion business is placed with a single firm. The specialist in conversion performs this service at a fixed rate of interest (6 per cent at the time the interviews were made).

Suppose that a Put and Call broker has an opportunity to sell a Call at a certain price and that he does so, filling the order through purchase of a Straddle which he is able to secure on favorable terms. He now has a surplus Put. The Put and Call broker has two choices in regard to this Put. He may either hold it and advertise it for sale, or he may convert it into a Call for which there is a present demand. The second choice may be the more desirable for a broker with limited funds.

Put and Call brokers may not desire to convert if they have sufficient financial resources to finance an inventory of surplus options. Most surplus options arise through the purchase of a Straddle and subsequent sale of only one side to a customer. According to brokers, this is the only manner of consequence in which an inventory of options comes into the hands of the typical broker. However, another possibility exists. Since options are negotiable instruments, a broker often has an opportunity to buy an option at a favorable price. The owner of the Put or Call may have lost interest in it because the situation for which he purchased it no longer exists, or because an anticipated market movement did not take place. Prior to the expiration date he may sell the option back to the Put and Call broker provided the latter sees an opportunity to dispose of it profitably, either directly or through conversion.

Option arbitrage can be carried on also by an individual investor of sufficient financial standing. Suppose he feels that there is an unduly large difference between the asking price for a Put and the bid price for a Call on the same stock, the Call price being the higher. If he does not already own the stock he can purchase it and then sell the Call. Simultaneously, he buys the Put in order to protect himself from a decline in the market price of the stock during the period for which he must hold it in case it is called for. His arbitrage profit is the difference in price between the Call and the Put minus commissions and taxes on the necessary transactions. Thus conversion may be performed by the option maker, by the option broker, or by a conversion specialist.

REGULATION OF THE OPTIONS BUSINESS

The Put and Call business is largely self-regulated, but a great deal of the aura of secrecy which surrounds this activity seems to stem from the early 1930's when the threat of strict regulation or even legislative extermination haunted the entire options trade. Testimony before the Senate Committee on Banking and Currency in 1932 and 1933 disclosed that many of the financial abuses of the 1920's were related to the use of options. A favorite device of large stockholders was to grant options without cost to a pool which would then attempt to make these profitable by "churning" activities designed to bring the general public in as buyers of the stock. In addition, long-term and even unlimited-period option warrants were issued frequently in connection with new stock issues. The possibilities of profiteering in the style of the 1920's through the use of options seem to have been greatly reduced by the right to require the reporting of options granted to the Securities and Exchange Commission.

To date no significant rules or regulations on Puts and Calls have been promulgated by the Securities and Exchange Commission. The only rule devised by the Securities and Exchange Commission in recent years which applied directly to the Put and Call business is one which was recommended to and adopted by the several securities exchanges. The rule as suggested by the Securities and Exchange Commission reads as follows:

> No member, while on the floor, shall initiate the purchase or sale on the exchange for his own account or for any account in which he, or the firm of which he is a partner or any partner of such firm, is directly or indirectly interested of any security, classified for trading as a stock by the exchange, in which he holds or has granted any Put, Call, Straddle, or Option, or in which he has knowledge that the firm of which he is a partner or any partner of such firm holds or has granted any Put, Call, Straddle, or Option.

Although regulation of the Put and Call business by the Securities and Exchange Commission is not at all stringent, the power to increase the scope of regulation exists. Several provisions of the Securities Exchange Act of 1934 could be applied to the business if this were deemed necessary by the Securities and Exchange Commission. Need of detailed Securities and Exchange Commission regulation has been diminished by extensive self-regulation. In part the rules are based on those suggested by the Securities and Exchange Commission.[4]

THE DETERMINATION OF PRICE

Statistical investigation of the factors affecting the price of Puts and Calls is difficult because of the unavailability of data as to actual prices at which options are sold. This would be an interesting and useful field for a large-scale study if data could be secured from records of the brokers.

The writers have made a preliminary investigation of the relation between stock prices and the prices of ninety-day Calls and ninety-day Puts for a single day, October 17, 1955. For this purpose, "offering" prices for these options as reported by one options broker were utilized; these can differ from actual prices at which the options were sold, but constitute the only sort of price data readily available on Puts and Calls. Closing prices for the thirty-eight associated stocks as reported by the New York Stock Exchange were used. Included in the thirty-eight stocks were those of four steel companies, five railroads, five oil companies, three automobile producers, two airlines, six aircraft producers, and others.

Graphic investigation indicated a linear relationship between both Call prices and Put prices and the price of the associated stock. Consequently, linear regressions were computed in order to secure equations for estimating option prices from stock prices. These linear regressions are shown in Fig. 1, which also includes the observations to which the curves were fitted. Letting Y be the price of a ninety-day option on one hundred shares, and X be the closing price of the associated stock on the day specified, the regression equations were:

$$\text{For Calls, } Y = 63.44 + 7.81X \tag{1}$$

$$\text{For Puts, } Y = 89.11 + 5.83X \tag{2}$$

[4]These rules are too voluminous to be set forth profitably here. They are available in a document entitled *Explanation of Rules and Practices Governing Dealings in Stocks on the New York Stock Exchange* (Department of Floor Procedures, New York Stock Exchange, March 12, 1951), pp. 39–40.

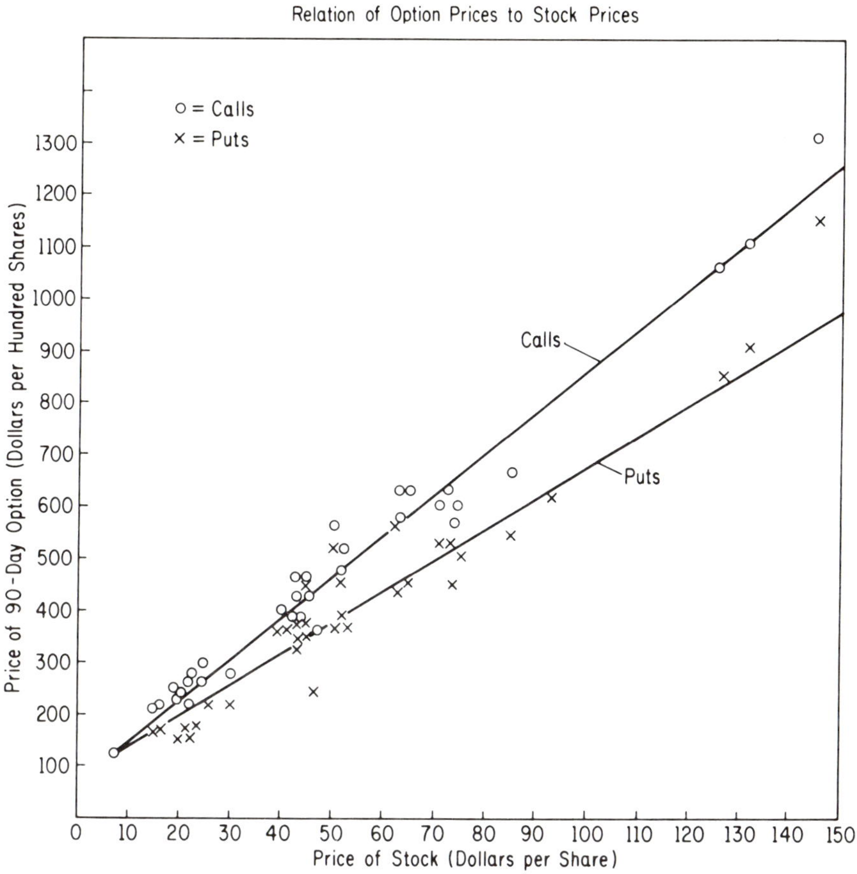

Fig. 1

In both cases coefficients of correlation were high and standard errors of estimate quite low, the fit being somewhat better for Calls than for Puts. Deviations of actual from estimated option prices were compared with "volatility" of stock prices (measured as the spread between the 1955 high and low price). While there was some evidence of a positive correlation between volatility and these deviations (a high volatility causing actual option prices to exceed estimates) the relation was not close.

This highly preliminary statistical study suggests that Put and Call prices vary closely with the price of the associated stock. Call prices exceed Put prices in almost every case, apparently reflecting the chronic bullishness of most stock-market speculators. From the buyer's point of view both Puts and Calls seem to be priced more favorably on high-priced stocks. For very low-priced stocks both Puts and Calls are apt to sell for the standard minimum price of \$137.50. (This floor on option prices must be kept in mind in connection with use of the regression equation cited earlier.) Consequently option prices are apt to be favorable to sellers but not to buyers for very low-priced stocks. The ratio of the price of a Call to the price of 100 shares of stock decreases as the price of the stock increases. For example, at a price of $20 per share a Call sells for about 11 per cent of the value of the one hundred shares which it controls. A Put sells for about 10 per cent of the stock value. At $50 per share a Call and Put sell respectively at 9 per cent and 7.6 per cent. At $100 per share the percentages are 8.4 for a Call and 6.7 for a Put.

TABLE 3
Put and Call Prices* and Stock Prices
October 17, 1955

Name of Stock	Closing Price of Stock	90-Day Put	90-Day Call
U.S. Steel	$ 54.75	$ 375.00	$ 475.00
Bethlehem Steel	146.75	1150.00	1300.00
Armco Steel	44.75	375.00	425.00
Republic Steel	48.00	375.00	425.00
N.Y. Central R.R.	45.50	350.00	387.50
Can. Pacific R.R.	31.25	225.00	287.50
North. Pac. R.R.	66.50	450.00	625.00
Southern Pac. R.R.	54.75	387.50	475.00
B. & O. R.R.	44.88	350.00	450.00
Cities Service	54.50	450.00	525.00
Sinclair Oil	52.52	375.00	450.00
Standard Oil, N.J.	126.62	850.00	1050.00
Phillips Petro.	73.88	450.00	625.00
Royal Dutch	76.75	500.00	600.00
Chrysler	93.12	625.00	800.00
General Motors	131.50	900.00	1100.00
Stud.-Packard	9.62	137.50	137.50
Amer. Airline	21.88	187.50	237.50
Pan-American Air	17.88	175.00	212.50
Boeing Airplane	64.50	425.00	575.00
General Dynamics	52.12	525.00	575.00
Douglas Aircraft	71.88	525.00	600.00
Lockheed Aircraft	47.88	375.00	375.00
Northrop Aircraft	25.00	250.00	300.00
Republic Aviation	40.75	350.00	400.00
Celanese	20.25	200.00	250.00
Textron	23.00	162.50	250.00
Pepsi Cola	21.00	162.50	225.00
Anaconda Copper	63.50	550.00	625.00
Amer. Smelt. & Ref.	45.62	425.00	450.00
Molybdenum Corp.	24.50	250.00	275.00
Int. Tel. & Tel.	27.12	225.00	262.50
RCA	43.50	375.00	387.50
Western Union	24.75	175.00	225.00
General Electric	48.25	250.00	350.00
Montgomery Ward	86.12	550.00	675.00
Amer. Tobacco	75.75	525.00	575.00
Natl. Distillers	19.12	175.00	225.00

*"Offerings" as quoted by Godnick and Son.

SUMMARY AND CONCLUSIONS

While the market for Puts and Calls cannot be considered to be a highly important one to the economy, these options seem to be increasing in popularity both absolutely and in relation to total stock traded. There is a decided trend toward longer-term options, with six-month-and-ten-day options increasingly popular due to the capital gain and loss provisions of the federal income tax law.

Put and Call brokers emphasize the usefulness of these options for hedging. This seems to be based on the general public acceptability of all sorts of "insurance." Actually the evidence indicates that most options are bought instead for speculative purposes. They constitute a way of controlling stock on a small margin, with the possible loss limited to the cost of the option plus fees and taxes. The far greater volume of Calls compared with Puts, and the higher prices at which the former sell, indicate that most of the purchases are not for purposes of hedging except in the unlikely circumstance that short sellers are much more active in hedging their commitments than buyers on the long side.

From the point of view of the buyer, Puts appear usually to be better bargains than Calls. For both Puts and Calls, options against the higher-priced stocks seem to be more favorable to the buyer than those against low-priced stocks. The usual minimum price of $137.50 for both Puts and Calls causes their prices to constitute a high percentage of the price of the lower-priced stocks.

In general, the sale of Puts and Calls appears to offer opportunities of substantial income at a cost of sacrificing possible capital gains while still retaining the possibility of loss. The main problem of the Put and Call brokers seems to be that of finding buyers rather than sellers, suggesting that these options tend to be overpriced. This apparent overpricing is due in part to the lack of an organized market and lack of adequate information, especially on the part of option buyers.

From the point of view of promoting stability of stock prices there is something to be said for options. The existence of Put options would tend to cushion a sharp break in stock prices, since holders of Puts would enter the market as buyers in order to exercise their profitable options. Unlike short sellers, buyers of Puts do not first enter the market as sellers; consequently, there is no danger that the purchase of Put options will in itself be a cause of a stockmarket decline. Similarly, the purchase of Calls does not in itself tend to cause a rise in the stock market, as does the outright purchase of stock. The stabilizing effect of a well-developed options market on stock prices would seem to be the main social virtue of this financial device. A second, though presently quite unimportant, economic function of options is the provision of a means of hedging both long and short positions in the stock market.

29

Stop Loss Orders: A Technician Gives Some Tips on How To Use Them*

James Dines

At one time or another, nearly everybody, in the stock market, whether short or long, is faced by a large loss, at least on paper. When this happens to an investor it often converts him into a trader; when it happens to a trader, it often turns him into a nervous wreck. Yet, one need not suffer the agony of watching a stock drop from say 74 to 19, since there is a safe way to prevent it: the stop technique. Some people manage to bungle this procedure because they do not know how to use it correctly. The key to correct usage is to grasp the method not only intellectually but also emotionally, surely the hardest part.

Accordingly, let us lay down some emotional guide lines. First, it is necessary to reach the stage where one is unafraid to take a small loss. Refusing to take a loss implies an expected profit on every trade, in other words, perfection. To those who still have this complex, we wish good luck. But most hard-nosed businessmen know that not every transaction works out, and that the first loss is usually the best loss.

VIRTUES OF GROPING

Second, it should be clear that the best way to achieve a sizable gain is to buy a stock before a major advance, and then not to sell prematurely. Both steps are more difficult than they sound, and involve considerable groping, Groping, in turn, involves many small profits equaled by many small losses, a few big winners and absolutely no big losses. This approach rules out people who take a few points profit whenever possible, and who do not comprehend that one big loss frequently will wipe out all the small gains. Nor is it for people who are obsessed with tax considerations or dividends. Never let Uncle Sam decide your buying or selling; dividends are miniscule compared with capital gains.

Third, we rule out people who are unwilling to put in some hard work. Those who view the stock market as a glorified casino, to be handled mainly by guesswork and hunches, are bound to be disillusioned. One can guess, and even be lucky, but this is no real substitute for hard work and strict observance of

*From *Barron's* (December 17, 1962), p. 9. Reprinted by courtesy of *Barron's National Business and Financial Weekly*.

percentages. The crack trader should buy graph paper and chart every investment daily.

Fourth, the stop-loss is not intended to be triggered. When you buy fire insurance for your house you do not want a fire. But if fire occurs, protection prevents a major loss. If you ever used a proper stop and thereby took small losses, but then ceased using it, you did not wait for the law of averages to bail you out.

Fifth, you must no longer try to buy-low-sell-high. Understand why a stock can be a buy at say 50, and a sale at 45. Buy-low-sell-high presupposes a long level trading range, whereas we are interested in long sustained uptrends. Our rule is to buy-high-sell-higher.

Let us turn now to the mechanics of the stop technique. Starting from basics, a stop order is nothing more than an order to be executed automatically if a certain price is reached. For example, you buy a stock at 50 and place the order to "sell at 48 stop." If and when the stock declines to 48, the order will be automatically executed as a market order. Or, if a stock sells at 50 and you want to buy only if and when it rises to 53, you order "buy at 53 stop." Your order to buy automatically becomes a market order only should the stock sell at 53. (If the "limit" is added to the above two orders it means that instead of a market order being placed, it will be limited to the price you specify.)

As for the short sale side, stops can be used in exactly the same way, only inverted. In other words, if a stock is shorted at 50, place the order "cover at 53 stop." Only on an advance to 53 will you be stopped out, making the maximum loss around 3 points. It is especially important to use the stop technique on shorts, for uncontrolled short sales can develop into real catastrophes. So much for the emotional and practical basics.

Yet even those who grasp all of the above often fall down on the next and most important step: where to place the stop order. In determining the proper place for a stop order, beginners frequently try the clumsy approach of using a fixed number of points, or an absolute percentage, apparently on the theory that they are unable to afford a larger loss than that. In other words, stops are placed one, two or even more points (or percent) below the purchase price. The market, of course, is utterly unconcerned with what you can or cannot afford. Even worse, the approach does not distinguish in every case between meaningless variations and the true trend reversal. It is too rigid and dogmatic, for each stock requires a separate decision; only the lazy will use the fixed stop technique, because it is easier. There is but one place for a proper stop depending on whether you use the breakout or trendline method, and both involve toil. Making money on Wall Street is just as hard as making money anywhere else.

BASIC CHART THEORY

All stops are dependent on basic chart theory, which should be reviewed at this point (see *Barron's* June 18, 1962). Briefly, stocks are either in unfolding trends, or locked within limited neutral trading ranges. When concentrating on trading ranges, remember that a move of one point above a trading range shifts percentages from neutrality to favoring a near-term uptrend.

There are three types of stops: buy, long sales and short sales. In Example 1, the proper place for a breakout buy-stop is just one point above the trading range (A) AT 60, developing from either a prior uptrend or downtrend.

There is another type of buy stop. A practical example would be to buy the theoretical stock of Example 1 as close to the bottom of the trading range (B) as possible. The moment the order is executed, a long-sale stop should be placed just below (B), at say 49. This process is called a bottom-guessing buy stop. If there is no downside breakout, purchase will have been made at rock bottom, and if it does not work out, the loss is minimal. Note that placement of the stop is the same whether the stock was bought at 51 or 59, illustrating the inherent weakness in using predetermined numbers of points for stops. Assuming fundamentals and other factors point upward, the trading risks are highly acceptable. The main weakness here is that stocks often spend tediously long periods of time in trading ranges. While not objectionable to investors, traders prefer more speed.

EXAMPLE 1

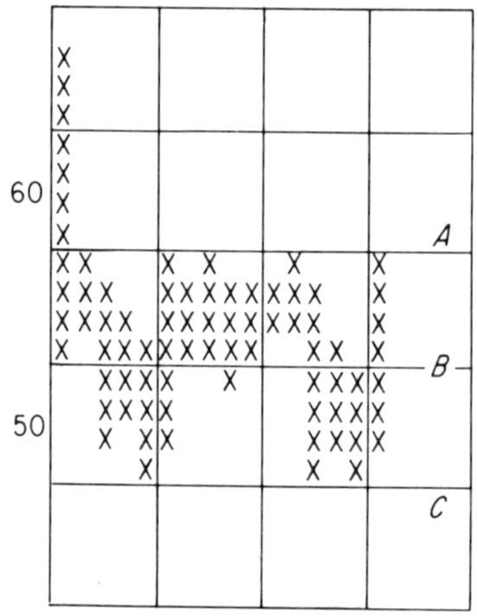

Traders should use the breakout-buy stop. Place the order to "buy at 60 stop, good until cancelled," and forget it. Eventually, if there is an upside breakout, your buy order will be placed automatically. The main weakness here is that the stop loss still must be placed no higher than (C) and the potential loss is larger, although still limited. The trader thus sacrifices safety for speed, although the stop is not intended to be triggered and is only a protective device.

LONG-SALE STOP

The long-sale is simple. For stocks already held, place the stop just below

(B), in (C), at say "sell 49 stop, good until cancelled." Or, sell at the top of the trading range, and repurchase only if there is an upside breakout (or use the breakout-buy stop).

The short-sale stop is meant mainly for traders, and reverses all of the above rules. The stock should be shorted as high in trading range (B) as possible, and the stop loss cover placed just above the trading range in (A) at 60. This process is called a top-guessing short. Or, traders may place the order to "sell short at 49, good until cancelled," but the stop loss must still be placed in (A). While this breakout-short stop is more likely to drop, the potential loss is higher, because the nearest cover is quite high. Again, a sacrifice of safety for speed.

With these properly placed stops, true trend reversals are guarded against, while minor unimportant fluctuations are correctly ignored. One important refinement would be to vary the depth in (A) and (C) for the stop orders. So long as they are in (A) and (C), they are correctly placed, and while agressive traders may use 1/8 of a point, the cautious often use two points as increased protection against an occasional false breakout. We use a one point variation because it normally works out well.

Before we go on, an important exception to the use of stops should be pointed out. When intrinsic value is so great, or a stock is already so deeply depressed that it is well below intrinsic value, stop losses should not be used. Or, when fundamentals are so overpowering that technical patterns are virtually ignored in a decision to buy or hold, then fundamental methodology is also used in the sale.

Stop loss orders are mainly for stocks that are moving up, or at such high levels that the risk of a major down-trend is present. Here, pure chartists often fail: they fail to blend fundamentals into technical thinking. The essence of our approach is using the two as crosschecks. The exception to blending is close trading, because a slight variation in the price-earnings ratio alone can account for a minor move, making fundamentals virtually worthless in gauging short-term trading timing. This is where technical techniques are unquestionably superior. As a declining stock becomes really cheap on fundamentals, pay less and less attention to charts and move to fundamentals. As a stock gets higher and higher, pay less and less attention to fundamentals and more to charts. Be more and more aggressive with stops as an advance extends to the point where a stock is outrageously high on fundamentals.

Now let us assume that the stock in our example has been bought at the bottom of either (A) or (B) and has not dipped into (C), and thus still is held long. It then has a move to 66 followed by a normal breakout pullback to 62, as in Example 2.

SELLING TOO SOON

Percentages have shifted to the upside, and the next problem is not selling too soon. This involves raising the stop loss, but still placing it properly. In Example 2, the stop is still properly placed at 49. The next rule is: when the pullback is at least three points, followed by another rise of at least three points,

EXAMPLE 2

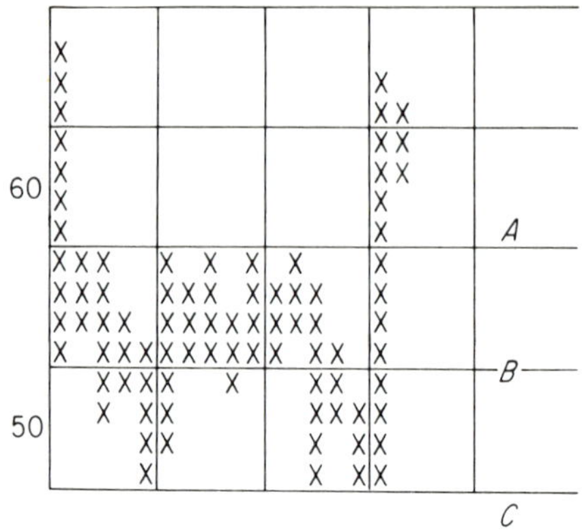

raise the stop to just below the low ebb of the pullback. In example 3, the stop is thus properly raised to 61. The stop is similarly raised on each leg of the advance. So long as there is an uptrend (rising lows), the stock will not be sold. But when the trend reverses, the stock will be sold automatically to protect accrued profits. On the short side, the whole procedure is reversed, with stop covers placed just above the previous rally high in a series of descending highs.

EXAMPLE 3

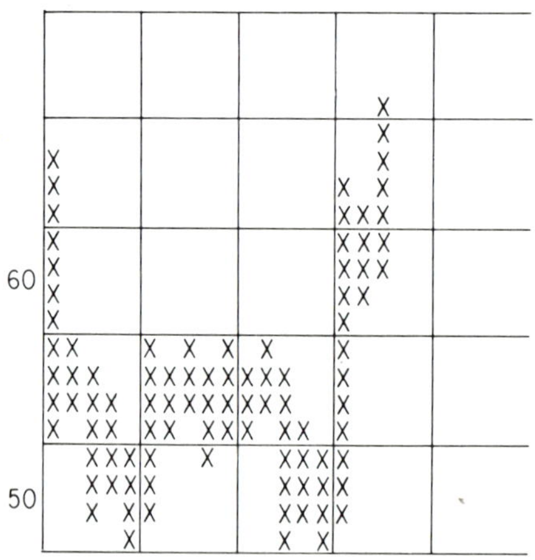

The trendline stop is a highly sensitive technique, and so complex that it is advised only for full-time professionals. For those who have mastered the fine art of drawing trendlines, it is largely a matter of placing the stop so that only a broken trend could trigger it (Example 4). The "X's" show where stops are progressively placed just below the uptrendline as the stock advances, until it is finally stopped out (E) when the trend does reverse. The advantage of the

EXAMPLE 4

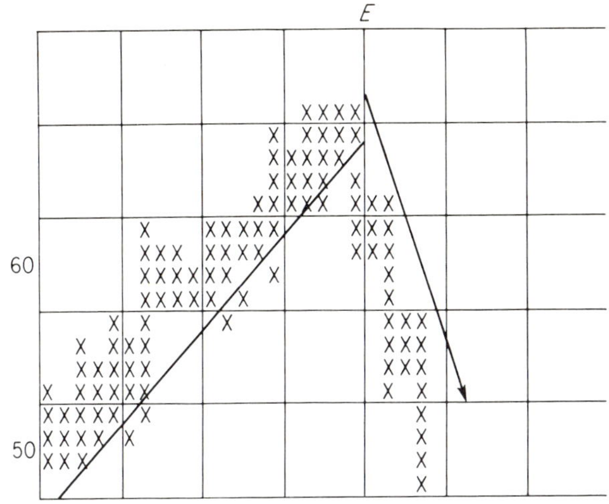

trendline stop is that a broken trend reveals itself sooner than for breakout stops, and some points are saved.

To follow these techniques, it is necessary to have up-to-the-minute charts available. Several services sell them. Or, to economize, buy some K&E 358-16 graph paper and do it yourself. Each box in the graph paper is divided into eight squares vertically (8 eighths to the point) and five squares laterally (for the five trading days).

Those few tape-watchers endowed with iron-nerved discipline can dispense with actually placing the stop order. The advantage is that a slightly higher price normally ensues when a cluster of stops is triggered. However, the first time you fail to sell on the ensuing rally, revert to actually placing the stop orders.

30

The Third Market: Its Past, Present, and Future*

Douglas A. Campbell

The Third Market is the trading of securities listed on a national exchange over-the-counter. In contrast, the primary market is the trading of listed stocks on national stock exchanges—principally the New York Stock Exchange which accounts for over 80% of the total primary market; the secondary market is the trading of the stocks of corporations which do not fulfill the listing requirements of an exchange or who wish to be bought or sold over-the-counter, (See Table 1). In the Third Market, an investor wanting to buy General Motors common, which is listed on many national exchanges, can do so either through a member of the New York Stock Exchange (or one of the other national exchanges where the stock is listed) or by dealing with an over-the-counter firm. Frequently the investor can save money on the purchase by negotiating a lower net price in the Third Market than the last sale plus commission on one of these stock exchanges.

The real significance of the Third Market only came into prominence with the publication of the Securities and Exchange Commission's *Report of Special Study of Securities Markets*. This five volume (3,182 pages) report, released in mid-1963, indicated that in the period 1941-1961 the Third Market had increased in size more than 20 times (from an estimated dollar volume of $84,000,000 in 1941 to an estimated $2 billion 20 years later) and represented almost 4% of New York Stock Exchange dollar trading volume in 1961. This compares with a tenfold increase in the corresponding volume of the New York Stock Exchange over the same period. The Special Study concluded in its findings that, "The rapid growth in recent years of an off-board market for the trading of listed common stocks had made this an increasingly important segment of the national securities markets" and that "under existing circumstances, it appears that the over-the-counter market for listed stock has been beneficial to investors and the public interest."

ORIGIN

The Third Market had its origin in the 1920s when blocks of bonds, listed

*From *Investment Dealers' Digest* (February 6, 1967), pp. 30–32. Reprinted by permission of *Investment Dealers' Digest*.

on exchanges, began to be traded over-the-counter. Banks and other financial institutions discovered that they could save on commission costs by dealing in the Third Market while certain non-member brokers found the business profitable since they did not have to raise the capital required to join the New York Stock Exchange.

After World War II, as common stock oriented financial institutions, such as mutual funds and pension funds, began to expand, the same non-member firms started to make markets in listed stocks. These firms found a demand on the part of institutions to reduce the costs of transacting block brokerage business, improve the market for large blocks of common stock, and provide a certain degree of privacy.

Per-share transaction costs on the New York Stock Exchange were (and still are) the same on a 10,000 share trade as on a 100 share trade, even though the larger transaction certainly involves far less than 100 times the cost and/or effort. More important, sale or purchase of a large block on the exchange often results in the stock specialist significantly dropping or raising the price of the stock because member brokers are not accustomed to crossing blocks and often show them to the specialist. Finally, since each exchange transaction is printed on the ticker tape, an institution buying or selling a block on the exchange, by so doing, draws attention to activity in the stock which may in turn adversely effect the same institution.

By dealing off the exchange floor in the Third Market, institutional investors found that they were less susceptible to the adverse effects of price fluctuations caused by their own buying or selling activity. This is because Third Market dealers normally do not go to the stock exchange specialist, but either buy or sell the block themselves or cross it with another institution without public knowledge of the transaction. An additional incentive to trading in the Third Market is the usually lower commissions charged by Third Market dealers.

Since the Special Study, the SEC has begun to collect and publish quarterly figures on Third Market transactions. These figures are shown in the Appendix (Table 2) both in absolute share volume and dollar value and as a percentage of the corresponding New York Stock Exchange volume. It is evident that the most rapid growth in the Third Market (relative to the primary–New York Stock Exchange–market) took place prior to issuance of the Special Study (See Table 2). The quarterly figures included in this table indicate a declining percentage since 1965. On the other hand, the absolute Third Market volume has shown a substantial increase from 1962 to 1965, and from the first quarter of 1965 to the second quarter of 1966. It is possible that the relative (to the New York Stock Exchange) decrease in Third Market volume may therefore have represented increased public and decreased institutional market participation. The dollar volume of the Third Market may therefore resume its growth relative to the exchange. Subsequent SEC quarterly releases on Third Market trading volume should be watched with care.

EFFECT ON INSTITUTIONS

As previously stated, it was the post World War II growth of common stock oriented financial institutions that originally brought about the growth of the Third Market. From 1949 to Dec. 31, 1965, these institutions increased their holdings of common stocks from $9.7 to $109.8 billion, over a tenfold increase. Institutional holdings as a percentage of (the value of) all stocks listed on the New York Stock Exchange increased from 12.7% at year-end 1949 to 20.4% at the end of 1965. As a per cent of trading (share volume) on the New York Stock Exchange, institutions accounted for 17.5% on a randomly selected day in December, 1954, and 31.4% on a randomly selected day in March, 1965, almost a 90% increase.

TABLE 1
Estimated over-the-Counter and Actual Exchange Sales of Outstanding Corporate Stocks for Selected Years (1929–61) in the United States
(Billions of Dollars)

Year	OTC Sales	Sales On All Exchanges	OTC As % Ex. Sales
1929	$22.0	$135.0	16%
1935	2.1	15.4	14
1937	5.6	21.0	27
1939	3.4	11.4	30
1946	10.5	18.7	56
1948	6.7	12.9	52
1949	4.9	10.7	46
1955	14.2	37.9	37
1961	38.9	63.8	61
Total	108.3	326.8	33

Sources: 1929–48 data is from Friend, Hoffman & Winn "The Over-The-Counter Securities Markets," p. 109 (1958) (35); 1949–1961 data derived from the SEC Questionnaire OTC-3. Report of Special Study of the Securities & Exchange Commission, Congress 1st Session, House Document No. 95, U.S. Government Printing Office, 1962.

Two types of institutions accounted for approximately half the total increase in stock holdings. Mutual fund holdings of stocks listed on the New York Stock Exchange rose from $1.4 billion in 1949 to $21.8 billion at the end of 1965, while corporate pension fund holdings increased from about $500,000,000 to $35.4 billion. At least 70 of the funds hold common stock in their portfolios worth $100,000,000 or more. By far the most active group of institutions, in terms of transactions, are the mutual funds.

"Special Study" and the increasing publicity surrounding the Third Market's growth resulted in a series of legal suits taken against mutual funds by their shareholders. These suits alleged that certain mutual funds could have traded with a Third Market broker with consequent commission savings to the fund shareholders. Additionally, the publication of the Wharton School Study of mutual funds in mid-1963 brought "the commission problem" into even greater focus; to understand this problem it is necessary to understand how mutual fund shares are sold.

Mutual fund shares have generally been sold either by investment brokers (and dealers) or through a sales company specially organized to sell the shares and usually owned by the investment advisor to the fund. The first method (through brokers) usually involves commission rebates or so-called "give-ups." In order to sell one fund as opposed to another, investment brokers and dealers who make such sales have commanded a part of the commission business which the fund itself generates through its portfolio management. This is in addition to a commission (about 8.5% on an average fund) on sale of the fund shares themselves. As sales of mutual funds became more competitive the practice of "give-ups" became more pronounced and stock brokers and dealers began to pressure the funds for higher "give-ups." Regional stock exchanges also permit "give-ups," but the maximum per cent is limited by the particular exchange.

NO "GIVE-UPS" INVOLVED

Third Market brokers and dealers generally have not been willing to "give-up" since their commissions are usually smaller than corresponding member firm commissions. Furthermore, most mutual funds have considered Third Market "give-ups" a dangerous practice to engage in because of the shareholders' suits that could be taken on the basis that they can openly negotiate lower commissions in the Third Market since commission rates are not fixed as on an exchange.

The study of mutual funds prepared by the SEC and made public on Dec. 2, 1966, particularly criticized the "give-up" as detrimental to the shareholders of a mutual fund. The commission furthermore stated that under existing law it has adequate authority to deal with this problem. Thus, it appears that the "give-up," at least in its current form, is likely to be changed and with it the necessity for mutual funds sold through brokers and dealers to do as much business with member firms in order to generate "give-ups." Furthermore, volume discounts on the exchange were also recommended in the same mutual fund report. The report stated that: "The commission has advised the exchanges that re-examination and changes in their commission rate structures are necessary."

"Give-up" problems are far less important where directly owned sale forces sell the fund's shares. Such "directly sold funds" may request "give-up" as payment to another broker for a research study; "give-ups" in return for selling a fund's shares are obviously not required, however.

To take advantage of the brokerage commissions which they nevertheless do generate and have to pay out, and because they are not dependent on brokers for selling their fund shares, at least three of the management companies of directly sold funds have gone into the brokerage business and joined the Pacific

Coast Stock Exchange. Other exchanges have rules which effectively preclude mutual fund membership. It is understood that the management companies of several other (directly sold) funds have applied for membership to the Pacific Coast Stock Exchange. However, the rules for becoming a member of this exchange have been tightened considerably since the first fund was accepted. Whether profits on a brokerage subsidiary of a mutual fund will accrue to the management company or to the fund's shareholders is still to be determined. The Third Market would probably benefit if "give-ups" were eliminated and will face an increased challenge from the establishment of fund associated exchange member brokerage houses and probable volume discounts.

SPECIALISTS RULE ON NYSE

As already mentioned, the New York Stock Exchange often was unable to cross or take positions in blocks of stocks because specialists did not have the experience or capital to handle them without raising or lowering prices significantly. Partly in order to offset this weakness, the New York Stock Exchange changed the capital requirements of the specialists. As of Dec. 17, 1953, and through Jan. 4, 1965, a specialist was required to have sufficient capital to take a position of 400 shares in each stock in which he made a 100 share market. Thereafter, the specialist was required to have sufficient capital to take a position of 1,200 shares, and after Jan. 1, 1966, the capital requirements were raised to 2,000 shares of each stock for which he was the registered specialist. Regional exchanges also tightened the capital requirements of their specialists.

Above and beyond trading rules, members and specialists of all stock exchanges have become far more aware of the problems posed by large blocks. With the continuous increase in institutional business, most major member firms have established block trading departments which, instead of going directly to a specialist for or with a block, first look for the other side of the transaction. In many cases members have positioned the blocks themselves. Specialists have also become more keenly aware of "block problems" and more aware of potential block buyers and sellers; they are thus in a better position to cross large orders without having to drastically disturb the price.

As a consequence several Third Market firms have joined (or were planning to join) the New York Stock Exchange. Blyth & Co. became members in 1965 (mainly because of its growing retail business). In 1966 Harriman Ripley & Co. merged with Drexel & Co. who already were members. Allen & Co. said that it planned to join in 1967. Then came the change in rule 394.

It became apparent that although the New York Stock Exchange specialists have been forced to take larger positions in block stock trades and have in general become "more aware" of block trading, certain Third Market dealers maintain even larger positions in the same stocks and provide relatively more attractive markets. However, until Nov. 7, 1966, Rule 394 of the New York Stock Exchange prohibited members from trading securities off the exchange

TABLE 2

Third Market and New York Stock Exchange Trading Volume Compared

Year And/ Or Quarter	Over-the-Counter Trading of Securities Listed on the NYSE		Primary Trading of Securities Listed on the NYSE		Ratio of:	
	Number of Shares	Dollar Value	Number of Shares	Dollar Value	Column 1 to Column 3	Column 2 to Column 4
1961	....	$2,000,000,000	....	$52,698,552,000	......	3.8%
1965/1	12,851,000	669,424,000	410,035,000	16,188,254,000	3.1%	4.1
1965/2	11,209,000	581,033,000	405,386,000	16,692,313,000	2.8	3.5
1965/3	10,736,000	555,775,000	401,237,000	16,382,788,000	2.7	3.4
1965/4	13,515,000	694,184,000	592,692,000	23,936,642,000	2.3	2.9
Total 1965	48,351,000	2,500,416,000	1,809,350,000	73,199,997,000	2.7	3.4
1966/1	15,549,000	798,560,000	627,825,000	27,797,992,000	2.5	2.9
1966/2	14,173,000	769,686,000	591,052,000	27,465,600,000	2.4	2.8

Source: SEC Statistical Bulletin and *The 1963 Special Study.*

floor without the explicit permission of the exchange; this was rarely forthcoming. A Third Market dealer could of course be treated as a non-member client of an exchange member and be charged full commission; but this charge is prohibitive and effectively prevented trading. On Nov. 7, 1966, as a result of a threatened antitrust suit, existing stockholder suits, and a great deal of pressure from the SEC, the New York Stock Exchange reluctantly amended Rule 394 (Rule 394 B) to permit member firms to engage in net trading with Third Market dealers under certain circumstances, which are as follows: A member firm wishing to deal outside of the Exchange must: (a) make a "diligent effort" to execute the order on the Exchange floor before going to a Third Market dealer; (b) clear going off-board with a floor governor of the Exchange and make certain verbal and written reports; (c) once a Third Market dealer's bid/offer price has been ascertained the member firm must take this off-board quote back to the Exchange floor where it can be replaced by other bids or offers, if these are better. In other words, off-board bids are obtained on a block of stock and the Exchange bidder, if the loser, is given a second chance. The SEC has, on its part, passed a rule which requires Third Market dealers to register with the commission the stocks in which they maintain markets and to demonstrate adequate financial capacity by having a minimum net worth of $1,500,000 or $250,000,000 per security in which they maintain a (third) market. Since Rule 394 has been modified, the amount of business done under the modified rule does not appear to have been great.

Many institutions balk at the higher exchange commissions, the tendency of the exchange specialists to vary prices in spite of their greater ability to take positions, and the ticker tape announcement that accompanies exchange dealings. Thus, the environment for Third Market business appears to have been little affected by the several recent developments discussed above. The continued growth of financial institutions and the crack in the modification of Rule 394 should, on the other hand, contribute to the breadth of the Third Market in particular and the securities markets in general.

FUTURE OF THE THIRD MARKET

It is now apparent that the Third Market is a major bourse for trading securities listed on the New York Stock Exchange and on other major stock exchanges. In size, it was bigger than the Pacific Coast and 13 other regional stock exchanges in 1965 (See Tables 1 and 2). In the same year it challenged the Midwest Stock Exchange with its volume of $2.5 billion, was almost one third of the American Stock Exchange volume, and 3.4% of New York Stock Exchange volume. The exchanges have tightened specialist capital requirements and have helped to make both members and specialists more aware of block trading.

The lower commissions, (potentially) greater stock availability, and less publicity from crossing blocks off-the-board still makes the Third Market attractive to institutional investors. The increasing volume of brokerage business generated by financial institutions should continue to contribute to Third Market growth. Keith Funston, president of the New York Stock Exchange, has estimated that institutional brokerage could account for 50% of all the business done on the New York Stock Exchange in the 1970s, compared to a recent figure of 31.5%. The probable end to sales and research "give-ups" also means that these institutions will have greater flexibility to deal in the Third Market. On the other hand, where fund-associated exchange member brokerage houses exist, and if and when volume discounts come to pass on these exchanges, listed business will be encouraged. On balance, these factors should at least maintain the relative position of the Third Market, although profit margins could be squeezed.

Over the longer run, the exchanges will undoubtedly further increase specialist capital requirements. At the same time there is also good reason to believe that Rule 394 will be relaxed to permit greater intermarket block trading. It is believed that the SEC wishes to encourage such a move. The Commission is expected to pressure the New York Stock Exchange to allow exchange members to seek the best market for a block without getting a low off-board bid and then showing it to the specialist. Additionally, smaller Third Market firms may be allowed to operate with the exchange through a qualified and registered market maker who will in turn take a clearing fee profit. Thus, the able Third Market dealer appears destined to at least hold his own, and the Third Market should continue to flourish.

31

Rise and Fall? Prospering Regional Exchanges May Face Tough New Rules*

David A. Hoddeson

Chicago–The Windy City ordinarily takes bad weather in stride, but last month's mile-a-minute winds and two-foot snowfall proved too much. The January 27-28 blizzard, Chicago's worst ever, stopped snowplows cold, choked main traffic arteries with so many stalled vehicles they remained plugged for days. Mail and newspaper deliveries were cancelled, the world's busiest airport closed down, and the Board of Trade, the Internal Revenue Service, and 20 General Motors plants suspended operations. National Guardsmen, called out to halt looting, couldn't reach their rendezvous points.

There remained one center of conspicuous activity, however–the Midwest Stock Exchange. The nation's third-biggest bourse foresightedly found downtown rooms for employes through the storm's first night; next day enough of a work force was on hand, according to Secretary John Withers, to open "almost every trading unit." With banks closed and most brokers and businessmen unable to get to their desks, trading was unusually light. All the same, when the Midwest closed its books for the week, it had added 680,000 shares to executions during the stormbound days–volume that otherwise might have escaped to its Eastern arch-rival, the New York Stock Exchange.

NOT AWED BY NYSE

Midwest's hardy reaction to the snowstorm was typical of today's bustling, up-to-date regional exchanges. Not in the least awed by the monolithic NYSE, they compete handily, utilizing more flexible rules and devising conveniences and trading economies unknown to the Big Board itself. Among them: intercity wire and phone hookups between trading floors; centralized "back-office" bookkeeping and billing subsidiaries, to which dozens of NYSE members subscribe (the Big Board does not yet offer equivalent aid to its cost-burdened brokers); and crosses executed at half-price. Most importantly (and also very much in the news of late, thanks to recent Securities and Exchange Commission objections to the practice), the regionals' relaxed rules which permit big institu-

*From *Barron's* (February 6, 1967). Reprinted by courtesy of *Barron's National Business and Financial Weekly*.

tional traders to split commissions among favored non-members, have sharply enlarged their trading.

Logically enough, the regionals have been flourishing. Their trading activity grew 40% faster than the NYSE in the first half of the current decade. Now, however, the government is preparing to put a severe crimp in their new-found prosperity. The Securities and Exchange Commission, in its long-delayed December "Report" on mutual funds, proclaimed a firm intention to forbid giveups—the aforementioned commission-splitting among brokers. It would also cut commissions on blocks, and reduce mutual fund sales "loads." Last week, the New York Stock Exchange, apparently discomfited by the regionals' increasingly lively competition, made political bedfellows with the SEC, and aligned itself against the give-up practice. Estimates of the probable impact of such actions on the regional exchanges therefore has become the subject of increasingly heated debate.

The consensus of opinion is that if the SEC's multiple blow falls, it will go hard with the regionals. Even the SEC, which has reason to play down the effects, has admitted the possibility of "irreparable" harm. At such a critical juncture, a close look at the regionals and the ends they serve in today's trading arena is in order.

DO WHOPPING VOLUME

The importance of the regional exchanges can be readily documented. The seven most active boosted their total business 140% in the 1960–65 span, to $7.4 billion annually—a respectable 8.3% of all trading done on all exchanges. (NYSE pre-empted 78.7% of the total exchange dollar volume in the first half of 1966, the Amex 13.4%. Offboard or third-market transactions came to 3.4% of NYSE trading.) Moreover, last year the big seven regionals probably boosted their collective activity about 35%, to some $10 billion.

The Midwest still ranks as the biggest, with trading last year up one-third to $3.9 billion. Pacific Coast, by virtue of a 61% gain to $3.5 billion, came in a good second. Next in line stood Philadelphia-Baltimore-Washington, which posted a 40% gain, to perhaps $1.4 billion. Detroit and Boston were neck-and-neck. The former grew from $630 million to over $706 million, while Boston spurted from $382 million to $718 million. Estimates on Cincinnati show a one-fourth increase to nearly $98 million, while Pittsburgh achieved a one-third increase to $55 million or so.

The regionals' growth, by and large, chiefly reflects the increasing use of their facilities by big institutional traders. For the regionals offer such traders inducements that the Big Board cannot match. To be sure, commission rates and payment regulations are nearly identical with those on the Big Board. But there is one major exception: most regionals permit cash giveups, or fee splitting, not only among exchange members, but with outsiders as well. By contrast, the NYSE permits such sharing only among its members.

MIDWEST A HOLD-OUT

Midwest, it should be noted, follows the Big Board's lead. But Pacific permits its members to split up to 25% of their commissions with outsiders, and all the others allow 40%.

The practice of fee-splitting became important with the expansion of mutual fund trading. Today mutual funds are believed to account for as much as one-half of New York Stock Exchange round-lot business. Customarily, they trade in large blocks. Since it costs no more, but pays a broker 100 times as much, to execute an order for 50,000 shares as for 500, the funds soon found dealers willing to execute their big trades while giving up part of the regular commission to whomever the mutuals designated. By that means, the funds were able to reward other brokers who provide them with selling and research services, yet still have their highly confidential, often unwieldy orders executed quietly, by a few skilled hands.

The regionals' crucial contribution to these complex arrangements lies in providing avenues to a far wider group of potential recipients–typically, any member of the National Association of Securities Dealers. On the Big Board, by contrast, emoluments to deserving non-members can be handed out only by fragmentation of the actual trading, or by clumsier non-cash rewards.

THEY'RE BIG BOYS NOW

The sheer mass of this new business not only has bulged regional volume; it also has transformed its character. In the past, the regionals served chiefly as a seasoning and proving ground for untried securities, or for local issues of merit but little national appeal. Today, such trading counts for little. Even the Midwest, which continues to cultivate local equities, now derives only a fraction of its volume from them. Elsewhere, the contribution of such "exclusives" is negligible.

Most of the regionals' business currently stems from so-called "duals"–New York and American Exchange issues which are listed on the regionals as well. Such duplicate listings have come to account for 98% of the regionals' total dollar volume. In consequence, the most active issues traded on regional exchanges often read like carbon copies of the equivalent NYSE-Amex rosters.

The regionals' leniency in the matter of giveups, for the most part, is new-minted, although old-timers point to a Pacific Coast "wire discount" or "western rate," a custom dating back to the 'Twenties, when Pacific Exchange members allowed a 25% discount to nonmembers to cover the additional expense of wiring transactions East. Detroit, with its 40% giveup rule, started the contemporary trend. It wasn't until the fall of 1965 that Pittsburgh, Boston, and Philadelphia-Baltimore all liberalized their giveup rules.

The rest, as the saying goes, is financial history. Detroit, having stolen a march on the others, enjoyed a threefold volume increase in the years 1960–65, triple the others' rate of gain. And, advancing with volume, the price of seats on the auto hub's exchange soared from a few thousand dollars to $18,000.

Last year, however, Detroit's precipitate growth was curbed by its imitators. Boston, in particular, took the play away. Its loosening of giveup rules stimulated an 85% volume jump in a single year, and boosted the price of its seats from below $2,000 to $12,800. (Detroit seat prices, meanwhile, fell to around $5,000–see table.)

Selling Prices of Seats on Regional Exchanges

	1965		1966		
	Low	High	Low	High	1967
Boston	$3,000	$11,000	$11,500	$13,000	$12,800
Cincinnati	$3,000*		5,000	5,700	5,500
Detroit	5,000	19,000	4,250	5,250	4,700
Midwest	9,500	13,000	13,500	22,000	......
Pacific	7,500	37,500	35,500	40,000	37,500
Phila-Balt-Wash	5,000	10,500	11,000	17,000	......
Pittsburgh	450	500	$1,000†		......

*Adjusted for 3-for1 split on October 1, 1965; Only sale in 1965.
†Only 1966 sale.

DEEPER ROOTS

Such spectacular fluctuations, though, tend to obscure the regionals' sound underlying growth. For that there are other, deeper roots than giveup tinkering. For one thing, powerful demographic trends back the regional exchanges–most notably, the westward migration of men and money. California now ranks first among states in the number of stockholders and contributes some 12% to NYSE trading. Another important element: the Pacific Coast board closes two hours later than the NYSE, which permits nimble traders both East and West to act on important financial news coming in after the New York close. Some 14% of Pacific Coast trades take place during that interval. Again, three mutual fund management companies–Investors Diversified Services, Waddell & Reed, and Imperial Services, Ltd.–have taken Pacific Coast seats. That commission-saving strategy is impossible on NYSE, which forbids memberships by publicly held companies.

Then there is the aforementioned shift in the character of stock market trading, away from the continuous stream of round-lot transactions and toward fewer, bigger deals. Big block business, which often is price-negotiated beforehand and crossed on exchange tapes as a formality, often is facilitated on a regional exchange. Regional specialists, less harassed by continuing streams of small orders, sometimes are better able to search out the opposite side of a large single transaction. This process may be all the easier since, according to Pacific Coast's president, Thomas Phelan, specialists there "take the trading side opposite their New York counterparts about 80% of the time."

BETTER TRADES MADE?

Similarly, Midwest's President Day insists that his exchange, for all its diminutive size and shallow liquidity when compared to the NYSE's bulk and depth, often makes better trades—if only by concentrating on issues other than the 400-odd wherein NYSE liquidity is deepest. Midwest reminds the visitor that about a year ago it crossed a 262,000 share block of Pennsylvania Railroad—the biggest single trade in the history of any exchange to that date.

Regional exchanges also offer substantial economies. Most obvious is the way they lighten traders' tax burdens. New York City transfer taxes now range well into five figures on big block trades, while markets outside the metropolitan area offer perfectly legal avenues with which to escape payment altogether. And on big-block crosses—those trades executed on both sides within a single brokerage firm—Midwest charges only a single commission, in contrast to the standard double fee levied elsewhere.

Again, the regionals are streamlining the methods by which equities are bought and sold. Innovations include Midwest's pioneering arrangements for clearances by mail, and its provision for direct wire access to the floor. Both Pacific Coast and Philadelphia-Baltimore interconnect and coordinate trading floors in their several cities. Pacific since 1962 has functioned as an amalgamation of the Los Angeles and San Francisco floors, which are joined by open telephone lines. Philadelphia-Baltimore now also holds Washington in similar electronic embrace and has "associate member" ties with Boston, and a private wire connection that extends to Montreal as well.

WHOLESALE BARGAINS

Regional techniques whereby wholesale bargains may be struck on large orders with non-member third market men also are held to be superior, despite the NYSE's recent liberalization of its Rule 394, which until last fall prohibited them outright. Even now, about one NYSE execution a month involves third market men; on the Midwest and other bourses, where the procedures are less cumbersome, such trades are frequent.

In sum, the effect of the regionals on equity trading markets has been salutary. "Even the little competitive irritants we provide," observes Midwest's genial Mr. Day, "may work to everyone's well-being in the end." Indeed, the Big Board itself has been prodded into following some of the regionals' innovations. Not least among them is the computerized back-room bookkeeping-and-billing service the NYSE will offer brokers starting next summer.

Equally important, the regionals, like the third market, often have provided supplementary trading outlets. By providing ancillary (and often surprisingly deep) puddles of liquidity to the NYSE's big pool, the regionals also have taken considerable strain from an auction market never designed to absorb the big, blockbusting transactions so frequent today.

Nevertheless, as noted, the regionals now face a grave regulatory threat. Last December 2, the SEC recommended the revision of mutual fund sale and management rates; the reduction of stock brokerage commissions on volume transactions; and the prohibition of cash giveups. So far, the regionals' attention has been riveted on the proposed giveup ban. Such a prohibition–and the SEC has the power to enforce it without further legislation–could halve Boston's trading volume and reduce Detroit to a fraction of its current size.

Other SEC proposals may prove equally harmful. Since the Midwest already forbids giveups, any SEC ban wouldn't hurt it. In common with other regionals, however, Midwest specializes in trading big blocks. Enforced discounts on big block trading, therefore, would do disproportionate injury.

Attrition within the regional brokerage communities stemming from lower income, undoubtedly would take place. The combined loss of cash giveups and the reduction in sales commissions on mutual funds business, in fact, probably would wipe out a significant number of small, local brokerage houses. At the same time, the destruction of giveup conduits would be likely to induce some large brokers to relinquish their regional seats; a goodly number first joined the regionals primarily for that reason. Finally, the snowballing effect of all these developments would shrink regional trade further still. As Pacific Coast's President Phelan observed recently (in a happier context), "Nowhere is it more true than in trading markets that volume begets volume, and success more success. It is in the nature of the business that this should be so." One might add, failure can beget failure.

It should be noted, however, that last week's NYSE-SEC agreement to ban giveups, as publicized by President Funston February 1, lends additional weight to forecasts that the practice indeed will be outlawed. Some of the supporting reasons Mr. Funston cites for his views make curious reading–among them is the clear implication that the regionals just compete too successfully, but the aid he has rendered to the SEC's giveup cause plainly is substantial.

Elsewhere on the regulatory front, there may be more hope. It remains to be seen, in fact, whether the SEC's other, multiple recommendations will be implemented. To many of them, the investment community has responded with cries of unadulterated anguish. Mutual fund representatives, the Association of Stock Exchange Firms, and the Investment Bankers Association all have entered vehement protests.

The SEC as yet has proposed no legislation, and the Senate Banking Committee's Chairman has observed that when any SEC bill does arrive, "it will require very careful study"–not to mention "extensive" hearings. Moreover, because of the complexity of the issues involved, the legislative decks will be cleared of other bills first. The regional exchanges, along with the rest of the securities industry, at least will have a period of grace to make their case.

Part V

Portfolio Management–Theory and Practice

INTRODUCTION

The first essay in this section concerning portfolio management presents the results of research conducted by Professors Fisher and Lorie at the Center for Research in Security Prices at the University of Chicago. This study is useful in that it establishes a benchmark for evaluating randomly selected portfolios. The authors computed rates of return for investments in common stock listed on the New York Stock Exchange for various time periods from 1926–1960. As stated in the article, the basic assumption in the computations is that, at the beginning of each time period studied, the investor commits an equal amount of funds to each common stock listed at that time on the exchange.

In the second paper, Professor William Sharpe expands one portion of Markowitz's work which deals with the analysis of probabilistic estimates of the future performance of securities to determine an efficient set of portfolios. He presents a model of the relationships among securities and describes how this model allows the portfolio analysis problem to be simplified.

Professor William Baumol, in an attempt to aid the non-professional portfolio manager, proposes a new efficiency criterion for the Markowitz portfolio selection approach. He demonstrates that the use of standard deviation as a measure of risk in the Markowitz analysis is misleading at times. Professor Robert Dince re-visits a concept that has recently been overshadowed by some of the more dramatic approaches to portfolio management as he demonstrates the profitability of formula planning. The rates of return generated by this approach are contrasted with those of Fisher and Lorie and those of Herzog.

George K. Freeman presents another automatic portfolio management system. He calls it the "10% rule." This plan explicitly deals with a technical principle that was encountered in Alexander's study; namely, that stock prices, having moved a certain distance in one direction, very likely will continue to move in that direction. In the concluding article in the section Paul F. Miller presents data which challenge the popular opinion that stocks with high price-earnings multiples have outperformed those stocks with low multiples. The results of this research covering the period 1948–1964 indicate that, growth reputation of the high-flyers notwithstanding, the purchase of stock with low price-earnings multiples will result in greatest price appreciation.

32

Rates of Return on Investments in Common Stocks*

L. Fisher
J. H. Lorie

This article presents data on rates of return on investments in common stocks. It answers the question of how much gain or loss an individual investor might have realized if he had bought all New York Stock Exchange common stocks—at five different dates and held them for varying lengths of time during the thirty-five years from 1926 through 1960, a total of twenty-two time periods. This work is the first to emerge from the Center for Research in Security Prices (sponsored by Merrill Lynch, Pierce, Fenner & Smith Inc.). For that reason we shall describe the facilities and plans of the Center before presenting the results and methods of its first research.

THE CENTER FOR RESEARCH IN SECURITY PRICES

Purpose

The sole purpose of the Center for Research in Security Prices is to conduct research and to disseminate the results throughout the academic and financial communities. This is what Merrill Lynch, Pierce, Fenner & Smith Inc. had in mind when they provided the funds to establish the Center, and this is what the Graduate School of Business had in mind when it sought support.

Despite the enormous quantities of available data on security prices and related things, the amount of scientific research based on these data is inadequate for many purposes. As a result, a number of controversies and unresolved issues about security prices have continued. For example, there is controversy

*From The *Journal of Business,* Vol. 37, No. 1 (January 1964), pp. 1–21. Reprinted by permission of The University of Chicago Press.

Funds to support the work reported in this article came primarily from Merrill Lynch, Pierce, Fenner & Smith Inc. Support also came from the Graduate School of Business through funds granted by the Ford Foundation. In addition, the work was supported by the National Science Foundation through their grant to the Computation Center of the University of Chicago. We also would like to acknowledge the invaluable help of Frederic J. Meier and Milton Davis in the collection of data and the direct assistance of at least nineteen computer programmers, most notably that of Sergius Kunitzky, Ann Walinski Loidl, Daniel I. Rosenfels, Lee H. Hook, and Haym L. Rabinovitz.

about whether successive changes in the prices of common stocks are statistically independent or are serially correlated. If the former is true, technical analysis such as that based on the Dow Theory is not likely to be helpful; if the latter is true, regularities in the patterns of change can be detected by appropriate analysis.

Another controversy revolves about the question of what effect, if any, dividends exert on stock prices. Some feel that only earnings matter and that payout ratios are therefore of no consequence. Others feel that the declaration of a dollar dividend affects the price of a stock differently from a dollar of earnings retained. This matter is of great consequence to American corporations, but the issue remains unresolved.

Another difficult problem is the subject of stock-market averages. Averages are a lot like the weather in that everyone talks about them—usually with dissatisfaction—but no one does anything. It is time that a serious effort be made to devise averages which do more than report descriptively the movement of some stock prices.

Many people would like to have more detailed and refined information regarding the relationship of movements in stock prices to changes of other sorts in the economy. More work needs to be done on the relationships between earnings and prices and on the relevance of balance-sheet data in understanding and predicting the financial fate of corporations.

The Center for Research in Security Prices will work on all of the problems mentioned above and many others. It is intended to be a permanent institution which will work as rapidly as financial resources and the imagination and abilities of research workers will permit. The facilities of the Center will be available not only to the faculty and graduate students of the University of Chicago but also to persons at other educational institutions and in the financial community who have serious problems for which the Center's facilities can be helpful. The Center's facilities will be described below.

Facilities

In March, 1960, Merrill Lynch, Pierce, Fenner & Smith Inc., made an initial grant of $50,000 to the University of Chicago to establish the Center for Research in Security Prices. The initial funds and additional resources equivalent to more than $150,000 have been used to establish a "laboratory" consisting of a very large volume of data on security prices and related things appropriately arranged and stored on computer tape. These data together with appropriate computer programs, make possible a large variety and number of analyses of security prices, of their determinants, and of their relationships to other things in the economy.

Security Prices. Monthly closing prices of all common stocks on the New York Stock Exchange from January, 1926, through December, 1960, have been placed on tape. Their accuracy has been appraised in several ways, and, after three years of checking and rechecking, it is estimated that the incidence of error is extremely low and that remaining errors do not bias the results.

Further, there are on tape—though at present in less useful form—daily high, low, and closing prices of all common stocks on the New York Stock Exchange from July 1, 1960, to the present. This information is being kept up to date, but has not yet been integrated with the file on monthly prices; and its accuracy has not been tested adequately.

Capital Changes. In order for the information on security prices to be useful for refined analyses, it is essential that information be recorded on all types of capital changes. This has been done. Such changes include, for example, cash dividends, stock dividends, stock splits, rights, exchanges of shares, etc. One way to summarize the data that have been placed on tape is to say that almost all pertinent information in the Commerce Clearing House series, *Capital Changes Reporter*, has been coded, checked for possible error, and placed on tape. The accuracy of these data has been exhaustively checked.

An additional comment is warranted on the treatment of cash dividends. Where available, four dates are recorded for each dividend: (1) the date of declaration, (2) the ex-dividend date, (3) the date of record, and (4) the date of payment. Further, the tax status for each dividend is recorded; there are seven different tax categories (see Appendix p. 403).

Other Data. A wide variety of national economic statistics has been coded and is ready to go on tape. These data cover such things as commodity prices, interest rates, industrial production, and national income.

For each period for which there is a security price, data on trading volume have also been recorded.

Data on earnings have been placed on IBM cards and ultimately will be transferred to tape. This information is in the form reported by the company and requires extensive adjustment before its use for refined analysis will be worthwhile.

Plans for the Future

It is planned to keep the basic file of information up to date and to include new data of various kinds, depending on the projects that the Center undertakes. Undoubtedly there will be experimentation with balance-sheet data, and certainly an effort will be made to include data on securities other than common stocks listed on the New York Stock Exchange. Priority will be given to research of general interest, but other projects will also be undertaken.

RATES OF RETURN ON INVESTMENTS IN COMMON STOCKS

It is surprising to realize that there have been no measurements of the rates of return on investments in common stocks that could be considered accurate and definitive. There have been many efforts, but each has been deficient in at least one crucial respect. Some have lacked comprehensiveness, having dealt only with a selection of individual securities such as those in one of the popular stock market averages. This study embraces all common stock listed on the New York Stock Exchange during the time periods covered—some seventeen hundred of them. Again, earlier studies have dealt only with one or two brief time periods in contrast to the twenty-two time periods within a thirty-five-year span covered here. Finally, all other studies have been deficient because they have ignored taxes and transaction costs. In this study actual New York Stock Exchange round-lot commission rates, as they existed on all purchase, sales and re-investment dates, have been included in the calculations; and all federal taxes, as they applied to income from dividends or capital gains at specific times in selected tax brackets, have been taken into consideration. As can be seen from Tables 1 and 2, taxes and commissions can have large effects on rates of return. This study has shortcomings, but we believe that they are less pronounced than those of previous work.

Rates of Return with Reinvestment of Dividends

Table 1 shows the results of investing an equal sum of money in each company having one or more issues of common stock listed on the New York Stock Exchange at the beginning of each period *and* of reinvesting dividends as received throughout the periods in the stock of the company making the payment. The results referred to thus include dividends and capital appreciation. Stocks listed at the beginning of any time period receive equal weight. A stock listed after the beginning and before the end of a particular time period is included whenever holders of other stocks receive its shares and also to whatever extent funds for reinvestment become available through the delisting of stocks that still possess value. To be more specific, when a stock is delisted, it is sold over the counter and the proceeds are spread evenly over all stocks listed on that date.

It should be emphasized that Table 1 represents the rates of return—or rates of capital appreciation—that result from the adoption of only one of a large number of possible investment policies. An illustrative alternative would be the allocation of investment funds in proportion to the value of shares outstanding.

Except for the large amount of double-counting involved, this latter policy, in contrast to the one underlying Tables 1 and 2, would indicate the rates of return available to all the investors considered together.[1] That is, new investors as a group might be able to allocate funds among securities in proportion to the value of shares outstanding but could not invest equal amounts in each security without changing many prices by a substantial amount.

The decision to invest equal amounts in each company with common stock listed on the Exchange was based on the desire to calculate rates of return that would on the average be available to the individual investor who selected stocks

[1] By "double counting" we mean the ownership by one company of stock in another listed company. For example, Du Pont owns large amounts of stock in General Motors. Allocation of investment funds in proportion to the value of Du Pont and General Motors stock outstanding involves counting some of the General Motors shares twice.

at random with equal probabilities of selection—that is, exercised no judgment. A policy of allocating funds in proportion to shares outstanding or according to any other criterion implies less neutrality of judgment in making investments.[2]

Since dividends constitute income, the results of reinvesting dividends would obviously vary with the individual investor's tax bracket. For the purpose of this study, three brackets were chosen, although any other set of tax rates could easily be substituted for those used.

The first category, "Tax Exempt," shows the rate of return that might have been realized by a tax-exempt institution.

Results in the $10,000 income class were computed in the following manner:

1. The marginal income tax rate as of 1960 was figured for a married man with standard deductions and an adjusted gross income of $10,000.

2. For each previous year, a tax rate was determined for a man who held the same relative position in the pattern of income distribution existing in those years as the man with $10,000 income in 1960.

3. The appropriate tax rate for such a married man was then applied in all preceding years.

A precisely analogous procedure was used in computing results in the third category, the $50,000 income class.[3]

For each period in each income class, two rates of return are shown. The first, "Cash-to-Portfolio," shows the after-tax rate of interest, compounded annually, which an individual would have had to get on a sum equal to the gross purchase price of the portfolio at the beginning of a period in order to equal the value of the portfolio at the end of the period. The second figure, "Cash-to-Cash," indicates the rate of interest, compounded annually, that would be required on the value of the initial portfolio in order to equal the value of the sum at the terminal date after selling the portfolio and paying the commissions and the capital gains tax applicable.

These rates of return speak for themselves and require little comment. The periods were chosen for obvious reasons. The period from 1926 to 1960 is a long span with booms and depressions—prime examples of each!—and war and peace.

[2]We made an estimate of the rates of return available from investing in proportion to the value of shares outstanding by using the Standard and Poor's Index of Common Stocks on the New York Stock Exchange—an index weighted according to the value of shares outstanding—and the Standard and Poor's dividend series. For three of the five starting dates covered in Table 1, the Standard and Poor's rate of return was generally higher; for two of the starting dates, the yield was lower. No systematic differences were detectable, and on the average the yields based on the two different investment policies were similar.

[3]For example, men with incomes of $10,000 or $50,000 in 1960 would have had incomes of $1,780 or $8,950, respectively, in 1933. The ranges of marginal tax rates were from 0 to 25 per cent for dividends for the $10,000 man and from 0 to 62 per cent for the $50,000 man. The capital gains tax rates ranged from 0 to 13 per cent for the $10,000 man and from 5 to 42 per cent for the $50,000 man.

TABLE 1
Rates of Return on Investment in Common Stocks Listed on the New York Stock Exchange with Reinvestment of Dividends*
(Per Cent per Annum Compounded Annually)

Period	Income Class					
	Tax Exempt		$10,000 in 1960		$50,000 in 1960	
	Cash-to-Portfolio†	Cash-to-Cash‡	Cash-to-Portfolio	Cash-to-Cash	Cash-to-Portfolio	Cash-to-Cash
1/26–12/60	9.0	9.0	8.4	8.2	7.4	6.8
1/26– 9/29	20.4	20.3	20.4	20.3	20.3	19.4
1/26– 6/32	–16.5	–16.8	–16.5	–16.8	–16.5	–13.4
1/26–12/40	2.4	2.3	2.4	2.4	2.2	2.4
1/26–12/50	6.8	6.8	6.3	6.1	5.5	5.1
9/29– 6/32	–48.4	–48.8	–48.4	–48.8	–48.2	–40.6
9/29–12/40	– 3.0	– 3.1	– 3.0	– 2.9	– 3.0	– 2.3
9/29–12/50	4.9	4.8	4.3	4.1	3.5	3.2
9/29–12/60	7.7	7.7	7.0	6.8	5.9	5.4
6/32–12/40	21.3	21.1	21.2	20.8	20.8	19.5
6/32–12/50	18.6	18.6	17.8	17.5	16.5	15.5
6/32–12/60	17.4	17.3	16.5	16.2	15.0	14.1
12/50–12/52	12.5	12.0	11.1	10.0	9.0	7.1
12/50–12/54	17.9	17.6	16.6	15.3	14.4	11.6
12/50–12/56	17.0	16.8	15.8	14.8	13.7	11.4
12/50–12/58	16.5	16.4	15.4	14.6	13.4	11.4
12/50–12/60	14.8	14.7	13.8	13.1	12.0	10.3
12/55–12/56	6.4	5.4	5.7	4.6	4.0	2.8
12/55–12/57	– 3.7	– 4.2	– 4.4	– 4.0	– 6.0	– 4.2
12/55–12/58	13.0	12.6	12.2	11.1	10.5	8.2
12/55–12/59	14.0	13.7	13.3	12.2	11.6	9.2
12/55–12/60	11.2	10.9	10.5	9.6	8.9	7.2

*The data underlying this table have been exhaustively checked. We are confident that any subsequent refinement or adjustment will do no more than change an occasional figure after the decimal point.

†"Cash-to-Portfolio" means the net rate of return which would have been realized after paying commissions and taxes (if any) on each transaction but continuing to hold the portfolio at the end of each period.

‡"Cash-to-Cash" means the net return which would have been realized after paying commissions and taxes (if any) on each transaction including the sale of the portfolio at the end of each period.

The periods beginning in September, 1929, were included to indicate the experience of those who invested at the height of the stock-market boom of the 1920's. The periods beginning in June, 1932, were included to show the results of investing at the nadir of this country's worst depression. The numerous brief, recent periods were included to bring details of postwar experience into sharp focus.

Aside from most periods ending in 1932 or 1940, the rates of return are surprisingly high. For half the twenty-two periods, the rates are above 10 per cent per annum compounded annually; and for two-thirds of the periods, the rates exceed 6 per cent.

Rates of Return Without Reinvestment of Dividends

Table 2 presents the rates of return on common stocks listed on the New York Stock Exchange with no reinvestment of dividends, that is, under the

TABLE 2

Rates of Return on Investment in Common Stocks Listed on the New York Stock Exchange without Reinvestment of Dividends*

(Per Cent per Annum Compounded Annually)

Period	Income Class					
	Tax Exempt		$10,000 in 1960		$50,000 in 1960	
	Cash-to-Portfolio†	Cash-to-Cash‡	Cash-to-Portfolio	Cash-to-Cash	Cash-to-Portfolio	Cash-to-Cash
1/26–12/60	6.9	6.9	6.7	6.5	6.2	5.8
1/26– 9/29	19.8	19.7	19.8	19.7	19.8	18.9
1/26– 6/32	–13.2	–13.4	–13.2	–13.4	–13.2	–10.8
1/26–12/40	1.6	1.6	1.6	1.7	1.6	1.8
1/26–12/50	5.1	5.1	4.9	4.7	4.5	4.2
9/29– 6/32	–48.2	–48.6	–48.2	–48.6	–48.1	–40.4
9/29–12/40	– 4.9	– 5.0	– 4.9	– 4.7	– 4.8	– 3.8
9/29–12/50	2.3	2.2	2.0	2.0	1.8	1.7
9/29–12/60	4.9	4.9	4.6	4.4	4.3	3.8
6/32–12/40	24.5	24.4	24.5	24.1	23.8	22.5
6/32–12/50	21.4	21.4	20.8	20.5	19.3	18.5
6/32–12/60	20.5	20.5	19.7	19.5	17.8	17.3
12/50–12/52	12.6	12.1	11.2	10.1	9.1	7.2
12/50–12/54	17.3	17.1	16.1	14.9	14.1	11.5
12/50–12/56	16.6	16.5	15.5	14.6	13.6	11.3
12/50–12/58	16.2	16.1	15.2	14.4	13.3	11.3
12/50–12/60	15.0	14.9	14.0	18.2	12.1	10.4
12/55–12/56	6.5	5.4	5.7	4.6	4.0	2.8
12/55–12/57	– 3.3	– 3.8	– 4.1	– 3.7	– 5.8	– 4.1
12/55–12/58	12.6	12.2	11.9	10.8	10.3	8.1
12/55–12/59	13.7	13.4	13.0	12.0	11.4	9.1
12/55–12/60	11.1	10.9	10.4	9.6	8.9	7.2

*The data underlying this table have been exhaustively checked. We are confident that any subsequent refinement or adjustment will do no more than change an occasional figure after the decimal point.

†"Cash-to-Portfolio" means the net rate of return which would have been realized after paying commissions and taxes (if any) on each transaction but continuing to hold the portfolio at the end of each period.

‡"Cash-to-Cash" means the net return which would have been realized after paying commissions and taxes (if any) on each transaction including the sale of the portfolio at the end of each period.

assumption that dividends are spent for consumers goods and services at the time they are received. The method of calculation is analogous to that used to compute the yield-to-maturity of a bond. The cost of the stock at the beginning of a time period is analogous to the purchase price of the bond; dividends are analogous to interest payments; and the value of the stock at the end of the period is analogous to the sum received by the holder of a bond when it matures. The rate of return is the rate of discounting which makes the stream of after-tax cash flows have a present value of zero.

At first, one might expect the rates in Table 2 to be significantly lower than in Table 1, whereas in fact the rates are quite similar for most of the periods. This similarity merely reflects the fact that the rate of appreciation in the prices of stocks after the receipt of dividends was on the average about the same as the rate of appreciation before the receipt of dividends. When the latter rate was higher, the rates in Table 2 are lower than those in Table 1 and vice versa. The individual who reinvests his dividends is obviously wealthier at an ending date than is the individual who spends them. On the average he also has a great deal more invested in his portfolio. Thus, some rates in Table 1 are higher than the corresponding rates in Table 2; some are lower; and several are the same.

Table 3 shows rate of capital appreciation or gain, ignoring dividends.

Comparison with Other Investment Media

Comparable data for other investment media are not available, but there is some information on realized rates of return on a *before-tax* basis. The most nearly complete data are for savings in commercial banks, mutual savings banks, and savings and loan associations. Savings in these institutions never earned as much as 6 per cent per annum for any of the twenty-two time periods listed in Table 1 and for most of the period 1926–60 earned less than 4 per cent.[4]

Data on mortgage loans made by commerical banks and life insurance companies on non-farm homes are available for 1920–47 and for some sub-periods.[5] When all types of mortgages are considered together, realized yields never exceeded 6 per cent, never fell below 4 per cent, and averaged about 5 per cent.

[4]Based on (1927-60) figures of U.S. Savings and Loan League *Fact Book,* 1955 and 1962 editions, whose sources are as follows: (1) (savings and loan associations) data of members of Federal Home Loan Bank System, (2) (mutual savings banks) Association of Mutual Savings Banks, (3) (commercial banks) data of Board of Governors of the Federal Reserve System and Federal Deposit Insurance Corporation. The yields for these years were computed by dividing the total cash and credited dividends or interest by the average of deposits at the beginning and end of each year.

1926 Figures: (savings and loan associations) R. W. Goldsmith, *A Study of Saving in the United States* (Princeton, N.J.: Princeton University Press, 1955), Vol. I, p. 447; and (savings and commercial banks) J. V. Lintner, *Mutual Savings Banks in the Savings and Mortgage Markets* (Boston, Mass.: Division of Research, Graduate School of Business Administration, Harvard University, 1948), p. 477.

[5]J. E. Morton, *Urban Mortgage Lending: Comparative Markets and Experience* (Princeton, N.J.: Princeton University Press, 1956), p. 114.

TABLE 3
Rates of Change in Value of Investment in Common Stocks Listed on the New York Stock Exchange, Ignoring Dividends*
(Per Cent per Annum Compounded Annually)

Period	Income Class					
	Tax Exempt		$10,000 in 1960		$50,000 in 1960	
	Cash-to-Portfolio†	Cash-to-Cash‡	Cash-to-Portfolio	Cash-to-Cash	Cash-to-Portfolio	Cash-to-Cash
1/26–12/60	3.9	3.8	3.9	3.6	4.0	3.3
1/26– 9/29	15.7	15.6	15.7	15.6	15.7	14.8
1/26– 6/32	–21.0	–21.2	–21.0	–21.2	–20.9	–17.8
1/26–12/40	– 2.8	– 2.9	– 2.8	– 2.8	– 2.7	– 2.4
1/26–12/50	1.3	1.3	1.4	1.2	1.5	1.1
9/29– 6/32	–51.5	–51.9	–51.5	–51.9	–51.3	–43.4
9/29–12/40	– 8.0	– 8.0	– 8.0	– 7.7	– 7.6	– 6.4
9/29–12/50	– .5	– .6	– .5	– .6	– .2	– .3
9/29–12/60	2.5	2.4	2.5	2.2	2.7	2.1
6/32–12/40	16.9	16.8	16.9	16.4	16.8	15.1
6/32–12/50	13.1	13.0	13.0	12.5	13.0	11.7
6/32–12/60	11.9	11.9	11.9	11.4	11.8	10.8
12/50–12/52	5.9	5.4	5.9	4.8	5.9	4.0
12/50–12/54	11.4	11.1	11.3	10.1	11.3	8.6
12/50–12/56	10.8	10.7	10.8	9.8	10.8	8.4
12/50–12/58	10.7	10.6	10.7	9.8	10.7	8.5
12/50–12/60	9.6	9.4	9.5	8.7	9.5	7.6
12/55–12/56	1.5	.4	1.4	.4	1.4	.2
12/55–12/57	– 8.3	– 8.8	– 8.3	– 7.9	– 8.3	– 6.6
12/55–12/58	8.0	7.6	8.0	6.9	8.0	5.8
12/55–12/59	9.3	9.0	9.3	8.2	9.3	6.9
12/55–112/60	6.7	6.5	6.7	5.8	6.7	5.0

*The data underlying this table have been exhaustively checked. We are confident that any subsequent refinement or adjustment will do no more than change an occasional figure after the decimal point.

†"Cash-to-portfolio" means the net rate of change which would have been experienced after paying commissions and taxes (if any) on each transaction but continuing to hold the portfolio at the end of each period.

‡"Cash-to-cash" means the net change which would have been experienced after paying commissions and taxes (if any) on each transaction including the sale of the portfolio at the end of each period.

Realized yields on municipal and U.S. government bonds, as indicated by Standard and Poor indexes, ranged from –7.0 to +7.8 per cent and averaged less than 4 per cent during the twenty-two time periods listed in Table 2.

Average realized yields on large issues of corporate bonds are available for 1900–58.[6] These yields ranged from –6 per cent to just over 15 per cent during

[6]W. B. Hickman, *Statistical Measures of Corporate Bond Financing Since 1900* (Princeton, N.J.: Princeton University Press, 1960), pp. 291, 298–301. Hickman's sample included all straight corporate bond issues of $5 million or more. See also David Durand, "A Quarterly Series of Corporate Basic Yields, 1952–57, and Some Attendant Reservations," *Journal of Finance*, Vol. XIII, No. 3 (September 1958).

periods from 1920–43. The very high yields were achieved during the recovery from the depression of 1929–32 when prices of industrial bonds, in particular, advanced sharply in price. During most periods, yields varied between 5 and 8 per cent and in recent periods have been lower.

The fact that many persons choose investments with a substantially lower average rate of return than that available on common stocks suggests the essentially conservative nature of those investors and the extent of their concern about the risk of loss inherent in common stocks. And yet their experience with mortgage foreclosures during the 1930's and the substantial rate of default on bonds during the same period shows that even such "conservative" investments carry considerable risks.

The Center for Research in Security Prices is currently at work on another study that will focus more sharply on this question of risk in common-stock ownership. While the present study is concerned with rates of return on common stocks for various periods, the above-mentioned study will seek to answer the questions of how often and how much the investor might have gained or lost on every stock listed on the New York Stock Exchange from 1926 to 1960.

CONCLUSIONS

During the entire thirty-five-year period, 1926–60, the rates of return, compounded annually, on common stocks listed on the New York Stock Exchange, with reinvestment of dividends, were 9.0 per cent for tax exempt institutions; 8.2 per cent for persons in the $10,000 income class; and 6.8 per cent for persons in the $50,000 income class.[7] These rates are substantially higher than for alternative investment media for which data are available. It is probably worth noting here that a dollar earning 9.0 per cent per annum, compounded annually, would be worth over $20 in 35 years.

The rates for the postwar periods are substantially higher than for the periods prior to the war except during the period of recovery after 1932. It will perhaps be surprising to many that the rates have consistently been so high. For the postwar period (1950–60), as a whole, rates have exceeded 10 per cent for all tax brackets considered, even after payment of capital gains taxes, and this has been true for most subperiods as well.

Rates of return without reinvestment of dividends varied from period to period above and below rates with reinvestments, but on the whole the rates

---

Basic yields, together with some discussion of the basic-yield concept, appeared in David Durand, *Basic Yields of Corporate Bonds, 1900-1942,* Technical Paper No. 3 (New York: National Bureau of Economic Research, 1942). The series was later brought up to date, with additional discussion, in David Durand and Willis J. Winn, *Basic Yields of Bonds, 1926-1947: Their Measurement and Pattern,* Technical Paper No. 6 (New York: National Bureau of Economic Research, 1947). Later basic-yield figures have appeared in the *Economic Almanac* and the *Statistical Abstract of the United States.*

[7] The specification of tax brackets and treatment of taxes are discussed on pp. 3, 6, 16, and 17.

were similar. This merely reflects the fact that, on the average, rates of appreciation in the prices of stocks after the receipt of dividends were similar to rates before the receipt of dividends.

APPENDIX: METHODOLOGY

DATA

Coverage of the Data

Definition of Common Stock. We have used a rather strict definition of common stock. To be considered a common stock, an issue must have residual rights to dividends. However, where the payment of a dividend is a liability for another company, which is the case for most guaranteed stocks, we do not consider the security to be a common stock. We ignore the matter of the voting power of the stock.

Initially we had the naive belief that it would be easy to distinguish between common stocks and other securities by using the designations employed in the lists in the *Bank and Quotation Record*. But as the study progressed we found over fifty ambiguous designations of securities. It was necessary in each such instance to examine more detailed descriptions to determine the rights of the security-holder and, thus, whether the security was a common stock.

If the company had only one issue of stock, this was almost always found to be common stock; but there were exceptions. For example, Green Bay and Western Railroad has a capital structure consisting of "Class A Income Debentures," "Class B Income Debentures," and "common stock." Class A income debentures and the common stock have rights ordinarily ascribed to first and second non-cumulative preferred stocks. The Class B income debentures have the residual rights to the income of the corporation. In our files, we treat the Class B income debentures as the common stock.

Another example is General Gas and Electric's "Class A common stock," which was listed on the New York Stock Exchange from 1925 to 1933. Until 1929, the company also had outstanding dividend certificates, which were traded over the counter. These certificates were entitled to share equally in dividends after the Class A and Class B common stock had each received 5 per cent dividends. For our purposes, General Gas and Electric Company had no common stock listed until 1929.

Radio-Keith-Orpheum had both "Class A" and "Class B common stocks" outstanding. The Class B stock was entirely owned by the Radio Corporation of America. Until April, 1931, the Class A stock was in fact a participating preferred stock under our definition; but then Radio Corporation of America waived its rights to dividends. Under our definition the Class A became common stock at that time.

Sometimes a company has several securities simultaneously listed, each of which we consider to be a common stock. Where all of these issues had a continuous series of price quotations, we treat each of them as a separate common stock. Occasionally voting trust certificates and stock have been traded simultaneously for a relatively short period. In such cases we take as the common stock the issue which has the largest dollar volume of trading.

List of Common Stocks. The common stocks included in the study are those listed and traded on the New York Stock Exchange during 1926–60. Our data cover stocks only during the period of their listing. Several issues which were seldom or never traded on the Exchange during the period have effectively been excluded from the study. Two of these issues were essentially worthless by 1926; one was the stock of a holding company whose only asset is included; the remainder are New York banks traded for a short time late in 1927 and early 1928 and delisted in 1928. Whenever a substantial amount of stock remained outstanding after a merger, this remainder is included under a different identification number as long as reasonably reliable price quotations are available.

Period of Time. Our study covers the period from January 30, 1926, through December 30, 1960. This period was selected for a variety of reasons. First, we wanted to include a substantial period of time prior to the great "bull" market of 1928–29. Second, we were limited in our efforts to go back to earlier periods by the difficulties of getting complete data for the period prior to 1926.

The data terminate in December, 1960, because of the amount of time needed to process the information included. We intend to bring the data up to date.

The Basic Data

We have included all data necessary for the determination of realized rates of return. Therefore our file includes price quotations; records of dividends and other distributions of cash and property to common stock holders; information on mergers and exchange offers affecting common stock holders; and, in the case of companies which were delisted during the period of the study, a record of the over-the-counter price shortly after the delisting.

Price Quotations. The prices consist of the last price on the last business day of the month, whenever such prices are available. When there was no trading of a particular stock on the last business day of the month, we use the mean of the bid-and-asked price or the bid price or the asked price.

In our file we have a price for each month that a stock was listed from January, 1926, through December, 1960—a total of more than 350,000 quotations. In addition to each price, we have recorded the transaction volume and the round-lot commission applicable at that time. We have also indicated our estimate of the quality of the price information. The overwhelming majority of prices are sales prices which are deemed to have been "good." We suspect errors in approximately 0.5 per cent of the prices in our file. A substantial proportion of these errors are believed to be caused by errors in our sources. All errors are believed to be small and unbiased.

Data on Distributions to Stockholders and Other Capital Changes. We have included data on thirty-nine kinds of distributions to stockholders and other capital changes. These data consist of information on cash dividends, stock dividends and splits, subscription rights, distributions of other stocks, mergers, exchange offers, and reorganizations.

Approximately 90,000 cash dividends are included. For each dividend we have recorded the amount payable (and in the case of liquidating dividends, the percentage liquidation which the dividend constitutes), the payment data, the date of record, and where available, the exdividend date on the New York Stock Exchange, and the date of declaration.

These dividends are classified according to their tax status as follows:

1. Ordinary cash dividends, i.e., dividends subject to
   a) Surtax only (1926–35)
   b) The same tax as other income (1936–July 31, 1954)
   c) The 4 per cent dividend credit (August 1, 1954–date)
2. Dividends not entitled to the 4 per cent dividend credit.
3. Dividends subject to both normal tax and surtax (1926–35)
4. Distributions of capital gains
5. "Dividends" which are paid in partial liquidation of a company
6. "Dividends" which are return of capital
7. "Dividends" which are reported capital gains retained by a regulated investment company

Dividends which are paid in property other than listed common stocks are also included. For these dividends we show the estimated fair market value of the dividend and classify them in the same manner as cash dividends.

For distributions of subscription rights, we have recorded the following information: the number of rights required to subscribe to one additional share (or unit), the subscription price, the market value of one right, the percentage of cost basis for tax purposes which may be allocated to the right, and the record date for the distribution of the rights. We have also classified subscription rights according to whether they were rights to subscribe to the same issue of common stock or rights to subscribe to something else such as preferred stock, stock of another company, bonds, etc.[8]

For each stock dividend, split, and reverse split, we have recorded the percentage change in the number of shares outstanding as a result of the split, and the change of par value occurring at the time of the split. We have also recorded the date of the dividend, or effective date of the split, as well as the record and ex dates.

[8] Where the subscription rights apply to "units" including the same issue of stock, we arrive at the subscription price per share by deducting the value of other securities making up the unit from the gross subscription price.

The information recorded on distribution of other listed common stocks depends on the taxability of the distribution. We have recorded the effective date of the distribution, ex and record dates, a number identifying the stock distributed and the number of shares receivable per share held. For distributions which are treated as non-taxable exchanges (spin-offs) we have also recorded the percentage of cost basis to be allocated to the stock received. For other distributions—those which are treated as dividends, taxable exchanges or returns of capital—we have recorded the fair market value of each share received.

Mergers in which the old and new securities are all listed are recorded at least twice. For the security or securities absorbed in the merger, the following information is recorded:

1. The effective date of the merger
2. A number identifying the successor security
3. The tax status of the merger, i.e., non-taxable exchange, taxable exchange, non-taxable exchange except that a portion of the proceeds may be taxable as income or as capital gain
4. The number of shares of the new security received for each share of the old
5. The dollar value of cash and other property (such as preferred stock and debentures)
6. The fair market value of each new common share except where the merger is a non-taxable exchange
7. Where the merger is a non-taxable exchange, the percentage of the cost basis to be allocated to the new common stock
8. Where a portion of the proceeds of the exchange of stock is taxable or may be taxable under a special rule, the maximum amount so taxable

Mergers are further classified into three categories: those which are probably deemed mergers in the legal sense; those effected through the voluntary exchange of stock where at least 50 per cent of the publicly held stock was exchanged under the terms of the offer; and exchange offers where less than half of publicly held stock is exchanged. Two other kinds of "merger" items are included in the file: reorganizations which are most easily handled by treating them as if they were mergers and occasional changes in security identification numbers to simplify the analytical programs.

For the emergent security, the date of the merger and the identity of the security or securities merged are recorded.

Data on Other Changes. When a security ceases to be traded on the New York Stock Exchange for any reason other than by being absorbed by a merger into another listed common stock, we have recorded the mean of the bid-and-asked prices over the counter at the end of the month in which the delisting occurs.[9]

[9]In a few cases the price recorded is the price on some other stock exchange rather than the over-the-counter price. Very occasionally a security had substantial value at the time of delisting, but we could find no over-the-counter price until several months after the delisting. In these cases we have used the first reasonable price available.

In order to facilitate reference to the file, we have recorded effective dates of changes of name and have generally noted reported reorganizations and bankruptcy proceedings.

Organization of the Data. The data have been arranged to facilitate the use of an electronic computer in making the calculations reported in the text. Our file is recorded on magnetic tape.[10] All data pertaining to a particular common stock are arranged chronologically within the records for that stock. The sequence of securities is essentially alphabetical within the restrictions imposed by two requirements: (1) stocks which have been delisted without being merged into another listed stock are at the beginning of the file arranged in the order of the dates of their delisting, and (2) stocks whose holders received another stock precede the other stock in the file. Each event—the price at the end of the month, the occurrence of the ex date of the dividend, the distribution of rights, etc.—constitutes an independent "record" which contains information pertinent to that event.

Unless the majority of the stock is exchanged, the data for a particular stock are kept together regardless of name changes. If the stock is still listed after an exchange, the remainder of the record for that stock constitutes information for another "security" in our file.[11]

Methods of Collection and Control[12]

The methods of collection and control are complicated. We have organized the material in the following section approximately in the chronological order in which the project progressed.

Strenuous efforts were made to keep all clerical procedures as simple as possible. This effort was made in order to reduce the amount of error in the file by making much of the work within the capacity of clerks and leaving for the computer that work for which it had superior efficiency. The first step in carrying out this policy was to get for each month a list of companies with stocks listed on the New York Stock Exchange. This was done by reference to the files of the Exchange.

Collection of Price Data. The list for each month was then arranged in alphabetical order and an IBM card for each listed company was punched and printed with the company name, the month and year, and an identifying number. These cards were believed to be in the same order as lines in the *Bank*

[10]The number of reels of tape occupied by the file depends on the particular use to be made of it the next time we use the data, e.g., when arranged for printing, it requires eight reels of magnetic tape; when arranged for the computations described in the text, two reels.

[11]Where we gathered information before discovering that a particular security is not a common stock for our purposes, we have nevertheless retained that information in our file and have placed special indicators on it. We have not, however, applied the error detection and correction procedures reported below to most of these data.

[12]Much of the material in this section is also presented in L. Fisher, "Use of Electronic Computers in the Quality Control of Financial Data" in *1963 Proceedings of the Business and Economics Section of the American Statistical Association* (Washington, D.C.: American Statistical Association, 1963), pp. 169–71.

and Quotation Record, which was the basic source of information on stock prices and volume of trading.[13] Clerks were instructed to write relevant data in prepared spaces on these specially designed punch cards. They were to fill out a card for each price quotation other than one which was specifically stated as being for preferred or preference stock. If there was a prepunched card it was to be used. If there was no prepunched card, a blank card was to be filled out. Prepunched cards for which no information was found were put in a special file. In addition to the information described in the preceding section, the clerk placed a code on each card designating the kind of stock (e.g., 1 for common stock: 2 for Class A; 3 for Class B; 4 for Class C; – for new or when-issued, etc.). Also recorded was the par value, which was useful as a quality-control device. Prices were recorded precisely as printed. When there was no sale price, the clerk recorded the bid price, the asked price, or if available, both. Conversions of fractions to decimals and computation of the means of bid and asked prices were later performed on the computer. A staff of approximately forty full-time and part-time clerks worked approximately 6 months to code these price data.

The punching of the partly prepunched cards was completed by one keypunch operator. Rather than check the accuracy of the keypunching alone by means of the usual methods of verification, the quality of both clerical recording of prices and the keypunching was checked by means of independent coding and punching a sample of 5,000 price quotations. We have relied on this sample check of the coding and punching and the consistency checks which will be discussed below.

The accuracy of the recording and punching of data was estimated from this sample, which had 100 clusters of 50 entries each. In all, 133 prices were found to be in error. Of these errors, approximately 79 per cent were of the sort which would be detected by the computer programs and corrected. Thus, approximately 0.5 per cent of the total number of prices would continue to be erroneous after all data-processing. By a coincidence which will not be described, it was found that the original data after correction through data-processing would be 99-44/100% pure. The errors which are not detectable by our data-processing procedures are small and unbiased.

We began with approximately 400,000 prepunched cards. Of these the clerks filled out 380,000, leaving 20,000 blank. In addition, the clerks found about 10,000 prices for which they had no prepunched cards. Many of these additional prices were for stocks which were not in the list obtained from the files of the New York Stock Exchange. The prepunched cards that had either sales or both bid-and-asked prices for issues designated as common stock in the *Bank and Quotation Record* were sorted by identification numbers and date and placed on magnetic tape. This file was called the "main file." All other cards were sorted in the same manner and listed before they were also placed on

[13]Prior to February, 1928, the basic reference was the predecessor of the *Bank and Quotation Record*, the "Bank and Quotation Section" of the *Commercial and Financial Chronicle*.

magnetic tape. This file was the "hold-out file." From this list the decision was made as to which of the stocks among those not specifically designated as common in the *Bank and Quotation Record* were common stocks for our purposes.

Initial Error Detection and Correction. The first correction procedure applied was the detection prices which were invalid on their face. Both files were checked to make certain that fractions were valid, that is, that the numerator was an odd number smaller than the denominator and that the denominator was a power of 2. Where both a bid and an asked price appeared, they were compared to make sure that the bid was less than the asked price. The "mail file" was also checked to make sure that each entry in fact contained either a sale price or both bid and asked prices. The same additional test was applied to the "hold-out file" except that the existence of only a bid price or only an asked price was ignored if the volume of trading was less than one thousand shares for the month. All errors detected by these procedures were corrected.

Collection and Initial Correction of Cash Dividends. Two different methods had to be used for the collection of cash dividends. For the period 1937–60, annual issues of *Moody's* or *Standard and Poor's Dividend Records* or the annual section of *Standard Corporation Records* were used, depending on which was in the University of Chicago Library. For the period 1926–36, *Moody's Quarterly Dividend Record* was used. Since the only known complete file of this last publication is in Moody's New York offices, the data from the earlier period were recorded by trainees working for the research division of Merrill Lynch, Pierce, Fenner & Smith Inc. For each dividend the data described above were recorded, and also recorded was a code to indicate whether the dividend was annual, quarterly, monthly, or extra, etc. As a crosscheck, annual total payments per share were taken from the appropriate *Moody's Manual*. The computer was then used to check the annual totals of the individual dividends taken from the dividend records against the annual totals from *Moody's Manuals*. All discrepancies were resolved.

Other Distributions to Stockholders, Mergers, Exchange Offers, Name Changes, and Reorganizations. After preliminary experiments, data on other distributions to stockholders, mergers, exchange offers, name changes, and reorganizations were taken from the Commerce Clearing House Corporation's *Capital Changes Reporter*.

Nine specially designed printed forms were used for this purpose. After the initial coding and punching, a printed list was made, classified by company name. This list was compared with the original source to make sure that the interpretation of the entries was correct and that capital changes had been collected for each company. For companies for which a list of capital changes did not appear in the *Capital Changes Reporter* or was incomplete, reference was made to a variety of sources including Prentice-Hall's *Capital Adjustments*, *Moody's Manuals*, the *Commercial and Financial Chronicle*, and *Poor's Daily Digest of Corporate News*.

At the same time that the list of capital changes was being checked against the source, the information it contained about mergers and name changes was used in conjunction with our now-corrected information on dates of trading to assign a new number to each new security so as to place it in the appropriate order within the file. When the errors detected by this check had been corrected, the file of capital changes was recorded on magnetic tape and the security identification numbers were placed in the file.

Because there were thirty-nine different kinds of records in this file, a computer program was written which decoded the information to provide a verbal description of each item. These verbal descriptions were then checked against the sources of data, and more errors were detected and corrected.

Tax Status of Distribution of Cash. Since the existence of a special tax status for a cash dividend is generally not shown in any of the dividend records, it was necessary to find out about any special tax status from other sources. We used the appropriate sections of the *Capital Changes Reporter* and *Capital Adjustments* for this purpose. However, we then found that our records of distributions of cash had come from three sources, each of which had only a portion of the information required. We therefore wrote and used computer programs to collate the information about the distributions from the three sources.

Editing and Detecting Additional Errors in the Price-Volume Files. The security numbers were applied to the two files of price and volume information by means of a computer program. Fractions were converted to decimals; bid and asked prices were averaged; the commission applicable to each price of each stock was computed, and the sums of the price and commission were inserted into the file. After correction for prices which had not been assiged new identification numbers with the original program, these files were sorted according to the new number and merged together.

Until this time the computer we used was the UNIVAC I at the University of Chicago. The file of prices then consisted of thirty-three reels of magnetic tape. The University was installing an IBM 7090 computer (which has since been converted to an IBM 7094). At this time the entire file was printed, and the UNIVAC I tapes were copied onto IBM tapes through the data conversion facilities of the Reader's Digest Association.

The error detection program designed to make price data "99-44/100% pure" was now written for the IBM 7074 computer owned by Merrill Lynch, Pierce, Fenner & Smith Inc. and used. The program performed the following tasks:

1. Except for securities we do not regard as common stock, price quotations were placed into two categories:[14]

   a) Sole quotations for a security for a month

   b) One of several quotations for a security for a month

[14] If there were identical quotations, all but one were deleted.

2. Quotations in category 1*b* were further broken down

a) The quotation with the highest product of price and trading volume for the month

b) All other

(If there was no trading the quotation with the highest price was placed in category 2*a*. If there was a tie, the first quotation in the file was placed in category 2*a*.)

3. Quotations in categories 1*a* and 2*a* were further divided into three subcategories each:

a) The magnitudes of the changes from both the preceding quotation in category 1*a* or 2*a* for this security to this quotation and from this quotation to the next such quotation exceed a point plus 10 per cent of the first quotation of the pair and the changes are of opposite sign—the price is "bad"

b) The price is not bad but one of these changes exceeds a point plus 25 per cent—it is "suspicious"

c) The price is neither bad nor suspicious—it is "good"

4. For each security, a one-to-three-line list of time periods for which a quotation falling into categories 1*a* or 2*a* is in the file for each month was prepared.

5. For each gap in the series of price quotations for a security, further action was taken. If the gap was for less than 12 months, dummy records were created. For longer gaps a special report was made.

6. A two-page summary of the price information for each common stock was prepared. For each month, January, 1926–December, 1960, this summary shows the category of the real or dummy quotation and the price.

The output from the program consisted of several files, each on one or more reels of magnetic tape:

1. The main file consisting of all good, suspicious, and duplicate (category 2*b*) quotations, and all quotations which were for other than common stock or which show a volume of trading but no price

2. A "bad and missing" file containing the dummy and bad quotations

3. A suspicious file[15]

4. A "multiple-price" file showing all quotations in category 2

5. A list of deletions

All of these files, except the main file, were printed and examined in order to make corrections and to revise our plans for the next steps in preparing the data. For January, 1926, and December, 1960, it was impossible for the program to call a price bad. Suspicious prices for these months were treated as if they were bad. A sample of the remaining suspicious items was checked. In almost every case the price agreed with a price in the *Bank and Quotation Record*.

For the calculations reported in the text we did not think it necessary to

[15] Files 2 and 3 were sorted by date and company name as well as by security number and date.

correct all the bad and missing items. We checked all quotations classified as bad and missing for the beginning or ending dates of the various periods studied. We further corrected all discrepancies for a number of other dates where, through printer's errors, prices had not been aligned with company names in the *Bank and Quotation Record* (in this case several consecutive prices had been attributed to wrong securities). In addition, all discrepancies were checked for a sample of 115 securities.

Construction of the Combined File. The separate files for prices, cash dividends, and ten groups of other events were rearranged to provide a convenient, common format and were merged together. The arrangement of the data is described in Appendix B. Critical discrepancies, discovered by checking the output of the error detection program just described were corrected and several thousand additions were made by means of special correction programs. This first application of the correction programs altered data for about 16,000 events.

Error Detection Procedure for the Combined File. The data in the combined file had come from several independent sources. Hence it was likely that inconsistencies would be found. For example, when a company's stock is split, this action must generally be approved by a meeting of the stockholders. The *Capital Changes Reporter* states the date the action was approved by the stockholders. Trading in the new (split) shares cannot take place until the stock exchange has been notified of the stockholders' action. Hence, the split may not actually be effective until the next month or even later. Thus it was necessary to search the file for further inconsistencies in the data.

A fairly elaborate program for the IBM 7094 was used for this purpose. This program, which we have called "Filter King," reports the following kinds of inconsistencies:

1. Some or all of the events for a security may be misplaced within the file if

a) Price quotations are missing for more than 12 consecutive months

b) Price quotations are available on the Exchange after the date at which we thought the stock had been exchanged through a merger or after the date for which we had collected an over-the-counter price

c) The information for a security was above that of a company whose stockholders received this security through merger or other distribution

2. Prices or capital changes may have been misrecorded if a price quotation is inconsistent with previous and/or subsequent quotations, adjusted for dividends, stock dividends, rights, etc.

The program also performs other functions: (1) If a stock is being traded with a stock dividend on and also on a when-issued basis, the program chooses the price consistent with the date of the stock dividend. (2) Visual reference to the information in the file is not convenient. When printed, the file takes about 22,000 pages of 11 × 15-inch paper. Therefore, Filter King produces a 2,500-page summary of the file. This summary contains the most recent name and the identification number of each security and part of the information about each event, that is, for prices, the year and month, whether the price is consistent with previous and subsequent prices and the price itself; for other events, the year and month of the ex date, the kind of event, and the most useful number pertaining to the event (the amount of a dividend; the size of a stock dividend, split, or reverse split; the value of one right; the number of shares received in a spin-off or merger); but other information is omitted.

Filter King was used twice to test the entire file before we made the computations reported here. Between the first and second runs about 13,000 changes were made in the file and about 4,000 changes after the second run. All possible inconsistencies in the arrangement of the file were investigated and action taken to correct them. All inconsistencies in price quotations which were near capital changes in time or which suggested the existence of an unrecorded capital change were also investigated. All inconsistent or missing price quotations for dates of sale or purchase of a portfolio were checked again.

Other inconsistencies were left until later. We are now investigating and correcting them. The process will be completed about the time this article is published.

Calculation of Rate of Return

In this section we describe the methods we have used to calculate rates of return. Since the programs for calculating rates of return with and without reinvestment of dividends use nearly identical procedures, we shall first describe the calculation of rates of return with reinvestment of dividends and then indicate the changes required to compute rates of return without reinvestment.

The calculation of average rate of return for all listed common stocks over a particular period of time requires that we know how much was invested at the initial date and what the value of the portfolio is at the final date. Since our investor is required to pay federal income taxes, we must also know what the cost basis for tax purposes (or simply "basis") is. The file is arranged by security and chronologically within each security. The computer program for calculating rate of return with reinvestment of dividends selects one item from the file at a time and then takes appropriate action. During the course of the computation several additional files are maintained internally:

1. A file of regular income tax rates—one entry for each month
2. A file of capital gains tax rates—one entry for each month
3. A file showing the current number of shares held, the cost of these shares, and the number of dollars available for reinvestment at the end of the current month. All of these items pertain to the security currently under consideration
4. A deferred file which shows the effective date, that is, payment date, of a distribution to stock holders or other capital change and its effect on the number of shares held, the cost of shares, and/or funds available for reinvestment. An entry is made in this file when the ex date for some distribution occurs and is maintained until the distribution date

5. A cross-reference file which contains the identification number of a security distributed as a result of a spin-off or merger, the identification of the security whose holders receive something as a result of a spin-off or merger, the effective date of the spin-off or merger, and the number of shares, their cost basis, and the amount of funds received. An entry is made in this file whenever a spin-off or merger occurs and is maintained until the program is processing information for the security received

6. A file showing the amount to be reinvested in each security each month through the proceeds of sales of securities over the counter

7. The running total of the initial investment in securities

8. Running totals of the value of the investment in each security at the ending date of the study. Three such totals are maintained: one showing the market value of the portfolio, one showing net proceeds from the sale of the portfolio before payment of the capital gains taxes, and one showing net proceeds after payment of capital gains taxes

An event may directly affect the number of shares held, the cost basis, or the funds available for investment. In general the computations are performed as follows: when the first event for a stock is read into the computer, the number of shares, basis, and funds are set to zero. When the price for a beginning date of the study comes up, we add $1,000 to the initial investment, place $1,000 into the basis, and divide $1,000 by the price plus commission to compute the number of shares held initially.[16]

Most dividends and other distributions to stockholders are based on the number of shares held on the day prior to the ex-dividend date and not on the number of shares held on the distribution date. Therefore dividends, etc., have been placed in the file according to their ex dates. When a new event is perceived, its key date is noted, the deferred file is scanned, and processing of all items in the deferred file with effective dates less than the current key date is completed. Completion of the processing requires that the change in shares be added to the current number of shares held, change in basis be added to the current basis, change in funds available be added to current funds available, and the entry in the deferred file be destroyed.

When a price is found, the next step is to determine whether the price is for an ending date of the study. If it is for an ending date, processing of all remaining items in the deferred file is completed, and the appropriate computation of the value of the interest in the security is made for each of the three assumptions about valuation of the proceeds and added to the running totals. If the price is not for an ending date for the study, the funds currently available are added to the current basis, funds are divided by price plus commission and the quotient added to the current number of shares, and funds are set to zero.

When a dividend is perceived, a new item is created in the deferred file. If

[16]If the company has more than one common stock at the beginning date, the $1,000 is divided equally among the common stock issues, i.e., if there are two common stocks the initial investment in each stock is $500.

the dividend is a cash dividend, current number of shares is multiplied by the amount of the dividend per share, the product is reduced by the amount of tax liability and placed in "change in funds." If the dividend causes a change in basis, the change in basis is also recorded.

When a stock dividend, split, or reverse split is perceived, a new item in the deferred file is created and the change in the number of shares held is recorded.

Perception of the description of a distribution of subscription rights requires the following action. If the subscription rights are for the same security, it is assumed that enough rights are sold so that after taxes the remaining rights may be exercised. The changes in number of shares held and basis are added to current number of shares and current basis. If the rights are not to the same security, they are treated as though they were dividends with the appropriate tax status and the current basis and funds currently available are adjusted.

When a spin-off occurs, both a deferred item and an item in the cross-reference file are created. The deferred item shows the change in basis. The cross-reference item shows the number of shares to be received after allowing for taxes and cost basis of these shares.

When a merger is perceived, processing of all items in the deferred file is completed and a cross-reference item is created. The cross-reference item shows the after-tax figures for the number of shares received, basis, and the funds received in exchange for the old stock. To funds in the cross-reference item, currently available funds are added. Current shares, basis, and funds are then reduced to zero.

The notation of the receipt of shares and/or funds as the result of a spin-off by another security or the merger of another security causes the cross-reference file to be searched. When the appropriate item is found, the shares, basis, and funds shown there are added to the respective current items; and the item in the cross-reference file is destroyed.

When an over-the-counter price is perceived, processing of the remaining items in the deferred file is completed; the current number of shares is multiplied by the over-the-counter price; and the product, adjusted for tax liability on credit, is added to current funds. The current funds are then added to the file of funds received through over-the-counter sales.

When the end of the file has been reached and the computations for the last security completed, the discount rates on investment are calculated. The calculation is performed by finding the ratio of the value of the portfolio or cash at the ending date by the total initial investment, taking the natural logarithm of the ratio and dividing it by the length of the period to find the rate of return, compounding continuously. This rate is then converted to the equivalent rate of return, compounding annually.[17]

[17]The actual computer program performs all of the calculations reported in Table 1 in one pass of the file. It can compute results for six starting dates, twelve ending dates, and three sets of tax rates (one of which is zero) in about 22 minutes.

Rates of Return Without Reinvestment of Dividends. The calculation of rates of return without reinvestment of dividends required several changes in the computer program. The deferred file must also show the amount of cash to be paid out. A file showing the amount of cash paid out each month must be maintained. Portions of the subprograms for handling cash dividends other than partial liquidations, rights to subscribe to other securities, mergers, and several housekeeping functions had to be altered to maintain the file of cash paid out. The major change, however, was in the actual computation of rate of return. The rate of return is the discount rate which makes the present value of the income stream purchased equal to the initial investment in the portfolio. This income stream consists of dividends received each month (assumed to be at midmonth) and the final value of the portfolio.

A new method of making successive approximations was used. This method requires about five to ten iterations, depending on the length of the period and the magnitude of the rate, to compute the rate of return to more than seven significant decimal digits. The program for making the computations shown in Table 2 required a total of 25 minutes on the IBM 7094.

33

A Simplified Model for Portfolio Analysis*

William F. Sharp †

This paper describes the advantages of using a particular model of the relationships among securities for practical applications of the Markowitz portfolio analysis technique. A computer program has been developed to take full advantage of the model: 2,000 securities can be analyzed at an extremely low cost—as little as 2% of that associated with standard quadratic programming codes. Moreover, preliminary evidence suggests that the relatively few parameters used by the model can lead to very nearly the same results obtained with much larger sets of relationships among securities. The possibility of low-cost analysis, coupled with a likelihood that a relatively small amount of information need be sacrificed make the model an attractive candidate for initial practical applications of the Markowitz technique.

1. INTRODUCTION

Markowitz has suggested that the process of portfolio selection be approached by (1) making probabilistic estimates of the future performances of securities, (2) analyzing those estimates to determine an *efficient set* of portfolios and (3) selecting from that set the portfolios best suited to the investor's preferences [1, 2, 3]. This paper extends Markowitz' work on the second of these three stages—*portfolio analysis*. The preliminary sections state the problem in its general form and describe Markowitz' solution technique. The remainder of the paper presents a simplified model of the relationships among securities, indicates the manner in which it allows the portfolio analysis problem to be simplified, and provides evidence on the costs as well as the desirability of using the model for practical applications of the Markowitz technique.

*From *Management Science*, Vol. 9, No. 2 (January 1963), pp. 277–293. Reprinted by permission of *Management Science*.

†The author wishes to express his appreciation for the cooperation of the staffs of both the Western Data Processing Center at UCLA and the Pacific Northwest Research Computer Laboratory at the University of Washington where the program was tested. His greatest debt, however, is to Dr. Harry M. Markowitz of the RAND Corporation, with whom he was privileged to have a number of stimulating conversations during the past year. It is no longer possible to segregate the ideas in this paper into those which were his, those which were the author's, and those which were developed jointly. Suffice it to say that the only accomplishments which are unquestionably the property of the author are those of authorship—first of the computer program and then of this article.

2. THE PORTFOLIO ANALYSIS PROBLEM

A security analyst has provided the following predictions concerning the future returns from each of N securities:

$E_i \equiv$ the expected value of R_i (the return from security i)
C_{i1} through C_{in}; C_{ij} represents the covariance between R_i and R_j (as usual, when $i = j$ the figure is the variance of R_i)

The portfolio analysis problem is as follows. Given such a set of predictions, determine the set of *efficient portfolios*; a portfolio is efficient if none other gives either (a) a higher expected return and the same variance of return or (b) a lower variance of return and the same expected return.

Let X_i represent the proportion of a portfolio invested in security i. Then the expected return (E) and variance of return (V) of any portfolio can be expressed in terms of (a) the basic data (E_i-values and C_{ij}-values) and (b) the amounts invested in various securities:

$$E = \sum_i X_i E_i$$

$$V = \sum_i \sum_j X_i X_j C_{ij}$$

Consider an objective function of the form:

$$\phi = \lambda E - V$$

$$= \lambda \sum_i X_i E_i - \sum_i \sum_j X_i X_j C_{ij}$$

Given a set of values for the parameters (λ, E_i's and C_{ij}'s), the value of ϕ can be changed by varying the X_i values as desired, as long as two basic restrictions are observed:

1. The entire portfolio must be invested:[1]

$$\sum_i X_i = 1$$

and 2. no security may be held in negative quantities:[2]

$$X_i \geqslant 0 \text{ for all } i$$

[1] Since cash can be included as one of the securities (explicitly or implicitly) this assumption need cause no lack of realism.

[2] This is the standard formulation. Cases in which short sales are allowed require a different approach.

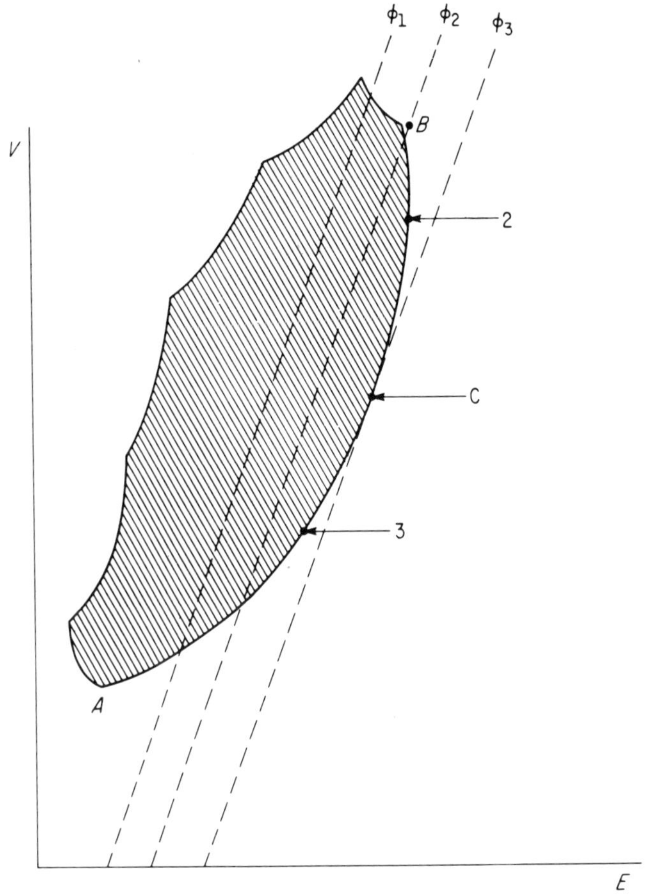

Fig. 1

A portfolio is described by the proportions invested in various securities–in our notation by the values of X_i. For each set of admissable values of the X_i variables there is a corresponding predicted combination of E and V and thus of ϕ. Figure 1 illustrates this relationship for a particular value of λ. The line ϕ_1 shows the combinations of E and V which give $\phi = \phi_1$, where $\phi = \lambda_k E - V$; the other lines refer to larger values of $\psi(\psi_3 > \phi_2 > \phi_1)$. Of all possible portfolios, one will maximize the value of ϕ;[3] in Fig. 1 it is portfolio C. The relationship between this solution and the portfolio analysis problem is obvious. The E, V combination obtained will be on the boundary of the set of attainable combainations; moreover, the objective function will be tangent to the set at that point. Since this function is of the form

$$\phi = \lambda E - V$$

[3]This fact is crucial to the critical line computing procedure described in the next section.

the slope of the boundary at the point must be λ; thus, by varying λ from $+\infty$ to 0, every solution of the portfolio analysis problem can be obtained.

For any given value of λ the problem described in this section requires the maximization of a quadratic function, ϕ (which is a function of X_i, X_i^2, and X_iX_j terms) subject to a linear constraint ($\Sigma_i X_i = 1$), with the variables restricted to non-negative values. A number of techniques have been developed to solve such *quadratic programming problems.* The critical line method, developed by Markowitz in conjunction with his work on portfolio analysis, is particularly suited to this problem and was used in the program described in this paper.

3. THE CRITICAL LINE METHOD

Two important characteristics of the set of efficient portfolios make systematic solution of the portfolio analysis problem relatively straightforward. The first concerns the relationships among portfolios. Any set of efficient portfolios can be described in terms of a smaller set of *corner portfolios*. Any point on the E, V curve (other than the points associated with corner portfolios) can be obtained with a portfolio constructed by dividing the total investment between the two adjacent corner portfolios. For example, the portfolio which gives E, V combination C in Fig. 1 might be some linear combination of the two corner portfolios with E, V combinations shown by points 2 and 3. This characteristic allows the analyst to restrict his attention to corner portfolios rather than the complete set of efficient portfolios; the latter can be readily derived from the former.

The second characteristic of the solution concerns the relationships among corner portfolios. Two corner portfolios which are adjacent on the E, V curve are related in the following manner: one portfolio will contain either (1) all the securities which appear in the other, plus one additional security or (2) all but one of the securities which appear in the other. Thus in moving down the E, V curve from one corner portfolio to the next, the quantities of the securities in efficient portfolios will vary until either one drops out of the portfolio or another enters. The point at which a change takes place marks a new corner portfolio.

The major steps in the critical line method for solving the portfolio analysis problem are:

1. The corner portfolio with $\lambda = \infty$ is determined. It is composed entirely of the one security with the highest expected return.[4]
2. Relationships between (a) the amounts of the various securities contained in efficient portfolios and (b) the value of λ are computed. It is possible to derive such relationships for any section of the E, V curve

[4] In the event that two or more of the securities have the same (highest) expected return, the first efficient portfolio is the combination of such securities with the lowest variance.

between adjacent corner portfolios. The relationships which apply to one section of the curve will not, however, apply to any other section.

3. Using the relationships computed in (2), each security is examined to determine the value of λ at which a change in the securities included in the portfolio would come about:
   a. securities presently in the portfolio are examined to determine the value of λ at which they would drop out, and
   b. securities not presently in the portfolio are examined to determine the value of λ at which they would enter the portfolio.
4. The next largest value of λ at which a security either enters or drops out of the portfolio is determined. This indicates the location of the next corner portfolio.
5. The composition of the new corner portfolio is computed, using the relationships derived in (2). However, since these relationships held only for the section of the curve between this corner portfolio and the preceding one, the solution process can only continue if new relationships are derived. The method thus returns to step (2) unless $\lambda = 0$, in which case the analysis is complete.

The amount of computation required to complete a portfolio analysis using this method is related to the following factors:

1. The number of securities analyzed

   This will affect the extent of the computation in step (2) and the number of computations in step (3).
2. The number of corner portfolios

   Steps (2) through (5) must be repeated once to find each corner portfolio.
3. The complexity of the variance-covariance matrix

   Step (2) requires a matrix be inverted and must be repeated once for each corner portfolio.

The amount of computer memory space required to perform a portfolio analysis will depend primarily on the size of the variance-covariance matrix. In the standard case, if N securities are analyzed this matrix will have ½ $(N^2 + N)$ elements.

4. THE DIAGONAL MODEL

Portfolio analysis requires a large number of comparisons; obviously the practical application of the technique can be greatly facilitated by a set of assumptions which reduces the computational task involved in such comparisons. One such set of assumptions (to be called the diagonal model) is described in this article. This model has two virtues: it is one of the simplest which can be constructed without assuming away the existence of interrelationships among securities and there is considerable evidence that it can capture a large part of such interrelationships.

The major characteristic of the diagonal model is the assumption that the returns of various securities are related only through common relationships with some basic underlying factor. The return from any security is determined solely by random factors and this single outside element; more explicitly:

$$R_i = A_i + B_i I + C_i$$

where A_i and B_i are parameters, C_i is a random variable with an expected value of zero and variance Q_i, and I is the level of some index. The index, I, may be the level of the stock market as a whole, the Gross National Product, some price index or any other factor thought to be the most important single influence on the returns from securities. The future level of I is determined in part by random factors:

$$I = A_{n+1} + C_{n+1}$$

where A_{n+1} is a parameter and C_{n+1} is a random variable with an expected value of zero and a variance of Q_{n+1}. It is assumed that the covariance between C_i and C_j is zero for all values of i and j $(i \neq j)$.

Figure 2 provides a graphical representation of the model. A_i and B_i serve to locate the line which relates the expected value of R_i to the level of I. Q_i indicates the variance of R_i around the expected relationship (this variance is assumed to be the same at each point along the line). Finally, A_{n+1} indicates the expected value of I and Q_{n+1} the variance around that expected value.

The diagonal model requires the following predictions from a security analyst:

1) values of A_i, B_i and Q_i for each of N securities
2) values of A_{n+1} and Q_{n+1} for the index I.

The number of estimates required from the analyst is thus greatly reduced: from 5,150 to 302 for an analysis of 100 securities and from 2,003,000 to 6,002 for an analysis of 2,000 securities.

Once the parameters of the diagonal model have been specified all the inputs required for the standard portfolio analysis problem can be derived. The relationships are:

$$E_i = A_i + B_i(A_{n+1})$$

$$V_i = (B_i)^2\,(Q_{n+1}) + Q_i$$

$$C = (B_i)\,(B_j)\,(Q_{n+1})$$

A portfolio analysis could be performed by obtaining the values required by the diagonal model, calculating from them the full set of data required for the standard portfolio analysis problem and then performing the analysis with the derived values. However, additional advantages can be obtained if the portfolio

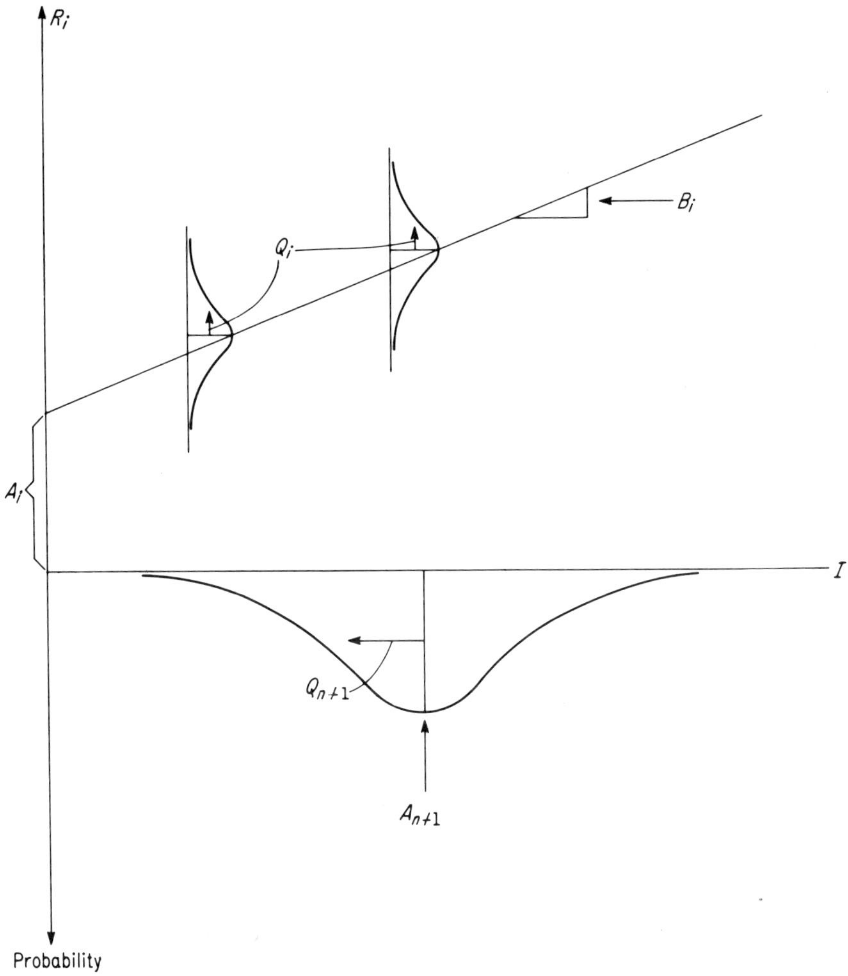

Fig. 2

analysis problem is restated directly in terms of the parameters of the diagonal model. The following section describes the manner in which such a restatement can be performed.

5. THE ANALOGUE

The return from a portfolio is the weighted average of the returns from its component securities:

$$R_p = \sum_{i=1}^{N} X_i R_i$$

The contribution of each security to the total return of a portfolio is simply X_iR_i or, under the assumptions of the diagonal model:

$$X_i(A_i + B_iI + C_i)$$

The total contribution of a security to the return of the portfolio can be broken into two components: (1) an investment in the "basic characteristics" of the security in question and (2) an "investment" in the index:

(1) $$X_i(A_i + B_iI + C_i) = X_i(A_i + C_i)$$

(2) $$+ X_iB_iI$$

The return of a portfolio can be considered to be the result of (1) a series of investments in N "basic securities" and (2) an investment in the index:

$$R_p = \sum_{i=1}^{N} X_i(A_i + C_i) + \left\{ \sum_{i=1}^{N} X_iB_i \right\} I$$

Defining X_{n+1} as the weighted average responsiveness of R_p to the level of I:

$$X_{n+1} \equiv \sum_{i=1}^{N} X_iB_i$$

and substituting this variable and the formula for the determinants of I, we obtain:

$$\begin{aligned} R_p &= \sum_{i=1}^{N} X_i(A_i + C_i) + X_{n+1}(A_{n+1} + C_{n+1}) \\ &= \sum_{i=1}^{N+1} X_i(A_i + C_i) \end{aligned}$$

The expected return of a portfolio is thus:

$$E = \sum_{i=1}^{N+1} X_iA_i$$

while the variance is:[5]

$$V = \sum_{i=1}^{N+1} X_i^2 Q_i$$

This formulation indicates the reason for the use of the parameters A_{n+1} and Q_{n+1} to describe the expected value and variance of the future value of I. It also indicates the reason for calling this the "diagonal model". The variance-covariance matrix, which is full when N securities are considered, can be expressed as a matrix with non-zero elements only along the diagonal by including an $(n + 1)$st security defined as indicated. This vastly reduces the

[5] Recall that the diagonal model assumes cov $(C_i\,C_j) = 0$ for all i and j $(i \neq j)$.

number of computations required to solve the portfolio analysis problem (primarily in step 2 of the critical line method, when the variance-covariance matrix must be inverted) and allows the problem to be stated directly in terms of the basic parameters of the diagonal model:

Maximize: $\lambda E - V$

Where:

$$E = \sum_{i=1}^{N+1} X_i A_i$$

$$V = \sum_{i=1}^{N+1} X_i^2 Q_i$$

Subject to: $X_i \geqslant 0$ for all i from 1 to N

$$\sum_{i=1}^{N} X_i = 1$$

$$\sum_{i=1}^{N} X_i B_i = X_{n+1}$$

6. THE DIAGONAL MODEL PORTFOLIO ANALYSIS CODE

As indicated in the previous section, if the portfolio analysis problem is expressed in terms of the basic parameters of the diagonal model, computing time and memory space required for solution can be greatly reduced. This section describes a machine code, written in the FØRTRAN language, which takes full advantage of the characteristics of the diagonal model. It uses the critical line method to solve the problem stated in the previous section.

The computing time required by the diagonal code is considerably smaller than that required by standard quadratic programming codes. The RAND QP code[6] required 33 minutes to solve a 100-security example on an IBM 7090 computer; the same problem was solved in 30 seconds with the diagonal code. Moreover, the reduced storage requirements allow many more securities to be analyzed: with the IBM 709 or 7090 the RAND QP code can be used for no more than 249 securities, while the diagonal code can analyze up to 2,000 securities.

Although the diagonal code allows the total computing time to be greatly reduced, the cost of a large analysis is still far from insignificant. Thus there is every incentive to limit the computations to those essential for the final selection of a portfolio. By taking into account the possibilities of borrowing and lending money, the diagonal code restricts the computations to those

[6]The program is described in [4]. Several alternative quadratic programming codes are available. A recent code, developed by IBM, which uses the critical line method is likely to prove considerably more efficient for the portfolio analysis problem. The RAND code is used for comparison since it is the only standard program with which the author has had experience.

absolutely necessary for determination of the final set of efficient portfolios. The importance of these alternatives, their effect on the portfolio analysis problem and the manner in which they are taken into account in the diagonal code are described in the remainder of this section.

A. The "Lending Portfolio"

There is some interest rate (r_l) at which money can be lent with virtual assurance that both principal and interest will be returned; at the least, money can be buried in the ground ($r_l = 0$). Such an alternative could be included as one possible security ($A_i = 1 + r_l$, $B_i = 0$, $Q_i = 0$) but this would necessitate some needless computation.[7] In order to minimize computing time, lending at some pure interest rate is taken into account explicitly in the diagonal code.

The relationship between lending and efficient portfolios can best be seen in terms of an E, σ curve showing the combinations of expected return and standard deviation of return ($= \sqrt{V}$) associated with efficient portfolios. Such a curve is shown in Fig. 3 (FBCG); point A indicates the E, σ combination attained if all funds are lent. The relationship between lending money and purchasing portfolios can be illustrated with the portfolio which has the E, σ combination shown by point Z. Consider a portfolio with X_z invested in portfolio Z and the remainder $(1 - X_z)$ lent at the rate r_l. The expected return from such a portfolio would be:

$$E = X_z E_z + (1 - X_z)(1 + r_l)$$

and the variance of return would be:

$$V = X_z^2 V_z + (1 - X_z)^2 V_l + 2X_z(1 - X_z)(\text{cov}_{zl})$$

But, since V_l and cov_{zl} are both zero:

$$V = X_z^2 V_z$$

and the standard deviation of return is:

$$\sigma = X_z \sigma_z$$

Since both E and σ are linear functions of X_z, the E, σ combinations of all portfolios made up of portfolio Z plus lending must lie on a straight line connecting points Z and A. In general, by splitting his investment between a portfolio and lending, an investor can attain any E, σ combination on the line connecting the E, σ combinations of the two components.

[7]Actually, the diagonal code cannot accept non-positive values of Q_i; thus if the lending alternative is to be included as simply another security, it must be assigned a very small value of Q_i. This procedure will give virtually the correct solution but is inefficient.

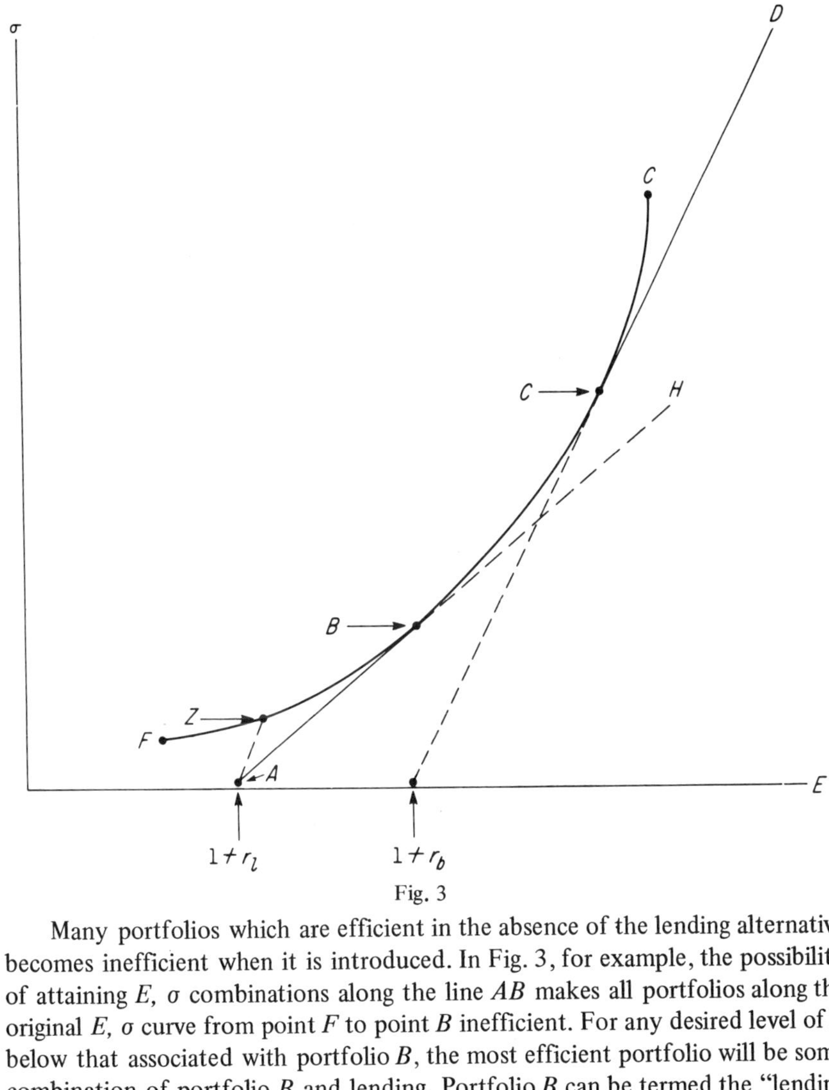

Fig. 3

Many portfolios which are efficient in the absence of the lending alternative becomes inefficient when it is introduced. In Fig. 3, for example, the possibility of attaining E, σ combinations along the line AB makes all portfolios along the original E, σ curve from point F to point B inefficient. For any desired level of E below that associated with portfolio B, the most efficient portfolio will be some combination of portfolio B and lending. Portfolio B can be termed the "lending portfolio" since it is the appropriate portfolio whenever some of the investor's funds are to be lent at the rate r_l. This portfolio can be found readily once the E, σ curve is known. It lies at the point on the curve at which a ray from ($E = 1 + r_l$, $\sigma = 0$) is tangent to the curve. If the E, σ curve is not known in its entirety it is still possible to determine whether or not a particular portfolio is the lending portfolio by computing the rate of interest which *would* make the portfolio in question the lending portfolio. For example, the rate of interest associated in this manner with portfolio C is r_b, found by extending a tangent to the curve down to the E-axis. The diagonal code computes such a rate of interest for each corner portfolio as the analysis proceeds; when it falls below the previously stated lending rate the code computes the composition of the lending portfolio and terminates the analysis.

B. The "Borrowing Portfolio"

In some cases an investor may be able to borrow funds in order to purchase even greater amounts of a portfolio than his own funds will allow. If the appropriate rate of such borrowing were r_b, illustrated in Fig. 3, the E, σ combinations attainable by purchasing portfolio C with both the investor's funds and with borrowed funds would lie along the line CD, depending on the amount borrowed. Inclusion of the borrowing alternative makes certain portfolios inefficient which are efficient in the absence of the alternative; in this case the affected portfolios are those with E, σ combinations along the segment of the original E, σ curve from C to G. Just as there is a single appropriate portfolio if any lending is contemplated, there is a single appropriate portfolio if borrowing is contemplated. This "borrowing portfolio" is related to the rate of interest at which funds can be borrowed in exactly the same manner as the "lending portfolio" is related to the rate at which funds can be lent.

The diagonal code does not take account of the borrowing alternative in the manner used for the lending alternative since it is necessary to compute all previous corner portfolios in order to derive the portion of the E, σ curve below the borrowing portfolio. For this reason all computations required to derive the full E, σ curve above the lending portfolio must be made. However, the code does allow the user to specify the rate of interest at which funds can be borrowed. If this alternative is chosen, none of the corner portfolios which will be inefficient when borrowing is considered will be printed. Since as much as 65% of the total computer time can be spent recording (on tape) the results of the analysis this is not an insignificant saving.

7. THE COST OF PORTFOLIO ANALYSIS WITH THE DIAGONAL CODE

The total time (and thus cost) required to perform a portfolio analysis with the diagonal code will depend upon the number of securities analyzed, the number of corner portfolios and, to some extent, the composition of the corner portfolios. A formula which gives quite an accurate estimate of the time required to perform an analysis on an IBM 709 computer was obtained by analyzing a series of runs during which the time required to complete each major segment of the program was recorded. The approximate time required for the analysis will be:[8]

$$\text{Number of seconds} = .6 + .114 \times \text{number of securities analyzed}$$

[8]The computations in this section are based on the assumption that no corner portfolios prior to the lending portfolio are printed. If the analyst chooses to print all preceding portfolios, the estimates given in this section should be multiplied by 2.9; intermediate cases can be estimated by interpolation.

+ .54 X number of corner portfolios
+ .0024 X number of securities analyzed X number of corner portfolios.

Unfortunately only the number of securities analyzed is known before the analysis is begun. In order to estimate the cost of portfolio analysis before it is performed, some relationship between the number of corner portfolios and the number of securities analyzed must be assumed. Since no theoretical relationship can be derived and since the total number of corner portfolios could be several times the number of securities analyzed, it seemed desirable to obtain some crude notion of the typical relationship when "reasonable" inputs are used. To accomplish this, a series of portfolio analyses was performed using inputs generated by a Monte Carlo model.

Data were gathered on the annual returns during the period 1940–1951 for 96 industrial common stocks chosen randomly from the New York Stock Exchange. The returns of each security were then related to the level of a stock market index and estimates of the parameters of the diagonal model obtained. These parameters were assumed to be samples from a population of A_i, B_i and Q_i triplets related as follows:

$$A_i = \overline{A} + r_1$$

$$B_i = \overline{B} + \psi A_i + r_2$$

$$Q_i = \overline{Q} + \theta A_i + \gamma B_i + r_3$$

where r_1, r_2 and r_3 are random variables with zero means. Estimates for the parameters of these three equations were obtained by regression analysis and estimates of the variances of the random variables determined.[9] With this information the characteristics of any desired number of securities could be generated. A random number generator was used to select a value for A_i; this value, together with an additional random number determined the value of B_i; the value of Q_i was then determined with a third random number and the previously obtained values of A_i and B_i.

Figure 4 shows the relationship between the number of securities analyzed and the number of corner portfolios with interest rates greater than 3% (an approximation to the "lending rate"). Rather than perform a sophisticated analysis of these data, several lines have been used to bracket the results in various ways. These will be used subsequently as extreme cases, on the presumption that most practical cases will lie within these extremes (but with no presumption that these limits will never be exceeded). Curve A indicates the average relationship between the number of portfolios and the number of

[9] The random variables were considered normally distributed; in one case, to better approximate the data, two variances were used for the distribution–one for the portion above the mean and another for the portion below the mean.

securities: average $(N_p/N_s) = .37$. Curve H_1 indicates the highest such relationship: maximum $(N_p/N_s) = .63$; the line L_1 indicates the lowest: minimum $(N_p/N_s) = .24$. The other two curves, H_2 and L_2, indicate respectively the maximum deviation above (155) and below (173) the number of corner portfolios indicated by the average relationship $N_p = .37\, N_s$.

In Fig. 5 the total time required for a portfolio analysis is related to the number of securities analyzed under various assumptions about the relationship between the number of corner portfolios and the number of securities analyzed. Each of the curves shown in Fig. 5 is based on the corresponding curve in Fig. 4; for example, curve A in Fig. 5 indicates the relationship between total time and number of securities analyzed on the assumption that the relationship between

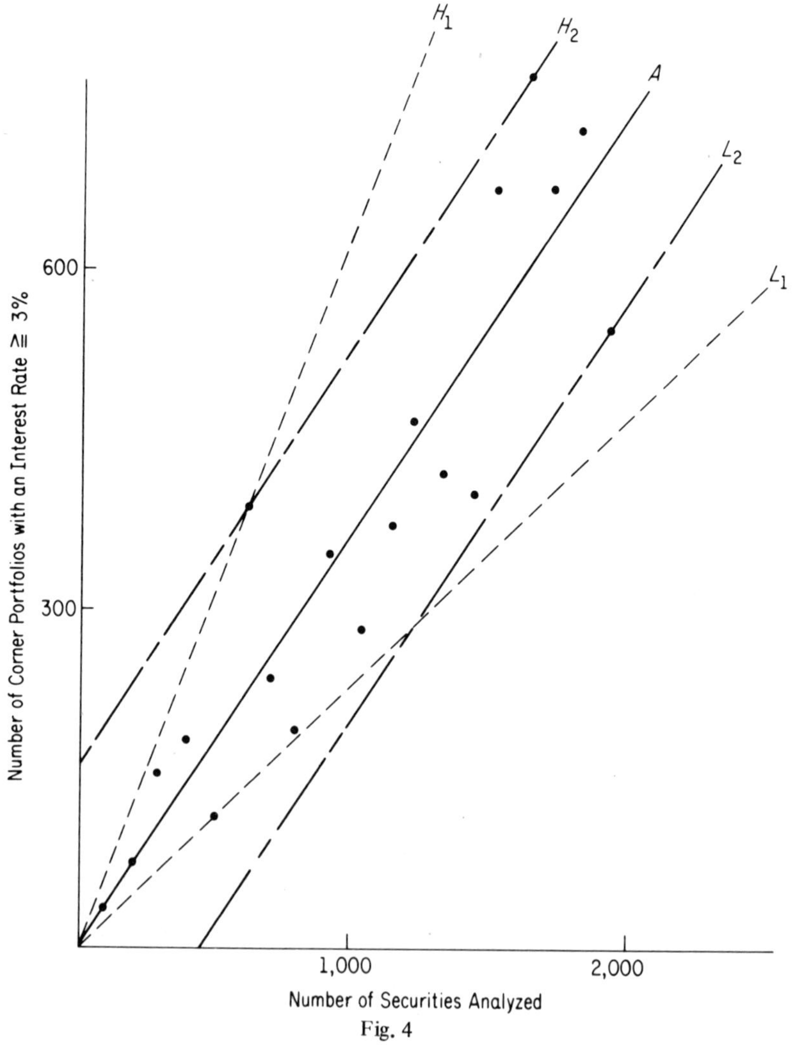

Fig. 4

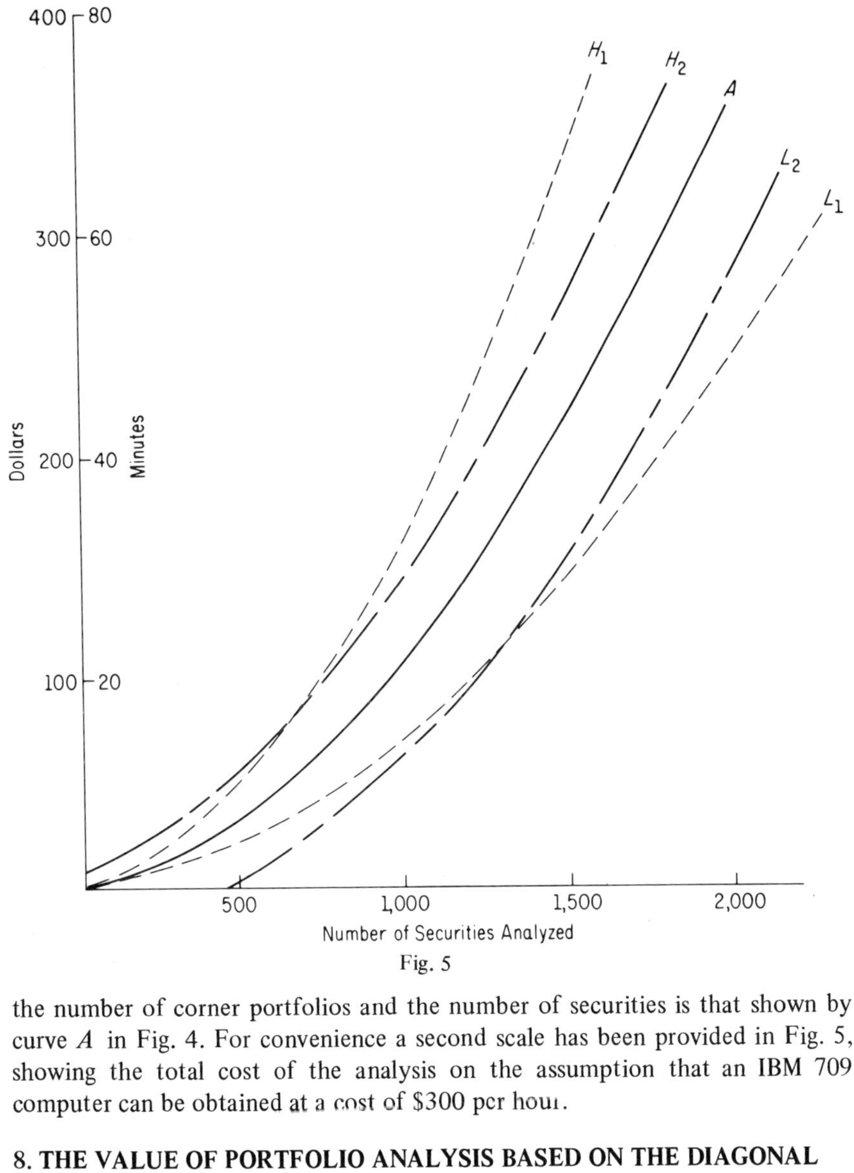

Fig. 5

the number of corner portfolios and the number of securities is that shown by curve A in Fig. 4. For convenience a second scale has been provided in Fig. 5, showing the total cost of the analysis on the assumption that an IBM 709 computer can be obtained at a cost of $300 per hour.

8. THE VALUE OF PORTFOLIO ANALYSIS BASED ON THE DIAGONAL MODEL

The assumptions of the diagonal model lie near one end of the spectrum of possible assumptions about the relationships among securities. The model's extreme simplicity enables the investigator to perform a portfolio analysis at a very small cost, as we have shown. However, it is entirely possible that this simplicity so restricts the security analyst in making his predictions that the value of the resulting portfolio analysis is also very small.

In order to estimate the ability of the diagonal model to summarize information concerning the performance of securities a simple test was performed. Twenty securities were chosen randomly from the New York Stock Exchange and their performance during the period 1940–1951 used to obtain two sets of data: (1) the actual mean returns, variances of returns and covariances of returns during the period and (2) the parameters of the diagonal model, estimated by regression techniques from the performance of the securities during the period. A portfolio analysis was then performed on each set of data. The results are summarized in Fig. 6a and 6b. Each security which entered any of the efficient portfolios in significant amounts is represented by a particular type of line; the height of each line above any given value of E indicates the percentage of the efficient portfolio with that particular E composed of the security in question. The two figures thus indicate the compositions of all the efficient portfolios chosen from the analysis of the historical data (Fig. 6b) and the compositions of all the portfolios chosen from the analysis of the parameters of the diagonal model (Fig. 6a). The similarity of the two figures indicates that the 62 parameters of the diagonal model were able to capture a great deal of the information contained in the complete set of 230 historical relationships. An additional test, using a second set of 20 securities, gave similar results.

These results are, of course, far too fragmentary to be considered conclusive but they do suggest that the diagonal model may be able to represent the

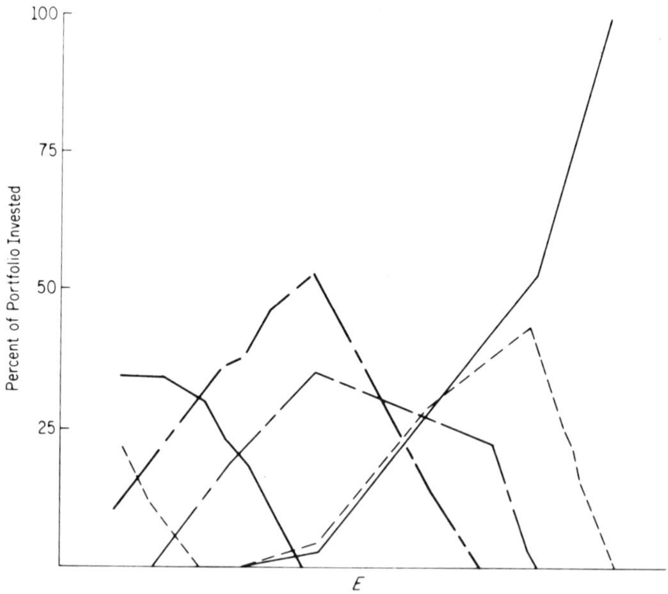

Fig. 6a Composition of efficient portfolios derived from the analysis of the parameters of the diagonal model.

relationships among securities rather well and thus that the value of portfolio analyses based on the model will exceed their rather nominal cost. For these reasons it appears to be an excellent choice for the initial practical applications of the Markowitz technique.

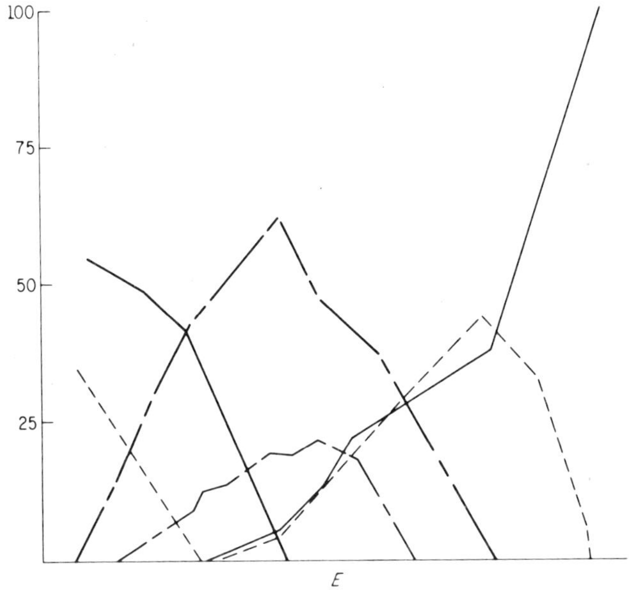

Fig. 6b. Composition of efficient portfolios derived from the analysis of historical data.

REFERENCES

1. Harry M. Markowitz. *Portfolio Selection, Efficient Diversification of Investments.* New York: John Wiley and Sons, Inc., 1959.
2. Harry M. Markowitz. "Portfolio Selection," *The Journal of Finance,* Vol. 12 (March 1952), 77–91.
3. Harry M. Markowitz. "The Optimization of a Quadratic Function Subject to Linear Constraints," *Naval Research Logistics Quarterly,* Vol. 3 (March and June 1956), 111–133.
4. Philip Wolfe. "The Simplex Method for Quadratic Programming," *Econometrica,* Vol. 27 (July 1959), 382–398.

34

An Expected Gain—Confidence Limit Criterion for Portfolio Selection*

William J. Baumol †

A new efficiency criterion is proposed for the Markowitz portfolio selection approach. It is shown that the use of standard deviation as a measure of risk in the original Markowitz analysis and elsewhere in economic theory is sometimes unreasonable. An Investment with a relatively high standard deviation (σ) will be relatively safe if its expected value (E) is sufficiently high. For the net result may be a high expected floor, $E - K\sigma$, beneath the future value of the investment (where K is some constant). The revised efficient set is shown to eliminate paradoxical cases arising from the Markowitz calculation. It also simplifies the task left to the investor. For it yields a smaller efficient set (which is a subset of the Markowitz efficient set) and therefore reduces the range of alternatives from among which the investor must still select his portfolio. The proposed criterion may also be somewhat more easily understood by the nonprofessional.

The economic literature has frequently sought to explain[1] and set up norms[2] for the selection of portfolios of stocks, bonds and other securities in terms of two standard statistical concepts which are taken to indicate the value of the portfolio to the investor. These variables are the expected return, E, representing the most likely net yield of the investment, and the standard deviation of that return, σ, representing, in some sense, the degree of undependability of the yield. The greater the standard deviation of the return the more risky the portfolio is generally assumed to be and, consequently, the less desirable from the investor's viewpoint.[3] This premise has led to the

*From *Management Science,* Vol. 10, No. 1 (October 1963), pp. 174–182. Reprinted by permission of *Management Science.*

†The author is grateful for their helpful comments to E. J. Kane, B. K. Malkiel and Harry Markowitz, to E. Zinbarg of the Prudential Insurance Company for first calling the problem to his attention, and to the National Science Foundation whose grant was so helpful in completion of this paper.

[1] See, e.g., Tobin [8] p. 71 ff. and Lintner [2] pp. 254–261 and 264–266. Both of these authors use variance rather than standard deviation, but the latter concept is more convenient for present purposes.

[2] See Markowitz [4] and [5].

[3] Because of the observed rate of increases of sample variances with the size of sample, and on a number of other statistical and heuristic grounds, some of the students of the data

argument that, given the value of E, any *ceteris paribus* increase in σ is undesirable.

More specifically, in his pathbreaking work on Portfolio Selection, Markowitz has on this basis defined a portfolio to be *efficient* if ". . . it is impossible to obtain a greater average [expected] return without incurring greater standard deviation; it is impossible to obtain smaller standard deviation without giving up return on the average." ([5] p. 22.) He goes on to imply that, in the absence of specific knowledge of the investor's preference structure one cannot say that one efficient portfolio is better than another. Only "judgment" can be "employed in choosing one of the set of all efficient portfolios" (*loc. cit.*)

Markowitz uses a diagram similar to Fig. 1 to illustrate the point.

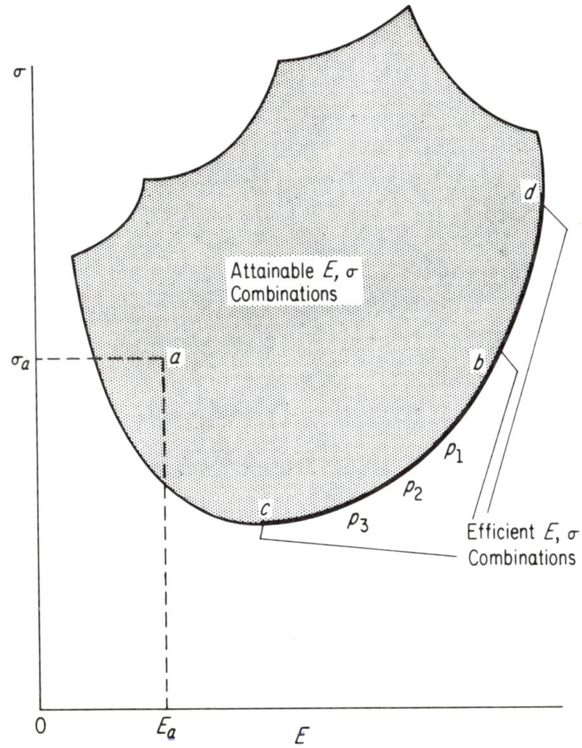

Fig. 1

---

have recently come to feel that many economic series, and particularly security yield and price statistics, are drawn from a sample of infinite variance. If this is so, the standard deviation of a sample, while necessarily finite, is not very meaningful and is certainly a poor measure of risk. This criticism is equally applicable to the Markowitz construction and to the alternative which is proposed in this paper. For a detailed discussion of the implications for economics of distributions with nonfinite variances by the leading investigator of the subject, see Mandelbrot [3].

Suppose some portfolio, A, offers an expected return E_a and a standard deviation σ_a. Then this portfolio can be represented by point a in the diagram. Assume all portfolios available with a fixed amount of money to be invested have been represented similarly and that the dots describing them constitute the shaded region in the figure. We see then that A is not an efficient portfolio because c which lies below and to the right of a offers a higher expected yield and a lower standard deviation. The locus of all efficient portfolios is the lower right hand segment of the boundary of the shaded region because these points represent all lowest σ-highest E combinations. This locus is the heavy arc *cbd*.[4]

Now I shall argue that this efficient set is very likely to contain portfolios which, many investors would agree, should be rejected out of hand. I shall suggest that the expected yield-standard deviation investment criterion [henceforth referred to as the (E, σ) criterion] does not accomplish quite what it is designed to do, and should be replaced by another closely related standard.[5] Fortunately, the criterion I shall propose calls for no extensive modifications of the arguments of the current literature. Indeed, all of the standard Markowitz analysis remains equally applicable, except that some unacceptable portfolios which do not satisfy the criterion have to be culled out of the Markowitz (E, σ) efficient set.

Before going further I must emphasize that my criticism of Markowitz's work is in no way meant to detract from his very significant contribution. Rather, I intend it to be regarded as an amendment which adds somewhat to the applicability of his approach, and which calls for no major change in his analytic and computational machinery.

1. UNACCEPTABLE (E, σ) EFFICIENT PORTFOLIOS

Consider two portfolios A and B which have the expected values and standard deviations shown in Table 1. Note that A and B may both be efficient—neither "dominates" the other because B has the better expected return but the poorer standard deviation. Yet we see that if we take $E + \sigma$ and $E - \sigma$ as a sort of upper and lower confidence limit, that is, if $E - \sigma$ is considered the (equally likely) lowest plausible outcome for each investment and $E + \sigma$ is the highest plausible outcome for each investment it may well be questioned whether anyone in his right mind would ever choose portfolio A. For the worst anticipated outcome associated with B, $E_b - \sigma_b = 11$ is better than the highest plausible outcome for $A = E_a + \sigma_a = 10$!

What has gone wrong here? The difficulty is that the investor is not interested in σ per se. He would prefer the danger of coming out \$10 short on a \$100 expected return as against an \$8 shortfall below a \$50 expected return.

[4]Markowitz points out ([5] pp. 152–3) that the efficient locus, cbd, will, in fact, be made up of arcs of hyperbolas.

[5]It should be mentioned that Markowitz does consider several other criteria. See, e.g., [5], pp. 15 and 187. However, he does not seem to think highly of them and does not pursue their analysis very deeply.

That is, while *for a given value of E* σ = \$10 is always worse than σ = \$8 this need no longer be the case when the value of E varies.

2. AN ALTERNATIVE EFFICIENT PORTFOLIO CRITERION

What alternative measure, then, should be employed to represent the investor's risk? One possibility is suggested by standard probability theory which tells us the following: If our basic random variable (the return on our investment) is normally distributed,[6] then there is only about a 16 percent

TABLE 1

	A	B
E	8	15
σ	2	4
$E+\sigma$	10	19
$E-\sigma$	6	11

probability that the realized return will ever fall below $E - \sigma$, there is only a 2 percent probability that it will ever be lower than $E - 2\sigma$, no more than a 0.1 percent probability that it will fall below $E - 3\sigma$, etc. Thus we may say that the risk involved in a given portfolio is represented by $E - K\sigma$ for some appropriately chosen value of K. Here $E - K\sigma$ may be considered the lower confidence limit for the investor's return.[7]

The situation may perhaps be made clearer with the aid of the following diagram (Fig. 2). On the horizontal axis we represent the expected values, E, of various efficient portfolios and on the vertical axis we represent the values of $E + K\sigma$, E and $E - K\sigma$ corresponding to these same portfolios.[8] Here the 45° line, as usual, describes the identity $E \equiv E$ so by adding or subtracting $K\sigma$ from the 45° line we obtain, respectively, the $E + K\sigma$ and $E - K\sigma$ curves.

Now, even though these portfolios are all efficient on the Markowitz (E, σ) criterion it is easy to see that the investor may readily reject some of them. For example, he will generally prefer portfolio A to portfolio C because $E_a > E_c$ and

[6]Markowitz ([5], p. 51–52) does consider some alternative efficiency concepts and recognizes their relationship in the normal distribution case. However, (though his concept is not clearly defined) he seems to be in error in arguing that a portfolio is (E, σ) efficient *if* and only if it is what he calls "mean-probability of loss efficient". The "only if" is valid, but the "if" is not, if I interpret him correctly.

[7]For a somewhat similar approach to utility theory, see Quandt [6]. Cf. also Roy [7]. The reader may prefer a decision theoretic approach to the matter in which the value of K is determined in terms of the *cost* of an erroneous choice, but this would complicate matters excessively for present purposes. Note also that this confidence limit approach, by ignoring all contingencies more remote than K standard deviations from the expected value, implicitly assumes a rather simple minded investor utility function.

[8]That is, the (E, σ) efficient locus cbd in Fig. 1 may be described by the equation $\sigma = f(E)$. The equation for the upper curve in Fig. 2 is then $L = E + kf(E)$, where E is the abscissa of any point on the curve and L is its ordinate. A similar equation, equation (1) below, holds for the lower curve in the figure.

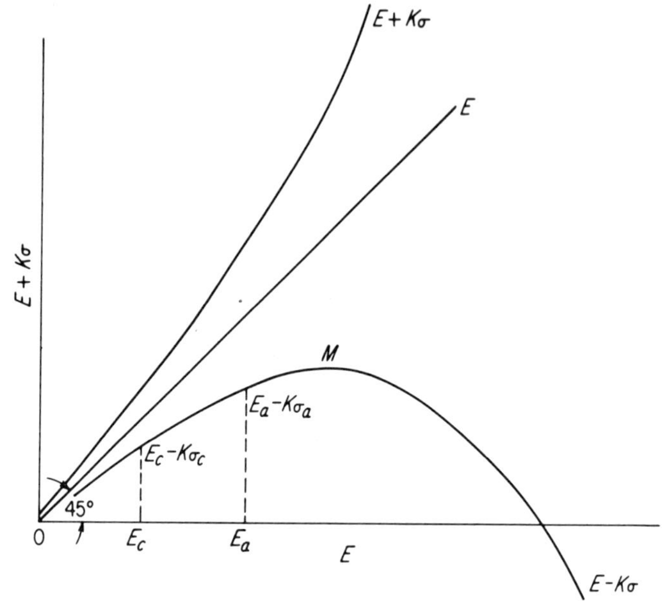

Fig. 2

$E_a - K\sigma_a > E_c - K\sigma_c$. That is, Portfolio A offers both a higher expected return and a higher floor on earnings ($E - K\sigma$). This is so because our $E - K\sigma$ curve has a positive slope between E_c and E_a—over this range of the curve portfolios with higher expected returns are also safer! Only to the right of point M, where the $E - K\sigma$ curve begins to turn down, do we get to portfolios which are efficient in terms of our alternative (E, L) criterion (where for brevity I write $L = E - K\sigma$ to designate the *lower* confidence limit). For only in this negatively sloping segment does the investor have to make up his mind in trading off greater expected return against reduced safety.[9]

3. RELATIONSHIP BETWEEN (E, L) EFFICIENCY AND (E, σ) EFFICIENCY

Let us see now how the set of (E, L) efficient portfolios is related to the Markowitz (E, σ) efficient set. It is easy to argue that *the former is a subset of the latter.*[10] That is, no portfolio can be (E, L) efficient without being (E, σ) efficient. For suppose portfolio A were not (E, σ) efficient because it is "(E, σ) dominated" by portfolio B, that is, because $E_b \geqslant E_a$ and $\sigma_b \leqslant \sigma_a$. Then we must have for our L figures $L_b \geqslant L_a$ since $L_b = E_b - K\sigma_b \geqslant E_b - K\sigma_a \geqslant E_a - K\sigma_a = L_a$. Hence (E, σ) inefficient portfolio A cannot be (E, L) efficient either, because

[9]Of course, I am defining a portfolio to be (E, L) efficient if there exists no other portfolio which offers a higher value of E without any reduction in L.

[10]Indeed, one may helpfully describe the (E, L) investment procedure as follows: the investor chooses on the basis of E and σ, but from his calculated (E, σ) efficient points he excludes from consideration all portfolios dominated in the (E, L) plane, i.e., he excludes all portfolios like portfolio A in Table 1.

as compared with B it involves both a lower expected return, E, and a smaller lower confidence limit, L.

We can go further and determine what portion of the (E, σ) efficient set *cbd* in figure 1 is also (E, L) efficient. For this purpose let the equation of the curve *cbd* be represented by $\sigma = f(E)$. Then we have

$$L = E - K\sigma = E - Kf(E) \tag{1}$$

But we have seen that for (E, L) efficient portfolios, portfolios offering larger expected values of E must be characterized by less high values of L, i.e., such efficient portfolios are represented by the negatively sloping segment of the $L = E - K\sigma$ curve in Fig. 2. Hence, (E, L) efficiency requires $dL/dE < 0$, so that, differentiating (1), we obtain

$$dL/dE = 1 - Kf'(E) < 0$$

or

$$f'(E) > 1/K \tag{2}$$

To see what this implies, in Fig. 1 let P_1, P_2, and P_3 represents the points on the (E, σ) efficiency locus *cbd* where the curve has slope unity, 1/2 and 1/3 respectively. Then since as the diagram is drawn, the slope of arc P_1bd is greater than unity throughout, (2) tells us that it is the locus of the (E, L) efficient set for $K = 1$. Similarly, arc P_2bd is the (E, L) efficiency locus for $K = 2$, etc. Thus we see that, normally,[11] *the* (E, L) *efficient set will be a proper subset of the* (E, σ) *set,* i.e., there will be many Markowitz efficient portfolios which are not efficient on the proposed (E, L) criterion. However, it is to be noted that the Markowitz (E, σ) efficient set is the limit of the (E, L) efficient set as K becomes larger and larger, i.e., as K approaches infinity. In other words the more conservative our confidence limit criterion–the more standard deviations below our expected outcome which we consider plausible, the more closely our (E, L) efficient set will approximate the Markowitz (E, σ) set.

This result is really not difficult to explain. The basic objection to the Markowitz criterion is that in the expression $L = E - K\sigma$ an increasing E may more than counterbalance an increase in σ, so that despite greater variability in the return from the portfolio with the larger E, it may be considered relatively safe because the lower confidence limit L is relatively high. But the larger the value of K in $E - K\sigma$ the more of a rise in E it will take to compensate[12] for a given fall in σ. When K is very large the $K\sigma$ becomes the overwhelmingly

[11] The only exception occurs if arc cbd in Fig. 1 is of slope greater than, say, unity throughout its length, with a kink at point c. In that case the (E, L) efficiency locus for $K > 1$ will also be cbd so that it will coincide with the (E, σ) efficient set.

[12] For example, in the case shown in Table 1, with a sufficiently large K investment B would yield a smaller value of L than does investment A. The borderline occurs where $K = 3.5$, at which $L_a = L_b = 1$.

important term in $L = E - K\sigma$ and so the behavior of L will be almost perfectly correlated with that of σ. Hence an (E, L) criterion will then not differ significantly from an (E, σ) criterion.[13]

4. THE (*E*, *L*) CRITERION IN APPLIED PORTFOLIO SELECTION

It can be claimed for the (E, L) criterion that it is a somewhat more easily interpreted measure of risk than is (E, σ). In fact, it is possible with the former to take explicit account of differing attitudes toward risk and to examine their consequences. Figure 3 shows a family of different $L = E - K\sigma$ curves for different values of K, and indicates the alternative (E, L) combinations which are available with different selections of the value of K. The higher the value of K chosen by the investor, the more conservative he must be considered since he must then be taking into account far less likely possibilities of loss. As is to be expected, Fig. 3 shows that an investor whose K is 4, and who must surely be considered extremely conservative on almost any standards, may plausibly be expected to accept relatively low values of E. For his is the lowest curve shown

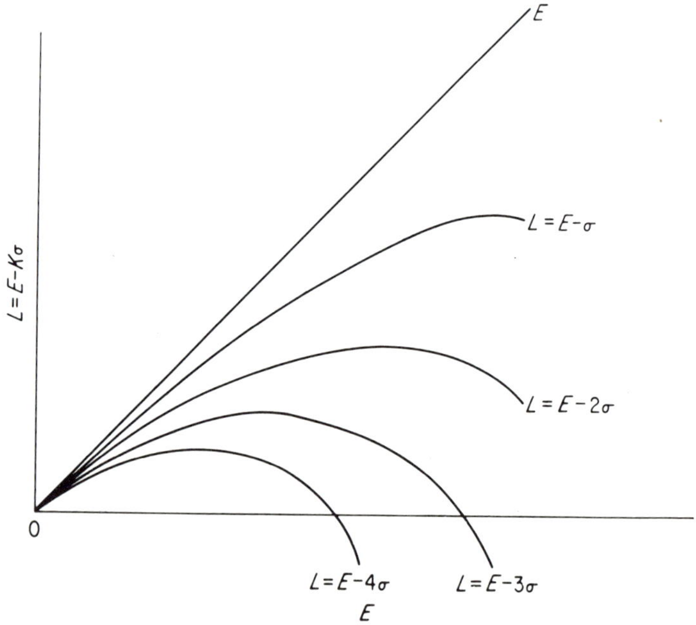

Fig. 3

[13] An alternative way of looking at the entire matter is to say that the choice of K depends on the investor's attitude toward risk, and that this psychological element determines the region within which one can expect to find points of tangency between the investor's indifference curves and the (E, σ) efficiency locus. The smaller the value of K the greater, *ceteris paribus*, will be the slopes of the indifference curves and, therefore, the further to the right on arc cbd must the possible tangency points lie.

in the figure, and the points where it turns down and crosses the E axis are well to the left of the corresponding points on the other curves shown in the diagram. This relationship is mentioned merely to illustrate the ready interpretability of our diagram.[14]

One disadvantage of the (E, L) approach is that it imposes on the user of the analysis yet another explicit judgment which takes a form to which he is little habituated.[15] For, to employ the method, the investor must first express his risk preferences by choosing a specific value for K. But even where the distribution cannot be assumed to be approximately normal this requirement is not totally unreasonable, because, with the aid of Chebyshev's inequality[16] any value of K can be assigned an interpretation in terms of the likelihood that observations will fall beyond $E \pm K\sigma$.

The preceding remarks are somewhat peripheral to the basic question of application to which this section is addressed. The purpose of the Markowitz analysis may be described in general terms as a procedure whereby, from among the astronomical number[17] of candidate portfolios, the vast majority of possibil-

[14] Another example of the interpretation which may be given Fig. 3 follows from our observation that (E, L) efficient points must lie on negatively sloping segments of our curves. We see in the diagram that, as K increases, the positively sloping (inefficient) segment of the curve grows shorter and shorter so that the efficient set grows more and more extensive, as we have already seen. In the limit, as K approaches infinity, the slope of the corresponding curve will be negative even at the origin, and every point on the curve will be (E, L) efficient.

[15] Here it may be appropriate to remark briefly on Markowitz' apparent reluctance to use historical data as a basis for estimation of the E and σ values needed in his calculation. No doubt it is true that extrapolation of these values from past history is a risky business and when there is specific information indicating changes in the operations of a particular company or in the performance of the economy as a whole, this should clearly be taken into account. But, particularly because investment management is not habituated to translating its experience into the language of expected values, variances, and covariances required for the computation, there is surely much to be said for providing these measures routinely by more or less mechanical statistical calculation, *but then having them examined and modified by the professional investors before they are used in the portfolio selection procedure.*

For this purpose it is probably not desirable to proceed as Markowitz does in his illustrative calculations ([5] Chapter 1) by dealing with a time series of annual returns data. This implies that investors are typically concerned with a one year experience and perhaps even that portfolios will characteristically be held for one year periods. Since securities will be held for varying lengths of time, it may well be preferable to collect data for much shorter time periods (say monthly) and then select a sample of time periods for the calculation of mean variances and covariances with the aid of a table of random numbers. That is, if one employs data about a security extending over a 36 month period, this approach might, for example, have us dealing with the return from month 3 to month 12, the return from month 8 to month 24, etc. Such a random sample of possible investor experience in holding the security in question may well be helpful to a potential purchaser who does not know in advance for how long a period he will keep it in his portfolio.

[16] Chebyshev's inequality (whose proof is quite elementary) states that for *any* distribution with given mean and variance, the probability of observations outside the range $E \pm K\sigma$ will be no greater than $1/K^2$! See, e.g., Feller [1], pp. 183–4.

[17] I assume here that expenditures on any security can be made only in discrete amounts so that the number of possible portfolios will be finite.

ities can be ruled out because they are not worth the investor's consideration (they are not in the efficient set). The goal of the approach is to present the investor (or his counsellor) with a much smaller and more tractable list of alternatives from among which he must still make up his mind, perhaps partly with the help of the E, σ data used in the calculation. The (E, L) procedure which has been proposed in this note, besides providing data which may be more meaningful intuitively and ruling out confusing paradoxical cases such as that described in Table 1, is helpful because it yields a smaller efficient set. This means that far fewer (and only more clearly relevant) alternatives are likely to be offered to the investor for comparison in the difficult and complex selection process. In effect, then, the proposed (E, L) approach may add efficacy to the pruning procedure which is the basic application of the Markowitz analysis.

REFERENCES

1. William Feller. *An Introduction to Probability Theory and Its Applications.* Vol. I. New York: Wiley, 1950.
2. John Lintner. "Dividends, Earnings, Leverage, Stock Prices and the Supply of Capital to Corporations," *Review of Economics and Statistics,* Vol. XLIV (August 1962).
3. Benoit Mandelbrot. "The Variation of Certain Speculative Prices." I.B.M. Research Note NC-87, March 26, 1962.
4. Harry Markowitz. "Portfolio Selection," *Journal of Finance,* Vol. VII (March 1952).
5. ——. *Portfolio Selection.* Cowles Foundation Monograph 16. New York: Wiley, 1959.
6. Richard E. Quandt. "A Contribution to the Pathology of Gambling," *Zeitschrift Für Nationalökonomie,* Vol. XX (1960).
7. A. D. Roy. "Safety First and the Holding of Assets," *Econometrica,* Vol. 20 (July 1952).
8. James Tobin. "Liquidity Preference as Behavior Toward Risk," *Review of Economic Studies,* Vol. XXV (February 1958).

35

Another View of Formula Planning*

Robert R. Dince†

I

Formula planning is often put forth as an investment technique for taking advantage of stock market fluctuations. Formula planning involves taking a position in a diversified list of common stocks (the aggressive portion) in combination with a position in non-volatile fixed income securities (the defensive portion).[1] The proportions invested in stocks or bonds are determined by the relative dearness or cheapness of the aggressive portion.

Traditional economic theory states that price and value are one and the same. But most analysts would agree that a stock price may or may not reflect its expected capital value. All of this leads to the proposition that stocks are sometimes overpriced and sometimes underpriced in terms of values determined by capitalization techniques. Once we have acknowledged the proposition that stock prices can be cheap or dear (under or overvalued), then it is the function of investment policy to take advantage of this fact. In retrospect, it is clear that the capitalization process can be tested only after the fact; errors can result because of price swings above or below price projections.

The purpose of this paper is to examine the effectiveness of a particular formula plan incorporating certain rigid assumptions. The basic assumption was made by Weston in 1956 when he stated that criteria for judging the level of common stock prices could be determined.[2] Weston sought specific criteria for determining secular trends in stock prices which would serve to identify cyclical or random swings. Weston posited a close economic relationship between Gross National Product (GNP) and aggregate sales; between aggregate sales and profits

*From *Journal of Finance,* Vol. 19, No. 4 (December 1964), pp. 678–688. Reprinted by permission of *Journal of Finance.*

†An earlier version of this paper was presented to the Southwestern Finance Association, March 27, 1964, at Dallas, Texas. Thanks are due to Dr. Mark Hanna for many helpful comments and Lois Shackleford and James Fortson of the University of Georgia's Computer Center for help in programming.

[1] Formula planning ignores the question of security analysis. Results would always be dependent on the investment analyst's judgement and the correctness of his analysis in selecting which securities to buy or sell.

[2] Weston, J. Fred, "The Stock Market in Perspective," *Harvard Business Review,* Vol. 34, No. 2 (March-April 1956), pp. 71–79.

before taxes; between profits and dividends; and between dividends and stock prices.[3] He tested the correlation between stock prices and GNP from 1868 through 1940 and derived the formula: Dow-Jones Industrial Average (DJIA) = 28.20 + .9675 GNP. With stock prices in 1955 rising sharply, Weston concluded that stock prices were roughly in line with what one would have expected on the basis of historical relationships.

In 1960, Weston commented on his prior work by writing that the continued growth of the economic base of the nation, as measured in the growth of GNP, would support rising levels of the stock market; but certain institutional changes in the demand for stocks was forcing the price of stocks to rise even faster than the economic base supporting these levels.[4] The growth of GNP sets a higher and higher floor below which the Dow-Jones Industrial Average is not likely to decline in the future. Further, an average rise in the DJIA beyond 5–8 per cent per annum "would be clearly in the category of excesses."[5]

Using Weston's earlier article as a base, the author attempted in 1961 to develop a formula plan incorporating Weston's regression equation for determining a flexible "central value."[6] Flexibility was emphasized, since the formula plans examined by Cottle and Whitman[7] seemed too rigid. If the formula could be made to work so that the relative cheapness or dearness of stocks could be related to a current economic statistic, then adjustments in proportions of stocks and bonds could be made in a more meaningful way. Using Weston's estimating equation as the determinant of the formula value for the DJIA, the formula plan achieved spectacular results. Starting at the end of 1929 with $100,000, the value of the portfolio by the end of 1959 had increased to $502,315. The purpose of this present paper is to update and retest that formula.

II

Instead of using Weston's original equation again, new equations were developed using standard computer correlation programs which automatically developed all major tests for statistical significance. Quarterly GNP statistics were the independent variable and the DJIA closing price for the end of the quarter was the dependent variable. The period used was 1929 to 1962 as opposed to Weston's period of 1868 to 1940. That the relationship is secular is clearly demonstrated by the new regression equation based on the period

[3]"Thus . . . stock prices can be linked directly to gross national product leaving out the intermediate steps. Therefore, as gross national product grows over the years, we would expect that the total value of stock prices will grow in the same proportion." *Ibid.*, p. 70.

[4]Weston, "A Not-So-New-Era in the Stock Market," *The Financial Analysts Journal,* Vol. 16, No. 6 (Nov.-Dec. 1960), pp. 57–64.

[5]*Ibid.*, p. 64.

[6]R. R. Dince, "Formula Planning," *The Financial Analysts Journal* Vol. 17, No. 2 (March-April 1961), pp. 59–64; reprinted in Lerner, Eugene (ed.) *Readings in Financial Analysis and Investment Management* (Irwin, 1963), pp. 454–462.

[7]C. S. Cottle and W. T. Whitman, *Investment Timing: The Formula Plan Approach* (McGraw-Hill, 1953), p. 83.

1929–1962; the new equation is remarkably similar to the older one developed by Weston. Weston's original formula was:

$$DJIA = 28.20 + .9675\ GNP$$

The new equation using quarterly data taken as annual totals is:

$$DJIA = 22.37 + 1.001\ GNP$$

Using a hypothetical value of $600 billion for GNP and substituting in both equations, the following values are received. Weston's formula predicts a DJIA of 608.70 as compared to a DJIA predicted level of 622.97 for the new formula. While the Dow Jones Average went through the 800 level when GNP was at $600 billion, both formulas agree that the *current* relationship between the variables is out of line with *predicted* levels, and by almost the same amount.

Using a computer simplifies the making of a series of correlations. While standard programs yield many different estimating equations,[8] for purposes of simplicity in calculation only two versions were used, the rectilinear version given above and a curvilinear regression equation with two terms which yield the highest possible coefficient of determination of all two term equations tested.

Equation I: DJIA = 22.37 + 1.001 GNP
R^2 = .767, t = 21.074 with 134 d. f., S_b = .190. At the 95 per cent confidence level, the term, (.190) (1.96) = ± .327 can be added to the b coefficient to give its range of values.

Equation II: DJIA = 116.59 + .02853 $(GNP)^2$
R^2 = .812, t = 24.090 with 134 d. f., S_b = .00118. At the 95 per cent confidence level, the term (.00118) (1.96) = ± .00231 can be added to the b coefficient to give its range of values. (GNP is used in its quarterly form.)

The second formula because of its mathematical qualities may seem more suitable for those who believe in an ever-rising market which continues to accelerate faster than the growth of the economy. But despite the fact that the curve describes a better fit for the data, using this formula as the determinant of the formula values for the plan yielded decidedly inferior results as compared to using the simpler straight line regression. (See Tables 1 and 2.) Assuming a $600 billion GNP as before, the predicted level of the DJIA would be 758.52 using Equation II. But in the depression, the high value of the constant and the resulting high predicted levels of the DJIA kept the plan more fully invested in stocks than the plan using the rectilinear equation. This can be seen by comparing the last columns in both Tables 1 and 2.

Departing from Weston's concept of a secular relationship between the

[8] If all other tests except the coefficient of determination are rejected then an estimating equation with six terms including log x and x^4 yielded a R^2 value of .875. Little can be gained by using the more complicated formula despite its slightly higher coefficient of determination.

TABLE 1

Year End Portfolio Value and Yields, Using Linear Equation

Year End	Total Value	Stock Value[1]	#Shares	DJIA	Income	Yield %[2]	Ratio S/D[3]
1929	$100,000	$ 20,000	80.500	286.10			20/80
1930	93,339	14,358	113.427	164.58	$ 5,085	5.26	20/80
1931	77,338	34,523	595.669	77.90	4,727	5.54	60/40
1932	81,935	45,620	957.027	59.93	4,542	5.70	70/30
1933	119,814	49,434	359.803	99.90	4,580	4.54	30/70
1934	122,691	63,837	471.709	104.04	4,201	3.46	40/60
1935	141,555	45,144	196.427	144.13	4,795	3.62	20/80
1936	147,916	32,541	166.291	177.90	5,035	3.48	20/80
1937	134,610	33,784	556.928	120.85	5,254	3.72	50/50
1938	151,434	48,340	195.702	154.76	5,633	3.94	20/80
1939	155,471	46,147	413.926	150.24	5,377	3.31	40/60
1940	149,395	59,348	569.645	131.13	6,010	3.94	50/50
1941	136,255	78,315	859.577	110.96	6,695	4.69	70/30
1942	145,958	119,994	977,944	119.40	6,924	4.91	80/20
1943	162,182	113,357	834.185	135.89	6,876	4.46	70/30
1944	175,809	124,029	814.266	152.32	6,842	4.05	70/30
1945	206,702	126,970	642.896	192.91	6,791	3.55	60/40
1946	199,929	121,266	789.787	177.20	6,623	3.26	70/30
1947	203,294	143,315	789.787	181.46	8,653	4.29	70/30
1948	200,180	139,889	903.237	177.30	10,325	5.12	80/20
1949	216,329	134,532	648.565	200.03	11,493	5.52	60/40
1950	238,741	145,482	608.491	235.41	12,504	5.67	60/40
1951	259,098	155,014	575.769	269.23	12,472	5.01	60/40
1952	272,151	168,067	559.405	291.90	11,855	4.46	60/40
1953	267,351	189,707	666.236	280.90	12,414	4.60	70/30
1954	332,782	175,948	411.462	404.39	13,435	4.48	50/50
1955	363,535	149,412	297.736	488.40	13,470	3.87	40/60
1956	368,969	189,069	369.361	499.47	13,500	3.68	50/50
1957	345,370	168,695	475.618	435.69	13,755	3.85	60/40
1958	398,287	168,232	272.963	583.65	14,555	3.91	40/60
1959	418,500	130,353	184.806	679.36	14,585	3.57	30/70
1960	407,438	168,656	264.618	615.89	14,632	3.54	40/60
1961	433,607	133,918	237.226	731.13	15,817	3.76	40/60
1962	431,249	229,406	330.662	652.10	16,162	3.74	50/50

[1] Before adjustment.
[2] On average portfolio.
[3] Ratio of stocks to defensive portion.

stock market and GNP, correlations were also run for the ten year interim periods, 1929-1938, 1939-1948, 1949-1958. Their values and significance levels are shown in Table 3. Perhaps, there is some question concerning the efficacy of this type of correlation analysis. If there are interim trends in the stock market, and the data are correlated on a quarterly basis, there is a possibility that autocorrelation results. It would have been possible to have correlated the first differences in the variables. However, the close approximation of the rectilinear regression equation for the total period to Weston's original equation makes the possibility of autocorrelation less probable. If, according to von Morgenstern, the variables move in random ways, then we can ignore this problem.[9]

[9] C. W. T. Granger and O. Morgenstern, "Special Analysis of New York Stock Market

TABLE 2

Year End Portfolio Value and Yields, Using Curvilinear Equation

Year End	Total Value	Stock Value[1]	#Shares	DJIA	Income	Yield %[2]	Ratio S/D[2]
1929	$100,000	$ 20,000	80.500	286.10			20/80
1930	93,339	14,358	170.140	164.58	$ 5,869	6.07	30/70
1931	68,866	37,698	618.816	77.90	4,426	5.46	70/30
1932	63,047	48,553	810.162	59.93	3,972	6.02	80/20
1933	97,056	58,647	587.058	99.90	3,494	4.36	60/40
1934	99,478	61,078	587.058	104.04	3,504	3.56	60/40
1935	119,335	62,307	441.188	144.13	4,060	3.71	40/60
1936	129,292	40,389	227.034	177.90	5,065	4.07	30/70
1937	114,504	39,233	473.744	120.85	4,890	4.01	50/50
1938	136,024	72,932	351.573	154.76	4,710	3.76	40/60
1939	137,179	54,372	361.903	150.24	5,043	3.69	40/60
1940	131,765	65,506	499.547	131.13	5,422	4.03	50/50
1941	120,230	69,204	758.479	110.96	5,997	4.74	70/30
1942	126,938	91,215	744.192	119.40	5,997	4.85	70/30
1943	139,298	83,412	717.557	135.89	5,569	4.18	70/30
1944	150,623	91,318	692.199	152.32	5,744	3.96	70/30
1945	173,121	89,149	448.710	192.91	5,668	3.50	50/50
1946	166,596	101,048	570.248	177.20	5,420	3.19	60/40
1947	169,025	103,477	558.884	181.46	6,768	4.03	60/40
1948	166,603	116,425	656.654	177.30	8,203	4.89	70/30
1949	177,913	93,050	444.493	200.13	8,742	5.07	50/50
1950	193,361	98,576	418.740	235.41	9,302	5.01	50/50
1951	207,168	103,214	383.368	269.23	9,260	4.62	50/50
1952	217,612	134,710	447.302	291.90	9,117	4.29	60/40
1953	212,800	130,020	454.538	280.90	9,714	4.51	60/40
1954	258,402	136,622	319.496	404.39	10,013	4.25	50/50
1955	279,460	114,857	328.878	488.40	10,309	3.83	40/60
1956	284,707	145,891	285.009	499.47	10,380	3.77	50/50
1957	266,497	130,170	367.000	435.69	10,612	3.70	60/40
1958	307,329	129,812	263.282	583.65	10,971	3.45	50/50
1959	327,904	135,439	193.066	679.36	11,272	3.49	40/60
1960	318,105	163,807	258.240	615.89	11,365	3.52	50/50
1961	344,028	141,075	235.271	731.13	12,362	3.73	50/50
1962	338,472	213,336	311.429	652.10	12,489	3.66	60/40

[1] Before adjustment.
[2] On average portfolio.
[3] Ratio of stocks to defensive portion.

III

Operating the formula plan is an essentially mechanical process easily handled by the computer. Table 1 shows the results of using the first equation for determining the theoretical value of the DJIA. This value is then divided into the actual value to give a percentage. Applying the percentage to Table 4, the proportion that should be invested in stocks is determined. The remainder is invested in the defensive portion. The process is continued each quarter. If the

Prices," *Kyklos,* Vol. 16, No. 1 (1963), pp. 1–27. See especially p. 17–18. M. D. Godfrey, C. W. T. Granger, and O. Morgenstern, "The Random-Walk Hypothesis of Stock Market Behavior," *Kyklos,* Vol. 17, No. 1 (1964), pp. 1–30, and O. Morgenstern, *On the Accuracy of Economic Observations* (Princeton, 1950), pp. 73–85.

signal is to buy, then defensive funds are liquidated and put into stocks at the prevailing price of the DJIA. Switches are made at the end of any quarter regardless of the market's fluctuations and provided that the total switch demanded by the formula is greater than $2,000. No provision is made for brokerage commissions.

TABLE 3

Regression Equations, Quarterly GNP and DJIA
1929–1938, 1939–1948, 1949–1958

Year	Equation	R_2	t	S_b	(S_b) (1.96)
	Rectilinear Regressions				
1929–38	$Y_c = -182.38 + 16.96(X)$	.724	9.981	1.696	±3.324
1939–48	$Y_c = 94.52 + 1.26(X)$	.411	5.149	.245	± .480
1949–58	$Y_c = 133.09 + 5.50(X)$	.826	13.44	.493	± .966
Curvilinear Regressions	Curvilinear Regressions				
1929–38	$Y_c = 53.65 + .0053(X)^4$	.806	12.611	.0000427	± .00008
1939–48	$Y_c = 117.88 + .015(X)^2$	.442	5.492	.00273	± .005
1949–58	$Y_c = 156.50 + .00024(X)^3$	.850	14.632	.000017	± .00003

$t = 1.96$ at 95 per cent confidence level with 38 d.f.

TABLE 4

Relationship of Percentage Difference Between Actual Dow-Jones Industrial Average and Formula Value as Related to Zones Determining Variable Ratios of Stocks and Defensive Portion

Dow-Jones as a % of Formula Value	Zones	Stocks	% Ratio	Defensive
141 or more	I	20	–	80
126–140	II	30	–	70
111–125	III	40	–	60
90–110	IV	50	–	50
75–89	V	60	–	40
50–74	VI	70	–	30
59 or less	VII	80	–	20

Source: Marshall Ketchum, "Investment Management Through Formula Timing Plans," *Journal of Business* (July 1947), p. 159.

In an earlier test of this formula plan, a very elaborate scheme for handling the defensive portion of the portfolio was attempted. The Cottle-Whitman method of using the product of a current bond average times the defensive portfolio was rejected. Instead a system was devised where the bonds were assumed to have a twelve and a half year maturity. Then, when bonds were sold, the dollar amount of bonds sold was distributed proportionally through all the maturities held. This produced an elegant but complicated technique. As pointed out in the previous article, the portfolio manager attempting to maximize portfolio income would not have liquidated high-yield bonds arbitrarily.[10]

In order to eliminate completely the problem of bond trading in the current experiment, the defensive portfolio was assumed to have been invested in a savings and loan account receiving the average yield for the period concerned. Cash dividends were those paid out quarterly on the DJIA. The income was computed by multiplying the DJIA dividend rate times the number of shares held at the the beginning of the quarter and adding to this subtotal the product of the average savings and loan dividend times the quarterly balance of defensive funds held. Table 1 shows year-end income results using the linear equation. Table 2 shows the corresponding results using the curvilinear equation.

In comparing the original formula plan using Weston's equation with the present plans, certain interesting differences are apparent. First, neither of the two present methods yielded as high a result as the former study. However, the two studies are not identical. The most important difference is that unlike dates for selecting the DJIA were used. In the 1961 study, closing prices were taken on a semi-annual basis as opposed to the quarterly basis in the present study. Related to the difference is the enforced quarterly adjustment of the portfolio as opposed to semi-annual switching.

The lower total under a plan which required more frequent adjustments in the securities held leads to some interesting thoughts on the operation of formula plans. Cottle and Whitman demonstrated effective methods of operating a formula plan under severe restrictions to prevent overtrading.[11] One simple method used in both the present and the prior study is to prohibit shifts unless the net change is greater than a $2,000. Cottle and Whitman also advocated strongly prohibiting trading when the formula is in certain zones. If stocks are undervalued, according to the formula used to determine "central value", then stock should never be sold in Zones V, VI, VII. (See Table 4.) Similarly, stocks should never be bought in Zones I, II, III when they are overvalued even though the automatic formula calls for adjustment. Earlier research showed that restricting trading in the manner described by Cottle and Whitman resulted in a total portfolio of $444,331 at the end of 1957, as compared to a total of $409,325 without these restrictions. Under these same restrictions, the portfolio managed under the updated rectilinear equation totaled $495,812 by the end of 1962; this was a gain of $64,563 over trading every quarter. Using the curvilinear formula, the results were increased $92,705, a gain of 28 per cent, to a total of $431,177. In both cases, no trades were made in over half the possible quarters.

A simple test of the proposition that "the less trading, the better the results" was attempted by multiple runs of the data through the computer.

[10] R. R. Dince, *op. cit.*, p. 64

[11] Cottle and Whitman, *op. cit.*, pp. 16–18.

Trading was done only on the first and third quarters, the second and fourth quarters, and then for each quarter through the year assuming that trades were not made on the remaining three quarters. The summary results, including the earlier study, are shown in Table 5.

TABLE 5

Results of $100,000 Invested by Formula Beginning at the End of 1929

Formula Used	Year End Results		
	Dec. 1957	Dec. 1959	Dec. 1962
Weston, semi-annual	$405†	$502†	$n.a.†
Weston, restricted	444	n.a.	n.a.
Dince, curvilinear, quarterly	266	328	338
Dince, curvilinear, restricted	343	422	431
Dince, linear, quarterly	345	419	431
Dince, linear, restricted	401	486	496
Dince, linear, 1st and 3rd quarters	316	365	361
Dince, linear, 2nd and 4th quarters	266	328	338
Dince, linear, 1st quarter	421	480	498*
Dince, linear, 2nd quarter	531	607	637*
Dince, linear, 3rd quarter	264	307	304*
Dince, linear, 4th quarter	319	408	408

*1962 results carried to year end.
†000 eliminated.

The results are perplexing. Testing of the data shows that it is not always the lack of trading which creates the better result. Rather, it is the quarter chosen. The basis of the second quarter yielding such superior results over other quarters can be traced to 1932. In that quarter, the portfolio held 80 per cent in the defensive portion. When the DJIA fell to 42.84 the formula called for a shift to 80 per cent stock. The combination of having a substantial liquid reserve and being able to buy large quantities of stock at a low price (an enormous number of shares, 1351) was the basis of the better performance of the second quarter. No other plan was able to combine this liquidity with an almost record low DJIA.

The conclusion that "the less trading, the better the results" is only partly borne out. The average of the results ending in 1962 shows that trading only once a year yields better results than any other method. Yet, quarterly adjustments using the rectilinear formula produce better results than semi-annual trading.

These confusing conclusions prompted still another test. Perhaps the results are random. If the portfolio were managed by a completely irrational investor—i.e., one who bought the most stock only when prices were high and sold when prices were low—then the hypothesis might be that the final results using this form of portfolio management would be no worse than the formula plan used in this experiment. The data was again processed by the computer with the zones inverted. If the formula plan called for 80 per cent in stock and 20 per cent in the defensive portion, this was reversed to 20 per cent in stock and 80 per cent in the defensive position. The results for the same period 1929–1962 equaled only $87,746. One may assume that reasoned formula planning is better than unreasoned planning.

IV

There are two important conclusions to be drawn from all of this. The first is that the secular relationship described by Weston still has validity. Even though a GNP of $610 billion in the summer of 1964 predicts a DJIA of 633, the 30 per cent discrepancy between the predicted and the actual DJIA seems to bear out Weston's feeling that the rise has taken on the "characteristic of speculative excesses."[12] The formula at the end of the second quarter of 1964 would place only 30 per cent in stocks and 70 per cent in the defensive portion, signifying that stocks are overpriced. Yet, the second formula estimates a DJIA of 802 which would place the portfolio in a 50/50 position. Readers are reminded that the curvilinear equation states mathematically that every change in the GNP is associated with a greater than proportional change in stock prices. If the second formula more accurately defines the relationship between GNP and stock prices, then it is possible that there is a "new era" of stock prices.

The second conclusion deals with the general usefulness of formula planning techniques. One way to compare investment results is to demonstrate the formula-managed portfolio's rate of return as opposed to investing in stocks alone. For the period tested, the discounted rate of return for both formulas appears to be superior to stocks alone as an investment vehicle. Lorie's study shows that from 1929 through 1960 the compounded rate of return in common stocks, assuming all dividends and distributions are paid out in cash and selling the portfolio at the end of the period but including all brokerage commissions paid, is 4.9 per cent.[13] Herzog's paper shows the rate of return from 1929 to 1962 as 5.7 per cent and from 1930 to 1962 as 6.6 per cent.[14] Herzog's study makes no allowance for commissions and taxes which makes his study similar to the formula plan results. Since the present study starts with December 31, 1929, perhaps Herzog's 1930–1962 period is the correct one to use for comparison purposes. Notwithstanding the fact that Lorie's study used all stocks on the New York Stock Exchange, Herzog's paper used Moody's 125 Stock Average, and the present paper used the Dow Jones Industrial Average, there is a sufficient basis for comparisons. Using the familiar discounted rate of return technique employed by both Lorie and Herzog, (the discounted rate of return which makes

[12] Weston, *op. cit.*, 1960, p. 64

[13] L. Fisher and J. H. Lorie, "Rates of Return on Investments in Common Stock," *Journal of Business*, Vol. 37, No. 1 (January 1964), pp. 5, 15–17.

[14] J. P. Herzog, "Investor Experience in Corporate Securities: A New Technique for Measurement," *Journal of Finance*, Vol. 19, No. 1 (March 1964), pp. 51–3.

the present value of the income stream plus the sale of all holdings at the end of period equal to the initial capital amount invested), Plan I had a discounted yield of 8.66 per cent and Plan II had a 7.62 per cent yield.

The formula plans employed here have produced significant capital gains and increasing money income. The rates of return using both formulas during the period are greater than for stocks alone. But as Herzog points out so clearly,[15] the final yields for an investment program are dependent on when the program was started; the same is true for formula plans.

[15] *Ibid.*, p. 58.

36

The 10% Rule: It Furnishes a Simple Formula for Catching Broad Market Swings*

George K. Freeman

The great surge of equity prices over the past year has brought into sharp focus the investor's eternal dilemma—how to realize the market's full potential, yet avoid exceptional risks. At today's peak levels, of course, the hazards loom larger than ever. Still, the specter of inflation and the powerful recovery in business and corporate earnings hold out the prospect that stocks will push up to still loftier heights. One resolution for all but the most speculative minds is the "10% rule."

Of the numerous "automatic" market systems, the 10% rule adjusts perhaps most quickly and accurately to swift and unforeseen changes. Thus, as the accompanying table illustrates, the technique has demonstrated its effectiveness quite handsomely in the shifting markets of the 'fifties. Clearly, any investment approach which has withstood the tests posed by the market vagaries of recent years deserves a careful look.

Although mechanical in application, the 10% rule is not strictly a formula plan. What it does essentially is formalize a basic technical principle: that stock prices, having moved a certain distance in one direction, very likely will continue to move in that direction. Most experienced investors will accept this premise. The problem is to recognize which moves are worth following and which represent only ripples in the major trend. The 10% rule assumes the burden of decision. At the cost of being slightly late, it promises to identify the really significant changes in the course of equity prices.

• • • • •

Not the least of its attributes is that the technique is simple to apply. Unlike some of the true formulas, the 10% rule involves no value judgments or complicated calculations. Instead, the stockholder need only calculate the value of his account at each week's closing prices—something he might very well do in any case.

At the end of each month, the weekly figures are averaged and recorded. So long as the monthly average continues to rise or holds relatively steady, a fully

*From *Barron's* (March 16, 1959), p. 9. Reprinted by courtesy of *Barron's National Business and Financial Weekly.*

TABLE 1

The 10% Rule in Operation. Model Portfolio, 5 Leading Industrial Stocks[1]

Value of Account[2]

Jan. 1946 Account established; also monthly high	$100,000	
Sep. 1946 Down 10%: Sell	81,300	
May 1947 Monthly low	76,300*	
Jul. 1947 Up 10%: Buy	81,300	
Jun. 1948 Monthly high	95,300	
Nov. 1948 Down 10%: Sell	85,800	
Jun. 1949 Monthly low	72,400*	
Sep. 1949 Up 10%: Buy	85,800	
Jan. 1953 Monthly high	182,100	
Sep. 1953 Down 10%: Sell; also, monthly low	163,000	
Dec. 1953 Up 10%: Buy	163,000	
Feb. 1955 Monthly high	277,700	
Mar. 1955 Fulbright reaction	262,400†	
Sep. 1955 Monthly high	348,000	
Oct. 1955 Eisenhower reaction	336,400†	
Apr. 1956 Monthly high	398,300	
May 1956 Reaction low	384,000†	
Aug. 1956 Monthly high	413,000	
Mar. 1957 Down 10%: Sell	368,000	
Dec. 1957 Monthly low	312,300*	
Jun. 1958 Up 10%: Buy	368,000	
Jan. 1959 New monthly high	442,100	12%/year
Dow-Jones 30 Industrials	**Value of account (2)**	
Jan. 1946 Account established	$100,000	
Jun. 1946 Monthly high	104,000	
Sep. 1946 Down 10%: Sell	90,100	
May 1947 Monthly low	86,900*	
May 1948 Up 10%: Buy	90,100	
Jun. 1948 Monthly high	91,600	
Jun. 1949 Down 10%: Sell; also, monthly low	80,900	
Oct. 1949 Up 10%: Buy	80,900	
Jul. 1957 Monthly high	223,600	
Oct. 1957 Down 10%: Sell	191,700	
Dec. 1957 Monthly low	189,000*	
Jul. 1958 Up 10%: Buy	191,700	
Feb. 1959 New monthly high	233,300	6.5%/year

[1]U.S. Steel, General Motors, Standard Oil (New Jersey), International Paper, United Aircraft.

[2]Monthly average of weekly closing prices.

*Assuming account still fully invested.

†10% selling signal not registered.

invested position is maintained. However, when the average falls 10% below a previous high, all holdings promptly are sold. No new buying is undertaken until the 30-day average for the former holdings rises 10% above a monthly lowpoint. At that time, the account is fully invested once more.

At first glance, the practice of going all-out for every market move of this size may seem reckless. Indeed, it might appear better suited to a trader than a long-term investor. In fact, however, a leeway of 10% proves amply conservative, particularly since monthly averages, rather than absolute highs and lows, are used as standards. What must be borne in mind is that the objective of the plan is to ascertain only the major moves of the market and to distinguish these from the minor fluctuations.

Herein lies the chief strength of the 10% rule: It places the investor on the right side of the market for the really big swings. As every tapewatcher knows, stock prices usually maintain their direction longer than is reasonable by most yardsticks. In gearing itself to this tendency, the 10% rule has a marked advantage over the buy-and-hold approach as well as over the standard formula plans.

At present, to be sure, the theory of buying "good" stocks and holding them indefinitely has a large and vocal following. The longer prices continue to rise, the more prudent an imperturbable long-term policy appears to be. However, unless it is assumed that the market henceforth will be a one-way street, such "a buy-and-forget" approach is open to grave doubts.

The well-known formula plans also contain a flaw, which ultimately may impair their effectiveness nearly as much as a bear market could set back a buy-hold investor. Invariably, adherents of these techniques act too soon, rather than too late, in both buying and selling stocks. Notwithstanding J. P. Morgan's dictum to the effect that the way he grew rich in the stock market was by selling too soon, premature action can prove highly unrewarding. During extended market moves, only a trend method, with its slightly laggard confirmation signals, can cope with the unexpected or unprecedented.

This is not to say that dollar averaging and other formula plans do not have definite merits. One of their purposes is to cushion the effect of a market break, and, in this regard, they are more or less successful. For novice investors and managers of very large funds, such techniques are extremely useful, possibly even essential. But for the investor who can afford a more aggressive approach, the 10% rule may offer as much safety, with less sacrifice of capital appreciation.

By itself, of course, a trend system can not assure good market results. Like any investment policy, the 10% rule places a premium on stock selection. To illustrate, the 10% rule applied to five of the strongest Dow Industrial stocks would have produced far better returns since 1946 than applied to the Industrial Average as a whole. Thus, a $100,000 portfolio of U. S. Steel, General Motors, Jersey Standard, International Paper and United Aircraft, between January, 1946 and October, 1958, would have grown to $432,800, or at a rate of 12.09% per year. An account made up of all 30 Industrials, on the other hand, would have increased only 6.05% annually, to $212,600.

Moreover, timing signals will vary considerably, depending on the component stocks. The "Average" account rode fully invested through the 1953 decline, while the selected five-stock portfolio was out of the market from September to December, 1953. Similarly, the reversal of the 1953–57 uptrend was signaled in March, 1957, for the five stocks, but not until October of that year for the Average. The latest reinvestment signal came in June, 1958, for the model portfolio, a month earlier than for the full 30-stock list.

Although it makes allowances for individual decision, the 10% rule also has attractive automatic features. For example, it correctly assessed the short-run emotional reactions of 1955–56. The shocks which accompanied the Fulbright investigation, the President's heart attack, his subsequent relapses, and the Mid-East crises, scarcely showed up in the monthly average figures.

Obviously, one of the prime virtues of any formula plan is the restraining hand it places on its user in times of emotional stress. In the case of the 10% rule, the monthly calculation feature forces one to wait. By that time, temporary fears and enthusiasms quite often have been dispelled, and the outlook can be appraised more realistically.

Unfortunately, no market formula can lay claim to infallibility, each has its weakness. The prime defect of the 10% rule is its proclivity to produce whipsaws in a tightly restricted market. In the 1946–49 period, when the Industrial Average fluctuated within a 53-point range, the 10% slack was too great for such a narrow market. For that reason, the unpropitious 1946 starting time was used in the above computations. It provides the stiffest conceivable test for the 10% rule, and it did produce some whipsaws. Happily, such markets are rare; in fact, no other market in this country's history compares to it, except possibly that of 1911–14.

Another fault of the 10% rule is the uneven tax burden it imposes on its user. In part, this drawback can be overcome by regular changes in the portfolio, with appropriate adjustments in the base monthly average for each change (new additions of capital require the same adjustment). However, in any case, the technique is flexible enough so that tax considerations need not intrude on basic investment considerations.

In sum, for the investor who hopes to follow the market's major uptrends to their conclusion, and yet avoid the serious downtrends, the 10% rule appears to offer some real advantages. Obviously, any method works best when supplemented with sound investment judgment. Particularly today, however, a rigid, objective formula can prove an invaluable aid for even the keenest investor.

37

A Basic Research Study on the Relationship of Price–Earnings to Future Stock Price Performance*

Paul F. Miller, Jr.

INTRODUCTION

From time to time over the last seven years, Drexel & Co. has conducted basic research studies aimed at investigating the importance of price-earnings ratios as a tool for stock selection and portfolio management.

The best known of these studies were done in 1963 and covered the 30 issues comprising the Dow-Jones Industrial Average for the period 1936 to 1962. These studies together with others covering 62 blue chip issues, published in April and June of 1964, indicated that there has been a strong price performance bias operating in favor of the low price-earnings ranges of the market.

By necessity, the size of our samples in these studies was limited by the tremendous volume of hand calculations. Now with the aid of Standard & Poor's Compustat tapes and a computer, we have been able to significantly expand the study of this area. Of interest is the fact that this study involved approximately 18,000 pieces of data and about 35,000 manipulations and calculations. The total machine time used was about twenty minutes.

Our methodology, and the summary of the results of this new study are described below:

METHODOLOGY

Time Span

The study covered time segments from 1948 through 1964.

Sample

Industrial companies covered in Compustat with sales of over $150 million in a given year. The actual number of companies grew consistently during the

*From *Institutional Service Report-Monthly Review* (November 1965), Drexel and Company. Reprinted by permission of Drexel Harriman Ripley, Incorporated, Philadelphia Pennsylvania.

period from 110 which had sales over $150 million in 1948 to 334 in 1964. Companies with deficits were eliminated in the years that the deficits occurred. The sample was confined to companies with fiscal year-ends of September 30 to January 31.

Computation of Price-Earnings Ratios

Price-earnings ratios were computed using year-end prices and calendar year earnings (or fiscal year earnings as long as the fiscal year ended between September 30 and January 31). This procedure assumed that the market had relatively accurate knowledge of calendar year earnings as of each year-end. While this assumption may be open to some question, we feel that the number of companies whose earnings may have differed significantly from the expectations of the market was quite limited. In any event, our subsequent procedure of ranking the stocks into quintiles by price-earnings ratios gives us confidence that the composition of the *quintiles* could not have been altered substantially by earnings surprises.

Ranking of Stocks by Price-Earnings Ratios and Division of the Sample into Quintiles

As of each year-end the companies that qualified on the basis of sales size were ranked by ascending order of price-earnings ratios and then divided into quintiles from the lowest price-earnings ratio quintile to the highest.

Examination of Price Performance

The price performances of the qualifying companies were computed for all one-year periods following the year-end price-earnings ratio calculations. Then an *average price* performance was computed for each *P/E* quintile. In a like manner price performances of the quintiles were computed for all three-year periods and all five-year periods in the 1948–1964 span.

SUMMARY OF RESULTS

Performance of Stocks Ranked in Quintiles by *P/E* at Each Year-End During Subsequent One-Year Periods (1948–1964 incl.)

	Number of Years in Which Price Performance Ranked:				
P/E Quintile	First	Second	Third	Fourth	Fifth
First (High *P/E*)	1	3	2	3	8
Second	1	1	2	11	2
Third	1	5	7	1	3
Fourth	2	7	4	2	2
Fifth (Low *P/E*)	12	1	2	0	2

As can been seen from the above summary, the lowest price-earnings ratio quintile had an average price performance which ranked *first* among all quintiles in 12 out of 17 years, or approximately 71% of the time. The highest price--earnings ratio quintile ranked *last* in one-year price performance in 8 out of 17 years, or 47% of the time.

The channel which has been drawn on the table is the perfect rank correlation channel. That is, if each quintile had had a price performance which correlated in an exact correlative way (inverse to the height of the price-earnings ratio), the numbers appearing in this channel would have been 17. In other words, the fifth quintile would have performed best in the 17 years, the fourth quintile would have performed second best in 17 years, the third quintile would have performed third best in 17 years, etc. While the correlation is not perfect, note that the largest numbers in every column fall within this correlation channel.

If we examine the average price gain per year for each quintile, we find that here too there is a strong tendency for price performance to vary inversely with the height of the price-earnings ratio. These figures are given below:

Average Price Gain Per Year

P/E Quintile	
First (High *P/E*)	7.7%
Second	9.2
Third	12.0
Fourth	12.8
Fifth (Low *P/E*)	18.4

Interestingly, while each quintile experienced an average loss in 5 out of the 17 years, the average loss *per loss year* did not vary significantly among the various price-earnings quintiles, as seen below.

Average Loss Per Loss Year

P/E Quintile	
First (High *P/E*)	12.1%
Second	10.7
Third	9.4
Fourth	9.5
Fifth (Low *P/E*)	10.1

Out of curosity we examined the number of years out of the 17 covered that each quintile outperformed the Dow-Jones Industrial Average.

No. of Years (out of 17) Quintile Outperformed D-J Industrials

P/E Quintile	
First (High *P/E*)	5
Second	7
Third	8
Fourth	7
Fifth (Low *P/E*)	11

As shown, the purely mechanical approach of confining a portfolio to the lowest price-earnings ratio quintiles would have achieved performances better than the Dow-Jones in 11 out of 17 years.

Turning now to the performance over each of 15 three-year periods included in the time span, the same strong bias in favor of low price-earnings ratio quintiles is demonstrated. The low price-earnings quintile was the best performing group in 10 out of 15 periods, whereas the highest price-earnings quintile was the worst performing group in 9 out of 15 periods. Just as the study of one-year periods showed, the perfect inverse correlation channel contained the largest number of periods in each column.

Performance Over 15 Three-Year Periods

P/E Quintile	Number of Periods in Which Price Performance Ranked: First	Second	Third	Fourth	Fifth
First (High *P/E*)	2	1	1	2	9
Second	0	1	0	10	4
Third	1	3	8	2	1
Fourth	2	8	3	1	1
Fifth (Low *P/E*)	10	2	3	0	0

Again the average price gain per period correlated perfectly in an inverse manner with the level of the price-earnings ratio.

Average Price Gain Per Three-Year Periods

P/E Quintile	
First (High *P/E*)	27.6%
Second	29.1
Third	38.1
Fourth	42.2
Fifth (Low *P/E*)	58.5

For five-year periods, the results continued in the same pattern with the low price-earnings quintile ranking first in 10 out of 13 periods, and the high price-earnings quintile ranking last in 8 out of 18 periods. Once again the perfect inverse correlation channel contains the largest number in every column and the average price gain per period again showed the same perfect bias toward the low price-earnings ratio groups.

Average Price Gain Per Five-Year Periods

P/E Quintile	
First (High *P/E*)	55.7%
Second	59.8
Third	67.7
Fourth	75.2
Fifth (Low *P/E*)	93.5

EXAMINATION OF RESULTS

When we first did similar work with the Dow-Jones Industrials, we were criticized for the small sample and the attention we gave to one-year periods. We were also criticized, probably justifiably, for using June 30 prices and calendar year earnings in the computation of price-earnings ratios. This objection was based on the theory that many of the stocks which were classified as low price-earnings stocks each June 30 based on calendar year earnings were probably stocks which turned out to be low price-earnings stocks as a result of surprisingly good earnings in the last half of the year. (We dealt with this criticism in our April 1963 *Monthly* Review.) We think we have effectively eliminated these objections in this study.

It was thought by some that if we gave consideration to a larger sample and to longer time periods than one year, the earnings growth of the high price-earnings stocks would have had time to work to the price advantage of the high price-earnings issues. Judging from the results of the study of three and five-year periods, this does not appear to be the case.

We have asked ourselves whether a handful of issues might have accounted for the superior price performance of the lower price-earnings ratio stocks. Consequently, we have examined the distribution of the price performances within the lowest and highest price-earnings ratio quintiles. In so doing we calculated the number of stocks in the lowest and highest quintiles which had a price performance exceeding the average price performance of the quintile.

Summary of Companies in Highest and Lowest Quintiles—
Exceeding Average Price Performance of Quintile

	Lowest Quintile	Highest Quintile
1 Year	44.5%	48.1%
3 Year	40.4	42.8
5 Year	39.5	41.1

As can be seen, there is some tendency for the lowest quintile to have a slightly more skewed distribution than the highest quintile. We believe, however, that the differences are quite insignificant.

CONCLUSION

We think that the results of this study support our continuing contention that price-earnings ratios are indeed an important consideration in portfolio management and research direction. However, much further work needs to be done to determine why this bias has been so consistently present in favor of low price-earnings ratio groups. Among the first jobs we have undertaken is a study of the correlation or lack of it, that exists between price-earnings ratios and subsequent earnings growth. This work is now in process and will be reported on in the near future.

Part **VI**

Institutional Investors—Philosophy and Performance

INTRODUCTION

The objective of the editors in this section is to introduce the student to the institutional investor. Institutions like mutual funds, pension funds, and banks now own some forty per cent of all common and preferred stocks.

In the first article, Mr. Morton Smith examines the bases for changes in trust investment policy that have occurred in the past half century.

Professors Edward Gill and Edward Reed examined the investment performance of common stock common trust funds. They found that during the four-year period covered, the average performance of common stock common trust funds was equivalent to that of the general stock market as measured by the Standard and Poor's 500 stock index. During this same four-year period through the end of 1964 and the three-year period through the end of 1964, the average performance of common stock common trust funds was superior to that of common stock mutual funds as measured by Wiesenberger's Indexes.

In the third article, Mr. Jack Treynor and Kay Mazuy examine the ability of mutual fund managers to anticipate major turns in the stock market. As the authors state, it is commonly believed that one of the advantages of investing through mutual funds is the quality of the management. The authors devised a statistical test for measuring the success of mutual funds in anticipating major turns in the stock market. The test was applied to the performance record of fifty-seven open-end mutual funds and the authors found no evidence to support the belief that mutual fund managers can outguess the market.

38

Changing Concepts of Trust Investment Policy*

Morton Smith

There is no such thing as a safe trust investment. That is to say, there is no way to determine by legislative action or otherwise that what looks like a safe trust investment today will be safe tomorrow, or next year. Massachusetts recognized this 121 years ago when the Supreme Judicial Court in *Harvard College v. Amory*[1] stated, "Do what you will, the capital is at hazard"; but it took the legal list States 100 years to discover it. The realization has led to two important changes in trust investment policies: (1) the widespread adoption of the prudent-man rule; and (2) the realization that during a period of inflation trustees may have a duty to preserve not only the "dollar value" of the funds committed to their care, but also their "real" or "purchasing power value."

This discussion concerns itself with the second of these changes. It will try to answer two questions: (1) Why has it come about? (2) What should corporate trustees do about it?

CONSERVATION OF DOLLAR VALUES UNDER THE GOLD STANDARD

The answer to the first question is, broadly speaking, contained in the one word inflation, but, as a glance at the chart shows, inflation is nothing new–the inflation of commodity prices preceding and accompanying the First World War was at least as great as that which occurred during the period embracing the Second World War. Not only did commodity prices rise materially from 1897 to 1920, but bond prices declined, while stock prices held fairly steady.[2]

This combination of events, however, appears to have had little or no effect on institutional investment policies, which all during the 1920's continued to concentrate mainly on bonds and real estate mortgages. A book on *Investment Analysis* written in 1921 by Professor Lagerquist of Northwestern University

*From *Trust Bulletin*, Vol. 37, No. 1 (September 1957), pp. 11–77. Reprinted by permission of *Trust Bulletin*.

[1] 9 Pick. 446 (1830).

[2]

	12/31/1902	Low–1920
Atchison, Topeka & Sante Fe. Gen. Mtge. 4%, 1995	103	69
Dow-Jones Industrial Average	64.29	66.75

CHART 1

Wholesale Prices (Bureau of Labor Statistics Index, 1947–49=100)

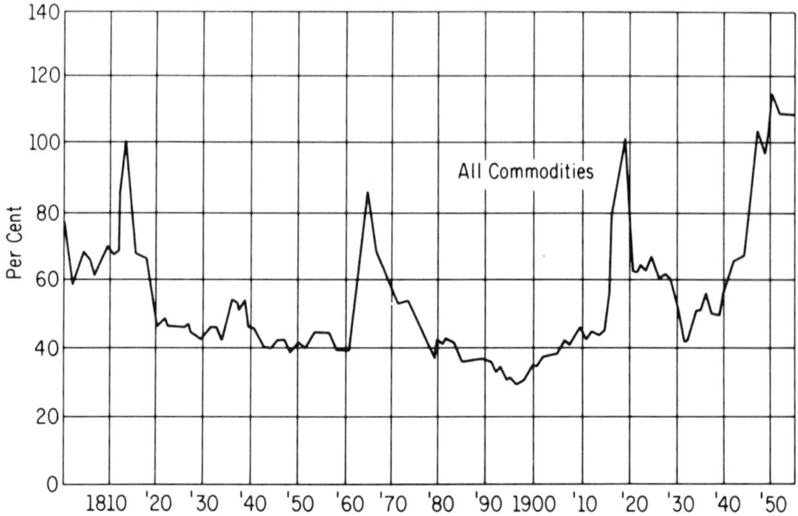

contained no reference at all to common stock investments and Edgar Lawrence Smith in his famous work *Common Stocks As Long Term Investments* written in 1924 stated that "in the minds of most investors bonds hold an unassailable position, common stocks are rarely even mentioned." At the Eleventh Mid-Winter Trust Conference in February 1930, six out of seven speakers stated that they never bought common stocks in trust accounts unless they were directed to do so in the instrument. The only exception was, as might be expected, a gentleman from a Boston bank who admitted that his institution bought common stocks as a matter of considered policy. In 1934 Professor Riddle of Ohio State University in his book *The Investment Policies of Trust Institutions* traced the investments of 196 separate trusts administered by institutions in leading financial centers from Boston to St. Louis during the years from 1919 to 1932. He found that during this period the book value of the bond portfolios increased from 23 per cent to 34 per cent, real estate mortgages from 16 per cent to 24 per cent, while the book value of common stocks decreased from 35 per cent to 32 per cent.

The failure of trustees and other conservative investors to think in terms of common stocks and conservation of purchasing power following the inflation of 1897 to 1920 may be explained as follows:

1. During the '20's the country was firmly on the gold standard and most bonds and mortgages were payable in gold coin of the then existing weight and fineness.

2. As reference to the chart will disclose, commodity prices after reaching a peak in 1920 declined precipitately and within a year had lost about 50 per cent

of the wartime rise. Thereafter until 1929 commodity prices fluctuated within a narrow range at about the new level and no one was much concerned over the possibility of any further increase.

3. The government pursued orthodox fiscal policies and retirement of the public debt was steady and substantial.

4. Adequate yields were available on bonds and taxes were lower.

5. Equities had a predominantly speculative background, as is illustrated by the fact that the total number of shares traded on the New York Stock Exchange in 1901 was more than three times the number of shares listed. In 1919 the ratio was still one and one-half times, while in 1956 all the stock transactions on the New York Stock Exchange were equivalent to only 13 per cent of the total number of shares listed.[3] In other words, during the first 20 years of this century common stocks were used primarily as a medium for making short-term trading profits, while more recently they have been purchased for yield and long-term gains.

While bonds remained the most widely accepted medium for investing trust funds, common stocks were acquiring a degree of respectability they had never previously enjoyed. Edgar Lawrence Smith's book, a milestone in investment analysis, compared the results which could have been achieved by investing in selected lists of stocks and bonds, objectively chosen without benefit of hindsight, during the period from 1866 to 1922. In the great majority of cases the stock lists outperformed the bonds by a substantial margin, due, in Mr. Smith's opinion, to the compounding effect of plowed back earnings.

In 1928 Dwight Rose, a partner of Scudder, Stevens, and Clark, in his book entitled *A Scientific Approach to Investment Management* compared the investment results achieved by the principal fire insurance companies from 1903 to 1926. The company with the best investment performance had an average of 38 per cent in common stocks whereas the company with the poorest investment performance had an average of only 11 per cent invested in equities.

Both Smith and Rose advocated a balanced investment policy as between stocks and bonds and both pointed out the danger of buying stocks regardless of price, but Smith's book, in particular, was used as an argument for doing just that. As a consequence, when the market collapsed, Smith's reputation collapsed with it at precisely the time when application of his theory would have paid off handsomely.

CONSERVATION OF "REAL" VALUES AND MANAGED MONEY

1. *Depression–Recovery–Recession* (1929–1940). From 1929 to 1932 the high-grade bond market gave an excellent account of itself relative to other forms of investment. True, Atchison General 4s sold down from 95 to 75, but there was no interruption of income. In the meantime wholesale commodity

[3] *New York Stock Exchange Fact Book*, 1957.

prices had declined from 62 to 42 so that the income beneficiary was actually better off in 1932 than he had been in 1929. Stocks, on the other hand, performed very poorly. The Dow-Jones Industrial Average declined from 381 to 41, and dividends on that average declined from $12.75 to $4.62. However, at precisely the time when truly high-grade bonds had proved their value, two factors came into play to undermine investor confidence in fixed-income securities and the theory of conservation of dollar value:

a. Widespread defaults in two areas which had hitherto been regarded as the safest repositories for conservative funds—railroad bonds and real estate mortgages.

b. Departure of the United States from the gold standard in April, 1933—not because of a shortage of gold but for the deliberate purpose of inflating the price level. This action touched off spectacular advances in common stock prices which in the words of the *Commercial and Financial Chronicle*, were "paralleled only by the wild speculation of 1928–1929." Two years later, in 1935, the United States Supreme Court in the so-called "Gold Cases"[4] held that Congress had the right, in pursuance of its authority to control the currency, to abrogate clauses in private contracts calling for payment in gold.

These events were a severe shock to investor confidence. Together with government-fostered "pump priming" and low interest rates they provided the background for the inflationary psychology which has been such an important market factor ever since. In the middle 1930's the courts began to adopt a more liberal attitude toward trust investments. In Pennsylvania, for example, a lower court decided in 1937 that a common stock was a "security." Said Judge Bok of the Philadelphia Orphans Court, "The modern stock market offers opportunities for investment substantially as safe as mortgage bonds."[5] The movement to liberalize the investment statutes of legal list states got under way at about this time, and corporate trustees started to buy common stocks as a matter of policy—my own bank, for example, set up its first "approved list" of common stocks in 1935. It should be noted, however, that all of these trends were actuated more by the desire to maintain the income of the life beneficiary during a period of declining interest rates than by fear of a depreciating dollar.

However, the move into equities in the 1930's did not go very far. In a country whose productive capacity was far in excess of effective demand, an increase in money supply brought about by revaluing gold and by deficit spending was not enough to insure for long either rising prices or general prosperity. Business confidence remained at a low ebb and in 1937 there was a severe collapse. Once again high-grade bonds returned to favor. Atchison General 4s declined from 116 in 1937 to 98 in 1938, while the Dow-Jones Average declined from 194 to 98, and the dividends on the Dow-Jones stocks declined

[4] Norman v. Baltimore & Ohio Railroad Co., 294 U. S. 240; Nortz v. United States, 294 U. S. 317.

[5] Carwithen's Estate, 28 D & C 66.

from $8.78 to $4.98. In the meantime high-grade bonds coupons continued to be paid in full.

Another negative factor was apparent in the pre-World War II period. The 1930's were occupied with the "mature economy" theory. The United States had reached the last frontier, population growth was slowing down and would soon stop entirely, and capital was accumulating faster than outlets for its productive employment could be developed. Consequently, it seemed to many intelligent people that the only way to keep things going was for the government to take over the responsibility for making capital investment and maintaining employment.

In sum, the pre-World War II policies of the government were highly inflationary, but they were carried out in an atmosphere which was unfriendly to business and pessimistic as to the future of the country's economy. As a result wholesale commodity prices recovered only about 60 per cent of the 1929–1932 decline, and by the time World War II broke out trustee inclination to hedge against a depreciating dollar had increased very little since the initial shocks to the dollar conservation theory in 1933–35.

2. *War and Postwar Inflation (1941–1957).* During the war the development of normal investment policies was obscured by the necessities of the time. Although war is inflationary and theoretically favorable to stocks, investors do not, as a rule, regard it as a good background against which to buy equities—at least, until war's end appears to be in sight. For a number of reasons, including the scarcity of corporate bonds, U. S. Governments and particularly Series "G" bonds were a favorite medium for investors' funds from 1941 to 1945.

It was not until the end of World War II that the inflationary policies of the previous twelve years began to have their greatest effect on the investment practices of corporate trustees. Although the inflation of commodity prices had been approximately the same at the end of both World Wars, the effect on investment sentiment was wholly different for the following reasons:

a. In contrast to World War I, interest rates had been pegged and trustees found themselves with large funds invested at 2½ per cent at a time when commodity prices had doubled and beneficiaries were clamoring for "real" grocery store income. Common stocks yielding 5–6 per cent or more were a natural, indeed the only practical, answer to this problem. But other factors besides the need for income emphasized the importance of conserving "real" (as distinct from dollar) values.

b. The United States was deeply shocked by the Russian invasion of Iran in 1946 and the subsequent activities of the Communists. We were faced with the fact that the war had not ended in 1945, but had, in effect, started all over again with a more dangerous enemy than the ones we had just defeated. There is little doubt that the Cold War and the Korean War had a lot to do with preventing the postwar deflation of commodity prices which had always previously taken place when farms and factories were converted from producing goods to be wasted to producing goods for which markets had to be found among willing buyers who could use them and had the money to pay for them. (Reference to the Commodity Price Chart shows that when the periods embracing the War of 1812, the Civil War, the First World War, the Second World War, and the Cold War are eliminated, there is little evidence of long-term inflation of wholesale commodity prices in the United States.) United States Government expenditures, which had dropped from a wartime high of $95-billion to $36-billion in 1948, climbed back again to $75-billion in 1953 after the Korean War, and commodity prices, far from collapsing, exceeded their wartime highs.

As a consequence, trustees again started to buy stocks not only for immediate income but because they believed they provided a long-term hedge against a declining dollar. The Cold War might go on for a generation, or it might end suddenly in a holocaust of atom bombs. In either event, oil or coal or ownership of productive enterprises looked like better means of conserving "real" values than promises to pay paper money. It should be noted, however, that there is another possibility which, although slight, seems worthy of some consideration, although at the moment it appears to be receiving none. That is that the United States and Russia will work out some sort of *modus vivendi*, which will materially reduce the threat of a suicidal atomic war and restore the international temperature to a commercially comfortable level. Any such development could have considerable impact on the theory of inevitable inflation.

c. Added to the risk of continuing armament inflation has been the threat of long-term peacetime inflation implicit in the Full Employment Act of 1946. If budgetary deficits and deliberate inflation of the money supply are to be the answers to any future depression, this does not furnish a good argument for buying bonds.

d. The steady inflation of costs and wages forced on industry by the power of the labor unions, operating on an inadequate labor supply, has provided further impetus to the preference for common stocks, on the theory (which may be dubious) that industry will be able to pass along the increased costs to the consumer and maintain reasonable profit margins.

e. To these, on the whole, negative reasons for buying stocks, there has been added a positive one. The "mature economy" theory of the tired 1930's had been replaced by the "growing economy" theory of the dynamic 1950's. This attractive proposition has 150 years of United States history to back it up. It provides the final and perhaps the most convincing reason for preferring stocks to bonds. It should be noted, however, that while the reasons for it change, the theory itself is not new. Note, also, that it has few, if any, adherents during periods of low economic visibility. Accepted as gospel in 1929, rejected as nonsense in the 1930's, it is embraced once again as gospel in 1957.

In describing the reasons which have led trustees, consciously or unconsciously, to seek conservation of purchasing power as well as dollar values, one question remains unanswered. What will be the attitude of the courts towards a trustee who makes no attempt to conserve "real" values, on the one hand, or on the other hand, a trustee who makes one attempt and fails? A Michigan Court in the Dodge[6] case last year refused to surcharge a trustee in the first of these situations, and indeed it is difficult to see how a standard could be set up to measure the damages arising out of a trustee's failure to conserve "real" values, assuming that he had the power to do so. Stocks per se are not the answer to conservation of "real" values. It has been entirely possible to buy high-grade stocks which have not maintained "dollar" values, let alone "real" values. Forty per cent of all the stocks listed on the New York Stock Exchange sold at lower prices in 1956 than the highs of 1946, including such high-grade issues as American Telephone & Telegraph, Abbott Laboratories, and Woolworth.

But, surcharge or not, it is the duty of a trustee to act as a reasonable man. To what extent he has a duty to hedge against inflation is perhaps a matter of degree. To put an extreme case, if the United States ever experienced a German-type inflation where a million dollars wouldn't buy a postage stamp, no one would say that a trustee deserved the confidence of the public, if, under a broad investment power, he had invested only in bonds.

FUNCTION OF DIVERSIFICATION UNDER TODAY'S CONDITIONS

1. *Bonds*. In the light of what has been said, is a policy of diversification between bonds and common stocks desirable? Assuming long-term inflation is inevitable, would not beneficiaries be better off if trustees bought nothing but high-grade common shares? The common practice of keeping a balanced position of perhaps 50 per cent in bonds and 50 per cent in commons gives a trustee the feeling that no matter what happens he cannot be criticized, but, aside from this, does diversification by type of security have any positive advantages? I think it does for the following reasons:

a. Conservation of dollar values is still the duty of a trustee, and the public and the courts are not likely to settle for anything less. If the commodity price level should, by any chance, drop by 50 per cent, a trustee who had lost half the principal of a trust in the stock market would not receive a very sympathetic reaction either from his beneficiaries or from the courts by pointing out that he had done a very good job of conserving "real" values even though dollar values had been cut in half. While inflation is a long-term risk against which a trustee should seek protection, experience shows that deflation can be a serious short-term risk against which bonds form a useful hedge. This is particularly true of short-term trusts set up during periods of high stock prices.

b. Bonds are also useful for the purpose of providing reserve buying power for stocks. Most trusts do not have a continuous flow of funds of a type which makes "dollar averaging" practicable, and, as a consequence, a trust which is placed wholly in common stocks at a given time is not in a flexible position to take advantage of changes in business conditions and market sentiment.

[6]Horace E. Dodge Estate, Probate Court, Wayne County, Michigan, October 6, 1955.

c. The function of tax-exempt bonds in preserving real values in high-tax bracket accounts under today's conditions should not be overlooked. With good grade tax-exempts selling to yield about 3½ per cent, the yield to a beneficiary in a 50 per cent or higher tax bracket is roughly three times the present income on many growth stocks. The beneficiary can obtain now a rate of return for which he will have to wait from five to ten years in the leading growth stocks, assuming continuance of present tax rates and the same rate of dividend increase as has occurred during the last ten years of unprecedented boom. In addition to this many tax-exempt bonds are selling at substantial discounts to afford a virtually certain prospect of substantial capital appreciation if held to maturity.

2. *Preferred Stocks*. Preferred stocks have not been popular as trust investments aside from states like Pennsylvania where they enjoy a considerable advantage over most bonds because of the exemption of a wide list of high-grade preferred stocks from the personal property tax. Preferred stocks have frequently been dismissed from consideration as trust investments on the grounds that "they are neither fish, flesh, nor fowl," having none of the advantages of a common stock and none of the protection of a bond. However, a comparison of the price record of truly high-grade preferred stocks over a 30-year period with high-grade long-term bonds will show that issues such as National Biscuit 7% Preferred, du Pont 4½% Preferred, and Consolidated Edison 5% Preferred have fluctuated little more than the bonds from the highs to the lows of the price cycle, and in the meantime they have yielded an average of about 1 per cent more over a long period of years.

Two risks, however, are present in preferred stocks which are not present in bonds. The first is that the price is completely at the mercy of interest rates (unless the issue has a sinking fund), having no maturity which will insure the holder a particular price at a fixed date. The second is, that, when a company or an industry loses investor acceptance to any degree, the price of a preferred stock may be permanently affected even if there is no interruption of dividends or even any risk thereof. A good rule to follow in buying preferred stocks is to buy them only when money rates are high, and then to purchase the issues of those companies whose common stocks enjoy widespread investment acceptance and are likely to continue to do so.

3. *Common Stocks*. Although common stocks are widely regarded as the best and only practicable hedge against inflation, it has already been pointed out that a large number of good stocks have made no progress in the past ten years despite inflation and unprecedented prosperity. However, it is still true that almost any well diversified list of common stocks purchased in 1946, which would doubtless have included such issues as du Pont, Standard Oil of New Jersey, and General Electric, would, on the average, have performed very well even though it included some of the poorer acting stocks previously mentioned. A well diversified list of common stocks has, in fact, been a good inflation hedge, even though many individual stocks have not, because diversification applied to equities tends to be a positive factor insuring profits whereas in the

case of bonds its only purpose is to insure against loss. A rise of 200 per cent in du Pont, for example, will more than offset a 50 per cent decline in two or three other stocks.

There is a tendency on the part of trustees to think of equities either as "growth" stocks or as "defensive" stocks, but growth stocks which have no defensive characteristics and defensive stocks with no growth characteristics are equally suspect as trust investments. For most investors a growth stock is one which goes up and a defensive stock is one which does not go down. From the standpoint of results, and that is what we are interested in, these definitions are satisfactory, but they do not help in the selection of the investment to begin with.

A good definition of a growth company is one where (a) sales are growing at a faster rate than the economy as a whole, (b) a substantial proportion of the earnings are being plowed back into the business, and (c) the business is earning a better than normal rate of return on its invested capital. (It is the plow back and the rate of return on it which Edgar Lawrence Smith recognized in 1924 as being the principal reason why common stocks have outperformed bonds over the years.) However, such a company must have sufficiently stable earnings to be able to pay some dividend when times are bad.

By contrast, a defensive stock may be described as one whose earnings and dividends will fluctuate less than the average during poor business conditions, and which can be depended upon to pay a reasonable rate of return on the purchase price even when times are bad. Such a stock, however, is not likely to be a good inflation hedge unless the company has some prospect of increasing the stockholders' equity, as a business never stands still for long, and if it does not grow at all, it will decline.

PRICE RISK IN BUYING COMMON STOCKS

Although at the top of any market the only price risk which gives people much concern is the risk that if they don't buy a stock it will be higher next week, the experience of the past 25 years shows that the downside risk in purchasing almost any stock is very real when purchases are made after a long rise. However, the characteristics of the market have changed greatly during this period. There was a time when virtually all stocks went up and down together; but just as the economy has been marked by "rolling readjustments" in one industry after another, so the stock market has been characterized by over-valuation in some shares and under-valuation in others in terms of price times earnings ratios and yields. "Formulas" for determining under-valuation and over-valuation have proved to be of doubtful value, and as a consequence a tendency has grown up on the part of trustees to buy "good" stocks, particularly "good growth stocks," almost regardless of price on the theory that investment judgment has done all that it can when it has selected a good company in a good industry with good growth prospects and that the price that is paid for such a company's stock is a matter of opinion and does not lend itself to analysis. It is suggested, however, (i) that not much investment judgment is required to arrive at the conclusion that I.B.M., Minneapolis Honeywell, Minnesota Mining, and General Electric are high-grade companies with good growth prospects, and (ii) that there is a limit to what should be paid for growth. Air Reduction was widely regarded as a growth company in 1937 when its earnings reached an all-time high. In that year the company earned \$2.85 a share and the price of its stock ranged between 45 and 80. In 1950 the company earned \$3.15 a share but it had lost its growth "halo" and the shares ranged from 21 to 29. Even though earnings per share had increased by about 10 per cent, the return on capital had declined from 20 per cent to 10.4 per cent and the dividend had been cut from \$3.00 to \$1.00. In 1957 the stock has sold as high as 66 on the basis of 1956 earnings of \$4.20 per share and it is again being recommended as a growth stock. This performance has been very disheartening to anyone who purchased Air Reduction in 1937 on the theory that it was a good growth stock and that price didn't matter. On the other hand those who bought the shares in 1950 when they were out of favor and selling at a reasonable price in relation to earning have done very well.

The point is that while a trustee is required to observe what prudent men are doing in the way of investing their funds, he isn't required to follow the crowd. He should take into account the actions of others, but if, based on his own investigations, he arrives at a conclusion which differs from the majority, he is acting prudently if he follows his own judgment. It needs no argument to show that if all prudent men constantly buy and sell the same stocks at the same times, the results will not bring credit on the prudent-man rule.

The theory that any price is a good price to pay for a good stock is extremely dangerous. But the fact that no one can say what is a prudent price to pay for a stock does not mean that trustees should not make the attempt. A given price may be prudent in a long-term trust where current income is of no importance and imprudent in a short-term trust where income is essential. Discrimination between what is a good value and what is not, as applied to particular trust accounts, is essential. Informed independent judgment plus common sense can be relied upon to produce reasonably good results.

In conclusion, there is a sound basis for the emphasis trustees have placed on conserving real values through the purchase of common stocks. But the duty to conserve dollar values as well still remains. The perpetual inflation argument may not be flawless—at least inflation in this country has not been a continuous process, and there have been long periods when there was none at all. Consequently, bonds and preferred stocks continue to have an important place in trust portfolios, particularly where they yield significantly more than equities. As to common shares, diversification, is, as a general rule, the key to good investment performance. Every reader of this article can cite instances from his own experience of spectacular results which have been achieved by breaking this rule, but absent special circumstances, the rule is still a good one. Finally, in a free society diversity of opinion among prudent men is healthy and desirable. The prudent trustee should not seek the false sense of security which comes from doing what everybody else is doing. If he has made a careful analysis of a security and has taken the opinion of others into account, it is his duty to be guided by his own judgment even though it is contrary to that of the majority.

39

The Investment Performance of Common Stock Common Trust Funds*

Edward K. Gill
Edward W. Reed

The number of common trust funds and their total market value have grown significantly in recent years. From the end of 1960 to the end of 1965, the number of such funds increased from 420 to 1016, and the number of commercial banks and trust companies operating them increased from 327 to 464. The total market value of these funds advanced during the same period from $2.8 to $7.5 billion.[1] There has been little information publicly available concerning the performance of common trust funds. The objective of this study is to provide some evidence of this performance.[2]

The elements of performance which we shall consider are: appreciation, yield, and stability. We shall first compare a composite of common trust funds with Standard and Poor's 500 Stock Index and with several mutual fund indexes prepared by Arthur Wiesenberger and Company.[3] Then, we shall attempt an analysis of relative performance among common stock common trust funds. For this purpose, simple coefficients of correlation are developed between measures of appreciation, yield, and stability. The period covered is from the end of 1960 through the end of 1964, though some deviations were necessary.

I. SOURCE OF DATA

Data for this study were obtained through questionnaires sent to the 207 trust institutions which, according to a list provided by the Office of the

*From *The National Banking Review,* Vol. 4, No. 2 (December 1966), pp. 159–166. Reprinted by permission of *The National Banking Review.*

[1] Stanley Silverberg, "Bank Trust Investments in 1965," *The National Banking Review,* 3 (June 1966), p. 492.

[2] When classified according to asset composition, common trust funds fall into three broad categories: fixed income funds, equity or common stock funds, and diversified funds. The latter are composed of portfolios of common stocks and debt instruments combined, and are expected to provide some appreciation while yielding a more stable income than is provided by common stock funds.

[3] Arthur Wiesenberger and Company, *Investment Companies* (New York: Arthur Wiesenberger and Company, 1965).

Comptroller of the Currency, operated common stock funds as of late 1964. There were 146 respondents to the questionnaire, a 71 percent return. This is sufficiently high to permit analysis, but it should be kept in mind that bias might exist. For example, reluctance to return the questionnaires might have been greater among those institutions whose funds performed poorly. Possibilities such as this cannot be disproved.

II. COMMON TRUST FUND INDEXES

In order to make the comparisons with the Standard and Poor's 500 Stock Index, and the mutual fund indexes, the data for the common trust funds were combined into indexes. Because of the lack of correlation between the various funds' valuation dates, four indexes were prepared. Regulation 9 of the Comptroller of the Currency, which provides the ruling for the operation of common trust funds, requires only that they be valued once each quarter. Most funds hold to the quarterly valuation, though some are valued monthly. Fortunately for this study, most of the funds (124 of those which provided data, or 85 percent) use the last business day of their chosen month or quarter. Therefore, one index of monthly-valued funds, and three of quarterly-valued funds, were readily feasible.

The indexes were given a base of 100 on their first valuation date. Funds begun after this date were added to the indexes in the same manner that new issues are added to a common stock index. Values of the Standard and Poor's 500 Stock Index and the mutual fund indexes were converted to a base of 100 on the dates which make up the first valuation dates of the common trust fund indexes.

III. COMPARISON WITH STANDARD AND POOR'S 500 STOCK INDEX

The common trust funds are compared with Standard and Poor's 500 Stock Index in Charts 1 through 4, and with the mutual fund indexes in Charts 5 through 8. Since three different base dates are used, the charts can be compared to each other only to a limited extent.

The yields on the common trust fund indexes and the Standard and Poor's 500 Stock Index are compared in the lower part of each chart. Yield percentages for the Standard and Poor's Index were available only for quarters ending March 31, June 30, September 30, and December 31. As a result, the yield comparisons in Charts 3 and 4 are not for exactly corresponding quarters. However, the discrepancy is not considered to be sufficient to hide any significant variations in yields. All yield figures are rounded to the nearest tenth of a percent.

The composite performance of common trust funds was not greatly different from that of the Standard and Poor's 500 Stock Average during the first two and one-half years of the four-year period. As the 1963–1964 bull market continued, however, the price performance of the common trust funds was

Prices and Yields: Standard and Poor's 500 Stock Index and Common Trust Fund Indexes

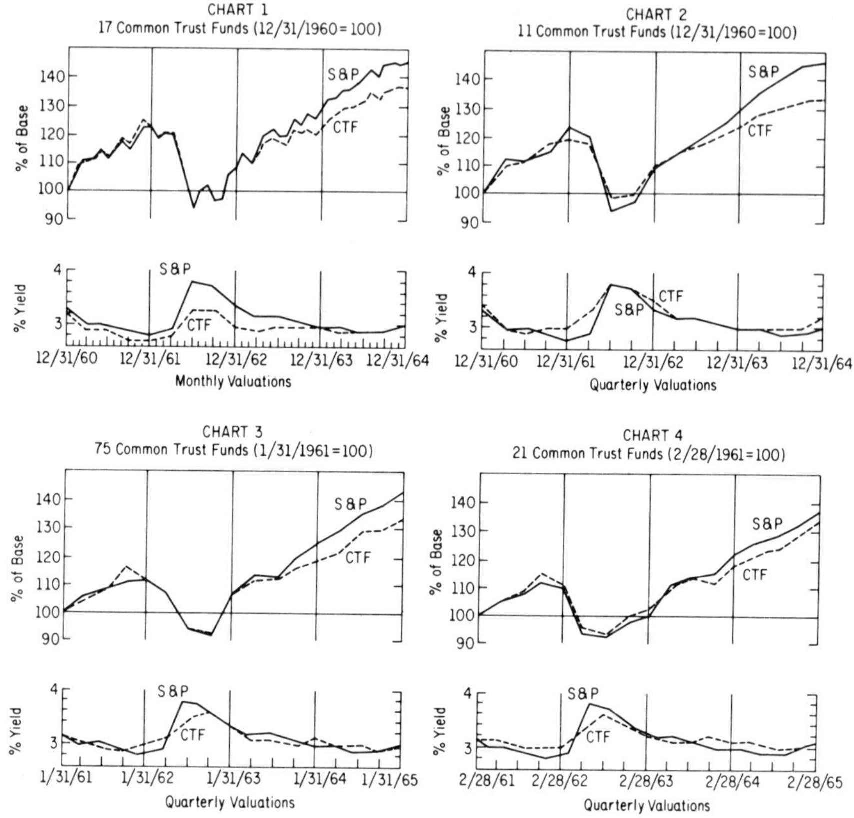

inferior to that of the general market. Yield performance was very similar, except during the low period of 1962. The yield on the Standard and Poor's Index increased about 33 percent during early 1962, as the value of the index declined roughly 25 percent.[4] Common trust funds lost almost as much value as did the Standard and Poor's Index, but the yields did not rise as sharply during the decline. It may be that some common trust fund managers were switching part of their stocks to short-term government securities during the latter part of the decline. This would have prevented the common trust funds from receiving the mid-year dividends on the stocks sold. The interest on any government bills acquired in the late phases of the decline would not have been received until well past the middle of the year, and this interest would not have fully offset the lost dividends. Yields on government bills were about 2.6 percent during this period, as compared with about 3.8 percent on the Standard and Poor's Index.

[4]This movement reflects the fact that dividend payout by corporations did not decline in 1962, even though stock prices dropped sharply. If a stock declined 25 percent in value, its yield would increase 33 percent with no change in dividend rate, for example.

Stability performance, which can be judged from the graphs only by the size of the fluctuations from valuation date to valuation date, appears to be very similar for the common trust fund indexes and the Standard and Poor's 500 Stock Index. The yield performances are also very nearly equal, and price performance favors the Standard and Poor's Index only after mid-1963.

Common trust funds have several disadvantages, however. They must pay brokerage and other expenses. The temporarily idle cash which they hold will restrict their price performance in periods of rising stock prices. Moreover, the newer funds did not, in general, perform as well as the older funds in the indexes. Of the 75 funds in Chart 3, 40 were in operation at the beginning of the four years. The average annual appreciation of these was 8.6 percent, while that for the entire index was 7.3 percent.

Although some allowance should be made for these limitations, its exact value would be difficult to determine. We assume that such an allowance would make up the differences in price performance between the common trust fund indexes and the Standard and Poor's Index. This assumption is not unrealistic and does not greatly alter the conclusion to be drawn from this section. It allows us to state that: During the four-year period covered, the average performance of common stock common trust funds was equivalent to that of the general stock market as measured by the Standard and Poor's 500 Stock Index.

IV. COMPARISON WITH MUTUAL FUND INDEXES

Two indexes of mutual fund performance for each of two categories of funds composed entirely of common stock–classified as "growth" and "growth-with-income"–are published in an annual survey by Arthur Wiesenberger and Company.[5] These four mutual fund indexes will be compared with the common trust fund indexes. Two of these mutual fund indexes are not designated as such by Wiesenberger's, but since they are averages of the performance of virtually every major mutual fund in each category, they are considered here to be general indexes of performance.

In computing the performance measure for each mutual fund in each of these general indexes, it is assumed that capital gains and income are reinvested. The value at the end of the period, and the start of the period is divided into the value at the end of the period, and the resulting percentage increase or decrease is the measure of that fund's performance. The common trust fund price and value indexes were constructed exclusive of income distributions, so in order to allow exact comparisons it was necessary to assume that income was not paid out but was held and reinvested. Two common trust fund indexes which are valued on December 31, were reconstructed on this basis. The valuation dates of the other two did not correspond exactly to the dates on which the mutual fund performance figures were computed.

[5] Arthur Wiesenberger and Company, *op. cit.*

The important results of these comparisons can be stated briefly. From the end of 1960 through the end of 1964, the growth mutual fund index appreciated 39 percent, and the corresponding growth-with-income index increased 47 percent. The two common trust fund indexes, with income assumed to be reinvested, grew by 51.1 percent and 49.8 percent. During 1962, a year of major decline, the growth mutual fund index dropped by 19 percent, the growth-with-income index declined 12 percent, and the common trust fund indexes as compared here declined 9.5 percent and 6.1 percent.

The second pair of mutual fund indexes is set forth in graphical comparison with the four common trust fund indexes in Charts 5 through 8. These mutual fund indexes are designated as Wiesenberger's Indexes in the annual investment company report of Wiesenberger and Company. Each index consists of the average values of five mutual funds, each fund selected for homogeneity of objective. Quarter-by-quarter values for these indexes were available only from the end of 1961 on; therefore, these charts cover three years rather than four. Yield comparisons on an annual basis are set forth in the lower right corner of Chart 5.

Prices: Wiesenberger's Growth and Growth-with-Income Mutual Fund Indexes and Common Trust Fund Indexes

CHART 5
17 Common Trust Funds (12/31/1961 = 100)

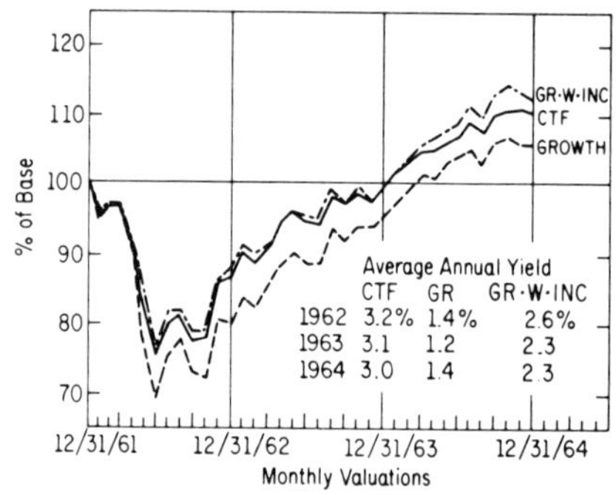

CHART 6
11 Common Trust Funds (12/31/1961 = 100)

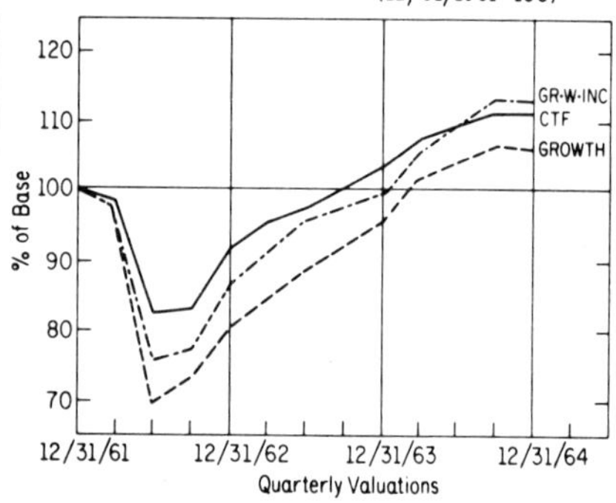

CHART 7
75 Common Trust Funds (1/31/1962 = 100)

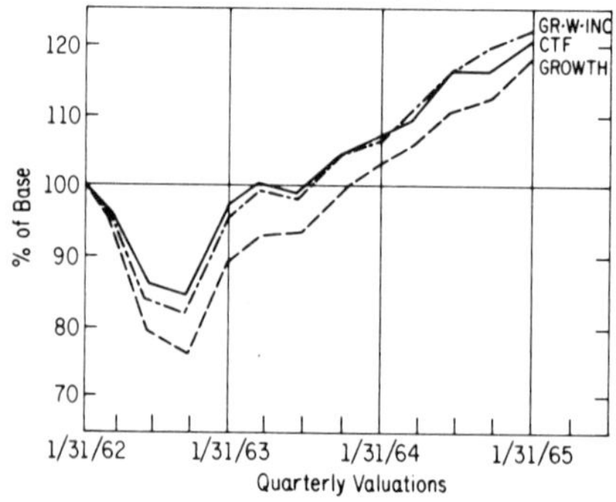

CHART 8
21 Common Trust Funds (2/28/1962 = 100)

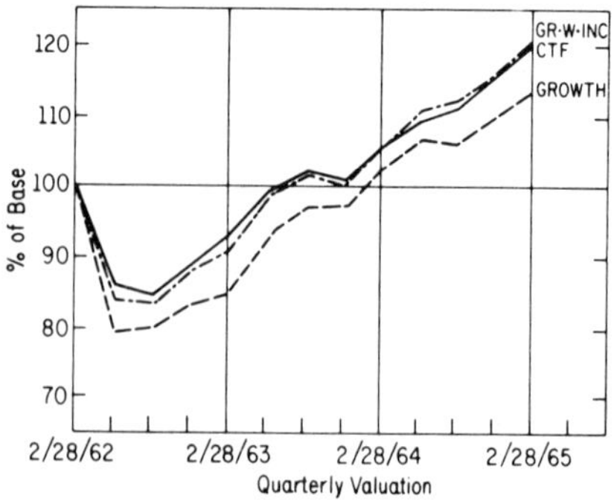

The charts indicate that the price performance of the common trust funds was quite similar to that of the growth-with-income index. Particular notice should be given to Chart 7 regarding this point, since it contains 60 percent of the common trust funds in all the common trust fund indexes. Common trust funds were somewhat more stable in the 1962 decline than was the growth-with-income mutual fund index, but they did not grow as rapidly after mid-1962. Common trust funds were clearly more stable and provided more appreciation during the three years than did the growth mutual fund index. Yield performance of common trust funds was vastly superior to that of either mutual fund index.

The comparisons in Charts 5 through 8 produce results similar to those of the earlier four-year comparisons with the general mutual fund indexes. On this basis, it may be concluded that: The investment performance of common stock common trust funds was superior to that of common stock mutual funds, as reflected by the Wiesenberger Indexes, for the four-year period ended December 31, 1964, and for the three-year period ended December 31, 1964.

V. SIMPLE CORRELATION ANALYSIS OF COMMON TRUST FUND PERFORMANCE

In this section, we deal with the relative performance of the funds. Forty funds, in operation throughout the four-year period ending January 31, 1965, are analyzed. Three measures of performance for each fund were computed: one for appreciation, one for yield, and one for stability. The appreciation, or growth, measure is the change in value from January 31, 1961 to January 31, 1965, expressed as a percent of the January 31, 1961 value. The yield measure is the mean quarterly yield. The quarterly yields were computed by dividing the total past year's income for the fund by its value at the end of each quarter. The stability measure is the July 31, 1962 value of the fund expressed as a percent of its January 31, 1962 value. This is an arbitrary measure, but since the early 1962 market decline was very sharp in its effect and encompassed the entire market for common stocks, it was a good test of the stability of common stock portfolios.

Coefficients of correlation were computed for each pair of performance measurement series and were found to be as follows:

Between growth and yield	.0680
Between growth and stability	.3778
Between yield and stability	.5271

The usual tests of the null hypothesis of no correlation (which assume normally distributed populations) indicate that the first coefficient is not significant, and the second and third coefficients are significant at the 2 percent and .1 percent levels, respectively.

The nature of the relationship between the three pairs of series is clearer in

CHART 9

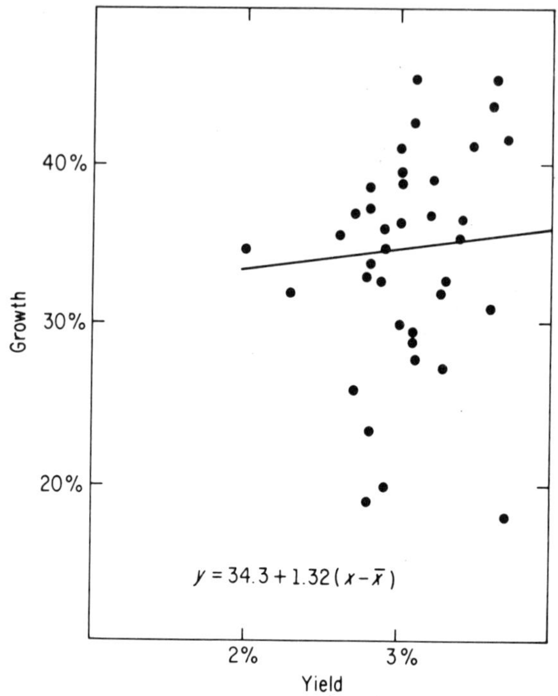

CHART 10

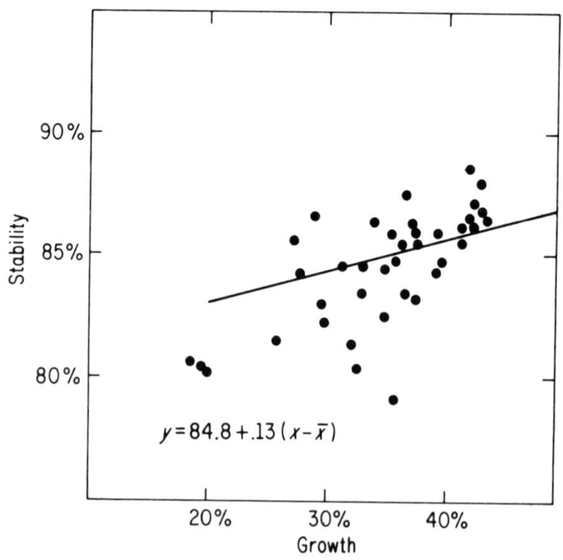

Charts 9 through 11. The various points of growth-yield, growth-stability, and yield-stability are plotted, and the least squares line of best fit has been computed for each. It must be pointed out that this section is not based on regression analysis, even though the lines are computed by finding regression coefficients. Regression analysis assumes a causal effect of one of the variables on the other, while correlation analysis simply seeks a degree of association. The nature of any causal relationships between the variables dealt with here would be very difficult to define, so correlation analysis seems most appropriate.

CHART 11

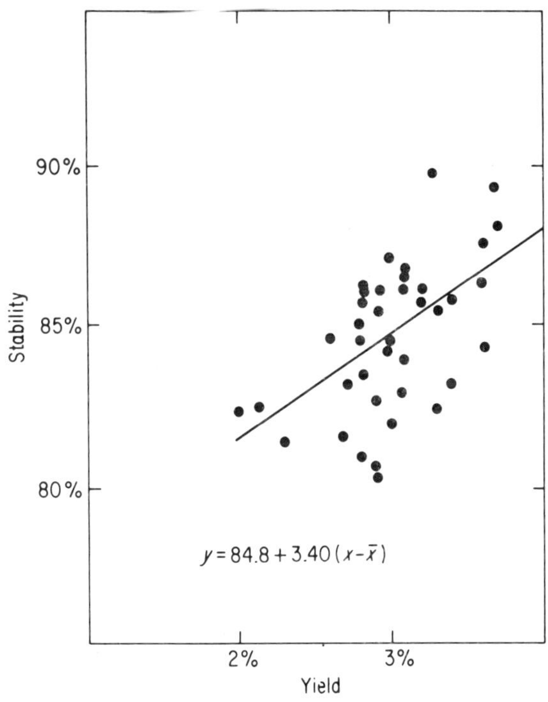

The first coefficient of correlation indicates no significant relationship between growth and yield. The funds which grew most produced yields at least as high as did the slower growing funds. This result is important, since it would normally be expected that rapid growth would be accompanied by low yields and slow growth by higher yields. The low positive correlation between growth and yield indicates that the selection of stocks primarily for growth may not have been fruitful during the four-year period studied. This same lack of success in the case of mutual funds was apparent in the previous section. Those mutual funds with rapid growth objectives did not advance as much during the four years as did the growth-with-income funds which place more emphasis on providing reasonable yields.

The second coefficient of correlation indicates a strong positive relationship between growth and stability. By the measures used here, the funds which grew most over the four years declined least during early 1962. Of course, there is some build-in bias here, because those funds which fell least in early 1962 did not have as far to go to reach new highs during the subsequent period. Nonetheless, the opposite result, that is, a negative correlation between growth and stability, would normally be expected, because lack of stability is characteristic of the so-called growth stocks.

The third coefficient reveals a high positive correlation between yield and stability. This meets with normal expectations. It means that the higher-yielding funds, which apparently seek reasonable income returns, were most stable. The most successful common trust funds during the four years, then, as well as the most successful mutual funds, appear to be those which sought reasonable yields and did not invest primarily in the so-called growth stocks. In fact, it may be that common trust fund managers would have been in error to invest primarily for growth, at the expense of income, at any time in the recent past. The general performance record of growth stocks in the 1940's and 1950's is slightly inferior to the performance of Standard and Poor's 500 Stock Index.[6] IBM was the outstanding exception to this record, but as the Wharton Study pointed out, IBM shares made up only about one-half of one percent of the value of common stock holdings of mutual funds just prior to the period of its rapid growth.[7]

VI. TWO FUNDS COMPARED

A number of trust institutions operate more than one common stock fund. An opportunity to compare a "growth" fund with a "growth-with-income" fund is provided in one situation where the two funds were started on the same date, by the same institution, with the same management of both funds. These funds were started near the market high of 1961. By the end of 1964, the growth fund had appreciated 3 percent, the growth-with-income fund 8 percent. During that period, the growth fund provided an average yield of 1.8 percent, the growth-with-income fund 3.8 percent. From February 28, 1962 to May 30, 1962, the growth fund declined 23 percent while the growth-with-income fund declined 14 percent.

VII. SUMMARY AND CONCLUSIONS

The objective of this study was to provide some evidence of the investment performance of common stock common trust funds. The following are our conclusions:

[6]Benjamin Graham *et al, Security Analysis* (New York: McGraw-Hill, 1962), p. 535.

[7]U.S. Securities and Exchange Commission, *A Study of Mutual Funds,* Report of the Committee on Interstate and Foreign Commerce, 87th Congress, 2d Session, 1962.

1. During the four-year period from the end of 1960 through the end of 1964, the average performance of common stock common trust funds was equivalent to that of the general market as measured by the Standard and Poor's 500 Stock Index.

2. During the four-year period through the end of 1964 and the three-year period through the end of 1964, the average performance of common stock common trust funds was superior to that of common stock mutual funds as measured by Wiesenberger's Indexes.

3. During the four-year period ending January 31, 1965, the common stock common trust funds which appreciated most were also the most stable and produced yields equal to those of the slower-growing, less-stable funds.

40

Can Mutual Funds Outguess the Market?*

Kay K. Mazuy
Jack L. Treynor

Are mutual fund managers successfully anticipating major turns in the stock market? There is a widely held belief that they are. Whether investment managers themselves actually share this belief is hard to say. At one time or another in promoting their services, however, a number of mutual funds have used the claim that they can anticipate major stock market movements.

We have devised a statistical test of mutual funds' historical success in anticipating major turns in the stock market. Applying this test to the performance record of 57 open-end mutual funds (as reported in this article), we find no evidence to support the belief that mutual fund managers can outguess the market.

DEBATED RESPONSIBILITIES

The question we have studied has an important bearing on the responsibilities which investment managers can properly be asked to assume. For instance, today almost everyone agrees that the market was dangerously high in early 1929 and that stocks were a bargain in the 1950's. On hindsight, laymen are tempted to think that these extremes should have been "obvious" to fund managers at the time, and that they should have sold or bought common stocks accordingly. In actuality, of course, fund managers did *not* always sell in 1929 and buy in the 1950's.

What position should the fund manager take to protect himself against accusations that he should have anticipated market movements in this way? More broadly, what does the shareholder have a right to expect from the fund manager? Is the fund manager speculating if he attempts to anticipate major market movements? Or is he negligent if he fails to try? It seems to us that the answers to these questions depend in part on whether or not investment managers actually have the *ability* to anticipate major turns in the stock market.

Because a mutual fund's performance in each succeeding year is readily measured, widely published, and easily compared with that of other mutual funds, managers in this industry are perhaps particularly sensitive to the effect

*From *Harvard Business Review*, Vol. 44, No. 4 (July-August 1966), pp. 131–136. Reprinted by permission of *Harvard Business Review*.

on their funds' performance of a market decline or market rise during the year. We believe that our findings may have significance not only for mutual fund managers, but also for pension, trust, and endowment fund managers—despite the fact that their objectives vary widely. If it is generally true that investment managers cannot outguess the market, then it may be necessary to revise certain conceptions about the responsibilities of investment management across the board.

ANALYTICAL APPROACH

It is well known that there is a definite tendency for the prices of most common stocks to move up and down together. Because this tendency exists, it is meaningful to talk about fluctuations in the "market." It is also well known that some common stocks are more volatile (i.e., sensitive to market fluctuations) than others.

Thus, when we talk about investment managers outguessing the market, we mean anticipating whether the general stock market is going to rise or fall and adjusting the composition of their portfolios accordingly. That is, if they think the market is going to fall, they shift the composition of the portfolios they manage from more to less volatile securities (including bonds). If they think the market is going to rise, they shift in the opposite direction. The result of such shifts is a change in effective *portfolio* volatility. (A simple graphical measure of portfolio volatility was developed by one of the authors in a previous HBR article,[1] and is reviewed in some detail later in this article.)

In order to test whether or not a mutual fund manager has actually outguessed the market, we ask, in effect: *Is there evidence that the volatility of the fund was higher in years when the market did well than in years when the market did badly*? This is the question that was applied to the 57 funds we studied. Of course, we did not know that *all* of them were trying to outguess the market, but that does not matter. Unquestionably, some of them were trying to do this and thought they had the ability.

Performance Data Used

Data for the mutual funds in our sample were obtained from *Investment Companies 1963*, by Arthur Wiesenberger Company.[2] For open-end investment companies, Wiesenberger employs the following formula to compute rate of return: "To asset value per share at the end of the period, adjusted to reflect reinvestment of all capital gains distributions, add dividends per share paid during the period from investment income, similarly adjusted; divide the total by the starting per share asset value."[3]

[1] Jack L. Treynor, "How to Rate Management of Investment Funds," *HBR* (January-February 1965), p. 63.

[2] Port Washington, New York: Kennikat Press, Inc., 1963.

[3] *Ibid.*, p. 99.

The resulting rate-of-return figure is only approximate, since it disregards subtleties relating to (1) the timing within the period of dividend distributions and (2) the relative after-tax value to the shareholder of market appreciation, on the one hand, and of dividend-interest income, on the other. We feel, however, that the measure is probably adequate for our purpose, even though these effects are disregarded.

The Characteristic Line

If, year by year, the rate of return for a managed fund is plotted against the rate of return, similarly defined, for a suitable market average–such as the Dow-Jones Industrial Average or the Standard & Poor's 500-Stock Index–the result is the kind of patterns shown in Exhibit 1. A line fitting the pattern is called the characteristic line. If the line has the same slope for years in which the market goes up as for years in which the market goes down, the slope of the line is constant; the line is straight. When this is so, a single number–the tangent of the slope angle of the line–is sufficient to characterize the sensitivity of the fund in question to market fluctuations, and we can talk meaningfully about "the" volatility of the line.

The fund shown in Part A of Exhibit 1 has kept a constant volatility over the years included in the sample. For such funds, the degree of scatter around the characteristic line is a measure of how well diversified the fund is. The more nearly perfect the diversification of the fund, the less scatter around the characteristic line, because the more accurately the fund reflects the stocks in the market average.

Outguessing the Market

What happens, however, if a fund management tries continually to outguess the market by oscillating between two characteristic lines, one of which has a high volatility and the other, a low volatility?

Part B of Exhibit 1 illustrates the extreme case in which management is able to outguess the market at every turn. Whenever management has elected the highly volatile composition demonstrated by characteristic line *C-D*, the market has risen; whenever management has elected the low-volatility line *A-B*, the market has fallen. It is clear in this case that the characteristic line is no longer straight.

If, on the other hand, fund management guesses wrong as often as it guesses right, then we have the kind of picture shown as Part C of Exhibit 1. Here the fund's performance traces out the undesirable points *H, G, F, and E* as frequently as it traces out the desirable points *A*, *B*, *C*, and *D*. The result is considerable scatter in the characteristic-line pattern, *but no curvature*.

Probably no fund management would claim to be able to anticipate the market perfectly. Let us assume, however, that management has some prediction powers. Then, the better the market performs, the more likely management is to have anticipated good performance and to have increased fund volatility appropriately; and the larger, on the average, the chosen volatility is likely to be. The

EXHIBIT 1

Illustrative Characteristic Lines

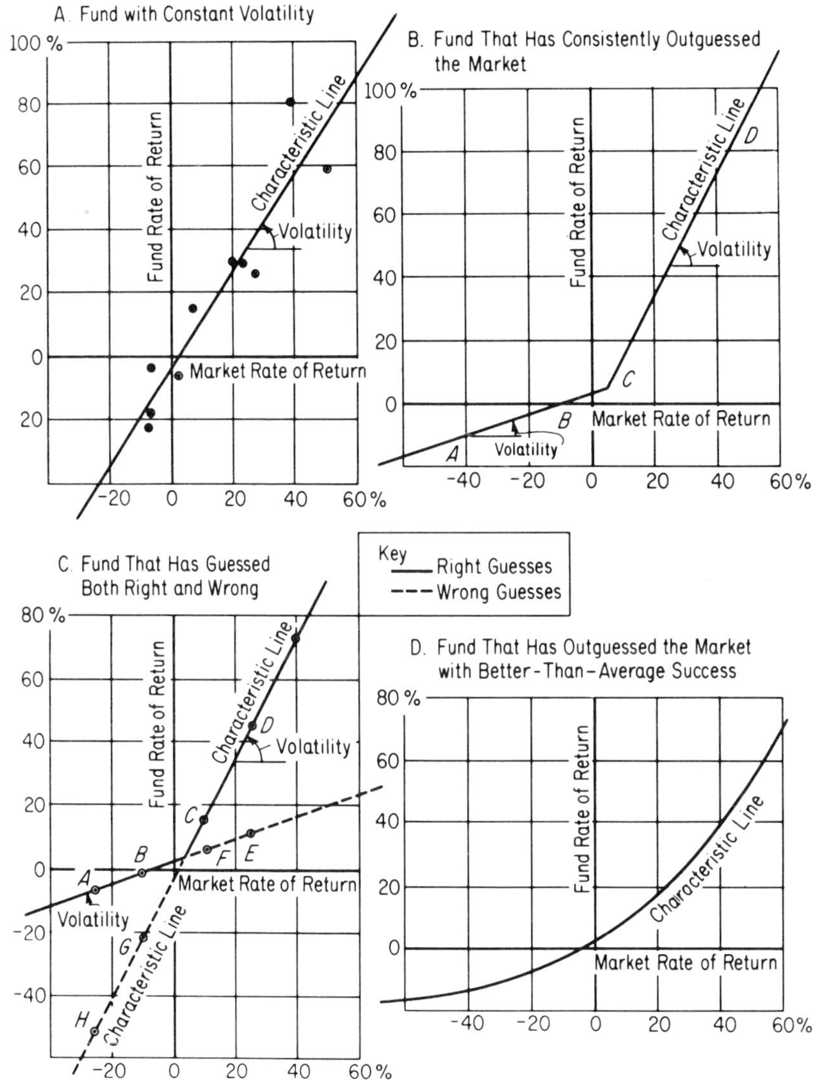

result will be a gradual transition of fund volatility from a flat slope at the extreme left of the characteristic-line diagram to a steep slope at the extreme right, with the slope varying more or less continuously in between, producing a smoothly curved characteristic line pattern with a certain amount of scatter resulting from management's bad predictions (see Part D of Exhibit 1) rather than the kinked pattern associated with the policy illustrated in Exhibit 1-B.

The key to our test for successful anticipation is simple: the only way in which fund management can translate ability to outguess the market into a benefit to the shareholder is to vary the fund volatility systematically in such a fashion that the resulting characteristic line is concave upward, as in Exhibit 1-D. If fund management has correctly anticipated the market more often than not, then the characteristic line will no longer be straight. (And we can add, for the more mathematically inclined reader, that whether the characteristic line is smoothly curved or kinked, a least-squares statistical fit of a characteristic line to the performance data for the fund will be improved by inclusion of a quadratic term in the fitting formula.)

Choice of Funds

If the management of a balanced fund elects to change the fund's volatility, it can shift the relative proportions of debt and equity, or change the average volatility of the equity portion, or both. However, stock funds and growth funds, which are commonly considered to consist primarily of equity securities, are obviously not free to alter their volatilities by shifting the relative proportions of debt and equity (although they can alter the average volatility of the common stocks held). For this reason, it is sometimes argued that a balanced fund is more likely to make frequent changes in fund volatility. To allow for this possibility, we divided our sample in roughly equal proportions between balanced and growth funds.

EXHIBIT 2

Breakdown of Sample by Size and Type of Funds

Market Value of Assets*	Number of Funds		
	Growth	Balanced	Total
Less than $20	7	10	17
$20-$99	7	13	20
$100-$500	10	7	17
More than $7,500	1	2	3
Total	25	32	57

*In millions of dollars as of December 31, 1962

In addition, it is sometimes argued that smaller funds will have less difficulty in changing their portfolio composition quickly when a change in volatility is desired. To account for this, we included in our sample of 57 mutual funds a wide range of fund sizes. Exhibit 2 shows the distribution of our sample among fund sizes and between balanced funds and growth funds.

Time Period Studied

The period covered in the study includes the ten years beginning in 1953 and ending in 1962. One may ask if our findings would have been different if another time period had been selected for study. We do not think so. Subject to the various sources of random scatter in characteristic-line patterns discussed previously, the characteristic-line pattern remains invariant over time, regardless of the behavior of the market, unless and until basic management policies or abilities change. (In fact, management policies and abilities are probably drifting slowly as individual men in the management team mature and as the composition of the management team changes, but these effects are usually small, compared to the effects on the year-to-year rate of return caused by market fluctuations.)

As mentioned earlier, if management is right more often than wrong in its attempts to outguess the market, the characteristic-line pattern will be curved. The degree of curvature depends on how heavily management bets on its expectations—that is, the degree to which management changes fund volatility when its expectations regarding the market change. So long as management policy continues roughly constant in this regard, the degree of curvature manifested in the characteristic line will remain unchanged.

The only criterion for the time period selected for a curvature study is that during the period the market should have exhibited wide and frequent swings both upward and downward, so that the characteristic-line data are not confined to a segment in the middle of the pattern which, because of its shortness, is indistinguishable from a straight line.

The period 1953–1962 contains one year in which the Dow-Jones Industrials demonstrated a rate of return of 50%, and three years in which the return was negative by substantial amounts. We feel that this is a suitable period for our study because it is long enough to cover a variety of ups and downs in the general market, short enough to avoid serious problems resulting from the gradual drift of fund policies over time, and recent enough to reflect modern mutual fund management practices and policies. The fact that the market was generally rising throughout the period has no effect on the characteristic line, and hence in no way invalidates our findings.

We have used yearly data because we feel that even the smaller mutual funds would be reluctant to make the changes in portfolio composition necessary to change fund volatility much more often than once a year. Based as it is on yearly data, however, the study cannot detect any success that fund managements may have had with more frequent changes in volatility.

FINDINGS

What does the study show? It shows no statistical evidence that the investment managers of any of the 57 funds have successfully outguessed the market. More precisely, we find no evidence of curvature of the characteristic lines of any of the funds.

Here are some of the more technical aspects of our study:

In order to test for the presence of curvature, we used the methods mentioned earlier. (A least-squares regression technique was employed to fit characteristic-line data for the 57 open-end mutual funds in our sample. That is, for each of the funds we calculated the constants for the equation which "best" describes the performance data of the mutual fund for the Standard & Poor's Composite Price Index as a quadratic function of the performance.)

Exhibit 3 summarizes our results. The value of the F statistic, plotted along the horizontal axis, is a measure of the degree of curvature of the fund (and is normalized to allow for variations in the amount of random scatter observed). The vertical axis shows the number of funds which had F values equal to the F value given on the horizontal axis. As the magnitude of an F value increases, the higher the probability that the amount of curvature seen for the fund is real, i.e., is greater than we would expect by random chance. The vertical dotted line marks the F value (5.6) corresponding to the amount of apparent curvature which even those funds that have no real curvature would display one time in twenty. A fund should show an F value greater than 5.6 in order to be considered to have real curvature.

EXHIBIT 3

Distribution of Funds According To F Value

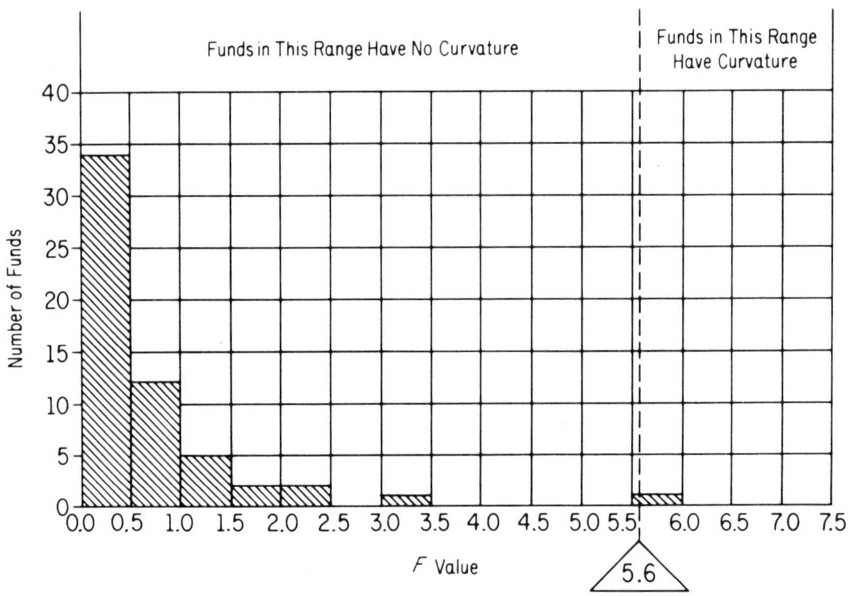

In our sample of 57 managed funds, only one displayed even an F value of 5.6 This fund's curve and also the actual data points are given in Exhibit 4.

In other words, our findings show that for the mutual funds in our sample, at least, it is safe to assume that their characteristic lines are straight. Actual funds tend to resemble the fund in Exhibit 1-A rather than the funds in Exhibits 1-B and 1-D. Our results suggest that an investor in mutual funds is completely dependent on fluctuations in the general market. This is not to say that a skillful fund management cannot provide the investor with a rate of return that is higher

EXHIBIT 4

Characteristic Line of the Fund Which Has the Greatest F Value

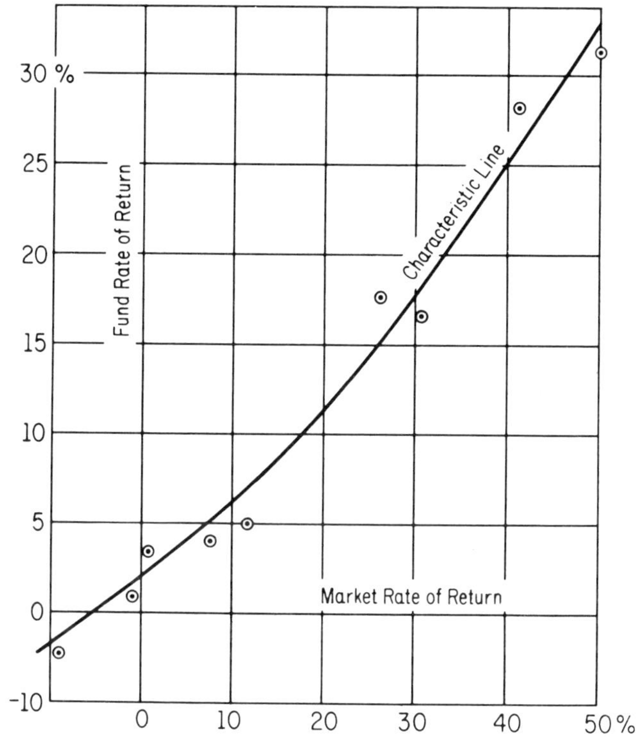

in both bad times and good than the return provided by the market averages, but it does suggest that the improvement in rate of return will be due to the fund manager's ability to identify underpriced industries and companies, rather than to any ability to outguess turns in the level of the market as a whole.

The fact that only one of the 57 mutual funds in our sample has a characteristic line suggesting curvature indicates that perhaps no investor–professional or amateur–can outguess the market. This finding has clear significance for the man in the street managing his own portfolio, for the man with fiduciary responsibility for a private estate, for the president of a manufacturing company responsible for its pension fund, and for a college treasurer managing an endowment. It means that probably the best assumption they can make is that investment managers have no ability to outguess the market and should not try to. It also means they should not hold fund managers responsible for failing to foresee changes in market climate.

List of Contributors

Armen Alchian	Professor of Economics, University of California at Los Angeles
Sidney Alexander	Professor of Management, School of Industrial Management, Massachusetts Institute of Technology
Stephen L. Allison	Graduate School of Business, University of California at Berkeley
Leo Barnes	Professor and Chairman of the Department of Finance, Hofstra University
William J. Baumol	Professor of Economics, Princeton University
Douglas A. Campbell	President, D. A. Campbell Company
John C. Clendenin	Professor of Finance, University of California at Los Angeles
Marshall Colberg	Professor of Economics, Florida State University
David T. Crary	Assistant Professor of Finance, Graduate School of Business, University of Southern California
Robert R. Dince	Professor of Finance, University of Georgia
James Dines	Analyst and author of *The Dines Letter*
David Durand	Professor of Management, School of Industrial Management, Massachusetts Institute of Technology
David K. Eiteman	Associate Professor of Finance, University of California at Los Angeles
Eugene F. Fama	Assistant Professor of Finance, Graduate School of Business, University of Chicago
Lawrence Fisher	Associate Professor of Finance, Graduate School of Business, University of Chicago
Charles B. Franklin	University of Florida
George K. Freeman	Analyst and Investment Adviser, New York City
William Freund	Chief Economist, Prudential Insurance Company of America and Adjunct Professor of Finance, New York University
Edward K. Gill	Instructor, Department of Finance, University of Oregon
David Green, Jr.	Graduate School of Business, University of Chicago
A. James Heins	Associate Professor of Finance, University of Illinois

David A. Hoddeson	Analyst and Investment Adviser, New York City
Charles C. Holt	Professor of Economics, University of Wisconsin
Estelle James	Assistant Professor of Economics, San Francisco State College
Ralph James	Lecturer, Department of Economics and School of Business, University of California at Berkeley
Reuben Kessel	Associate Professor of Economics, University of Chicago
William Kurtz	Valuation Analyst, Institutional Research Department, Hornblower Weeks-Hemphill, Noyes, New York.
J. H. Lorie	Professor of Business Administration, Graduate School of Business, University of Chicago
K. Mazuy	Member of Operations Research Staff of Arthur D. Little, Inc., Cambridge, Massachusetts
Paul F. Miller, Jr.	President, Drexel Harriman Ripley, Inc., Philadelphia, Pennsylvania
Thomas Gale Moore	Michigan State University
Anelise N. Mosich	Associate Professor of Accounting, University of Southern California
John K. Pfahl	Professor of Finance, College of Administrative Sciences, The Ohio State University
Edward W. Reed	John B. Rogers Professor of Banking and Finance, University of Oregon
Harry V. Roberts	Professor of Statistics, Graduate School of Business, University of Chicago
Joel E. Segall	Graduate School of Business, University of Chicago
Daniel Seligman	Analyst and Columnist, *Fortune*
Joseph J. Seneca	Research Fellow at the Economics Research Services Unit of the University of Pennsylvania
William Sharpe	Associate Professor, Graduate School of Business, University of Washington
Morton Smith	Vice President, Girard Trust Corn Exchange Bank, Philadelphia, Pennsylvania
George J. Stigler	Charles R. Walgreen Distinguished Service Professor, Department of Economics and Graduate School of Business, University of Chicago
J. L. Treynor	Member of Operations Research Staff of Arthur D. Little, Cambridge Massachusetts
Maurice Van Cleave	Graduate School of Business, University of California at Los Angeles
Roman L. Weil, Jr.	Graduate School of Business, University of Chicago

Robert E. Weintraub	Associate Professor of Economics, City College of New York
Paul Wendt	Professor of Finance, Graduate School of Business, University of California at Berkeley
J. Fred Weston	Professor of Business Economics and Finance, Graduate School of Business, University of California at Los Angeles
Edward Zinbarg	Adjunct Professor of Finance, Bernard M. Baruch School of Business and Public Administration, The City University of New York